UNDERSTANDING PATENT LAW

Understanding Patent Law

Amy L. Landers
Professor of Law
University of the Pacific, McGeorge School of Law

Print ISBN: 978-0-7698-5276-8

eBook ISBN: 978-0-3271-8118-7

Library of Congress Cataloging-in-Publication Data

Landers, Amy L.

Understanding patent law / Amy L. Landers.

p. cm.

Includes bibliographical references and index.

ISBN 978-0-7698-5276-8 (softbound)

1. Patent laws and legislation--United States. I. Title.

KF3114.L36 2012

346.7304'86--dc23

2012024160

NOTE TO USERS: To ensure that you are using the latest materials available in this area, please be sure to periodically check the LexisNexis Law School web site for downloadable updates and supplements at www.lexisnexis.com/lawschool.

Editorial Offices

121 Chanlon Rd., New Providence, NJ 07974 (908) 464-6800

201 Mission St., San Francisco, CA 94105-1831 (415) 908-3200

www.lexisnexis.com

MATTHEW◆BENDER

Preface

Patent law is an important, fascinating, and rapidly changing field. Built on an incentive structure, this area of the law is intended to encourage the development of new solutions. The topic can be provocative. For those interested in a system developed to create the future, the study of patent law can be eminently rewarding.

Over the past few years since the first edition was published, there have been numerous substantive changes in the law. Both the U.S. Supreme Court and the Court of Appeals for the Federal Circuit have issued several key decisions. In enacting the America Invents Act of 2011, the U.S. Congress has passed some of the most significant changes in patent law in the past sixty years. The U.S. Patent & Trademark Office has been active in implementing these changes, and instituting other changes to improve the field. This book incorporates these modifications. Where the former law has continued relevance, both the old and new versions are presented.

For those who are new to patent law, a word of advice: Patience. Even if you have prior legal experience, the terminology, history, and science described in the major cases can be new and complicated. The rules and statutes present intellectual challenges. This book is intended to provide a roadmap for your exploration of the law and theory, and to explain the more difficult areas of the law and the science. This should enable you to more fully understand this intriguing field.

Frequent Citations and Abbreviations

"The 1952 Patent Act" refers to all amendments to 35 U.S.C. that were enacted in 1952 including the former version of 35 U.S.C § 102.

The "AIA" refers to the America Invents Act of 2011, enacted at 35 U.S.C.

"House report" is the document titled AMERICA INVENTS ACT, H.R. Rep. No. 112-98 (2011).

"MANUAL OF PATENT EXAMINING PROCEDURE" is the United States Patent and Trademark Office, MANUAL OF PATENT EXAMINING PROCEDURE. This document is available at http://www.uspto.gov/web/offices/pac/mpep/index.htm, and in many law libraries.

"Patent Act" is the statute set forth in 35 U.S.C.

"TRIPS" is the Agreement on Trade-Related Aspects of Intellectual Property Rights, administered by the World Trade Organization. A copy is available at http://www.wto.org/english/tratop_e/trips_e/t_agm0_e.htm.

"U.S. PTO" used throughout refers to the United States Patent and Trademark Office.

Statutory citations refer to those under Title 35, U.S. Code unless otherwise specified.

Citations to the Code of Federal Regulations refer to those under Title 37 unless otherwise specified.

Table of Contents

Chapter 1   **INTRODUCTION TO THE PATENT SYSTEM** 1

§ 1.01   THE PATENT RIGHT 1
§ 1.02   HISTORY AND ORIGINS OF THE PATENT RIGHT 2
   [A]   Early European Patent Systems 2
   [B]   The British Patent System and the Statute of Monopolies 3
§ 1.03   U.S. CONSTITUTIONAL BASIS: ADOPTION OF THE COPYRIGHT AND
        PATENT CLAUSE 5
   [A]   The Patent System and the U.S. Constitution 5
   [B]   Congressional Adoption of the Patent System 7
   [C]   Current Events: The America Invents Act of 2011 8
§ 1.04   FOUNDATIONS OF MODERN U.S. PATENT LAW 9
   [A]   The Legal Foundation of Patent Rights 9
   [B]   Patent Rights as an Appropriation Mechanism 11
   [C]   Incentives and Patent Law 13
§ 1.05   HOW DOES THE PATENT "RIGHT TO EXCLUDE" OPERATE? 14
§ 1.06   WHAT DOES ONE DO WITH A PATENT? 15
§ 1.07   CONCLUSION 16

Chapter 2   **THE U.S. PTO: OBTAINING A PATENT** 19

§ 2.01   INTRODUCTION 19
§ 2.02   PATENT APPLICATIONS: PRE-FILING CONSIDERATIONS 21
§ 2.03   THE PATENT APPLICATION 22
   [A]   Provisional v. Non-provisional Patent Applications 22
   [B]   Non-provisional Utility Patent Applications 23
   [C]   Some Details: A Closer Look at a Patent Specification 25
§ 2.04   PATENT PROSECUTION AND INFORMATION SHARING 26
   [A]   Patent Application Secrecy and Publication 26
   [B]   Communication with the U.S. PTO 27
   [C]   International Applications and Work Sharing 28
§ 2.05   EXAMINATION PROCEDURES 28
   [A]   Intake and Examination 28
   [B]   Final Office Actions 30
     [1]   Allowance 30
     [2]   Rejection and Appellate Options 30
   [C]   Continuation Applications 31
§ 2.06   INTERNATIONAL CONSIDERATIONS AND THE PCT APPLICATION
        PROCESS 32
§ 2.07   CONCLUSION 34

Table of Contents

Chapter 3   **POST-GRANT ADMINSTRATIVE PROCEEDINGS** **35**

§ 3.01   INTRODUCTION 35

§ 3.02   RE-ISSUE 37

    [A]   Background to Reissue Proceedings 37

    [B]   Defining "Error" for Purposes of Reissue 38

    [C]   Limitations on Reissue 40

      [1]   Two Year Limit on Broadening Reissue 40

      [2]   The Rule Against Recapture 40

§ 3.03   THE DOCTRINE OF INTERVENING RIGHTS 41

§ 3.04   CERTIFICATE OF CORRECTION 44

§ 3.05   REEXAMINATION 46

    [A]   Generally 46

    [B]   *Ex Parte* Reexamination 46

    [C]   The Former *Inter partes* Reexam 48

§ 3.06   POST-GRANT REVIEW 49

§ 3.07   *INTER PARTES* REVIEW 52

§ 3.08   SUPPLEMENTAL EXAMINATION 53

§ 3.09   DETERMINING INVENTORSHIP 55

§ 3.10   CONCLUSION 56

Chapter 4   **CLAIMS** **57**

§ 4.01   BACKGROUND 57

§ 4.02   WHAT IS A CLAIM LIMITATION? 60

§ 4.03   THE ANATOMY OF A CLAIM 60

    [A]   The Preamble 61

    [B]   The Transition 61

    [C]   The Body of the Claim 62

§ 4.04   TYPES OF CLAIMS 62

    [A]   Independent Claims, Dependent Claims and Multiple Dependent Claims 62

    [B]   Apparatus Claims 63

    [C]   Process and Method Claims 63

    [D]   Product-By-Process Claims 64

    [E]   Composition Claims 65

    [F]   Combination Claims 65

    [G]   Means-Plus-Function Claims 65

    [H]   Markush Claims 66

    [I]   *Jepson* Claims 67

§ 4.05   CONCLUSION 68

Table of Contents

Chapter 5   **PATENT TYPES** **69**

§ 5.01   INTRODUCTION 69
§ 5.02   UTILITY PATENTS 69
§ 5.03   DESIGN PATENTS 70
§ 5.04   PLANT PATENTS 73
§ 5.05   PLANT VARIETY PROTECTION ACT CERTIFICATE 74
§ 5.06   CONCLUSION 75

Chapter 6   **ADJUDICATION OF PATENT DISPUTES WITHIN THE**
                 COURT SYSTEM **77**

§ 6.01   INTRODUCTION 77
§ 6.02   U.S. DISTRICT COURT ACTIONS 78
  [A]   Subject Matter Jurisdiction 78
  [B]   Standing to Sue for Infringement 81
  [C]   Declaratory Judgment Jurisdiction 81
  [D]   Personal Jurisdiction and Venue 82
§ 6.03   THE U.S. COURT OF APPEALS FOR THE FEDERAL CIRCUIT 84
  [A]   Background 84
  [B]   The Jurisdiction of the Federal Circuit 85
§ 6.04   PATENT LITIGATION IN THE INTERNATIONAL TRADE
           COMMISSION 86
§ 6.05   CONCLUSION 87

Chapter 7   **OVERVIEW: THE DISCLOSURE REQUIREMENTS OF**
                 § 112 .... **89**

§ 7.01   INTRODUCTION 89
§ 7.02   HISTORY AND POLICY OF PATENT DISCLOSURE 90
§ 7.03   ASSESSING THE ADEQUACY OF THE DISCLOSURE
           REQUIREMENTS 91
§ 7.04   CONCLUSION 92

Chapter 8   **ENABLEMENT** **93**

§ 8.01   INTRODUCTION 93
§ 8.02   THE ENABLEMENT ANALYSIS 94
  [A]   Generally 94
  [B]   The Historic Perspective: *O'Reilly v. Morse* 95
  [C]   Edison's Light Bulb: *Consolidated Electric Light Co. v. McKeesport Light
             Co.* 96
  [D]   A Comparison: Bell's Telephone Patent 97
§ 8.03   ENABLEMENT AND CLAIM SCOPE 97

Table of Contents

§ 8.04   UNDUE EXPERIMENTATION   100

  [A]   The Modern Foundation of Undue Experimentation: The *Wands*
         Factors   100

§ 8.05   ENABLEMENT, PRIORITY AND TIMING   103

  [A]   The Relevant State of the Art   103

  [B]   Enablement and Priority   103

  [C]   Enablement and Patent Enforcement   104

§ 8.06   ENABLEMENT AND UTILITY   105

§ 8.07   A BRIEF NOTE: SOME ECONOMIC CONSIDERATIONS   107

§ 8.08   CONCLUSION   108

Chapter 9   **WRITTEN DESCRIPTION** **109**

§ 9.01   INTRODUCTION   109

§ 9.02   GENERAL PRINCIPLES   110

§ 9.03   *ARIAD*: THE CURRENT LEGAL STANDARD   111

§ 9.04   APPLICATION OF THE POSSESSION TEST   114

  [A]   Amendments During Prosecution   114

  [B]   Benefit Of An Earlier Filing Date   116

  [C]   Biological and Chemical Subject Matter   118

§ 9.05   COMPARISON: WRITTEN DESCRIPTION AND ENABLEMENT . . .   120

§ 9.06   CONCLUSION   122

Chapter 10   **DEFINITENESS** **123**

§ 10.01   INTRODUCTION   123

§ 10.02   "PARTICULARLY POINT OUT AND DISTINCTLY CLAIM"   124

  [A]   General Rules   124

  [B]   Differing Definiteness Standards: Patent Applications v. Issued
         Patents   125

  [C]   Assessing Whether a Claim is Definite   125

  [D]   Indefiniteness and Means Plus Function Claims   126

  [E]   Terms of Degree   127

  [F]   Remedy: Should an Indefinite Claim Be Invalidated?   128

§ 10.03   "APPLICANT REGARDS:" THE INVENTOR'S DEFINITION   129

§ 10.04   CONCLUSION   131

Chapter 11   **BEST MODE** **133**

§ 11.01   OVERVIEW   133

§ 11.02   THE BEST MODE STANDARD   134

§ 11.03   APPLICATION OF THE BEST MODE STANDARD   135

  [A]   First Prong: The Inventor's Subjective Intent   136

Table of Contents

[B]   Second Prong: Objective Examination of the Patent Disclosure 137

§ 11.04   IMPACT OF A BEST MODE VIOLATION 140

§ 11.05   CONCLUSION 141

Chapter 12   OVERVIEW OF § 102: NOVELTY, STATUTORY BARS AND DERIVATION 143

§ 12.01   INTRODUCTION 143

§ 12.02   TERMINOLOGY RELEVANT TO A § 102 ANALYSIS 144

§ 12.03   THE PRE-AIA VERSION OF SECTION 102 145

[A]   The Structure of the Former Version of § 102 145

[B]   The Historic Underpinnings of the Pre-AIA Statute 147

§ 12.04   NOVELTY AND THE AMERICA INVENTS ACT 149

§ 12.05   SECTION 102's "STRICT IDENTITY" REQUIREMENT 153

§ 12.06   INHERENCY 156

[A]   Defining Inherency 156

[B]   Accidental Inherency and Knowledge of an Inherent Property 158

[C]   Inherency and "New Use" Patents 160

§ 12.07   THE AIA: TAX STRATEGIES 162

§ 12.08   CONCLUSION 163

Chapter 13   PUBLIC KNOWLEDGE AND USE AS PRIOR ART . . . 165

§ 13.01   INTRODUCTION 165

§ 13.02   TERRITORIALITY RESTRICTIONS: "KNOWN" OR "USED" 166

§ 13.03   PRIOR KNOWLEDGE 167

[A]   Prior Knowledge Must Be "Publicly Known" 167

[B]   Knowledge Must Be Enabling 168

§ 13.04   PRIOR USE 169

[A]   What is a "Public Use"? 169

[B]   Private vs. Public Uses 172

§ 13.05   THE EXPERIMENTAL USE EXCEPTION 174

§ 13.06   PROVING PRIOR KNOWLEDGE AND USE 175

§ 13.07   CONCLUSION 178

Chapter 14   PATENTS AND PRINTED PUBLICATIONS 179

§ 14.01   INTRODUCTION 179

§ 14.02   PRINTED PUBLICATIONS 181

[A]   Background: What is a "Printed Publication" under § 102? 181

[B]   "Printed Publications" and Public Accessibility 184

[1]   Development of the "Public Accessibility" Standard 185

[2]   The Current Standard: *In re Klopfenstein* 186

Table of Contents

§ 14.03   PRIOR PATENTS   188
§ 14.04   CONCLUSION   190

Chapter 15   PRIOR SALES AND OFFERS FOR SALE   191

§ 15.01   INTRODUCTION   191
§ 15.02   ON-SALE AND THE "READY FOR PATENTING" STANDARD   193
   [A]   Introduction   193
   [B]   The U.S. Supreme Court's *Pfaff v. Wells Electronics, Inc.*   194
   [C]   Applying the Pfaff "Ready for Patenting" Standard   196
§ 15.03   DEFINING AN "OFFER FOR SALE" OR "SALE"   197
§ 15.04   LICENSES AND ON-SALE ACTIVITY   199
§ 15.05   CONCLUSION   200

Chapter 16   ABANDONMENT AND THE PRE-AIA 35 U.S.C.
                    § 102(c)   203

§ 16.01   INTRODUCTION   203
§ 16.02   HISTORIC BACKGROUND OF ABANDONMENT   204
§ 16.03   PATENTEE DELAY   205
§ 16.04   ABANDONED INVENTION v. ABANDONED APPLICATION   206
§ 16.05   DISCLOSED BUT UNCLAIMED SUBJECT MATTER   206
§ 16.06   CONCLUSION   207

Chapter 17   PRIOR PATENTS   209

§ 17.01   INTRODUCTION   209
§ 17.02   OPERATION OF THE PRE-AIA 35 U.S.C. § 102(d)   210
§ 17.03   IDENTIFYING PRIOR ART THAT IS "PATENTED"   211
§ 17.04   CLAIM SCOPE AND VALIDITY OF THE FOREIGN PATENT   212
§ 17.05   WHEN IS A FOREIGN INVENTION "PATENTED?"   214
§ 17.06   DISTINCTION BETWEEN § 102(d) AND THE "PATENTED"
           PROVISIONS OF §§ 102(a) & (b)   215
§ 17.07   CONCLUSION   215

Chapter 18   EARLIER FILED PATENTS AND APPLICATIONS . . .   217

§ 18.01   INTRODUCTION   217
§ 18.02   U.S. PATENT APPLICATIONS   218
   [A]   Origins of U.S. Patents as Prior Art   218
   [B]   *In re Hilmer*: Prior U.S. Patents and Foreign Filings   221
§ 18.03   PATENT APPLICATIONS FILED UNDER THE PATENT COOPERATION
           TREATY   224
§ 18.04   PUBLISHED PATENT APPLICATIONS   225

Table of Contents

§ 18.05   CONCLUSION 225

Chapter 19   DERIVATION AND INVENTORSHIP 227

§ 19.01   INTRODUCTION 227
§ 19.02   INVENTORSHIP 228
   [A]   Who is an Inventor under the Patent Act? 228
   [B]   Joint Inventors and Ownership 230
   [C]   Filing a Patent Application: The Inventor's Oath 231
§ 19.03   WHAT IS "DERIVATION"? 231
   [A]   The Legal Standard for Derivation 231
   [B]   Application of § 102(f)'s Two-Prong Test 232
§ 19.04   DERIVATION ACTIONS UNDER THE AIA 234
§ 19.05   CORRECTION OF INVENTORSHIP 235
§ 19.06   CONCLUSION 236

Chapter 20   THE FIRST TO INVENT SYSTEM 237

§ 20.01   INTRODUCTION 238
§ 20.02   STRUCTURE AND OPERATION 239
§ 20.03   CONCEPTION AND REDUCTION TO PRACTICE 240
   [A]   Conception 240
      [1]   Complete Conception 241
      [2]   Conception: Inventor Recognition and Appreciation of the
             Invention 242
      [3]   Utility is Not Required to Establish Conception 243
      [4]   Conception's Corroboration Requirement 243
   [B]   Reduction to Practice 244
      [1]   Actual Reduction to Practice 244
      [2]   Reduction to Practice: All Elements Requirement 244
      [3]   Reduction to Practice: Demonstrating that the Invention Works for Its
             Intended Purpose 245
      [4]   Inventor's Appreciation and Recognition of the Invention's Utility . . 246
      [5]   Constructive Reduction to Practice 247
   [C]   Simultaneous Conception and Reduction to Practice 248
§ 20.04   PRIORITY RULES UNDER § 102(g) 249
   [A]   General Rule: The First to Reduce to Practice Has Priority 249
   [B]   Diligence and the First to Conceive 249
§ 20.05   "ABANDONED, SUPRESSED OR CONCEALED" 252
   [A]   Overview of the Doctrine and Policy 252
   [B]   Intentional Abandonment, Suppression or Concealment 252
   [C]   Patentee Delay and an Inference of Abandonment, Suppression or
          Concealment 253

Table of Contents

[D]   Patentee's Resumed Activity Negating a Finding of Abandonment,
        Suppression or Concealment   254
§ 20.06   CONCLUSION   255

Chapter 21   NONOBVIOUSNESS   257

§ 21.01   INTRODUCTION   257
§ 21.02   THE ORIGINS OF THE NONOBVIOUSNESS REQUIREMENT   259
[A]   Patentability Standards Prior to the Enactment of § 103   259
[B]   Origins of the Secondary Considerations of Nonobviousness   261
[C]   The Former "Flash of Creative Genius" Standard   261
§ 21.03   NONOBVIOUSNESS ANALYTIC FRAMEFORK: *GRAHAM v. JOHN
        DEERE*   263
§ 21.04   HOW IS PRIOR ART USED UNDER § 103?   265
§ 21.05   BACKGROUND: COMBINING MULTIPLE REFERENCES   266
§ 21.06   CURRENT LAW: *KSR INT'L CO. v. TELEFLEX INC.*   268
§ 21.07   OBVIOUS TO TRY: *IN RE KUBIN*   272
§ 21.08   DETERMINING THE SCOPE AND CONTENT OF THE PRIOR ART .   273
[A]   What is "Prior Art" Under § 103?   273
[B]   A Reference Must Constitute Analogous Art   276
§ 21.09   SECONDARY CONSIDERATIONS OF NONOBVIOUSNESS   278
§ 21.10   NONOBVIOUSNESS AND COMBINATION CLAIMS   281
§ 21.11   CONCLUSION   282

Chapter 22   UTILITY   283

§ 22.01   INTRODUCTION   283
§ 22.02   OPERABLE UTILITY   285
§ 22.03   SPECIFIC OR PRACTICAL UTILITY   286
[A]   The Historical Context for the Modern Utility Standard   286
[B]   U.S. Supreme Court Sets § 101's Utility Standard: *Brenner v. Manson* .   288
[C]   Subsequent Development of the *Brenner* Utility Standard   289
§ 22.04   MORAL UTILITY   292
§ 22.05   SOME ECONOMIC CONSIDERATIONS RELATING TO THE UTILITY
        REQUIREMENT   294
§ 22.06   CONCLUSION   295

Chapter 23   STATUTORY SUBJECT MATTER   297

§ 23.01   INTRODUCTION   297
§ 23.02   PRODUCTS OF NATURE   298
[A]   History: Products of Nature and Natural Phenomenon   299
[B]   Products Made from Living Things: *Parke-Davis & Co. v. H.K. Mulford*

Table of Contents

	Co.	300
[C]	Products of Nature v. Living Things: The Supreme Court's *Diamond v. Chakrabarty*	301
[D]	Claims Derived from Nature: *Mayo v. Prometheus*	303
[E]	Emerging Issues: The *Myriad* Case	305
§ 23.03	ABSTRACT SUBJECT MATTER, BUSINESS METHODS AND SOFTWARE	307
[A]	Introduction	307
[B]	*Gottschalk v. Benson*	308
[C]	*Parker v. Flook*	309
[D]	*Diamond v. Diehr*	310
[E]	Patentable Subject Matter at the Federal Circuit	311
[F]	The Federal Circuit's Restrictive Approach	313
§ 23.04	THE SUPREME COURT'S *BILSKI* OPINION	314
[A]	*Bilski* and the Prohibition on Abstract Subject Matter	314
[B]	*Bilski's* Progeny	316
§ 23.05	CONCLUSION	317

Chapter 24   PROCEDURES FOR CLAIM CONSTRUCTION   319

§ 24.01	INTRODUCTION	319
§ 24.02	COMPARISON: CLAIM INTERPRETATION AT THE U.S. PATENT & TRADEMARK OFFICE AND IN THE COURTS	321
§ 24.03	CLAIM INTERPRETATION IN THE COURTS	322
[A]	Former Law: Claim Construction Procedures	322
[B]	Current Law: *Markman v. Westview Instruments, Inc.*	323
[1]	*Markman's* Aftermath	325
§ 24.04	IMPLEMENTING *MARKMAN*	326
§ 24.05	CLAIM CONSTRUCTION AND THE ACCUSED DEVICE	328
§ 24.06	CONCLUSION	329

Chapter 25   HOW TO INTERPRET PATENT CLAIM TERMS   331

§ 25.01	INTRODUCTION	331
§ 25.02	HISTORY: FORMER APPROACHES TO CLAIM CONSTRUCTION	332
§ 25.03	THE CURRENT APPROACH: THE FEDERAL CIRCUIT'S EN BANC DECISION IN *PHILLIPS v. AWH CORP*	334
[A]	The *Phillips* Claim Construction Methodology	334
[B]	Application of the *Phillips* Claim Construction Methodology	338
§ 25.04	A CLOSER LOOK AT THE INTERACTION OF THE SPECIFICATION AND CLAIM TERMS	338
[A]	Putting a Claim Construction Analysis Together	338
[B]	The Patentee as Lexicographer: *SciMed*	340

Table of Contents

§ 25.05   CLAIM CONSTRUCTION AND VALIDITY 341

§ 25.06   CANONS OF CLAIM CONSTRUCTION 342

[A]   The Doctrine of Claim Differentiation 342

[B]   Construction of Terms in the Preamble 342

[C]   Additional Canons of Claim Construction 344

§ 25.07   CONCLUSION 345

Chapter 26   AN INTRODUCTION TO PATENT INFRINGEMENT . 347

§ 26.01   INTRODUCTION 347

§ 26.02   VIOLATION OF THE PROVISIONAL RIGHT 348

§ 26.03   OVERVIEW OF INFRINGEMENT THEORIES 349

[A]   Direct and Indirect Infringement 349

[B]   Literal Infringement and Infringement under the Doctrine of
Equivalents 350

§ 26.04   CONCLUSION 351

Chapter 27   DIRECT INFRINGEMENT 353

§ 27.01   INTRODUCTION 353

§ 27.02   TYPES OF CLAIMS AND DIRECT INFRINGEMENT 354

[A]   Product, Device and Apparatus Claims 354

[B]   Process and Method Claims 356

§ 27.03   ACTS THAT CONSTITUTE INFRINGEMENT UNDER § 271(a) 358

[A]   "Makes" 358

[B]   "Uses" 359

[C]   "Offers to Sell" 360

[D]   "Sells" 361

[E]   "Imports into the U.S." 362

§ 27.04   MULTIPLE INFRINGERS: DIVIDED INFRINGEMENT 362

§ 27.05   CONCLUSION 364

Chapter 28   PRIOR USE RIGHTS 365

§ 28.01   INTRODUCTION 365

§ 28.02   IMPLEMENTING THE PRIOR USE RIGHTS UNDER THE AIA 366

[A]   Prior Law 366

[B]   Prior use Rights Under the AIA 367

[1]   Subject Matter Scope 367

[2]   Who is a Prior User? 368

[3]   Effect of the Defense 369

[4]   The University Exclusion 369

§ 28.03   CONCLUSION 369

Table of Contents

Chapter 29   **INFRINGEMENT UNDER THE DOCTRINE OF EQUIVALENTS** **371**

§ 29.01   INTRODUCTION 371

§ 29.02   *WINANS v. DENMEAD*: THE HISTORIC FOUNDATIONS OF THE DOCTRINE OF EQUIVALENTS 373

§ 29.03   THE DEVELOPMENT OF THE CURRENT DOCTRINE OF EQUIVALENTS: *GRAVER TANK & MFG. CO. v. LINDE AIR PRODUCTS CO* 375

§ 29.04   THE U.S. SUPREME COURT'S REFINEMENT OF THE DOCTRINE OF EQUIVALENTS: *WARNER-JENKINSON CO. v. HILTON DAVIS CHEMICAL CO* 376

     [A]   Factual Background of the *Warner-Jenkinson* Opinion 376

     [B]   *Warner-Jenkinson's* Affirmation of the Doctrine of Equivalents 377

     [C]   *Warner-Jenskinson* and the Principle Prosecution History Estoppel ... 378

     [D]   The Doctrine of Equivalents and After-Arising Technology 379

§ 29.05   TESTS FOR INFRINGEMENT IN A POST-*WARNER-JENKINSON* ERA 380

§ 29.06   PUTTING THE DOCTRINE TOGETHER: AN EXAMPLE OF THE APPLICATION OF THE *WARNER-JENKINSON* STANDARD 383

§ 29.07   THE REVERSE DOCTRINE OF EQUIVALENTS 384

§ 29.08   CONCLUSION 385

Chapter 30   **RESTRICTIONS ON THE DOCTRINE OF EQUIVALENTS** **387**

§ 30.01   INTRODUCTION 387

§ 30.02   PROSECUTION HISTORY ESTOPPEL: THE *FESTO* CASES 388

     [A]   Overview of the Doctrine of Prosecution History Estoppel 388

     [B]   *Festo*: The Ground Rules of Prosecution History Estoppel 389

     [C]   *Festo*: The Federal Circuit's Refinement 392

     [D]   Putting the *Festo* Analysis Together: Application of the Doctrine of Prosecution History Estoppel 393

§ 30.03   ADDITIONAL RESTRICTION ON THE DOCTRINE OF EQUIVALENTS: AN EQUIVALENT CANNOT ENCOMPASS THE PRIOR ART 394

§ 30.04   THE PUBLIC DEDICATION RULE 395

§ 30.05   THE DOCTRINE OF EQUIVALENTS CANNOT VITIATE AN ENTIRE CLAIM ELEMENT 396

§ 30.06   CONCLUSION 397

Chapter 31   **CLAIM CONSTRUCTION OF MEAN PLUS FUNCTION CLAIM TERMS** **399**

§ 31.01   INTRODUCTION 399

§ 31.02   IDENTIFYING A "MEANS PLUS FUNCTION" CLAIM TERM 401

Table of Contents

§ 31.03   EXAMPLE: CLAIM CONSTRUCTION UNDER § 112, ¶ 6 402

§ 31.04   LITERAL INFRINGEMENT ANALYSIS FOR MEANS PLUS FUNCTION CLAIMS 404

   [A]   Literal Infringement of Claims Governed by § 112, ¶ 6 405

   [B]   Literal Infringement and After-Arising Technologies 407

   [C]   Application of the Literal Infringement Standard for Claims Governed by § 112, ¶ 6 Governing Rules: *Al-Site Corp. v. VSI Int'l, Inc.* 407

§ 31.05   INFRINGEMENT OF A MEANS PLUS FUNCTION CLAIM UNDER THE DOCTRINE OF EQUIVALENTS 408

   [A]   Doctrine of Equivalents and Functional Claims 408

   [B]   A Comparison of "Equivalent Structure" for § 112, ¶ 6 Limitations: Literal and Doctrine of Equivalents Infringement 410

§ 31.06   CONCLUSION 411

Chapter 32   EXPERIMENTAL USE **413**

§ 32.01   INTRODUCTION 413

§ 32.02   COMMON LAW EXPERIMENTAL USE 414

   [A]   The Origins of Common Law Experimental Use 414

   [B]   Current Standards: Common Law Experimental Use 415

§ 32.03   STATUTORY EXPERIMENTAL USE: 35 U.S.C. § 271(e) 418

   [A]   The Background and Structure of Statutory Experimental Use 418

   [B]   Statutory Experimental Use and the FDA Approval Process 419

   [C]   The Supreme Court's Construction of Statutory Experimental Use: *Merck KGaA v. Integra Lifesciences I, Ltd.* 420

§ 32.04   CONCLUSION 421

Chapter 33   CONTRIBUTORY INFRINGEMENT **423**

§ 33.01   INTRODUCTION 423

§ 33.02   POLICY ISSUES RELATING TO CONTRIBUTORY INFRINGEMENT 425

§ 33.03   "A MATERIAL PART OF THE INVENTION" 426

§ 33.04   KNOWLEDGE OF USE FOR INFRINGEMENT 426

§ 33.05   SUBSTANTIAL NONINFRINGING USES 427

§ 33.06   DIRECT INFRINGEMENT 430

§ 33.07   CONCLUSION 431

Chapter 34   ACTIVE INDUCEMENT **433**

§ 34.01   INTRODUCTION 433

§ 34.02   INTENT TO INDUCE INFRINGEMENT 435

§ 34.03   CONDUCT THAT INDUCES INFRINGEMENT 437

§ 34.04   DIRECT INFRINGEMENT BY ANOTHER 437

Table of Contents

§ 34.05   CONCLUSION 438

Chapter 35   **EXTRATERRITORIAL ACTIVITY AND PATENT**
                        INFRINGEMENT **439**

§ 35.01   INTRODUCTION 440
§ 35.02   SECTION 271(a) AND EXTRATERRITORIAL ACTIVITY 441
   [A]   Infringing Uses: *NTP, Inc. v. Research in Motion, Ltd.* 441
   [B]   The Locus of an Infringing Offer to Sell and Infringing Sales 443
      [1]   Offers for Sale and Sales Outside the U.S. 443
      [2]   Extra-Territorial Activity Directed toward the U.S. 444
§ 35.03   EXPORTING COMPONENTS FROM THE U.S. 444
   [A]   "Makes" and Extraterritorial Activity: *Deepsouth Packing Co. v. Laitram
          Corp.* 444
   [B]   The Enactment of Section 271(f): Closing the *Deepsouth* Loophole . . . 446
   [C]   Interpretation of Section 271(f): What is a "Component of a Patented
          Invention"? 447
      [1]   Designs and Plans 448
      [2]   Tangible Items and Section 271(f): Software 448
      [3]   Method Claims and Section 271(f) 450
§ 35.04   SECTION 271(G) AND THE IMPORTATION OF PRODUCTS
          INCORPORATING U.S. PATENTED INVENTIONS 451
   [A]   The Enactment of Section 271(g) 451
   [B]   The Operation of Section 271(g) 452
§ 35.05   INFRINGEMENT ACTIONS BEFORE THE U.S. INTERNATIONAL
          TRADE COMMISSION 455
   [A]   The Jurisdiction of the International Trade Commission 455
   [B]   The International Trade Commission Process 455
   [C]   Section 271(g) and Patent Infringement in the International Trade
          Commission 457
§ 35.06   CONCLUSION 458

Chapter 36   **INEQUITABLE CONDUCT AND THE DUTY TO**
                        DISCLOSE **459**

§ 36.01   INTRODUCTION 459
§ 36.02   INEQUITABLE CONDUCT: HISTORY AND POLICY 460
   [A]   Origins in Equity 460
   [B]   Development of Inequitable Conduct 463
§ 36.03   THE CURRENT STANDARD FOR INEQUITABLE CONDUCT 464
   [A]   *Therasense*: Intent to Deceive 465
   [B]   A Closer Examination of the Materiality Standard 466
   [C]   Application of the *Therasense* Standard 466

Table of Contents

§ 36.04   REGULATION OF ATTORNEY CONDUCT BY THE U.S. PATENT &
           TRADEMARK OFFICE 467
§ 36.05   SUPPLEMENTAL EXAMINATION AND INEQUITABLE
           CONDUCT 469
§ 36.06   CONCLUSION 469

Chapter 37   PATENT MISUSE 471

§ 37.01   INTRODUCTION 471
§ 37.02   THE ORIGINS OF THE PATENT MISUSE DOCTRINE 472
   [A]   Early Common Law Roots 472
   [B]   The *Mercoid* Cases: Patent Misuse and Contributory Infringement ... 474
§ 37.03   THE 1952 PATENT ACT: *DAWSON CHEMICAL v. ROHM & HAAS* .. 475
§ 37.04   THE 1988 AMENDMENTS TO THE PATENT ACT: REFUSALS TO
           LICENSE AND MARKET POWER 476
§ 37.05   INCREASING THE TEMPORAL SCOPE OF A PATENT LICENSE .. 478
§ 37.06   TYING AND PATENT POOLS 480
§ 37.07   CONCLUSION 482

Chapter 38   PATENTS AND ANTITRUST LAW 483

§ 38.01   INTRODUCTION 483
§ 38.02   TYING CLAIMS 485
   [A]   Defining the Relevant Terminology: Tying, Per Se Illegality and the Rule of
              Reason 485
   [B]   The Evolving Jurisprudence of Patent Tying Cases 487
§ 38.03   UNILATERAL REFUSALS TO LICENSE A PATENT 489
§ 38.04   SETTLEMENTS AND REVERSE PAYMENTS 492
§ 38.05   PATENT INFRINGEMENT LITIGATION AND THE SHAM
           EXCEPTION 495
   [A]   Background: Anticompetitive Patent Infringement Litigation: *Handgards,
              Inc. v. Ethicon, Inc.* 495
   [B]   The First Amendment and *Noerr-Pennington* Immunity 496
   [C]   The Sham Exception to *Noerr-Pennington* Immunity 496
§ 38.06   FRAUDULENT PROCUREMENT OF A PATENT: *WALKER PROCESS*
           CLAIMS 498
§ 38.07   CONCLUSION 500

Chapter 39   EXHAUSTION AND THE FIRST SALE DOCTRINE ... 501

§ 39.01   INTRODUCTION 501
§ 39.02   FIRST SALE AND EXHAUSTION 502
§ 39.03   EXHAUSTION: UNAUTHORIZED AND FOREIGN SALES 505
§ 39.04   POST SALE RESTRICTIONS 505

Table of Contents

§ 39.05   THE DOCTRINE OF REPAIR/RECONSTRUCTION   507

[A]   The Analytic Framework   507

[B]   The Sequential Replacement of Parts   508

§ 39.06   REPLACEMENTS THAT ARE "AKIN TO REPAIR": *HUSKY INJECTION MOLDING SYSTEMS, LTD. v. R & D TOOL ENGINEERING CO*   509

§ 39.07   CONCLUSION   510

Chapter 40   PROSECUTION LACHES **511**

§ 40.01   INTRODUCTION   511

§ 40.02   THE HISTORIC FOUNDATIONS OF PROSECUTION LACHES   514

§ 40.03   THE CURRENT STANDARD   515

[A]   Delay   515

[B]   Prejudice   517

§ 40.04   CONCLUSION   518

Chapter 41   REMEDIES FOR PATENT INFRINGEMENT **519**

§ 41.01   INTRODUCTION   520

§ 41.02   INJUNCTIVE RELIEF   521

[A]   Permanent Injunctive Relief   521

[1]   Statutory Basis and Former Law   521

[2]   The Current Standard: *eBay v. MercExchange*   522

[3]   Application of the *eBay* Standard   523

[5]   Compensation for Ongoing Infringement   525

[B]   Preliminary Injunctions   525

§ 41.03   MONETARY RELIEF: STATUTORY BACKGROUND   526

§ 41.04   MONETARY RELIEF: LOST PROFITS   527

[A]   The *Panduit* Test: Proof of a Causal Relationship to Infringement   527

[B]   Spotlight on the Second *Panduit* Factor: Availability of Non-Infringing Alternatives   529

[C]   Lost Profits: Price Erosion   530

[D]   Market Share Calculation of Lost Profits   530

§ 41.05   MONETARY RELIEF: REASONABLE ROYALTY   532

[A]   Established Royalty   532

[B]   The Analytic Approach   533

[C]   The Reasonable Royalty Based on a Hypothetical Negotiation   533

§ 41.06   MONETARY RELIEF: ADDITIONAL CONSIDERATIONS   536

[A]   The Entire Market Value Rule   536

[B]   Patentee Delay and the Ability to Recover Monetary Relief   538

[C]   Actual and Constructive Notice/Marking   539

§ 41.07   WILLFUL INFRINGEMENT AND EXCEPTIONAL CASES   540

§ 41.08   PREJUDGEMENT INTEREST   542

Table of Contents

§ 41.09   CONCLUSION   542

Chapter 42   **INTERNATIONAL TREATIES AND THE
                      GLOBALIZATION OF PATENTS** **543**

§ 42.01   INTRODUCTION   543
§ 42.02   THE PARIS CONVENTION OF 1883   544
§ 42.03   COORDINATION OF PATENT APPLICATION FILING: THE PATENT
           COOPERATION TREATY AND THE EUROPEAN PATENT
           CONVENTION   545
§ 42.04   TRIPS: THE WORLD TRADE ORGANIZATION AND THE AGREEMENT
           ON TRADE-RELATED ASPECTS OF INTELLECTUAL PROPERTY
           RIGHTS   546
§ 42.05   CONCLUSION   548

           GLOSSARY **549**

TABLE OF CASES **TC-1**

INDEX **I-1**

Chapter 1

INTRODUCTION TO THE PATENT SYSTEM

SYNOPSIS

§ 1.01   THE PATENT RIGHT

§ 1.02   HISTORY AND ORIGINS OF THE PATENT RIGHT

   [A]   Early European Patent Systems

   [B]   The British Patent System and the Statute of Monopolies

§ 1.03   U.S. CONSTITUTIONAL BASIS: ADOPTION OF THE COPYRIGHT AND PATENT CLAUSE

   [A]   The Patent System and the U.S. Constitution

   [B]   Congressional Adoption of the Patent System

   [C]   Current Events: The America Invents Act of 2011

§ 1.04   FOUNDATIONS OF MODERN U.S. PATENT LAW

   [A]   The Legal Foundation of Patent Rights

   [B]   Patent Rights as an Appropriation Mechanism

   [C]   Incentives and Patent Law

§ 1.05   HOW DOES THE PATENT "RIGHT TO EXCLUDE" OPERATE?

§ 1.06   WHAT DOES ONE DO WITH A PATENT?

§ 1.07   CONCLUSION

§ 1.01   THE PATENT RIGHT

A *patent* is a right granted by the government that allows the patent owner to exclude others from practicing the invention during its term. This right is grounded in the U.S. Constitution, which has authorized Congress to create protection for inventive works. Pursuant to this power, Congress has enacted legislation, set forth at Title 35 of the U.S. Code, which provides the foundation for an inventor's ability to obtain patent protection for new and useful ideas.

To obtain a utility patent, one must submit an application to the U.S. Patent & Trademark Office (the "U.S. PTO"), the federal agency responsible for patent examination.[1] The U.S. PTO's review considers whether the application includes all

---

[1] The U.S. Patent & Trademark Offices issues three types of patents: 1) utility patents; 2) plant patents; and 3) design patents. Of these, utility patents are by far the most prevalent and are the primary focus of patent law courses and this book. *See generally* Chapter 5 (describing the different types of patents).

information required by the Patent Act. Such information includes a detailed *disclosure* of the invention including how the invention can be made and used by others in the field.[2] This disclosure must demonstrate the invention's *utility*.[3] In addition, the applicant must include at least one *claim* that provides notice of the elements of the asserted invention.[4] The claimed invention must be *novel*[5] and must fall within the purview of the Patent Act's *statutory subject matter*[6] — that is, the invention must be among the types of advances that are authorized for protection under the patent system. Further, the claimed invention must meet the *nonobviousness*[7] requirement, such that the application does not claim subject matter that would be obvious to those in the art.

If the requirements of patent law are met and the U.S. PTO issues a patent based on the application, the right becomes enforceable against infringers. A patentee may then choose to assert the right, for example by filing an infringement action in a U.S. District Court. If successful, the owner may obtain monetary relief and, under certain conditions, an injunction against further infringement. Subject to certain exceptions, under current law a patent has an effective life of twenty (20) years from the application's filing date.[8]

§ 1.02 HISTORY AND ORIGINS OF THE PATENT RIGHT

[A] Early European Patent Systems

Some early patent systems existed well before U.S. patent law was contemplated. The earliest patent statute was passed in 1474 in the City of Venice. This statute provided a right to "every person who shall build any new and ingenious device in this City, not previously made in our Commonwealth," upon notice that the invention "has been reduced to perfection so that it can be used and operated."[9] Such inventions appeared to have been subject to an examination procedure to determine compliance with statutory requirements.[10] If the right was infringed, the inventor was entitled to a penalty of one hundred ducats and an order that the infringing device be destroyed.[11]

---

[2] 35 U.S.C. § 112 (2000); *see generally* Scott Paper Co. v. Marcalus Mfg. Co., 326 U.S. 249, 254 (1945) ("The [patent] grant is conditioned upon the filing of an application in the patent office describing the invention and the manner of making and using it."). *See also infra* Chapters 7-11 (describing patent disclosure requirements).

[3] 35 U.S.C. § 101; *see infra* Chapter 22.

[4] 35 U.S.C. § 112; *see infra* Chapter 10.

[5] 35 U.S.C. § 102; *see infra* Chapter 12.

[6] 35 U.S.C. § 101; *see infra* Chapter 23.

[7] 35 U.S.C. § 103; *see infra* Chapter 21.

[8] 35 U.S.C. § 154(a)(2).

[9] *Reproduced in* Edward C. Walterscheid, *The Early Evolution of the United States Patent Law: Antecedents (Part 1)*, 76 J. Pat. & Trademark Off. Soc'y 697, 709 (1994).

[10] Frank D. Prager, *A History of Intellectual Property from 1545-1787*, 26 J. Pat. Off. Soc'y, 711, 716 (1944).

[11] Walterscheid, *supra* note 9, at 709.

During the late fifteenth and sixteenth centuries, a number of other European countries developed the practice of issuing patents.[12] For example, an early French patent system provided the rights holder a "privilege to operate according to his invention,"[13] and an additional right that prohibited others from copying. Also, the French instituted an examination procedure that called for scientific evaluation of a proposed invention, although in practice it appeared that a number of patents were granted without taking advantage of this resource.[14] As another example, during the sixteenth and seventeenth centuries, the Netherlands instituted a patent custom that, at certain times in its history, required a written specification or model as proof of the invention's existence.[15]

The existence of early European systems was not without controversy.[16] Some nations resisted enacting any form of patent protection until the latter part of the nineteenth century.[17] However, nations that adopted early systems included features that have become central to the U.S. patent system. These include a requirement that the inventor had created a solution to a practical problem, an examination system, and the principle that a patent signified a legal right to exclude others from practicing the invention.

[B] The British Patent System and the Statute of Monopolies

In several important respects, the U.S. patent system was crafted to reflect lessons learned from an earlier system implemented by Great Britain. As background, the term "patent" was used in that country to refer to more than the rights granted to inventors. As to its derivation, "[p]atent, the adjective, means 'open,' and patent, the noun, is the customary abbreviation of 'open letter.' "[18] In Elizabethan times, "letters patent" — a translation of the Latin term *litterae patentes* — referred to all types of directives that were openly and publicly made, in contrast to "letters close" which were kept private.[19] Letters patent included a

---

[12] *Id.* at 711.

[13] Prager, *supra* note 10, at 724.

[14] *Id.* at 725. For more about the development of the French patent system, see Gabriel Galvez-Behar, *Was the French Patent System Democratic?*, Institut de Recherches Historiques du Septentrion (IRHiS) (2008).

[15] Walterscheid, *supra* note 9, at 714. Although in 1869 the Netherlands repealed this practice under the view that "a good law of patents is an impossibility," the country reinstated a patent system some years later in 1910. STAFF OF S. SUBCOMM. ON PATENTS, TRADEMARKS, AND COPYRIGHTS, 85TH CONG., AN ECONOMIC REVIEW OF THE PATENT SYSTEM 4-5 (Comm. Print 1958) [hereinafter "Economic Review"] (prepared by Fritz Machlup).

[16] John F. Duffy, *Harmony And Diversity In Global Patent Law*, 17 BERKELEY TECH. L.J. 685, 713 (2002); *See generally* ERICH KAUFER, THE ECONOMICS OF THE PATENT SYSTEM 1, 8-10 (1989) (detailing an anti-patent movement in Europe during the 1800's)k.

[17] *See* F.M. Scherer, *The Political Economy of Patent Policy Reform in the United States*, 7 J. TELECOMM. & HIGH TECH. L. 167, 168-69 (2009).

[18] ECONOMIC REVIEW, *supra* note 15, at 1.

[19] Walterscheid, *supra* note 9, at 700-01 ("letters patent, that is, open letters, *literae patentes*: so called, because they are not sealed up, but exposed to open view, with the great seal pendant at the bottom; and are usually directed or addressed by the king to all his subjects at large", *quoting* WILLIAM

variety of rights and privileges issued as a matter of royal prerogative,[20] such as grants of office, pardons, rights, titles or monopolies.[21]

Between 1561 and 1600, Elizabeth I granted at least 51 patents of monopoly.[22] Although some appeared to have been granted to protect novel inventions, a number were granted to bring knowledge and skills developed in other regions to benefit Great Britain's local economy.[23] The crown granted the latter type to foster importation of foreign industries that could be practiced within the realm. In return for these monopoly grants, the recipient was expected "not only to introduce the new art, trade or industry within England but also to practice or 'work' it within the country."[24]

In addition, Elizabeth I granted a number of monopoly patents to her courtiers for trades and industries that were already practiced domestically. These patents, which became known as odious monopolies, included the right to control long-established businesses such as white soap, ovens and furnaces, salt, mining certain metals and ores, playing cards and ale.[25] As a consequence, rights holders were able to charge high prices for these commodities.[26] Because of its effect on the nation's citizens, Elizabeth I's practices led to considerable friction between the Queen and Parliament.

In 1601, Parliament raised its strongest challenge to the odious monopolies by introducing legislation that had the potential to curtail the Queen's broad power. Elizabeth attempted to protect her authority in all spheres while accommodating Parliament's specific concerns about these problematic patents. She asked that the legislation be withdrawn in exchange for her concession that her patents could be submitted to "a Tryal according to law for the good of the People."[27] Parliament accepted this compromise, thereby subjecting the Queen's patents to the scrutiny of the common law courts. One of the most famous of these court challenges was the *Case of Monopolies (Darcy v. Allen)*,[28] which examined a challenge to a patent for playing cards. In result, the court found in favor of the accused infringer.[29] According to one report of the case, the patent was found to violate Parliament's laws that had been enacted "for the advancement of the freedom of trade and

---

BLACKSTONE, 2 COMMENTARIES ON THE LAWS OF ENGLAND 316-317 (1768)).

[20] The royal prerogative in this context refers to the crown's practice of exercising broad discretion in the grant and modification of rights with respect to commerce. *See generally* THEODORE F.T. PLUCKNETT, TASWELL-LANGMEAD'S ENGLISH CONSTITUTIONAL HISTORY, 318 (11th ed. 1960).

[21] Walterscheid, *supra* note 9, at 700-01; *see also* KAUFER, *supra* note 16, at 1.

[22] Edward C. Walterscheid, *The Early Evolution of United States Patent Law: Antecedents (Part 2)*, 76 J. PAT. & TRADEMARK OFF. SOC'Y 849, 853 (1994)

[23] Adam Mossoff, *Rethinking the Development of Patents: An Intellectual History, 1550-1800*, 52 HASTINGS L.J. 1255, 1260-61 (2001).

[24] Walterscheid, *supra* note 22, at 857.

[25] *Id.* at 854 n.14.

[26] PLUCKNETT, *supra* note 19, at 318.

[27] Walterscheid, *supra* note 22, at 866.

[28] Jacob I. Corré, *The Argument, Decision and Reports of Darcy v. Allen*, 45 EMORY L.J. 1261 (1996) (provides a comprehensive review of the decision and recognizes the uncertain grounds on which it rests).

[29] *Id.* at 1263.

traffic."[30] This description appeared to have been an effort to limit the royal prerogative against the grant of odious monopolies in favor of control by Parliament. Nonetheless, the court did not issue a written opinion and, lacking a definitive basis for the ruling, the *Case of Monopolies* did not fully end the matter.[31]

After Elizabeth's death, her successor James I continued to grant similar monopolies to members of his court.[32] In 1623, Parliament enacted the Statute of Monopolies, which declared "all monopolies and . . . letters patent heretofore made or granted . . . contrary to the laws of this realm, and so are and shall be utterly void and of none effect."[33] Significantly, the Statute specifically allowed a grant of a patent "to the true and first inventor" for "the sole working or making of any manner of new manufactures within this realm" for a maximum term of fourteen years.[34] Additionally, the Statute required that such patents "be not contrary to the law nor mischievous to the state by raising prices of commodities at home, or hurt of trade, or generally inconvenient."[35] In this manner, the Statute of Monopolies drew a distinction between odious monopolies and those that provided a public benefit by encouraging invention and new industries. By prohibiting the former and allowing the latter, the Statute of Monopolies resolved the patent controversy of the Elizabethan era.

As discussed in the next section, the principle that patents should issue for genuine contributions became a cornerstone of the American patent system. Great Britain's experience with odious monopolies demonstrated the danger of allowing rights to issue as a matter of governmental favor. The U.S. would not repeat this experience.

§ 1.03   U.S. CONSTITUTIONAL BASIS: ADOPTION OF THE COPYRIGHT AND PATENT CLAUSE

[A]   The Patent System and the U.S. Constitution

Between 1776 and 1789 when the U.S. Constitution was adopted, a number of the U.S. states issued patents that were enforceable within their borders. However, one historian estimates that these patents were few in number.[36] State patent practice ceased as a unified federal patent system developed. The Constitution's Patent and Copyright Clause, which was unanimously adopted at the

---

[30] The Case of Monopolies (Darcy v. Allen), (1603) 77 Eng. Rep. 1260, 1265.

[31] John F. Duffy, *Inventing Invention: A Case Study Of Legal Innovation*, 86 TEX. L. REV. 1, 26 (2007).

[32] Walterscheid, *supra* note 22, 76 J. Pat. & Trademark Off. Soc'y at 871.

[33] Statute of Monopolies, 1623, 21 Jac. 1, c. 3, sec. 1, (Eng.).

[34] *Id.* at sec. 6.

[35] *Id.*

[36] Edward C. Walterscheid, *The Early Evolution of the U.S. Patent Law: Antecedents (5, Part II)*, 78 J. PAT. & TRADEMARK OFF. SOC'Y 665, 668 (1996) (noting that "it is difficult to know precisely how many state patents were actually granted, but it is unlikely that the total exceeded forty").

Constitutional Convention of 1787,[37] authorized Congress to create a federal copyright and patent system with the express purpose:

> . . . . [t]o promote the Progress of Science and useful Arts, by securing for limited Times to Authors and Inventors the exclusive Right to their respective Writings and Discoveries.[38]

James Madison, writing in support of the clause in The Federalist Papers, noted that "the right to useful inventions seems . . . to belong to the inventors," and that the "States cannot separately make effectual provision" for such a right.[39]

In contrast, while the Constitution was under consideration for ratification by the states, Thomas Jefferson detailed his thoughts in a number of writings that have become influential to the current conception of U.S. patent law. As summarized by the U.S. Supreme Court:

> Jefferson, like other Americans, had an instinctive aversion to monopolies. It was a monopoly on tea that sparked the Revolution and Jefferson certainly did not favor an equivalent form of monopoly under the new government. His abhorrence of monopoly extended initially to patents as well. From France, he wrote to Madison (July 1788) urging a Bill of Rights provision restricting monopoly, and as against the argument that limited monopoly might serve to incite "ingenuity," he argued forcefully that the "benefit even of limited monopolies is too doubtful to be opposed to that of their general suppression."[40]

Despite these early statements, by 1807, Jefferson expressed his support for a U.S. patent system in a letter to Oliver Evans, stating "[c]ertainly an inventor ought to be allowed a right to the benefit of his invention for some certain time . . . Nobody wishes more than I do that ingenuity should receive a liberal encouragement."[41] In all, Jefferson's writings have been seen as framing an issue which is the subject of ongoing concern that continues to exist today — that is, the extent to which "the underlying policy of the patent system that 'the things which are worth to the public the embarrassment of an exclusive patent,' as Jefferson put it, must outweigh the restrictive effect of the limited patent monopoly."[42]

In 1792, Alexander Hamilton issued a report to Congress that included a suggestion that patents issue for inventions that were imported into the U.S., as formerly permitted under British law.[43] Under this suggestion, patent rights could

---

[37] *See* Tyler T. Ochoa and Mark Rose, *The Anti-Monopoly Origins of the Patent and Copyright Clause*, 84 J. Pat. & Trademark Off. Soc'y 909, 922 (2002).

[38] U.S. Const. art I, § 8.

[39] The Federalist No. 43 (James Madison).

[40] Graham v. John Deere Co., 383 U.S. 1, 8-9 (1966), *quoting* V Writings of Thomas Jefferson, at 47 (Ford ed., 1895)).

[41] *Graham*, 383 U.S. at 9 *quoting* Jefferson, *supra* note 41, at 75-76. For an analysis of Jefferson's correspondence of the Copyright and Patent Clause, *see* Justin Hughes, *Copyright And Incomplete Historiographies: Of Piracy, Propertization, And Thomas Jefferson*, 79 S. Cal. L. Rev. 993 (2006).

[42] *Graham*, 383 U.S. at 10-11.

[43] *See* P.J. Federico, *The Patent Act of 1793*, 18 J. Pat. Off. Soc'y (Special Issue) 77, 79 (1936) ("The

be granted to "the introducer as well as to the inventor."[44] Hamilton's suggestion was not adopted. Rather, the minimum standard for patentability that has been developed over the history of U.S. patent law requires that an invention be novel[45] and "evidence more ingenuity and skill than that possessed by an ordinary mechanic acquainted with the business."[46] Invention is required; mere importation is insufficient.

[B]   Congressional Adoption of the Patent System

The U.S. Constitution's Copyright and Patent Clause did not expressly create the U.S. patent system, but rather empowered the legislature to do so. Acting under this grant, Congress enacted the first Patent Act in 1790, soon after U.S. government operations began. Since that time, patent law has been exclusively federal.

The system established under the 1790 Patent Act was quite rudimentary. To obtain a patent under the first Act, an inventor was required to petition a three-person panel that consisted of the Secretary of State, the Secretary for the Department of War, and the Attorney General of the United States.[47] The Act contained explicit disclosure requirements, including that the petition must "describe the said invention or discovery, clearly, truly and fully."[48] The applicant was required to file a written specification and submit models to both "distinguish the invention or discovery from other things before known and used," and describe the invention sufficiently to enable others skilled in the art "to make, construct, or use the same."[49] Any two members of the panel could grant the petition if the invention was deemed "sufficiently useful and important."[50] Where these conditions were met, the President would "cause the seal of the United States to be thereto affixed."[51]

In 1793, the Patent Act was amended again.[52] According to one historian, those charged with examining patents were too occupied with their other duties to appropriately examine patents.[53] The 1793 amendment eliminated patent

---

encouragement of new inventions and discoveries at home is among the most useful and exception act which could govern the country. This privilege should be extended to the introducer as well as to the inventor") (quoting Hamilton's report).

[44] *Id.*

[45] *See* 35 U.S.C. § 102 (setting forth novelty requirements under current law).

[46] Graham v. John Deere Co. 383 U.S. 1, 11 (1966) (describing patentability standard established in Hotchkiss v. Greenwood, 52 U.S. 248 (1851)).

[47] Patent Act of 1790, ch. 7, § 1, 1 Stat. 109-112 (April 10, 1790). The three-person panel was known as the "Commissioners for the Promotion of Useful Arts." *Graham*, 383 U.S. at 7. As the then-Secretary of State, Thomas Jefferson was a member of this group.

[48] Patent Act of 1790, § 1.

[49] *Id.*, § 2.

[50] See *id.*, § 1.

[51] *Id.*

[52] Patent Act of 1793, ch. 11, § 1, 1 Stat. 318-323 (February 21, 1793).

[53] P.J. Frederico, *The Patent Act of 1793*, 18 J. Pat. Off. Soc'y 77 (1936) (Special Issue).

examination and allowed patents to issue upon registration.[54] Under this scheme, the Patent Office (which was established in 1802) lacked any statutory authority to examine applications on the merits.[55]

Within a few decades, Congress became concerned about the quality of granted patents and an increase in patent litigation. Because patents were issued without any meaningful assessment, the courts bore the entire burden of applying the patentability requirements.[56] In 1836, a report to the Senate observed that forty years without any examination process had resulted in "[a] considerable portion of some of the patents granted are worthless and void," and that "a great number of law suits arise, which are daily increasing in an alarming degree, onerous to the courts, ruinous to the parties, and injurious to society."[57]

That same year, Congress amended the Patent Act to authorize the Patent Office to substantively examine applications.[58] The 1836 Act directed the Patent Office to reject an application if the subject matter had been previously invented in this country, had been previously patented or described in a patent publication in this or any other country, or had been previously in public use or on sale with the applicant's consent. Additionally, the revised Patent Act authorized the creation of a board to hear administrative appeals of Patent Office rejections. Further, the Patent Office was authorized to decide interference actions to determine the rightful owner of a patent where more than one inventor claimed the same invention.[59]

The 1836 amendments had a lasting significance. By formalizing and supporting an administrative examination system, the 1836 Act laid the foundation for an application process based on specified statutory criteria. Certainly by 1836, the U.S. patent system bore little resemblance to the patent system established in Elizabethan times. The Patent Office, which began with a half dozen patent examiners,[60] now exceeds 6,000 examiners at the U.S. PTO today.[61]

[C] Current Events: The America Invents Act of 2011

Congress has amended the patent statute numerous times since it was first enacted in 1790. Some of these revisions have been minor, while others are quite significant. Recently, the America Invents Act of 2011 was passed and introduces

---

[54] *Id.*

[55] *See generally* P.J. Frederico, *The Patent Act of 1836*, 18 J. PAT. OFF. SOC'Y 91 (1936) (SPECIAL ISSUE).

[56] Oren Bracha, *The Commodification Of Patents 1600-1836: How Patents Became Rights And Why We Should Care*, 38 LOY. L.A. L. REV. 177, 228 (2005) ("the 1793 system shifted the real gravity center to ex-post review in the courts. While the issuing authority was deprived of any meaningful role, all substantive decisions regarding patents were now to be made by the courts whenever a conflict was laid at their doors.").

[57] This report is quoted in P.J. Frederico, *supra* note 55 at 93.

[58] Patent Act of 1836, ch. 357, 5 Stat. 117, § 7 (July 4, 1836).

[59] *Id.* § 8.

[60] P.J. Frederico, *Organization and Function of the Patent Office*, 18 J. PAT. OFF. SOC'Y 209 (1936).

[61] U.S. Patent & Trademark Office, *Performance and Accountability Report: Fiscal Year 2010*, at 9, available at http://www.uspto.gov/about/stratplan/ar/2010/U.S.PTOFY2010PAR.pdf.

some major shifts in patent law. A few of these include:

- A transition from a first-to-invent system to a modified first-to-file priority system;

- Modified procedures for issued patents to be administered by the U.S. PTO; and

- A prior user right defense to a charge of infringement has been implemented.

References to these and additional changes are noted throughout this book. The America Invents Act has numerous effective dates throughout. Some provisions are effective immediately; others are not scheduled to take effect for more than a year after the law's enactment.

Where relevant, both the old and new has been described throughout this book. This is because both will be practiced during the next several years. As one example, it is expected that a patent with an effective filing date on or before March 16, 2013, will be assessed under the former first-to-invent standard. However, applications filed after March 16, 2013, will be assessed under the new modified first-to-file standard. Those working with patents during the coming years will encounter patents that fit into both categories. The areas of concurrent treatment are noted in the chapters that follow.

§ 1.04   FOUNDATIONS OF MODERN U.S. PATENT LAW

What is the nature of a patent right under U.S. law? At its inception, the patent system was adopted by the Framers of the Constitution without resolution of its deeper theoretical underpinnings. Today, these questions are the subject of political and scholarly debate. A few of these issues are discussed, below.

[A]   The Legal Foundation of Patent Rights

During the 19th century, some European scholars had discussed patent rights as grounded on the theory of *natural rights*[62] for the protection of inventions. For example, in 1791 the French Constitutional assembly adopted a patent statute that adopted a natural rights theory as its theoretical foundation:

---

[62] *See generally* Fritz Machlup & Edith Penrose, *The Patent Controversy in the Nineteenth Century*, 10 J. Econ. Hist. 1, 11-17 (May 1950) (citing and summarizing various commentator's natural right justifications for patent rights). Perhaps the most prevalent natural right theory associated with intellectual property is John Locke's labor-desert theory, which was conceptualized in the context of traditional property rights. Locke's theory holds that the state should recognize a natural property right where one had labored with respect to a thing. As Locke explains:

> The "labour" of his body and the "work" of his hands, we may say, are properly his. Whatsoever, then, he removes out of this state that Nature hath provided and left it in, he hath mixed his labor with it, and joined to it something that is his own, and thereby makes it his property.

John Locke, Two Treatises on Government 12 (3d ed. 1698). For an application of this theory to modern intellectual property law cases, *see, e.g.*, Wendy J. Gordon, *A Property Right In Self-Expression: Equality And Individualism In The Natural Law Of Intellectual Property*, 102 Yale L.J. 1533 (1993).

. . . that every novel idea whose realization or development can become useful to society belongs primarily to him who conceived it, and that it would be a violation of the rights of man in their very essence if an industrial invention were not regarded as the property of its creator.[63]

Some early references to a natural law justification for U.S. patent law also exist.[64] Taking a contrary position, in 1813, Thomas Jefferson wrote:

Stable ownership is the gift of social law, and is given late in the progress of society. It would be curious then, if an idea, the fugitive fermentation of an individual brain, could, of natural right, be claimed in exclusive and stable property.[65]

Jefferson's statements were resurrected in the U.S. Supreme Court's 1966 *Graham v. John Deere Co.*, which defined patent rights in utilitarian terms, as a system intended to grant a patent as "a reward, an inducement, to bring forth new knowledge."[66] The *Graham* Court underscored that Jefferson had rejected a natural rights basis for the patent system in favor of the "social and economic rationale of the patent system."[67] Thus, regardless of the amount labor invested in an invention, according to the Court "[o]nly inventions and discoveries which furthered human knowledge, and were new and useful, justified the special inducement of a limited private monopoly."[68]

The principle that the patent right is a government grant, rather than a natural right, is a prevalent theme of current law. The U.S. Supreme Court in the 1834 decision *Wheaton v. Peters* considered a related point.[69] The issue presented in *Wheaton* concerned whether an author possessed a perpetual common law copyright that was enforceable in equity. To determine the dispute, the Court considered whether such authors and inventors had rights that were pre-existent under the common law or instead had been created pursuant to federal statutory law as authorized by the Constitutional grant. Focusing on the term "securing"[70] in the Copyright and Patent Clause, *Wheaton* found the rights purely statutory in creation, explaining:

---

[63] Quoted in Malchup & Penrose, *supra* note 62, at 11 (citing Law of January 7, 1791, in ANTON SCHULLER, HANDBUCH DER GESETZE UBER AUSSCHLIESSENDE PRIVILEGIEN AUF NEUE ERFINDECKUNGEN UND VERBESSERUNGEN IM GEBIETE DER INDUSTRIE (Vienna, 1843).

[64] *See* Frederico, *supra* note 53 at 80-81 (describing legislative debates, including the statements of Mr. Murray "that an inventor has a natural right to the inventions he may make"). For an argument that the early development of American patent law was guided by natural rights principles, *see* Adam Mossoff, *Who Cares What Thomas Jefferson Thought About Patents? Reevaluating the Patent 'Privilege' in Historical Context*, 92 CORNELL L. REV. 953 (2007).

[65] Graham v. John Deere Co. 383 U.S. 1, 9 n.2 (1966), *quoting* VI WRITINGS OF THOMAS JEFFERSON, at 180-181 (Washington ed.).

[66] *Id.*

[67] *Id.* at 8-9.

[68] *Id.* at 9.

[69] *See* 33 U.S. 591 (1834).

[70] The Copyright and Patent Clause reads that Congress has the power "To promote the Progress of Science and useful Arts, by securing for limited Times to Authors and Inventors the exclusive Right to their respective Writings and Discoveries." U.S. CONST. Art. I, Sec. 8 (emphasis added).

. . . [n]o one can deny that when the legislature are about to vest an exclusive right in an author or an inventor, they have the power to prescribe the conditions on which such right shall be enjoyed; and that no one can avail himself of such right who does not substantially comply with the requisitions of the law.[71]

Although *Wheaton* considered the issue in deciding an issue of copyright law, the case has been read to firmly establish the federal statutory nature of the patent right.[72]

[B] Patent Rights as an Appropriation Mechanism

Why is legal protection needed to "secure[e] for limited Times to . . . Inventors the exclusive Right to their respective . . . Discoveries"?[73] To some degree, the answer lies in the problem raised by the intangible nature of inventions. As a practical matter, rights to tangible goods, such as real or personal property, have attributes that permit the disposition of ownership and exclusion based on principles that are well established in the law. These rules seem less suited to regulating ideas and information.

This is because tangible goods are rivalrous — that is, possession of a good by one prevents possession by another. Thus, many of the rules for tangible property operate to resolve rival claims to the same thing. For example, under established legal rules, one with the right to possess real property can fence out trespassers or otherwise obtain a court order of exclusion. Similarly, disputes about possession of an item of tangible personal property — such as a valuable painting — can be resolved by a court decision that orders transfer of the painting to the rightful possessor.

Intangibles do not easily fit within this construct because they are non-rivalrous — that is, one person's possession of the idea does not diminish another's ability to share and possess that same idea. Simply stated, one cannot "fence out" another from using an idea after the information has been disclosed. Jefferson eloquently recognized this in a letter dated 1807:

. . . . the action of the thinking power called an idea, which an individual may exclusively possess as long as he keeps it to himself; but the moment it is divulged, it forces itself into the possession of every one, and the receiver cannot dispossess himself of it. Its peculiar character, too, is that no one possesses the less, because every other possesses the whole of it. He who receives an idea from me, receives instruction himself without lessening mine; as he who lights his taper at mine, receives light without darkening me.[74]

---

[71] *Wheaton*, 33 U.S. at 663-64.

[72] *See e.g.*, Sears, Roebuck & Co. v. Stiffel Co., 376 U.S. 225, 229 n. 5 (1964).

[73] U.S. CONST. art I, § 8.

[74] *Graham*, 383 U.S. at 9 n.2, *quoting* Letter to Oliver Evans (May 1807), V WRITINGS OF THOMAS JEFFERSON, at 75-76 (Washington ed.).

As this passage makes clear, information can easily be given away at low or no cost.[75] This is particularly true today, when methods for reverse engineering products have become sophisticated. For example, one who develops and discloses a substance that can prevent the common cold can expect that others who learn of the formula to desire to sell a competing copy. In the absence of patent protection, disclosing the formula, even once, might destroy the information's entire value and deprive the inventor of the cost of its research and development.[76]Unlike tangible property, many people can use the same information at the same time. However, it might be expected that one would never invest in formulating the solution in the first instance if doing so gives the inventor no advantage in the market.

Patents are thought to solve some of these problems by acting as an appropriation mechanism. In operation, the patent system creates a legally enforceable right to protect ideas similarly to the manner in which a fence surrounds real property.[77] The patent right allows inventors and inventing firms to exclude others from practicing the invention disclosed in the patent by providing the patent owner with the ability to assert the right against infringers.[78] The right to enforce preserves the value of the information, because although one learns the information from reading the patent, one cannot practice the patent without infringing the right.

Another dimension to the nonrivalrous nature of information has been recognized in Arrow's Information Paradox.[79] This insight recognizes that those interested in purchasing information cannot ascertain its value without full disclosure, but once full disclosure has been made the purchaser has learned the information without making any payment. For example, one who wishes to purchase a formula to a drug to prevent the common cold will want to examine the information to determine the appropriate price. However, once the interested purchaser learns the information, she no longer has an incentive to pay for what has already been freely revealed. Appropriability assists in resolving Arrow's Information Paradox. That is, the patent right permits owners to share a fully disclosed invention with a potential purchaser, such that both parties can attempt to fully assess the value of the right while mitigating the concern that disclosure will lead to the devaluation of the idea.

In addition, some patents claim inventions for which there are few or no economic substitutes. For the owners of such patents, the patent right translates into the ability to charge more for products that incorporate these inventions. As one court has explained, "[p]atentees value the right to exclude in part because the ability to

---

[75] Suzanne Scotchmer, *Standing on the Shoulders of Giants: Cumulative Research and the Patent Law*, 5 J. ECON. PERSP. 29, 35 (1991); *see also* Kenneth J. Arrow, *Economic Welfare and the Allocation of Resources for Invention*, *in* THE RATE AND DIRECTION OF INVENTIVE ACTIVITY 609, 614-615 (National Bureau of Economic Research, 1962), available at www.nber.org/chapters/c2144.pdf ("The cost of transmitting a given body of information is frequently in many cases very low. If it were zero, then optimal allocation would obviously call for unlimited distribution without cost.").

[76] *Id.*

[77] *See* KAUFER, *supra* note 16, at 19.

[78] *See generally* Kenneth W. Dam, *The Economic Underpinnings Of Patent Law*, 23 J. LEGAL STUD. 247 (1994) (recognizing that "if a firm could not recover the costs of invention because the resulting information were available to all, then we could expect a much lower and indeed suboptimal level of innovation.").

[79] This theory was explained in ARROW, *supra* note 75, at 615.

foreclose competitors from making, using, and selling the invention may allow them an opportunity to obtain above-market profits during the patent's term."[80] Thus, part of the patent law's incentive includes the financial return anticipated if a patented product is successful. An underlying assumption of the patent system is that "[t]he patent owner expends resources in expectation of receiving this reward."[81]

[C]   Incentives and Patent Law

What are the specific incentives contemplated by the patent system? One critical purpose of patent law is to provide an incentive to *invent*. As the U.S. Supreme Court has observed, unlike the odious monopolies granted in Elizabethan times,"[p]atents are not given as favors," but granted only for an application that demonstrates "a genuine invention" that amounts to an advance in a technological art.[82] The U.S. patent right is intended to provide an incentive to inventors and to those who support invention with the ultimate goal of providing a public benefit. As explained by the Supreme Court:

> The patent laws promote this progress by offering a right of exclusion for a limited period as an incentive to inventors to risk the often enormous costs in terms of time, research, and development. The productive effort thereby fostered will have a positive effect on society through the introduction of new products and processes of manufacture into the economy, and the emanations by way of increased employment and better lives for our citizens.[83]

A further purpose of the patent system is to provide an incentive to *disclose* inventions that might otherwise remain a trade secret.[84] The patentee's disclosure is said to be the *quid pro quo* for the government grant of exclusivity.[85] The purpose of the disclosure is to enrich the art by adding to the total available information in the field, and also to provide a roadmap for others to practice the invention once the patent term expires and the invention becomes part of the public domain. Consequently, no patent will issue if the invention disclosed in the application is already known to the public or obvious to those of skill in the art.[86]

---

[80] Biotechnology Indus. Org. v. District of Columbia, 496 F.3d 1362, 1372 (Fed. Cir. 2007).

[81] King Instruments Corp. v. Perego, 65 F.3d 941, 950 (Fed. Cir. 1995).

[82] Sears, Roebuck & Co. v. Stiffel Co., 376 U.S. 225, 230 (1964).

[83] Kewanee Oil Co. v. Bicron Corp., 416 U.S. 470, 480 (1974).

[84] *See* Brenner v. Manson, 383 U.S. 519, 534 n.21 (1966) ("As a reward for inventions and to encourage their disclosure, the United States offers a seventeen-year monopoly to an inventor who refrains from keeping his invention a trade secret.") (quotation and citation omitted).

[85] Kewanee Oil Co., 416 U.S. at 481. ("When a patent is granted and the information contained in it is circulated to the general public and those especially skilled in the trade, such additions to the general store of knowledge are of such importance to the public weal that the Federal Government is willing to pay the high price of 17 years of exclusive use for its disclosure, which disclosure, it is assumed, will stimulate ideas and the eventual development of further significant advances in the art.").

[86] *See generally* Eldred v. Ashcroft, 537 U.S. 186, 216 (2003); 35 U.S.C. §§ 102-03 (providing the statutory basis for application rejections based on a failure to meet the novelty and nonobviousness requirements).

Another purpose to the patent system is to provide an incentive to *design around* to others in the same field. Generally, "designing around" refers to efforts to create an implementation that falls outside the scope of a claim to avoid infringing another's patent. For example, one attempting to avoid infringing a patent claim for a table requiring "at least four support members" may create a table supported by only one support post. This result has a favorable public benefit because the total amount of new inventions has increased — now, two table options exist rather than only the first. Designing around is said to bring "a steady flow of innovations to the marketplace"[87] and therefore benefits the public.

One further purpose served by the patent system is the incentive to *commercialize* the invention. The right can be used to "stimulate the investment of risk capital in the commercialization of useful patentable inventions so that the public gets some benefit from them, which may not occur in the absence of some patent protection."[88] As the Supreme Court has stated, inventive activity fostered by the patent system "will have a positive effect on society through the introduction of new products and processes of manufacture into the economy, and the emanations by way of increased employment and better lives for our citizens."[89]

§ 1.05 HOW DOES THE PATENT "RIGHT TO EXCLUDE" OPERATE?

A patentee's violation of the right to exclude is an *infringement*. One infringes a patent when one engages in the unauthorized making, using, offering to sell, selling or importing into the United States any patented invention within the patent's term. The scope of a patentee's right to exclude is embodied in one or more *claims* that define the invention. That is, when another person makes, uses, offers to sells, sells or imports that which is within the scope of a patent's claim without authorization, one infringes that claim.[90]

Just as some pieces of land are larger than others, every claim has a scope.[91] A *broad* claim will be infringed by conduct that concerns more implementations than a *narrow* claim. For example, a patent for a table that includes a broad claim for "an apparatus with a horizontal surface and at least one supporting member" will be infringed by both a four-legged table and a table relying on a single support post. On the other hand, a patent which includes a narrower claim as an "apparatus comprising a horizontal surface *and four supporting legs*" is infringed by another who makes, uses, offers to sell or sells, or imports a table with four legs without the authorization of the patent owner. However, one who makes a table with a *single* support post does *not* literally infringe this narrower claim because that implemen-

---

[87] State Indus., Inc. v. A.O. Smith Corp., 751 F.2d 1226, 1236 (Fed. Cir. 1985).

[88] Rohm & Haas Co. v. Crystal Chem. Co., 722 F.2d 1556, 1571 (Fed. Cir. 1983).

[89] *Kewanee Oil Co.*, 416 U.S. at 480.

[90] *See* 35 U.S.C. § 271(a).

[91] *See* Robert P. Merges and Richard R. Nelson, *On the Complex Economics of Patent Scope*, 90 COLUM. L. REV. 839 (1990) ("[t]he economic significance of a patent depends on its scope: the broader the scope, the larger the number of competing products and processes that will infringe the patent."). For more about claim scope, see Chapter 4.

tation does not have the "four supporting legs" as recited.

A few observations are warranted. Note that the infringement inquiry is performed by comparing the accused device, process or method to the patent claim. The infringer's state of mind is *not* part of this inquiry. Rather, direct patent infringement can be found where there is no intent to infringe, and even where the infringer is entirely unaware of the patent's existence. Additionally, there is no requirement that the infringer copy the invention. Thus, infringement can be found where the accused device, process or method has been independently developed by another.

§ 1.06   WHAT DOES ONE DO WITH A PATENT?

Although the patent system as a whole is intended for public benefit, a patent inures as a private right to an individual patent owner. Private ownership has been said to implement the principle that "[t]he economic philosophy behind the clause empowering Congress to grant patents and copyrights is the conviction that encouragement of individual effort by personal gain is the best way to advance public welfare through the talents of authors and inventors in 'Science and useful Arts.' "[92]

Patent owners use these privately held rights in a variety of ways. For example, some organizations obtain patents that cover key products in order to assert the patent right *offensively* against any rivals who attempt to make and sell competing products that incorporate that invention. In doing so, the organization can attempt to protect the research and development expenses that were used to develop the invention and to obtain a profit if the product is successful. For example, one who develops a novel preventative medication for the common cold may patent its formulation. If a rival attempts to make or sell a drug that has the formulation claimed in the patent, the patentee can assert the claim in court against the rival to pursue monetary relief (such as lost profits) and injunctive relief (to prevent future infringement).

Because U.S. patent law does not require patent owners to practice their inventions, other uses of patents are possible.[93] For example, one may file or otherwise acquire patent rights throughout an entire technology field. Using our previous example, a patentee may attempt to patent *all* effective formulations for preventing the common cold. During the life of these patents, the patent holder can prevent potential competitors from entering the market for common cold preventatives entirely. Unless a competitor can design around the patents by creating an effective compound that has not been already claimed, the patent holder can prevent the introduction of all rival products.

Other uses of patents include *defensive* uses — that is, a company may refrain from asserting its patent rights unless needed to defend against a charge of

---

[92] Mazer v. Stein, 347 U.S. 201, 219 (1954).

[93] *See generally* Amy L. Landers, *Let the Games Begin: Incentives to Innovation in the New Economy of Intellectual Property Law*, 46 Santa Clara L. Rev. 307 (2006) (detailing various strategic uses of patents).

infringement of another's patent. Assume that a patentee A makes four-legged tables and holds a number of related patents in that field. Further assume that a rival table maker B owns a patent with a broad claim to a table, and accuses A's products of infringing B's patents. At that juncture, A may examine B's products to determine whether any infringe A's patents. If A so finds, A may attempt to use A's patents as leverage to negotiate a *cross-license* with B. If those negotiations are successful, A can avoid a patent infringement lawsuit brought by B.

Cross-licensing raises other opportunities. For example, some industries are composed of a limited number of companies, who engage in open-ended cross-licenses among them. This allows all those under such agreements *freedom to operate* — that is, each company protected by such agreements can make and sell any manner of technological variations within that field without concern that another within the industry will sue for patent infringement.

Additionally, patentees may raise revenue by *licensing* their patents to others who manufacture and sell products. One may do so if one is unconcerned about creating competition for use of the invention. For example, an inventor who does not make or sell products may obtain licensing revenue from those who practice the patent. Companies that have patented their inventions, but have elected not to commercialize all of them, may obtain licensing fees from their unused patents.

Some individuals and companies purchase patents invented by others with the goal of obtaining profits through the creation of a licensing revenue stream. Because many of these companies do not create or sell products, they have been labeled as "non-practicing entities," and sometimes with the derogatory term "patent troll." This term was coined to refer to ". . . somebody who tries to make a lot of money from a patent that they are not practicing, have no intention of practicing and in most cases never practiced."[94] A number of debates about patent reform and policy have centered on a debate about this practice, with some claiming that those who do not invent or commercialize patents are harming subsequent innovators through these practices.[95]

§ 1.07 CONCLUSION

The patent right is granted pursuant to Congressional authority that derives from power enumerated in the Constitution. The U.S. patent right can trace its roots in former European patent systems. The U.S. Supreme Court has viewed the U.S. patent right as utilitarian in its focus. Patents are intended to provide incentives to invent, encourage disclosure to enrich knowledge in various fields, support commercialization of inventions and advance the creation of new implementations for those that design around existing patent claims.

---

[94] The term "patent troll" was coined by Peter Detkin, then in-house counsel for Intel Corp. *See* Brenda Sandburg, *Inventor's Lawyer Makes a Pile from Patents*, THE RECORDER, July 30, 2001; *and* Peter N. Detkin, *Leveling The Patent Playing Field*, 6 J. MARSHALL REV. INTELL. PROP. L. 636 (2007).

[95] For a contrary view of this issue, *see* Raymond P. Niro, *Who Is Really Undermining The Patent System — 'Patent Trolls' Or Congress?*, 6 J. MARSHALL REV. INTELL. PROP. L. 185 (2007).

As a general matter, patent law is a complex field that offers significant protections for inventors. The appropriability of the patent right, coupled with Congressional authority to assign and license these rights,[96] serve as incentives to "build and create by bringing to the tangible and palpable reality around us new works."[97] Quoting legal philosopher Jeremy Bentham, the Federal Circuit has stated with respect to the grant of patent rights, "[i]t is supposed that men will not labor diligently or invest freely unless they know they can depend on rules which assure them that they will indeed be permitted to enjoy a substantial share of the product as the price of their labor or their risk of savings."[98]

---

[96] *See* 35 U.S.C. § 261.

[97] KSR Intern. Co. v. Teleflex Inc., 127 S. Ct. 1727, 1746 (2007).

[98] Patlex Corp. v. Mossinghoff, 758 F.2d 594, 599 (Fed. Cir. 1985), *quoting* J. Bentham, Theory of Legislation, chs. 7-10 (6th ed. 1890).

Chapter 2

THE U.S. PTO: OBTAINING A PATENT

SYNOPSIS

§ 2.01 INTRODUCTION

§ 2.02 PATENT APPLICATIONS: PRE-FILING CONSIDERATIONS

§ 2.03 THE PATENT APPLICATION

    [A] Provisional v. Non-provisional Patent Applications

    [B] Non-provisional Utility Patent Applications

    [C] Some Details: A Closer Look at a Patent Specification

§ 2.04 PATENT PROSECUTION AND INFORMATION SHARING

    [A] Patent Application Secrecy and Publication

    [B] Communication with the U.S. PTO

    [C] International Applications and Work Sharing

§ 2.05 EXAMINATION PROCEDURES

    [A] Intake and Examination

    [B] Final Office Actions

        [1] Allowance

        [2] Rejection and Appellate Options

    [C] Continuation Applications

§ 2.06 INTERNATIONAL CONSIDERATIONS AND THE PCT APPLICATION PROCESS

§ 2.07 CONCLUSION

§ 2.01 INTRODUCTION

The *United States Patent & Trademark Office* ("U.S. PTO") is the federal administrative agency to which Congress has delegated the power to issue patents.[1] The U.S. PTO, a part of the U.S. Department of Commerce, may exercise this delegated authority so long as it acts in a "reasonable manner not inconsistent with the existing statutory scheme."[2] The U.S. PTO has a number of statutory powers and obligations. For example, the agency may advise other branches of government

---

[1] 35 U.S.C. § 2 (2000).

[2] Stevens v. Tamai, 366 F.3d 1325, 1333 (Fed. Cir. 2004).

about intellectual property policy and disseminate information about patents to the public.[3]

For many patent practitioners, the U.S. PTO's most visible role is in connection with the examination of patent applications and the conduct of proceedings relating to issued patents. Since 1836, the agency has been responsible for examining patent applications. As of 2010, it employed over 6,000 patent examiners.[4] That same year, the U.S. PTO received over 500,000 utility, plant, and reissue applications and granted over 264,000 of these.[5] The average time that a utility patent application was pending before the agency was just under three years.[6] Examiners perform related tasks, such as examining petitions to correct errors in previously issued patents.[7]

In addition to patent examiners and an administrative structure, the agency includes the *Patent Trial and Appeals Board* ("PTAB"), which will replace the current Board of Patent Appeals and Interferences ("BPAI"). The PTAB includes administrative law judges who are appointed to consider: 1) appeals from adverse decisions of patent examiners; 2) reexamination proceedings; 3) derivation proceedings; 4) inter partes review; and 5) post-grant review.[8] The U.S. PTO "has broad authority to govern the conduct of proceedings" and the attorneys practicing before it[9] and is also empowered to impose reasonable procedural requirements for patent applications.[10] To that end, the PTO has promulgated procedures for obtaining patents set forth in *Title 37 of the Code of Federal Regulations.* In addition, the PTO publishes the *Manual of Patent Examining Procedure* (referred to as the *"MPEP"*) to apprise patent examiners, patent applicants and attorneys of the practices and procedures used for the examination of patent applications. These documents are publicly available in a number of locations, including without charge on the U.S. PTO website.[11]

The U.S. PTO's power does not include substantive rulemaking authority.[12] This means that Congress and the courts are the final interpreters of substantive patent

---

[3] *See generally* 35 U.S.C. §§ 2-13.

[4] U.S. Patent & Trademark Office, *Performance and Accountability Report: Fiscal Year 2010,* at 9, available at http://www.uspto.gov/about/stratplan/ar/2010/index.jsp

[5] United States Patent and Trademark Office, Performance and Accountability Report Fiscal Year, 125 (2010)

[6] *Id.*

[7] 35 U.S.C. §§ 256, 257.

[8] The Board of Patent Appeals and Interferences conducted another type of proceeding, called an interference proceeding, which will be phased out over the next few years. For more about interference proceedings, see Chapter 20.

[9] Lacavera v. Dudas, 441 F.3d 1380, 1383 (Fed. Cir. 2006).

[10] *In re Bogese,* 303 F.3d 1362, 1368 (Fed. Cir. 2002) ("The PTO has inherent authority to govern procedure before the PTO, and that authority allows it to set reasonable deadlines and requirements for the prosecution of applications").

[11] The U.S. Patent & Trademark Office website is located at http://www.uspto.gov/.

[12] *See e.g.,* Merck & Co., Inc. v. Kessler, 80 F.3d 1543, 1549-50 (Fed. Cir. 1996) ("the broadest of the PTO's rulemaking powers-35 U.S.C. § 6(a)-authorizes the Commissioner to promulgate regulations directed only to 'the conduct of proceedings in the [PTO]'; it does NOT grant the Commissioner the

law. Therefore, the U.S. PTO's construction of the governing statutes is not granted administrative deference; rather, the agency's interpretations may be adopted based on "the thoroughness of its consideration and the validity of its reasoning, *i.e.*, its basic power to persuade . . . ."[13] Moreover, the U.S. PTO does *not* have the authority to decide infringement or to grant any relief for any violation of a patentee's rights. Primarily, such disputes are decided in civil actions filed in a federal district court.[14]

§ 2.02 PATENT APPLICATIONS: PRE-FILING CONSIDERATIONS

Generally, the process of filing an application and pursing a patent is called *patent prosecution.* In many cases, a U.S. patent application is filed through an attorney or patent agent who is admitted to practice before the U.S. PTO. If she so chooses, an inventor may personally file and prosecute an application pro se.

A patentee may consider a number of issues before filing a patent application. Although not required to do so, one may conduct a search of the pre-existing art in the relevant field to determine whether the application meets the patentability requirements. The goal of such a search is to determine whether there is any *prior art* — that is, any relevant invention, discovery or technology that may bear on the application's novelty or nonobviousness. This search may avoid the waste associated with filing a patent application that will not likely succeed. It can also provide valuable information about how broadly the claim can be drafted and still avoid the prior art.[15]

Timing presents an additional consideration. Based on the America Invents Act, for patent applications with an effective filing date after March 16, 2013, priority is given to the *first inventor to file* an application or to the first inventor to disclose the invention to the public, assuming the inventor then files the application within one year of the disclosure. This is an important consideration that generally counsels in favor of filing an application as early as practicable, because if another files an application claiming the same invention a single day earlier then the opportunity to obtain a patent is lost. Product makers have an added incentive to obtain patent protection at the earliest opportunity. Some may take advantage of programs for accelerated examination offered by the U.S. PTO.[16]

---

authority to issue substantive rules.") (emphasis in original) (citation omitted).

[13] *Id.* at 1550.

[14] As an alternative, a patentee who is seeking to exclude the importation of infringing products may adjudicate infringement before the administrative court in the International Trade Commission ("ITC"). *See generally* 19 U.S.C. § 1337. Relief in the ITC is largely limited to issuing an order excluding the infringing goods from importation into the U.S. Therefore, a patentee who seeks monetary damages or an injunction that prevents the practice of a patent within the U.S. will file suit in a U.S. federal district court either as an alternative or in parallel with an ITC action.

[15] However, even the best search of the pre-existing art cannot absolutely ensure the patentability of an application. Prior art encompasses information that is available world-wide and some that is not publicly available.

[16] *See* 76 Fed. Reg. 6369 & 18399 ("Changes To Implement the Prioritized Examination Track (Track I) of the Enhanced Examination Timing Control Procedures").

For patent applications with an effective filing date before March 16, 2013, priority is given to the person who is *first to invent.* Yet even first inventors must consider that the right to patent can be lost under these rules. For example, a claim may be time barred where the inventor waits longer than one year after making an offer to sell a product that incorporates the invention.[17] Moreover, under the first to invent system, the filing date of a patent application serves as the presumptive date of invention for the claims stated therein.[18] In a dispute with a challenger, an early filing date allows the patentee to rely on this presumption rather than bearing the burden to demonstrate the earlier invention date.

On the other hand, a patent's term is based on the application's filing date.[19] All else being equal, an application that is filed sooner will expire sooner. Those patenting technologies that are not expected to experience commercial activity during the next decade (or more) may be inclined to delay filing. However, the risk of early patent expiration must be balanced against the possibility that another's independent invention might create a challenge to the patent's validity.

§ 2.03 THE PATENT APPLICATION

[A] Provisional v. Non-provisional Patent Applications

One who is considering filing a utility patent application may select from two types of patent applications. The first type is a *provisional patent application.*[20] Provisional patent applications are not examined. Rather, the application establishes an effective filing date as a "placeholder" to preserve an invention's priority for 12 months.[21] Also, this application allows for the use of the phrase "patent pending" to be applied to products or descriptions of the invention.

Twelve months after a provisional application is filed, the patentee must supplement the filing with a non-provisional application or otherwise seek permission to convert the application into one that is ready for examination.[22] If the patentee fails to act within that time period, the provisional patent application

---

[17] 35 U.S.C. § 102(b). There are a number of other time restrictions, explored in depth later in this book.

[18] *See e.g.,* Hyatt v. Boone, 146 F.3d 1348, 1352 (Fed. Cir. 1998).

[19] 35 U.S.C. § 154 ("such grant shall be for a term beginning on the date on which the patent issues and ending 20 years from the date on which the application for the patent was filed in the United States").

[20] 35 U.S.C. § 111(b) (A provisional application does not require the submission of a claim, oath or an information disclosure statement.).

[21] 35 U.S.C. § 119(e).

[22] *See* 37 C.F.R. § 1.53(c) (2007). The provisional application's specification must be sufficient to support the claim(s) subsequently added. *See* 35 U.S.C. § 112 (2000); and New Railhead Mfg., L.L.C. v. Vermeer Mfg. Co., 298 F.3d 1290, 1294 (Fed. Cir. 2002) ("the specification of the *provisional* must 'contain a written description of the invention and the manner and process of making and using it, in such full, clear, concise and exact terms,' 35 U.S.C. § 112, ¶ 1, to enable an ordinarily skilled artisan to practice the invention *claimed* in the *non-provisional* application") (emphasis added).

is considered abandoned.[23] Provisional applications are not required to be complete — for example, there is no claim requirement and an inventor's oath is not required. Therefore, their initial preparation costs tend to be lower. However, applicants must be careful to include a specification that will be sufficient to support any claims that will be added after the twelve month provisional period has expired.

The second type is the *non-provisional application.*[24] This type must meet all formal application requirements and is examined on the merits. Filing requirements for non-provisional utility applications are detailed in the next subsection.

Some applicants proceed with a provisional application for inventions that may be of dubious value at the outset, so that an applicant has up to a year to decide whether to pursue a full examination. Although a provisional application tends to be less costly initially, those savings may quickly dissipate when the application is converted or substituted into a form that will be examined. However, reliance on provisional applications may be a viable option for those who wish to get a quick, low-cost application on file to preserve priority under the newly-adopted first to file system. Ultimately, the decision of which option is best is a judgment made with a full assessment of the relevant circumstances.

[B] Non-provisional Utility Patent Applications

At a minimum, a non-provisional utility patent application filed at the U.S. PTO requires:

• *A specification, including at least one claim.* The patentee must provide a written, textual description that fully discloses the invention.[25] In addition, the specification must include one or more claims.

• *A drawing, if necessary.* A drawing must be submitted "where necessary for the understanding of the subject matter sought to be patented."[26]

• *An inventor's oath or declaration.* The application must be submitted with an inventor's oath that attests that the inventor believes him or herself to be the original and first inventor of the subject matter of the application.[27] For applications filed after September 16, 2012, an applicant may submit a substitute statement if the inventor is deceased, is under a legal

---

[23] Because abandonment occurs six months before the provisional application is published, it will not become prior art.

[24] *See* 35 U.S.C. § 111(a).

[25] 35 U.S.C. § 112, ¶ 1.

[26] 35 U.S.C. § 113 (2000).

[27] Additional information that must be set forth in the inventor's declaration is stated as 37 C.F.R. § 1.63 (The oath or declaration must "(1) identify the application to which it is directed; (2) state that the person making the oath or declaration has reviewed and understands the contents of the application . . . ; and (3) state that the person making the oath or declaration acknowledges the duty to disclose to the Office all information known to the person to be material to patentability as defined in § 1.56.").

incapacity, cannot be found, or is under an obligation to assign the invention and refuses to make the oath.[28]

• *Filing fees.* Each patent application must be submitted with a supporting amount that includes a filing fee, a search fee and an examination fee.[29] The amount increases with the number and types of claims submitted in an application. For example, fees increase for applications with more than twenty (20) total claims or with more than three (3) independent claims.[30] Fees are reduced for certain types of inventors, such as small entities and micro entities.[31]

There are additional documents filed with the application.[32] Some applications include an *Information Disclosure Statement* (or "IDS") listing any prior art known to the patentee together with an explanation of the relevance of the submitted information.[33]

Together, the original filing becomes part of the *prosecution file history*, which will ultimately contain all written communications between the agency and the patentee concerning the prosecution of a particular application. The prosecution file history acts as the official record of the proceedings that relate to the prosecution of the application from the initial filing by the applicant through a final decision by the U.S. PTO or abandonment. Prosecution file histories for all issued patents and all published patent applications are available for public inspection.[34] For many patents, this file can later establish important evidence to ascertain the scope and meaning of the claimed invention. In addition, the file may disclose discrepancies that might demonstrate that the patent should not have been granted or should be rendered unenforceable. Thus, if one seeks to assess the potential strength, value and scope of any particular patent, its file history should be obtained and evaluated.

---

[28] 35 U.S.C. § 115.

[29] Updated information about filing fees are available from the U.S. PTO and periodically published in the Federal Register.

[30] As of late 2011, the filing fee for a non-provisional utility application with under twenty total claims and fewer than three independent claims was over $1,000. *See* U.S. Patent and Trademark Office Fee Schedule, available at http://www.uspto.gov/web/offices/ac/qs/ope/fee092611.htm#patapp (effective Sept. 26, 2011).

[31] *See* 35 U.S.C. § MPEP § 509.02.

[32] These documents are: 1) a Utility Patent Application Transmittal Form (PTO/SB/05) or a comparable Transmittal Letter; 2) a Fee Transmittal Form (PTO/SB/17); and 3) an Application Data Sheet (see 37 C.F.R. § 1.76). For certain types of inventions, a Nucleotide and/or Amino Acid Sequence Submission must also be submitted. *See* U.S. Patent and Trademark Office, A GUIDE TO FILING A NON-PROVISIONAL (UTILITY) PATENT APPLICATION, http://www.uspto.gov/web/offices/pac/utility/utility.htm (last visited October 28, 2011). Forms and additional information are available on the U.S. PTO's website.

[33] *See* MPEP § 1.98.

[34] *See* 37 C.F.R. § 1.11(a).

[C]   Some Details: A Closer Look at a Patent Specification

Absent amendment, the content of an application's written specification becomes the content of the written specification of the patent (if issued).[35] The U.S. PTO suggests that a non-provisional utility patent specification include the following information in the following order:[36]

i) ***Title of Invention and Preliminary Information.*** The U.S. PTO suggests that the patent specification include a title. In addition, the U.S. PTO suggests that certain background information, such as the inventor's name and residence, be included. If issued, this information will appear on the first page of the patent.

ii) ***Cross-reference to related applications.*** Inventors may protect their invention in more than one patent application, whether domestically or in one or more foreign jurisdictions. An applicant may seek the benefit of the earliest filing date among related applications. To obtain this benefit, the application must include a reference to the earlier U.S. and/or foreign application(s), including the application number(s), the filing date(s), and the relationship of the applications.

iii) ***Background of the Invention.*** This background is a statement of the field of endeavor to which the invention pertains. This may include an overview of the state of the art.

iv) ***Brief Summary of the Invention.*** This portion of the application provides an overview of the invention and may include a description of the features that distinguish the claimed invention from the state of the art.

v) ***Brief Description of Drawings***: If the application includes drawings, the application must include a list of figures along with an explanation of the content.

vi) ***Detailed Description of the Invention.*** This section includes certain statutorily required information, including: 1) a *written description* of the invention;[37] 2) sufficient information to *enable* one of ordinary skill in the art to make and use the claimed invention;[38] and 3) the *best mode* contemplated by the inventor of carrying out the invention.[39] In addition, some written specifications disclose alternative *embodiments* — that is, a description of the different ways that the invention can be made or implemented. An inventor may label one of these the *preferred embodi-*

---

[35] As used in this book, the term "written specification" refers to all descriptive information in a patent or patent application that appears prior to the claims (including all text and drawings).

[36] 37 C.F.R. § 1.77(b) (providing that, if applicable, the specification should also disclose: 1) the disposition of rights of inventions conceived of, or reduced to practice, using federal funds; and 2) a list of any information submitted on compact disc that is submitted with the specification, such as a computer program, a gene sequence listing or a table of data that would comprise more than 50 pages if printed on paper.).

[37] *See* Chapter 9, *infra.*

[38] *See* Chapter 8, *infra.*

[39] *See* Chapter 11, *infra.*

ment. Note that, in many cases, any embodiments disclosed in the detailed description are considered illustrative of the invention's use but do not necessarily limit the scope of patent protection.

vii) ***Claim.*** The patent application must contain "one or more claims particularly pointing out and distinctly claiming the subject matter which the applicant regards as his invention."[40] This portion of the specification defines the scope of the patent right.

viii) ***Abstract of the Disclosure.*** The abstract provides a brief (shorter than 150 words) explanation of the nature of the invention, including what is new in the art. If the application is approved, the abstract will typically appear on the front page of the issued patent for easy reference by the U.S. PTO and the public.

There are additional requirements that apply in particular circumstances. For example, inventions made with federal funds must include a statement to that effect.

§ 2.04 PATENT PROSECUTION AND INFORMATION SHARING

[A] Patent Application Secrecy and Publication

Formerly, all U.S. patent applications were kept secret until issued.[41] Examination was performed entirely in confidence between a patent examiner and the applicant, and no member of the public was aware of the specifics of their discussions. This permitted a patentee to hold the invention as a trade secret in the event that the U.S. PTO rejected the application.

During the late 1960's, a number of foreign countries began to require publication of patent applications eighteen months after the filing date.[42] Generally, the purpose to pre-issue publication was a "desire to enhance domestic industrial development through early disclosure of technology."[43] By the 1990's, U.S. law was harmonized with other countries through the *American Inventors Protection Act of 1999* (or "*AIPA*"). The AIPA requires the U.S. PTO to publish all non-provisional utility patent applications eighteen (18) months after the application's filing date.[44] This requirement applies to all pending patent applications filed in the U.S. on or after November 29, 2000.

An applicant may affirmatively request exclusion from the automatic publication requirement if the invention has *not* been described in an application that has been

---

[40] 35 U.S.C. § 112.

[41] 35 U.S.C. § 122. A limited exception to this rule existed for "special circumstances," such as the need to reveal the contents of the application to another who contested first inventorship.

[42] *See* Paul A. Ragusa, Note, *Eighteen Months to Publication: Should the United States Join Europe and Japan by Promptly Publishing Patent Applications?*, 26 Geo. Wash. J. Int'l L. & Econ. 143, 144-45 & n.7 (1992-93) (listing countries with publication requirements for patent applications).

[43] *Id.*, at 144-45; 147-48.

[44] 35 U.S.C. § 122(b).

filed in another country that requires publication. Thus, patentees who file for patent protection *only* in the U.S. can apply to opt out of the application's publication. To the extent that a U.S. application requires a broader disclosure than a foreign filing, an applicant may submit a redacted U.S. application that corresponds to the foreign filing.[45]

The automatic publication requirement exposes some applications to public disclosure without any assurance that any patent will be ultimately granted. Once published, the details relating to the invention are open for public inspection, including to the applicant's competitors, and any assertions of trade secret protection of disclosed information is lost. In theory, this allows competitors to access the applicant's disclosure in order to copy the invention.

To alleviate some of this concern, the AIPA allows for a *provisional remedy* in the form of monetary damages for a reasonable royalty where the following conditions are met:[46]

- Another practices the invention claimed in the published patent application;

- The other party has actual notice of the published patent application and if the basis is an international application that designates the U.S., has a translation in the English language;

- The invention claimed in the application is substantially identical to the claim in a patent which issues from that application;

- The patentee seeks relief in an action no longer than six (6) years after the patent issues.

If all requirements are met, the patentee can obtain damages for an infringement that occurs prior to the patent's issue date. For infringement after the patent issues, traditional patent infringement remedies are available for any infringement during the patent's term.[47]

[B] Communication with the U.S. PTO

Formerly, nearly all communications about a pending patent application and the U.S. PTO were ex parte. As a general rule, third parties were not entitled to actively participate in the process or to comment on the patentability of pending applications. As a limited exception, a third party was permitted to submit a copy of a relevant patent or printed publication in connection with another's pending application.[48] However, the third party was not permitted to include any explanation, information or argument in connection with the submission. Perhaps as a result of this limitation, this procedure was rarely used.

---

[45] *Id.* at § 122(b)(2)(B)(v).

[46] 35 U.S.C. § 154(d).

[47] For more about remedies for patent infringement, see Chapter 41.

[48] 37 C.F.R. § 1134.01.

Beginning September 16, 2012, any third party may submit a patent, published patent application or printed publications to the U.S. PTO relevant to another's pending published application.[49] Unlike the former procedure, this new section permits the third party to concisely describe the relevance of the submitted information.[50]

Other initiatives to open the patent prosecution process include the voluntary Peer to Patent program, which was formed between the U.S. PTO and New York Law School. Although not currently active in the U.S., this program gave applicants the option to submit applications for disclosure to the public on the Peer to Patent website. Participating applications received expedited examination. Further, the website allowed registered members of the public to discuss the patentability of the applications and to submit relevant information for agency consideration.

As alternatives, private initiatives have recently emerged as repositories and/or sources of relevant prior art, including IP.com[51] and Article One Partners.[52] Unlike the Peer to Patent project, these private alternatives have no formal association with the U.S. PTO.

[C]   International Applications and Work Sharing

Sometimes a patent office will not share information with the public, but may share information with a patent office located in another country. Many applicants file applications in more than one jurisdiction that are directed to the same invention. Where this circumstance occurs, more than one patent office is examining a similar application at roughly the same time. To avoid duplication of effort, a patentee may elect to take advantage of the U.S. PTO's *Patent Prosecution Highway* program if a patentee has received a notice of allowance from any of the many patent offices that are part of this program. Under this program, an applicant who receives a ruling from the office in which the application is first filed can obtain fast track treatment in another jurisdiction. This election allows the office in which the application was later filed to use the granting office's work product to streamline examination.

§ 2.05   EXAMINATION PROCEDURES

[A]   Intake and Examination

Patent prosecution begins with the filing of a patent application. Upon receipt, a patent application is reviewed for completeness by the Office of Initial Patent Examination. Each application is assigned a patent application number and assigned a technology center that possesses expertise in the relevant field.

---

[49] 35 U.S.C. 122(e).

[50] 35 U.S.C. 122(e)(2).

[51] IP.com is located at http://ip.com/.

[52] Article One Partners is located at http://www.articleonepartners.com/.

The assigned examiner will review the submission and may perform independent research into the state of the art to determine whether the proposed claims are patentable. The examiner and the applicant may have an initial interview. An examiner might grant the application if it meets all requirements. However, in most cases, an examiner issues an *office action* that rejects the application.[53] This office action is transmitted to the patentee, along with a document that specifies the examiner's reasons. For example, the examiner may identify prior art that demonstrates that a claim or claims in the application fail the novelty requirement.[54] An applicant then has a limited amount of time to reply. If the applicant fails to do so, the application is deemed abandoned.[55]

The applicant who wishes to proceed with the application will file a reply to the examiner's ground(s) for rejection. In some case, a patentee may amend the patent claims to overcome the rejection. For example, an applicant may submit a redrafted claim that excludes the prior art relied upon by the examiner in order to demonstrate that the application satisfies novelty. Although she may amend the application's claims, the applicant cannot add any new matter to the application's written specification after the initial filing.[56]

An examiner may grant the application based on the patentee's response. In some instances, the examiner may issue an additional office action either because the applicant's response is insufficient or because the examiner has identified another ground for rejection. Alternatively, an examiner may object to the form of a submitted claim, in which case a patentee may submit a further amended claim.[57] An examiner may request any information from the applicant "as may be reasonably necessary to properly examine or treat the matter."[58]

In addition, an examiner may find that an application includes more than one independent and distinct invention.[59] In that event, the examiner may issue a *restriction*, which requires the patentee to elect one of the inventions for examination in the application. The patentee is permitted to file one or more *divisional* applications for the remaining inventions excluded from the earlier application.[60]

---

[53] 35 U.S.C. § 132; *see generally*, MPEP § 706.

[54] 35 U.S.C. § 102. "Prior art" refers to a prior patent, publication, instance of public use, knowledge or other specified type of information that demonstrates that the invention claimed in an application is not novel, and therefore does not meet the requirements to issue as a patent.

[55] *Id.*, § 1.105(c).

[56] *Id.* § 132 ("No amendment shall introduce new matter into the disclosure of the invention."). Generally, "new matter" is a new invention or a new part of an existing invention which was not originally disclosed in a patent application.

[57] *See id.*, § 706.01.

[58] 37 C.F.R. § 1.105 (2007).

[59] *See* MPEP § 802.01 (according to the U.S. PTO, "independent" in this context can be understood as "unconnected in design, operation, and effect. For example, a process and an apparatus incapable of being used in practicing the process are independent inventions.").

[60] 35 U.S.C. § 121 (2000). *See generally* 35 U.S.C. § 120 (The patentee can claim the benefit of the filing date of the original application.).

[B]   Final Office Actions

[1]   Allowance

If the U.S. PTO decides to grant the application, the agency will send the applicant a *notice of allowance*.[61] Upon the patentee's payment of a fee, the patent will issue and become an enforceable right. With the exception of a violation of the provisional right, a patent cannot be infringed until its effective date.

A patent may be subject to invalidation during its term (because of this, some refer to a patent right as a probabilistic right). For example, a patent may be challenged in a re-examination proceeding before the U.S. PTO or invalidated in court litigation. Although patents are presumed valid, some patents cannot withstand an evidentiary showing or argument demonstrating that one or more claims fail at least one of the patentability criteria.

Once issued, patents are effective for twenty (20) years measured from the filing date.[62] Those seeking to extend the patent term must seek a *patent term adjustment* with the agency for one of several available reasons.[63] These include the U.S. PTO's failure to issue the patent within three years from the actual filing date or to meet another enumerated deadline. Other extensions can be based on time needed to resolve an interference proceeding[64] and/or the time period attributable to successful appellate review.

In addition, the Patent Act authorizes the owners of certain types of patents to enlarge the patent term while awaiting premarket government approval.[65] For example, a drug maker may seek to enlarge a pharmaceutical patent's term for the time needed for the U.S. Food and Drug Administration's review and approval of the patented drug.

[2]   Rejection and Appellate Options

If the U.S. PTO does not issue a notice of allowance, it will issue a *final office action* that rejects one or more claims and states the examiner's reasons for the rejection. At that point, a patentee may elect to abandon the application and go no further.[66]

Alternatively, a patentee may appeal the rejection of any claims to the PTAB.[67] If the PTAB's decision affirms the rejection, the patentee has two avenues for appeal. First, the applicant may file a civil action in the U.S. District Court for the

---

[61]   37 C.F.R. § 1.311.

[62]   35 U.S.C. § 154.

[63]   See generally 37 CFR §§ 1.702-1.705; 1.710.

[64]   For more about interference practice, see Chapter 20.

[65]   35 U.S.C. § 156; *see also* MPEP §§ 2750 *et seq.*

[66]   *See e.g.*, MPEP § 711.01.

[67]   35 U.S.C. § 6(b) ("The Board of Patent Appeals and Interferences shall, on written appeal of an applicant, review adverse decisions of examiners upon applications for patents").

Eastern District of Virginia.[68] If the district court agrees with the patentee that the rejection was erroneous, the district court will order the Director to issue the patent.[69] If the district court's decision affirms the rejection, the patentee may appeal this decision to the U.S. Court of Appeals for the Federal Circuit (the "Federal Circuit").[70] In the alternative, the patentee can appeal an adverse decision of the PTAB directly to the Federal Circuit.

In either circumstance, the Federal Circuit's final decision can be considered only by discretionary review by a writ of certiorari in the U.S. Supreme Court. This type of review is extremely limited as a practical matter, as the Court accepts only a very limited number of petitions per year.

[C] Continuation Applications

A patentee has the alternative to file a *request for continued examination* (or "*RCE*") for an application that is under a final rejection.[71] This submission may address the examiner's ground and may include new evidence, new arguments or an amendment.[72] Under this procedure, an applicant may continue the examination.

If the application is still in prosecution, a patentee may obtain further consideration of a rejected claim by filing a *continuation* application. The continuation may claim priority to the earlier application (called the "parent" application). Continuation applications must meet the following requirements:[73]

- The continuation must be filed before the earlier application is issued or abandoned;

- The earlier application must be a non-provisional application;

- Both the earlier application and the continuation must have at least one (1) inventor in common;

- The disclosure for both applications should be the same, such that there is no *new matter*[74] in the later application;

- The continuation application must reference the earlier application; and

---

[68] 35 U.S.C. § 145.

[69] *Id.*

[70] 35 U.S.C. § 141.

[71] *See* 35 U.S.C. § 132 and 37 C.F.R. § 1.114.

[72] 37 C.F.R. § 1.114(c); *see also* Robert Bahr, *Request for Continued Examination (RCE) Practice*, 82 J. Pat & Trademark Off. Soc'y 336, 337 (2000). However, the PTO advises that new evidence or arguments are not *required* to support an RCE. *See* U.S. Patent and Trademark Office, Request for Continued Examination (RCE) Questions and Answers (updated May 5, 2003), http://www.uspto.gov/web/offices/dcom/olia/aipa/rcefaq.htm ("The fact that the previously submitted arguments were not found persuasive does not preclude them as a submission").

[73] *See* Mpep § 201.07.

[74] New matter is subject matter that has not been expressly or inherently disclosed in the original application. 35 U.S.C. § 132 ("[N]o amendment shall introduce new matter into the disclosure of the invention."); *see also* Schering Corp. v. Amgen Inc., 222 F.3d 1347 (Fed. Cir. 2000). For more about inherency, see Chapter 12.

- The earlier application must comply with the disclosure requirements of the first paragraph of 35 U.S.C. § 112.[75]

Under some circumstances, an applicant may file successive continuation applications that claim priority back to a prior application back through a chain of filings. Thus, an applicant may claim priority to an application filed prior to a parent, and so forth, so long as all of the continuation requirements have been met along the chain.

In contrast, a *continuation-in-part* application includes a substantial amount of an earlier disclosure and adds new matter that was not disclosed in the earlier application.[76] Because it represents a combination of both already-disclosed and new matter, a continuation-in-part application may have different priority dates for different claims.[77] Claims based on matter disclosed in an earlier application may rely on the filing date of the prior application. In contrast, claims based on new matter must rely on the filing date of the continuation-in-part application.

§ 2.06 INTERNATIONAL CONSIDERATIONS AND THE PCT APPLICATION PROCESS

One consideration for patentees is geographic. As an initial matter, it bears emphasis that there is no such thing as an international patent — that is, no patent system exists which will provide patent protection simultaneously in all countries throughout the world. For example, U.S. patent protection is territorial to the U.S. To the extent one seeks to protect an invention in more than one jurisdiction, a patentee might individually prepare and file applications that comply with each foreign agency's requirements. The applicant must prosecute each individually through the patent offices located in each country in which protection is sought. One benefit of filing a foreign patent is that one may obtain an early priority date that assists the U.S. application. Specifically, under 35 U.S.C. § 119, a patentee may obtain a priority date based on a *foreign* filing where the U.S. application is filed within twelve months of the foreign application.[78]

An alternative filing system exists under the *Patent Cooperation Treaty* ("*PCT*"), which was enacted in 1970 and became effective in 1978.[79] The PCT, which is administered by the World Intellectual Property Organization ("WIPO"), authorizes a patentee to file a single patent application that can ultimately be designated

---

[75] 35 U.S.C. § 120 (limiting applicability to "an invention disclosed in the manner provided by the first paragraph of section 112 of this title in an application previously filed in the United States"); Bayer AG v. Schein Pharmaceuticals, Inc., 301 F.3d 1306, 1313 (Fed. Cir. 2002) ("by its terms, section 120 applies only if the earlier-filed application . . . complies with the requirements of section 112.").

[76] *See* MPEP § 201.08.

[77] *See* Applied Materials, Inc. v. Advanced Semiconductor Materials America, Inc., 98 F.3d 1563, 1579-80 (Fed. Cir. 1996).

[78] 35 U.S.C. § 119 (2000).

[79] Patent Cooperation Treaty, June 19, 1970, 28 U.S.T. 7645, 1160 U.N.T.S. 231 (entered into force Jan. 24, 1978), available at http://www.wipo.int/pct/en/texts/pdf/pct.pdf. More information about PCT applications is available from World Intellectual Property Organization, PCT Resources, http://www.wipo.int/pct/en/ (last visited Jan. 17, 2008). *See also* MPEP § 1801.

for patenting in over 100 member countries as well as under identified regional patent treaties. Note that the PCT does not harmonize the substantive patent law of all of the member nations but it does create an important procedural mechanism for obtaining patent protection in multiple countries with a single filing. In operation, a U.S. resident or national can elect to file a single PCT application in the U.S. PTO that establishes an effective filing date in all PCT member states.[80] Likewise, a patent applicant in another PCT member country may file an application in a foreign receiving office that will be considered an effective filing in the U.S.

After a PCT application is filed, the prosecution proceeds in two sequential phases: first, the *international phase*, and second, the *national phase*. During the *international phase*, an International Searching Authority ("ISA", or "receiving office") will examine the application and conduct a search for relevant patents and technical literature. The results of this search are incorporated into an international search report and a written opinion.[81] The opinion, which is non-binding on the contracting states, provides an initial assessment of the likely success of the application.[82]

In addition, the patentee may demand that the receiving office conduct an *international preliminary examination*.[83] In response, the ISA may issue one or more written opinions that consider the application's patentability. This process adds to the time that the application is pending in the international phase. As with the first opinion, these preliminary examination opinions are not binding on the member nations. Nations are free to vary their substantive requirements that are consistent with obligations under other international treaties.

If the patentee elects to go forward with prosecution after the completion of the international phase, the patentee must begin the *national phase* of the PCT application process. In most PCT countries, this must be undertaken within thirty (30) months of the initial filing. At the national stage, the applicant must submit the application and fees to any local patent offices in which protection is sought, provide translations of the application, if required, and appoint a local patent agent or attorney according to local law. Each national office then begins an individualized examination of the application to determine whether to grant or deny the application based on the laws of the respective jurisdiction.

There are a number of advantages to the PCT process. In addition to the convenience of a single filing, the PCT process permits the patentee to allow some months to pass (30 months in many countries) to make decisions about which countries warrant the expense of local translation and filings. During that time, the

---

[80] 35 U.S.C. § 361(a).

[81] *See generally* World Intellectual Property Organization, Regulations Under the Patent Coopera-tion Treaty, as in force from April 1, 2007, Rule 43 *bis*, http://www.wipo.int/pct/en/texts/rules/r43bis.htm#_43bis.

[82] After receiving this information, a patentee may amend the claims once and file a brief statement in explanation. Patent Cooperation Treaty, supra note 26, Art. 19.

[83] *Id.* at Art. 31. *See generally id.* at Art. 34(2)(b) (A patentee who elects this procedure will have an opportunity "to amend the claims, the description, and the drawings").

patented product might be tested in those markets or the patentee may identify licensees during this time period. These actions may inform whether seeking patent protection in each identified jurisdiction is appropriate.

§ 2.07 CONCLUSION

The U.S. PTO is the agency responsible for examining and issuing U.S. patents together with related proceedings. The agency has enacted a number of rules governing procedures for the examination of patent applications. Patent applications are subject to a number of requirements, all of which must be met for a patent application to be granted.

A patent applicant must make a number of decisions concerning the filing of an application, including the jurisdictions in which the patentee will seek protection, the type of patent application filed and the timing of the filing. The alternatives include the filing of a PCT application, which can lead to patent protection in various countries who are members of the treaty.

Formerly, patent applications were maintained as secret by the U.S. PTO. Under the AIPA, patent applications filed on or after November 29, 2000 are subject to automatic publication after eighteen (18) months unless a patentee petitions the agency to bar publication under certain circumstances. The AIPA provides for provisional monetary remedies where various conditions are met, such as infringement by one with knowledge of the application.

The U.S. PTO's decision to grant a patent application results in the issuance of a patent upon payment of a fee by the patentee. Once issued, the patent right becomes an enforceable right that can be asserted against an infringer. If the U.S. PTO denies a patent application, the patentee has a number of procedural options to obtain a review or reconsideration of that determination. These include appeal and continuation practice.

Chapter 3

POST-GRANT ADMINSTRATIVE PROCEEDINGS

SYNOPSIS

§ 3.01   INTRODUCTION

§ 3.02   RE-ISSUE

    [A]   Background to Reissue Proceedings

    [B]   Defining "Error" for Purposes of Reissue

    [C]   Limitations on Reissue

        [1]   Two Year Limit on Broadening Reissue

        [2]   The Rule Against Recapture

§ 3.03   THE DOCTRINE OF INTERVENING RIGHTS

§ 3.04   CERTIFICATE OF CORRECTION

§ 3.05   REEXAMINATION

    [A]   Generally

    [B]   *Ex Parte* Reexamination

    [C]   The Former *Inter partes* Reexam

§ 3.06   POST-GRANT REVIEW

§ 3.07   *INTER PARTES* REVIEW

§ 3.08   SUPPLEMENTAL EXAMINATION

§ 3.09   DETERMINING INVENTORSHIP

§ 3.10   CONCLUSION

§ 3.01   INTRODUCTION

The U.S. PTO's role continues after a patent has been granted. Some matters are routine, such as the agency's collection of maintenance fees.[1] Other activity requires more involvement. As some examples, the U.S. PTO provides a forum that reexamines, corrects and reissues patents, and resolves disputes relating to inventorship. Notably, with the enactment of the 2011 America Invents Act, the U.S. PTO's role is in transition. Some procedures have been newly instituted, modified or discontinued. Because continuity is necessary for an accurate understanding of the

---

[1]   37 C.F.R. § 1.362 (2007) (Maintenance fees for a utility patent are due at 3 ½, 7 ½ and 11 ½ years from the date the patent is granted.).

agency's post-grant activity, a review of all currently relevant activity is discussed in this chapter.

To begin the overview of these procedures, the agency will *reissue* a patent if the patentee has made an error that rendered the patent either wholly or partially inoperative or invalid.[2] In addition, the agency may authorize and conduct *reexamination* proceedings (also called "reexam"), in which a claim may be corrected, modified or cancelled.[3] The U.S. PTO may issue a *certificate of correction* to fix a clerical or typographical error in an issued patent.[4]

Recently, the America Invents Act added several new procedures that allow the U.S. PTO to consider the validity of issued patents. One is *post-grant review*, which offers a "first window" for third party challenges on any grounds during the first nine months of its term. Conducted by a panel of three administrative law judges of the Patent Trial and Appeal Board, the proceeding allows consideration of a wide range of evidence. After this nine-month window has closed, a second, more limited, window opens. This procedure, called *inter partes review*, is restricted to the examination of whether a patent meets the novelty and nonobviousness requirements based solely on prior art patents and printed publications. In addition, the America Invents Act created a specialized procedure, a *transitional post-grant review*, as a short-term program to clear out problematic business method patents.

In addition, the America Invents Act created *supplemental examination* to allow patentees to request the agency to consider, reconsider or correct information relating to an issued patent. Information that the agency reviews through this procedure cannot be used to hold the patent unenforceable due to inequitable conduct. Thus, supplemental examination can be sought by a patentee to cleanse any past misconduct and to ensure that material omitted during the initial prosecution will not cloud the patent's enforceability.

Several procedures allow the patentee to modify the claim scope or substitute claims. These changes can create prejudice to third parties. Some safeguards have been developed to prevent or minimize this impact. For example, the ability to broaden claims through a certificate of correction is extremely circumscribed. In addition, claims cannot be broadened in reissue unless an application is filed within two years after the original patent issues. The *doctrine of intervening rights* has been developed to authorize courts to grant relief to protect the legitimate expectations of those who might be prejudiced from claim amendments or substitutions.

For patents issued under the first to invent standard, the U.S. PTO will conduct an *interference proceeding* to decide a dispute between two inventors, each of whom claims to be the first inventor of at least one patent claim. As the U.S. moves from the first to invent system to a first to file system under the America Invents Act, interference proceedings are expected to become less frequent and will eventually cease entirely. Instead, patents issued under the first to file system are subject to

---

[2] 35 U.S.C. § 251 (2000).

[3] 35 U.S.C. §§ 302-311.

[4] 35 U.S.C. § 255 (2000).

derivation proceedings. This mechanism ensures that a patent applicant can to obtain a remedy where an earlier-filed application was derived from a later applicant. In this way, derivation proceedings ensure that the patent will list the name of a true inventor.

§ 3.02   RE-ISSUE

[A]   Background to Reissue Proceedings

It is frequently stated that the claim defines the invention. However, on occasion, there is a drafting error and the resulting claim fails to adequately capture the subject matter that the inventor sought to patent. As the U.S. Supreme Court has recognized, a patent specification and its claims "constitute one of the most difficult legal instruments to draw with accuracy."[5]

Courts have long recognized that the patent office has the authority to reissue a patent to correct a patentee's errors. For example, in the 1832 U.S. Supreme Court decision *Grant v. Raymond*, the Court acknowledged, "[t]hat sense of justice and of right which all feel, pleads strongly against depriving the inventor of the compensation thus solemnly promised, because he has committed an inadvertent or innocent mistake."[6] In the 1892 landmark decision *Topliff v. Topliff*, the Supreme Court explained the operation and underlying policies of reissue:[7]

> . . . it would be manifestly unjust to deny [the inventor] the benefit of a reissue to secure to him his actual invention . . . . The object of the patent law is to secure to inventors a monopoly of what they have actually invented or discovered, and it ought not be defeated by a too strict and technical adherence to the letter of the statute, or by the application of artificial rules of interpretation.[8]

In *Topliff*, the Court found that the agency could reissue a patent to modify either the claims or specification to align the subject matter of the patent with the patentee's actual invention. In addition, *Topliff* acknowledged that reissue could result in either narrowing or broadening of the original patent's claims. However, where a *broadening* reissue is sought, to minimize prejudice to the public, the Court held that the patentee must act with due diligence to discover the mistake, and that "the lapse of two years will ordinarily, though not always, be treated as evidence of an abandonment" of the ability to obtain a reissue.[9] Further, the Court noted that the ability to obtain reissue would be lost if the patentee acts with "fraud or deception."[10]

---

[5]   Topliff v. Topliff, 145 U.S. 156, 171 (1892).

[6]   Grant v. Raymond, 31 U.S. (6 Pet.) 218, 242 (1832).

[7]   *Topliff*, 145 U.S. at 171.

[8]   *Id.*

[9]   *Id.* (A broadened claim must be supported by the original specification); Superior Fireplace Co. v. The Majestic Products Co., 270 F.3d 1358, 1371 (Fed. Cir. 2001) (§ 271 requires that the broadened claim be supported by the original specification).

[10]   *Topliff*, 145 U.S. at 170.

In 1952, Congress codified this practice in § 251 of the Patent Act. The statute authorizes the U.S. PTO to reissue a patent where, because of a defective specification, drawing or claim, has been rendered "wholly or partly inoperative or invalid."[11] Because a reissued patent cannot contain new matter, modified claims cannot be changed in a manner that lacks support in the original written specification of the original patent.[12] To consider an absurd example, the PTO would not reissue a claim to time travel based on a specification that described travel via an airplane. This rule limits the extent that a patentee can obtain a reissue claim to an invention that was never contemplated at the time of the original filing.

Although the original 1952 section provided that the error must have been made "without deceptive intent," this clause has been stricken as part of the America Invents Act. This change appears to have been enacted to minimize inquiry into the state of mind of applicants. This version of the reissue statute is expected to apply to patents with an effective filing date after March 16, 2013.

[B] Defining "Error" for Purposes of Reissue

What type of error justifies reissue? Courts have found that a broad range of conduct qualifies as the statute is "based on fundamental principles of equity and fairness, and should be construed liberally."[13] Error may include inadvertence, accident, or mistake, including a prosecuting attorney's misunderstanding of the scope of the invention when prosecuting the original patent application.[14]

In *In re Wilder*,[15] the Federal Circuit considered a reissue application for a patent directed to an improved dictating machine. In support of the application, the prosecuting attorney explained that the original patent was drafted more narrowly than the true scope of the invention, a problem that was discovered after a discussion with the inventor that revealed that the attorney had a flawed assumption about the prior art.[16] The *Wilder* court held that the patent should be reissued. Construing the term "error" liberally, the court noted that an attorney's failure to appreciate the full scope of the invention was a common source of defects that warranted relief. *Wilder* explained, "[t]he fact that the error could have been discovered at the time of prosecution with a more thorough patentability search or with improved communication between the inventors and the attorney does not, by itself, preclude a patent owner from correcting defects through reissue."[17]

The reissue statute, 35 U.S.C. § 251, allows reissue if a patent is rendered "wholly or partly inoperative or invalid." As with the other portions of this statute, this phrase is construed broadly to allow reissue in a wide variety of circumstances.

---

[11] 35 U.S.C. § 251; *See also* P.J. Federico, *Intervening Rights in Patent Reissues*, 30 Geo. Wash. L. Rev. 603, 605 (1962).

[12] 35 U.S.C. § 251; *See also Superior Fireplace*, 270 F.3d at 1371.

[13] *In re* Weiler, 790 F.2d 1576, 1579 (Fed. Cir. 1986).

[14] Hester Indus. v. Stein, Inc., 142 F.3d 1472, 1479 (Fed. Cir. 1998), *cert. denied*, 525 U.S. 947 (1998).

[15] *See e.g., In re* Wilder, 736 F.2d 1516, 1518-19 (Fed. Cir. 1984).

[16] *Id.* at 1519 (as a threshold matter, the court found that the reissue application, which sought to broaden the claims, was timely filed within two years of the original patent grant).

[17] *Id.* at 1520.

Generally, the term "inoperative" means that a patent (or any portion of the patent) is incapable of adequately protecting the invention.[18] This can occur where a claim is drafted either too broadly or too narrowly. One example of this circumstance occurred in *In re Tanaka*.[19] There, the court considered whether an attorney's failure to add narrower claims met this standard. The *Tanaka* court found that it did and explained that the addition of a narrow claim acted as a hedge against invalidity if the broader claim was later found to be unpatentable in light of the prior art. Therefore, under *Tanaka*, the word "inoperative" includes errors that "fail[ ] to protect the disclosed invention to the full extent allowed by law."[20]

Despite the remedial purpose of reissue, the courts have cautioned that "[t]he reissue statute was not enacted as a panacea for all patent prosecution problems, nor as a grant to the patentee of a second opportunity to prosecute *de novo* his original application."[21] For example, reissue will not be granted where the discrepancy arose through a patentee's deliberate or strategic choice, rather than an inadvertent error. *In re Serenkin* illustrates this distinction.[22] There, the prosecuting attorney filed a U.S. patent application on January 29, 1997. The attorney then requested international filing treatment for the application under the Patent Cooperation Treaty.[23] On February 17, 1998, the attorney sought to add some drawings to support the application's disclosure. In response, the patent office gave the attorney a choice: First, the agency would accept the drawings but the priority date would be considered February 17, 1998, when the drawings were received. Alternatively, the attorney would be permitted to proceed without the drawings but retain the original January 29, 1997 filing for priority purposes. The attorney chose the first option, with the later priority date and allowance to submit the drawings.

Serenkin examined the patentee's assertion that reissue should be granted to allow the original January 1997 filing date. The patentee argued that the prosecuting attorney made an erroneous procedural choice during prosecution to select the later filing date. *Serenkin* held that reissue was not available, because the so-called "error" was a deliberate decision to obtain an advantage — here, the ability to submit drawings to support the disclosure. The court explained that "an applicant who intentionally and knowingly surrendered his right to a claim of priority, in exchange for a benefit, and now is unhappy with his choice"[24] was not entitled to reissue as a remedy. Thus, although the reissue standard is tolerant of miscommunications as grounds for reissue, obtaining relief based on a knowing choice is not permitted.

---

[18] *See In re* Handel, 312 F.2d 943, 946 n.2 (C.C.P.A. 1963).

[19] *In re* Tanaka, 640 F.3d 1246 (Fed. Cir. 2011).

[20] *Id.* at 1251.

[21] *In re* Weiler, 790 F.2d 1576, 1582 (Fed. Cir. 1986).

[22] *In re* Serenkin, 479 F.3d 1359 (Fed. Cir. 2007).

[23] For more information about the Patent Cooperation Treaty, see Chapters 2 and 42.

[24] *Id.* at 1364.

[C] Limitations on Reissue

[1] Two Year Limit on Broadening Reissue

Even where the requirements for reissue are met, patentees must consider some limitations. For example, the two year suggested time limit discussed in the Supreme Court's *Topliff* decision has been incorporated as a bright-line rule in § 251, as follows:

> No reissued patent shall be granted enlarging the scope of the claims of the original patent unless applied for within two years from the grant of the original patent.

Under this provision, any broadening reissue that occurs more than two years after the original patent issued results in an invalid claim.[25]

[2] The Rule Against Recapture

An important limitation to reissue is the rule against *recapture* of subject matter, which "prevents a patentee from regaining through reissue the subject matter that he surrendered in an effort to obtain allowance of the original claims."[26] If a patentee narrows or cancels a claim to avoid an examiner's rejection during the initial prosecution, these actions operate as the patentee's admission that the claim is not patentable. Under these circumstances, recapture prevents a reissue that incorporates the subject matter of the previously cancelled claim. As the Federal Circuit explained, "[i]t is precisely because the patentee amended his claims to overcome prior art that a member of the public is entitled to occupy the space abandoned by the patent applicant."[27] Because the recapture rule applies primarily to claims that are subject to broadening amendments during reissue, the issue typically arises for claims that are modified within the first two years after the patent issues.

The recapture rule barred a reissue application in *In re Mostafazadeh*, which considered an effort to broaden claims relating to semiconductor chip packaging.[28] The claims included a description of the chip mounted on a frame and supported by a die attach pad, to which solder balls are attached. The examiner rejected the claims during the initial prosecution based on prior art. To overcome the rejection, the applicant narrowed the claims by specifying that the die attach pad in the amended claims were circular and arguing to the agency that this particular shape did not exist in the prior art.[29] After the patent issued, the patentee filed a reissue application seeking to omit the word "circular" in the claim. The proposed amended

---

[25] *See e.g.*, Forest Laboratories, Inc. v. Ivax Pharmaceuticals, Inc., 501 F.3d 1263, 1270 (Fed. Cir. 2007).

[26] *In re* Clement, 131 F.3d 1464, 1468 (Fed. Cir. 1997).

[27] *See e.g.*, Mentor Corp. v. Colorplast, Inc., 998 F.2d 992 (Fed. Cir. 1993).

[28] *In re* Mostafazadeh, 643 F.3d 1353 (Fed. Cir. 2011).

[29] The portion of the claim added states: "each of said elongated leads including a circular portion formed as an attachment pad," and the proposed reissue claim read, "wherein each of the contacts includes a portion that forms an attachment pad." *See Mostafazadeh*, 643 F.3d at 1357.

claim instead included the element "an attachment pad" that was sufficiently broad to read on any pad shape.

The *Mostafazadeh* opinion affirmed denial of the application, highlighting that the circular shape of the attachment pad had been added specifically to overcome the examiner's rejection. The court found that this limitation could not be eliminated through reissue without violating the recapture rule. The court reasoned that omitting the word "circular" in the claim would broaden the limitation to an attach pad of any shape, which included shapes in the prior art.

The steps of a recapture analysis are as follows:

First, one must determine whether and in what aspect the reissue claims are broader than the original patent claims;

Second, one must identify the extent to which the broader aspects of the proposed claim relate to the surrendered subject matter; and

Third, determine whether surrendered subject matter has been substantially or fully re-introduced by the proposed reissue claim.[30]

If the answer to the last question is "yes," the reissue application will be denied.

Does the patentee's subjective intent to surrender — or not to surrender — matter? The answer is that it does not; the Federal Circuit has framed the standard as an objective one — that is, the question is "whether an objective observer viewing the prosecution history would conclude that the purpose of the patentee's amendment or argument was to overcome prior art and secure the patent."[31] Thus, the application's file history become central in determining whether the recapture rule bars a proposed claim in reissue.

§ 3.03   THE DOCTRINE OF INTERVENING RIGHTS

When a patent is reissued, the original patent is surrendered[32] and therefore "[a]n original patent cannot be infringed once a reissue patent has issued."[33] Under the former law, the patent owner of a reissue patent could not bring an action based on *any* infringing activity that occurred prior to the reissue, because "before the reissue patent issued . . . no patent existed upon which one could allege infringement."[34] Under this now-superseded rule, a patentee entirely forfeited the ability to obtain damages from any infringement of the original patent accruing prior to the reissue.

When the reissue statute was added to the Patent Act in 1952, Congress changed these rules. Under the new rule, the statute allows continuity between "substantially identical" claims in the originally issued patent and the reissued patent. Now

---

[30] *Id.* at 1358.

[31] Yoo Ja Kim v. ConAgra Foods, Inc., 465 F.3d 1312, 1323 (Fed. Cir. 2006).

[32] 35 U.S.C. § 252.

[33] Seattle Box Co., Inc. v. Industrial Crating and Supply, 731 F.2d 818, 827 (Fed. Cir. 1984) ("Seattle Box I").

[34] *Id.*

a patentee can recover for all infringing activity that occurred since the date of the commencement of the original patent's term if there is substantial identity between the claims.[35] However, current law provides that where substantial identity is lacking, "[t]he original claims are dead."[36] In other words, the ability to reach back to the original claims exists only for claims that have not significantly changed.

Note that by the time that a reissue claim is granted, a third party may already be practicing, or preparing to practice, the invention that has become the subject of a reissue claim. As previously discussed, if the reissue claim is identical, or substantially identical, to the original claim, the reissue statute allows a patentee to sue for both pre- and post-reissue activity. Where the claim has been significantly modified, the *doctrine of intervening rights* can protect the third party activity that infringes the newly reissued claim. Essentially, this allows a " 'personal intervening right' to allow the third party to continue activity that would otherwise infringe.[37]

There are two types of intervening rights. An *absolute intervening right* applies to products that have already been made. The right allow one who has "made, purchased, offered to sell, or used within the United States, or imported into the United States" an existing product or service to continue to do so after the reissue is granted.[38] In this way, this right cuts off a patentee's recourse against existing products.

An *equitable intervening right* applies to products that are not yet in existence at the time of reissue, whether because they are still in development or they are not-yet-manufactured products in an existing line.[39] This right authorizes courts to exercise discretion to prevent prejudice to third parties who have already begun preparations. In applying this discretion, courts may authorize the third party to move forward to production and sale without liability.[40] Because the right is based in equity, a court may decline to allow one to practice a claim if that individual has engaged in unclean hands by willfully infringing.[41]

The leading cases describing the doctrine of intervening rights are the Federal Circuit's *Seattle Box* cases ("*Seattle Box I*" and "*Seattle Box II*").[42] In *Seattle Box I*, the court considered a patent directed to spacers used to stack pipes in several tiers. These spacers permitted the pipes to withstand shipment without damage by preventing the weight of upper pipes from crushing the lower pipes. As originally issued, the patent claimed spacers with a height "*greater than the diameter of the*

---

[35] *Id.*

[36] *Id.*

[37] Seattle Box Co., Inc. v. Industrial Crating and Supply, 756 F.2d 1574, 1579 (Fed. Cir. 1985) ("Seattle Box II").

[38] 35 U.S.C. § 252; BIC Leisure Products, Inc. v. Windsurfing Intern., Inc., 1 F.3d 1214, 1220-21 (Fed. Cir. 1993).

[39] *See e.g.*, Shockley v. Arcan, Inc., 248 F.3d 1349, 1360 (Fed. Cir. 2001).

[40] *Seattle Box I*, 731 F.2d at 830; *BIC Leisure Products*, 1 F.3d at 1221.

[41] Shockley v. Arcan, Inc., 248 F.3d 1349, 1361 (Fed. Cir. 2001).

[42] *Id.* at 827; *Seattle Box II*, 756 F.2d at 1579.

pipe."[43] The reissued claim specified a spacer "of a height *substantially equal to or greater than* the thickness of the tier of pipe length."[44]

The infringer made spacer blocks that were slightly shorter (1/16") than the pipe diameter, an effort that the court found was an attempt to design around the original patent. Although the accused implementations did not infringe the *original* claim (which required a height "greater than" the pipe diameter), the accused product did infringe the *reissue* claim (because the reissue claimed encompassed a spacer "substantially equal" to the pipe diameter). The patent holder filed suit on both the original and the re-issue patent.

As an initial matter, the *Seattle Box I* court determined that the reissued claim was not "substantially identical" to the original as that term is used in the reissue statute.[45] In doing so, the court noted that there was a substantive difference between the two — specifically, the addition of the term "substantially equal to" broadened the subject matter of the original claim. On this basis, the court found that the claims of the first patent had been rendered ineffective by the reissue and could not be infringed. *Seattle Box I* remanded the case to the district court to fashion an appropriate remedy with respect to the reissue claim.

After remand, the Federal Circuit decided the subsequent *Seattle Box II*.[46] In an example of the doctrine of absolute intervening rights, the Federal Circuit determined that the patentee could not recover for the infringer's post-reissue sales of items that had been in the infringer's inventory on the date the reissue patent was granted. Further, under the doctrine of equitable intervening rights, the court authorized the infringer to fulfill orders taken before the reissue date, explaining, "the remedy of intervening rights is calculated to protect an infringer's preexisting investments and business. Prior business commitments, such as previously placed orders, are one such example."[47]

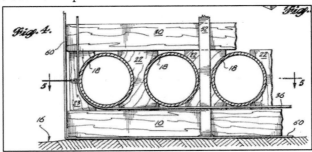

---

[43] *Seattle Box I*, 731 F.2d at 821, *quoting* U.S. Patent No. 4,099,617 (filed Feb. 17, 1977) (emphasis added).

[44] *Id., quoting* U.S. Patent No. Re. 30,373 (filed Dec. 1, 1978) (emphasis added).

[45] 35 U.S.C. § 252 (where the claims are substantially identical, the patent holder can recover for all damages.); Kaufman Co., Inc. v. Lantech, Inc., 807 F.2d 970, 978 (Fed. Cir. 1986) (The doctrine of intervening rights applies *only* where the reissued claim is *not* substantially identical to the originally issued claim.).

[46] *Seattle Box II*, 756 F.2d at 1579.

[47] *Id.* at 1580.

§ 3.04 CERTIFICATE OF CORRECTION

Under 35 U.S.C. § 255, the U.S. PTO may issue a certificate of correction to remedy a patentee's good faith mistake "of a clerical or typographical nature, or of minor character."[48] Unlike other post-issue procedures, certificates of correction lack safeguards that prevent prejudice to third parties such as the two-year limitation for broadening corrections or the doctrine of intervening rights.[49] For this reason, correction that results in the modification of a claim is available only under a very narrow set of circumstances.

In *Superior Fireplace Co. v. The Majestic Products Co.*, the Federal Circuit held that a broadening correction is allowed only where the error is clearly evident from the patent's public record.[50] There, the court examined a certificate of correction that had issued to modify a claim directed at an improved gas fireplace. The originally issued claim stated that the invention included a firebox that included "*rear walls*," in plural, which would require the presence of at least two walls. After the patent issued, the patentee obtained a certificate of correction, which modified the formerly plural "rear walls" to the singular "rear wall." This modification had the effect of broadening the claim, because a device using a single rear wall implementation was sufficient to meet the "rear wall" limitation, although a single-walled implementation was outside the scope of the original claim.[51]

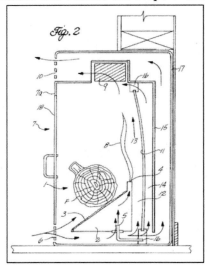

---

[48] 35 U.S.C. § 255 (2000); *See also* 35 U.S.C. § 254 (2000) (A certificate of correction for errors made by the U.S. PTO is available pursuant to this section).

[49] Superior Fireplace, Co. v. Majestic Products, Co., 270 F.3d 1358, 1371 (Fed. Cir. 2001).

[50] *Id.*

[51] *See* Central Admixture Pharmacy Services, Inc. v. Advanced Cardiac Solutions, P.C., 482 F.3d 1347, 1353 (Fed. Cir. 2007) ("to answer the question of whether a claim has been broadened through correction requires interpreting the old and new versions of that claim, and then determining whether the new version covers territory the old one did not.").

The *Superior Fireplace* court observed that there were three potential types of errors under the correction statute. First, the court explained that some mistakes are "immediately apparent and leave no doubt as to what the mistake is," "such as the use of 'frane' instead of 'frame,' for example."[52] Second, some mistakes are not evident to the public, such as an error using a properly spelled word that is logically consistent in its context. Third, in some instances "it is apparent that a mistake has been made, but it is unclear what the mistake is," such as "those that create inconsistent terms, but leave unclear which of the conflicting terms is in error."[53] The *Superior Fireplace* court expressed concern about potential prejudice to the public from the latter two, as "[i]t is not evident to the reader of the public record how to appropriately correct mistakes of the second and third categories."[54]

Superior Fireplace held that a certificate of correction could broaden a claim only for the first type, where the error and the manner in which it should be corrected are clearly evident from the specification, drawings, and prosecution history. Applying this standard, the court found that the correction was improper and that the claim in its original state should be restored. The court found that the singular term "rear wall" appeared correct in the context of the patent, which could be read as applying to either the singular or the plural, and neither the asserted error nor the manner of correcting the error were clearly evident from original patent or the prosecution history. *Superior Fireplace* held that the certificate should not have issued.[55] As *Superior Fireplace* demonstrates, a certificate of correction permits only very limited changes to an issued patent. Correction cannot be used as a substitute for reexamination or reissue. Broadening corrections raise the most serious public notice problems that have the potential for prejudice to the public, and their grant is therefore quite limited.

Beyond this, correction will not be permitted if the applicant attempts to add new matter or the change is significant such that reexamination is required.[56] A request for a correction that requires a material change in the patent's meaning or claim scope will not be granted.[57]

---

[52] *Superior Fireplace*, 270 F.3d at 1370.

[53] *Id.*

[54] *Id. But see* Arthrocare Corp. v. Smith & Nephew, Inc., 406 F.3d 1365 (Fed. Cir. 2005) (A certificate of correction broadening a claim was properly issued where the specification and prosecution history were clear as to how the typographical error in the original claims should have been corrected.).

[55] *Superior Fireplace*, 270 F.3d at 1375 (The court further held that an error could not be considered "minor" under § 255 if the effect of the correction was to broaden the claim.).

[56] *See* MPEP § 1481.

[57] *Id.*; see also In re Arnott, 19 U.S.P.Q.2d 1049 (Com'r Pat. & Trademarks 1991).

§ 3.05 REEXAMINATION

[A] Generally

The Patent Act authorizes the administrative *reexamination* of an issued patent during its effective term to assess a patent's validity.[58] Generally, this procedure began in 1980 to allow administrative consideration of patent validity. As the legislative history explains:

> Reexamination will permit efficient resolution of questions about validity of issued patents without recourse to expensive and lengthy infringement litigation . . . . A new patent reexamination procedure is needed to permit the owner of a patent to have the validity of his patent tested in the patent office where the most expert opinions exist and at a much reduced cost.[59]

Formerly, there were two types of reexamination procedures — *ex parte reexam* and *inter partes reexam.* Both required a threshold showing that a substantial new question of patentability existed for one or more claims. Where this showing was met, the reexamation was ordered and the U.S. PTO conducted a second examination. Although there were similarities in the purposes and procedures for both, a third party who elected to use the *inter partes* procedure had additional opportunities for substantive participation and the right to appeal. Although ex parte reexam is still available, the 2011 America Invents Act eliminated *inter partes* reexam and instituted two new procedures called *post-grant review* and *inter partes review.* These are examined in more detail in the following subsections.

[B] *Ex Parte* Reexamination

Currently, three categories of individuals may request ex parte reexamination of an issued patent. First, the *patentee* may do so. One might question why a patentee would pursue reexamination of her own patent after obtaining approval in the initial examination. The reasons are myriad, but a primary explanation is that new information may have become available that throws doubt on the patent's validity, sometimes through a third party. Unlike a validity challenge in court, ex parte reexams are less expensive, have procedural advantages for patentees, and are not adversarial if brought by the patentee. Moreover, a patentee may amend or substitute claims in reexamination and can, through that process, preserve some of the original claim coverage. In contrast, a patentee who loses a court challenge will have the subject claim invalidated entirely.

Second, any *third party* may file a request for an ex parte reexam on any issued patent. This broad standard allows challenges by anyone who would have standing to challenge the patent in court, as well as those who do not.[60] Indeed, the public interest group The Electronic Frontier Foundation has had a number of requests

---

[58] *See* 35 U.S.C. §§ 302-318.

[59] H.R. Rep. No. 96-1307, at 4 (1980).

[60] *See generally* MedImmune, Inc. v. Genentech, Inc., 546 U.S. 1169 (2007) (describing standing requirements for court validity challenges).

for reexamination granted by the U.S. PTO.[61]

Third, the *U.S. PTO Director* may commence a reexam on his own initiative.[62] The office's statistics indicate that these instances are rare. As of September 2011, the Director's requests numbered only 1% of the total.[63]

The applicant must support a request for an ex parte reexam with a showing that demonstrates "a substantial new question of patentability" for one or more claims.[64] The evidentiary foundation for the request is limited to patents and printed publications.[65] Under an amendment created by the America Invents Act, an applicant may submit any statements of the patent owner that bear on claim scope, if such statements have been filed in either a Federal Court proceeding or to the U.S. PTO.[66] However, these statements can only be considered to assist in the construction of the claims and not to establish a foundation to demonstrate a substantial new question of patentability.[67]

If the U.S. PTO grants the request for an *ex parte* reexam, the patent owner may file a statement in response. The patentee's response may include a proposed amendment to the patent and new claims drafted to avoid the prior art. If a third party filed the original reexam request, this party may file a statement in reply to the patent owner's response.[68] According to the rules governing *ex parte* reexaminations, the third party requester's "reply may include additional prior art patents and printed publications and may raise any issue appropriate for reexamination."[69] As a strategic matter, a patentee who refrains from filing a response at this stage can preclude the third party's substantive participation in an *ex parte* reexamination entirely. If the third party does have the opportunity to submit a reply, the third party requester's participation in the *ex parte* proceedings then ends. There are no additional opportunities for a third party to provide substantive information or argument to the U.S. PTO.

From this point forward, the U.S. PTO's reexamination is conducted in a similar manner as the prosecution of the original application.[70] For example, the agency may issue one or more office actions.[71] During this proceeding, the patent is not presumed valid.[72] This is because "the intent underlying reexamination is to 'start

---

[61] These efforts are detailed on The Electronic Frontier Foundation's Patent Busting website at https://w2.eff.org/patent/.

[62] 35 U.S.C. § 303.

[63] United States Patent and Trademark Office, Ex Parte Reexamination Filing Statistics — September 30, 2011, available at http://www.uspto.gov/patents/EP_quarterly_report_Sept_2011.pdf.

[64] *Id.* at §§ 302, 303.

[65] 35 U.S.C. §§ 301, 302.

[66] 35 U.S.C. § 301

[67] *Id.* at § 301(d).

[68] *Id.* at § 1.535.

[69] MPEP § 2251.

[70] 35 U.S.C. § 305.

[71] *See e.g.,* MPEP § 2260-2266.

[72] *In re* Etter, 756 F.2d 852, 857 (Fed. Cir. 1985).

over' in the PTO with respect to the limited examination areas involved, and to re examine the claims, and to examine new or amended claims, as they would have been considered if they had been originally examined."[73] A patentee may respond to these office actions and file proposed new claims or proposed amendments to existing claims.[74] However, it is important to note that claims cannot be broadened during an ex parte reexam.[75]

At the close of these proceedings, the U.S. PTO will issue a reexamination certificate that either: 1) cancels an unpatentable claim; 2) confirms claims that have been found patentable; or 3) incorporates amended or new claims that had been modified or added during the proceeding. Until a certificate is issued, the original patent may be enforced according to its existing claims.

Patent owners who obtain an adverse decision in an ex parte reexam may appeal.[76] However, the Patent Act does not include any provision that authorizes a third party a right to an appeal.

[C]   The Former *Inter partes* Reexam

The former *inter partes* reexam was designed for participation by third parties. Unlike an *ex parte* reexam, the third party requester's opportunities to participate did not end with a reply to the patent owner's initial statement. Rather, the third party could file a submission *each time* that the patent owner responded to an office action.[77] A further distinction related to the right to appeal. Under *ex parte* procedures, only the patent holder could appeal.[78] For *inter partes* reexam, the third party requester gained these same rights.[79] The U.S. PTO appeared more likely to cancel claims in *inter partes* proceedings, when compared to the cancellation rate in *ex parte* reexaminations.[80] Despite its advantages, a third party who obtained *inter partes* reexam was subject to a broad estoppel provision. Specifically, the third party was estopped from asserting an invalidity defense in litigation based on the same prior art that was raised — or could have been raised — in the earlier reexamination proceedings.[81]

Generally, *inter partes* reexam has not been as successful as originally envisioned. When first enacted, the procedure was intended to provide third parties with an inexpensive alternative to court challenges. However, the limited type of

---

[73] *Id.*

[74] 35 U.S.C. § 395.

[75] 35 U.S.C. § 305; MPEP 2258; see also Quantum Corp. v. Rodime, PLC, 65 F.3d 1577, 1582 (Fed. Cir. 1995).

[76] 35 U.S.C. § 306.

[77] *See* 35 U.S.C. § 314(b); *See also* 37 C.F.R. 1.947 (2007) and Mpep § 2666.05.

[78] 35 U.S.C. § 306.

[79] 35 U.S.C. § 315(b).

[80] *See generally* Roger Shang & Yar Chaikovsky, *Inter Partes Reexamination Of Patents: An Empirical Evaluation*, 15 Tex. Intell. Prop. L.J. 1, 11-12 (2006) (Study finding that claims were cancelled in 57% of the *inter partes* reexaminations, compared to a 10% cancellation rate in *ex parte* proceedings.).

[81] 35 U.S.C. § 315(c).

information that could be considered (patents and printed publications) constrained the procedure's usefulness. Further, the estoppel provisions may have chilled third parties' willingness to use the procedure. Since 1999, there have been fewer than 1,400 ex parte reexam requests filed, and 70% of these concerned a patent that was already in litigation.[82]

Although students of patent law will continue to see references to *inter partes* review in case law and patent literature, the 2011 American Invents Act has eliminated *inter partes* reexam going forward. In its place, the Act instituted two new procedures. The first, *post-grant review*, offers the opportunity for third parties to challenge during the first nine months after a patent is issued. This "first window" allows consideration of a broad range of patentability issues and types of evidence. The second, called *inter partes review*, offers a "second window" that occurs after the initial nine-month post-grant review period ends. By comparison, *inter partes* review is more limited in scope than post-grant review. Unlike court challenges which require a demonstration of invalidity by clear and convincing evidence, these new proceedings can be successful under the preponderance of the evidence standard. Both of these are examined in detail in the following two sections.

§ 3.06   POST-GRANT REVIEW

The America Invents Act institutes post-grant review, a new procedure that authorizes broad agency evaluation for a brief window of time after a patent issues. According to a Judiciary Committee Report:

> The intent of the post-grant review process is to enable early challenges to patents, while still protecting the rights of inventors and patent owners against new patent challenges unbounded in time and scope. The Committee believes that this new, early-stage process for challenging patent validity and its clear procedures for submission of art will make the patent system more efficient and improve the quality of patents and the patent system.[83]

A post-grant review proceeding may be brought by any person who is not the owner of the patent at issue. The third party standing requirements are broad; that is, any person who is not the owner of the subject patent may bring a challenge.[84] This allows challenges far beyond the class of individuals who have standing to challenge a patent in court.[85]

In contrast to the limited grounds available in reexam, the scope of a post-grant review challenge is broader, encompassing all grounds that could be asserted to render a patent invalid or unenforceable. The Act allows petitioners to submit more

---

[82] *See* United States Patent & Trademark Office, Inter Partes Reexamination Filing Data — September 30, 2011, available at http://www.uspto.gov/patents/stats/Reexamination_Information.jsp.

[83] House Report, at 47-48.

[84] 35 U.S.C. § 321(a).

[85] *See generally* MedImmune, Inc. v. Genentech, Inc., 546 U.S. 1169 (2007) (describing standing requirements for court validity challenges).

than the patents and printed publications that are the sole evidentiary foundation to invalidate claims in reexam. Instead, post-grant review allows a wide range of evidence to support of the request including expert opinion.[86] However, unlike reexamination, a third parties' ability to file for post-grant review is limited to a "first window" — that is, the petition must be brought during the first nine months after a patent issues.

For a petition to move forward, the submission must meet a threshold showing that it is more likely than not that one or more claims is not patentable.[87] Alternatively, the showing may be met if the petition "raises a novel or unsettled legal question that is important to other patents or patent applications."[88] This is a higher standard than the "substantial new question of patentability" showing required to commence an ex parte reexam and the former *inter partes* standard.

The proceedings are conducted by a three-member panel of administrative judges from the Patent Trial and Appeal Board.[89] At a minimum, post-grant review procedures permit discovery, authorize protective orders against the disclosure of confidential information, and provide the right to an oral hearing.[90] Unlike court proceedings, which require invalidation to be proven by clear and convincing evidence, invalidation in post-grant review is subject to a preponderance of the evidence standard.[91] The office has discretion to consolidate or transfer related proceedings and to join related parties.[92] Further, a patentee may move once as of right to amend the patent, in order to cancel the challenged claim and/or to substitute other claims, so long as the proposal does not broaden the existing claims or add new matter.[93]

Unless the proceeding is settled or dismissed, the Board will issue a final written decision.[94] In addition, the Board will issue a certificate that will either cancel or affirm the existing claim(s), and if appropriate will incorporate any new claims or amendments that were accepted during the proceedings.[95] A post grant review proceeding is presumed to last no longer than one year.[96] Any party has the right to appeal an adverse ruling in the Board's final written decision to the Federal Circuit.

---

[86] *Id.* at § 322(a)(3).

[87] *Id.* at § 324(a).

[88] *Id.*

[89] 35 U.S.C. § 6(c).

[90] *Id.* at § 326(a).

[91] *Id.* at § 326(e).

[92] *Id.* at § 325(c) and (d).

[93] *Id.* at § 326(d).

[94] *Id.* at § 328.

[95] *Id.* at § 328(b).

[96] 35 U.S.C. § 326(a)(11). The agency may extend the time for an additional six months on a showing of good cause.

The doctrine of intervening rights applies to claims that have been modified or substituted during post-grant review.[97] To prevent re-litigation, post-grant review is subject to a strong estoppel provision. Specifically, if the review proceeds to a final decision, the petitioner is estopped from bringing a subsequent request based on any grounds that were, or could have been, raised during the first review.[98] Further, the petitioner cannot raise any of grounds that were, or could have been, raised to invalidate the patent in any court or ITC action. However, this estoppel effect does not apply if the parties settle the *inter partes* review prior to a decision on the merits.[99]

The Act includes a complex series of provisions to regulate dual actions in court and in post-grant review before the agency. For example, one cannot file a petition for post-grant review if one has already filed a declaratory judgment action seeking a determination of invalidity in court.[100] A petitioner cannot escape this rule by filing a declaratory judgment action after seeking post-grant review, because the statute requires that the court action will be automatically stayed.[101] The stay will be lifted only if any of the following occur: 1) the patent owner moves to lift the stay; 2) the patent owner files a civil action or counterclaim alleging infringement; or 3) the petitioner moves to dismiss the court action. However, a petitioner is not barred from filing for post-grant review if the petitioner's invalidity challenge is asserted in a counterclaim against a complaint that alleges infringement.[102]

As a new procedure, the post-grant review procedure will undoubtedly be subject to refinement over the coming years. As conceived, it offers a broad opportunity for an accelerated determination by a three-judge panel comprised of patent experts. This section seeks to stabilize the patent system by allowing challenges to patents that are likely to have been erroneously issued. By offering abbreviated discovery and a hearing, the agency will have the opportunity to consider arguments brought by those who have identified the most problematic patents. Once this first window is closed, patent owners can be assured that future challenges are limited to those brought in court and to the more limited *inter partes* review performed by the agency.

In addition, the America Invents Act includes a post grant review procedure that is specific to business method patents, intended to clear those issued in the 1990's and early 2000's, when the agency had nascent expertise and limited access to prior art in the business method field. To obtain this type of review, a petitioner must have been accused of, or sued for, infringement of the business method patent. The successful petition will show that the patent lacks novelty or is obvious under the law that existed just prior to the America Invents Act. The procedures parallel those

---

[97] *Id.* at § 328(c).

[98] The inter partes review estoppel provisions for both court and agency actions applies to the inter partes petitioner, as well as to any real party in interest and any person in privy with the petitioner. *See* 35 U.S.C. § 325(e).

[99] 35 U.S.C. § 327.

[100] 35 U.S.C. § 325(a).

[101] *Id.* at § 325(a)(2).

[102] *Id.* at § 325(a)(3).

used for post-grant review. This section of the Act sunsets eight years after the date that U.S. PTO's governing regulations governing post grant review for business method patents become effective. After that time, there would have been little need for this special procedure. Certainly, business method patents issued under the new law will be subject to the same post-grant review as all other types of patents.

§ 3.07 *INTER PARTES* REVIEW

The 2011 American Invents Act has made several significant changes to *inter partes* practice, now called "*inter partes* review." The former *inter partes* reexam has been changed into an adjudicatory proceeding conducted by a panel of three administrative judges.[103] This new form of review acts as a limited "second window" for post-issue challenges to issued patents. To file an application for *inter partes* review, an applicant must wait until the post-grant review period is terminated whether by the expiration of nine months or the conclusion of a post-grant proceeding (whichever is later). Unlike post grant review, the grounds for *inter partes* review are limited to lack of novelty and nonobviousness. The grounds for these challenges are restricted to patents and printed publications.

There are several similarities between post-grant review and the new *inter partes* review. As with post-grant review, the procedure can be commenced only by a third party — that is, "a person who is not the owner of a patent."[104] As with post-grant review, to obtain *inter partes* review the application must demonstrate that there is a "reasonable likelihood of success that the requester would prevail" for at least one of the claims in the challenged patent.[105] The assessment is made based on the application, the submitted prior art and the patentee's preliminary response. As with post-grant review, each party has the right to request an oral hearing. There are limited rights to discovery, such as the depositions of witnesses who have submitted sworn statements and the ability to request additional discovery under the "interest of justice" standard. Additionally, the Patent Act allows the patentee to move once as of right to amend the patent to cancel the challenged claim and/or to substitute claims, so long as the proposal does not broaden the existing claims or add new matter.[106] The doctrine of intervening rights applies to claims that have been modified or substituted in during reexam.[107]

Unless the proceeding is settled or dismissed, the Board will issue a full written decision and certificate at the conclusion of the proceeding. As with ex parte reexam, the certificate will either cancel or affirm the existing claim(s), and incorporate any new or modified claims that were adopted during the proceedings. The America Invents Act provides that *inter partes* review actions are presumed to conclude within one year.[108] Either party has the right to appeal to the Federal Circuit.

---

[103] 35 U.S.C. § 6(c).

[104] 35 U.S.C. § 311(a).

[105] 35 U.S.C. § 312.

[106] 35 U.S.C. § 316(d).

[107] *Id.* at § 318(c).

[108] *Id.* at § 316(a)(11). The agency may extend the time for an additional six months on a showing of good cause.

As with post-grant review, the new statute includes a rather complex series of limitations that govern the interaction between court litigation and *inter partes* review. A request for an *inter partes* review cannot be filed if the petitioner has previously filed a court action seeking a declaration of the patent's invalidity. If the *inter partes* review petitioner files a court declaratory judgment action for an invalidity ruling after filing for an *inter partes* review, the court action is automatically stayed.[109] A person accused of infringement cannot file a request for *inter partes* review more than one year after being served with a complaint alleging infringement of the subject patent.[110]

The estoppel provisions are similar to those implemented for post-grant review. If the *inter partes* review proceeds to a final written decision, the petitioner is estopped from bringing a subsequent request based on any grounds that were, or could have been, raised during the first review.[111] As with the prior *inter partes* estoppel provision, the petitioner is barred in any court or ITC action from asserting an argument that was, or could have been, raised during the agency proceedings. However, this estoppel effect does not apply if the parties settle the *inter partes* review prior to a decision on the merits.[112]

Through this structure, *inter partes* review is intended to provide a forum that allows expeditious, expert agency adjudication of potentially invalid patents. By requiring a high threshold showing before an action is instituted, patent owners are assured of some protection from nuisance actions. At the same time, discovery and an opportunity for a hearing before three administrative adjudicators optimizes the potential for challenges to receive thorough consideration.

§ 3.08 SUPPLEMENTAL EXAMINATION

The America Invents Act establishes a new procedure called a *supplemental examination*, which allows the U.S. PTO to consider, reconsider, or correct information that is believed to be relevant to an issued patent.[113] Proceedings are instituted by the patent owner and are conducted in a manner that is similar to an ex parte reexam. Similar to the threshold assessment made for an ex parte reexam, the U.S. PTO will respond to the request for a supplemental examination by indicating whether the information in support demonstrates a substantial new question of patentability. If the agency finds that it does, it will conduct a reexamination of all claims that are the subject of the request.

There are a few notable distinctions between the two procedures. First, a supplemental examination allows the PTO to consider "information" submitted by

---

[109] *Id.* at § 315(a). This code section provides that the stay can be lifted if: 1) the patent owner files a motion to lift the stay; 2) the patent owner files a complaint or counterclaim alleging that the inter partes petitioner infringes the patent; or 3) the inter partes petitioner moves to dismiss the civil action.

[110] *Id.* at § 315(b). This bar applies to a real party in interest and those in privity with the petitioner.

[111] The inter partes review estoppel provisions for both court and agency actions applies to the inter partes petitioner, as well as to any real party in interest and any person in privy with the petitioner. *See* 35 U.S.C. § 315(e).

[112] 35 U.S.C. § 317.

[113] 35 U.S.C. § 257.

the patent owner and, unlike ex parte reexam, this term is not expressly limited to patents and printed publications.[114] Second, a patentee does not have the right to submit a response or seek to amend the patent or to substitute any new claim(s).

Third, the supplemental examination statute can act as an "amnesty program" for patentees who are concerned that the omitted information could lead to a finding of inequitable conduct.[115] That is because the statute establishes the general rule that "[a] patent shall not be held unenforceable on the basis of conduct relating to information that had not been considered, was inadequately considered, or was incorrect in a prior examination of the patent if the information was considered, reconsidered, or corrected during a supplemental examination of the patent."[116] In other words, the information considered in a supplemental examination cannot later be used to hold the patent unenforceable on the grounds that the patentee has engaged in inequitable conduct.

The supplemental examination allows patentees to air concerns about potential charges of inequitable conduct in the agency, rather than in the courts. What are the reasons that justify this treatment? Recently, some prominent studies have found that the patent system is "hampered by provisions that require courts to divine the difficult-to-prove subjective intent of individuals in patent disputes" including the inequitable conduct defense.[117] A recent Federal Circuit cases has observed that the assertion of these inequitable conduct defense has become "a significant litigation strategy" in infringement actions that has been invoked to:

> . . . cast a dark cloud over the patent's validity and paint the patentee as a bad actor. Because the doctrine focuses on the moral turpitude of the patentee with ruinous consequences for the reputation of his patent attorney, it discourages settlement and deflects attention from the merits of validity and infringement issues.[118]

Further, "the remedy for inequitable conduct is the 'atomic bomb' of patent law" — that is, a finding that such conduct has occurred renders the entire patent unenforceable.[119] Avoiding this result may lead risk adverse patent attorneys to provide examiners with a plethora of irrelevant information. Supplemental examination provides patents attorneys with an alternative to clear the patent of any potential prior art clouds by authorizing the agency to determine that the information would not have affected the original prosecution.

There are two primary exceptions to the rule that information considered in a supplemental examination cannot be used as the foundation for an inequitable conduct defense. First, the patentee cannot obtain this advantage where an

---

[114] 35 U.S.C. § 257(a).

[115] *See generally* Jason Rantanen and Lee Petherbridge Ph.D., *Toward a System of Invention Registration: The Leahy-Smith America Invents Act*, 110 Mich. L. Rev. First Impressions 24 (2011).

[116] 35 U.S.C. § 257(c).

[117] House Report, at 50, citing the National Academy of Sciences and the Federal Trade Commission as prominent critics of legal standards that rest on subject states of mind. For more about inequitable conduct, see Chapter 36.

[118] Therasense, Inc. v. Becton, Dickinson and Co., 649 F.3d 1276, 1288 (Fed. Cir. 2011) (en banc).

[119] *Id.*

inequitable conduct defense has already been properly asserted in litigation before the request for a supplemental examination has been filed.[120] Second, this exemption does not apply for section 337 actions filed in the International Trade Commission, unless the supplemental examination has been completed before the action is filed.[121] Further, if the office believes that the patentee has engaged in fraud, the statute specifically authorizes the PTO Director to refer the matter to the U.S. Attorney General for appropriate action.[122]

In summary, supplemental examination allows patentees to seek guidance from the PTO about information that was omitted during prosecution. It is possible that the system could lead to abuse if patent prosecutors withhold information with the view that later absolution is possible under the supplemental examination procedure.[123] At present, only time will tell whether this is likely to occur. Overall, Congress opted to prioritize the reduction of inequitable conduct litigation, thus providing supplemental examination as an option for those in doubt about the nature of omitted information.

§ 3.09   DETERMINING INVENTORSHIP

For patents governed by the first to invent standard, the U.S. PTO's Board of Patent Appeals and Interferences (the "BPAI"), conducted proceedings to determine priority between two or more inventors in an *interference action*.[124] An interference action adjudicates *priority* between two inventors who dispute first inventorship of at least one claim[125] in a pending application or unexpired patent. To resolve such challenges, the BPAI's Trial Division considers the parties' evidence and arguments to determine who is the first inventor and therefore entitled to the ownership of the contested claim(s).

Under the America Invents Act, applications filed after March 16, 2013, will be assessed under the new modified first-to-file standard. Under that system, the first inventor who files a patent application will be entitled to the patent.[126] This priority system eliminates the need for interference proceedings for all patents issued

---

[120] 35 U.S.C. § 257(c)(2)(a) (stating that the immunity afforded by supplemental examination is not applicable where the allegation has already been pled with particularity in a court action or under 21 U.S.C. § 355(j)(2)(B)(iv)(II) (a notice of opinion that a patent is invalid, unenforceable or not infringed under the Federal Food, Drug and Cosmetic Act).

[121] For more information about patent infringement actions based on section 337 and filed in the International Trade Commission, see Chapter 6, section 6.04.

[122] 35 U.S.C. § 257(e).

[123] *See* Rantanen and Petherbridge, supra note 115, at 30 (describing scenarios that suggest that the quality of information disclosed to the patent examiner will be reduced, resulting in more low quality patents).

[124] *See* 35 U.S.C. §§ 102(g)(1).

[125] A claim is a single sentence definition of the invention and at least one must be included in a patent application. The claim(s) is what determines the scope of the patent, that is, what the owner of the patent has the right to exclude others from making, using and selling. *See* 35 U.S.C. § 112.

[126] 35 U.S.C. § 102(a). An exception exists for inventors who discloses information about the invention and files an application within one year after the disclosure. *Id.* at § 102(b). For more about the first to file system, see Chapter 12.

under its terms. In other words, in cases of near-simultaneous independent inventions, one only need to consult the filing date on the face of the application (or on the face of each patent, if issued) to determine which inventor is entitled to the patent.

However, first filing dates do not always tell the whole story. There is a concern that a patent should not issue to one who has merely taken another's idea and used that information to quickly file a patent application ahead of a true inventor. To address that concern, the America Invents Act has instituted *derivation proceedings* to determine petitions claiming that a first-filed application derived the invention from the petitioner without authorization.[127] These proceedings, conducted by the Patent Trial and Appeal Board, will determine whether the petitioner's later-filed application is entitled to priority, and correct inventorship if appropriate. A petition must be filed within one year from the date of publication of the second-filed application that contains at least one claim that is substantially similar to the earlier filed application. The derivation proceeding ensures that the first to file system does not deprive true inventors of the patent right merely because a first filer jumped ahead of the true inventor.

§ 3.10   CONCLUSION

After a patent issues, the U.S. PTO has jurisdiction to consider various matters relating to issued patents. In addition to routine matters such as the collection of maintenance fees and correction, the office decides substantive matters. These include matters brought by patent owners, including applications for reissue, reexamination and supplemental examination. The agency considers challenges brought by third parties, such as petitions for *inter partes* review, post-grant review, and derivation proceedings. In the course of these proceedings, the issue patent's claims may be modified. In those instances, the doctrine of intervening rights may preserve the interests of third parties who may otherwise be prejudiced by such changes.

---

[127] 35 U.S.C. § 135.

Chapter 4

CLAIMS

SYNOPSIS

§ 4.01 BACKGROUND

§ 4.02 WHAT IS A CLAIM LIMITATION?

§ 4.03 THE ANATOMY OF A CLAIM

    [A] The Preamble

    [B] The Transition

    [C] The Body of the Claim

§ 4.04 TYPES OF CLAIMS

    [A] Independent Claims, Dependent Claims and Multiple Dependent Claims

    [B] Apparatus Claims

    [C] Process and Method Claims

    [D] Product-By-Process Claims

    [E] Composition Claims

    [F] Combination Claims

    [G] Means-Plus-Function Claims

    [H] Markush Claims

    [I] *Jepson* Claims

§ 4.05 CONCLUSION

§ 4.01 BACKGROUND

A utility patent's *claims* are the most important part of the document. This is because the claim defines the invention. Although one may consult the patent's title, diagrams or examples to gain a familiarity of the patent's general subject matter, the operative legal effect of the patentee's right to exclude depends on the words of the claim. As has been pithily stated by a prominent patent jurist, "the name of the game is the claim."[1]

---

[1] *In re* Hiniker Co., 150 F.3d 1362, 1369 (Fed. Cir. 1998) (" 'The U.S. is strictly an examination country and the main purpose of the examination, to which every application is subjected, is to try to make sure that what each claim defines is patentable. To coin a phrase, the name of the game is the claim,' " *quoting* Giles Sutherland Rich, *Extent of Protection and Interpretation of Claims-American Perspectives*, 21 INT'L REV. INDUS. PROP. & COPYRIGHT L. 497, 499 (1990).

When the Patent Act was initially enacted in 1793, the statute did not require applicants to submit a claim.[2] At that time, infringement was determined by comparing the accused device with the patent's written specification. In 1836, the Patent Act was amended to require applicants to "particularly specify and point out the part, improvement, or combination, which he claims as his own invention or discovery."[3] Some applicants began to include claims that summarized the most important features of an invention and used words such as "substantially as set forth" in the patent.[4] This manner of claiming — called *central claiming* — referred the reader back to the written specification to ascertain the contours of the invention. At this time, claims were rarely consulted to determine infringement; rather, infringement was typically determined by comparing the accused device to the written specification.[5]

In 1870, the Patent Act was amended to expressly require claims by directing applicants to "particularly point out and distinctly *claim*" the invention.[6] This amendment precipitated a shift from the former central claiming practice to the current rule of *peripheral claiming*.[7] Under this practice, the claim must describe the boundaries of the invention through the use of claim terms that set the "metes and bounds" of the patentee's right to exclude.[8] As described by one court, "[a] claim is a group of words defining only the boundary of the patent monopoly."[9] A device, process or method that has a one-to-correspondence with all of the claim terms will be found to literally infringe the claim. This is true even if the device, process or method does not look like the diagrams in the written specification or match the examples provided in the written specification. The key to infringement is whether there is a match between the words of the claim and the accused device, process or method.

The present claim requirement is stated in 35 U.S.C. § 112, which states, "[t]he specification shall conclude with one or more claims particularly pointing out and distinctly claiming the subject matter which the applicant regards as his invention." Today, a utility patent with a claim that refers the reader back to the specification by using a phrase such as "substantially as set forth in the patent" will likely be considered invalid because it is considered indefinite under current standards.[10]

---

[2] Pennwalt Corp. v. Durand-Wayland, Inc., 833 F.2d 931, 957-58 (Fed. Cir. 1987) (Newman, J. commentary).

[3] Patent Act of July 4, 1836, ch. 357, § 6, 5 Stat. 117, 119 (1836).

[4] *Pennwalt*, 833 F.2d. at 958.

[5] Karl B. Lutz, *Evolution of the Claims of U.S. Patents*, 20 J. Pat. & Trademark Off. Soc'y 134, 147 (1938).

[6] Patent Act of 1870, ch. 23, 16 Stat. 198, 201 (1870) (emphasis added).

[7] Markman v. Westview Instruments, Inc., 517 U.S. 370, 379 (1996); Hilton Davis Chem. Co. v. Warner-Jenkinson Co., 62 F.3d 1512, 1566 (Fed. Cir. 1995) (en banc) (Nies, J., dissenting) ("the Act of 1870 . . . while a small language change, was interpreted to effect a major change from central to peripheral claiming"); *see also*, Dan L. Burk & Mark A. Lemley, *Fence Posts or Sign Posts? Rethinking Patent Claim Construction*, 157 U. Pa. L. Rev. 1743, 1767 (2009) (explaining central claiming).

[8] *See e.g., Ex parte* Fressola, 27 U.S.P.Q. 2d (BNA) 1608 (B.P.A.I. 1993).

[9] *In re* Vogel, 422 F.2d 438, 442 (C.C.P.A. 1970).

[10] *Id.*

Under the prevailing view, peripheral claims are thought to best serve the *public notice* of the patent system. As described by one court:

> The claim is a statutory requirement, prescribed for the very purpose of making the patentee define precisely what his invention is; and it is unjust to the public, as well as an evasion of the law, to construe it in a manner different from the plain import of its terms.[11]

As a result of the shift from central claiming to peripheral claiming, the role of the specification has changed from central to supportive. Under peripheral claiming practice, patent "[c]laims must be read in view of the specification, of which they are a part."[12] The specification is considered highly relevant to an understanding of ambiguous or disputed claim terms, and indeed according to the Federal Circuit, the specification is the "single best guide to the meaning of a disputed term."[13] Under current law, the claim is unmistakably the centerpiece of an analysis to define the scope of the patent right.

Different claims may have different legal effects depending on the specificity of the terms used to define the invention. This concept is more formally referred to as *claim scope*.[14] Broad claims encompass a greater range of implementations than narrow claims. A broad claim to "a chair with legs" will describe (or, as the patent bar sometimes says, *"read on"*)[15] more implementations than a comparatively narrow claim such as "a chair made of wood with four legs."

Because claims define the scope of the patent right, claim drafting can be a challenging task. As one court has recognized, "[o]ften the invention is novel and words do not exist to describe it. The dictionary does not always keep abreast of the inventor. It cannot."[16] A claim drafter must balance several considerations that can affect claim scope. For example, a claim should be broad enough to capture the invention and any later developed embodiments that might infringe. However, a claim that is stated too broadly may be invalid because it reads on the prior art, or a nonobvious variant of the prior art. Further, a claim must meet the requirements as to form required by the Patent Act, the applicable decisional law and the U.S. PTO's regulations. Because one cannot predict how the U.S. PTO or a later court will evaluate the claims, applicants usually include multiple claims of varying scope to increase a patent's prospects of being held both valid and infringed.

---

[11] White v. Dunbar, 119 U.S. 47, 50 (1886).

[12] Markman v. Westview Instruments, Inc., 52 F.3d 967, 979 (Fed. Cir. 1995), *aff'd*, 517 U.S. 370 (1996).

[13] *See* Phillips v. AWH Corp., 415 F.3d 1303 (Fed. Cir. 2005) (en banc). The role of the specification in determining claim scope is explored in more detail, *infra* Chapter 25.

[14] A foundational article describing the importance of claim scope is Robert P. Merges & Richard R. Nelson, *On the Complex Economics of Patent Scope*, 90 Colum. L. Rev. 839 (1990).

[15] The term "read on" means that all limitations of a claim are present in a device, process or other type of reference. Essentially, whether a claim reads on something is determined by performing a direct infringement analysis. *See infra*, Chapter 29. However, note that not every claim that reads on a device, process or reference is infringing in fact. For example, where a claim reads on a device, process or reference that *pre-dates* the claimed invention, the device, process or method is said to *anticipate* (rather than infringe) the claim.

[16] Autogiro Co. of America v. United States, 384 F.2d 391, 397 (Ct. Cl. 1967).

§ 4.02 WHAT IS A CLAIM LIMITATION?

Claim *limitations* are the terms used in a patent claim that have the legal effect of defining the invention. For example, the claim limitations of a process claim define the steps or acts to be performed to recreate the invention.[17] If another performs these steps, she has infringed. As a further example, claim limitations in an apparatus claim define discrete physical structures or materials used to create the invented device. Another who makes, uses, offers to sell, sells, or imports a device with the structure defined by the claim infringes this apparatus claim.

Patent cases and other authorities sometimes use the term *"element"* or *"limitation"* to refer to claim language that defines the invention. The Federal Circuit has expressed a preference that the word "limitation" is used to refer to claim language, and that the word "element" is used to refer to a corresponding portion of an accused device or invalidating reference.[18] Despite the court's advice, this preference has not been uniformly adopted and one can expect to see both terms "limitation" and "element" to refer to definitional portions of a patent claim.

§ 4.03 THE ANATOMY OF A CLAIM

The portion of the patent that contains the claim (or claims) is at the end of the specification, and typically starts out with the phrase, "I claim . . . ." "[w]e claim, . . . " or "the invention claimed is . . . ."[19] If there is more than one claim, subsequent claims follow in consecutively numbered sentences, usually beginning with the broadest claim and ending with the narrowest. Additionally, the U.S. PTO requires that each individual claim consist of a single sentence, beginning with a capital letter and ending in a period.[20] An example of a patent claim and its parts follows:

A cup and holder combination for drinking comprising:

a cup; and

a holder comprising a band encircling the cup with an inner surface with a plurality of discreet, spaced-apart depressions that create an air gap between the band and the cup.

A typical utility claim has three parts: the *preamble*, the *transition* and the *body*. Each is discussed in more detail below.

---

[17] *See* MPEP § 2106.

[18] *See* Raj. S. Davé, *A Mathematical Approach to Claim Elements and the Doctrine of Equivalents,* 16 HARV. J.L. & TECH. 507, 532 n.133 (2003).

[19] *See* MPEP § 608.01.

[20] *Id.*

[A] The Preamble

The claim starts with a *preamble* that typically provides a general description of the purpose, type or nature of the claimed invention.[21] One issue that may arise is whether language in the preamble can be read as a limitation. In the above example, if the preamble read "for drinking *hot* liquids" mean that a cup and holder for drinking *cold* liquids does not infringe? As a general rule, where a patentee defines a structurally complete invention in the claim body, the language in the preamble is not considered a limitation.[22]

However, there are some exceptions to this general rule. Where the preamble is "necessary to give life, meaning and vitality" to the claim, the preamble will be found to be a limitation.[23] The distinction is made by examining "the entire[ ] . . . patent to gain an understanding of what the inventors actually invented and intended to encompass by the claim."[24] This issue is explored in more detail *infra*, in Chapter 25. In addition, a preamble to a Jepson claim is a limitation. That exception is addressed later in this Chapter.

[B] The Transition

Following the preamble is a *transition* word or phrase that has legal effect. For example, the transition word "comprising" presumptively means that the claim is *open* — that is, the claim limitations can be infringed even if the infringing device adds unclaimed features.[25] For example, the transition "comprising" in a claim to a three-legged stool signifies that a stool may infringe even if it includes an additional, unclaimed feature such as a padded top.

In contrast, a claim that uses the phrase "consisting of" is presumptively *closed*, which limits the reach of the claim to implementations that include the claimed elements and nothing further.[26] Thus, a claim to a three-legged stool that states that the invention "consists of" a horizontal surface and three legs is not infringed by a device that includes a third, unclaimed element such as a vertical back support. The "consisting of" transition is very common in the chemical arts.

Other transitional phrases may be construed as either open, closed or a hybrid between them.[27] For example, phrases such as "consisting entirely of" and

---

[21] *Id.* Generally, a preamble that merely describes the field of the invention does not limit the claim scope. However, in some cases, a claim can include limitations in the preamble. *See e.g., In re* Stencel, 828 F.2d 751 (Fed. Cir. 1987).

[22] Rowe v. Dror, 112 F.3d 473, 478 (Fed. Cir. 1997).

[23] Pitney Bowes, Inc. v. Hewlett-Packard Co., 182 F.3d 1298, 1305 (Fed. Cir. 1999).

[24] Catalina Marketing Int'l, Inc. v. Coolsavings.com, Inc., 289 F.3d 801, 808 (Fed. Cir. 2002).

[25] *See* Crystal Semiconductor Corp. v. Tritech Microelectronics Int'l, Inc., 246 F.3d 1336, 1348 (Fed. Cir. 2001); *see also,* MPEP § 2111.03. Other phrases that are presumptively open ended are transitions such as "including," "containing" and "characterized by."

[26] *See Ex parte* Davis, 80 U.S.P.Q. (BNA) 448, 450 (Bd. App. 1948) ("consisting of" defined as "closing the claim to the inclusion of materials other than those recited except for impurities ordinarily associated therewith.").

[27] *See generally* MPEP § 2111.03.

"composed of" have been held in certain cases to be a hybrid between an open and closed construction.[28] A hybrid claim allows a construction that is open to include unclaimed features that do not affect the basic and novel characteristics of the claimed composition.

[C]   The Body of the Claim

After the transition, the *body* is the portion of the claim that describes the limitations of the invention and how they interact. For example, a typical apparatus claim will list the claimed elements of the apparatus and their orientation to each other. Similarly, a process claim will list each individual step of the claimed process. Interpretation of the body of a patent claim has generated a significant amount of decisional law. The process and methods for claim interpretation (also called *claim construction*) are discussed more extensively in Chapters 24 and 25.

§ 4.04   TYPES OF CLAIMS

[A]   Independent Claims, Dependent Claims and Multiple Dependent Claims

35 U.S.C. section 112, paragraph 3 states, "A claim may be written in independent or, if the nature of the case admits, in dependent or multiple dependent form."

An *independent claim* is self-contained and complete onto itself. It is a full and complete description of an operative invention. A *dependent claim* refers back to an earlier claim and adds a limitation.[29] A dependent claim is interpreted to include all limitations of the independent claim on which the dependent claim depends plus the added limitation.[30] An example of a dependent claim that refers to an independent claim to a three-legged stool is, "An apparatus according to claim 1, further comprising legs that are attached with locking hinges."

The Patent Act authorizes claiming in a *multiple dependent claim*, which refers in the alternative to more than one previous claims in the same application.[31] For example, a claim that includes the phrase "an apparatus according to claims 3 or 4, comprising . . . ." is in proper multiple dependent claim format.[32] However, there is a limit — that is, a multiple dependent claim cannot be used to support another

---

[28] AFG Industries, Inc. v. Cardinal IG Co., 239 F.3d 1239, 1245 (Fed. Cir. 2001).

[29] *See* 37 C.F.R. § 1.75 (2007).

[30] 35 U.S.C. § 112, ¶ 4 (2000) (". . . a claim in dependent form shall contain a reference to a claim previously set forth and then specify a further limitation of the subject matter claimed. A claim in dependent form shall be construed to incorporate by reference all the limitations of the claim to which it refers.").

[31] 35 U.S.C. § 112, ¶ 5 (2000).

[32] *See* MPEP § 608.01(n). Although referring to alternative claims is permitted, cumulative claiming is not permitted. Therefore, a claim stating "A machine according to claim 3 *and* 4, further comprising . . . ." is not a proper claim. *Id.*

multiple dependent claim.[33]

[B]   Apparatus Claims

An *apparatus claim* is directed to a device's structure. An example of an apparatus claim for a three-legged stool for sitting follows:

A sitting apparatus comprising:

a board with a substantially flat surface; and

at least three legs, each having a first end and a second end, the first ends connected to the bottom of said substantially flat surface; and

said legs being placed in a substantially perpendicular position to said board.

Infringement is determined by whether the claim's structural limitations exist in the accused apparatus.[34] Because as a general rule the preamble is not a limitation, a table, chair or stool with a flat surface and at least three legs infringes this claim. However, any method of manufacturing the stool is *not* protected by this apparatus claim. Thus, a device that incorporates all of the structural elements of an apparatus claim will infringe even though the device is made by an entirely different process than that described in the patent's written specification.[35]

Because an apparatus claim protects structure, a device can fall within the scope of an apparatus claim where all of the *structural* elements of the claim are met, even if the *function* of the accused device is entirely different.[36] For example, a three-legged stool with a substantially flat seat infringes the above example even though the stool is being used to hold a plant rather than for sitting.

[C]   Process and Method Claims

A *process* or *method claim* describes a series of steps to achieve a result. A process is an act, or a series of acts, performed upon the subject-matter to be transformed and reduced to a different state or thing.[37] An example of a simple process claim is:

A method for making a sitting device comprising:

cutting a wooden object into a substantially flat piece with a power cutting tool; and

attaching at least three legs to the bottom of said substantially flat surface using glue.

---

[33] *Id.*

[34] *See* Hewlett-Packard Co. v. Bausch & Lomb, Inc., 909 F.2d 1464, 1468 (Fed. Cir. 1990) ("[A]pparatus claims cover what a device is, not what a device does.").

[35] *In re* Pilkington, 411 F.2d 1345, 1348 (C.C.P.A. 1969).

[36] *See e.g.*, *Michlin*, 256 F.2d. at 319.

[37] Gottschalk v. Benson, 409 U.S. 63, 70 (1972).

The subject matter of such claims is the list of actions or steps and not the product that is the end result. Therefore, a process or method claim does not protect the product, only the process described in the claim. A three-legged stool made by any other method or process, such as hand sanding the wood into the proper shape rather than using a power tool, does not infringe this process claim.

[D] Product-By-Process Claims

The *product-by-process* claim describes a product by the process by which the product is made. This practice was originally created to facilitate protection for a product that defies description by any way except for the manner in which the product was made.[38] Typically, such claims are prevalent in nascent arts that are operating with an underdeveloped vocabulary to describe structural characteristics with words. For example, product by process claims became prevalent for claims in the chemical arts during the years that chemical structures were not easily described.[39] However, the governing rules do not limit product-by-process claims to any particular fields or subject matter. An example of a product-by-process claim is:

A chemical compound XYZ prepared by the process comprising the steps of:

combining substance A with substance B;

cooling said combined substance below 0° C until individual layers form; and

separating the top layer from the remaining layers to obtain the chemical compound XYZ.

This example includes a product (chemical compound XYZ) as well as process steps to create the chemical (for example, "combining," "cooling" and "separating").

The interpretation of product-by-process claims was once subject to considerable controversy.[40] Under one reading, the operative limitation of the product-by-process claims was limited to the product.[41] The portions of the claim describing the process limitations were not considered in the infringement analysis. To apply this framework to our example claim, any chemical compound XYZ would have been considered infringing even if made by an alternative process. In contrast, another line of authorities held that both the product and process elements of the claim were operative limitations.[42] Under this second view, only compounds XYZ made by the use of the claimed process are held to infringe.

---

[38] *See In re* Thorpe, 777 F.2d 695, 697 (Fed. Cir. 1985).

[39] *See generally* 1 MOY'S WALKER ON PATENTS § 4:74 (4th ed.) (noting that "The structure of some chemicals, especially those including elaborate polymer chains, cannot be accurately determined.").

[40] *Id.*

[41] SmithKline Beecham Corp. v. Apotex Corp., 439 F.3d 1312, 1317 (Fed. Cir. 2006) ("Regardless of how broadly or narrowly one construes a product-by-process claim, it is clear that such claims are always to a product, not a process."); Scripps Clinic & Research Foundation v. Genentech, Inc., 927 F.2d 1565 (Fed. Cir. 1991).

[42] Atlantic Thermoplastics Co. v. Faytex Corp., 970 F.2d 834 (Fed. Cir. 1992).

In 2009, the Federal Circuit resolved this conflict in an en banc opinion that adopted the second approach.[43] There, the court held that the process terms in a product-by-process claim serve as a limitation in determining infringement. Under current law, the proper construction of our example claim would hold that only a chemical compound XYZ made by the process that is articulated in the claim would be found to infringe. Others can make, use, offer to sell, sell or import compound XYZ made by other methods that are not described in the claim without infringing.

[E]   Composition Claims

A *composition claim* includes two or more combined substances or composite articles, made either chemically or mechanically.[44] Such claims can include compositions of all types of substances such as gases, fluids, powders, solids or otherwise. A composition claim protects the claimed substance created by the listed elements.[45]

[F]   Combination Claims

A *combination claim* unites elements that are previously known in an art, or combines previously known elements with novel elements. Combination claims may also be apparatus, process, composition or another type of claim. The label "combination claim" refers to the fact that the claim is made of pre-existing things or already-known actions that are combined in a novel and nonobvious way. The fact that a claim is built on disparate prior art elements does not present any bar to patentability. As one court explained:

> Claim limitations may, and often do, read on the prior art, particularly in combination patents. That all elements of an invention may have been old (the normal situation), or some old and some new, or all new, is however, simply irrelevant. Virtually all inventions are combinations and virtually all are combinations of old elements.[46]

Note that combination claims must meet all patentability criteria. Therefore, if a combination claims simply arranges old elements with each performing the same function it had been known to perform and yields no more than one would expect from such an arrangement, the combination is likely invalid as obvious.[47]

[G]   Means-Plus-Function Claims

Under 35 U.S.C. section 112, paragraph 6, authorizes patentees to claim certain limitations in a *means-plus-function* format, stating, "[a]n element in a claim for a combination may be expressed as a means or step for performing a specified

---

[43] Abbott Laboratories v. Sandoz, Inc., 566 F.3d 1282 (Fed. Cir. 2009).

[44] Diamond v. Chakrabarty, 447 U.S. 303, 308-09 (1980).

[45] *In re* Crish, 393 F.3d 1253, 1258 (Fed. Cir. 2004).

[46] Environmental Designs, Ltd. v. Union Oil Co., 713 F.2d 693, 698 (Fed.Cir.1983).

[47] *See generally* KSR Int'l Co. v. Teleflex, Inc., 127 S. Ct. 1727 (2007). This issue is discussed in detail *infra*, in Chapter 21.

function without the recital of structure, material, or acts in support thereof . . . ." Thus, one might use the term "means for fastening" as a claim element rather than a structural limitation such as "a nail," or "glue." A means-plus-function limitation describes the element's *function* (that is, what that element does), rather than the *structure* (the physical aspects of that element of the invention).

Section 112, paragraph 6 specifically limits the scope of means-plus-function claims, requiring that "such claim shall be construed to cover the corresponding structure, material, or acts described in the specification and equivalents thereof." In order to understand the scope of a means-plus-function claim, the court must first determine the function described in the claimed element.[48] Second, the court identifies the corresponding structure in the written description that performs that function. Taken together, these rules define the scope of a means-plus-function claim as the claimed function plus the corresponding structure in the written description plus any equivalents of the described structure.

The use of the word "means" creates a presumption that § 112, ¶ 6 applies.[49] This presumption can be rebutted, for example by demonstrating that the claim recites sufficient structure to perform the stated function.[50] Likewise, a claim which uses the word "means," but specifies no corresponding function for the "means," does not implicate section 112.[51] Conversely, omitting to use the word "means" creates a presumption that § 112, ¶ 6 does not apply.

Chapter 31 is devoted to examining means-plus-function claims.

[H] Markush Claims

Some patent claims contain a *Markush group*, which is a list of specified alternatives that form a group, such as "wherein R is a material selected from a group consisting of A, B, C and D."[52] An applicant can also use the word "or" in describing a group.[53]

A Markush group must be stated in a "closed" format — that is, such claims should use the phrase "consisting of," instead of "comprising" or "including."[54] Where the applicant tries to claim a Markush group, the PTO will require the transition phrase "group consisting of" to limit its construction to the listed

---

[48] JVW Enterprises, Inc. v. Interact Accessories, Inc., 424 F.3d 1324, 1329 (Fed. Cir. 2005).

[49] Personalized Media Commc'n, L.L.C. v. Int'l Trade Com'n, 161 F.3d 696, 703-04 (Fed. Cir. 1998).

[50] *See* Sage Prod. v. Devon Indus., Inc., 126 F.3d 1420, 1427-28 (Fed. Cir. 1997) ("[W]here a claim recites a function, but then goes on to elaborate sufficient structure, material, or acts within the claim itself to perform entirely the recited function, the claim is not in means-plus-function format" even if the claim uses the term "means") (omitted citing cases).

[51] *Id.* at 1427.

[52] *See* MPEP § 21703.5(h); Abbott Laboratories v. Baxter Pharm. Prod., Inc., 334 F.3d 1274, 1280 (Fed. Cir. 2003).

[53] *See* 37 C.F.R. § 2173.05(h) (2007).

[54] *Abbott*, 334 F.3d, at 1280-81, *quoting* STEPHEN A. BECKER, PATENT APPLICATIONS HANDBOOK § 2:17 (9th ed. 2000).

items.[55]

[I] *Jepson* Claims

A *Jepson claim* is a type of combination claim in which an applicant claims an improvement by providing a general description of the prior art in the preamble together with the novel aspects of the invention in the body of the claim linked by the phrase "the improvement comprising . . . ."[56] An example of a Jepson claim follows:

In an instrument marker pen body including an ink reservoir and means for receiving a writing tip, *the improvement comprising*:

a pen arm holding means consisting of an integrally molded hinged member adapted to fold against a surface of the pen body and to be locked against said surface by engageable locking means and to receive and secure in place against said surface a pen arm when said hinged member is in its folded and locked position.[57]

The scope of a Jepson claim includes both the preamble and the improvement described in the body of the claim.[58] Thus, the preamble of a Jepson claim acts as a limitation.

One issue that a Jepson claims poses is the extent to which the art described in the claim is considered as prior art that might invalidate the invention as a whole. In *In re Fout*,[59] the court considered this question relevant to a preamble that described a process for decaffeinating coffee or tea, called the "Pagliaro process." The *Fout* applicants did not dispute that they were not the inventors of the decaffeination process summarized in the claim's preamble. Rather, the *Fout* applicants argued that the preamble process could not be used as prior art for failure to meet the formal requirements of 35 U.S.C. § 102 that are necessary for the prior art process to be considered as invalidating.[60] The *Fout* court rejected the patentee's argument and found that the preamble's description of the process in the claim preamble constituted a binding admission that could be used to find the entire claim invalid.[61]

However, courts view the issue differently where the art described in a Jepson preamble is the patentee's *own invention*. For example, in *Reading & Bates*

---

[55] Gillette Co. v. Energizer Holdings, Inc., 405 F.3d 1367, 1372 (Fed. Cir. 2005).

[56] *See* 37 C.F.R. § 1.75(e) (2007).

[57] This example is based on the claim at issue in Pentec, Inc. v. Graphic Controls Corp., 776 F.2d 309, 312 (Fed. Cir. 1985), *quoting* U.S. Patent No. 3,983,569 (filed Oct 6, 1975) (emphasis added).

[58] *Id*, at 315; *see* MPEP § 608.01(m) ("The preamble of this form of [Jepson] claim is considered to positively and clearly include all the elements or steps recited therein as a part of the claimed combination.").

[59] *In re* Fout, 675 F.2d 297 (C.C.P.A. 1982).

[60] *Id.* at 299 (applicant argues that the process described in the preamble, ". . . were not patented or described in a printed publication in this or a foreign country, nor were they publicly known or practiced in this country, more than one year prior to the effective filing date of this application.").

[61] *Id.* at 301.

Construction Co. v. Baker Energy Resources Corp.,[62] the court considered the question of whether prior art could encompass a Jepson preamble's description of art from the same inventor as the patent in suit. Noting that there was an important distinction to be drawn where the patentee cites his own work, the court found that the material in the Jepson preamble is not considered prior art by admission. The *Reading* court explained, "where the inventor continues to improve upon his own work product, his foundational work product should not, without a statutory basis, be treated as prior art solely because he admits knowledge of his own work."[63]

§ 4.05 CONCLUSION

The most important portion of a patent is the claim, which sets the scope of the patent right to exclude. An understanding of the claim is a necessary part of the framework to address additional problems that arise in determining issues of validity, enforceability, infringement and a number of defenses to a patent infringement suit. An understanding of the invention is a critical foundational issue that must be answered before one can analyze almost any other question that arises in patent law.

---

[62] Reading & Bates Constr. Co. v. Baker Energy Res. Corp., 748 F.2d 645, 649-50 (Fed. Cir. 1984); *In re* Ehrreich, 590 F.2d 902 (C.C.P.A. 1979).

[63] *Id.*

Chapter 5

PATENT TYPES

SYNOPSIS

§ 5.01 INTRODUCTION

§ 5.02 UTILITY PATENTS

§ 5.03 DESIGN PATENTS

§ 5.04 PLANT PATENTS

§ 5.05 PLANT VARIETY PROTECTION ACT CERTIFICATE

§ 5.06 CONCLUSION

§ 5.01 INTRODUCTION

There are three different types of patents authorized by the Patent Act and administered by the U.S. PTO: 1) utility patents; 2) design patents and 3) plant patents to protect asexually reproduced plants. In addition, the U.S. Department of Agriculture is authorized to issue Plant Variety Protection Act Certificates, a type of patent-like protection that applies to sexually reproduced plants.

§ 5.02 UTILITY PATENTS

The U.S. PTO grants a utility patent for any new, nonobvious and useful process, machine, manufacture, or composition of matter.[1] Utility patents are by far the most prevalent type of patent, making up approximately 90% of the patents issued by the agency over the past several years.

As the name implies, utility patents protect *useful* inventions that have a practical application, such as an apparatus, process, compound or method. A utility patent application is subject to the U.S. PTO examination process to determine whether all patentability criteria are met.[2] These requirements include a textual description of the invention and an enabling disclosure.

Unlike the enforcement of a copyright, a patentee does not need to demonstrate that one copied an invention to establish patent infringement. Thus, a patent owner may assert a patent against another who has independently developed the accused product. A utility patent becomes enforceable upon issuance from the U.S. PTO.

---

[1] 35 U.S.C. § 101 (2000).

[2] An detailed overview of the U.S. PTO examination process is described *supra* in Chapter 2.

For applications filed on or before June 8, 1997, a patent has a term of 20 years from the application's filing date.[3]

A utility patent's claim defines the scope of the patentee's right. A device, process or method that has a one-to-correspondence with all of the elements of the claim terms will be found to literally infringe. When issued, a patent grants the owner the right to exclude others from making, using, selling, offering to sell or importing goods which are encompassed by at least one claim of an issued, valid patent.[4]

§ 5.03   DESIGN PATENTS

Design patent protection is available from the U.S. PTO for a design that is "new, original, and ornamental."[5] A design patent protects the visual appearance of a functional product.[6] Generally, the subject matter of a design patent relates to either configuration, shape or surface ornamentation, or some combination of these.[7] Unlike a utility patent application, a design patent application does not require a textual description.[8] In contrast to utility patents that last for twenty (20) years from the date of filing, design patent protection lasts for fourteen (14) years from the date that the design patent is granted.[9]

---

[3] 35 U.S.C. § 154(a)(2); *see also*, 35 U.S.C. § 154(b) (The term is subject to the payment of maintenance fees and can be extended under certain circumstances.); and 35 U.S.C. § 154(c) (For applications filed before June 8, 1995, the patent term is either 17 years from the date of issuance or 20 years from the filing date, whichever is greater.).

[4] 35 U.S.C. §§ 154, 271.

[5] 35 U.S.C. § 171.

[6] *See* L.A. Gear, Inc. v. Thom McAn Shoe Co., 988 F.2d 1117, 1123 (Fed. Cir. 1993).

[7] *See e.g.*, MPEP § 1502.

[8] *Id.*, § 1503.01 (noting that a textual description is neither required nor prohibited).

[9] 35 U.S.C. § 173.

US00D638854S

(12) **United States Design Patent**   (10) Patent No.:   **US D638,854 S**

Andre et al.   (45) **Date of Patent:**   ** **May 31, 2011**

(54) **MEDIA DEVICE**

(75) Inventors: **Bartley K. Andre**, Menlo Park, CA (US); **Daniel J. Coster**, San Francisco, CA (US); **Daniele De Iuliis**, San Francisco, CA (US); **Richard P. Howarth**, San Francisco, CA (US); **Jonathan P. Ive**, San Francisco, CA (US); **Steve Jobs**, Palo Alto, CA (US); **Duncan Robert Kerr**, San Francisco, CA (US); **Shin Nishibori**, Portola Valley, CA (US); **Matthew Dean Rohrbach**, San Francisco, CA (US); **Douglas B. Satzger**, Menlo Park, CA (US); **Calvin Q. Seid**, Palo Alto, CA (US); **Christopher J. Stringer**, Woodside, CA (US); **Eugene Antony Whang**, San Francisco, CA (US); **Rico Zorkendorfer**, San Francisco, CA (US)

(73) Assignee: **Apple Inc.**, Cupertino, CA (US)

(**) Term: **14 Years**

(21) Appl. No.: **29/379,225**

(22) Filed: **Nov. 16, 2010**

Related U.S. Application Data

(60) Continuation of application No. 29/361,026, filed on May 4, 2010, now Pat. No. Des. 627,367, which is a continuation of application No. 29/343,120, filed on Sep. 8, 2009, now Pat. No. Des. 616,899, which is a division of application No. 29/334,452, filed on Mar. 26, 2009, now Pat. No. Des. 601,172, which is a division of application No. 29/296,899, filed on Oct. 30, 2007, now Pat. No. Des. 589,530, which is a continuation of application No. 29/265,521, filed on Sep. 1, 2006, now Pat. No. Des. 560,228.

(51) LOC (9) Cl. **14-03**

(52) U.S. Cl. **D14/496**

(58) **Field of Classification Search** .... D14/496, D14/401, 435, 474, 483, 217, 137, 138, 160, D14/168, 356, 203.1–203.8, 507; 345/156, 345/169, 173–179, 905; 715/727–729, 864; 710/1, 5, 8; 713/1, 600; 455/1.1, 1.7, 73, 455/344–347, 93, 95, 3.01–3.06, 550.1, 573.1; 370/342–344; 369/1, 2, 6–12; 463/43–47; 273/148 B

See application file for complete search history.

(56) **References Cited**

U.S. PATENT DOCUMENTS

5,825,408 A   10/1998   Yuyama et al.

(Continued)

FOREIGN PATENT DOCUMENTS

CN   3260632D   10/2002

(Continued)

OTHER PUBLICATIONS

"ASCII" weekly publication issued on Jul. 29, 2003, No. 450, Design of USB Memory Audio Player (JPO publicly known design No. HA15013509) received by the National Center for Industrial Property Information on Jul. 15, 2003.

(Continued)

Primary Examiner — Prabhakar Deshmukh

(74) Attorney, Agent, or Firm — Sterne, Kessler, Goldstein & Fox PLLC

(57)   **CLAIM**

The ornamental design for a media device, as shown and described.

DESCRIPTION

FIG. 1 is a front perspective view of a media device showing our new design.

FIG. 2 is a front elevational view thereof;

FIG. 3 is a rear elevational view thereof;

FIG. 4 is a top plan view thereof;

FIG. 5 is a bottom plan view thereof;

FIG. 6 is a left side elevational view thereof; and,

FIG. 7 is a right side elevational view thereof.

The dashed broken lines in the Figures show portions of the media device which form no part of the claimed design. The dot-dash broken lines in the Figures show unclaimed boundary lines and form no part of the claimed design.

1 Claim, 4 Drawing Sheets

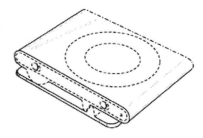

A design patent is limited to a single claim, which typically refers to the drawing or drawings as the primary description. For example, in this patent issued to Apple Inc. for the design of a media player, the claim reads "The ornamental design for a media device, as shown and described."

A design patent claim protects only the article's overall appearance and not its utilitarian features.[10] Design that is primarily functional is not protectable. Some factors used to determine whether a design is primarily ornamental — rather than functional — include whether alternative designs might serve the same function, whether alternative designs would affect the article's utility, whether a utility patent covers the same article, how the ornamental features are advertised and whether some design elements are clearly not dictated by any function.[11]

A design patent can be granted for the ornamental features of a useful product. For example, a design patent can be granted for an athletic shoe's overall visual appearance if that look is primarily driven by ornamentation.[12] As one example, a decision held that design protection for a key blade was denied where the shape of the blade was dictated by the need to properly fit into a corresponding lock.[13] As the court explained, "[a]ny aesthetic appeal of the key blade design shown in the . . . patent is the inevitable result of having a shape that is dictated solely by functional concerns."[14]

Both design and utility patents may be obtained on the same article where the design and utility patents protect different features of the same device.[15] For example, one may wish to obtain a design patent for the overall visual appearance of a portable media player and a utility patent for a novel and nonobvious improvement of the memory device inside. However, obtaining both a design and utility patent for the identical feature — such as the MP3 player's ergonomic design — is problematic. This is because the existence of a utility patent for the device's appearance may demonstrate that its design is functional rather than primarily ornamental.

The focus of the infringement inquiry is on the design patent's visual depiction.[16] Infringement of a design patent is based on whether an ordinary observer who is familiar with the prior art would be deceived into believing that the accused product is the same as the patented design.[17] The focus is on the overall design, not the features in isolation. If the designs are plainly dissimilar, a patentee cannot succeed. If the designs are close, an ordinary observer should consider the claimed design against the relevant prior art. When doing so, it is expected that the "differences between the claimed and accused design that might not be noticeable in the abstract can become significant."[18] Thus, if a claimed design does not exhibit many differences from the prior art, "small differences between the accused design and

---

[10] *L.A. Gear*, 988 F.2d at 1123.

[11] PHG Technologies, LLC v. St. John Companies, Inc., 469 F.3d 1361, 1366-67 (Fed. Cir. 2006).

[12] *L.A. Gear*, 988 F.2d at 1123 (finding design patent protection appropriate where "[i]t was not disputed that there were other ways of designing athletic shoes to perform the functions of the elements of the [patented] design.").

[13] Best Lock Corp. v. Ilco Unican Corp., 94 F.3d 1563 (Fed. Cir. 1996).

[14] *Id.* at 1565.

[15] MPEP § 1502.01.

[16] Crocs, Inc. v. ITC, 598 F.3d 1294, 1303 (Fed. Cir. 2010).

[17] Egyptian Goddess, Inc. v. Swisa, Inc., 543 F.3d 665 (Fed. Cir. 2008).

[18] *Id.* at 678.

the claimed design assume more importance to the eye of the hypothetical ordinary observer."[19]

§ 5.04 PLANT PATENTS

Under the Plant Patent Act, the U.S. PTO may grant a patent to one who "invents or discovers and asexually reproduces any distinct and new variety of plant."[20] The legislation was originally enacted in 1930, to "afford agriculture, so far as practicable, the same opportunity to participate in the benefits of the patent system as has been given to industry" and to provide plant breeders with incentives to undertake development work with plants.[21]

The legislative history of the Plant Patent Act defines "asexual reproduction" as reproduction by "grafting, budding, cuttings, layering, division, and the like, but not by seeds."[22] Sexually reproduced plants are not subject to plant patent protection. As one court described, "Asexual reproduction is the heart of the present plant patent system: the whole key to the 'invention' of a new plant is the discovery of new traits plus the foresight and appreciation to take the step of asexual reproduction."[23]

Plant patents have a relaxed written description requirement particularly compared to utility patents. The specification of a plant patent application need only set forth the subject matter of the application in a way that is "as complete as is reasonably possible."[24] Under this standard, the specification must describe the plant and the characteristics that distinguish the plant from related known varieties and describe the manner of asexual reproduction.[25] Like design patents, plant patents are limited to a single claim.[26]

The Plant Patent Act grants the patentee the right to exclude others from the following activities that involve the patented plant: 1) asexual reproduction; 2) use; 3) offers for sale, or 4) sales.[27] To establish infringement, the patentee must demonstrate that one of these acts occurred with respect to an accused plant that

---

[19] *Crocs*, 598 F.3d at 1304.

[20] 35 U.S.C. § 161. At the time that that Plant Patent Act was passed in 1930, protection was limited to asexually reproduced plants because new plant varieties could not be reproduced true-to-type through sexual reproduction. Diamond v. Chakrabarty, 447 U.S. 303, 312 (1980). By 1970, that circumstance had changed and protection for sexually reproduced plants was extended in Plant Variety Protection Act ("PVPIA"). *Id.* at 313. The PVPIA is discussed later in this Chapter.

[21] *See* Imazio Nursery, Inc. v. Dania Greenhouses, 69 F.3d 1560, 1562 (Fed. Cir. 1995) (describing legislative history and quoting S. Rep. No. 315, 71st Cong., 2d Sess. 3 (1930)).

[22] *Imazio*, 69 F.3d at 1566, *quoting* S. Rep. No. 315, 71st Cong., 2d Sess. 3 at 1 (1930).

[23] Yoder Bros., Inc. v. California-Florida Plant Corp., 537 F.2d 1347, 1380 (5th Cir. 1976) ("Asexual reproduction is literally the only way that a breeder can be sure he has reproduced a plant identical in every respect to the parent.").

[24] 35 U.S.C. § 162; *see generally, Chakrabarty*, 447 U.S. at 312 ("Because new plants may differ from old only in color or perfume, differentiation by written description was often impossible.").

[25] 37 C.F.R. § 1.163(a) (2007); *Imazio*, 69 F.3d at 1564.

[26] 37 C.F.R. § 1.163(c)(10).

[27] 35 U.S.C. § 163 (2000).

is an asexual progeny of the patented plant, or part of the plant invented or discovered by the applicant.[28] The Federal Circuit has emphasized that the reach of a plant patent is narrow — that is, "[t]he statute requires asexual reproduction of the patented plant for there to be infringement."[29] A critical distinction between a plant patent and a utility patent is that independent development of the plant is a complete defense to an allegation of infringement of a plant patent.[30] Although plant patents and utility patents are distinct, one may seek to protect a single plant under either (or both) systems.[31]

§ 5.05 PLANT VARIETY PROTECTION ACT CERTIFICATE

Under the Plant Variety Protection Act ("PVPA"), 7 U.S.C. § 2321 et seq., the U.S. Department of Agriculture[32] may award a certificate of protection that lasts for 20 years for most crops and 25 years for trees, shrubs, and vines. The PVPA was passed by Congress in 1970 to provide developers with "adequate encouragement for research, and for marketing when appropriate, to yield for the public the benefits of new varieties."[33] The PVPA extends a patent-like protection to novel varieties of sexually reproduced plants (that is, plants grown from seed) which parallels the patent protection for asexually reproduced plant varieties under the Patent Act.[34]

Under the PVPA, owners, breeders or discoverers of certain sexually reproduced or tuber propagated plants may acquire "the right . . . to exclude others from selling the variety, or offering it for sale, or reproducing it, or importing it, or exporting it, or using it in producing . . . a hybrid or different variety therefrom"[35] so long as the plant is:

- new, such that the variety has not been sold or disposed to other persons, for longer than one (1) year prior in the U.S. or longer than four (4) years outside the U.S. (or six (6) years for a tree or vine);

- distinct, as a variety that "is clearly distinguishable from any other variety the existence of which is publicly known or a matter of common knowledge at the time of the filing of the application";

---

[28] See generally Vincent G. Gioia, Plant Patents — R.I.P, 79 J. Pat. & Trademark Off. Soc'y 516 (1997).

[29] Imazio Nursery, Inc. v. Dania Greenhouses, 69 F.3d 1560, 1570 (Fed. Cir. 1995).

[30] Id.

[31] J.E.M. AG Supply Inc. v. Pioneer Hi-Bred Int'l, Inc., 534 U.S. 124, 145 (2001) (". . . we hold that newly developed plant breeds fall within the terms of § 101, and that neither the PPA nor the PVPA limits the scope of § 101's coverage").

[32] The U.S. Department of Agriculture has established a division called the "Plant Variety Protection Office," to examine PVPA applications and to issue PVPA certificates. See 7 U.S.C. § 2321. The U.S. Department of Agriculture's Plant Variety Protection Office is distinct from the U.S. Department of Commerce's Patent & Trademark Office, which examines and issues utility and plant patents.

[33] 7 U.S.C. § 2581.

[34] Asgrow Seed Co. v. Winterboer, 513 U.S. 179, 181 (1995).

[35] See generally Syngenta Seeds, Inc. v. Delta Cotton Co-operative, Inc., 457 F.3d 1269 (Fed. Cir. 2006), quoting 7 U.S.C. § 2483(a)(1) (2004) (describing rights under the Plant Variety Protection Act).

- <u>uniform</u>, such that any variations are describable, predictable, and commercially acceptable; and

- <u>stable</u>, and will remain unchanged with regard to the essential and distinctive characteristics of the variety with a reasonable degree of reliability.[36]

Unlike utility patents, the PVP examination does not have a nonobviousness requirement or require a written disclosure.[37] The PVPA allows certificate holders to sue for infringement, authorizing the awards of both injunctive and monetary damages.[38] Infringing acts include, *inter alia*, selling or marketing the protected variety, sexually multiplying the variety as a step in marketing, using the variety in producing a hybrid, or dispensing the variety without notice that the variety is protected.[39]

Unlike a patent right, a PVP certificate is subject to a number of exceptions. These include a provision that allows a farmer to save and replant seed on the farmer's own acreage.[40] In addition, the statute includes a research exception for plant breeding or other bona fide research,[41] as well as an exception for private, noncommercial uses of protected seed.[42]

§ 5.06 CONCLUSION

By far, utility patents are the most numerous of all three types issued by the U.S. PTO. Fundamentally, utility patents protect useful inventions, such as an apparatus or process that performs a function or results in the creation of another thing. By contrast, design patents protect a product's ornamental features.

In addition, two different types of plant protection exist. The first is under the 1930 Plant Patent Act, which authorizes the U.S. PTO to issue a patent for distinct and new varieties of asexually produced plants. The second is the 1970 Plant Variety Protection Act, administered by the U.S. Department of Agriculture, which protects novel asexually reproduced plants.

---

[36] 7 U.S.C. § 2402.

[37] *See* Mark D. Janis & Jay P. Kesan, *U.S. Plant Variety Protection: Sound And Fury . . . ?*, 39 HOUS. L. REV. 727, 748 (2002).

[38] 7 U.S.C. § 2561.

[39] 7 U.S.C. § 2541(a); *see also* J.E.M. AG Supply Inc. v. Pioneer Hi-Bred Int'l, Inc., 534 U.S. 124, 140 (2001).

[40] 7 U.S.C. § 2543; see also Asgrow Seed Co. v. Winterboer, 513 U.S. 179 (1995).

[41] 7 U.S.C. § 2544.

[42] *Id.* at § 2541(e).

Chapter 6

ADJUDICATION OF PATENT DISPUTES WITHIN THE COURT SYSTEM

SYNOPSIS

§ 6.01   INTRODUCTION

§ 6.02   U.S. DISTRICT COURT ACTIONS

   [A]   Subject Matter Jurisdiction

   [B]   Standing to Sue for Infringement

   [C]   Declaratory Judgment Jurisdiction

   [D]   Personal Jurisdiction and Venue

§ 6.03   THE U.S. COURT OF APPEALS FOR THE FEDERAL CIRCUIT

   [A]   Background

   [B]   The Jurisdiction of the Federal Circuit

§ 6.04   PATENT LITIGATION IN THE INTERNATIONAL TRADE COMMISSION

§ 6.05   CONCLUSION

§ 6.01   INTRODUCTION

The U.S. court system is the primary forum for the litigation of patent infringement disputes.[1] In connection with resolving these actions, courts serve a vital function by scrutinizing the validity and enforceability of issued patents.[2] Judicial review of patents, which has existed since the first Patent Act was instituted in 1790, is an important compliment to the U.S. PTO's ability to issue patents in the first instance:

> Public policy requires that only inventions which fully meet the statutory standards are entitled to patents. This policy is furthered when the validity

---

[1]   35 U.S.C. § 281; 28 U.S.C. § 1338.

[2]   35 U.S.C. § 282; Lear, Inc. v. Adkins, 395 U.S. 653, 670 (1969) ("[T]he Patent Office is often obliged to reach its decision in an *ex parte* proceeding, without the aid of the arguments which could be advanced by parties interested in proving patent invalidity."). For more on this issue, *see* Jay P. Kesan & Andres A. Gallo, *Why "Bad" Patents Survive in the Market and How Should We Change? — The Private and Social Costs of Patents*, 55 EMORY L.J. 61, 70 (2006) (describing how "incorrectly issued patents can survive in the market without judicial review, even when the invention is neither novel nor nonobvious," in part due to the high cost of court challenges).

of a patent, which was originally obtained in *ex parte* proceedings in the PTO, can be challenged in court.[3]

In the course of performing this work, the courts have developed substantive patent law and key interpretations of the Patent Act.[4] In addition, U.S. District Courts have jurisdiction to consider any claim asserted by a plaintiff where the right to relief requires resolution of a substantial question of patent law.[5] District Courts examine other patent related matters. As one example, the court in the Eastern District of Virginia has jurisdiction to consider civil actions filed by patent applicants seeking review of U.S. PTO rejections of claims in a patent application.[6]

Since 1982, appeals from U.S. District Court infringement actions have been taken to the U.S. Court of Appeals for the Federal Circuit (most commonly referred to as the "Federal Circuit"), a Federal appellate court that was formed to promote uniformity in patent cases. Beyond this, the U.S. Supreme Court may grant discretionary review of the Federal Circuit's final judgments through a writ of certiorari.

The International Trade Commission ("ITC") is an administrative court that adjudicates actions brought to prevent the U.S. importation of infringing goods. Specifically, the ITC may grant orders preventing the exclusion of infringing goods and requiring that further infringement cease and desist. However, the ITC lacks authority to award monetary damages.

§ 6.02   U.S. DISTRICT COURT ACTIONS

[A]   Subject Matter Jurisdiction

28 U.S.C. section 1338 provides that "district courts shall have original jurisdiction of any civil action arising under any Act of Congress relating to patents . . . ." Under this section, the U.S. District Court's subject matter jurisdiction to resolve infringement disputes depends on whether the face of the complaint raises an issue of patent law under the well-pleaded complaint rule.[7] In other words, the district court's jurisdiction is established where patent law creates the cause of action or the plaintiff's right to relief necessarily depends on resolution of a substantial question of patent law. Certainly, a plaintiff's patent infringement

---

[3] *See* Constant v. Advanced Micro-Devices, Inc., 848 F.2d 1560, 1564 (Fed. Cir. 1988); *see also* Mark A. Lemley, *Rational Ignorance at the Patent Office*, 95 Nw. U. L. Rev. 1495, 1497 (2001) (arguing that court validity determinations are economically preferable to expending resources at the U.S. PTO to ensure that all issued patents are valid "[b]ecause so few patents are ever asserted against a competitor, it is much cheaper for society to make detailed validity determinations in those few cases than to invest additional resources examining patents that will never be heard from again.").

[4] *See generally* Craig Allen Nard, *Legal Forms and the Common Law of Patents*, 90 B.U.L. Rev. 51 (2010).

[5] *See, e.g.*, Warrior Sports, Inc. v. Dickinson Wright, P.L.L.C., 631 F.3d 1367 (Fed. Cir. 2011).

[6] 35 U.S.C. § 145.

[7] *See* 28 U.S.C. § 1338; Holmes v. Vorando Air Circulation Systems, Inc., 535 U.S. 826 (2002); Christianson v. Colt Indus. Operating Corp., 486 U.S. 800 (1988). See generally Franchise Tax Board v. Construction Laborers Vacation Trust, 463 U.S. 1 (1983) (explaining the well-pleaded complaint rule).

complaint against an accused infringer satisfies this requirement. Similarly, jurisdiction may be found where patent infringement is a necessary element of the patentee's state law claim.[8]

However, the mere presence of a patent issue in the case, such where as a complaint asserts a breach of contract claim based on a failed patent assignment, does not support federal jurisdiction.[9] As one court explained, "[i]t may seem strange at first blush that the question of whether a patent is valid and infringed ordinarily is one for federal courts, while the question of who owns the patent rights . . . [is] exclusively for state courts. Yet that long has been the law."[10] As another example, a non-patent cause of action is not easily transformed into a basis for federal patent jurisdiction simply by inserting an allegation somewhat relating to patents into another cause of action. Thus, in *Christianson v. Colt Industries*,[11] the Supreme Court examined whether an antitrust claim could confer patent-based jurisdiction where the specific allegations required proof that the defendant's patents were invalid. The Court held that the plaintiff's theory, which indisputably rested on a demonstration of the invalidity of the defendant's patents, did not "arise under" patent law, explaining, "just because an element that is essential to a particular theory might be governed by federal patent law does not mean that the entire monopolization claim 'arises under' patent law."[12] *Christianson* underscores that, to establish patent-based jurisdiction, patent law must be an essential element to a plaintiff's claim.

When the well-pleaded complaint rule is applied under section 1338, a patent issue that exists solely in a defendant's counterclaim is not sufficient.[13] This circumstance can occur where a plaintiff asserts a state law cause of action against a defendant, such as a state breach of contract claim, and the defendant counterclaims with a cause of action for patent infringement. Under former law, the defendant could not use the patent infringement counterclaim as the basis to remove the entire case to the U.S. district court. This is because the federal court's patent jurisdiction must be based on a well-pleaded complaint (because a counterclaim is not a complaint, it is insufficient). In this example, the defendant might attempt to file a separate federal action for patent infringement, and thereby effectively convert the state court counterclaim into a federal court complaint. For factually related claims, this creates litigation in two separate courts in a manner that raises the specter of inconsistent findings and wasteful duplication.

The recently enacted America Invents Act attempts to resolve this dilemma through a series of provisions. First, the Act prevents state courts from hearing

---

[8] See *Warrior Sports, Inc. v. Dickinson Wright, P.L.L.C.*, 631 F.3d 1367 (Fed. Cir. 2011) (in a legal malpractice action, the requirement that the plaintiff show probable success on the merits of a patent infringement case was sufficient to establish subject matter jurisdiction).

[9] See, e.g., *Beghin-Say Int'l, Inc. v. Ole-Bendt Rasmussen*, 733 F.2d 1568 (Fed. Cir. 1984) (no federal jurisdiction under § 1338, where the complaint asserted a breach of contract claim against a defendant for failure to assign U.S. patents pursuant to the parties' agreement).

[10] *Jim Arnold Corp. v. Hydrotech Sys., Inc.*, 109 F.3d 1567, 1572 (Fed. Cir. 1997).

[11] *Christianson*, 486 U.S. at 805-06.

[12] *Id.* at 811.

[13] *Id.* at 808.

any patent law claims, including any asserted via counterclaim by a defendant, in those courts.[14] Second, the Act allows a defendant to file a new suit as a plaintiff in federal court under the well-pleaded complaint rule.[15] Third, any party may rely on a defendant's patent counterclaim as the basis to remove an entire action to federal court.[16]

Because section 1338's "arising under" language has been preserved in the America Invents Act, the well-pleaded complaint rule remains applicable to that section. As a general rule in federal practice, removal does not typically confer subject matter jurisdiction.[17] Given that this section expressly divests state courts of jurisdiction to hear patent claims, is such removal proper? Or does this series of statutory amendments mean that a defendant's counterclaim for patent infringement has no forum in which it can be determined unless filed as a separate federal action?

Some patent reform legislative history suggests that an action with a state law claim and a patent counterclaim might proceed as a single case in a federal district court.[18] As a predicate, one must assume that a plaintiff has filed a state court action and that the sole patent claim raised in the case is in the defendant's counterclaim. Subject matter jurisdiction for the removed action might be based on the newly amended removal statute.[19] Because no court has issued an authoritative interpretation on this point, district court jurisdiction for a patent counterclaim is presently not certain.

---

[14] The amended 28 U.S.C. § 1338 now includes the sentence "No State court shall have jurisdiction *over any claim for relief arising under* any Act of Congress relating to patents, plant variety protection, or copyrights." (emphasis added).

[15] 28 U.S.C. § 1338 ("The district courts shall have original jurisdiction of any civil action arising under any Act of Congress relating to patents . . . .").

[16] 28 U.S.C. § 1454 ("A civil action in which any party asserts a claim for relief arising under any Act of Congress relating to patents . . . may be removed to the district court of the United States for the district and division embracing the place where the action is pending.") (as amended Sept. 16, 2011).

[17] Jim Arnold Corp. v. Hydrotech Systems, Inc., 109 F.3d 1567, 1571 (Fed. Cir. 1997).

[18] The testimony that explains this scenario is, in relevant part, excerpted here:

> With respect to State court jurisdiction, I think the best approach is the most direct. What we want to do is to assure that State courts are precluded from hearing claims under the patent and copyright laws. It seems to me the simplest way to do that is to say that, and the place to say that is in the second sentence of 1338(a) that is the exclusive jurisdiction provision. . . .
> Now, there is one difficulty with that. If you do that alone, a patent or copyright counterclaim brought in State court would have to be dismissed, and the defendant would have to file a new suit in Federal court. So you end up with the parties litigating two suits, even though the claims are closely related or perhaps even interdependent. That's just not very efficient. To avoid that, Congress could enact a statute that would authorize removal on the basis of a patent or copyright counterclaim.

HOLMES GROUP, THE FEDERAL CIRCUIT, AND THE STATE OF PATENT appeals, HEARING BEFORE THE SUBCOMM. ON COURTS, THE INTERNET, AND INTELLECTUAL PROPERTY OF THE H. COMM. ON THE JUDICIARY, 109th Cong. 33 (2005), available at http://www.access.gpo.gov/congress/house/pdf/109hrg/20019.pdf (testimony of Prof. Arthur D. Hellman); *see also* H.R. Rep. No. 112–98, at 54 (2011) affirming and adopting H.R. Rep. No. 109-407 (2006).

[19] *Id.* To do so, the section might be construed in a manner consistent with the officer's removal statute, 28 U.S.C. § 1441 et seq. See generally Jefferson County, Ala. v. Acker, 527 U.S. 423 (1999) (explaining the officer removal section as an exception to the well pleaded complaint rule).

[B] Standing to Sue for Infringement

A patent infringement action can be filed by any patentee.[20] The Patent Act defines "patentee" as the one to whom the patent was issued and also any successors in interest such as an assignee of the patent.[21] In addition, an exclusive licensee who holds all substantial rights to the patent may also bring suit for infringement.[22] However, a non-exclusive licensee or one who otherwise lacks all substantial rights to the patent cannot sue to enforce a patent.[23]

[C] Declaratory Judgment Jurisdiction

In a typical lawsuit, the injured party files suit against the wrongdoer to obtain relief. In a patent case, this correlates to a patentee filing suit against an accused infringer. However, some who learn about another's patent may wish to file a lawsuit rather than wait to be sued. To do so, the accused infringer must file suit under the Declaratory Judgment Act.[24] This procedure is geared to prevent the scenario such as that described below:

> Guerrilla-like, the patent owner attempts extra-judicial patent enforcement with scare-the-customer-and-run tactics that infect the competitive environment of the business community with uncertainty and insecurity. Before the [Declaratory Judgment] Act, competitors victimized by that tactic were rendered helpless and immobile so long as the patent owner refused to grasp the nettle and sue.[25]

By using the Act, one is not left with a choice between incurring potential infringement liability or discontinuing sales or manufacture of the accused product. Instead, one can "clear the air by suing for a judgment that would settle the conflict of interests."[26] Such actions can assert non-infringement, invalidity or unenforceability, among other things.

Declaratory Judgment jurisdiction is limited. Thus, one who is merely selling a product that might be covered by another's patent does not have a sufficient interest to invoke a federal court's jurisdiction.[27] As one opinion explains, "[t]he mere existence of a potentially adverse patent does not cause an injury nor create an imminent risk of an injury; absent action by the patentee, a potential competitor is

---

[20] 35 U.S.C. § 281 (2000).

[21] 35 U.S.C. § 100(d).

[22] Textile Prod., Inc. v. Mead Corp., 134 F.3d 1481, 1483-84 (Fed. Cir. 1998).

[23] *Id.* at 1484. There is a limited exception where a licensee may sue when "necessary to prevent an absolute failure of justice, as where the patentee is the infringer, and cannot sue himself." *Id.* (citing Waterman v. Mackenzie, 138 U.S. 252, 255 (1891)).

[24] 28 U.S.C. § 2201(a). *See* Sony Elecs., Inc. v. Guardian Media Technologies, Ltd., 497 F.3d 1271 (Fed. Cir. 2007).

[25] Arrowhead Indus. Water, Inc. v. Ecolochem, Inc., 846 F.2d 731, 735 (Fed. Cir. 1988).

[26] *Id.*

[27] Prasco, LLC v. Medicis Pharmaceutical Corp., 537 F.3d 1329, 1338 (Fed. Cir. 2008) ("the existence of a patent is not sufficient to establish declaratory judgment jurisdiction").

legally free to market its product in the face of an adversely held patent."[28] Similarly, infringement allegations that are leveled against a seller's customers are not sufficient unless it can be shown that the seller's actions independently infringe.[29]

On the other hand, the standard is easily met where, for example, a patentee threatens another with an infringement lawsuit, identifies the relevant claims and provides notice of the products alleged to be infringing.[30] However, relief is not limited to those with a reasonable apprehension that a patent lawsuit is imminent. Rather, one may sue under the Declaratory Relief Act whenever the parties have a dispute that is "definite and concrete, touching the legal relations of parties having adverse legal interests."[31] Under these circumstances, one may sue where the parties have "taken adverse positions with regard to their obligations, each side presenting a concrete claim of a specific right" relating to patent infringement.[32]

To determine whether the jurisdiction exists, the court examines the totality of the parties' relationship. It is present where discussions indicate that it is reasonable to believe that the patentee will file suit if the accused infringer indicates a readiness to engage in the allegedly infringing activity.[33] Additionally, a party who continues to pay royalties under protest may meet this standard where the parties' discussions establish that the licensee contends that the patent is invalid and royalties are no longer due.[34]

[D]　Personal Jurisdiction and Venue

Personal jurisdiction in patent cases is based on the same principles that are well established in all other areas of the federal practice.[35] Where the constitutional "minimum contacts" test is applied, personal jurisdiction for a patent infringement claim is established where a defendant ships an accused product through an established distribution channel located in a particular state.[36] Under this standard, "any company that operates in national commerce is likely subject to

---

[28] *Id.* (rejecting that "paralyzing uncertainty" from the potential for an infringement lawsuit was sufficient to establish jurisdiction, explaining that fear of future harm is not sufficient).

[29] Creative Compounds LLC v. Starmark Laboratories, 651 F.3d 1303, 1316 (Fed. Cir. 2011). Note that the result might be different in the presence of a seller indemnification agreement or a suggestion that the seller would be indirectly liable for the customer's infringement.

[30] *See Sony*, 497 F.3d at 1285-86 (parties' ongoing negotiations did not render the dispute nonjusticiable, where one party determined that further negotiations would not be productive).

[31] MedImmune, Inc. v. Genentech, Inc., 549 U.S. 118, 127 (2007).

[32] SanDisk Corp. v. STMicroelectronics, Inc., 480 F.3d 1372, 1379 (Fed. Cir. 2007).

[33] See Revolution Eyewear, Inc. v. Aspex Eyewear, Inc., 556 F.3d 1294, 1299 (Fed. Cir. 2009).

[34] *MedImmune*, 549 U.S. at 128.

[35] Beverly Hills Fan Co. v. Royal Sovereign Corp., 21 F.3d 1558, 1565 (Fed. Cir. 1994) ("due process requires . . . that in order to subject a defendant to a judgment *in personam*, if he be not present within the territory of the forum, he have certain *minimum contacts* with it such that the maintenance of the suit does not offend 'traditional notions of fair play and substantial justice," *quoting* International Shoe Co. v. Washington, 326 U.S. 310, 316 (1945).

[36] *Id.*; see also Nuance Communications, Inc. v. Abbyy Software House, 626 F.3d 1222 (Fed. Cir. 2010).

personal jurisdiction in many possible districts."[37]

Under 28 U.S.C. § 1440, *venue* is proper in any U.S. district court "where the defendant resides, or where the defendant has committed acts of infringement and has a regular and established place of business." The Federal Circuit has construed this language expansively, finding that venue is proper wherever personal jurisdiction exists.[38]

Although a wide range of available choices exist to litigate patent actions where the accused infringer sells product throughout the U.S., most patent cases tend to be concentrated in specific regions. For example, one study noted that "patent cases are not dispersed evenly throughout the ninety-four judicial districts nor dispersed according to the relative size of the court's civil docket generally, but rather consolidated in a few select jurisdictions. This suggests that patent holders actively select particular forums."[39] This same source suggests that patentees chose particular forums for strategic reasons, including speed of adjudication, the opportunity to take a case to trial and a view that a district's juries are disposed to favor patentees.[40]

One jurisdiction that has become very popular in recent years is the Eastern District of Texas.[41] There have been reports that plaintiffs file actions there because of a perception that juries in that forum favor patent owners.[42] In response, some defendants have filed a motion to transfer venue out of the district, particularly in cases where the sole connection is based on the sale of infringing products and the parties, witnesses and documents are elsewhere. These motions to transfer are based on 28 U.S.C. section 1404(a), which allows a district court to transfer the case to another venue "[f]or the convenience of parties and witnesses." Although formerly such motions had been routinely denied by the district courts, the Federal Circuit has begun to reverse some of those denials as an abuse of discretion.[43] Thus, where such procedures are invoked, a litigant's strategic choice of forum is not unconstrained by court oversight.

---

[37] Kimberly A. Moore, *Forum Shopping in Patent Cases: Does Geographic Choice Affect Innovation?*, 83 J. Pat. & Trademark Off. Soc'y 558, 563 (2001).

[38] Trintec Indus., Inc. v. Pedre Promotional Prods., Inc., 395 F.3d 1275, 1280 (Fed. Cir. 2005).

[39] Moore, *supra* note 37, at 561.

[40] *Id.* at 568-69, 594.

[41] Julie Cresswell, *So Small a Town, So Many Patent Suits*, The New York Times (Sept. 24, 2006) (noting that "[m]ore patent lawsuits will be filed here [in the Eastern District of Texas] this year than in federal district courts in San Francisco, Chicago, New York and Washington.").

[42] *Id.* (noting that patentees favor the Eastern District of Texas because of rules that shorten the time to trial and "the fact that they usually win. Three-fourths of the cases that come to trial in Marshall are decided in favor of the plaintiffs, compared with less than half in New York."); *see generally* Yan Leychkis, *Of Fire Ants and Claim Construction: An Empirical Study of the Meteoric Rise of the Eastern District of Texas as a Preeminent Forum for Patent Litigation*, 9 Yale J.L. & Tech. 193 (2007).

[43] *See* In re Genentech, Inc., 566 F.3d 1338 (Fed. Cir. 2009); In re TS Tech U.S.A Corp., 551 F.3d 1315 (Fed. Cir. 2008); In re Zimmer Holdings, Inc., 609 F.3d 1378 (Fed. Cir. 2010). These cases apply the law applicable in the Fifth Circuit.

§ 6.03   THE U.S. COURT OF APPEALS FOR THE FEDERAL CIRCUIT

[A]   Background

From 1891 through 1982, an appeal of a patent case from district court litigation was taken to the circuit court assigned to that district court's geographic region. Appeals challenging the administrative decisions of the U.S. PTO were taken to the Court of Customs and Patent Appeals, a court which no longer exists.

During the 1960's and 1970's, concerns began to arise that disagreements among the circuit courts had created splits of authority that created a " 'jurisprudential disarray' [that] threatens to become 'an intolerable legal mess.' "[44] Although review in the U.S. Supreme Court was theoretically available to resolve such conflicts, it was observed that the Court's "capacity to do so is limited by the sheer volume of adjudications, not to speak of its other major tasks."[45] As a practical matter, the uniformity of patent law was threatened and such uncertainty was thought to devalue patents and potentially harm this incentive system.

A number of studies were conducted to address solutions. One was performed by the Hruska Commission, a group formed by Congress in 1972.[46] The group's report:

> . . . confirmed what has long been asserted: the perceived disparity in results in different circuits leads to widespread forum shopping. "[M]ad and undignified races," Judge Henry Friendly describes them, "between a patentee who wishes to sue for infringement in one circuit believed to be benign toward patents, and a user who wants to obtain a declaration of invalidity or non-infringement in one believed to be hostile to them."[47]

Identified problems included a number of inter-circuit conflicts.[48] Other evidence indicated that, in at least one instance, a patent was held valid in one circuit and invalid in another.[49] As a result of the work performed by the Office for Improvements in the Administration of Justice, bills were submitted to Congress to merge two previously existing courts — namely, the appellate division of the Court of Claims and the Court of Customs and Patent Appeals — to create a nationwide

---

[44] *See* COMMISSION ON REVISION OF THE FEDERAL COURT APPELLATE SYSTEM STRUCTURE AND INTERNAL PROCEDURES, RECOMMENDATIONS FOR CHANGE, 67 F.R.D. 195, 206 (1975) [hereinafter HRUSKA COMMISSION REPORT].

[45] *Id.*

[46] *Id.* Another was undertaken by the Office for Improvements in the Administration of Justice, created by the U.S. Department of Justice in 1978. *See generally* Daniel J. Meador, *Origin of the Federal Circuit: A Personal Account*, 41 AM. U. L. REV. 581 (1992).

[47] HRUSKA COMMISSION REPORT, *supra* note 44, at 220.

[48] *Id.* at 228.

[49] *See generally* Paul M. Janicke, *To Be or Not to Be: The Long Gestation of the U.S. Court of Appeals for the Federal Circuit (1887-1982)*, 69 ANTITRUST L. J. 645, 646 (2002) (citing Graham v. John Deere Co., 383 U.S. 1 (1966), which considered a patent held valid in the Fifth Circuit but invalid in the Eighth).

court that would determine all patent appeals as part of its purpose.[50]

In 1982, Congress adopted a version of these proposals by enacting the Federal Courts Improvement Act which created the Federal Circuit. A Senate Report in support of the Act explained that the court was intended to "provide[ ] a forum that will increase doctrinal stability in the field of patent law."[51] This Report noted that "[u]niformity in the law will be a significant improvement from the standpoint of the businesses that rely on the patent system . . . . This can have important ramifications upon our economy as a whole."[52]

The Federal Circuit began operations on October 1, 1982. Those studying patent law should be cognizant of the shift that occurred after that date. Today, after the U.S. Supreme Court, the precedential opinions of the Federal Circuit are the most significant under the current federal court structure. Upon its formation, the Federal Circuit adopted all prior holdings of the Court of Claims and the Court of Customs and Patent Appeals as the precedent "most applicable to the areas of law within the substantive jurisdiction" of the court.[53] Thus, patent decisions of those two former courts retain viability to extent those rulings are not in conflict with later holdings of the Federal Circuit. Patent decisions of the regional circuit courts of appeals prior to October 1, 1982 are not considered binding on the Federal Circuit, although such cases may have some persuasive influence.[54]

[B]   The Jurisdiction of the Federal Circuit

Since its formation in 1982, all patent appeals from the U.S. District Courts are taken to the Federal Circuit Court of Appeals. Unlike other U.S. Courts of Appeals, the Federal Circuit's jurisdiction is based on subject matter rather than geography.[55] All appeals from patent cases decided in any of the U.S. District Courts throughout the U.S. are heard by the Federal Circuit. In addition, the Federal Circuit has exclusive jurisdiction over appeals of patent cases decided by the ITC.[56] The Federal Circuit reports that, in total, approximately 31% of its cases concern intellectual property matters, nearly all of which involve patent matters to some degree.[57]

---

[50] Meador, *supra* note 46, at 606-07.

[51] S. Rep. No. 97-275, at 5 (1981).

[52] *Id.* at 6.

[53] South Corp. v. United States, 690 F.2d 1368, 1370 (Fed. Cir. 1982).

[54] *See, e.g.*, SmithKline Beecham Corp. v. Apotex Corp., 403 F.3d 1331, 1353 (Fed. Cir. 2005) (referring to decisions of "our sister circuits, whose rulings on patent law prior to 1982 do not bind this court but retain persuasive value . . . .").

[55] 28 U.S.C. § 1295(a)(1) (2000).

[56] 28 U.S.C. § 1295(a)(6).

[57] *See* United States Court of Appeals for the Federal Circuit: About the Court, http://www.cafc.uscourts.gov/about.html (last visited Nov. 3, 2011). The largest percentage of the court's cases are those involving administrative law (55%), for example cases involving federal personnel and veterans claims. *Id.* Additionally, the court hears matters involving money damages brought against the U.S. (11% of its caseload), such as claims asserting unlawful takings, tax refund appeals, government contract cases and other types of pay cases. *Id.*

28 U.S.C. § 1295(a), the statutory basis for the court's jurisdiction over patent cases, formerly held that the Federal Circuit's jurisdiction for patent appeals depended on the U.S. district court's subject matter jurisdiction.[58] Just as this circumstance created a problem for patent counterclaims in the district courts, section 1295 created a subject matter jurisdiction "gap" where the federal patent claim was raised in a counterclaim. This is because a counterclaim, which is not a complaint, cannot satisfy the well-pleaded complaint rule that governed.[59] This raises a concern that uniform patent policy cannot be supported where patent litigation must be resolved in both state and federal courts.[60]

In 2011, the America Invents Act was amended to fill the gap. Specifically, the statute now expands the Federal Circuit's jurisdiction to include any civil action in which a party has asserted a compulsory counterclaim arising under federal patent law.[61]

§ 6.04 PATENT LITIGATION IN THE INTERNATIONAL TRADE COMMISSION

In addition to federal court, patent litigation is decided in the International Trade Commission ("ITC"), a federal administrative agency that both investigates and adjudicates matters relating to international trade.[62] Under 19 U.S.C. § 1337, the ITC investigates unfair importation activities, which include the importation of articles that infringe a valid and enforceable U.S. patent. The ITC's investigation commences either on the ITC's own initiative or based on the filing of a verified complaint that establishes factual grounds for relief. Typically, such complaints are filed by a patentee who must identify the infringing goods that are subject to importation into the U.S. In addition, the ITC has the authority to adjudicate these disputes to resolution.

One unique aspect of litigation in the ITC is that the complainant must demonstrate harm to a *domestic industry*, which is not a requirement for patent infringement actions filed in the federal courts.[63] Harm to a domestic industry may be shown, for example, where a patentee has a significant investment in plant and equipment located in the U.S., has significant employment of labor or capital in the U.S. or a substantial investment in the patent's exploitation within the U.S., including engineering, research and development, or licensing.[64]

---

[58] Holmes Group, Inc. v. Vornado Air Circulation Systems, Inc., 535 U.S. 826 (2002).

[59] *Id.*

[60] *Cf.* Christopher A. Cotropia, *Counterclaims, The Well-Pleaded Complaint, And Federal Jurisdiction*, 33 Hofstra L. Rev. 1, 39 (2004) ("The exclusion of certain cases from a federal district court's jurisdiction due to the well-pleaded complaint rule frustrates the purposes behind federal question jurisdiction--particularly the goal of uniformity.").

[61] 28 U.S.C. § 1295(a)(1) (as amended Sept. 16, 2011).

[62] For more information about patent litigation in the ITC, see *infra*, Chapter 35.

[63] 19 U.S.C. § 1337(a) (2000).

[64] 19 U.S.C. § 1337(a)(3); John Mezzalingua Associates, Inc. v. International Trade Comm'n, 660 F.3d 1322 (Fed. Cir. 2011) (litigation expenses to enforce a patent do not count toward demonstrating substantial investment for purposes of demonstrating the domestic industry requirement).

ITC cases proceed on a highly accelerated schedule. Although this forum may appear ideal for a patentee who seeks an expeditious resolution of a patent dispute, the relief available from the ITC is limited in scope. If the Commission decides that relief is appropriate, it may issue an *in rem* exclusion order that prevents the importation of infringing goods.[65] In addition, the Commission may issue a cease-and-desist order that prevents further unfair competition, such as prohibiting the sale of infringing goods out of U.S. inventory.[66] However, the ITC has no authority to award monetary damages. Patentees pursuing relief before the ITC frequently file a parallel action in the U.S. district court to preserve the ability to obtain monetary relief.

§ 6.05   CONCLUSION

The federal court system is the primary forum for the litigation of patent disputes. A party may bring suit where subject matter jurisdiction exists and personal jurisdiction and venue are proper. Where the parties have a definite and concrete dispute about a patent right, an accused infringer may file suit under the Declaratory Judgment Act. The Federal Circuit, created in 1982 to promote a uniform system of patent law, has jurisdiction to hear appeals based on federal patent infringement actions and compulsory patent counterclaims.

In addition, the ITC investigates and adjudicates investigations against unfair competition based on activity that infringes a U.S. patent. Although the ITC may initiate an investigation, a patentee may file a complaint to seek an *in rem* order excluding the importation of infringing products and/or an order that prevents continued infringement.

---

[65] 19 U.S.C. § 1337(d).

[66] 19 U.S.C. § 1337(f).

Chapter 7

OVERVIEW: THE DISCLOSURE REQUIREMENTS OF § 112

SYNOPSIS

§ 7.01 INTRODUCTION

§ 7.02 HISTORY AND POLICY OF PATENT DISCLOSURE

§ 7.03 ASSESSING THE ADEQUACY OF THE DISCLOSURE
REQUIREMENTS

§ 7.04 CONCLUSION

§ 7.01   INTRODUCTION

The four patent disclosure requirements are set forth in the first two paragraphs of 35 U.S.C. § 112. The first paragraph of § 112 includes the first three of the disclosure requirements:

> The specification shall contain a *written description* of the invention, and of the manner and process of making and using it, in such full, clear, concise, and exact terms as to *enable* any person skilled in the art to which it pertains, or with which it is most nearly connected, to make and use the same, and shall set forth the *best mode* contemplated by the inventor of carrying out his invention.[1]

Specifically, these three are: 1) the *written description* requirement ("The specification shall contain a written description of the invention"); 2) the *enablement requirement* ("and of the manner and process of making and using it, in such full, clear, concise, and exact terms as to enable any person skilled in the art to which it pertains, or with which it is most nearly connected, to make and use the same"); and 3) the *best mode* requirement (". . . and shall set forth the best mode contemplated by the inventor of carrying out his invention.").[2]

The second paragraph of section 112 states the fourth disclosure requirement-- that is, that patents must conclude with at least one claim that *particularly points out and distinctly claims the subject matter* and that the claim correlate to *what the applicant regards as the invention.*[3] The requirement that a patent application include a clear and precise claim allows patentees to set the scope (sometimes called

---

[1] 35 U.S.C. § 112 (2000).

[2] *Id.*

[3] *Id.*

the "metes and bounds") of their invention.

Each of these four statutory requirements must be met before the U.S. PTO will grant the patentee's application. Once the patent has issued, the patent may be invalidated if the challenger proves that *any single* requirement has not been met. An invalid patent has no legal effect and cannot be infringed.

§ 7.02 HISTORY AND POLICY OF PATENT DISCLOSURE

When the foundation of the early English patent system rested on the discretion of the crown, no specification was required.[4] One historian posits that no description was required "to protect the royal prerogative to its fullest extent" by eliminating any grounds that the English courts might use to invalidate a patent granted by the monarch.[5] Later, "[s]ometime after the beginning of the eighteenth century the law officers began to require a written specification as a condition of the patent grant and thereafter came to make this a routine requirement."[6]

Court enforcement of the specification requirement has been traced to *Liardet v. Johnson,* a case which was tried in the English courts in 1778.[7] In *Liardet,* Judge Mansfield explained to a jury that the patentee must show:

> . . . whether the specification is such as instructs others to make it. For the condition of giving encouragement is this: that you must specify upon record your invention in such a way as shall teach an artist, when your term is out, to make it — and to make as well by your directions; for then at the end of the term, the public shall have the benefit of it.[8]

These policies form the foundation for the disclosure requirements of U.S. patent law today. In return for the government granted patent right, the patentee must publicly disclose detailed information relating to the inventor's claims. As explained by the U.S. Supreme Court:

> When a patent is granted and the information contained in it is circulated to the general public and those especially skilled in the trade, such additions to the general store of knowledge are of such importance to the public weal that the Federal Government is willing to pay the high price of 17 years of exclusive use for its disclosure, which disclosure, it is assumed,

---

[4] Edward C. Walterscheid, *The Early Evolution of the United States Patent Law: Antecedents (Part 2),* 76 J. Pat. & Trademark Off. Soc'y 849, 860-62 (1994).

[5] *Id.* at 861-62; *see also* Adam Mossoff, *Rethinking the Development of Patents: An Intellectual History, 1550-1800,"* 52 Hastings L.J. 1255, 1267 (2000) (tracing the origins and history of the royal prerogative, including the statement of Queen Elizabeth who described the issuance of letters patent as "the chiefest flower in her garden and principal and head pearl in her crown and diadem").

[6] Edward C. Walterscheid, *The Early Evolution of the United States Patent Law: Antecedents (Part 3),* 77 J. Pat. & Trademark Off. Soc'y 771, 780 (1995).

[7] *See* John N. Adams & Gwen Averley, *The Patent Specification: The Role of* Liardet v. Johnson, 7 J. Legal Hist. 158, 162-67 (1986).

[8] Walterscheid, *supra* note 6, at 796; *see also* Boulton & Watt v. Bull, 126 Eng. Rep. 651 (1795) ("The specification is the price which the patentee is to pay for the monopoly.").

will stimulate ideas and the eventual development of further significant advances in the art.[9]

As it was under eighteenth century English law, today disclosure is viewed as a *quid pro quo* for the exclusionary right granted to the inventor.[10] The patent right acts as an incentive to disclose information that might otherwise be maintained as a trade secret. If those in the art have no way of knowing how the initial inventor solved a particular problem, they might engage in duplicative experimentation to reach a similar result. The disclosure requirements are intended to provide a critical public benefit of new ideas in order to advance scientific knowledge.[11]

The government right provides the patentee the right to exclude others in return for the patentee's disclosure of the invention. This disclosure informs others how to practice the invention after the patent has expired and enables those in the art to seek a license from the patentee.[12] The patent informs others of the patentee's advancements in the art so that others can design around the patent's claims.[13] Further, the specification tells the public what the invention is, so that there is adequate public notice of the scope of the patentee's rights.

§ 7.03   ASSESSING THE ADEQUACY OF THE DISCLOSURE REQUIREMENTS

Although the four disclosure requirements include different substantive requirements, there are a number of considerations that are common to each. First, an analysis of the sufficiency of these requirements requires an understanding of the claimed invention. In other words, one cannot determine whether the enablement or best mode requirements have been met for any particular patented invention unless one understands the metes and bounds of the patent claims.[14] Where the relevant claim terms cannot be given their ordinary meaning, a claim construction analysis may be required before adequacy under § 112 is determined.[15] Second, whether a patent or application is deemed to have an adequate disclosure is assessed from the perspective of one of ordinary skill in the art.[16]

---

[9] Kewanee Oil Co. v. Bicron Corp., 416 U.S. 470, 481 (1974); *see also* Festo Corp. v. Shoketsu Kinzoku Kogyo Kabushiki Co., Ltd., 535 U.S. 722, 731 (2002) ("the patent laws require inventors to describe their work in "full, clear, concise, and exact terms," as part of the delicate balance the law attempts to maintain between inventors, who rely on the promise of the law to bring the invention forth, and the public, which should be encouraged to pursue innovations, creations, and new ideas beyond the inventor's exclusive rights.") (citation omitted).

[10] Eldred v. Ashcroft, 537 U.S. 186, 216 (2003) (referring to the patent disclosure obligation as "exacted from" the patentee as "the price paid for the exclusivity secured").

[11] Some question the extent to which the public benefits from disclosures. *See e.g.*, Katherine J. Strandburg, *What Does The Public Get? Experimental Use And The Patent Bargain* 2004 Wis. L. Rev. 81 (2004); Timothy R. Holbrook, *Possession In Patent Law*, 59 Smu L. Rev. 123 (2006).

[12] *See generally* Univ. of Rochester v. G.D. Searle & Co., Inc., 358 F.3d 916, 922 (Fed. Cir. 2004).

[13] Strandburg, *supra* note 11, at 91-92 (describing the policies of disclosure obligations).

[14] *See e.g., In re* Warmerdam, 33 F.3d 1354, 1360 (Fed. Cir. 1994).

[15] For more information about construing patent claims, see Chapter 25.

[16] Phillips v. AWH Corp., 415 F.3d 1303, 1313 (Fed. Cir. 2005) ("The descriptions in patents are not

Third, a specification does not have to describe every possible implementation of the claimed subject matter to meet § 112's requirements. Rather, a patentee can describe a single embodiment to support a broad claim if the specification would "reasonably convey to a person skilled in the art that the inventor had possession of the claimed subject matter at the time of filing," and would "enable one of ordinary skill to practice the full scope of the claimed invention."[17] If this standard is met, a claim can be infringed by a device or process that is not described in the patent's specification so long as the claim's limitations are met either literally or under the doctrine of equivalents.

§ 7.04   CONCLUSION

The disclosure requirements of § 112 are: 1) the written description requirement; 2) the enablement requirement; 3) the best mode requirement; and 4) the requirement that the patentee particularly point out and distinctly claim the subject matter. A failure to meet any one of them may result in invalidation of the patent. These disclosure requirements, which have significant historic roots, are viewed today as an important *quid pro quo* for granting an inventor the patent right.

---

addressed to the public generally, to lawyers or to judges, but, as section 112 says, to those skilled in the art to which the invention pertains or with which it is most nearly connected.") (citation omitted).

[17] LizardTech, Inc. v. Earth Res. Mapping, Inc., 424 F.3d 1336, 1346 (Fed. Cir. 2005).

Chapter 8

ENABLEMENT

SYNOPSIS

§ 8.01   INTRODUCTION

§ 8.02   THE ENABLEMENT ANALYSIS

   [A]   Generally

   [B]   The Historic Perspective: *O'Reilly v. Morse*

   [C]   Edison's Light Bulb: *Consolidated Electric Light Co. v. McKeesport Light Co.*

   [D]   A Comparison: Bell's Telephone Patent

§ 8.03   ENABLEMENT AND CLAIM SCOPE

§ 8.04   UNDUE EXPERIMENTATION

   [A]   The Modern Foundation of Undue Experimentation: The *Wands* Factors

§ 8.05   ENABLEMENT, PRIORITY AND TIMING

   [A]   The Relevant State of the Art

   [B]   Enablement and Priority

   [C]   Enablement and Patent Enforcement

§ 8.06   ENABLEMENT AND UTILITY

§ 8.07   A BRIEF NOTE: SOME ECONOMIC CONSIDERATIONS

§ 8.08   CONCLUSION

§ 8.01   INTRODUCTION

35 U.S.C. § 112, ¶ 1 provides the foundation of the *enablement* requirement, as follows: "The specification shall contain . . . the manner and process of making and using [the invention], in such full, clear, concise, and exact terms as to enable any person skilled in the art to which it pertains, or with which it is most nearly connected, to make and use the same."[1] Enablement is met by a disclosure that teaches one of ordinary skill in the art how to make and use the full scope of the claimed invention without undue experimentation according to the state of the art on the effective filing date.[2]

---

[1] 35 U.S.C. § 112 (2000) (emphasis added).

[2] Liquid Dynamics Corp. v. Vaughan Co., Inc., 449 F.3d 1209, 1224 (Fed. Cir. 2006).

Considered part of the *quid pro quo* for the patent right, this patentability requirement serves two primary purposes. First, enablement has been said to effectuate a teaching function.[3] That is, the disclosed information can be used to introduce new information into a field and advance an art. This information is useful to design around a patent's claims or to innovate through non-infringing conduct. To the extent that a teaching remains technologically relevant beyond the patent's life, enabling information can be used to practice and use the invention after expiration of the patent's term.[4] Second, the enablement requirement demonstrates that the invention is sufficiently concrete to warrant a patent. As one court stated, "[p]atent protection is granted in return for an enabling disclosure of an invention, not for vague intimations of general ideas that may or may not be workable."[5] In other words, enablement prevents a patentee from obtaining a right before demonstrating that the invention has been fully realized.[6]

§ 8.02 THE ENABLEMENT ANALYSIS

[A] Generally

To assess enablement, one examines the relationship between the specification, the claims, and the knowledge of one of ordinary skill in the art as of the effective filing date.[7] The sufficiency of the disclosure is based on an objective examination of the four corners of the patent. An inventor is not required to demonstrate any subjective comprehension of how the invention works by disclosing the invention's underlying scientific principles.[8] Because enablement is targeted to teach those with ordinary skill in the art, a patent does not need to disclose what is already known to those in the field.[9]

---

[3] *See generally* Warner-Lambert Co. v. Teva Pharmaceuticals USA, Inc., 418 F.3d 1326, 1336-37 (Fed. Cir. 2005) ("The purpose of this [enablement] requirement is to ensure that the public knowledge is enriched by the patent specification to a degree at least commensurate with the scope of the claims.") (internal quotation and citation omitted). Professor Holbrook has questioned the extent to which an art actually benefits from patent disclosures. *See* Timothy R. Holbrook, *Possession in Patent Law*, 59 S.M.U. L. REV. 123, 146 (2006) ("while stating that patents never serve a teaching function is too strong of a statement, the courts have grossly overstated the true extent of this function.").

[4] *See* Lowell v. Lewis, 15 F. Cas. 1018, 1020 (C.C. Mass. 1817) ("Unless . . . such a specification was made, as would at all events enable other persons of competent skill to construct similar machines, the advantage to the public, which the act contemplates, would be entirely lost, and its principal object would be defeated.").

[5] *See* Genentech, Inc. v. Novo Nordisk A/S, 108 F.3d 1361, 1366 (Fed. Cir. 1997).

[6] *See* Holbrook, *supra* note 3, at 147 ("the best evidence of possession [of an invention] would be either the inventor physically creating the invention or, at least, providing a description that is clear enough to enable someone else to build it.").

[7] National Recovery Technologies, Inc. v. Magnetic Separation Systems, Inc., 166 F.3d 1190, 1196 (Fed. Cir. 1999).

[8] Fromson v. Advance Offset Plate, Inc., 720 F.2d 1565 (Fed. Cir. 1983); Newman v. Quigg, 877 F.2d 1575, 1581 (Fed. Cir. 1989) ("it is not a requirement of patentability that an inventor correctly set forth, or even know, how or why the invention works".).

[9] Hybritech Inc. v. Monoclonal Antibodies, Inc., 802 F.2d 1367, 1384 (Fed. Cir. 1986).

Furthermore, an applicant is not required to actually reduce the invention to practice prior to filing.[10] The relevant question is whether the specification enables one of ordinary skill to have made the invention, not whether the invention has been made. The specification may, but is not necessarily required, to include examples.[11]

[B] The Historic Perspective: *O'Reilly v. Morse*

In the 1853 *O'Reilly v. Morse*,[12] the U.S. Supreme Court considered a patent issued to Samuel Morse for the invention of the telegraph. The Court's analysis focused on claim 8, which described "electro-magnetism, however developed, for making or printing intelligible characters, letters or signs, at any distances . . ."[13] The *O'Reilly* Court found that claim 8, which was not limited to any specific implementation or machinery, was invalid. The Court found that Morse's "however developed" language amounted to an attempt to obtain the right to use something which Morse had not described in the patent.

The court explained that the level of detail provided in the Morse patent could not support a claim to all machinery that used electricity to print characters remotely. The opinion observed that to make the claim operative, the electricity "must be combined with, and passed through, and operate upon, certain complicated and delicate machinery, adjusted and arranged upon philosophical principles, and prepared by the highest mechanical skill."[14] Because the disclosure did not evidence that Morse had invented *all* mechanisms for transmitting electricity to transmit characters at a distance, claim 8 was too broad to be sustained:

> The evil is the same if he claims more than he has invented, although no other person has invented it before him. He prevents others from attempting to improve upon the manner and process which he has described in his specification and may deter the public from using, it, even if discovered. He can lawfully claim only what he has invented and described, and if he claims more his patent is void.[15]

There are a few important concepts to observe. First, the Court's analysis is focused on the objective disclosure within the four corners of the specification. The inventor's own subjective thought processes are not controlling. Second, Morse was entitled to patent protection for any claims that were narrowly tailored and supported by the patent's specification. Third, *Morse* illustrates that the enablement doctrine is used to enforce the teaching function of the disclosure requirement

---

[10] *See* Mpep § 2164.02.

[11] In patent law parlance, there are at least two types of examples. A "working" example is one that describes work that has actually been performed. A "prophetic" example is based on predicted results, rather than results that have been actually achieved. Mpep § 2164.02.

[12] O'Reilly v. Morse, 56 U.S. 62, 114 (1853).

[13] *Id.*

[14] *Id.* at 117.

[15] *Id.* at 120-21.

and the proscription against allowing claims to inventions that have not been fully developed.

[C] Edison's Light Bulb: *Consolidated Electric Light Co. v. McKeesport Light Co.*

In 1892, the Supreme Court decided *Consolidated Electric Light Co. v. McKeesport Light Co.*[16] This case examined an invalidity challenge to a patent (the "Sawyer and Man patent," named after the two listed inventors) to an incandescent light bulb. The challenge was brought by the real party in interest, Edison Electric Light Co., which had been founded by Thomas A. Edison.

The Sawyer and Man patent claimed a bulb with a filament made of a "carbonized fibrous or textile material."[17] This broad claim term encompassed numerous substances, including the carbonized bamboo used by the defendant Edison Electric that had been developed by Edison. However, the Sawyer and Man patent specification acknowledged that the inventors had experimented only with carbonized paper and wood carbon. The specification did not explain how any other substances that fit within the claim could be used to make a working light bulb. Instead, the specification stated that "[n]o especial description of making the illuminating carbon conductors . . . is thought necessary, as any ordinary methods . . . in practice before the date of this improvement, may be adopted in practice thereof by any one skilled in the arts."[18]

The *Consolidated Electric Light* opinion held that the narrow disclosure to carbonized paper and wood were insufficient to support "a monopoly of all fibrous and textile materials for incandescent conductors."[19] Although noting that broad claims are not per se objectionable, the Court observed that the broad claims at issue encompassed thousands of substances that failed to achieve the patent's purpose. The Court explained:

> [H]ow would it be possible for a person to know what fibrous or textile material was adapted to the purpose of an incandescent conductor, except by the most careful and painstaking experimentation? . . . If Sawyer and Man had discovered that a certain carbonized paper would answer the purpose, their claim to all carbonized paper would, perhaps, not be extravagant; but the fact that paper happens to belong to the fibrous kingdom did not invest them with sovereignty over this entire kingdom, and thereby practically limit other experimenters to the domain of minerals.[20]

The *Consolidated Electric Light* opinion illustrates the rule that a claim will not be upheld where one must conduct undue experimentation to practice the claims. To underscore the point, the Court detailed Edison's efforts to locate his solution using carbonized bamboo that had resulted in his commercially viable bulb. In an early

---

[16] Consol. Elec. Light Co. v. McKeesport Light Co., 159 U.S. 465 (1895).

[17] *Id.* at 468 quoting U.S. Patent No. 317,076 (filed Jan. 8 1885).

[18] *Id.* at 467.

[19] *Id.* at 472.

[20] *Id.* at 475-76.

effort to describe undue experimentation, the opinion details that Edison's own work required months of trial and error, including testing dozens of possible solutions before the location of one species that was uniquely suited for this use.

[D] A Comparison: Bell's Telephone Patent

A comparison of *O'Reilly* and *Consolidated Electric Light* with *Dolbear v. American Bell Tel. Co.*[21] ("American Bell") is useful. In *American Bell*, the Supreme Court considered the validity of a patent invented by Alexander Graham Bell. The patent claimed a "method of, and apparatus for, transmitting vocal or other sounds telegraphically, as herein described, by causing electrical undulations, similar in forms to the vibrations of air accompanying the said vocal or other sounds, substantially as set forth."[22] The Court determined that the disclosure included a sufficiently clear and accurate description that would permit a mechanic to successfully reproduce the claims. Distinguishing the open-ended claim 8 invalidated in *O'Reilly*, the *American Bell* Court explained that Bell had:

> . . . described clearly and distinctly his process of transmitting speech telegraphically, by creating changes in the intensity of a continuous current or flow of electricity, in a closed circuit, exactly analogous to the changes of density in air occasioned by the undulatory motion given to it by the human voice in speaking. He then pointed out two ways in which this might be done.[23]

Read together, *O'Reilly*, *Consolidated Electric Light Co.*, and *American Bell* form the foundation of the modern enablement requirement. Today, enablement requires that patentees disclose sufficient information in the specification to teach of one of ordinary skill how to make and use the invention without undue experimentation. This serves both a teaching function, as well as imposing a requirement that an invention be concretely developed before a right will be granted.

§ 8.03 ENABLEMENT AND CLAIM SCOPE

Undertaken on a claim-by-claim basis, an enablement analysis relies on an examination of the information in the written specification, the knowledge within the state of the art, and the claim. As a general rule, a patentee is not required to provide an encyclopedia of descriptive information that enables every plausible implementation that is encompassed by the claims. Such a result would bloat applications, raise patenting costs, and duplicate information that already exists. Further, such a rule might force patentees to file narrow claims that are easy to design around in a manner that might devalue patenting. As *American Bell* stated about Bell's telephone, "a patent for such a discovery is not to be confined to the

---

[21] Dolbear v. American Bell Tel. Co. (American Bell 1), 126 U.S. 1 (1888); *see also* U.S. v. American Bell Tel. Co., 128 U.S. 315 (1888).

[22] *Id.* at 353.

[23] *Id.* at 536.

mere means he improvised to prove the reality of his conception."[24]

However, consider that any invention can be stated at various levels of specificity. Patentees have an incentive to draft the broadest possible claim of sustainable validity. For example, one who invents a four-legged wooden chair might attempt to claim "any sitting device with a horizontal plane." Such a broad claim would encompass devices made from wood, plastic or stuffed fabric. Under section 112 and *O'Reilly*, shouldn't a patentee be required to include sufficient information to enable all three?

The answer is that a specification must provide sufficient information to enable the *full claim scope*, but is not required to describe knowledge that is already part of the relevant art. As the courts recognize, the enablement doctrine must permit practice of all facets of a claim but:

> . . . [t]hat is not to say that the specification itself must necessarily describe how to make and use every possible variant of the claimed invention, for the artisan's knowledge of the prior art and routine experimentation can often fill gaps, interpolate between embodiments, and perhaps even extrapolate beyond the disclosed embodiments, depending upon the predictability of the art.[25]

Sitrick v. Dreamworks[26] illustrates how this rule applies to a technology that can be implemented in different media. The *Sitrick* court examined an invalidity defense based on lack of enablement brought by a film company accused of infringement. The claims concerned a system that allowed the integration or substitution of user-generated images for pre-existing images of characters. The patent's claims were broad enough to encompass both video games and movies. Significantly, the patent's disclosure did not explain how the claim could be implemented outside of video gaming. More specifically, the written specification taught the use of a system that intercepted electronic signals coming from a game card or storage card that corresponded to a pre-defined character. The specification described that the claimed system could modify these signals to replace the original character with another that was chosen by an end-user.

The defendant film company Dreamworks was accused of infringement because it generated and modified characters when creating special effects in films, not video games.[27] The *Sitrick* court noted that video games and films use fundamentally different technologies, given that films generate the illusion of movement by slightly varying a character's image within an individual frame, which is then displayed together in a continuous sequence with others. The court noted that films do not have separate signals for each character that can be intercepted and changed. The court found that the patent's written disclosure did not teach one of

---

[24]   *Id.* at 539.

[25]   AK Steel Corp. v. Sollac and Ugine, 344 F.3d 1234, 1244 (Fed. Cir. 2003).

[26]   Sitrick v. Dreamworks, LLC, 516 F.3d 993 (Fed. Cir. 2008).

[27]   One important point about *Sitrick* should be noted. Although the invalidity challenge was raised by a film company, the result in the case would have been the same if the accused infringer's product was a video game. As a general matter, invalidity challenges do not have a standing requirement that limits a challenge based on the nature of the accused product.

ordinary skill how to implement the claims in film. On that basis, the *Sitrick* court invalidated the claims.

The *Sitrick* case demonstrates that enabling a single claimed implementation is not sufficient for claims that can be implemented in technologically disparate products. In those cases, the specification must include sufficient textual support to enable all unless knowledge and ordinary skill can fill in the gaps. Furthermore, *Sitrick* underscores that enablement serves a function in addition to enriching the state of the art. In particular, the enablement doctrine reigns in broad claims that reach beyond that which has been realized by the inventor.[28]

Another example is *Liebel-Flasheim Co. v. Medrad, Inc.*,[29] which considered the patentability of a claim to a medical syringe. When the application to the patent was originally filed, it enabled and claimed an implementation that used a pressure jacket to allow the syringe to withstand the force of motor powered injection. The specification recognized that the jacket was thought necessary to effectuate the invention and described a jacketless implementation as "impractical."[30]

After a competitor subsequently developed a jacketless syringe, the patentee amended the original claims to eliminate any reference to a requirement for a jacket. Invalidating the claims for lack of enablement, the court held that the disclosure taught only how to make a syringe with a pressure jacket and failed to inform one of ordinary skill to solve all of the technical problems associated with making the syringe without a pressure jacket. In result, the patentee was precluded from attempting to claim advances which were not developed at the time that the patent was filed. In summary, in *Liebel-Flasheim*, the enablement doctrine was used to invalidate claims that had been broadened to cover the competitor's later solution that had eluded the patentee.

More broadly, *Sitrick* and *Liebel-Flasheim* illustrate the principle that the full claim scope must be enabled. Although patentees are not required to provide a teaching for every conceivable implementation encompassed by the claims, the application must have a sufficient teaching to reach technologically distinct implementations.[31]

---

[28] For an additional example, see Automotive Tech. Int'l v. BMW, 501 F.3d 1274 (Fed. Cir. 2007).

[29] Liebel-Flarsheim Co. v. Medrad, Inc., 481 F.3d 1371 (Fed. Cir. 2007).

[30] *Id.* at 1379, quoting U.S. Patent No. 5,456,660 (filed Nov 30, 1993).

[31] *See also* Automotive Technologies Intern., Inc. v. BMW, 501 F.3d 1274 (Fed. Cir. 2007) (claim to an airbag sensor that encompassed both mechanical and electronic implementations was invalid for the specification's failure to enable electronic sensors).

§ 8.04   UNDUE EXPERIMENTATION

[A]   The Modern Foundation of Undue Experimentation: The *Wands* Factors

The courts have explored the level of experimentation that is acceptable and, therefore, results in a patentable claim. In 1988, in the *In re Wands* decision, the Federal Circuit promulgated a set of factors (known as the "*Wands* factors") to assess whether experimentation in any particular case is undue.[32] The *Wands* factors are:

(1)   the quantity of experimentation necessary,

(2)   the amount of direction or guidance presented,

(3)   the presence or absence of working examples,

(4)   the nature of the invention,

(5)   the state of the prior art,

(6)   the relative skill of those in the art,

(7)   the predictability or unpredictability of the art, and

(8)   the breadth of the claims.

According to the Federal Circuit, the *Wands* factors are illustrative and their use is not mandatory in all cases.[33] Nonetheless, they offer useful considerations to determine whether a disclosure requires undue experimentation for the practice of a claim.

The *Wands* opinion illustrates the application of these factors. There, the patentee claimed a method to detect a hepatitis B surface antigen[34] through the use of particular monoclonal antibodies[35] that have a high affinity[36] for binding with the hepatitis B antigen. The method of detecting antigens by using antibodies is called "immunoassay."[37] The PTO had rejected several claims on the basis that the unpredictability and unreliability of the art required those of ordinary skill to engage in undue experimentation to practice the invention.

As the *Wands* opinion describes, the applicant had undertaken to *deposit* one cell line capable of producing antibodies sufficient to practice the claim. This

---

[32] *In re* Wands, 858 F.2d 731, 737 (Fed. Cir. 1988).

[33] Amgen, Inc. v. Chugai Pharmaceutical Co., 927 F.2d 1200, 1212 (Fed. Cir. 1991).

[34] An "antigen" is a molecule that may generate an immune response from the body.

[35] According to the *Wands* court, "antibodies" "are a class of protein (immunoglobulins) that help defend the body against invaders such as viruses and bacteria." *Id.* at 733. The body generates antibodies against any particular disease after exposure to its antigen. "Monoclonal" antibodies are identical because they are all derived from (i.e., clones) of a single parent cell.

[36] According to the court, "[a]ffinity is a quantitative measure of strength of antibody-antigen binding." *Id.* Furthermore, "[u]sually, an antibody with a higher affinity will be more useful for immunological diagnostic testing than one with a lower affinity." *Id.*

[37] *Id.*

deposit procedure permits patentees to satisfy any of § 112's disclosure requirements by submitting microorganisms to authorized cell depositories located worldwide to support the patent application.[38] After the patent issues, the depository will provide samples of the material to any member of the public who wishes to understand the patent's disclosure. Here, the patentee's submission of the single cell line was adequate to satisfy the best mode[39] requirement. However, the deposit was arguably inadequate to enable the full scope of the broad claims at issue, which contemplated the use of antibodies from more than one cell line to perform the claimed immunoassays.[40]

Considering whether these claims could be replicated by those in the art using the information in the application's written description, the court explained:

> The determination of what constitutes undue experimentation in a given case requires the application of a standard of reasonableness, having due regard for the nature of the invention and the state of the art. The test is not merely quantitative, since a considerable amount of experimentation is permissible, if it is merely routine, or if the specification in question provides a reasonable amount of guidance with respect to the direction in which the experimentation should proceed.[41]

Here, the patentee submitted evidence that a commercially available kit had been used to screen for the most likely monoclonal antibodies cells. This was followed by a second screening procedure that was well known in the art. The application's disclosure included working examples. Further, the patentee demonstrated that the entire procedure had been performed three times, and that each time yielded at least one antibody that satisfied all claim limitations and a much larger percentage that did not. Nonetheless, the PTO and the board found the specification inadequate based on evidence that the patentee's overall yield from the screening procedure was low, thus demonstrating that one of ordinary skill must undertake undue experimentation to practice the claims.

Applying the above-described *Wands* factors, the Federal Circuit reversed and held that the written specification was sufficient to enable the applicant's broad claims. The decision noted that the claimed steps that related to isolation, cloning and analysis were known in the art. With respect to the yield, the court determined that the PTO's characterization of the inventor's yield as "low" misconstrued the legal standard. In particular, the opinion noted that testing a high volume of cell lines did not necessarily render the claims unpredictable, noting that six subsequent tests had resulted in a usable product that was within the scope of the claims.

The *Amgen* court identified that the specification provided specific direction on the practice of the invention and a number of working examples. Further, the

---

[38] Such deposits may be necessary where the starting material (for example, living biological cells) are not readily available to the public and/or the disclosure requirements cannot otherwise be met by a written description within the specification. *See* Mpep § 2404.

[39] For more information about best mode, *see infra* Chapter 11.

[40] It was undisputed that the claimed immunoassays could be made from readily available starting materials using methods known in the art. *See In re* Wands, 858 F.2d 731, 736 (Fed. Cir. 1988).

[41] *Id.* at 737.

Wands court noted that "[t]here was a high level of skill in the art at the time that the application was filed, and all methods needed to practice the invention were well-known."[42] Under *Wands*, the specification's description, the patentee's deposit and the knowledge that was known in the art at the time of filing supported the court's conclusion that the claims were enabled.

The Federal Circuit came to a contrary conclusion in *Amgen, Inc. v. Chugai Pharmaceutical Co.*[43] There, the court considered a broad claim for a recombinant DNA[44] version of erythropoietin (EPO), which is used to stimulate the production of red blood cells. The *Amgen* court noted that the enablement doctrine did not preclude a claim that required some experimentation to practice the claim so long as the level is not undue.

One claim encompassed any substitute (or "analog") for the natural EPO protein that caused bone marrow cells to increase production of red blood cells. The *Amgen* court noted that the number of EPO analogs that might be created was "potentially enormous," given that the gene was extremely complex and there were a large number of potential nucleotide modifications that might be made.[45] Finding that the disclosure included only one working example, the court explained that the inventor's inability to determine which analogues increased production of red blood cells was fatal to the claim:

> Considering the structural complexity of the EPO gene, the manifold possibilities for change in its structure, with attendant uncertainty as to what utility will be possessed by these analogs, we consider that more is needed concerning identifying the various analogs that are within the scope of the claim, methods for making them, and structural requirements for producing compounds with EPO-like activity. It is not sufficient, having made the gene and a handful of analogs whose activity has not been clearly ascertained, to claim all possible genetic sequences that have EPO-like activity.[46]

Although the court acknowledged that, as a general matter, a patent applicant could obtain protection for a broad generic claim by providing one or a few enabling examples, *Amgen* cautioned that this was possible only where the requirements of § 112 had been fully met — a circumstance that was not present given the breadth of the claims, as well as the complexity and unpredictability of the technology at issue.

The reasonableness standard, as articulated in the *Wands* factors, rests on considerations such the relationship between the amount of knowledge available in the art, the predictability of the invention, the amount of information disclosed in the specification and the nature of the claim. Generally, the more unpredictable and

---

[42] *Id.* at 740.

[43] Amgen, Inc. v. Chugai Pharmaceutical Co., 927 F.2d 1200 (Fed. Cir. 1991).

[44] Recombinant DNA is created by joining together one or more DNA strands joined with another. Typically, the resulting combination would not occur in the same maner naturally.

[45] *Amgen*, 927 F.2d at 1213.

[46] *Id.* at 1214.

nascent arts require more disclosure in comparison to the more established and predictable arts, where an explanation of a single embodiment may be sufficient.[47]

§ 8.05 ENABLEMENT, PRIORITY AND TIMING

The relevant date for measuring enablement is the effective filing date of the patent application.[48] The state of knowledge in any particular art changes over time. A specification submitted in the early stages of the development of an art will necessarily require more detail than an application drafted for a well-developed art. The prosecution of a patent may take a number of years. These circumstances have an impact on the substantive application of the enablement standard.

[A]   The Relevant State of the Art

The relevant state of the art may progress since the time of the claim's effective filing date. As a general rule, later-developed documentation cannot be used to "fill in" information that was missing from the application when originally filed.

This rule was explored in *In re Glass*,[49] where the Federal Circuit examined the rejection of an application for an invention for "whiskers," which are long, needle-like linear crystals used for strengthening refractory materials. The patentee attempted to demonstrate enablement by relying on four patents owned by a third party, Lexington, as representative of the state of the art. The *Glass* applicant attempted to establish that details omitted in the Glass application — including proper temperature, pressure, and vapor saturation conditions — were established in the art at the time of filing. Notably, the applications supporting the Lexington patents were filed prior to the *Glass* application and maintained as secret in the PTO until after the *Glass* application's filing date.

The *Glass* court held that the Lexington patents could not be used to support a rejection of the claim because such information was not publically available at the time of filing and therefore could not demonstrate the knowledge available in the art on that date. In summary, *Glass* establishes that information that becomes available after a patent's filing date cannot be used to supplement information that was lacking in the originally filed specification.

[B]   Enablement and Priority

Enablement is measured as of the application's effective filing date. *In re Hogan*[50] provides a good example of how this rule implicates both the enablement standard and patent priority. Claiming a chemical polymer, the *Hogan* application was filed in 1971 and claimed priority through a series of applications dating back

---

[47] *See* Spectra-Physics, Inc. v. Coherent, Inc., 827 F.2d 1524, 1533 (Fed. Cir. 1987) ("If an invention pertains to an art where the results are predictable, e.g., mechanical as opposed to chemical arts, a broad claim can be enabled by disclosure of a single embodiment").

[48] *Id.*

[49] *In re* Glass, 492 F.2d 1228 (C.C.P.A. 1974).

[50] *In re* Hogan, 559 F.2d 595 (C.C.P.A. 1977).

to one that had been originally filed in 1953. Unquestionably, the state of the relevant art had advanced over those many years.

The U.S. PTO Examiner had rejected the 1971 application based on third-party references dating between 1955 and 1971. All references dated after the original parent application had been filed in 1953, and disclosed a new implementation — amorphous polymers — that were not in existence as of the original 1953 filing date. The examiner, who has the burden of proof, argued that these references demonstrated that the claimed polymers were not enabled. Specifically, the examiner attempted to use post-1953 documentation to show that the 1971 application claims were broad genus claims that encompassed amorphous polymers that lacked support in an enabling disclosure.

The court found that the post-1953 references were not the proper basis of a rejection. The court relied on § 120, which provides that subsequent patent applications that disclose the same invention as a previously filed application naming the same inventors "shall have the *same effect* . . . . as though filed on the date of the prior application." *Hogan* found the Examiner's reliance on information that did not exist in 1953 application was improper under the statute, finding that a contrary ruling would "render the 'benefit' of 35 U.S.C. § 120 illusory."[51] Thus, references cannot be used by the PTO to demonstrate non-enablement with facts that were not in existence at the time that the priority application is filed.

Note that the *Hogan* rule is subject to a limitation. That is, the mere fact that a document has been *generated* after an application's filing date does not automatically preclude its use. For example, the courts have approved the use of post-filing documents that *describe the former state of the art* that existed at the time of the applicant's original filing date to demonstrate a lack of enablement.[52] An article published in 2007 that describes the state of the art in the year 2005 may be used to demonstrate a lack of enablement for an application filed in that same art in the same year of the invention (in this case, 2005).

Taken together, *Glass* and *Hogan* underscore the principle that the critical time for assessing enablement is the effective filing date. This rule invokes the state of knowledge existent at the time of filing, both for purposes of assessing the adequacy of the disclosure and the references that can be used to demonstrate the lack of enablement.

[C]   Enablement and Patent Enforcement

The interplay between the enablement doctrine and the infringement standard leads to the phenomenon that an inventor may capture a judgment against an implementation that was not envisioned at the time of filing. This is because although the application's disclosure is measured on the effective filing date, liability for use of a patent claim is determined as of the time of infringement. Because many technology sectors evolve within a period of years, this change in the scope of coverage may be significant. As Professor Mark Lemley writes:

---

[51] *Id.* at 604.

[52] *See id.* at 605 & n.17.

If the original inventor has at that time enabled the use of an entire class of products, a claim covering that entire class is warranted. But if the class subsequently expands to include other species not conceived at the time of the first patent, the generic claim language will allow the first inventor to capture those new species within the scope of his claim.[53]

For example, assume that in the year 2000 a patentee files an application with a claim to a personal listening device with a "rechargeable battery." Further assume that the specification fully enables one of ordinary skill to recreate the device using a rechargeable battery that relies on an AC charger, which is the prevalent technology for that era. Over the next decade, a rival develops a personal listening device with a rechargeable battery that relies on solar energy. A factfinder may determine that the enablement requirement is met for the claim term "battery powered" according to the technology existent at the time of filing. Nonetheless, the factfinder could find that a device using solar power to recharge the battery is met by the "rechargeable battery" claim term because the phrase is construed as of the date of infringement.

§ 8.06 ENABLEMENT AND UTILITY

The enablement requirement of section 112 requires the inventor to disclose sufficient information so that one of ordinary skill in the art can use the invention. The "how to *use*" component of enablement necessarily fails if the patent specification fails to disclose practical *utility* as required under 35 U.S.C. § 101.[54] If a claim has no useful application, then an inventor cannot enable anyone to use the invention. As described by one court, "compliance with [section] 112 requires a description of how to use presently useful inventions; otherwise an applicant would anomalously be required to teach how to use a useless invention."[55]Thus, a claim may be enabled as of its original filing date, and reach forward over implementations that were not imagined by the original inventor. In part, this is because a claim that is enabled can, though the principles of claim construction, encompass later developed implementations

This point was examined in *Janssen Pharmaceutica N.V. v. Teva Pharmaceuticals*.[56] The patent at issue in *Janssen* claimed a method using an already existent chemical, called galanthamine, to treat Alzheimer's disease.[57] The specification cited papers in which galanthamine had been administered to humans or animals. The human studies demonstrated that galanthamine crossed the blood-brain barrier and therefore could have some effect on the human brain. The animal studies suggested some positive effects on the memory of animals that had amnesia, and others that demonstrate a positive effect on short-term memory. The patent

---

[53] Mark A. Lemley, *The Economics of Improvement in Intellectual Property Law*, 75 Tex. L. Rev. 989, 1009 (1997).

[54] *In re* Fisher, 421 F.3d 1365, 1378-79 (Fed. Cir. 2005).

[55] *In re* Kirk, 376 F.2d 936, 942 (C.C.P.A. 1967).

[56] Janssen Pharmaceutica N.V. v. Teva Pharmaceuticals, 583 F.3d 1317 (Fed. Cir. 2009).

[57] Alzheimer's disease is a form of progressive dementia in which memory and mental abilities steadily decline.

application asserted that these studies demonstrated that galanthamine would have a positive impact on patients with Alzheimer's disease. The PTO rejected the application as obvious.

In response, the applicant explained that the cited studies were conducted under "circumstances having no relevance to Alzheimer's disease," because they had been conducted on animals and individuals who were normal, rather than those who had been physiologically affected by Alzheimer's.[58] The applicant noted that experiments had commenced to prove a connection between galanthamine and Alzheimer's treatments, and promised to submit the results to the agency. Although the applicant never submitted the studies, the PTO issued the patent.

The *Janssen* court held the patent invalid for failing to meet the enablement standard. The Federal Circuit observed that, "[i]f a patent claim fails to meet the utility requirement because it is not useful or operative, then it also fails to meet the how-to-use aspect of the enablement requirement."[59] The *Janssen* court confirmed that clinical trials are not required to meet this standard in all cases and that animal studies or lab experiments may be sufficient. Nonetheless, the specification for the patent at issue failed. As the court explained:

> . . . neither in vitro test results nor animal test results involving the use of galanthamine to treat Alzheimer's-like conditions were provided. The results from the '318 patent's proposed animal tests of galanthamine for treating symptoms of Alzheimer's disease were not available at the time of the application, and the district court properly held that they could not be used to establish enablement.[60]

The *Janssen* court rejected the argument that utility could be established by inference from the existing research, based on the effect of the chemical on certain receptors in the brain. This argument was based on the proposition that those of ordinary skill would have understood that a connection between galanthamine and Alzheimer's disease existed based on the material provided in the specification and the state of the art. It is interesting to note that, if this inference had been sufficient, the PTO's original nonobviousness rejection might have been the correct disposition of the application. In that case, the specification's summary of research might have led one of ordinary skill to recreate the invention by exercising ordinary creativity.[61]

However, given the state of the record, the *Janssen* court explained that the patent did "no more than state a hypothesis and proposed testing to demonstrate the accuracy of the hypothesis."[62] In summary, *Janssen* illustrates the application of the rule that enablement is not met in the absence of a specification that demonstrates operable utility.

---

[58] *Janssen*, 583 F.3d at 1322.

[59] *Id.* at 1324 quoting Process Control Corp. v. HydReclaim Corp., 190 F.3d 1350 (Fed. Cir. 1999).

[60] *Id.* at 1325.

[61] For more about the nonobviousness standard, see Chapter 21.

[62] *Id.* at 1327.

§ 8.07   A BRIEF NOTE: SOME ECONOMIC CONSIDERATIONS

As has been explored by Professors Merges and Nelson, decision makers have some discretion in applying the enablement doctrine in individual cases.[63] One open question is the amount of information that is required to obtain protection within an zart. Typically, if the enablement standard requires a higher level of disclosure, a patentee must more fully develop a solution before obtaining a patent. This development can add both time and cost to the development of the original idea. Conceivably, a prohibitively high level might dissuade individuals from patenting and perhaps investing in research and development. An inventor who lacks resources may rely solely on trade secret protection rather than face a high disclosure standard.

On the other hand, one who obtains protection under a very low enablement standard has the potential to obtain a reward for a broad range of later implementations. This circumstance may impact sequential invention. That is, if earlier inventors are allowed patents to nascent technology that has not yet materialized, later researchers will have little incentive to develop improvements.

Which standard is preferable — a more lenient or more rigorous standard? One theory, known as Kitch's Prospect Theory, argues in favor of erring on the side of early patent protection to first inventors.[64] This theory suggests that a low enablement standard is preferable in order to protect early inventor's incentives. Analogizing the patent system to mining claims granted to encourage stakeholders to work the property interest, the Prospect Theory holds that the first patent owner is in a good position "to coordinate the search for technological and market enhancement of the patent's value so that duplicative investments are not made and so that information is exchanged among searchers."[65]

On the other hand, Professors Merges and Nelson argue that, "[w]ithout extensively reducing the pioneer's incentives, the law should attempt at the margin to favor a competitive environment for improvements, rather than an environment dominated by the pioneer firm."[66] This view militates in favor of a more stringent application of the enablement doctrine, forcing inventors who seek broad protection to more fully develop their inventions to justify the reach of far-reaching claims.

Economic considerations such as these underlie the question of whether broad claims may be sustained under the enablement doctrine, although such problems do not appear to garner any explicit discussion in the enablement cases. Nonetheless, such consequences may have a real world impact on research incentives.

---

[63] Robert P. Merges & Richard R. Nelson, *On the Complex Economics of Patent Scope*, 90 COLUM. L. REV. 839, 852 (1990).

[64] *See* Edmund W. Kitch, *The Nature and Function of the Patent System*, 20 J.L. & ECON. 265 (1977).

[65] *Id.* at 276.

[66] Merges & Nelson, *supra* note 63, at 843-44.

§ 8.08   CONCLUSION

Under 35 U.S.C. § 112, a patentee must disclose sufficient information in a patent application to enable one of ordinary skill in the art to make and use the invention without undue experimentation. The relevant time is fixed at the effective filing date of the claim. This requirement ensures that a patent disclose information to the public about the invention and also confirms that the claims submitted to the PTO have been sufficiently developed beyond the stage of an abstract idea.

Determining whether the enablement requirement is met can be performed by examining the following:

1. Identify the nature and scope of the relevant claim

2. Identify the specification disclosure informing one of ordinary skill how to make and use the invention

3. Identify the state of the relevant art

4. Combine the specification's disclosure with the state of the art, and determine whether one of ordinary skill in the art would have to perform undue experimentation to make the invention, using the *Wands* factors if appropriate

5. Consider whether the specification demonstrates sufficient information to allow one of ordinary skill to use the invention.

A lack of enablement will prevent a claim from issuing or, if a challenge is brought in litigation, result in the invalidation of an already-issued claim. A patentee need not disclose information that is already known in the art or that can be ascertained through a reasonable level of routine experimentation. Enablement may be readily met for simpler, predictable technologies by the description of a single mode of implementation. For uncertain, complex or nascent arts, more information is necessary.

Chapter 9

WRITTEN DESCRIPTION

SYNOPSIS

§ 9.01   INTRODUCTION

§ 9.02   GENERAL PRINCIPLES

§ 9.03   *ARIAD*: THE CURRENT LEGAL STANDARD

§ 9.04   APPLICATION OF THE POSSESSION TEST

    [A]   Amendments During Prosecution

    [B]   Benefit Of An Earlier Filing Date

    [C]   Biological and Chemical Subject Matter

§ 9.05   COMPARISON: WRITTEN DESCRIPTION AND ENABLEMENT

§ 9.06   CONCLUSION

§ 9.01   INTRODUCTION

According to the *written description* requirement of 35 U.S.C. section 112(1), an application must identify the invention in a manner sufficient to demonstrate to a person of ordinary skill in the art that the inventor had *possession* of the subject matter on the patent's effective filing date. This requirement applies to all claims, including those filed with the original application, those that are added or amended during prosecution, and any asserting entitlement to the benefit of an earlier priority date.[1]

The written description requirement played a particularly important role at the inception of the U.S. patent system.[2] This is because early U.S. patent system did not formally require claims and so a complete written description in the patent specification was necessary to provide notice of the scope of the right.[3] Today, although all non-provisional patent applications must include at least one claim,

---

[1] *See* University of Rochester v. G.D. Searle & Co., Inc., 358 F.3d 916, 923-24 (Fed. Cir. 2004); *see generally* Guidelines for Examination of Patent Applications under the 35 U.S.C. 112, ¶ 1 "Written Description" Requirement, 66 Fed. Reg. 1099, 1106 (Jan. 5, 2001); MPEP § 2163.

[2] Vas-Cath v. Mahurkar, 935 F.2d 1555, 1560-61 (Fed. Cir. 1991) (describing the history of the written description requirement).

[3] *See* Evans v. Eaton, 20 U.S. 356, 434 (1822) (noting that the specification must "put the public in possession of what the party claims as his own invention, so as to ascertain if he claim any thing that is in common use, or is already known, and to guard against prejudice or injury from the use of an invention which the party may otherwise innocently suppose not to be patented.").

written description remains an independent patentability requirement based in the current statute.

§ 9.02 GENERAL PRINCIPLES

The legal standard for the written description is whether the specification includes sufficient information to establish that the patentee was in possession of the invention at the time that the patent application is filed.[4] A specification may rely on words, structures, figures, diagrams, formulas, or other information set forth in the disclosure. Whether this standard is met is considered an issue of fact.[5]

The claim and written description requirements both direct the patentee to identify the invention. As the widely invoked maxim states, "[i]t is a bedrock principle of patent law that the claims of a patent define the invention to which the patentee is entitled the right to exclude."[6] In other words, the written description requirement may be difficult to justify in an era where the application must claim the invention.

There is recognition that a claim may be sufficient to satisfy the written description requirement.[7] Perhaps this eliminates some concerns by prosecutors about the overlap because the same text — the claim — might sometimes be sufficient to meet both requirements. However, there are circumstances where the written description requirement maintains independent relevance. First, written description may be lacking for a broad genus claim that appears to patent future inventions that are not yet developed. In those cases, the written specification is not adequate to support the broad claim because the inventor cannot describe species that have not yet been envisioned. Second, written description may be lacking if there is a significant variation between a written specification and an original claim, perhaps due to unskilled drafting.

Third, a written description problem may arise for claims that have been significantly amended or modified after the initial application has been filed. To illustrate, assume that a patentee filed an application that describes a straight, tube-shaped florescent light bulb that must be used in a housing that supplies electricity from opposite ends of the tube. While the application is pending, a market emerges for a spiral-shaped florescent light bulb that can be screwed into a standard household socket designed for incandescent light. Further assume that the patentee wishes to add or amend the application's claims to encompass spiral-shaped bulbs, so that the patentee can capture a monopoly within this new market. The written description requirement bars the patentee's ability to do so, because the application's disclosure does not support an inference that the inventor

---

[4] Enzo Biochem v. Gen-Probe Inc., 323 F.3d 956, 969 (Fed. Cir. 2002).

[5] Capon v. Eshhar, 418 F.3d 1349, 1357 (Fed. Cir. 2005).

[6] Phillips v. AWH Corp., 415 F.3d 1303, 1312 (Fed. Cir. 2005) (en banc) (citing cases and internal quotations omitted).

[7] Ariad Pharmaceuticals, Inc. v. Eli Lilly and Co., 598 F.3d 1336 (Fed. Cir. 2010) ("Although many original claims will satisfy the written description requirement, certain claims may not."); MPEP, § 2163 ("There is a strong presumption that an adequate written description of the claimed invention is present when the application is filed" citing *In re* Wertheim, 541 F.2d 257, 263 (C.C.P.A. 1976)).

had fully conceptualized — or "possessed" — a spiral bulb with a single base when the original application was filed. As the Federal Circuit has explained, an applicant must "recount his invention in such detail that his *future* claims can be determined to be encompassed within his *original* creation."[8] The written description requirement requires the patentee to commit to a particular invention as articulated in the application's initial written specification. One who claims too broadly or shifts the subject matter of the claims during prosecution risks rejection or invalidation of a claim.

One might ask whether a patentee can circumvent this circumstance by amending the specification's disclosure during prosecution by adding support at a later time. The answer to this question is "no," because under 35 U.S.C. § 132, an applicant is prohibited from introducing any *new matter* to the disclosure after an application's filing date.[9] Under this section, one cannot add subject matter that materially changes a written specification beyond that expressly or inherently disclosed in the original filing.

§ 9.03   *ARIAD*: THE CURRENT LEGAL STANDARD

In the 2010 en banc opinion *Ariad Pharmaceutical v. Eli Lilly*, the Federal Circuit reconfirmed the existence of the written description requirement and established guidelines for application of the standard. Because of the importance of *Ariad* to the present written description law, attention to the specifics of the case are warranted.

As has been recognized as far back as 1822, patent law requires the application to describe the invention.[10] When claiming became routine, the U.S. Supreme Court began to recognize that the claim must correspond to the specification.[11] For example, in a 1938 decision, the Court invalidated a claim that had been amended during prosecution to add an element that was not described in the written specification, stating "the application for patent cannot be broadened by amendment so as to embrace an invention not described in the application as filed, at least when adverse rights of the public have intervened."[12] The modern written description requirement has been traced to the 1967 court decision, *In re Ruschig*.[13] Considering a priority question, the court invalidated a broad genus claim that had

---

[8] Amgen Inc. v. Hoescst Marion Roussel Inc., 314 F.3d 1313, 1330 (Fed. Cir. 2003) (emphasis added).

[9] 35 U.S.C. § 132 ("No amendment shall introduce new matter into the disclosure of the invention"). A similar statutory provision prohibits the introduction of new matter for re-issue. 35 U.S.C. § 251 ("No new matter shall be introduced into the application for reissue."). Examples of attempting to introduce new matter include adding subject matter that was not expressly or inherently disclosed in the original application, adding or changing specific percentages of compounds or adding or omitting an entire step from a method. MPEP, § 706.03(o); *see generally* Glaxo Wellcome, Inc. v. Impax Laboratories, Inc., 356 F.3d 1348, 1354 (Fed. Cir. 2004) (explaining "the new matter doctrine ensures the temporal integrity of the amendment process in the Patent Office").

[10] *See* Evans v. Eaton, 20 U.S. 356, 434 (1822).

[11] Cleveland Trust Co. v. F.E. Rowe Sales Co., 305 U.S. 47 (1938) (construing 35 U.S.C. § 33, which has now been replaced by 35 U.S.C. § 112).

[12] *Cleveland Trust Co.*, 305 U.S. at 57.

[13] *In re* Ruschig, 379 F.2d 990 (1967).

been added to a previously-filed application during an interference. Finding that the written specification lacked sufficient examples to demonstrate possession, the *Ruschig* court stated:

> It is an old custom in the woods to mark trails by making blaze marks on the trees. It is no help in finding a trail or in finding one's way through the woods where the trails have disappeared — or have not been made, which is more like the case here- to be confronted simply by a large number of unmarked trees. Appellants are pointing to trees. We are looking for blaze marks which single out particular trees. We see none.[14]

Controversy over written description developed in 1997, when the Federal Circuit decided *University of California v. Eli Lilly and Co. ("Eli Lilly")*.[15] *Eli Lilly* has been recognized as the first decision to apply the written description requirement to originally-filed claims.[16] Consider this dissent from a Federal Circuit jurist, describing the impact of the *Eli Lilly* decision:

> . . . the *Lilly* opinion does not test a later claim amendment against the specification for priority, but asserts a new free-standing disclosure requirement in place of the statutory standard of enablement. Based on the absence of a nucleotide-by-nucleotide recitation in the specification of the human insulin cDNA, the court determined that the applicant had not adequately described the invention. For the first time, this court purported to apply [written description] without any priority question.[17]

This dissent criticized the doctrine as incoherent, continuing, that the "[r]eplacement of enablement doctrine with an ill-defined general disclosure doctrine of [written description] imperils the integrity of the patent system."[18] Additionally, some justices expressed the view that the written description requirement should be limited to policing the prohibition against adding new matter.[19]

One jurist wrote that *Eli Lilly* had created confusion by creating a "new validity doctrine" within 35 U.S.C. § 112, beyond enablement and best mode."[20] At the core of this controversy is § 112's text, which was argued to fold the statutory term "written description" into the enablement requirement — that is, that "written description" is merely prefatory to an entire phrase that concerns enablement.[21] In

---

[14] *Ruschig*, 379 F.2d at 995.

[15] University of California v. Eli Lilly & Co., 119 F.3d 1559 (Fed. Cir. 1997).

[16] *See generally* Mark D. Janis, *On Courts Herding Cats: Contending with the 'Written Description' Requirement (and Other Unruly Patent Disclosure Doctrines)*, 2 WASH. U.J.L. & POL'Y 55, 60, 70, 83 (2000).

[17] Enzo Biochem, Inc. v. Gen-Probe Inc., 323 F.3d 956, 980 (Fed. Cir. 2002) (Radar, J., dissenting).

[18] *Id.* at 982.

[19] *See Enzo Biochem.*, 323 F.3d at 979-80 (Radar, J., Gasarja, J. and Linn, J. dissenting).

[20] University of Rochester v. G.D. Searle & Co., Inc., 375 F.3d 1303, 1309 (Fed. Cir. 2004) (Radar, J., Gasarja, J. and Linn, J. dissenting).

[21] 35 U.S.C. § 112, which states:

> The specification shall contain a written description of the invention and of the manner and process of making and using it, in such full, clear, concise, and exact terms as to enable any person skilled in the art to which it pertains, or with which it is most nearly connected . . .

other words, the first portion of the paragraph is read as a single prepositional phrase that is interpreted as requiring an "enabled description that is written." Since deciding *Eli Lilly*, the Federal Circuit received several appellate challenges to the written description requirement's existence and scope.[22] The court accepted one of these challenges when granting en banc review in *Ariad.*

In result, the *Ariad* court reaffirmed that the written description requirement is an additional patentability requirement that is separate from enablement. Finding support in the Supreme Court precedent from 1938, the *Ariad* court declined to disrupt the "settled expectations of the inventing community, which has relied on it in drafting and prosecuting patents, concluding licensing agreements and rendering validity and infringement opinions."[23] As a matter of statutory construction, the court found that this interpretation avoided rendering any portion of § 112 surplusage.

Further, the *Ariad* opinion reconfirmed that written description applies to all claims, including claims that issue as originally filed. Noting that nothing in the statutory language restricted the requirement, the court stated that the written description requirement served a purpose that claims do not:

> Although many original claims will satisfy the written description require-
> ment, certain claims may not. For example, a generic claim may define the
> boundaries of a vast genus of chemical compounds, and yet the question
> may still remain whether the specification, including original claim lan-
> guage, demonstrates that the applicant has invented species sufficient to
> support a claim to a genus.[24]

Ariad confirmed that written description nullifies claims that are broader than the inventive concept can support. As the opinion notes, peripheral claims may be improperly drafted to sweep in more than the inventor conceived, such as those implementations "that have not been invented, and thus cannot be described."[25]

The *Ariad* court clarified the controlling legal standard for written description, phrased as "possession as shown in the disclosure."[26] This requires an objective analysis of the four corners of the specification from the perspective of the person of ordinary skill in the art. A fact-specific test, the specification's disclosure must describe an invention in a way that is understandable to the skilled artisan and sufficient to show that the inventor actually invented the invention claimed. The *Ariad* opinion notes that the relevant time frame is the time of filing, and that the level of detail required depends on the nature and scope of the claims, as well as the complexity and predictability of the relevant technology.

See also In re Barker, 559 F.2d 588, 594-95 (C.C.P.A. 1977) (Markey, J., dissenting) (interpreting phrase as a whole).

[22] *See* LizardTech, Inc. v. Earth Res. Mapping, Inc., 433 F.3d 1373 (Fed. Cir. 2006); Univ. of Rochester v. G.D. Searle & Co., Inc., 375 F.3d 1303 (Fed. Cir. 2004); Enzo Biochem., Inc. v. Gen-Probe, Inc., 323 F.3d 956 (Fed. Cir. 2002).

[23] *Id.* at 1346 citing Schriber-Schroth Co. v. Cleveland Trust Co., 305 U.S. 47 (1938).

[24] *Ariad*, 598 F.3d at 1349.

[25] *Id.* at 1352.

[26] *Id.* at 1351.

Relevant to genus claims, the *Ariad* opinion declined to provide a bright-line rule for any precise number of species that must be described. Rather, *Ariad* suggested that a patentee must disclose either a representative number of species or structural features common to genus members so that one of skill in the art could "visualize or recognize" its members.[27] To apply this standard, the *Ariad* court examined the claims at issue. The patent in suit claimed a method of regulating gene expression by reducing the activity of a particular protein, NF-êB, in cells. *Ariad* recognized that these claims were genus claims that encompassed all substances that could be used to reduce the activity of these cells, although the patent disclosed only one figure which disclosed a single sequence that accomplished that function. Noting that the figure had not been included until two years after the patent's priority date, the court found the patent had an inadequate written description. Although the originally filed disclosure did include a series of "decoy molecules" that could be used to accomplish the claimed methods, the court found that the four corners of the patent lacked any descriptive link between the decoy molecules and the claimed functionality.[28]

In summary, the Federal Circuit's en banc *Ariad* decision: 1) reconfirmed the existence of the written description requirement; 2) affirmed that all claims are subject to the requirements; 3) clarified that the possession test must be met on an objective basis based on the four corners of the patent; and 4) elucidated the standard for genus claims, suggesting that it may be met by a representative number of species or structural features common to all members of the genus.

§ 9.04   APPLICATION OF THE POSSESSION TEST

[A]   Amendments During Prosecution

As previously described, the written description requirement can limit the patentee's ability to amend or add claims that are a significant shift from the original disclosure while attempting to rely on the original filing date for purposes of maintaining priority. One example of this principle in operation is *Gentry Gallery, Inc. v. Berkline Corp.*[29]

The claims at issue in *Gentry Gallery* were directed to a sectional sofa that allowed different sections of the sofa to independently recline. The invention featured control buttons that released the reclining sections. The patent's written specification featured the location of these control buttons on the *console portion* of the sofa, which is located between the different reclining sections. Significantly, the disclosure stated that the invention was *limited* to a specific location of the controls on the console of the sofa ("the only possible location") and described the invention as a sofa "with a *console* . . . that accommodates the controls for both the reclining

---

[27] *Id.* at 1350.

[28] The *Ariad* opinion includes additional views filed by Judge Newman, Judge Gajasa's concurring opinion, and two additional opinions dissenting-in-part and concurring-in-part by Judges Radar and Linn.

[29] Gentry Gallery, Inc. v. Berkline Corp., 134 F.3d 1473 (Fed. Cir. 1998).

seats."[30] The inventor testified that "locating the controls on the console is definitely the way we solved it [the problem of building a sectional sofa with parallel recliners] on the original group [of sofas]."[31]

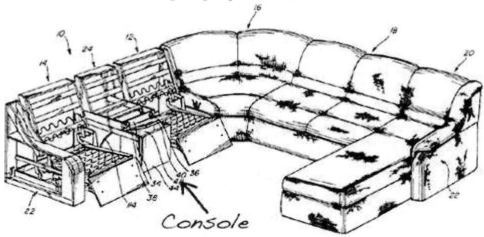

Console

Despite this emphasis on console placement in the original filing, the patentee had amended the application to include claims that located the controls on the seat sofa section. The *Gentry Gallery* court held that these claims failed to meet the written description requirement. The opinion noted that the patent's written specification made clear that "locating the controls anywhere but on the console is outside the stated purpose of the invention."[32] This presented a fatal disconnection between the restricted subject matter of the disclosure and the claim scope. Particularly where clear, specific limiting statements appear in a patent's disclosure, a patent that attempts to claim *significantly broader* or *different* subject matter than the inventor set forth in the written specification supports a finding that the requirement is not met.[33]

One point warrants particular attention. The patent application at issue in *Gentry Gallery* was drafted to emphasize that locating the button on the console was an essential element of the invention. However, applications need not be drafted in such a restrictive manner, and most are not. The Federal Circuit has underscored that in *Gentry Gallery* "we did not announce a new 'essential element' test mandating an inquiry into what an inventor considers to be essential to his invention and requiring that the claims incorporate those elements."[34] Indeed, the *Gentry Gallery* decision may be a cautionary tale to patent drafters about strong

---

[30] *Id.* at 1479.

[31] *Id.* at 1478.

[32] *Id.*

[33] *See* Johnson Worldwide Associates, Inc. v. Zebco Corp., 175 F.3d 985, 993 (Fed. Cir. 1999) (noting that *Gentry Gallery's* holding may be limited to where patent's disclosure "makes crystal clear that a particular (i.e., narrow) understanding of a claim term is an 'essential element of [the inventor's] invention.' ").

[34] Cooper Cameron Corp. v. Kvaerner Oilfield Products, Inc., 291 F.3d 1317, 1321 (Fed. Cir. 2002).

commitment to specific implementations in the written specification.

[B] Benefit Of An Earlier Filing Date

How does the written description standard apply to continuation applications that claim priority to an earlier parent? As a general rule, to obtain the benefit of an earlier filing date, the claims of the later-filed application must be supported by the written description in the earlier-filed application.[35] The Federal Circuit applied this rule in *Vas-Cath v. Mahurkar*[36] to claims in a continuation application filed under § 120, which states:

> An application for patent for an invention disclosed *in the manner provided by the first paragraph of section 112* of this title in an application previously filed in the United States . . . which is filed by an inventor or inventors named in the previously filed application shall have the same effect, as to such invention, as though filed on the date of the prior application[37]

This italicized language requires that section 112's disclosure requirements must be met in the original application that is relied upon to establish priority. In the *Vas-Cath* case, the patent claimed a catheter that used a pair of tubes (called a "double lumen catheter") designed to allow blood flow to and from an artery. The invention offered a smaller puncture area than prior art coaxial catheters carrying the same quantity of blood. The inventor filed a number of patent applications, including: 1) an early U.S. design patent (the '081 design application) filed on March 8, 1982 that had been abandoned; 2) a Canadian application that issued as a patent on August 9, 1982 (the '089 patent); 3) a U.S. utility patent (the '329 patent) filed on October 1, 1984; and 4) a U.S. utility patent (the '141 patent) filed on January 29, 1986. A timeline that summarizes this procedural history follows:

Vas-Cath, Inc. v. Mahurkar

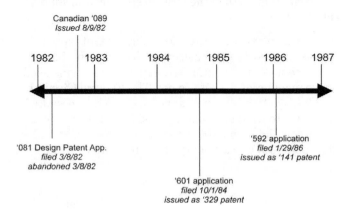

---

[35] Anascape, Ltd. v. Nintendo, 601 F.3d 1333, 1335 (Fed. Cir. 2010).

[36] Vas-Cath, Inc. v. Mahurkar, 935 F.2d 1555 (Fed. Cir. 1991).

[37] 35 U.S.C. § 120 (emphasis added).

In *Vas-Cath*, the patentee sought to rely on the March 1982 filing date of '081 design patent application. Presumably, this was because otherwise the patentee's Canadian patent would have barred the subsequent '601 and '592 applications. To determine the merits of this assertion, the court considered whether the diagram in the design application '081 design patent sufficiently disclosed the subject matter of the claims of the '329 and '141 patents. Applying the possession test, *Vas-Cath* accepted that the written description requirement need not be satisfied with text; rather, a sufficient diagram could meet the standard.[38] Here, the court determined that the patentee avoided summary judgment based on evidence that one of ordinary skill could have determined possession of the claimed subject matter based on the '081 diagram.

As *Vas-Cath* illustrates, to establish priority to an earlier filing date, the claim must be supported by an adequate written description in the earlier specification. The test for determining if an earlier patent can be used to set priority is whether the earlier application reasonably conveys a written description for the claims in the later patent. Further, *Vas Cath* demonstrates that the possession test can be met without a recitation in words, but rather can be satisfied through diagrams alone.

Anscape Ltd. v. Nintendo[39] applies these principles to the electronic arts. There, the validity of the later patent[40] (the " '700 patent") depended on whether its claims were supported by a written description in an earlier-filed patent (the " '525 patent").[41] The '700 claims were directed to hand-operated computer game controllers with multiple inputs. However, the '525 patent specification contained twenty references to single input controllers, and none to multiple input controllers. The court concluded that the earlier '525 specification could not support the claims of the later '700 patent, finding that:

> . . . the only reasonable reading of the '525 specification is that it is directed to and describes only a controller having a single input member operable in six degrees of freedom. In contrast, the '700 specification and claims were enlarged to cover more than single input members operable in six degrees of freedom.[42]

On this basis, the court ruled that the '700 patent was not entitled to rely on the '525 filing date for priority purposes.

---

[38] *See also* Cooper Cameron Corp. v. Kvaerner Oilfield Products, Inc., 291 F.3d 1317, 1322 (Fed. Cir. 2002) ("Drawings constitute an adequate description if they describe what is claimed and convey to those of skill in the art that the patentee actually invented what is claimed").

[39] Anascape Ltd. v. Nintendo of America, Ltd., 601 F.3d 1333 (Fed. Cir. 2010).

[40] U.S. Patent No. 6,906,700 (filed Nov 16, 2000).

[41] U.S. Patent No. 6,222,525 (filed July 6, 1996).

[42] *Anascape*, 601 F.3d at 1340.

[C] Biological and Chemical Subject Matter

One post-*Ariad* decision, *Boston Scientific v. Johnson & Johnson*,[43] demonstrates the level of specificity that is required in the chemical arts to satisfy the written description requirement. In *Boston Scientific*, the claims at issue concern a drug eluting stent, which is used to treat coronary heart disease. The claimed stent, a medical device that is inserted into an artery of the heart to keep the passageway open, was designed to release a chemical to prevent scarring. The patents at issue derived from a provisional application that was originally filed in 1997. These patents relied on a drug using rapamycin as an active ingredient. In 2006, the patentee added the phrase "macrocyclic lactone analogs" of rapamycin to the claims.

The *Boston Scientific* court considered whether these analogues were supported by the 1997 provisional application. The 1997 specification referenced the macrocyclic lactone analogue. The Federal Circuit held that the claims failed for an inadequate written description as a matter of law. Following *Eli Lilly*, the *Boston Scientific* court observed that the mere mention of the analogues was not sufficient. The court noted that the lack of any examples or experiments concerning a claimed sub-genus (here, macrocyclic lactone analogs) warranted invalidation, particularly because "the universe of potential compounds that are structurally similar to rapamycin and classifiable as macrocyclic lactones is potentially limitless."[44]

Significantly, the *Boston Scientific* court noted that prior art patents that disclosed some species did not cure the written description defects. Specifically, these disclosures did not rise to a level that "represented existing knowledge in the art," so as to excuse the patentee from objectively disclosing possession of sufficient information about the claimed analogues.[45] Fundamentally, the disclosure of a small number of analogues in prior art references was no substitute for the "tens of thousands of possible macrocyclic lactone analogues" that were unexplored when the provisional application was filed in 1997.[46] The *Boston Scientific* court noted that functional claim language can support the written description requirement for chemical claims where the art establishes a correlation between structure and function. In reasoning that highlights the *Ariad* court's emphasis on the objective nature of the written description inquiry, the *Boston Scientific* court found this rule inapplicable where the relevant disclosures explicitly acknowledged the uncertain and unpredictable state of the art.

The *Boston Scientific* decision is consistent with the pre-*Ariad* decision *Fujikawa v. Wattanasin*.[47] There, the Federal Circuit found that the mere mention of a compound was insufficient to support a claim to that same compound placed in a molecular structure at a specific location. The court drew a distinction between *disclosing* a compound used to make the claimed invention and a disclosure that

---

[43] Boston Scientific v. Johnson & Johnson, 647 F.3d 1353 (Fed. Cir. 2011).

[44] *Id.* at 1364.

[45] *Id.*

[46] *Id.* at 1365.

[47] Fujikawa v. Wattanasin, 93 F.3d 1559 (Fed. Cir. 1996).

leads one of ordinary skill to use the constituent parts to make the claimed subject matter. The *Fujikawa* court noted that a contrary rule was unacceptable for this technology, as otherwise "a 'laundry list' disclosure of every possible moiety for every possible position would constitute a written description of every species in the genus."[48]

Another post-*Ariad* decision, *Billups v. Rothenberg v. Associated Regional and University Pathologists*, illustrates that the "the written description requirement exists to ensure that inventors do not attempt to preempt the future before it arrives."[49] In *Billups*, the claim covered a test for a medical condition that is characterized by excessive iron absorption. The application, filed in 1994, was based on the detection of the mutation of a particular gene sequence, known as C282Y. The application failed to disclose the precise gene sequence, the sequence of the mutation, and described only the general location of the relevant mutation "within less than a 300 base pair region of a defined exon of a well studied multi-gene family."[50] The *Billups* court found the written description insufficient, finding that the patentee did not possess the mutation necessary for diagnosis, but rather had only disclosed a "research plan."[51]

Billups represents a rule common to claims to genetic material — that is, the level of detail that is typically necessary to satisfy the written description requirement for DNA is either 1) a description of the DNA itself; or 2) a description of the DNA's function together with knowledge in the art of a correlation between the function and a specified structure. Neither was present in the record in this case, and therefore the claims were invalid. Further, the *Billups* opinion underscores a second rule — that is, an inadequate written description cannot be cured by a later disclosure. Applying this rule, the court held that the sequence's disclosure by independent researchers two years later was irrelevant. The time to measure of the adequacy of the written description is at the time of filing.

In contrast, in *Amgen, Inc. v. Hoecst Marion Roussel*, the court considered the validity of a patent directed to the production of a naturally-occurring hormone that relied on recombinant DNA technology.[52] *Amgen* noted that the invention at issue was directed to biological materials that were already known to those of ordinary skill in the art and that the identification of these materials in general terms "readily convey distinguishing information concerning their identity such that one of ordinary skill in the art could visualize or recognize the identity of the members of the genus."[53] *Amgen* explained that, "the claim terms at issue here are not new or unknown biological materials that ordinarily skilled artisans would

---

[48] *Id.*

[49] *Billups Rothenberg v. Associated Regional and University Pathologists*, 642 F.3d 1031, 1036 (Fed. Cir. 2011).

[50] *Id.* quoting U.S. Patent No. 5,674,681. Generally, an "exon" refers to a section of DNA.

[51] *Id.* at 1037.

[52] Amgen Inc. v. Hoechst Marion Roussel, 314 F.3d 1313 (Fed. Cir. 2003).

[53] *Id.* at 1332.

easily miscomprehend."[54] In result, *Amgen* affirmed the trial court's rejection of the invalidity defense.

To assist patentees in meeting this standard for lesser known substances, the U.S. PTO has promulgated regulations which permit applicants to deposit biological material to satisfy section 112's disclosure requirements.[55] These deposits, which are made available to the public, must be referenced in the written specification. This procedure was examined in *Enzo Biochem, Inc. v. Gen-Probe Inc.*[56] In *Enzo*, the patentee had made a proper deposit of three DNA sequences and referenced the deposit in the disclosure. For the first set of claims that were identical to the deposited material, the *Enzo* court held that the possession test was met under those circumstances. For the second set of broader genus claims, *Enzo* noted that "because the deposited sequences are described by virtue of a reference to their having been deposited, it may well be that various subsequences, mutations, and mixtures of those sequences are also described to one of skill in the art."[57] *Enzo* remanded the question of the validity of the broader claims to the district court, which was asked to consider whether the deposited sequences were sufficiently representative of the genus claims such that one of skill in the art would understand that the patentee had possession of the invention for the broader genus claims. Thus, the *Enzo* case clarifies that a functional description of genetic material is not fatal, so long as the written description is met through another means such as a deposit.

Taken together, these authorities demonstrate a notable level of specificity for uncertain and unknown technology where a functional description cannot demonstrate possession. Further, if one of ordinary skill in the art has an understanding of the biological material based on the information provided in the specification and knowledge in the art, the written description requirement can be met on that basis alone. For lesser-known materials, the standard can be met by a detailed description or a reference to a biological deposit, so long as one of ordinary skill in the art is able to ascertain the inventor's possession of the invention from the deposited materials.

§ 9.05   COMPARISON: WRITTEN DESCRIPTION AND ENABLEMENT

As *Ariad* established, written description is a separate and additional requirement to the enablement requirement.[58] How are the standards different?

---

[54] *Id.* at 1332.

[55] *See* MPEP § 2404; 37 C.F.R. 1.801–1.809. The deposit process gives the public access to biological material at certain deposit sites located throughout the world. According to the U.S. PTO, such a deposit may be necessary, "[w]here the invention involves a biological material and words alone cannot sufficiently describe how to make and use the invention in a reproducible manner." MPEP § 2402.

[56] Enzo Biochem v. Gen-Probe Inc., 323 F.3d 956 (Fed. Cir. 2002).

[57] *Enzo Biochem*, 323 F.3d at 966.

[58] Ariad Pharmaceutical, Inc. v. Eli Lilly, 598 F.3d 1336, 1340 (Fed. Cir. 2010).

Enablement considers whether the specification describes sufficient information to enable one of ordinary skill in the art to make and use the invention, measured as of the filing date of the patent application. In contrast, the written description discloses sufficient information to allow one of ordinary skill in the art to reasonably conclude that the inventor had possession of the invention at the time that the application was filed. In other words, enablement requires disclosure of the inventor's best recipe for making and using the invention, while written description requires an identifying disclosure that demonstrates what the patentee actually invented.

According to *Ariad*, written description serves a different purpose from enablement:

> A description of the claimed invention allows the United States Patent and Trademark Office ("PTO") to examine applications effectively; courts to understand the invention, determine compliance with the statute, and to construe the claims; and the public to understand and improve upon the invention and to avoid the claimed boundaries of the patentee's exclusive rights.[59]

For some inventions, the two requirements may rise or fall together. As recognized by the Federal Circuit, "a recitation of how to make and use the invention across the full breadth of the claim is ordinarily sufficient to demonstrate that the inventor possesses the full scope of the invention, and vice versa."[60] However, it is possible that a patentee can satisfy one requirement and not the other. For example, a patentee may satisfy the written description requirement by describing the invention but fail enablement by omitting to provide one of ordinary skill sufficiently detailed information that describes how to make and use the invention. This might occur where the specification discloses that the invention includes compounds of either A, B or C, but fails to disclose how each of those three compounds can be obtained, made or used.

Likewise, a patentee may meet the enablement requirement but fail to meet the written description requirement. For example, a written specification may discuss compound A but not inform one of ordinary skill that the technology can be applied elsewhere.[61] In this example, assume that the specification contains sufficient information about compound A that permits one of ordinary skill to make and use compounds B and C, but does not specifically mention or inherently disclose either compound B or C. This disclosure would satisfy the enablement requirement for all three compounds, but fail the written description requirement for a claim for a class consisting of A, B and C.[62]

---

[59] *Id.* at 1345.

[60] LizardTech, Inc. v. Earth Resource Mapping, Inc., 424 F.3d 1336, 1345 (Fed. Cir. 2005).

[61] This example is based on a discussion from *In re* Di Leone, 436 F.2d 1404, 1405 n.1 (C.C.P.A. 1971).

[62] *Id.* at 927 n.1.

§ 9.06 CONCLUSION

Section 112's written description requirement compels patentees to describe the invention and demonstrate possession of the invention at the time that the patent application is filed. In addition to performing a teaching function, written descriptions pin the application to a particular invention on the filing date, which limits that patentee's ability to later shift or broaden the subject matter of the patent in the claims, or through amendment during prosecution. A patentee may meet this requirement through text, diagrams or other information stated in a specification. The sufficiency of a disclosure is based on the material within the four corners of the patent application examined through the understanding of one of ordinary skill in the art.

The courts have looked for specificity in a disclosure, particularly for inventions relating to biological material. Nonetheless, patentees have been able to satisfy these requirements by making a deposit pursuant to the U.S. PTO's regulations or where the claims at issue are in areas known to those in the art. The written description requirement is enforced in both issued patents and for patents seeking to claim priority back to a parent application. In the latter instance, the written description must be sufficient to demonstrate possession of the claims in the later applications.

Chapter 10

DEFINITENESS

SYNOPSIS

§ 10.01 INTRODUCTION

§ 10.02 "PARTICULARLY POINT OUT AND DISTINCTLY CLAIM"

[A] General Rules

[B] Differing Definiteness Standards: Patent Applications v. Issued Patents

[C] Assessing Whether a Claim is Definite

[D] Indefiniteness and Means Plus Function Claims

[E] Terms of Degree

[F] Remedy: Should an Indefinite Claim Be Invalidated?

§ 10.03 "APPLICANT REGARDS:" THE INVENTOR'S DEFINITION

§ 10.04 CONCLUSION

§ 10.01 INTRODUCTION

The *definiteness requirement* is stated in 35 U.S.C. § 112, paragraph 1, which provides, "[t]he specification shall conclude with one or more claims particularly pointing out and distinctly claiming the subject matter which the applicant regards as his invention."[1] This places the obligation of defining the invention on the patentee through the use of one or more claims.

A primary purpose of definiteness is to provide public notice of the scope of the claimed patent right.[2] Public notice allows others within the same field to ascertain whether their practices infringe and to have the opportunity to design around the patent where practicable. As the U.S. Supreme Court has explained, "This clarity is essential to promote progress, because it enables efficient investment in innovation. A patent holder should know what he owns, and the public should know what he does not."[3] The definiteness requirement is intended to protect against chilling the efforts of others from engaging in activity outside the scope of the patent claims.[4]

---

[1] 35 U.S.C. § 112 (2000).

[2] Oakley, Inc. v. Sunglass Hut Int'l, 316 F.3d 1331, 1340 (Fed. Cir. 2003).

[3] Festo Corp. v. Shoketsu Kinzoku Kogyo Kabushiki Co., 535 U.S. 722, 730-31 (2002).

[4] United Carbon v. Binney & Smith Co., 317 U.S. 228, 236 (1942).

An additional purpose of the definiteness requirement is to aid in determining whether other patentability requirements have been met, such as patent eligible subject matter, originality, novelty, utility, and non-obviousness.[5] For example, only a properly defined claim can be meaningfully evaluated as to whether it is sufficiently separate — and therefore novel and nonobvious — over the prior art.[6]

The statutory requirement for a definite claim has not always been part of the U.S. patent law; indeed, there has not always been a requirement for a claim at all. Its origins can be seen in the 1822 case, *Evans v. Eaton*,[7] where the Supreme Court pronounced that patentees are obligated to describe their inventions "in such full, clear, and exact terms, as to distinguish the same from all other things before known." Because the *Evans* court did not expressly require that this information be in a "claim" format, patentees could meet the *Evans* requirement by providing a textual description of the invention in the written specification.

By 1870, the Patent Act had been amended to expressly require the patentee to "particularly point out and distinctly claim the part, improvement or combination that he claims as his invention or discovery."[8] In the current Act, definiteness can be broken into two distinct conceptual components. First, claims must particularly point out and distinctly claim the subject matter. Second, the claim must set forth what the applicant regards as her invention.

§ 10.02   "PARTICULARLY POINT OUT AND DISTINCTLY CLAIM"

[A]   General Rules

In order to meet the requirement that a claim particularly point out and distinctly claim the subject matter, a claim must reasonably apprise those skilled in the art of its scope.[9] Generally, the standard is met if the claim at issue is sufficiently precise to allow one to determine whether or not she is infringing.[10] Definiteness is determined as a matter of law by the court.[11]

---

[5] Leeds v. Comm'r of Patents and Trademarks, 955 F.2d 757, 759 (D.C. 1992).

[6] *See, e.g.*, W.L. Gore & Assoc., Inc. v. Garlock, Inc., 721 F.2d 1540, 1548 (Fed. Cir. 1983) ("[I]t is the claims that measure and define the invention").

[7] Evans v. Eaton, 20 U.S. (7 Wheat.) 356, 380-81 (1822).

[8] Patent Act of July 8, 1870, ch. 230, § 26 16 Stat. 198 (emphasis added); *see generally* Pennwalt Corp. v. Durand-Wayland, Inc., 833 F.2d 931, 957-960 (Fed. Cir. 1987) (Newman, J., concurring) (describing the history of the patent claim requirement).

[9] Amgen, Inc. v. Chugai Pharm. Co., 927 F.2d 1200, 1217 (Fed. Cir. 1991).

[10] Morton Int'l., Inc. v. Cardinal Chem. Co., 5 F.3d 1464, 1470 (Fed. Cir. 1993).

[11] Exxon Research and Eng'g Co. v. U.S., 265 F.3d 1371, 1376 (Fed. Cir. 2001).

[B]   Differing Definiteness Standards: Patent Applications v. Issued Patents

According to the Federal Circuit, the standards for assessing definiteness differ depending on whether the patent is in prosecution before the PTO or has been issued.[12] Specifically, claims examined in prosecution are subject to more exacting scrutiny.[13] The court has explained that the more demanding standard for claims in prosecution permits applicants to remove ambiguities through claim amendment, which can be readily done when the application is pending in order to "fashion claims that are precise, clear, correct and unambiguous."[14]

In contrast, the Federal Circuit applies a statutory presumption of validity when examining claim definiteness after the patent has issued.[15] When the issue is examined in court litigation, close questions of indefiniteness for an issued patent are resolved in favor of finding the claim valid. For example, in *Exxon Research v. U.S.*, the court determined that the patentee's failure to specify numerical limits for factors such as time or quantity were not indefinite where the limitation was not critical to patentability.[16] *Exxon Research* relied on the ability of one of ordinary skill in the art to ascertain these limitations from the information disclosed in the specification. In its decision, the *Exxon Research* court stated that for already-issued patents, the Federal Circuit "has held claims definite even when some degree of experimentation was necessary, as long as the claims otherwise met the enablement requirement."[17]

[C]   Assessing Whether a Claim is Definite

For claims assessed in court, a claim term that is not defined in the specification does not necessarily render the claim indefinite. If the person of ordinary skill can ascertain a construction from the word's ordinary meaning, the prior art, knowledge within the art, and/or the specification, the claim is not indefinite.[18] A review of the leading cases illustrates the manner in which this standard is applied.

One is *Oakley, Inc. v. Sunglass Hut Int'l.*,[19] which considered the claim term "vivid colored appearance" as directed to a claim to colored reflective sunglass lenses. The specification described that a vivid colored appearance could be created on lenses where there was a "differential effect in intensity, of reflected light" on the lens.[20] The accused infringer asserted that the use of the word "vivid" was indefinite.

---

[12] *Id.* at 1379-80.

[13] 35 U.S.C. § 282 (2000 & Supp. IV 2004) ("A patent shall be presumed valid.").

[14] *In re* Zletz, 893 F.2d 319, 322 (Fed. Cir. 1989).

[15] *Exxon*, 265 F.3d at 1380.

[16] *Id.* at 1379-80.

[17] *Id.*

[18] *See* MPEP § 2173.02.

[19] Oakley, Inc. v. Sunglass Hut Int'l, 316 F.3d 1331 (Fed. Cir. 2003).

[20] *Id.* at 1335, *quoting* U.S. Patent No. 5,054,902 (filed Nov 1, 1989).

The *Oakley* court rejected this argument, finding that one of ordinary skill in the art could ascertain specific values that would yield a "vivid" effect from numerical ranges of differential effects described in the specification. The court reasoned that "because the language of the claim associates vividness with the differential effect, and the specification presents examples of numerical values of the differential effect that either qualify as vivid or do not,"[21] the claim met the standard.

In contrast, in *Datamize, LLC v. Plumtree Software, Inc.*,[22] the court found the claim term "aesthetically pleasing" rendered a claim indefinite. There, the claims were directed toward a software program for the creation of user interfaces for electronic kiosks. The court explained that the claim limitation, which required that the display be "aesthetically pleasing," was "completely dependent on a person's subjective opinion":[23]

> A purely subjective construction of "aesthetically pleasing" would not notify the public of the patentee's right to exclude since the meaning of the claim language would depend on the unpredictable vagaries of any one person's opinion of the aesthetics of interface screens. While beauty is in the eye of the beholder, a claim term, to be definite, requires an objective anchor.[24]

A similar issue was examined in *Halliburton Energy Services, Inc. v. M-1 LLC*,[25] which considered a patent to oil field drilling fluids. The patentee Halliburton had inserted into claims the term "fragile gels," which are substances that change from gels to fluids with very slight movement or pressure and then re-form into a gel when these conditions cease. A spectrum of substances that might fit this definition existed, including some in the prior art. The court held the term indefinite because the specification failed to disclose how much more quickly the claimed gels broke or to describe the parameters that distinguished the claimed fragile gels from the prior art fragile gels. Finding the claims invalid, the court explained that adopting the patentee's construction "could retard innovation because cautious competitors may steer too far around that which Halliburton actually invented, neglecting improvements that otherwise might be made."[26]

[D] Indefiniteness and Means Plus Function Claims

Indefiniteness is sometimes invoked for means plus function claims. As background, 35 U.S.C. § 112, paragraph 6 authorizes applicants to describe a claim limitation by its function rather than a specific structure. Referred to as a *means plus function* limitation, these descriptors can be very broad on their face. For example, rather than describing scissors, knives or blades in a claim directed to a device for cutting paper, a claim can use the phrase "cutting means" to encompass

---

[21] *Id.*

[22] Datamize, LLC v. Plumtree Software, Inc., 417 F3d 1342 (Fed. Cir. 2005).

[23] *Id.* at 1350.

[24] *Id.*

[25] Halliburton Energy Services, Inc. v. M-I LLC, 514 F.3d 1244 (Fed. Cir. 2008).

[26] *Id.* at 1254.

multiple ways to accomplish that limitation.

One important feature of a means plus function limitation is that, under § 112, paragraph 6, the function limitation is "construed to cover the corresponding structure, material, or acts described in the specification and equivalents thereof." Therefore, the specification must disclose a structure that corresponds to the functional element. In other words, in return for the ability to claim functionally, the patentee must indicate the structure that constitutes the means in the written specification.

To take our paper cutter example, the written specification must include the specific instruments (or "structure," in patent parlance) such as scissors, knives, blades or other implements that can be used to accomplish the "cutting means" limitation.

It is important to note that the failure to include a corresponding structure to support a functionally-defined element renders the claim indefinite.[27] For more information about indefiniteness and means plus function claims, see Chapter 31.

[E]   Terms of Degree

Terms of degree — such as "likely," "substantially," "relatively" or "about" — may raise an indefiniteness issue. However, such terms used in lieu of more precise numerical limitations do not necessarily render a claim indefinite if the claim can be understood by one of ordinary skill.[28] Under this standard, similar claim terms can yield different results depending on the context. For example, the term "about" referring to the stretch rate of plastic was held definite where the meaning could be ascertained by one of ordinary skill using a stopwatch.[29] However, in the context of a different patent, claims using the phrase "at least about" were held invalid for indefiniteness where there was close prior art and no other source of information permitted one of ordinary skill in the art to ascertain the range that the term "about" might cover.[30]

As an additional example, *In re Jolly*[31] considered claims that included the terms "sufficient," "insufficient," and "substantial proportion" to indicate minimum and maximum time periods for chemical reactions.[32] The application's specification described that this time period was critical to the invention and was dependent on other factors such as temperature, degree of agitation, and the amount of chemical used. The *Jolly* court found that claims including these terms indefinite, explaining,

---

[27] *See, e.g.,*

[28] *See, e.g.,* MPEP § 2173.05(b).

[29] W.L. Gore & Assoc., Inc. v. Garlock, Inc., 721 F.2d 1540, 1557 (Fed. Cir. 1983).

[30] Amgen, Inc. v. Chugai Pharm. Co., 927 F.2d 1200, 1218 (Fed. Cir. 1991).

[31] *In re* Jolly, 172 F.2d 566 (C.C.P.A. 1949). The claim language which was the focus of the court's analysis was: " 'for a time sufficient to produce a substantially homogenous product but insufficient to cause the formation of a substantial proportion of oil-insoluble reaction products."

[32] *Id.* at 570. The claim language which was the focus of the court's analysis was: " 'for a time sufficient to produce a substantially homogenous product but insufficient to cause the formation of a substantial proportion of oil-insoluble reaction products."

"considerable experimentation, on the part of one seeking to carry out the process, would be required to determine time limits" described in the claims.[33] Because the specification failed to disclose sufficient information from which the time period limitation could be ascertained to one of ordinary skill, the court affirmed the rejection.

In the final analysis, a claim must "inform the public during the life of the patent of the limits of monopoly asserted, so that it may be known which features may be safely used or manufactured without a license and which may not."[34] Although absolute clarity is not required, the meaning of a claim term must be discernable such that the public is notified of the scope of the patentee's right to exclude based on information reasonably available to those in the art.[35]

[F]   Remedy: Should an Indefinite Claim Be Invalidated?

In *Exxon Research and Engineering Co. v. United States*,[36] the Federal Circuit stated that a claim in an issued patent will be invalidated only where the "claim is insolubly ambiguous, and no narrowing construction can properly be adopted." Where possible, a court may elect to construe a claim narrowly rather than to impose the more drastic remedy of invalidation.

One example of claim narrowing can be seen in *Athletic Alternatives, Inc. v. Prince Manufacturing, Inc.*[37] In that case, the Federal Circuit examined a claim directed to splayed strings[38] for a tennis racquet. Defendant Prince sold a racquet (the "vortex"), which included strings splayed from the central plane at two, and only two, distinct offset distances: a distance of 2 millimeters at the upper and lower corners, and a distance of 4.5 millimeters along the sides of the frame.

Claim 1 of the asserted patent included the following limitation for the racquet strings:

> where *said distance di varies between a minimum distance* for the first and last string ends in said sequence *and a maximum distance* for a string end between (3rd intermediary distance) said first and last string ends in said sequence.[39]

The Federal Circuit found that the "varies between" claim language was susceptible to two meanings: one that required three offset distances (i.e., a minimum, a maximum, and at least one intermediate value) and a broader meaning that required only two offset distances (a minimum and a maximum). The Federal Circuit further found no resolution to the construction of this term in the patent

---

[33] *Id.*

[34] Permutit Co. v. Graver Corp., 284 U.S. 52, 59 (1931).

[35] Datamize, LLC v. Plumtree Software, Inc., 417 F.3d 1342 (Fed. Cir. 2005).

[36] Exxon Research and Eng'g Co. v. U.S., 265 F.3d 1371, 1375 (Fed. Cir. 2001).

[37] Athletic Alternatives, Inc. v. Prince Mfg, Inc., 73 F.3d 1573 (Fed. Cir. 1996).

[38] *Id.*, at 1574. According to the case, "splayed" strings are those that attach to the racquet frame alternately above and below its central plane. *Id.*

[39] *Id.* at 1577, *quoting* U.S. Patent No. 5,037,097 (filed Aug 18, 1988) (emphasis added).

specification, the prosecution history or by using the doctrine of claim differentiation.[40]

To resolve the issue, the *AAI* court adopted the narrower interpretation requiring three offset distances. The *AAI* court explained that a contrary finding that accepted the broader proposed interpretation would "undermine the fair notice function of the requirement that the patentee distinctly claim the subject matter disclosed in the patent."[41] The *AAI* court's decision to narrow the claim (rather than to invalidate) was discussed by a concurring Judge Neis, who stated disagreement with the majority's resolution on that basis, because "[n]arrowness can not be equated with definiteness."[42] Nonetheless, the Federal Circuit has indicated that issued claims should be construed to avoid invalidity so long as the claim is amenable to construction.[43] An issued claim will be invalidated only if it is insolubly vague.

§ 10.03 "APPLICANT REGARDS:" THE INVENTOR'S DEFINITION

The second paragraph of § 112 requires that the "specification shall conclude with one or more claims particularly pointing out and distinctly claiming the subject matter *which the **applicant regards** as his invention*."[44] Although there are few cases on point, this aspect of the definiteness requirement ensures that the claim is commensurate with the subject matter created by the inventor.

An example of the applicant regards analysis is *In re Prater*.[45] There, the claim was directed to a method for analyzing spectrographic data. The Examiner had rejected the claim based on a construction that the claimed steps could be performed in the mind — which the examiner believed was outside the scope of patentable subject matter under the "mental steps" doctrine.[46]

On appeal from the rejection, the applicant argued that the claim should be read to include a limitation that the analytic method must be performed on a machine. If successful, under the law at the time this interpretation might have assisted to avoid the mental steps bar to patentability. In support of the argument, the applicant pointed out that all implementations that were described in the specification were

---

[40] *Id.* at 1579-81. As the Federal Circuit has explained, claim differentiation ". . . means that an interpretation of a claim should be avoided if it would make the claim read like another one." Laitram Corp. v. Rexnord, Inc., 939 F.2d 1533, 1538 (Fed. Cir. 1991). Note that "[c]laim differentiation is a guide, not a rigid rule," and that claims that are only capable of identical construction must be construed as such.

[41] *Athletic Alternatives*, 73 F.3d at 1581.

[42] *Id.* at 1583 (Neis, J., concurring).

[43] Exxon Research and Eng'g Co. v. U.S., 265 F.3d 1371, 1375 (Fed. Cir. 2001).

[44] 35 U.S.C. § 112 (2000).

[45] *In re* Prater, 415 F.2d 1393 (C.C.P.A. 1969).

[46] *Id.* at 1398; *see generally, In re* Meyer, 688 F.2d 789, 794-95 (C.C.P.A. 1982) (explaining the "mental steps" doctrine, stating "[t]he presence of a mathematical algorithm or formula in a claim is merely an indication that a scientific principle, law of nature, idea or mental process may be the subject matter claimed and, thus, justify a rejection of that claim under 35 U.S.C. § 101) and *infra* Chapter 23.

performed on a computer. Notably, the claim did not include an express limitation to execution on a computer. Rather than reach the mental steps rejection, the *Prater* court examined the claim invalid for conformance with the "applicant regards" requirement. The court noted the distinction between the applicant's proposed claim construction that limited the claim's meaning to computer-implemented methods and the broad claim in the application which encompassed calculation in the human mind. Based on this disparity, the court found that the claims failed to reflect the subject matter that the applicant regarded as his invention.

Notice that the *Prater* court considered arguments in the applicant's brief to arrive at a conclusion that the "applicant regards" requirement was not met. What other types of evidence can be considered? In *Solomon v. Kimberly-Clark Corp.*,[47] the Federal Circuit drew a distinction between claims in prosecution and those examined in invalidity litigation. Specifically, *Solomon* explained that consideration of evidence outside the patent specification — such as the inventor's statements to the PTO — could be considered during prosecution because claims can be amended and ambiguities clarified during the prosecution period. According to the *Solomon* court, this was appropriate to "achieve a complete exploration of the applicant's invention and its relation to the prior art."[48]

However, after a patent is issued, the *Solomon* court directed that the claim should be construed in light of the understanding of the person of ordinary skill.[49] At that stage, the *Solomon* court stated that "a more limited range of evidence should be considered in evaluating validity."[50] Specifically, *Solomon* held that the court could not consider an inventor's deposition testimony about the scope of the claimed invention that had been submitted by a challenger who argued that the testimony established a failure to meet the applicant regards requirement, explaining:

> While presumably the inventor has approved any changes to the claim scope that have occurred via amendment during the prosecution process, it is not unusual for there to be a significant difference between what an inventor thinks his patented invention is and what the ultimate scope of the claims is after allowance by the PTO.[51]

The rule barring extrinsic evidence from modifying the patent is well supported by the principle that claim meanings should not change after a patent issues. Modifying an issued claim's coverage through testimony created after the patent issues might create unwarranted uncertainty. Thus, although the "applicant regards" requirement uses language that suggests subjectivity, there are stringent

---

[47] Solomon v. Kimberly-Clark, 216 F.3d 1372 (Fed. Cir. 2000).

[48] *Id.* at 1378.

[49] *Id.* *See generally*, Oakley, Inc. v. Sunglass Hut Int'l, 316 F.3d 1331, 1340-41 (Fed. Cir. 2003) (in determining definiteness of an issued patent, court construes the claim as one skilled in the art would understand them in light of the specification).

[50] *Solomon*, 216 F.3d at 1379.

[51] *Id.* at 1380.

limits on after-the-fact evidence that can be used to demonstrate a disparity after a patent issues.

§ 10.04   CONCLUSION

The second paragraph of § 112 requires the patent applicant to include a claim, stating that "[t]he specification shall conclude with one or more claims particularly pointing out and distinctly claiming the subject matter which the applicant regards as his invention." The requirement can be viewed as two conceptually distinct — but related — subparts. First, a patentee must draft a claim with sufficient precision that clearly and distinctly sets forth the subject matter when read by one of ordinary skill in light of the specification. Second, the patentee's claim must be commensurate with the subject matter that the inventor regards as the invention. The remedy for an indefiniteness violation for an issued claim may be invalidation, or if feasible through a narrow construction of the claim.

Chapter 11

BEST MODE

SYNOPSIS

§ 11.01 OVERVIEW

§ 11.02 THE BEST MODE STANDARD

§ 11.03 APPLICATION OF THE BEST MODE STANDARD

    [A] First Prong: The Inventor's Subjective Intent

    [B] Second Prong: Objective Examination of the Patent Disclosure

§ 11.04 IMPACT OF A BEST MODE VIOLATION

§ 11.05 CONCLUSION

§ 11.01 OVERVIEW

35 U.S.C. § 112 requires that the inventor disclose the *best mode* of the invention.[1] Satisfying the best mode requirement is considered part of the quid pro quo to obtain the patent right.[2] The patentee obtains the right to exclude others from practicing the claimed invention for a limited time, and the public receives knowledge of the preferred methods to practice the claimed invention. The U.S. is one of the few nations that impose this requirement.

Some patent applicants are reluctant to disclose preferred formulae and techniques in a patent application and seek to retain such information as a trade secret. That alternative would be very appealing to an intellectual property holder. A trade secret can be maintained indefinitely, so long as the information remains valuable and subject to reasonable efforts to maintain secrecy. In contrast, a patent right has a limited term. If a strategy to obtain the benefits of both trade secret and patent law is successful, the patentee could obtain the benefits of both intellectual property systems without providing the public with the full benefit of information disclosure. As one court stated, the best mode requirement is aimed to "to restrain inventors from applying for patents while at the same time concealing from the public preferred embodiments of their inventions which they have in fact conceived."[3]

---

[1] 35 U.S.C § 112, § 112 ("The specification . . . shall set forth the best mode contemplated by the inventor of carrying out his invention.").

[2] *Id.* at 1210.

[3] *In re* Gay, 309 F.2d 769, 772 (C.C.P.A. 1962).

Nonetheless, reliance on best mode in litigation has come under scrutiny in recent years. The major criticisms include: 1) the expense associated with litigating the issue in court, because proving a best mode violation requires testimony and documentary evidence of the inventor's subjective state of mind; 2) the defense creates uncertainty, because a patent's vulnerability to a best mode challenge cannot be ascertained from the face of the document; and 3) the costs on international patent applicants who must modify their disclosures to conform with U.S. law.[4] To address some of these concerns, recent U.S. legislation has removed best mode as a grounds to invalidate, cancel or render unenforceable a patent claim in litigation. Notably, Congress did not remove best mode entirely from section 112's disclosure requirements. Therefore, the best mode remains a statutory obligation although the ability to enforce the requirement is limited.

§ 11.02   THE BEST MODE STANDARD

Generally, whether the best mode requirement has been met requires a two-part examination.[5] The first inquiry examines the inventor's *subjective state of mind* and asks whether, at the time the inventor filed her patent application, she contemplated a best mode of practicing her invention. If she did, that best mode must be disclosed in the specification. Because the best mode standard is based on the inventor's subjective preference, a best mode need not be the optimal way to accomplish the invention on an objective basis. Rather, the best mode inquiry is based on the inventor's preference as of the patent's effective filing date.[6] There can be no best mode if the inventor did not know, or did not appreciate, any preferred method.[7]

If the best mode does exist, the analysis turns to the second question, which examines whether the best mode has been *adequately disclosed*. This step requires an objective examination of whether the inventor's patent disclosure is adequate to inform one of ordinary skill the best mode or the best way to practice the claim. Such information can include information, materials and methods developed by third parties.

Best mode is distinct from enablement. The enablement requirement requires sufficient information to enable one of ordinary skill to make and use the invention.[8] In contrast, best mode requires disclosure of known, specific instrumentalities and techniques that are subjectively preferred by the inventor as the best way of carrying out the invention. It is entirely possible to enable a claim yet fail to disclose the best mode. This can occur where a patentee discloses a method for making the invention but fails to disclose the inventor's preferred technique for doing so. Thus, "[i]f . . . the applicant develops specific instrumentalities or techniques which are

---

[4] *See* COMMITTEE ON INTELLECTUAL PROPERTY RIGHTS IN THE KNOWLEDGE-BASED ECONOMY, NATIONAL RESEARCH COUNCIL, A PATENT SYSTEM FOR THE 21ST CENTURY (STEPHEN A. MERRILL, ET AL., EDS. 2004).

[5] Amgen, Inc. v. Chugai Pharm. Co., Ltd., 927 F.2d 1200, 1209 (Fed. Cir. 1991) (setting forth the standard).

[6] Northern Telecom Ltd. v. Samsung Electronics Co., Ltd., 215 F.3d 1281, 1286 (Fed. Cir. 2000).

[7] *See* MPEP § 2165; Benger Laboratories Limited v. R. K. Laros Co., 209 F. Supp. 639, 644 (E.D. Pa. 1962).

[8] Glaxo Inc. v. Novopharm Ltd., 52 F.3d 1043, 1050 (Fed. Cir. 1995).

recognized at the time of filing as the best way of carrying out the invention, then the best mode requirement imposes an obligation to disclose that information to the public as well."[9]

§ 11.03   APPLICATION OF THE BEST MODE STANDARD

According to § 112, best mode is keyed to those methods of carrying out the invention. The "invention" referred to in this section is defined by the scope of the patent claims.[10] The relevant information must relate to the inventor's preferred method of practicing the claim as well as any information that materially affects the properties of the claimed invention.[11] Notably, this may include steps that are not specifically claimed if necessary to implement the invention.[12] On the other hand, § 112 does not require an inventor to disclose subject matter that is beyond the claim scope.[13]

For example, in *United States Gypsum Co. v. National Gypsum Co.*,[14] the court considered whether the best mode requirement was met for a compound used to join wallboards together in the construction of building walls and ceilings. In 1982, an inventor at United States Gypsum ("U.S.G") obtained a silicon-treated substance called "Sil-42" from a third party to use as filler when creating a joint compound. The inventor found that this compound delivered numerous advantages compared to other fillers, including the facts that using Sil-42 simplified the manufacturing process and delivered a smoother product that was lightweight, easy to sand, resisted cracking and adhered well. The U.S.G inventor did not know the chemical manufacture or method of manufacture for Sil-42, because the third party maintained this information as a trade secret.

The claims were directed to a joint compound that included a silicon treated substance. The *United States Gypsum* court found that the failure to name Sil-42 was a violation of the best mode requirement. Specifically, the court found that the record demonstrated that the inventor believed that Sil-42 was essential to improving the invention. Thus, although the claim was not limited to Sil-42, the claim expressly included a silicon treated substance. Therefore, the specific, known substance preferred by the inventor should have been disclosed along with the name of the supplier and the trade name of the substance so that others in the art could locate it.

---

[9] Spectra-Physics, Inc. v. Coherent, Inc., 827 F.2d 1524, 1533 (Fed. Cir. 1987).

[10] Bayer AG v. Schein Pharmaceuticals, Inc., 301 F.3d 1306, 1320 (Fed. Cir. 2002).

[11] *See* Bayer AG v. Schein Pharmaceuticals, Inc., 301 F.3d 1306 (Fed. Cir. 2002).

[12] Chemcast Corp. v. Arco Indust. Corp., 913 F.2d 923, 927 (Fed. Cir. 1990).

[13] DeGeorge v. Bernier, 768 F.2d 1318 (Fed. Cir. 1985) (directions for creating a word processor is not necessary where the claim was directed to an electronic circuit designed to be used with a word processor; disclosure of word processor modifications to accommodate the circuit was sufficient).

[14] United States Gypsum Co. v. National Gypsum Co., 74 F.3d 1209 (Fed. Cir. 1996).

[A]   First Prong: The Inventor's Subjective Intent

As a threshold matter, it must be determined whether at the time the patent application was filed the inventor actually knew of superior specific instrumentalities and techniques needed to practice the claimed invention.[15] *Glaxo Inc. v. Novopharm Ltd.*[16] drives home the point that the inventor's subjective preference controls the best mode inquiry. In that opinion, the Federal Circuit considered claims to the chemical compound ranitidine hydrochloride, an anti-ulcer medication. In April, 1980, a Glaxo scientist, Derek Crookes, developed a "Form 2 salt" crystalline ranitidine hydrochloride that had different and improved chemical properties from the original. In 1981, Glaxo filed a patent application on Crooke's Form 2 salt that issued as the '431 patent. Because Crook's Form 2 proved difficult to measure and dispense, other Glaxo scientists developed a novel chemical separation process (called "azeotroping") that enabled the Form 2 product to be much more easily made into a commercial product. Glaxo did not disclose the details of azeotroping in the application that led to the issuance of the '431 patent. Glaxo's decision was made despite the concerns expressed by Glaxo's in-house counsel, who had recommended that Glaxo refrain from seeking any patent protection on Form 2 salt for fear of violating the best mode requirement.[17]

Accused infringer Novopharm asserted that Glaxo's failure to disclose azeotroping violated best mode. The Federal Circuit rejected the argument based on statutory construction of § 112, which specifies that the inventor's obligation is limited to information "contemplated *by the inventor.*"[18] Accepting testimony that Crookes did not know about azeotroping when the application was filed, the Federal Circuit determined that the knowledge of other Glaxo scientists and officials should not be imputed to Crookes. Novopharm argued that the knowledge of officials at Glaxo aware of the separation process as the best mode of making Form 2 salt should be imputed to the inventor Crookes. Rejecting this argument, the *Glaxo* court found the company's nondisclosure to the PTO legally irrelevant.

As *Glaxo* suggests, documents or testimony that evidences the inventor's preference is frequently considered essential to demonstrate a best mode violation. Patent applicants have little incentive to develop and submit such evidence to the PTO to support the grant of a patent right. For that reason, a best mode violation would be extremely difficult to detect during patent prosecution. Indeed, the PTO Manual for Patent Examination Procedure instructs that examiners assume that the best mode requirement has been met when reviewing application.[19] Further, the agency notes that "[i]t is extremely rare that a best mode rejection properly would be made in ex parte prosecution."[20]

---

[15]   Chemcast Corp. v. Arco Industries Corp., 913 F.2d 923, 928 (Fed. Cir. 1990).

[16]   Glaxo Inc. v. Novopharm Ltd., 52 F.3d 1043, 1050 (Fed. Cir. 1995).

[17]   *Id.* at 1046. Glaxo had filed for British patent protection for the azeotroping process that was abandoned before the process was disclosed to the public. *Id.*

[18]   *Id.* at 1049.

[19]   MPEP § 2165.03.

[20]   *Id.*

Glaxo underscores that the first prong of the best mode inquiry is controlled by the inventor's subjective state of mind *at the time that the patent application is filed.* What happens if the inventor develops a subjective preference for a material part of the claim after the filing date? The answer is that the inventor is not required to do anything. There is no requirement that the inventor update an application that has already been filed while the patent is in prosecution, or at any time thereafter.[21]

As a side note, what happens where an application lists multiple inventors? Although there is little authority on this point, one Federal Circuit opinion suggests that the subjective preferences of all inventors must be disclosed.[22]

[B]   Second Prong: Objective Examination of the Patent Disclosure

Chemcast Corp. v. Arco Industries Corp.,[23] is a foundational case that considered the objective adequacy of the specification's disclosure. The claim was directed to a reinforcing grommet used in the automotive industry, which included a locking mechanism that was made of a very rigid material that could be formed through the use of a cast. The inventor preferred using a particular material called "R-4467" for this purpose, which he purchased from a third-party supplier who held the substance's formula as a trade secret. This supplier sold R-4467 exclusively to the patentee.

The *Chemcast* court held that the failure to include R-4467 was a best mode violation. The court acknowledged that the inventor could not have divulged the formula to R-4467, given that this information was a third-party trade secret. Nonetheless, because the characteristics of the material were needed to satisfy a claim element, the best mode requirement compelled disclosure of the specific supplier and trade name of the preferred material. The *Chemcast* opinion noted that no material comparable to R-4467 was described in the specification and those in the art would not have known of the existence of the material. Although R-4467 was not commercially available to those in the art, the court noted that an exclusive sales contract, "cannot control the extent to which [the inventor] must disclose his best mode."[24]

The court reached the opposite result in *Randomex, Inc. v. Scopus Corp.*[25] The patent in suit described a system for cleaning a stack of computer memory discs. The claimed system included a means to spray a cleaning fluid on a brush designed

---

[21] In Transco Products Inc. v. Performance Contracting, Inc., 38 F.3d 551 (Fed. Cir. 1994), the could held that, for purposes of determining the best mode, a continuation application was entitled to rely on the filing date of the original parent application for all common subject matter.

[22] Wellman, Inc. v. Eastman Chemical Co., 642 F.3d 1355, 1364 (Fed. Cir. 2011) (suggesting that the best mode subjectively possessed by "at least one inventor" must be disclosed).

[23] Chemcast Corp. v. Arco Industries Corp., 913 F.2d 923 (Fed. Cir. 1990).

[24] *Id.* at 930. The court reasoned that, if the rule were to the contrary, inventors "could readily circumvent the best mode requirement by concluding sole-user agreements with the suppliers of their preferred materials." *Id.*

[25] Randomex, Inc. v. Scopus Corp., 849 F.2d 585 (Fed. Cir. 1988).

to pass over discs during cleaning. The fluid was not a claim element, although using an appropriate fluid was necessary to practice the claim.[26] The specification stated that the cleaning solution "should be adequate to clean grease and oil from the disc surfaces, such as a 91 percent alcohol solution or a non-residue detergent solution such as Randomex Cleaner No. 50281." The inventor, an employee of the patentee Randomex, preferred using Randomex Cleaner No. 50281 in connection with the claimed invention.

Addressing the adequacy of the disclosure, the court noted that the "91 percent alcohol solution" was actually the "worst mode" because that substance was subject to explosion. Nonetheless, this did not provide an adequate ground for invalidation, given that the alcohol solution was a readily obtainable prior art alternative that could conceivably be used as a cleaning agent. Second, the court considered whether the phrase "non-residue detergent solution such as Randomex Cleaner No. 50281" was problematic given that the formula was not disclosed. Ultimately, the court found the disclosure sufficient on the grounds that the use of the phrase "non-residue detergent solution" referred to any number of easily available commercial solutions. The court reasoned that the reference to Randomex Cleaner No. 50281 was mere surplusage. As *Randomex* suggests, the inventor is not required to flag the preferred method when a series of options is disclosed.

Together, *Chemcast* and *Randomex* demonstrate that inventions that rely on off-the-shelf or pre-existing components must disclose sufficient information to allow one of ordinary skill to obtain or create the necessary components either based on the knowledge of one of ordinary skill or the patent's disclosure.[27] An inventor need not disclose how to make a commercially available product so long as the inventor discloses all available information about the material, preferably so that one of ordinary skill can obtain the item or its equivalent. As one court explained:

> For example, if one should invent a new and improved internal combustion engine, the best mode requirement would require a patentee to divulge the fuel on which it would run best. This patentee, however, would not be required to disclose the formula for refining gasoline or any other petroleum product. Every requirement is met if the patentee truthfully stated that the engine ran smoothly and powerfully on Brand X super-premium lead free "or equal."[28]

The best mode requirement relates only methods for practicing the invention and not to production details used to commercialize an end product that incorporates the invention. Generally, production details encompass two types of information: first, commercial considerations that do not relate to the nature or quality of the invention, such as the equipment on hand or prior relationships with suppliers. Second, the phrase refers to routine details already known to those of ordinary skill in the art. For this second type, an omitted detail may constitute a best mode but

---

[26] As one example, the patent's first claim reads in relevant part, "means for spraying a fluid against the brush to clean contaminants from the brush . . . " U.S. Patent. No. 3,803,660 (filed Apr. 27, 1972).

[27] *See, e.g.*, Bayer AG v. Schein Pharmaceuticals, Inc., 301 F.3d 1306, 1322-23 (Fed. Cir. 2002).

[28] *Randomex*, 849 F.2d at 590 n.1.

the disclosure is deemed adequate because it is already well known.[29] If one of ordinary skill would already know to take a particular step in order to practice the claim, then disclosure of that step is not required.[30]

Great Northern Corp. v. Henry Molded Products, Inc.,[31] explores this topic. There, the court considered whether the best mode requirement was met for an invention that used molded pulp to support large-diameter rolls for cushioning and support. The alleged infringer asserted invalidity on the grounds that the patent did not disclose diamond-shaped indentations that provided strength to the pulp. The *Great Northern* court held that the failure to disclose the diamond indents was a violation of the best mode, as these indents were more than mere production details and were "critical to practicing the claimed invention."[32] In particular, the diamond shapes were necessary to provide structural support to achieve the purpose of the invention to store heavy paper rolls.

In contrast, in *Wahl Instruments, Inc. v. Acvious, Inc.*,[33] the court considered whether an inventor had disclosed a sufficient level of detail relating to a temperature — sensitive egg timer. The inventor's application disclosed that the device was made in two parts and described various methods for joining them together. However, the specification did not disclose embedment molding, which is a low-cost method of joining the pieces together known to and used by the inventor in manufacturing the egg timers. The inventor had testified that the embedment molding process was "the best technique for the manufacture of the egg-timer."[34] Because the choice of embedment molding did not affect how the invention worked, the *Wahl* court held that the inventor had not violated the best mode. Because it was a method of manufacture of a commercial embodiment as distinguished from a mode of carrying out the invention as claimed in the patent, embedment molding was a mere production detail. The *Wahl* court noted that a patent need not cover the selection of steps and material involved in a process of manufacture, as "to do so would turn a patent specification into a detailed production schedule, which is not its function."[35]

Many patentees satisfy the best mode requirement by designating the best mode as the "preferred embodiment." Although adequate, a written example is not necessarily required.[36]

---

[29] Great Northern Corp. v. Henry Molded Products, Inc., 94 F.3d 1569, 1572 (Fed. Cir. 1996).

[30] For software, it is generally sufficient if the functions of the software are disclosed because the creation of the specific source code is typically within the skill of the art. Robotic Vision Systems, Inc. v. View Engineering, Inc., 112 F.3d 1163, 1166 (Fed. Cir. 1997); Fonar Corp. v. General Elec Co., 107 F.3d 1543, 1549-50 (Fed. Cir. 1997) (". . . . normally, writing code for such software is within the skill of the art, not requiring undue experimentation, once its functions have been disclosed. It is well established that what is within the skill of the art need not be disclosed to satisfy the best mode requirement as long as that mode is described").

[31] Great Northern Corp. v. Henry Molded Products, Inc., 94 F.3d 1569, 1571 (Fed. Cir. 1996).

[32] *Id.* at 1572.

[33] *See* Wahl Instruments, Inc. v. Acvious, Inc., 950 F.2d 1575 (Fed. Cir. 1991).

[34] *Id.* at 1581.

[35] *Id.*

[36] Mpep § 2165.01.

§ 11.04   IMPACT OF A BEST MODE VIOLATION

As a general matter, providing a best mode violation does not include establishing that the patentee acted with intent. Therefore, a best mode violation may be found regardless of whether an inventor actively concealed or acted inequitably. If the inventor possessed a best mode at the time of filing, that mode must be disclosed.

Until recently, litigated claims were subject to invalidation for the failure to include the best mode regardless of intent. One who acted with deceptive intent in omitting the best mode from an application might have been subject to a finding of inequitable conduct, which renders the subject claims unenforceable.

On September 16, 2011, the America Invents Act removed certain remedies for any violation of the best mode requirement. In that legislation, 35 U.S.C. § 282 was amended to state, "the failure to disclose the best mode shall not be a basis on which any claim of a patent may be cancelled or held invalid or otherwise unenforceable." Effective on the date of enactment, this amendment now precludes the former remedies for best mode violations.

A House Report that preceded an earlier version of the Act confirms that section 112's best mode requirement remains in force despite the lack of a strong enforcement mechanism through invalidation or claim rejection.[37] This circumstance reflects a congressional choice to require disclosure of the inventor's preferred methods of practicing the invention as a prerequisite to obtaining a patent right while removing the issue from litigation. This House Report states:

> Many have argued in recent years that the best mode requirement, which is unique to American patent law, is counterproductive. They argue that challenges to patents based on best mode are inherently subjective and not relevant by the time the patent is in litigation, because the best mode contemplated at the time of the invention may not be the best mode for practicing or using the invention years later.[38]

Consequently, it appears that an inventor might testify in patent litigation that a best mode was omitted from a patent application without concern that the court will invalidate the claim or hold the claim unenforceable. However, the amendment does not entirely remove the U.S. PTO's ability to act on such conduct. In particular, the PTO has authority to investigate misconduct, and if the violation is sufficiently egregious to refer the matter to the U.S. PTO's Office of Enrollment and Discipline or report the matter to the Attorney General to be handled as a criminal matter against the responsible parties.[39]

Under former law, a failure to disclose an inventor's best mode in a foreign application was required to establish an effective filing date based on the foreign filing under 35 U.S.C. § 119.[40] In addition, this was the case for provisional and

---

[37] H.R. Rep. No. 112-98, at 52 (2011).

[38] *Id.*

[39] *See* 18 U.S.C. § 1001 and 35 U.S.C. §§ 32, 257(e).

[40] *In re* Gosteli, 872 F.2d 1008,1010 (Fed. Cir. 1989) ("Under section 119, the claims set forth in a

continuation applications filed under §§ 119(e) (governing provisional applications) and 120 (governing continuation applications).[41] The AIA now provides that both provisional and continuation applications are entitled to the filing date of the first application (in this case, parent applications and provisional applications) even if the best mode has *not* been disclosed.[42] The AIA extends this rule to PCT applications that include a U.S. designation.

§ 11.05 CONCLUSION

The best mode requirement requires inventors to provide their best method of carrying out their invention. A patent will not be granted where the inventor has conceived of a preferred mode and concealed that information from the public. The focus of the best mode inquiry is whether information that is within the scope of the claimed invention was subjectively known by the inventor and omitted from the patent application when filed. The patent's written description is then examined to determine whether all of this relevant information has been disclosed. This assessment is made from the perspective of the person ordinarily skilled in the art.

United States application are entitled to the benefit of a foreign priority date if the corresponding foreign application supports the claims in the manner required by section 112, ¶ 1."); see also *In re* Wertheim, 541 F.2d 257 (C.C.P.A. 1976).

[41] 35 U.S.C. § 120.

[42] 35 U.S.C. §§ 119(e) & 120 (2011).

Chapter 12

OVERVIEW OF § 102: NOVELTY, STATUTORY BARS AND DERIVATION

SYNOPSIS

§ 12.01   INTRODUCTION

§ 12.02   TERMINOLOGY RELEVANT TO A § 102 ANALYSIS

§ 12.03   THE PRE-AIA VERSION OF SECTION 102

   [A]   The Structure of the Former Version of § 102

   [B]   The Historic Underpinnings of the Pre-AIA Statute

§ 12.04   NOVELTY AND THE AMERICA INVENTS ACT

§ 12.05   SECTION 102's "STRICT IDENTITY" REQUIREMENT

§ 12.06   INHERENCY

   [A]   Defining Inherency

   [B]   Accidental Inherency and Knowledge of an Inherent Property

   [C]   Inherency and "New Use" Patents

§ 12.07   THE AIA: TAX STRATEGIES

§ 12.08   CONCLUSION

§ 12.01   INTRODUCTION

The novelty provisions of the Patent Act are in a time of transition. Formerly, the system was grounded in first to invent principles embodied in 35 U.S.C. § 102. The major provisions of the original section were initially enacted in 1952.[1] That first version of § 102 represented a codification of the common law since the patent system's inception, with some variations that have been added and refined over the years. On September 16, 2011, the America Invents Act replaced the entire former version with an entirely new system based on first to file principles subject to a grace period triggered by an inventor's disclosure.

The change to a first to file system has been supported by several justifications. First, a filing date is clear and objective. The filing date appears on the front page of every U.S. patent application and every issued patent. In contrast, determining an invention date is a fact-intensive inquiry particularly where it is subject to dispute. Not only does it introduce uncertainty, but demonstrating an invention date

---

[1] 35 U.S.C. § 102 had been amended since 1952, however these amendments were consistent with a first to invent system. Throughout this Chapter, this is referred to as the "pre-AIA version of § 102."

adds the expense of obtaining witnesses and maintaining documentation in the event of a dispute. Second, the first to file system eliminates the need for interference proceedings, which can be expensive and burdensome to adjudicate. Third, a first to file system is used in all other patent systems worldwide and therefore simplifies matters for the many inventors who file for patent protection globally.

Both systems will be operational over the next two decades. Note that some significant terminology and principles of the older version have been carried forward into the new system, and therefore an understanding of these background principles is important to an understanding of the upcoming law. The next several chapters present law relevant to the pre-AIA and the AIA versions § 102. As a forewarning, some provisions of the AIA include ambiguities, and it can be expected that judicial interpretations of its provisions will greatly aid the patent community's understanding of this new statute.

According to the U.S. PTO, the AIA § 102 becomes effective on March 16, 2013.[2] Under the AIA's section 3n, this section of the statute applies to patents with an effective filing date "on or after" eighteen months after the Act was passed.[3] According to this direction, all patents with an effective filing date *prior* to March 16, 2013, are governed by the pre-AIA § 102. All patents with an effective filing date *on or after* March 16, 2013 are governed by the newly enacted § 102.

As with the other patentability requirements, the U.S. PTO examines patent applications to ensure compliance with § 102 before the patent is issued. However, the U.S. PTO may issue a patent unaware that the application fails to meet § 102's requirements in fact. In that event, compliance with § 102 can be litigated in reexamination before the PTO under certain circumstances. Alternatively, § 102 can be used to invalidate a patent in court proceedings.

§ 12.02   TERMINOLOGY RELEVANT TO A § 102 ANALYSIS

There are a few foundational terms used throughout the cases that bear on the interpretation and application of both versions of § 102.

A *reference* is an invalidating piece of prior art. For example, a previously issued patent or publicly available article that describes the same subject matter described in the claim is a reference that warrants rejection or invalidation of a claim so long as the effective date of that reference precedes the critical date of the claim. The *effective date* of the reference is the date upon which the reference became part of the art. For example, the effective date of a printed publication is the date that it becomes accessible to the public.

---

[2] U.S. PTO, America Invents Act Effective Dates (10/5/11), available at http://www.uspto.gov/aia_implementation/aia-effective-dates.pdf.

[3] There is some ambiguity. This section provides that the first to file provisions are slated to take effect "upon the expiration of the 18-month period beginning on the date of enactment of this Act . . ." That might be interpreted to mean "after March 16, 2013," rather than "on or after March 16, 2013." One who is risk averse and wishing to obtain any benefits of the first to invent system might ensure that her application is on file on March 15, 2013.

A claim's *critical date* is the last date upon which a prior art reference can destroy a claim. As one example, under pre-AIA law, the critical date for the novelty provisions is the date of invention. Under that rule, all references that precede the date of invention and describe the same subject matter demonstrate that the claim cannot issue.

There is no requirement that a patentee actually have any awareness of the reference or its effective date for the reference to invalidate the claim. Indeed, the patentee's subjective knowledge on this point is irrelevant.

§ 12.03   THE PRE-AIA VERSION OF SECTION 102

[A]   The Structure of the Former Version of § 102

Our analysis will begin with the pre-AIA version of § 102, which is begins with the statement that "a person shall be entitled to a patent unless . . ." is followed by a list of the various exclusions that, if any are applicable, prevent the issuance of the patent. The statutory structure thereby places the burden on the patent examiner to identify the basis for rejection.[4] If the examiner does so, the patentee then must demonstrate that the identified grounds should not prevent approval of the application. A patentee may do so with argument, amendment, or, if appropriate, the submission of additional information. In court, a patent is presumed valid. A party seeking to invalidate a claim must demonstrate the patentee's failure to comply with § 102 by clear and convincing evidence.[5]

The pre-AIA § 102 is a complex statute that can be broken down into three general categories — *novelty, statutory bar* and *derivation.* A single event that satisfies *any* one of these requirements is sufficient to destroy patentability. Additionally, § 102 provides criteria to determine who is entitled to a patent under the *first to invent* rules implemented by U.S. law. As will be discussed in the following several chapters, a number of these are subject to geographic restrictions. For example, the pre-AIA § 102(a) specifies that public knowledge and use must occur in the U.S.

First, the pre-AIA § 102(a),(e) and (g) set forth a number of grounds that render an application unpatentable for failure to satisfy the *novelty* requirement. This requirement ensures that patents are granted only for inventions that are new. For example, if a third party disclosed the same invention in a prior patent or a written publication before the date of invention of the subject claim, the novelty requirement prevents a later claim to the same subject matter.

Second, the pre-AIA § 102(b-d) incorporate *statutory bars*, which prevent a claim from being granted to an invention that the patentee or another has given over to the public for longer than a one-year grace period before the patent is filed. The statutory bar encourages an inventor to get a patent application on file within that time, or to forgo patent protection altogether.

---

[4] *In re* Warner, 379 F.2d 1011, 1016 (C.C.P.A. 1967).

[5] Microsoft Corp. v. i4i Ltd. Partnership, 131 S.Ct. 2238 (2011).

Third, the earlier § 102(f) prohibits a patentee from obtaining a patent on an invention that the applicant *derived* from another. As a constitutional requirement, U.S. law grants patents to *inventors* who have developed and disclosed inventions in a patent application. This requirement limits the patent right to the original and true inventor of the subject matter set forth in the application and will not be provided to one who has obtained the subject matter from another. To invalidate a claim, the pre-AIA section 102(f) requires a showing that the inventor derived an enabling description from another who actually conceived of the invention.

Fourth, the previous version of § 102(g) sets forth the order of *priority* between competing inventors. Under pre-AIA law, priority is determined based on who is first to invent, whereby the patent is granted to the inventor who is the first to conceive and diligently reduce the invention to practice. In addition, this subsection functions as a novelty provision to invalidate a patent during litigation where another has previously invented the subject matter of the claims, so long as the other has not abandoned, suppressed or concealed the invention.

Some distinctions between the three categories of novelty, statutory bar and the prohibition against derivation should be highlighted. First, the critical date for all novelty provisions is the *date of invention.* The date of invention is presumptively the filing date of the application; however, a patentee may establish an earlier date through appropriate evidence.[6] The critical date for the statutory bars is *one year prior to the effective filing date of the patent.*

Second, under § 102, the relevant activity that destroys *novelty* is *someone other than the inventor.* For example, subsection (a) states that a patent will not issue if the invention is "known or used *by others* . . . ." prior to the date of invention.[7] Thus, the inventor cannot destroy an invention's novelty, only another can. In one respect, this represents the logical application of a common sense principle — that is, an inventor cannot destroy a right to something before she has invented it. The primary focus of a novelty question is whether there is third party activity that occurred prior the date of invention. This occurs where another engages in any of the enumerated acts set forth in the novelty provisions with respect to the same invention as the subject claim. However, if the third party has obtained the invention from the true and first inventor, § 102(f)'s derivation provision can invalidate the third party's patent.

By contrast, either inventor or third party activity can trigger the statutory bars. Under this provision, a patentee who is entitled to the patent based on priority of invention is statutorily barred from doing so because the invention has passed to the public due to some activity that occurred before the one-year grace period that precedes the application's filing date. An example of a statutory bar includes a patentee's failure to file a patent application for more than one year after commencing sales of a product that incorporate the invention. Another is the

---

[6] Under 37 C.F.R. § 1.131 ("when any claim of an application or a patent under reexamination is rejected, the inventor of the subject matter of the rejected claim, the owner of the patent under reexamination . . . may submit an appropriate oath or declaration to establish invention of the subject matter of the rejected claim prior to the effective date of the reference or activity on which the rejection is based.").

[7] 35 U.S.C. § 102(a) (emphasis added).

inventor's publication of an article that discloses the invention more than one year prior to the filing date. The individual provisions of the pre-AIA § 102 are categorized as follows:

Novelty requirement: (3ʳᵈ party activity based on the date of invention) • Subsection (a) • Subsection (e) • Subsection (g)
Statutory bar: (either 3ʳᵈ party or inventor activity, based on 1 year prior to an application's filing date) • Subsection (b) • Subsection (c) • Subsection (d)
Derivation: • Subsection (f)

[B]   The Historic Underpinnings of the Pre-AIA Statute

The ability to obtain a patent has been conditioned on the creation of new solutions since the earliest days of the U.S. patent system. That system requires that one invent something that did not exist before. Unlike copyright law, where the subject matter must be original in the sense that it is the subjective expression of a creator, patent law requires that an invention represents an objectively novel advance.

As the U.S. Supreme Court held in the 1818 decision *Evans v. Eaton*,[8] a patent will not be granted to someone who has independently invented the subject matter of a patent if someone else has already developed the same thing. As the *Evans* Court explained:

> . . . if the thing was not *originally* discovered by the patentee, but had been in use, or had been described in some public work, anterior to the supposed discovery of the patentee, judgment shall be rendered for the defendant, and the patent declared void.[9]

---

[8] Evans v. Eaton, 16 U.S. 454, 514 (1818); *see also* Edward C. Walterscheid, *Novelty in Historical Perspective (Part II)*, 75 J. Pat. & Trademark Off. Soc'y 777, 790-91 (1993) (describing early interpretations of U.S. patent law).

[9] *Id.* at 549 (emphasis in original).

As the *Evans* Court describes, one cannot infringe a patent that is invalid because the claim does not describe a novel invention. In short, one's contribution must be novel to support a patent.

In contrast to the novelty requirement, the statutory bars derive from the principle that one who fails to file an application more than a year after the invention has been given to the public may forfeit the ability to obtain a patent even if the applicant is the first inventor. The Supreme Court explained this principle in the 1829 decision *Pennock v. Dialogue*,[10] where the Court considered whether one could obtain a patent for an invention that had been publicly used for a number of years by a third party before the inventor applied for a patent. Finding the patent invalid, the *Pennock* Court reasoned that an inventor's ability to obtain a patent was conditional:

> It has not been, and indeed cannot be denied, that an inventor may abandon his invention, and surrender or dedicate it to the public. This inchoate right, thus once gone, cannot afterwards be resumed at his pleasure; for, where givers are once made to the public in this way, they become absolute.[11]

Under this principle, even where an inventor is responsible for a novel invention, a statutory bar may arise to cut off the right to patent where the inventor fails to make a timely application. The pre-AIA § 102 statutory bars allow patentees to have a one year grace period to file an application after the triggering event.[12] For example, consistent with the *Pennock* Court's holding, one of these statutory bars arises to prevent the claim if either the inventor or a third party engages in a public use of the invention for longer than one year prior to an application's filing date.

The pre-AIA § 102(f) provides that a patent application is granted to the inventor and one cannot obtain a patent to an invention derived from another. As the Supreme Court stated in 1868, "No one is entitled to a patent for that which he did not invent."[13] Under the statute, a patent will not issue to one who files an application based on an enabling description obtained from a true inventor.[14]

With respect to determining invention under § 102(g), until the AIA was passed, the U.S. had awarded a patent based on a first to invent basis. One is considered to have completed the act of invention by reducing the subject matter to practice. As Justice Story observed in 1844:

> The law is, that whoever first perfects a machine, is entitled to the patent, and is the real inventor, although others may previously have had the idea, and made some experiments towards putting it in practice . . . [H]e is the

---

[10] Pennock v. Dialogue, 27 U.S. 1 (1829).

[11] *Id.* at 16.

[12] For information about the specific events which trigger the statutory bars, *see infra* Chapters 13, 14 and 15.

[13] Agawam Co. v. Jordan, 74 U.S. 583, 603 (1869).

[14] *Id.* ("where the suggestions go to make up a complete and perfect machine, embracing the substance of all that is embodied in the patent subsequently issued to the party to whom the suggestions were made, the patent is invalid, because the real invention or discovery belonged to another."); *see also* 35 U.S.C. § 102(f) (2000).

inventor, and is entitled to the patent, who first brought the machine to perfection, and made it capable of useful operation.[15]

The pre-AIA § 102 implemented the novelty, statutory bar, and derivation requirements in a manner that was consistent with these common law principles.[16] As one example, the roots of some of its provisions can be traced back to the earliest patent statute enacted in 1790, which stated the patentability requirement that the invention be "not before known or used."[17] The prior version of § 102(a) states in nearly identical terms that a patent will not be granted where the invention was "known or used by others in this country" before the date of invention. A significant number of principles have changed or modified under the newly enacted AIA.

§ 12.04   NOVELTY AND THE AMERICA INVENTS ACT

Like the pre-AIA version of § 102, the AIA § 102 begins with the statement that "a person shall be entitled to a patent unless . . ." followed by a list of exclusions that prevent the issuance of the patent. Also consistent with the prior version of this section, the burden is on the examiner to identify the basis for rejection. If the examiner does so, the patentee must demonstrate that the identified grounds should not prevent the claim from issuing.

The AIA presents a greatly simplified approach compared to the former version, although certainly the subtleties of the new provisions should be appreciated. As a starting point, priority is determined by *the first to file* a patent application, according to the patent's *effective filing date*.

What is the effective filing date of a U.S. prior art patent or published U.S. patent application? According to the AIA § 102(a)(2), it is the *earliest* of any of the following:

- The filing date of the first foreign application to which a later U.S. application establishes priority under § 119;

- The filing date of the first application to which a later continuation application has established priority under § 120;

- The filing date of the first U.S. application to which a later U.S. divisional application establishes priority under § 121;

- The filing date of the first PCT application to which a later U.S. application establishes priority under § 365(a, b);

- The filing date of the first PCT application to which a later U.S. continuation application establishes priority under § 365(c); or

- The application's actual filing date in the U.S. PTO.

The effective filing date for a reissued claim is the same filing date attributable to the patent for which the reissued claim was sought. In a contest to determine

---

[15] Washburn v. Gould, 29 F. Cas. 312, 317 (C.C. Mass. 1844).

[16] *See generally* H.R. Rep. No. 82-1923, at 6-7 (May 12, 1952).

[17] Patent Act of 1790, Ch. 7, 1 Stat. 109-112, § 1 (April 10, 1790).

whether a claimed invention has already been the subject of a prior U.S. patent or published U.S. patent application, the examined claim is compared to the disclosure of the earlier filed reference to determine whether strict identity exists, according to that which is expressly or inherently disclosed therein. If there is a match, the subject claim if later in time, will not be issued (or will be declared invalid).

A claim's novelty can be destroyed by a published patent application or a prior patent that discloses the same subject matter, names another inventor, and has an earlier effective filing date. Unlike the pre-AIA § 102, an inventor who files a patent application under the AIA cannot defeat this showing by demonstrating that she was first to invent. The effective filing date is determinative.

With respect to this subsection, one further point bears comment. For this section to apply, the patent application must "name another inventor."[18] However, according to the AIA's § 102(b)(2), patent applications filed by those within the same *inventive entity* are excluded. That is, if the patent is owned by the same person or subject to a joint obligation of an assignment, the patent will not be considered invalidating prior art. Joint ownership is broad enough to include those who are working under a joint research agreement.[19] Essentially, this new provision is an expansion of the previous Cooperate Research and Technology Enhancement Act of 2004 (the "CREATE Act").[20] In brief, the CREATE Act allowed the work of those within the same inventive entity to work on joint projects and file applications that would not render later patents filed by others within the same team to be rendered obvious. According to the CREATE Act's legislative history, "by disqualifying such background information from prior art, [it] will encourage communication among members of research teams, and patenting, and consequently public dissemination, of the results of 'team research.' "[21] The AIA applies this same principle to novelty for patent applications under the newly enacted § 102(a)(2). Indeed, the AIA has expressly adopted the CREATE Act's legislative purpose to "promote joint research activity."[22] To qualify under the AIA, the joint ownership or joint research arrangement must exist no later than the patent application's effective filing date.[23]

In addition to invalidating a claim through a prior patent, a separate section of the AIA, § 102(a)(1), establishes that prior art includes subject matter that was *"patented, described in a printed publication, or in public use, on sale, or otherwise available to the public"* before the claim's effective filing date.[24] Many of these terms have analogues in the former law, and will be more fully explored in the chapters that follow. The newly added language is the term "otherwise available to the public." This appears to open the door to *all* forms of public information, regardless of the mode in which it appears, so long as the information is available

---

[18] 35 U.S.C. § 102(a)(1) (2001).

[19] 35 U.S.C. § 102(c) (2011).

[20] This was codified at 35 U.S.C. § 103(c).

[21] "Section-By-Section Analysis of H.R. 6286, Patent Law Amendments Act of 1984," Cong. Rec. H10525 (October 1, 1984).

[22] 35 U.S.C. § 102(d)(2).

[23] *Id.* at § 102(b)(2)(C).

[24] *Id.*

to the public. This might capture some prior art that would have otherwise been eliminated through the deletion of "known or used" that appeared in the pre-AIA version of § 102(a).

There is some ambiguity to the phrase "or otherwise available to the public" in connection with the prior art categories that are listed in the same sentence of the AIA's § 102(a)(1). Specifically, statements made on the Senate floor prior to the enactment of this provision suggest that "available to the public" acts as a modifier to the other categories of prior art.[25] Under that interpretation, only publicly available sources of prior art qualify. This issue is particularly important for the terms "on sale," and "public use."[26] Under the interpretation proffered by this Senate floor discussion, a private sale of an invention (or a public use that did not meet the "publicly accessible" standard) would not qualify as prior art. However, under the prior case law that construed the pre-AIA version of § 102, prior art included inventions that were sold or publicly used even if those events are not publicly accessible. Whether the courts will accept the legislative history or the prior precedent's interpretation of those terms remains to be seen.

Notably, there is no geographic limitation on any of the AIA § 102(a)(1) categories of prior art. Therefore, information that can be linked to any of these categories from anywhere in the world qualifies. As will be discussed in later chapters, this represents a significant expansion of the available references. Furthermore, under the AIA, the critical date is the *effective filing date* of the claimed invention. The prior version of § 102, which relied on the date of either the date of invention or one year prior to the filing date, will not control under the AIA. Along with this change, determining priority and novelty according to the first to invent standard under the former § 102(g) has been eliminated.

Unlike the former law, the AIA's § 102(a)(1) does not limit prior art to any particular sources. Therefore, the activity of both inventors and third parties can result in invalidating prior art. However, AIA § 102(b)(1) creates a *one-year grace period* for two types of disclosures. First, any disclosure made one year or less before the effective filing date is not prior art if the disclosure has been made by the inventor, joint inventor, or another who obtained the subject matter disclosed directly or indirectly from the inventor or joint inventor.

Second, the AIA creates a one-year grace period for third party prior art that discloses the same subject matter that has already been publicly disclosed, "by the inventor or a joint inventor or another who obtained the subject matter disclosed

---

[25] As the bill's proponent Senator Leahy stated during that discussion:

> . . . subsection 102(a) was drafted in part to do away with precedent under current law that private offers for sale or private uses or secret processes practiced in the United States that result in a product or service that is then made public may be deemed patent-defeating prior art. That will no longer be the case. In effect, the new paragraph 102(a)(1) imposes an overarching requirement for availability to the public, that is a public disclosure, which will limit paragraph 102(a)(1) prior art to subject matter meeting the public accessibility standard that is well-settled in current law, especially case law of the Federal Circuit.

America Invents Act, 157 Cong. Rec. 1496 (March 9, 2011).

[26] Notably, under the pre-AIA § 102(d), a foreign patent that remained secret could create a statutory bar to a patent. Although the pre-AIA § 102(a) and (b) required that the patent be publicly accessible, this creates another arguable conflict for the interpretation of AIA § 102(a)(1).

directly or indirectly from the inventor or a joint inventor."[27] For this second type, an inventor's disclosure of the subject matter of the claim has a priority effect over all subsequent disclosures by others. In other words, an inventor's disclosure acts as prior art against all others and preserves the inventor's ability to file for a patent for one year thereafter. This second exception gives inventors a strong incentive to disclose inventions, and to follow through with a patent application within one year, to preserve the inventor's rights against others in the field.[28]

It is not clear whether there is symmetry between the prior art listed in § 102(a)(1) as "patented, described in a printed publication, or in public use, on sale or otherwise available to the public" and the "disclosures" listed in § 102(b). The language of each section is distinct, which suggests that the legislature used two different phrases to mean two different things. For example, the AIA's use of the term "disclosure" in § 102(b) suggests a broader set of conduct than the specific activity that is enumerated under § 102(a)(1). However, a colloquy between two of the Senate bill's sponsors, Senators Leahy and Hatch, on the Senate floor suggest a legislative intent to establish the same meaning for both.[29] As with the other ambiguities identified in the AIA, judicial interpretation of these provisions is expected to resolve the issue in the coming years.

In addition, the newly enacted AIA provides a mechanism to protect first inventors through a new procedure called a "derivation proceeding." Specifically, the AIA creates a remedy against those who file a patent application derived from an inventor without authorization. This allows ownership of a patent to inure to a true inventor.

---

[27] 35 U.S.C. § 102(b)(2)(A).

[28] This section applies to third party disclosures that "before such disclosure, had been publicly disclosed" by the inventor, joint inventor, or another who had obtained the invention from the inventor or joint inventor. 35 U.S.C. § 102(b)(1)(B). *See also* 35 U.S.C. § 102(b)(2)(B) (including similar language).

[29] This discussion states, in relevant part:

> Mr. LEAHY. . . . We intend that if an inventor's actions are such as to constitute prior art under subsection 102(a), then those actions necessarily trigger subsection 102(b)'s protections for the inventor and, what would otherwise have been section 102(a) prior art, would be excluded as prior art by the grace period provided by subsection 102(b). Indeed, as an example of this, subsection 102(b)(1)(A), as written, was deliberately couched in broader terms than subsection 102(a)(1). This means that any disclosure by the inventor whatsoever, whether or not in a form that resulted in the disclosure being available to the public, is wholly disregarded as prior art. A simple way of looking at new subsection 102(a) is that no aspect of the protections under current law for inventors who disclose their inventions before filing is in any way changed.

> Mr. HATCH. The Senator from Vermont is correct. For the purposes of grace period protection, the legislation intends parallelism between the treatment of an inventor's actions under subsection 102(a) that might create prior art and the treatment of those actions that negate any prior art effect under subsection 102(b).

America Invents Act, 157 Cong. Rec. 1496 (March 9, 2011).

§ 12.05   SECTION 102's "STRICT IDENTITY" REQUIREMENT

Both the prior version of § 102 and the AIA § 102 incorporate the principle that the subject matter of a novelty analysis is defined by the claim.[30] Under both authorities, a reference must have a *one-to-one correspondence*, or *strict identity*, between the limitations of the claim and the reference's disclosure. This standard is met where a single reference "expressly or inherently discloses each and every limitation of the claim."[31]

As a starting point, certainly one must understand what has been claimed. During prosecution, the PTO typically gives a claim its broadest reasonable construction. In litigation, the court will engage in claim construction of ambiguous or disputed claim terms. Once the scope of the claim under examination is understood, one determines whether each claim element literally exists in the proposed reference. The lack of a single claim element is sufficient to demonstrate that the proffered piece of prior art is inapplicable under § 102.[32] Determining whether this one-to-one correspondence exists follows the same standards as that used to determine literal infringement.[33] Indeed, it has long been said, "that which infringes, if later, would anticipate, if earlier."[34]

How does this standard apply under the 1952 version of § 102? Assume that a patent application is filed on May 1, 2004, directed to a toothbrush that claims a long handle, a curved head that hold the bristles and a removable toothpick that is inserted into the handle. Based on this filing date, the pre-AIA version of § 102 governs the analysis. Further assume that the date of invention for this application is May 1, 2003. Based on this assumption, the critical date for *both* novelty and the statutory bars is the same — May 1, 2003. This is because May 1, 2003 is the date of invention for purposes of assessing novelty. Also, May 1, 2003 is one (1) year prior the date that the application is filed and therefore the critical date for § 102's statutory bars.[35]

---

[30] The AIA defines "claimed invention" as "the subject matter defined by a claim in a patent or an application for a patent." 35 U.S.C. § 100(j) (2011).

[31] *See* EMI Group North America, Inc. v. Cypress Semiconductor Corp., 268 F.3d 1342, 1350 (Fed. Cir. 2001); RCA Corp. v. Applied Digital Data Systems, Inc., 730 F.2d 1440, 1444 (Fed. Cir. 1984).

[32] It should be noted that a reference which fails under § 102 might be used to render a claim nonobvious under § 103. For more about nonobviousness, *see supra* Chapter 21.

[33] Bristol-Myers Squibb Co. v. Ben Venue Laboratories, Inc., 246 F.3d 1368, 1378 (Fed. Cir. 2001) ("that which would literally infringe if later anticipates if earlier").

[34] Knapp v. Morss, 150 U.S. 221, 228 (1893) (citing Peters v. Manufacturing Co., 129 U.S. 530, 537 (1889)).

[35] There is no derivation issue presented by these facts, as nothing demonstrates that the applicant obtained any information from the earlier patent or any other source.

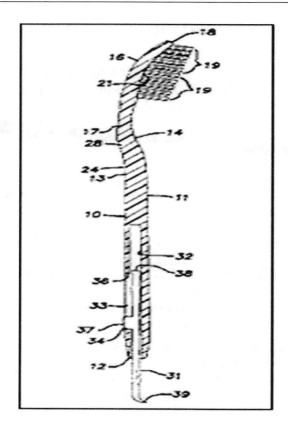

In considering whether strict identity is met, assume that a PTO examiner considers a third party's U.S. patent with an effective filing date *prior* to the application's May 1, 2003 critical date. Assume that this third party's patent discloses a toothbrush with a long handle and a curved head that holds the bristles but does *not* disclose any toothpick in the toothbrush handle. The examiner will conclude that the third party's patent does *not* anticipate the claims of the May 1, 2004 application under the pre-AIA § 102 because one-to-one correspondence is lacking — specifically, the application's claim limitation for a toothpick does not appear in the third party's patent and therefore a claim element is missing. If we assume the same set of facts to a patent filed under the newly enacted AIA, the result is the same based on the earlier filing date of the reference patent that fails to disclose every element of the claim.

However, if we change the disclosure of the third party's patent, we reach a different result. For example, assume that the third party's patent instead discloses a toothbrush with a long handle, a curved head that holds the bristles *and* a removable toothpick that can be inserted into the handle. Again, assume that the effective date of the third party's patent is prior to May 1, 2003, the application's critical date. This third party patent *would* constitute prior art because each limitation of the application's claims is present in a single reference prior to the application's critical date. Specifically, under the pre-AIA §§ 102(a), (b) and (e)(2), a patent cannot be granted if the invention has been disclosed in a previously issued

U.S. patent, as our hypothetical describes. If we assume the same set of facts to a patent filed under the newly enacted AIA, the result is the same based on the earlier filing date of the reference patent that discloses all of the elements of the claim.

Let's try a third hypothetical to demonstrate how anticipation interacts with infringement. For this, assume that *no* prior art exists. On that basis, on June 19, 2007, the examiner issues a patent based on the May 1, 2004 application. Assume that on July 1, 2007, a third party begins to make and sell to the public a toothbrush with a long handle, a curved head that holds the bristles and a removable toothpick that can be inserted into the handle. Because this activity post-dates the critical date of the patent, this toothbrush is *not* invalidating. Moreover, because this third party made and sold a toothbrush that includes all of the limitations of the invention claimed in the patent during the patent's effective term, the toothbrush literally infringes the patent.

Finally, let's apply the rule "that which infringes, if later, would anticipate, if earlier."[36] If this same toothbrush was known or used by the public *before the critical date* of May 1, 2003, then that toothbrush renders the claim invalid. This is so because a sale before the invention date renders the later invention unpatentable.[37] In addition, under the pre-AIA version of § 102(b), a patent cannot be granted where the invention has been in public use more than one year prior to the filing date of the application. Either ground is sufficient to invalidate the patent.

The anticipation standard requires that one find each claim element within a *single reference.* One cannot demonstrate that a claim is anticipated by combining disparate references. For example, one could *not* render the toothbrush patent invalid by relying on a patent for a toothbrush and then adding a separate patent for a toothpick, even if both individually existed prior to the critical date. As an exception to this rule, a single prior art document might be used if it properly incorporates other material by reference.[38]

To constitute prior art, a reference must be *enabled.* This enablement standard is met if "one of ordinary skill in the art could have combined the publication's description of the invention with his own knowledge to make the claimed invention."[39] A publication that describes each limitation of the claim does not prevent a claim from issuing unless the invention can be made by one of ordinary skill without undue experimentation.[40]

---

[36] *Id.*

[37] The result is the same under the AIA § 102(a)(1), which provides that sales of the patented device constitute prior art, if the sale occurs prior to the effective filing date of the patent.

[38] *See* Liebel-Flarsheim Co. v. Medrad, Inc., 481 F.3d 1371, 1381-82 & n. 3 (Fed. Cir. 2007) ("material not explicitly contained in the single, prior art document may still be considered for purposes of anticipation if that material is incorporated by reference into the document") (quotation and citation omitted).

[39] *In re* Donohue, 766 F.2d 531, 533 (Fed. Cir. 1985) (citations omitted).

[40] Elan Pharmaceuticals, Inc. v. Mayo Foundation for Medical Educ. and Research, 346 F.3d 1051 (Fed. Cir. 2003) ("The disclosure in an assertedly anticipating reference must be adequate to enable possession of the desired subject matter. It is insufficient to name or describe the desired subject matter, if it cannot be produced without undue experimentation").

The Federal Circuit has viewed the standard for enablement under § 102 somewhat differently than the enablement standard of § 112. That is, under § 112, a patentee must disclose sufficient information so that one of ordinary skill in the art can make *and use* the invention. By contrast, a reference can meet enablement for purposes of novelty and statutory bars by demonstrating how to make the invention disclosed in the claim, but there is no requirement that the reference disclose how *to use* the invention.[41] The distinction between was examined in *Rasmusson v. SmithKline Beecham Corp.*, where the court considered the validity of claims directed to a method of treating a type of prostate cancer by administering a chemical compound called finasteride.[42] A European patent application disclosed the use of this compound to treat prostrate cancer, but the European application failed to include any data demonstrating the effectiveness of this treatment. The Board of Patent Appeals and Interferences held that the European application did not constitute prior art, because one of ordinary skill would have no scientific basis to believe the compound was effective for the stated purpose. On appeal, the Federal Circuit reversed and remanded, explaining:

> . . . disclosure lacking a teaching of how to use a fully disclosed compound for a specific, substantial utility or of how to use for such purpose a compound produced by a fully disclosed process is, under the present state of the law, entirely adequate to anticipate a claim to either the product or the process and, at the same time, entirely inadequate to support the allowance of such a claim.[43]

Under *Rassumusson*, a reference does not need to demonstrate utility to anticipate under § 102. If the reference discloses sufficient information to enable one of ordinary skill to make the invention, an otherwise appropriate reference anticipates even though the reference does not fully disclose the invention's use.

§ 12.06   INHERENCY

[A]   Defining Inherency

The legal standard provides that "anticipation is established only when a single prior art reference discloses, expressly or *under principles of inherency*, each and every element of a claimed invention."[44] What is disclosure "under principles of inherency"?

Inherency provides that an invention, or the limitation of an invention, may be anticipated even where there is no express disclosure of that feature. Thus, "a prior art reference may anticipate without disclosing a feature of the claimed invention if that missing characteristic is necessarily present, or inherent, in the single anticipating reference."[45] The inherency doctrine is built on the principle that if

---

[41] Rasmusson v. SmithKline Beecham Corp., 413 F.3d 1318, 1325-26 (Fed. Cir. 2005).

[42] *Id.*

[43] *Id.* at 1325, *quoting In re* Hafner, 410 F.2d 1403, 1405 (C.C.P.A.1969).

[44] *See* RCA Corp. v. Applied Digital Data Systems, Inc., 730 F.2d 1440, 1444 (Fed. Cir. 1984).

[45] Schering Corp. v. Geneva Pharmaceuticals, 339 F.2d 1373, 1377 (Fed. Cir. 2003).

something already exists in the prior art then that feature is not novel, even where the presence of that feature has not been expressly stated.

Prima Tek II, L.L.C. v. Polypap, S.A.R.L., presents an example.[46] Prima Tek's patent described an apparatus and method for holding flowers without using a standard pot. One of the asserted claims described a substance to hold the flowers that was covered by a sheet of decorative material that included a "crimped portion in the sheet of material" having "at least one overlapping fold."

The *Prima Tek* court considered whether the invention was anticipated by a prior art reference (the "Charrin reference"), which was a published French patent application that described flowers inserted into wetted moss wrapped in a waterproof material. This cover was tied at the top with a cord passing through holes in the cover material. The Charrin reference described that the cord was then tightened to surround the wetted moss and the flowers. The district court had held that the Charrin reference did not invalidate the patent for the failure to describe the "crimped portion" and overlapping fold limitation of Prima Tek's patent. The Federal Circuit reversed, acknowledging that the Charrin reference did not expressly include either of those elements.

Nonetheless, *Prima Tek* noted that "a prior art reference may anticipate when the claim limitation or limitations not expressly found in that reference are nonetheless inherent in it."[47] The Federal Circuit found that the Charrin reference inherently disclosed a crimped portion and an overlapping fold, because, when the cord was tightened as described in Charrin, the waterproof cover material would necessarily and always be crimped and folds created. The *Prima Tek* opinion shows that inherency exists where the unstated feature is the *natural result* that *consistently flows* from the explicit disclosure.[48]

Anticipation by an inherent disclosure is limited to results that *necessarily* follow.[49] Thus, a result that is obtained occasionally or only under limited conditions is not an inherent disclosure. This issue was explored in *In re Robertson*, where the Federal Circuit considered the patentability of an invention directed to disposable diapers.[50] In *Robertson*, the claims described the use of two fasteners, each placed on the waist area to secure the diaper onto the wearer. In addition, the patent claimed a third fastener used only after the diaper was soiled. Specifically, the diaper was to be rolled and then securely held closed by this third fastener, to prevent leakage prior to disposal.

The Board of Patent Appeals and Interferences held that Robertson's application was anticipated by a reference (the "Wilson reference") that failed to expressly disclose the third fastening element. Instead, the Wilson reference "suggests that disposal of the used diaper may be 'easily accomplished' by rolling it

---

[46] Prima Tek II, L.L.C. v. Polypap, S.A.R.L., 412 F.3d 1284 (Fed. Cir. 2005).

[47] *Id.* at 1289.

[48] *See Schering*, 339 F.3d at 1379 ("In general, a limitation or the entire invention is inherent and in the public domain if it is the 'natural result flowing from' the explicit disclosure of the prior art.") (citation omitted).

[49] Transclean Corp. v. Bridgewood Servs., Inc., 290 F.3d 1364, 1373 (Fed. Cir. 2002).

[50] *In re* Robertson, 169 F.3d 743 (Fed. Cir. 1999).

up and employing the same fasteners used to attach the diaper to the wearer to form 'a closed compact package for disposal.' "[51]

The Federal Circuit found that the Wilson reference failed to inherently disclose the separate third fastener claimed in the application under review. *Robertson* reiterated that inherency is not present unless "the missing descriptive matter is necessarily present in the thing described in the reference."[52] The *Robertson* court found that the separate third fastening limitation was not necessarily or inevitably present by virtue of the Wilson reference's suggestion of what one *might* do. Rather, the court determined that this suggestion amounted to a mere probability or possibility that was insufficient to demonstrate inherency.

[B] Accidental Inherency and Knowledge of an Inherent Property

Can a feature that inherently exists in the prior art anticipate even where the feature is entirely unobserved and unobservable? If we assume that a pre-existing process necessarily — but undetectably — creates a particular side-effect, can that side-effect destroy novelty under § 102 as an inherent feature of the prior art?

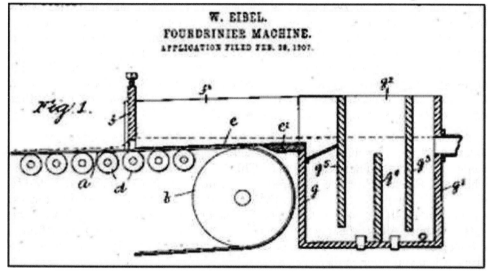

The earliest U.S. case analyzing inherency was the Supreme Court's 1880 decision *Tilghman v. Proctor*, which analyzed the validity of a patent claim for a method of forming free fatty acids and glycerine by heating fats with water at high pressure.[53] A reference authored by Perkins described the use of tallow and olive oil to lubricate the piston of a steam cylinder. The Perkins article noted that the steam generated by the cylinder caused this mixture to break down. The Court

---

[51] *Id.* at 745.

[52] *Id.*

[53] Tilghman v. Proctor, 102 U.S. 707 (1881).

considered whether the Perkins reference inherently anticipated the patent, because both used heat at high pressure to break down fats. The *Tilghman* Court rejected that Perkins invalidated the patent in suit, explaining:

> We do not regard the accidental formation of fat acid in Perkins's steam cylinder from the tallow introduced to lubricate the piston (if the scum which rose on the water issuing from the ejection pipe was fat acid) as of any consequence in this inquiry. What the process was by which it was generated or formed was never fully understood. Those engaged in the art of making candles, or in any other art in which fat acids are desirable, certainly never derived the least hint from this accidental phenomenon in regard to any practicable process for manufacturing such acids.[54]

Tilghman is read to establish the rule "that accidental, unappreciated results should not be regarded as anticipatory."[55]

Some years after *Tilghman*, the Supreme Court reaffirmed this principle in *Eibel Process Co. v. Minnesota & Ontario Paper Co.*[56] There, the Court considered the patentability of Eibel's improvement to a papermaking machine. The prior art consisted of a machine that permitted wet paper stock to fall onto a moving wire conveyer belt. The Eibel patent claimed an improvement that allowed the stock to fall onto the wire belt at the same rate of speed that the wire belt traveled, resulting in a more consistent quality finished paper product. This improvement consisted of raising the paper stock which caused the stock to fall faster and therefore match the speed of the moving conveyer.

The *Eibel* court considered a prior reference that raised the stock up above the wire belt to assist in draining the wet paper stock. This reference was argued to invalidate the Eibel patent, as the necessary effect of raising the stock achieved the same result. The Supreme Court rejected this argument on two grounds. First, the Court noted the lack of evidence that the reference had actually performed in the same way as the claimed invention. Second, the *Eibel* Court explained that "if it had done so under unusual conditions, accidental results, not intended and not appreciated, do not constitute anticipation."[57]

Tilghman and *Eibel* both refer to an unappreciated result as not invalidating. Over time, the courts began to incorporate the notion of "appreciation" into the legal standard for inherency. For example, in the Federal Circuit's 1991 decision *Continental Can Co. U.S.A, Inc. v. Monsanto Co.*, the legal standard for inherency required that the result "would be *so recognized by persons of ordinary skill*."[58]

However, the "appreciation" aspect of inherency was expressly disclaimed in a later Federal Circuit opinion before a three-judge panel, *Schering Corp. v. Geneva*

---

[54] *Id.* at 711.

[55] Mycogen Plant Science v. Monsanto Co., 243 F.3d 1316, 1336 (Fed. Cir. 2001).

[56] Eibel Process Co. v. Minnesota & Ontario Paper Co., 261 U.S. 45 (1923).

[57] *Id.* at 66.

[58] Continental Can Co. U.S.A., Inc. v. Monsanto Co., 948 F.2d 1264, 1268 (Fed. Cir. 1991) (emphasis added).

Pharmaceuticals.[59] The *Schering* case held that inherency can exist even where one of ordinary skill in the art would *not* have recognized the inherent disclosure. The *Schering* court reasoned that the critical question is whether the feature in fact exists in the prior art, not whether the feature would have been recognizable.

Under *Schering*, any inherent disclosure places the feature into the public domain. As the court has explained, "if granting patent protection on the disputed claim would allow the patentee to exclude the public from practicing the prior art, then that claim is anticipated."[60] *Schering* attempted to distinguish the Supreme Court's *Tilghman* and *Eibel*, stating that references to appreciation or recognition were mere *dicta.* Specifically, the Federal Circuit explained that *Tilghman* and *Eibel* turned on the fact that the record in both cases failed to demonstrate that the references had actually produced the claimed subject matter.[61]

Despite *Schering*, the issue of an "appreciation" requirement for inherent anticipation may not be entirely settled. In dissenting from an order denying rehearing en banc in *Schering*,[62] Justice Newman noted that the rule requiring recognition by one of ordinary skill was long-standing. Additionally, Justice Newman expressed concern over the ruling from a three-judge panel rather than by en banc review, stating "whether it is desirable new policy to bar the patentability of products that have not yet been discovered is a result I seriously doubt. The court should speak with one voice on this important question."[63] Despite Justice Newman's stated concerns, for the present the Federal Circuit panel decisions have followed *Schering.*[64] Although the Federal Circuit or U.S. Supreme Court may shift course, at present the trend in the case law does not require appreciation by one of ordinary skill for inherency to exist.

[C] Inherency and "New Use" Patents

Apparatus and composition claims protect *structure*, not function or use. Whether an apparatus or composition claim is anticipated depends on whether the *same structure* has been expressly or inherently disclosed in the prior art. A patentee cannot obtain a claim on structure disclosed in the prior art by simply changing its function or use. "It is well settled that the recitation of a new intended use for an old product does not make a claim to that old product patentable."[65]

However, an inventor of a new use can obtain a *method claim* where that new method is novel. The Federal Circuit explains:

---

[59] Schering Corp. v. Geneva Pharmaceuticals, 339 F.3d 1373 (Fed. Cir. 2003).

[60] *Id.* at 1379.

[61] *Id.* at 1378; *see also* Abbott Laboratories v. Geneva Pharmaceuticals, Inc., 182 F.3d 1315, 1319 (Fed. Cir. 1999) (distinguishing *Tilghman* and *Eibel* on the grounds that the cases produced "no useful or appreciated result").

[62] *See* Schering Corp. v. Geneva Pharmaceuticals, Inc., 348 F.3d 992 (Fed. Cir. 2003) (order denying rehearing and en banc rehearing).

[63] *Id.* at 995 (Newman, J., dissenting from denial of rehearing and rehearing en banc.).

[64] *See, e.g., In re* Omeprazole Patent Litigation, 483 F.3d 1364 (Fed. Cir. 2007) (following *Schering's* rule that recognition is not required for inherency).

[65] *In re* Schreiber, 128 F.3d 1473, 1477 (Fed. Cir. 1997).

Inventor A receives a patent having composition claims for shoe polish . . . . Suppose Inventor B discovers that the polish also repels water when rubbed onto shoes. Inventor B could not likely claim a method of using the polish to repel water on shoes because repelling water is inherent in the normal use of the polish to shine shoes. In other words, Inventor B has not invented a "new" use by rubbing polish on shoes to repel water. Upon discovering, however, that the polish composition grows hair when rubbed on bare human skin, Inventor B can likely obtain method claims directed to the new use of the composition to grow hair.[66]

The key to this analysis is that new properties of old uses are not patentable because those newly discovered properties are *inherently* existent in the old use. A straightforward application of *Schering* demonstrates that even properties that are not appreciable by one of ordinary skill are inherently anticipated by this scenario. However, a "new use" of a pre-existing structure is novel in the sense that, as a method, the inventor claims something that was not practiced before.

Perricone v. Medicis Pharmaceutical Corp. is an example of these principles in operation.[67] Perricone's patents claimed a method of treating skin damage through the topical application of Vitamin C in a fat-soluble form. The district court found Perricone's patent was anticipated by a prior patent granted to Pereira. The Pereira reference taught the use of fourteen different ingredients that delivered benefits to the skin when applied topically to a skin surface. The list of ingredients disclosed in Pereira included the ingredients that were in Perricone's claims.

The Federal Circuit affirmed that the Pereira patent anticipated several of Perricone's claims that described the application of the compound on exposed skin surfaces. However, the Federal Circuit explained that the Perricone's method claim for use of Vitamin C on sunburned skin was not anticipated, because that claim was a new use based on an existing composition and therefore novel. The *Perricone* court noted, "skin sunburn is not analogous to skin surfaces generally. Thus, there is an important distinction between topical application to skin for the purpose of avoiding sunburn, and the much narrower topical application to skin sunburn."[68] Because Pereira did not teach the use of any compound on sunburned skin, Perricone's claim to the use of the claimed compound for the new use was deemed novel.

The *Perricone* case demonstrates the principle that a patentee can claim a new use for an existing structure in the form of a method claim. However, one who does so may be required to obtain a license if the reference is a currently effective and valid patent to the structure that is used to implement the new use. This is because the patent right provides merely a right to exclude others from practicing the patent, but does not provide the patent holder the right to practice the invention to the extent that practice violates the patent rights of others.[69] If the holder of the

---

[66] Catalina Marketing International, Inc. v. Coolsavings.com, Inc., 289 F.3d 801, 809-10 (Fed. Cir. 2002).

[67] Perricone v. Medicis Pharmaceutical Corp., 432 F.3d 1368 (Fed. Cir. 2005).

[68] *Id.* at 1379.

[69] *Catalina Marketing*, 289 F.3d at 810.

"new use" patent therefore cannot practice the invention without using the structure claimed in the first patent, a license is required or infringement will be found.

§ 12.07 THE AIA: TAX STRATEGIES

The 2011 AIA includes a prior art provision directed to tax strategies.[70] Specifically, this section provides that for both novelty and nonobviousness, "any strategy for reducing, avoiding, or deferring tax liability" whether already known or completely unknown, "shall be deemed insufficient to differentiate a claimed invention from the prior art."[71] According to this code section, tax strategy claims can never meet the novelty or nonobviousness requirements regardless of the level of creativity employed at the time of invention or the effective date of filing. In essence, this prevents such patents from being granted. It defines "tax liability" broadly to encompass taxes of federal, state, local or foreign origin. The section became effective on the AIA's date of enactment, September 16, 2011.

This provision effectively eliminates the ability of patentees to obtain tax strategy patents going forward. As a House Report describes, "any future tax strategy will be considered indistinguishable from all other publicly available information that is relevant to a patent's claim of originality."[72] In doing so, Congress wished to allow tax strategists and preparers to share information in the public domain, so that interpretations of laws and regulations would be available to all. In addition, the House Report observed "Critics assert that it is not fair to permit patents on techniques used to satisfy a government mandate, such as compliance with the Internal Revenue Code."[73]

The reasons that the legislature chose to cut off patentability of tax strategies through novelty and nonobviousness, rather than directly addressing them more logically through patentable subject matter, is not clear. For example, the U.S. might have passed a statute deeming tax strategies non-technological subject matter without risking violation of the international Agreement on Trade-Related Aspects of Intellectual Property Rights (the "TRIPS Agreement"), which requires the U.S. as a member nation to grant patents "in all fields of technology."[74]

The section excludes from this limitation subject matter relating to the preparation or transmittal of tax information, as well as strategies that relate to financial management that are severable from tax strategies. Of course, for these exclusions the other patentability requirements must be met.

---

[70] America Invents Act, P.L. 112-29, § 14 (Sept. 16, 2011).

[71] *Id.* at § 14(a).

[72] H.R. Rep. No. 112-98, at 51 (2011).

[73] *Id.*

[74] TRIPS Agreement, Art. 27(1). For more information about TRIPS, see Chapter 42.

§ 12.08 CONCLUSION

Section 102 is in a state of transition. For the next several years, the patent system will be operating under two different regimes. The former § 102 is founded on first to invent principles. The subsections include novelty, statutory bar, and derivation sections. In contrast, the AIA is based on first to file principles, and further protects inventions that were subject to the inventor's disclosures up to one year prior to the effective filing date. Additionally, the AIA introduced a narrow provision designed to prevent patents directed to tax strategies from issuing.

Under both versions of § 102, an appropriate reference prevents a claim from issuing where there is strict identity between the claimed subject matter and the reference. To invalidate or prevent a claim from issuing, an anticipatory reference must disclose each limitation of the claim either expressly or inherently. In addition, the reference must be enabled to the extent that it must teach one of ordinary skill in the art how to make the invention, but is not required to disclose how the invention can be used.

Chapter 13

PUBLIC KNOWLEDGE AND USE AS PRIOR ART

SYNOPSIS

§ 13.01 INTRODUCTION

§ 13.02 TERRITORIALITY RESTRICTIONS: "KNOWN" OR "USED"

§ 13.03 PRIOR KNOWLEDGE

    [A] Prior Knowledge Must Be "Publicly Known"

    [B] Knowledge Must Be Enabling

§ 13.04 PRIOR USE

    [A] What is a "Public Use"?

    [B] Private vs. Public Uses

§ 13.05 THE EXPERIMENTAL USE EXCEPTION

§ 13.06 PROVING PRIOR KNOWLEDGE AND USE

§ 13.07 CONCLUSION

§ 13.01 INTRODUCTION

The version of the statute 35 U.S.C. § 102 that pre-dates the America Invents Act (AIA) enumerates prior *knowledge* or *use* of the invention as prior art. As one example, the pre-AIA § 102(a) states:

> A person shall be entitled to a patent unless —
>
> (a) the invention was *known or used* by others in this country . . . before the invention thereof by the applicant for patent . . .

There are several significant points about this version of § 102(a). First, the conduct must be undertaken "by another" — that is, a third party rather than the inventor. Indeed, it is not clear how an inventor could ever disclose her invention before the date of invention. Second, either "knowledge" or "use" can anticipate under this provision. Both of these terms have acquired a judicial gloss that excludes secret (or non-public) knowledge and uses. Third, the critical date for this subsection is the date of invention.

The second portion of the pre-AIA is a statutory bar of the pre-AIA § 102(b), which states that a patent will not be granted where:

> (b) the invention was . . . *in public use* . . . more than one year prior to the date of the application patent in the United States,

This subsection includes a statutory bar for a public use only, and excludes the term "known" that appears in the pre-AIA § 102(a). Moreover, under the pre-AIA § 102(b), a statutory bar can arise from a public use by *either* the inventor or a third party. The critical date for the statutory bar is one year prior to the patent application's filing date. More generally, both knowledge and use must be within the U.S. to qualify as a prior art reference.

The 2011 AIA uses a different approach that retains some of the former law. AIA § 102(a)(1), states that prior art includes subject matter that was *"in public use . . . or otherwise available to the public"* before the claim's effective filing date. Thus, the AIA expressly carries forward the "public use" of the former sections and omits the term "known." However, the AIA includes prior art that is as a separate category, "otherwise available to the public." The phrase encompasses a broad category of prior art regardless of its form, including publicly accessible knowledge.

As a general rule under the AIA, the critical date is the claim's effective filing date. Unlike the pre-AIA law, the AIA's first to file system does not allow an inventor to succeed by swearing behind the reference. Notably, there is *no* geographic limitation on any of the AIA § 102(a)(1) categories of prior art. In addition, both third party and inventor conduct can create an invalidating reference under the AIA.

AIA § 102(b)(1) creates a *one-year grace period* exception for: 1) any disclosure made one year or less before the effective filing date by the inventor, joint inventor, or another who obtained the subject matter disclosed directly or indirectly from the inventor or joint inventor; and 2) the subject matter disclosed has already been publicly disclosed, "by the inventor or a joint inventor or another who obtained the subject matter disclosed directly or indirectly from the inventor or a joint inventor." For this second type, an inventor's disclosure has a priority effect over all subsequent disclosures by others. These exceptions preserve the inventor's ability to file a patent application within one year after the disclosure even if a third party engages in conduct that would otherwise create prior art.

§ 13.02 TERRITORIALITY RESTRICTIONS: "KNOWN" OR "USED"

The pre-AIA § 102(a) and § 102(b) require that the invalidating conduct occur *within the United States.* Since the earlier part of the nineteenth century up to the present, foreign knowledge or uses did not invalidate or bar issuance of a patent. As the Supreme Court explained in the 1850 decision, *Gayler v. Wilder*:[1]

> . . . if the foreign discovery is not patented, nor described in any printed publication, it might be known and used in remote places for ages, and the people of this country be unable to profit by it. The means of obtaining knowledge would not be within their reach; and, as far as their interest is concerned, it would be the same thing as if the improvement had never been

---

[1] Gayler v. Wilder, 51 U.S. (10 How.) 477 (1850).

discovered. It is the inventor here that brings it to them, and places it in their possession.[2]

Gayler's 1850 restrictive view of the world is built on the assumption that foreign knowledge was difficult to obtain and therefore beyond the reach of those within the U.S. at that time. Additionally, evidence of unwritten practices or knowledge may have been thought to be too unreliable.[3]

This rule has been subject to criticism. One scholar, Professor Margo A. Bagley, writes, "the current geographical limitation on prior art allows the patenting of inventions in the public domain, it is unconstitutional and must be eliminated."[4] Prof. Bagley explains that in the modern world such knowledge has become knowable in the U.S. rendering § 102's geographic restrictions are beyond the constitutional grant of power that "prohibits the grant of patents on inventions in the public domain."[5] Additionally, Professor Toshiko Takenaka raised the concern that geographic restrictions may fail to comply with the Agreement on Trade Related Aspects of Intellectual Property Rights (TRIPS).[6] Further, Professor Takenaka argues that the geographic restriction may disadvantage U.S. inventors because "foreign activities do not trigger the grace period, which gives foreign applicants more time to exploit the invention prior to filing for a U.S. patent."[7]

These concerns are resolved by the newly enacted AIA, which eliminated the former territorial limitations to prior art. Therefore, information that is in public use or knowledge that is available to the public anywhere in the world can be used to demonstrate that a claim lacks novelty.

§ 13.03 PRIOR KNOWLEDGE

[A] Prior Knowledge Must Be "Publicly Known"

The pre-AIA § 102(a) provides that a third parties' public knowledge within the U.S. qualifies as prior art. As the Federal Circuit summarized in *Woodland Trust v. Flowertree Nursery, Inc.*[8]:

---

[2] *Id.* at 497.

[3] *See* Donald S. Chisum, *Foreign Activity: Its Effect on Patentability under United States Law*, 11 INT'L REV. INDUS. PROP. & COPYRIGHT L. 26, 36 (1980) ("The supposed evidentiary problems in proving prior foreign uses was undoubtedly influential" in excluding unpublished foreign uses from the statutory definition of prior art.).

[4] Margo A. Bagley, *Patently Unconstitutional: The Geographical Limitation On Prior Art In A Small World*, 87 MINN. L. REV. 679, 687 (2003) (footnote omitted).

[5] *Id.*

[6] Toshiko Takenaka, Ph.D., *The Best Patent Practice or Mere Compromise? A Review of the Current Draft of the Substantive Patent Law Treaty and A Proposal for a "First-To-Invent" Exception for Domestic Applicants*, 11 TEX. INTELL. PROP. L.J. 259, 305 (2003) ("[I]t is arguable that the geographical limitation on the prior art may violate the spirit of non-discrimination under TRIPS by conditioning the effect of prior art on the place of invention."). For more information about the patent-related aspects of TRIPS, *see* Chapter 42.

[7] *Id.* at 305-06.

[8] Woodland Trust v. Flowertree Nursery, Inc., 148 F.3d 1368 (Fed. Cir. 1998).

If the invention was known to or used by others in this country before the date of the patentee's invention, the later inventor has not contributed to the store of knowledge, and has no entitlement to a patent. Accordingly, in order to invalidate a patent based on prior knowledge or use, that knowledge or use must have been *available to the public.*[9]

The public knowledge requirement underscores that the *quid pro quo* of the patent system is the grant of the right to exclude to the first to invent, as well as to reward the inventor for the invention's disclosure. As the *Woodland* court observed, if the inventor's contribution is already in the public domain, there is no reason to grant a patent.

The AIA does not isolate knowledge as a separate category of prior art, although knowledge might be construed to be part of the broad catchall phrase, "or otherwise available to the public."[10] The pre-AIA prior art knowledge is "knowledge . . . which is accessible to the public."[11] If this similarity is carried forward, the AIA's version will receive more expansive treatment because the new law lacks the territorial restrictions. The interpretation of the AIA's "accessible to the public" is not entirely clear. On one hand, it might be interpreted in a manner consistent with the "publicly known" standard under Woodland Trust. On the other hand, the AIA's "accessible to the public" might be interpreted in a manner similar to the "publicly available" that is used for the pre-AIA "printed publication" provision. As described in more detail in the next Chapter, the phrase "publicly available" requires more exposure than a mere non-secret level of availability. Rather, the information under the "public availability" standard must be ascertainable to those interested in the art. It has been described as information that "has been disseminated or otherwise made available to the extent that persons interested and ordinarily skilled in the subject matter or art, exercising reasonable diligence, can locate it."[12] An authoritative answer to this interpretive ambiguity is not currently available.

[B] Knowledge Must Be Enabling

Knowledge must be enabling to constitute prior art. Generalized or superficial awareness of a solution is not sufficient, nor is a partial enablement. Rather, the known information must evidence sufficient detail to enable one of ordinary skill to make the invention as set forth in the claim.

This issue was examined in *Minnesota Mining and Manufacturing Co. v. Chemque, Inc.*[13] That court considered the validity of a patent directed to the use of certain compositions used to encapsulate connections for electronic or optical cables used to protect the connections from contamination. The defendant argued that the patent was invalid based on a two-part composition that apparently could be used to encapsulate connectors in the same manner described in the patent.

---

[9] *Id.* at 1370 (emphasis added).

[10] 35 U.S.C. § 102(a)(1) (2011).

[11] Carella v. Starlight Archery and Pro Line Co., 804 F.2d 135, 139 (Fed. Cir. 1986).

[12] In re Wyer, 655 F.2d 221, 226 (C.C.P.A. 1981) (quote and citation omitted).

[13] Minn. Mining & Mfg. Co. v. Chemque, Inc., 303 F.3d 1294 (Fed. Cir. 2002).

Samples of this composition had been sent out to various recipients prior to the patent's critical date.

The *Minnesota Mining* court ruled that this evidence lacked a sufficient foundation to anticipate for the failure to demonstrate enablement. Specifically, the court concluded that the record lacked any evidence that one of ordinary skill in the art would have known how to recreate the invention from the two-part composition sample. The court noted that the samples, by themselves, were not an enabling disclosure, absent some evidence such as instructions.

Although public knowledge does require enablement of the invention, the proponent does not need to show actual or constructive reduction to practice to satisfy the publicly known requirement.[14] Assume, for example, that the defendant in the *Minnesota Mining* case had submitted an enabling disclosure, such as an instruction sheet that accompanied the samples. Assuming this is enabled, the defendant would *not* need to show that any recipient had — in fact — followed those instructions to actually use the samples to encapsulate an electrical connection to demonstrate prior knowledge. So long as one of ordinary skill can make the invention from the information disclosed, the prior knowledge will meet § 102's requirements.

§ 13.04   PRIOR USE

[A]   What is a "Public Use"?

A landmark U.S. Supreme Court 1881 decision, *Egbert v. Lippmann*,[15] is cited for the proper application of the public use standard today.[16] Generally, the *Egbert* decision stands for the proposition that a public use is the "use of that invention by a person other than the inventor who is under no limitation, restriction or obligation of secrecy to the inventor."[17] In essence, this amounts to uses that are not secret. In addition, the courts have found that certain types of commercial uses constitute a public use, even if such uses have not been actually subject to public exposure.

In *Egbert*, the court considered an invalidity defense for a patent directed to an improvement for a corset spring to be used in women's undergarments. The case was analyzed under the predecessor statute to § 102(b), which at the time had a grace period of two years.[18] Because the application date was March 1866, the critical date for the statutory bar was in March 1864 according to the statute in

---

[14] *In re* Borst, 345 F.2d 851, 854-55 (C.C.P.A. 1965) (reduction to practice is not required, so long as the reference is enabled).

[15] Egbert v. Lippmann, 104 U.S. 333 (1881).

[16] *See, e.g.*, Motionless Keyboard Co. v. Microsoft Corp., 486 F.3d 1376, 1384-85 (Fed. Cir. 2007);

[17] *See, e.g.*, Eli Lilly and Co. v. Zenith Goldline Pharmaceuticals, Inc., 471 F.3d 1369, 1380 (Fed. Cir. 2006); Invitrogen Corp. v. Biocrest Mfg., L.P., 424 F.3d 1374, 1381 (Fed. Cir. 2005); *In re* Smith, 714 F.2d 1127, 1134 (Fed. Cir. 1983).

[18] The current statutory bar period is one (1) year. 35 U.S.C. § 102(b) (2002).

effect at the time.[19] The record demonstrated that the inventor had provided one set of prototypes to his fiancée Frances and then another some years later. Frances wore these prototypes sewn into the seams of her corset from 1855 forward. During these years, the inventor and Frances married. In 1863, the inventor showed the corset springs to another person, Sturgis, before the patent's critical date. To do so, Frances had to cut the springs out of the corset with scissors.

The issue presented for the *Egbert* Court was whether the use of the corset springs was a "public use" prior to the critical date that invalidated the patent. *Egbert* noted that one well-defined use of a single item that embodies the patented invention is sufficient to create a public use. Further, the *Egbert* decision established that an inventor who gives or sells a patented device to another person "without limitation or restriction, or injunction of secrecy, and it is so used, such use is public, even though the use and knowledge of the use may be confined to one person."[20] The *Egbert* Court emphasized that this rule applied to all inventions, even those which "by their very character [are] only capable of being used where they cannot be seen or observed by the public eye."[21] The *Egbert* case is frequently cited for the proposition that a use need not be visible to the public to constitute a public use.

With these rules in place, the *Egbert* Court found that the inventor had engaged in a public use by providing the corset springs to Frances in 1855, well before the critical date of the patent. Despite the nature of their close relationship, the court found that the inventor had provided the invention to Frances without any restriction or expectation of secrecy. On this basis, *Egbert* found that the inventor had let 11 years pass after this disclosure and thereby abandoned his right to a patent.

A public use as a statutory bar under § 102(b) applies in the same manner to a third party's public use. For example, in *Baxter Intern., Inc. v. COBE Laboratories, Inc.*,[22] the court held that a third party scientist's use of a centrifuge in a laboratory at the National Institute of Health ("NIH") prior to the critical date constituted a statutory bar to another's claims. Those working at the NIH did not have any obligation of confidentiality, and, indeed, the NIH had an anti-secrecy policy. The *Baxter* court held that the third party's use of the centrifuge in the NIH laboratory was non-secret and therefore a public use under § 102(b).[23]

Both *Egbert* and *Baxter* analyzed public use under § 102(b). *Rosaire v. Baroid Sales Division, Nat. Lead Co.*,[24] uses a similar analysis for public use invalidation under § 102(a). The invention at issue was a patent directed to a method for identifying the most likely locations for drilling for oil. The patentee asserted that

---

[19] *Egbert*, 104 U.S. at 334.

[20] *Id.*

[21] *Id.*

[22] Baxter Int'l Inc. v. COBE Laboratories, Inc., 88 F.3d 1054, 1058 (Fed. Cir. 1996).

[23] *Id.* at 1062 (noting that third party public use allows "unknown, private laboratory work to create a new bar to patentability.") (Newman, J. dissenting).

[24] Rosaire v. Baroid Sales Division, Nat. Lead Co., 218 F.2d 72 (5th Cir. 1955).

the date of invention for the two asserted patents took place in 1936. In response to infringement allegations, the defendant pointed to work that had been performed in 1935 and early 1936 by an unaffiliated third party, Teplitz, who performed the method in the U.S. The district court found that Teplitz's work was a reduction to practice of the patented method, and that it had been performed "without any deliberate attempt at concealment or effort to exclude the public and without any instructions of secrecy to the employees performing the work."[25]

Rosaire held that the Teplitz work was an invalidating third party use, even though the Teplitz work was never published or actually known to the public:

> While there is authority for the proposition that one of the basic principles underlying the patent laws is the enrichment of the art, and that a patent is given to encourage disclosure of inventions, no case we have found requires a holding that, under the circumstances that attended the work of Teplitz, the fact of public knowledge must be shown before it can be urged to invalidate a subsequent patent.[26]

The public does not need to actually view all of the details of a device's operation to demonstrate public use. For example, *Lockwood v. American Airlines* considered prior art relevant to a system claim for a series of airline reservation terminals, made of both software and hardware.[27] The defendant asserted invalidity based on the use of a system that had connected over one thousand reservation desks prior to the critical date and had been used by hotels, airlines, and car rental agencies. Although users were aware that the system possessed the capabilities of all elements in the claim, the public could not view the software structures that allowed those capabilities to operate. The *Lockwood* court held that the prior art system possessed all of the structures set forth in the claim, and therefore the "public use of the high-level aspects of the [prior art] system was enough to place the *claimed features*" of the patent in the public's possession.[28] The *Lockwood* case demonstrates that an enablement-type inquiry is not necessary for devices that operate in public, unlike documentary references such as patents and printed publications.[29]

A non-secret use of a claimed process in the usual course of producing articles for commercial purposes is a public use.[30] This rule applies even where no member of the public has actually viewed the invention's operation. For example, in *New Railhead Manufacturing v. Vermeer Manufacturing Co.*, the court held that the use of a drill bit underground on public land near an interstate highway was a public use.[31] The *New Railhead* court accepted that the record did not establish that any member of the public had actually seen the drill bit in operation as it was used underground. However, the court noted that the key determinant was the commercial nature of the use. On that basis, the *New Railhead* court found that this drilling

---

[25] *Id.* at 74.

[26] *Id.* at 75.

[27] Lockwood v. American Airlines, Inc., 107 F.3d 1565 (Fed. Cir. 1997).

[28] *Id.* at 1570 (emphasis in original).

[29] *In re* Epstein, 32 F.3d 1559, 1567-68 (Fed. Cir. 1994).

[30] W.L. Gore & Associates, Inc. v. Garlock, Inc., 721 F.2d 1540, 1558 (Fed. Cir. 1983).

[31] New Railhead Manufacturing v. Vermeer Manufacturing Co., 298 F.3d 1290 (Fed. Cir. 2002).

activity could serve as a reference to a method claim for the use of the bit.

Further, it has long been held that an *inventor* is statutorily barred under § 102(b) from obtaining a patent on a secret process if the inventor has sold a product made from that process before the critical date.[32] That the public cannot ascertain the details of the process by examining the product that has been sold to the public does not prevent the application of this principle. The key to this principle is that the inventor obtained a benefit from public exposure of the invention and is thereafter statutorily barred from obtaining the right after the grace period expires. However, where a *third party* sells a product made with a secret process, that third party's practice is not considered a public use that would bar a subsequent inventor's process claim.[33] In *W.L. Gore*, the court explained that inventor's commercialization is treated differently than a third party's in this context, because, "as between a prior inventor who benefits from a process by selling its product but suppresses, conceals, or otherwise keeps the process from the public, and a later inventor who promptly files a patent application from which the public will gain a disclosure of the process, the law favors the latter."[34] Note, however, that a third party's sale of goods made with a secret process would bar the inventor's ability to obtain a product or apparatus claim to the same invention. Whether this line of cases will have continued impact is unclear. Although it might be said that Congress did not evidence an intent to disturb this existing precedent when enacting the AIA, a plain meaning interpretation of the phrase "public use" in the AIA might be said to require actual public use of the claimed invention.

[B]   Private vs. Public Uses

A public use is "any use of that invention by a person other than the inventor who is under no limitation, restriction or obligation of secrecy to the inventor."[35] As the *Egbert* case illustrates, the courts have held that a single disclosure to one other person can constitute a public use.

In close cases, a court examines the totality of the circumstances to determine whether a particular use is public. These factors include an examination of the nature of the activity that occurred in public, the public access to and knowledge of the public use, and whether there was any confidentiality obligation imposed on persons who observed the use.[36]

In *Moleculon Research Corp. v. CBS, Inc.*,[37] the court assessed whether an inventor was statutorily barred from obtaining a patent for a puzzle designed with rotating cubes. The inventor showed a prototype of the puzzle to a few close colleagues, explained its use, and permitted one other person to use the game. The court found that, despite the lack of any express confidentiality agreement, all uses

---

[32] Metallizing Engineering Co. v. Kenyon Bearing & Auto Parts Co.,153 F.2d 516, 518 (2d Cir. 1946).

[33] *W.L. Gore*, 721 F.2d at 1550.

[34] *Id.*

[35] *In re* Smith, 714 F.2d 1127, 1134 (Fed. Cir. 1983).

[36] Bernhardt, L.L.C. v. Collezione Europa USA, Inc., 386 F.3d 1371, 1379 (Fed. Cir. 2004).

[37] Moleculon Research Corp. v. CBS, Inc., 793 F.2d 1261 (Fed. Cir. 1986).

were made with a legitimate expectation of privacy and confidentiality and were not therefore considered "public use." As part of this finding, *Moleculon Research* noted that the inventor did not act with any commercial motivation during the time that these uses occurred.

In *Beachcombers v. WildeWood Creative Products, Inc.*,[38] the court came to the opposite result on different facts. In *Beachcombers*, the inventor developed a kaleidoscope that used fluid to refract light patterns. This inventor held a party attended by 20 to 30 guests to generate discussion and obtain feedback for her device. She did not ask the guests to maintain confidentiality, and a number of guests picked up and used the kaleidoscope. The court found that this was a public use, as the inventor "did not retain control over the use of the device and the future dissemination of information about it."[39] The *Beachcombers* court distinguished *Moleculon Research*, where the inventor had maintained control over both the device and the disclosures had been made under an implied obligation of confidentiality.[40]

Similar to the *Beachcombers* case is *Netscape Communications Corp. v. Konrad*.[41] In *Netscape*, the invention was a system to allow a computer to search another computer from a remote location. The inventor set up workstations, but failed to monitor their use or to obtain confidentiality agreements. Significantly, the court held that the inventor could not establish these facts with reference to the confidentiality obligations of the Department of Energy, which had funded the work, stating, "[t]he onus is on him, as the inventor, to protect the confidentiality of his invention and its use by others before the critical date."[42] The *Netscape* court held that the inventor had relinquished the right to patent by failing to monitor or control others' use of the computers. Indeed, the inventor "would simply turn on the system and let people try it out."[43]

Whether a use is considered "public" depends on the degree to which the inventor relinquished control over the device, such that unfairness would result in granting a patent for subject matter that had been given over to the public prior to the critical date. On one hand, if the use is secret, then there is no public use. On the other hand, if the inventor or a third party relinquishes control of the practice of the invention in a manner that is non-secret prior to the critical date, a public use has occurred. The lack of an express confidentiality agreement is not dispositive, particularly if confidentiality can be implied from the circumstances or custom.

---

[38] Beachcombers v. WildeWood Creative Products, Inc., 31 F.3d 1154 (Fed. Cir. 1994).

[39] *Id.* at 1160.

[40] *Id.; see also Bernhardt*, 386 F.3d at 1380 (no public use where display was made at a showing where there was an industry-wide understanding that attendees were to hold in confidence the designs they viewed, and would result in a loss of reputation and trust in the industry for breach of that understanding).

[41] Netscape Commc'n Corp. v. Konrad, 295 F.3d 1315 (Fed. Cir. 2002).

[42] *Id.* at 1323.

[43] *Id.*

§ 13.05   THE EXPERIMENTAL USE EXCEPTION

An inventor may test the operation and qualities of an invention, to either perfect its operation or to determine whether the invention will serve its intended purpose. An inventor's use for these purposes is considered *experimental use,* and is not a "public use" under § 102 because such activity constitutes part of the process of reduction to practice. However, once the invention has been reduced to practice, the period of experimental use ends.

One of the most famous cases on experimental use is the U.S. Supreme Court's 1877 decision *City of Elizabeth v. American Nicholson Pavement Co.*[44] The inventor had developed wooden pavement that was intended to be very durable, "as to provide against the slipping of the horses' feet, against noise, against unequal wear, and against rot and consequent sinking away from below."[45] When accused of infringement, the defendant asserted the public use defense based on the inventor's installation of the pavement on a busy public street in Boston for several years before the patent's critical date. Despite the fact that the pavement had been — in the literal sense — used by the public for years, the *Elizabeth* court found no public use under patent law. The record demonstrated that the inventor had installed the pavement to test the invention's claimed properties, as heavily loaded vehicles going to a nearby mill frequently traveled the location. The inventor had inspected the pavement "almost daily" during this time period.

Finding that this use did not invalidate the patent, the Court explained:

> . . . if used under the surveillance of the inventor, and for the purpose of enabling him to test the machine, and ascertain whether it will answer the purpose intended, and make such alterations and improvements as experience demonstrates to be necessary, it will still be a mere experimental use, and not a public use, within the meaning of the statute.[46]

Under this ruling, the extent of the inventor's control over the use and testing of the device during the experimental use period is frequently a critical fact. In *Elizabeth,* the inventor had not given or sold his invention to Boston for installation throughout the city. Rather, the inventor had chosen a single location, where he installed the pavement at his own expense and which he tested almost daily.[47]

This dispositive element of control was found lacking in *Lough v. Brunswick Corp.*[48] There, the inventor developed an improved seal to prevent corrosion for inboard/outboard motors for use on boats. He made six prototype seals incorporating his invention. He installed one on his own boat, and three months later, gave a second prototype to a friend who used the device. The inventor then installed the

---

[44]   City of Elizabeth v. American Nicholson Pavement Co., 97 U.S. 126 (1877).

[45]   *Id.* at 127.

[46]   *Id.* at 135.

[47]   *Id.* at 133-34 (As the *Elizabeth* court observed, *public knowledge* of the invention could not destroy the novelty of the invention, because an inventor's own disclosures do not invalidate). 35 U.S.C. § 102(a) (2002) (a patent will not be granted where "the invention was known or used *by others* in this country" before the date of invention).

[48]   Lough v. Brunswick Corp., 86 F.3d 1113 (Fed. Cir. 1996).

other prototypes on the boats of his employer, a customer, and some longtime friends, all before the critical date. The inventor did not charge for the prototypes, nor did he ask for or receive any feedback.

Despite the lack of any commercial gain, the *Lough* court found that the inventor could not demonstrate experimental use. The court found that the inventor's failure to attempt follow through to obtain feedback on the operability of the devices, and the fact that one device was installed in a boat later sold to a stranger, indicated that the inventor "did not maintain any supervision and control over the seals during the alleged testing."[49] Further, *Lough* found that the inventor's subjective intent of experimental use had minimal value, particularly as that intent had only first been expressed after the litigation began.

To determine whether a use is experimental, the courts examine the factual circumstances to determine whether the use is "a *bona fide* effort to perfect the invention or to ascertain whether it will answer its intended purpose."[50] As *Lough* demonstrates, the failure to obtain a commercial benefit does not mean that a use is necessarily experimental. However, the inventor's commercial exploitation of the patented device is typically fatal. An exception has been recognized for a sale that is incidental to the experimentation.[51] The court explained that the primary purpose was testing the devices, the number of patients was small and the charge for the improved devices was not more than the typical charge for the prior art dental devices. Further, *TP Laboratories* observed that the inventor had retained control over the experimentation by virtue of the doctor-patient relationship with the subjects. By contrast, experimental use cannot be established where the primary intent of the experiment is to test the commercial market.[52]

The AIA does not explicitly discuss experimental use. However, the doctrine has longstanding precedential and policy support. It has been applied in U.S. law applying the 1952 Act, despite any textual support in the code for its existence. It can be expected that experimental use will be carried forward as an exception in the cases applying the AIA.

§ 13.06 PROVING PRIOR KNOWLEDGE AND USE

The courts have imposed requirements on the nature of proof that must accompany a showing of prior knowledge or use. As a general rule, corroboration of the oral testimony of an inventor, or the inventor's agents, affiliates, friends or other interested persons, is required. This rule arose from the U.S. Supreme Court's decision in the *Barbed Wire Patent Case*.[53] As the case name suggests, the asserted

---

[49] *Id.* at 1121.

[50] LaBounty Mfg., Inc. v. U.S. Int't Trade Comm'n, 958 F.2d 1066, 1071 (Fed. Cir. 1992).

[51] TP Labs., Inc. v. Prof'l Positioners, Inc., 724 F.2d 965 (Fed. Cir. 1984).

[52] *In re* Smith, 714 F.2d 1127 (Fed. Cir. 1983) (testing of carpet and room deodorizer was held to constitute a public use where the dominant purpose was to determine whether potential consumers would purchase the product and determine how much they would pay for it).

[53] Washburn & Moen Mfg. Co. v. Beat 'Em All Barbed-Wire Co. ("Barbed Wire Patent Case"), 143 U.S. 275 (1892).

patent in that case, which was issued in 1874, claimed an improvement to a barbed wire fence.

At the trial of the case, approximately twenty-four witnesses testified for the accused infringers that the same invention had been made by another and had been installed in a county fair in Iowa in 1858. For example, one witness testified that he had assisted in the fence's installation; another stated that he had hitched his horse to the fence, and noticed the horse's nose had become injured by the barbs. Another witness testified that a child, who had been injured by the fence, still retained scars on his face from being pushed onto the barbed wire while it was installed at the fair. One witness testified that he had obtained a piece of the wire from the previous inventor, had kept it over the years and submitted the wire in evidence to the trial court.

Nonetheless, the Supreme Court held the 1874 patent valid, explaining that this evidence, some of which was contradicted, was not sufficient to establish invalidity. The *Barbed Wire* Court laid down the following policy rationale that resonates through the invalidity cases today:

> Witnesses whose memories are prodded by the eagerness of interested parties to elicit testimony favorable to themselves are not usually to be depended upon for accurate information. The very fact, which courts as well as the public have not failed to recognize, that almost every important patent, from the cotton gin of Whitney to the one under consideration, has been attacked by the testimony of witnesses who imagined they had made similar discoveries long before the patentee had claimed to have invented his device, has tended to throw a certain amount of discredit upon all that class of evidence, and to demand that it be subjected to the closest scrutiny.[54]

This evidentiary issue was also dispositive of the invalidity defense asserted in *Woodland Trust v. Flowertree Nursery, Inc.*,[55] discussed earlier in the chapter, wherein the court considered an invention for preventing plants from freezing. There, the asserted prior art had been dismantled or destroyed twenty years before trial and no documentary evidence of the prior systems existed. *Woodland Trust* held that concerns over "the frailty of memory of things long past and the temptation to remember facts favorable to the cause of one's relative or friend," that the testimony was insufficient to meet that required clear and convincing evidentiary standard.[56] The *Woodland Trust* court listed a number of factors used to asses whether evidence is sufficient to establish invalidity:

(1) the relationship between the corroborating witness and the alleged prior user,

(2) the time period between the event and trial,

(3) the interest of the corroborating witness in the subject matter in suit,

---

[54] *Id.* at 284-85.

[55] Woodland Trust v. Flowertree Nursery, Inc., 148 F.3d 1368 (Fed. Cir. 1998).

[56] *Id.*

(4)   contradiction or impeachment of the witness' testimony,

(5)   the extent and details of the corroborating testimony,

(6)   the witness' familiarity with the subject matter of the patented invention and the prior use,

(7)   probability that a prior use could occur considering the state of the art at the time,

(8)   impact of the invention on the industry, and the commercial value of its practice.

These factors are incorporated into the *rule of reason*, a balancing test used to assess whether sufficient evidence exists to demonstrate invalidity. In addition, the Federal Circuit has held that "corroboration is required of *any* witness whose testimony alone is asserted to invalidate a patent, regardless of his or her level of interest."[57] Moreover, in all cases, courts have been cognizant of the presence (or absence) of the notes, invoices, notebooks, drawings or models that are typically generated by the inventive process when assessing whether the rule of reason standard has been met.[58]

As one example, in *Juicy Whip v. Orange Bang*,[59] the court considered whether particular testimony could demonstrate prior public knowledge of the patented invention. The asserted patent was a beverage dispenser with a clear top bowl. The bowl holds a colored liquid that the customer assumes is the drink for sale. In fact, a bottom portion of the device stores a flavored syrup that is mixed together with water to create the actual beverage that is consumed by the customer.

At trial, six witnesses testified about two prior art devices asserted to anticipate the claimed invention. In applying the rule of reason, the *Juicy Whip* court found these witnesses' testimony insufficient to invalidate the patent. Specifically, the court noted that the testimony came eight and twelve years, respectively, after the witnesses saw the allegedly invalidating dispensers. One had possessed the older machine for only one month, and another witness had kept another for less than three months. All witnesses were found to be interested in the outcome. Two were defendants in the case. Another was an operations manager for the defendant Orange Bang. The other witnesses were found to have either business or family relationships such that they were "sufficiently inter-connected to consider them 'interested witnesses.' "[60]

Further, the sole documentary evidence was drawings of the prior devices made by two of these interested witnesses during depositions. *Juicy Whip* found these documents insufficient, as neither had been created contemporaneously with the alleged prior invention. On these bases, the court held that "with the guidance of precedent cautioning against the reliance on oral testimony alone, we hold that the evidence of record did not provide the clear and convincing evidence necessary to

---

[57] Finnigan Corp. v. Int'l Trade Comm'n, 180 F.3d 1354, 1369 (Fed. Cir. 1999).

[58] *See id.*; *see also* Woodland Trust, 148 F.3d 1368 (Fed. Cir. 1998).

[59] *See* Juicy Whip, Inc. v. Orange Bang, Inc., 292 F.3d 728 (Fed. Cir. 2002).

[60] *Id.*

invalidate the patent for prior public knowledge."[61]

Thus, in addition to the standards for anticipation under § 102, *Barbed Wire* and the rule of reason impose strict evidentiary requirements to meet the clear and convincing burden of proof. To satisfy this standard, corroboration by documents created contemporaneously with the reference is typically important to the court's determination of whether witness testimony is sufficient.

§ 13.07 CONCLUSION

The pre-AIA § 102(a) provides that public knowledge of a patented invention in the U.S. prior to date of invention constitutes prior art. Public knowledge must be enabled under the standards for anticipatory enablement. Both the pre-AIA §§ 102(a) and (b) establish that public use can prevent the issuance of, or invalidate, a patent. As construed by the courts, public use amounts to a non-secret use, and can exist where the invention has been provided to one other person without restriction. Typically, the courts examine whether the inventor relinquished control of the invention to determine whether an invalidating use has occurred. However, an inventor who is engaged in experimental use does not lose the ability to patent.

If the prior knowledge or use is litigated at trial, the proponent of the defense must demonstrate anticipation by clear and convincing evidence. The courts have imposed a "rule of reason" to ensure that the later testimony of witnesses is sufficiently reliable to warrant invalidation of the patent. Under this rule, corroborating evidence of the invalidating event is typically required.

These concepts will be carried forward in the application of the AIA, which explicitly names public use as prior art. In addition, the AIA provides that an invention that has been made "otherwise available to the public" prior to the effective filing date can prevent a claim from issuing, which carries forward this same concept.

---

[61] *Id.*

Chapter 14

PATENTS AND PRINTED PUBLICATIONS

SYNOPSIS

§ 14.01 INTRODUCTION
§ 14.02 PRINTED PUBLICATIONS
    [A] Background: What is a "Printed Publication" under § 102?
    [B] "Printed Publications" and Public Accessibility
        [1] Development of the "Public Accessibility" Standard
        [2] The Current Standard: *In re Klopfenstein*
§ 14.03 PRIOR PATENTS
§ 14.04 CONCLUSION

§ 14.01 INTRODUCTION

The versions of 35 U.S.C. § 102(a) and (b) that pre-date the America Invents Act (AIA) have parallel provisions that state that a patent will be granted unless the invention is *"patented* or described in a *printed publication* in this or a foreign country." The pre-AIA § 102(a) is a novelty provision, and the pre-AIA § 102(b) is a statutory bar. The critical date for prior art under § 102(a) is the date of invention, and the critical date under the pre-AIA § 102(b) is one year prior to the filing date of the application. Inventor activity does not anticipate under § 102(a), but an inventor may generate prior art that bars her own U.S. patent under § 102(b).

As these subsections state, there are no territoriality restrictions for patents or printed publications. This rule is distinct from public use, on sale, and prior knowledge, which are all limited to events that occur in the U.S. under the pre-AIA law. Further, the global reach of patents to foreign jurisdictions under the pre-AIA §§ 102(a) and (b) stands in contrast to patents under the pre-AIA § 102(e), which is expressly limited to U.S. patents, published U.S. applications and PCT applications that designate the U.S. and are officially published in English.[1]

The 2011 AIA includes a similar provision in § 102(a)(1), which states that a patent will not be granted where the invention was "patented," or "described in a printed publication" before the effective filing date of the claimed invention. Like the pre-AIA version, the AIA includes no geographic restriction. Following standard rules of statutory construction, it can be expected that the courts construing the AIA will adopt certain aspects of the definitions of the terms

---

[1] For more about 35 U.S.C. § 102(e) and U.S. patents and applications as prior art, see Chapter 18.

"patented and described in a printed publication" that have been developed based on the prior version of the Act.

In addition, cases construing the phrase "printed publication" have developed a working definition of a related term — *publicly available* — that is important to the patent system's understanding of novelty for the new legislation. Specifically, the AIA uses a similar phrase *otherwise available to the public* in the newly enacted § 102(a)(1):

> A person shall be entitled to a patent unless —
>
> . . . the claimed invention was patented, described in a printed publication, or in public use, on sale, or *otherwise available to the public* before the effective filing date of the claimed invention.

In this subsection, the term "otherwise available to the public" constitutes a stand-alone category of prior art. In addition, the legislative history proposes that this phrase act as a qualifier on all categories of prior art, including printed publications, public uses, and on sale activity.[2] As one of the AIA's sponsors explained, "the new paragraph 102(a)(1) imposes an overarching requirement for availability to the public."[3] The statement suggests that the phrase "available to the public" is intended to have the same meaning as "the public accessibility standard that is well-settled in current law, especially case law of the Federal Circuit."[4] The authorities describing the public accessibility standard under the pre-AIA law is vital to understanding the scope of prior art under the AIA. If the legislative history is accepted, these precedents will impact the level of accessibility that is needed for any event (including on-sale activity) to become part of the prior art.

The overall structure of the pre-AIA §§ 102(a) and (b) sections have been modified. As described in Chapter 12, the AIA eliminated separate categories for "novelty" and "statutory bars." Alternatively, the AIA has created an inventor disclosure grace period.[5] Under its terms, the first to disclose has one year to file a patent application even if the invention is patented or the subject of a printed publication by a third party during that time. This will have a somewhat analogous effect as the grace period that existed under the pre-AIA § 102(b) statutory bar.[6]

---

[2] America Invents Act, 157 Cong. Rec. 1496 (statement of Senator Leahy).

[3] *Id.*

[4] *Id.*

[5] For more about the disclosure grace period, see Chapter 12, § 12.04.

[6] The legislative history states, in relevant part:

> Mr. LEAHY. . . . We intend that if an inventor's actions are such as to constitute prior art under subsection 102(a), then those actions necessarily trigger subsection 102(b)'s protections for the inventor and, what would otherwise have been section 102(a) prior art, would be excluded as prior art by the grace period provided by subsection 102(b) . . . .
>
> Mr. HATCH. The Senator from Vermont is correct. For the purposes of grace period protection, the legislation intends parallelism between the treatment of an inventor's actions under subsection 102(a) that might create prior art and the treatment of those actions that negate any prior art effect under subsection 102(b).

America Invents Act, 157 Cong. Rec. 1496 (March 9, 2011).

To qualify as prior art, both patents and printed publications must be enabled to the degree that each must inform a person of ordinary skill how to *make* the invention.[7] The case law has found that a reference does not require that one enable one of ordinary skill how to *use* to the invention.[8]

§ 14.02 PRINTED PUBLICATIONS

[A] Background: What is a "Printed Publication" under § 102?

Under current law, a document may be considered a printed publication if it "has been disseminated or otherwise made available to the extent that persons interested and ordinarily skilled in the subject matter or art, exercising reasonable diligence, can locate it."[9] The policy underlying this rule is that once the work has been made accessible to the public in a printed publication, "the invention has thereby been given to the public, and is no longer patentable by any one."[10] Purely private writings are not considered printed publications.[11] Whether a document is a "printed publication" is a legal conclusion reached after examining the reference and the circumstances of its dissemination in light of the legal standard.

Historically, the Patent Act's first recognition of this type of prior art appeared in the 1793 Patent Act, which authorized infringers to raise a defense based on subject matter that "had been described in some public work anterior to the supposed discovery of the patentee."[12] The term "public work" was construed as one of "a class of established publications or a book publicly printed and circulated."[13] The phrase "printed publication" first appeared in the 1836 Patent Act, which authorized the patent office to reject applications where the invention was previously "described in any printed publication in this or any foreign country."[14] The 1836 Act also authorized defenses in an infringement action for invalidity based on a prior "public work" or a "printed publication."[15] The phrase "printed publication" had a broader meaning than "public work," as a printed publication included "any description printed in any form and published or

---

[7] *See In re* Donohue, 766 F.2d 531, 533 (Fed. Cir. 1985) ("It is well settled that prior art under 35 U.S.C. § 102(b) must sufficiently describe the claimed invention to have placed the public in possession of it.").

[8] Rasmusson v. SmithKline Beecham Corp., 413 F.3d 1318, 1325-26 (Fed. Cir. 2005).

[9] *In re* Wyer, 655 F.2d 221, 226 (C.C.P.A. 1981) (quotation and citation omitted).

[10] Cottier v. Stimson, 20 F. 906, 910 (C.C.D. Or. 1884).

[11] *In re* Bayer, 568 F.2d 1357, 1360 (C.C.P.A. 1978) ("[p]rivate communications, although printed, do not come under this description, whether designed for the use of single persons or of a few restricted groups of persons"), *quoting* 1 WILLIAM C. ROBINSON, THE LAW OF PATENTS FOR USE INVENTIONS § 325 at 446-47 (Boston, Little, Brown, and Co. 1890).

[12] Patent Act of 1793, Ch. 11, 1 Stat. 318-323, § 6 (February 21, 1793).

[13] I.C.E. Corp. v. Armco Steel Corp., 250 F. Supp. 738, 740-41 (S.D.N.Y. 1966).

[14] Patent Act of 1836, Ch. 357, 5 Stat. 117, § 7 (July 4, 1836)

[15] *Id.* at § 15.

circulated to any extent."[16] Over time, the distinction between public works and printed publications was erased, and merged into use of the singular term "printed publication" exclusively.[17]

At one time, some courts analyzed whether a proposed reference was both "printed" and a "publication," as individual requirements.[18] This view held that Congress intended that the publication's text be "fixed or impressed on pages in contradiction to publication by such fugitive means as lectures, gestures, writing in longhand" or the like.[19] One example from this line of authority is *In re Tenney*, decided by the United States Court of Customs and Patent Appeals in 1958.[20] The *Tenney* court ruled that a microfilm of an unpublished German patent application on file in the U.S. Library of Congress was not "printed" and therefore did not bar the patent office from granting the patent. Although the court acknowledged that microfilm was a reproducible format, *Tenney* relied on the view that Congress intended to limit the term "printed" to formats that permitted the making of "a large number of copies so as to insure general distribution or publication:"[21]

> No one would dispute the fact that a wholly handwritten publication is not embraced within the phrase "printed publication." For one reason or other, Congress felt that such a publication would not be sufficient to establish that the invention sought to be patented was already in the public realm (or, as aforestated, was accessible to the public).[22]

Tenney, which is no longer good law, relied on a number of cases that had rejected typewritten documents as "printed publications," finding that "microfilm reproduction differs from normal printing methods" and was therefore not within the purview of § 102.

A second line of authority developed that did not read the term "printed" as a separate or restrictive requirement. For example, in *Philips Electronic & Pharmaceutical Industries Corp. v. Thermal & Electronics Industries*,[23] the court considered a reference quite similar to that considered in *Tenney* — that is, a German patent application that had been microfilmed and was available at the Library of Congress. *Philips* observed that "revolutionary developments in techniques for reproduction, printing and dissemination of documents and data" had

---

[16] *I.C.E. Corp.*, 250 F. Supp. at 740-41.

[17] *Id.* at 741.

[18] *See* J.B. Gambrell, *What is a Printed Publication Within the Meaning of the Patent Act?*, 36 J. Pat. Off. Soc'y 391, 398 (1954).

[19] *Id., quoting* Gulliksen v. Halberg, 75 U.S.P.Q. (BNA) 252, 253 (1937).

[20] *In re* Tenney, 254 F.2d 619, 622 (C.C.P.A. 1958) (holding that the court was "of the opinion that the microfilm is not 'printed.' ").

[21] *Id.* at 626 (citation and quotation omitted).

[22] *Id.* at 625; *see generally* Robert L. Coulter, *Typewritten Library Manuscripts are not 'Printed Publications*, 36 J. Pat. Off. Soc'y 258 (1954) (arguing that a typewritten thesis should not be considered a "printed publication," and stating that "it is a *non sequitur* to conclude that Congress had in mind a meaning so broad as to embrace a procedure that is clearly not a mode of printing but only a mode of handwriting").

[23] Philips Electronic & Pharmaceutical Industries Corp. v. Thermal & Electronics Industries, 450 F.2d 1164 (3d Cir. 1971).

emerged in recent years.[24] The *Philips* court rejected *Tenney's* restrictive definition of "printed" and held that the microfilmed reference constituted a printed
publication:

> To restrict our interpretation of Section 102(a)'s "printed" publication
> requirement solely to the traditional printing press would ignore the
> realities of the scientific and technological period in which we live and the
> underlying rationale of Section 102. We hold, therefore, that the term
> "printed" as used in Section 102 can include documents duplicated by
> modern methods and techniques, including the now well established
> process of microfilming.[25]

In the 1981 decision *In re Wyer*, the Court of Customs and Patent Appeals ruled
that the terms "printed" and "publication" should no longer be understood as two
separate requirements.[26] The *Wyer* court observed that the purpose of the
"printed" requirement had been to ensure that the invention was already given over
to the public, but that scrutinizing the manner of printing separately was not
necessarily meaningful or informative about the amount of public access to the prior
invention. Essentially, *Wyer* adopted the *Philips* approach, directing that the
method of creating the document — whether by handwriting, microfilm or printing
press — is analyzed under the unitary standard of whether the document is
"publicly accessible."

Applying this standard, the *Wyer* court considered whether a patent application
that was available for inspection at the Australian patent office constituted a printed
publication under § 102(b). The applicant had filed for patent protection in Australia
in 1972, four years before the applicant filed his U.S. application in the PTO. In
1974, any member of the public could view the Australian application by inspecting
microfilm in the Australian patent office, or by examining diazo copies of the
application distributed in five different sub-offices throughout Australia. Copies of
the application were also available for sale in the main Australian patent office.

Wyer held that the applicant's own prior Australian patent application constituted prior art as a printed publication to his U.S. patent under § 102(b). After
examining the fact that the Australian patent office had maintained records of
patent applications for public viewing, *Wyer* held that the properly indexed and
abstracted Australian application, on microfilm and diazo copy, was sufficiently
accessible to the public and to those interested in the art to qualify as a printed
publication.

Consistent with *Philips*, the microfilm and diazo print format of the patent
applications was not determinative to the *Wyer* court. Rejecting the *Tenney* court's
technical approach to the form of the document, the *Wyer* court based its
determination on whether members of the interested public would have had access
to sufficient information to locate the patent application as a reference. This
standard was met where the application had been laid open to the public, who could

---

[24] *Id.* at 1170.

[25] *Id.*

[26] *In re* Wyer, 655 F.2d 221 (C.C.P.A. 1981).

be guided to the document by the index and abstract.

[B]   "Printed Publications" and Public Accessibility

Since the time that the *Wyer* case was decided, the Federal Circuit has adopted *Wyer's* unitary view of printed publications, and the court's *public accessibility* standard as the benchmark for whether a reference constitutes a printed publication.[27] Certainly, a document that has been *actually* received by at least one member of the interested public will meet this standard.[28] However, the proponent of the reference is not required to demonstrate that anyone in fact received a copy of the document. Rather, a printed publication can be a prior art reference if the proponent shows that, prior to the critical date, the document could have been found by an interested member of the public exercising reasonable diligence.[29]

This standard does not require that a reference be permanently available in a formal, indexed repository. For example, in the 1928 *Jockmus v. Leviton*, the court considered whether a catalogue distributed generally to the trade in France could be considered as a reference.[30] At this time, some authorities had suggested that business circulars were insufficient to as prior art because a publication in a book was required.[31] Judge Learned Hand, writing for the *Jockmus* court, found that a catalogue met the standard nonetheless, comparing the circumstances to books, whereby, "[a] single copy in a library, though more permanent, is far less fitted to inform the craft than a catalogue freely circulated, however ephemeral its existence; for the catalogue goes direct to those whose interests make them likely to observe and remember whatever it may contain that is new and useful."[32]

On the other hand, the cases suggest that displays cannot be so ephemeral that permanence is entirely lacking. For example, in *University of California v. Howmedica, Inc.*, a district court suggested that slides projected at a lecture for a limited duration cannot constitute a printed publication.[33] The Federal Circuit has recently indicated approval for *Howmedica* in *In re Klopfenstein*, stating "the important proposition that the mere presentation of slides accompanying an oral presentation at a professional conference is not *per se* a 'printed publication'."[34] As

---

[27] *See, e.g.,In re* Klopfenstein, 380 F.3d 1345, 1348 n.2 (Fed. Cir. 2004).

[28] *See* MIT v. AB Fortia, 774 F.2d 1104, 1109 (Fed. Cir. 1985) (actual dissemination of paper without restriction to those interested in the art was found to constitute a printed publication).

[29] *See* Constant v. Advanced Micro-Devices, Inc., 848 F.2d 1560, 1568 (Fed. Cir. 1988).

[30] Jockmus v. Leviton, 28 F.2d 812 (2d Cir. 1928).

[31] *See, e.g.*, New Process Fermentation Co. v. Koch, 21 F. 580, 587 (E.D. Mich. 1884) ("It has been held generally, and perhaps universally, that business circulars which are sent only to persons engaged or supposed to be engaged in the trade, are not such publications as the law contemplates").

[32] *Id.* at 813-14.

[33] Regents of University of California v. Howmedica, Inc., 530 F. Supp. 846, 860 (D.N.J. 1981). The statement in *Howmedica* is arguably *dicta*, as the court also found that these slides failed to meet the standards for anticipatory enablement.

[34] *See In re* Klopfenstein, 380 F.3d 1345, 1349 n.4 (Fed. Cir. 2004). This statement may not have been necessary for the disposition of the issues presented in *Klopfenstein*, as the display at issue in the case appeared before those interested in the art on paper for a longer duration.

discussed later in this chapter, *Klopfenstein* provides a number of considerations to determine the more difficult cases.

[1] Development of the "Public Accessibility" Standard

The contours of the standard for public accessibility have been defined in a number of cases, including those considering whether a limited number of copies of a document — in some cases, a thesis or other unpublished work — existent in a single, discreet location, such as a library, meet the printed publication standard. Despite the *Jockmus* court's reference to "a single copy in a library" as permanent and likely accessible, not all documents available in a library have been held to constitute printed publications under § 102.

For example, in *In re Cronyn*, the court considered whether three college theses constituted printed publications.[35] A copy of each was available in the main library of a U.S. college prior to the applications' critical date, as well as in the library of the chemistry department where the students' work had been undertaken. The title and author of each of the theses were listed on individual cards, filed alphabetically by the author's name. There were approximately 6,000 different cards listing various theses in the main library, and in the chemistry department approximately 450 of such cards were contained in a shoebox. The information on these cards was not incorporated in the library's main catalogue. Both the cards and the theses themselves were available for public examination. The student authors of the three documents had not publicly presented or published any papers that would associate their names with the subject matter of their works.

The *Cronyn* court held these were not printed publications because they were not publicly accessible. The opinion reasoned that persons interested in the art would not have been able to locate them, explaining:

> . . . they had not been either cataloged or indexed in a meaningful way. Although the titles of the theses were listed on 3 out of 450 cards filed alphabetically by author in a shoebox in the chemistry department library, such "availability" was not sufficient to make them reasonably accessible to the public. Here, the only research aid was the student's name, which, of course, bears no relationship to the subject of the student's thesis.[36]

By contrast, in *In re Hall*, the Federal Circuit reached the opposite conclusion in a case that considered a single copy of a thesis that was located in a university library in Germany.[37] Unlike *Cronyn*, the thesis at issue in *Hall* had been indexed and catalogued in a special dissertations portion of the general users' catalogue. The *Hall* court found that the public accessibility standard was met — that is, interested members of the relevant public could have searched to obtain the information from the thesis in Germany if they had wanted to, because the library's indexing system would lead one who searched for the thesis at issue to find the document.

---

[35] *In re* Cronyn, 890 F.2d 1158 (Fed. Cir. 1989).

[36] *Id.* at 1161.

[37] *In re* Hall, 781 F.2d 897 (Fed. Cir. 1986).

In *Bruckelmyer v. Ground Heaters, Inc.*, the court considered the public accessibility of two diagrams in the patent file history of a Canadian application (the '119 application) available in a patent office in Quebec.[38] This Canadian application was not indexed. However, a patent that had issued from this application was both public and indexed, although the issued patent did not include the two figures at issue.

The *Bruckelmyer* court held that the issued patent was a sufficient indicator that would have led interested parties to find the figures in the Canadian file history. In so ruling, the court relied on a finding that the description in the Canadian patent closely tracked the use contemplated by the claimed methods of the patent in suit. *Bruckelmyer* explained, "[g]iven such a pertinent disclosure, we conclude that no reasonable trier of fact could find that a person of ordinary skill in the art interested in the subject matter of the patents in suit and exercising reasonable diligence could not locate the '119 application, including [the] figures . . . contained therein."[39] *Bruckelmyer*'s ruling was made over a dissent, which expressed disagreement that the Canadian patent provided sufficient guidance to lead members of the public to locate the two figures in the file history, pointing to "[t]he fact that an additional drawing, disclosing additional structure, is present in the application file is a matter of sheer happenstance nowhere indicated in the issued patent."[40]

Taken together, these cases demonstrate that a number of factors are considered to determine whether a document is a § 102 printed publication. Under *Cronyn*, an applicant is not charged with knowledge of all information located on any library shelf that could, in theory, only be found by wandering its stacks coupled with a good measure of luck. As *Wyer* and *Hall* illustrate, an index or abstract that is reasonably likely to draw those in the art to the prior document can establish the needed guidance to render the document publicly accessible. However, the *Bruckelmyer* majority suggests that the amount of information that needs to be provided to lead one to the reference is minimal and need not include a specific description of the information to be found.

[2] The Current Standard: *In re Klopfenstein*

In re Klopfenstein represents the Federal Circuit's recent guidance for applying the printed publication standard to a temporary display.[41] There, the court considered the PTO's rejection of a patent application that described the use of a double-extruded soy fiber to normalize cholesterol levels for mammals. The PTO's rejection was based on a reference (the "Liu reference"), presented by the applicants along with their colleague Liu, that was comprised of a series of fourteen printed slides that had been displayed on poster board twice prior to the application's critical date. The first display lasted two and one-half days at a conference that had been sponsored by an industry group. The second lasted less than one day at Kansas State University. Neither conference prohibited note-taking

---

[38] *See* Bruckelmyer v. Ground Heaters, Inc., 445 F.3d 1374 (Fed. Cir. 2006).

[39] *Id.* at 1379.

[40] *Id.* at 1381 (Linn, J., dissenting).

[41] *In re* Klopfenstein, 380 F.3d 1345 (Fed. Cir. 2004).

or copying. No copies of the Liu reference were disseminated, and they were apparently no longer available after these conferences ended.

On appeal, the applicant argued that the Liu reference did not constitute a printed publication, because the slides had not been indexed nor catalogued as had been required by the courts in *Cronyn* and *Hall.* The *Klopfenstein* court rejected that either indexing or abstracting were required in all cases, finding the "thesis in the library" cases inapposite to the facts presented here:

> . . . a public billboard targeted to those of ordinary skill in the art that describes all of the limitations of an invention and that is on display for the public for months may be neither "distributed" nor "indexed" — but it most surely is "sufficiently accessible to the public interested in the art" and therefore, under controlling precedent, a "printed publication."[42]

Klopfenstein provided a series of factors to be balanced in determining whether a temporarily displayed reference is a printed publication under § 102, as follows:

- the length of time the display was exhibited;

- the expertise of the target audience;

- the existence (or lack thereof) of reasonable expectations that the material displayed would not be copied; and

- the simplicity or ease with which the material displayed could have been copied.[43]

Applying this test, the *Klopfenstein* court held that the Liu reference constituted a printed publication. As to the first two considerations, the court found that Liu was displayed for approximately three days total to those interested in the art. Further, relevant to expectations of copying, the court found that Liu had been displayed without any protective measures to prevent reproduction, such as any non-disclosure agreement or even a statement of disclaimer prohibiting dissemination of the information in the slide pages. *Klopfenstein* found that the information displayed in the slides was in a relatively simplified format, using bullet points, and that "only a few slides presented would have needed to have been copied by an observer to capture the novel information."[44] On balance, the Federal Circuit found that the slides constituted a printed publication warranting rejection of the application.

Klopfenstein underscores that the touchstone of the printed publication requirement is public accessibility. Although *Klopfenstein* expressed concern that inventors might be chilled from participating in academic presentations or discussions, the court pointed to the inventor's ability to impose confidentiality obligations on participants, whether by agreement, norms in the relevant industry or disclaimer. Certainly, an inventor has the option of placing a patent application on file within one year after making any such presentation. Absent such measures, this subsec-

---

[42] *Id.* at 1348.

[43] *Id.* at 1350.

[44] *Id.* at 1351-52.

tion may cause the inventor's relinquishment of the ability to obtain a patent on information disseminated during a presentation.

It warrants observation that, in making a finding of public accessibility, the court is implementing an important aspect of patent policy. The court's conclusion that a work is publicly accessible amounts to a conclusion that the subject matter of the invention has become part of the public domain. Once that takes place, the same subject matter should not be pulled back into a private intellectual property rights sphere. As the Federal Circuit has explained, this public accessibility standard "is grounded on the principle that once an invention is in the public domain, it is no longer patentable by anyone."[45]

Additionally, as previously discussed, the prior cases that consider public accessibility will be highly significant to the meaning of "accessible to the public" in the newly enacted statute. The *Kloppenstein* decision (and others) should be carefully considered to determine the scope of available prior art with respect to any particular claim under the newly enacted law.

§ 14.03 PRIOR PATENTS

Both the pre- sections §§ 102(a) and (b) include provisions that block a U.S. patent where the invention has been "patented . . . in this or a foreign country" prior to the critical date. Under these subsections, a *previously issued patent*, whether issued in the U.S. or a foreign country, prevents a later patent from issuing.[46]

Under the pre-AIA §§ 102(a) and (b), a secret foreign patent does not qualify as a reference under either section — rather, the patent must be open to the public.[47] Given the AIA's legislative history favoring publicly accessible prior art, this is likely to be the standard under the new version of the statute. For the pre-AIA §§ 102(a) and (b), the effective date of a prior patent is the date that the patentee's rights become enforceable.[48] Using standard rules of statutory construction, the AIA is likely to be interpreted to incorporate these same rules.

In *Carlson*, the Federal Circuit considered the pre-AIA meaning of the word "patented" in the context of determining whether a German Geschmacksmuster met the requirements of § 102(a).[49] As background, a Geschmacksmuster is a registration system for industrial designs and models. To obtain protection, one files a registration with a drawing, photograph or sample of the article in a local deposit office. Some details of the registration are then published for distribution through-

---

[45] *In re* Lister, 583 F.3d 1307 (Fed. Cir. 2009).

[46] *See generally* IPXL Holdings, L.L.C. v. Amazon.com, Inc., 430 F.3d 1377 (Fed. Cir. 2005).

[47] *In re* Ekenstam, 256 F.2d 321, 323 (C.C.P.A. 1958) ("There seems to be no logical reason why the granting of a secret patent abroad should be a bar to patenting in this country. Such a foreign patent is of no value to persons in this country unless and until it is made available to the public.").

[48] *See In re* Monks, 588 F.2d 308, 311 (C.C.P.A. 1978) (finding that the effective date of a British patent is when the document is "sealed," that is, "the time when plaintiff's right to a patent is fixed and determined."). In contrast, the effective date of a § 102(e) reference is its filing date. *See* Chapter 18.

[49] *See In re* Carlson, 983 F.2d 1032 (Fed. Cir. 1992).

out Germany. Despite its resemblance to copyright protection, the *Carslon* court held that a Geschmacksmuster constitutes a "patent" under § 102(a), because the rights granted by the registration were both "substantial and exclusive." The *Carlson* court explained:

> We recognize that Geschmacksmuster on display for public view in remote cities in a far-away land may create a burden of discovery for one without the time, desire, or resources to journey there in person or by agent to observe that which was registered and protected under German law. Such a burden, however, is by law imposed upon the hypothetical person of ordinary skill in the art who is charged with knowledge of all the contents of the relevant prior art.[50]

Carlson relied on precedent establishing that a Geschmacksmuster constituted a patent for purposes of § 102(d),[51] and found no statutory distinction to vary the construction of the term "patented" for the pre-AIA § 102(a). Thus, a prior patent may be used as prior art where the patent is public, enabling, meets the all elements rule, and confers "substantial and exclusive rights" equal or akin to patent protection.

It is likely that the precedents interpreting the pre-AIA version of "patented" will be incorporated into the new version. However, the AIA § 102(a)(1) includes a provision that did not exist in the prior law. Although the AIA includes no statutory bars, there is the grace period based on the inventor's disclosure.

In some instances, § 102's prohibition on granting a U.S. patent where a prior patent exists might be redundant of other statutory provisions, such as the pre-AIA §§ 102(d) or (e).[52] However, there are important distinctions between each of these subsections, and therefore each patent must be evaluated individually. Here are some examples:

- The pre-AIA § 102(e) is limited to U.S. patents, published U.S. patent applications, and PCT applications that have been published by the World Trade Organization in English, and designate the U.S. However, the pre-AIA §§ 102(a) and (b) (as well as the AIA § 102(a)(1)) apply to both domestic and foreign patents.

- The effective date of a patent reference for patents under the pre-AIA §§ 102(a) and (b), is the date that the right becomes effective. This is likely to be the case for the AIA § 102(a)(1). In contrast, the effective date under the pre-AIA § 102(e) is the filing date. For the AIA § 102(b), it is the first effective filing date.

- The pre-AIA 35 U.S.C. § 102(d) provides that a patent will not be granted if the invention has been previously patented in a foreign country by the inventor more than twelve (12) months prior to the filing of an application for a U.S. patent. This section has been eliminated in the AIA.

---

[50] *Id.* at 1037.

[51] This precedent was *In re* Talbott, 443 F.2d 1397 (C.C.P.A. 1971).

[52] For a discussion of the comparison of patents under §§ 102(a) & (b) and § 102(d), *see* Chapter 17. Regarding 35 U.S.C. § 102(d), *see* Chapter 18.

Another area of overlap arises for issued patents that are publicly accessible, and therefore can be considered printed publications. Indeed, as *In re Wyer* established, publicly accessible patent *applications* may be considered printed publications under appropriate circumstances.[53]

§ 14.04   CONCLUSION

The prohibition on patenting subject matter that has been disclosed in a prior publication or a prior patent is intended to ensure that inventions which have already been made available to the public will not be subject to a patent. Further, the rule encourages inventors to place their patent applications on file expeditiously after any such disclosures have been made. Both inventor and third party activity can create prior art. Moreover, both domestic and foreign documents and patents can constitute prior art.

The touchstone of the prior publication requirement is whether the document at issue is publicly accessible to those interested in the art. As one court described, the inquiry is whether the document "could be located by persons interested and ordinary skilled in the subject matter or art exercising reasonable diligence."[54] This standard is certainly met where at least one member of the public has actually received and possesses the document, although that showing is not required. Reasonable diligence includes searches of foreign libraries and patent offices, even where only a single copy of the relevant document is located there, using the necessary and available tools to locate the reference. Likewise, the standard includes information that may be only temporarily displayed or available through a searchable database, so long as the balancing test of the *Klopfenstein* case has been met.

Section 102 further provides that no U.S. patent will issue where the invention has already been the subject of a U.S. or foreign patent. This provision is met where the prior patent is public, enabling, meets the all elements rule, and confers "substantial and exclusive rights" equal or akin to U.S. patent protection. The AIA has a similar provision, which precludes a claim from issuing where the invention has been previously disclosed in a prior patent or printed publication throughout the world.

---

[53] *In re* Wyer, 655 F.2d 221 (C.C.P.A. 1981). This principle was affirmed more recently in the Federal Circuit's Bruckelmyer v. Ground Heaters, Inc., 445 F.3d 1374 (Fed. Cir. 2006).

[54] *In re* Lister, 583 F.3d 1307, 1315 (Fed. Cir. 2009).

Chapter 15

PRIOR SALES AND OFFERS FOR SALE

SYNOPSIS

§ 15.01 INTRODUCTION

§ 15.02 ON-SALE AND THE "READY FOR PATENTING" STANDARD

    [A] Introduction

    [B] The U.S. Supreme Court's *Pfaff v. Wells Electronics, Inc.*

    [C] Applying the Pfaff "Ready for Patenting" Standard

§ 15.03 DEFINING AN "OFFER FOR SALE" OR "SALE"

§ 15.04 LICENSES AND ON-SALE ACTIVITY

§ 15.05 CONCLUSION

§ 15.01 INTRODUCTION

35 U.S.C. § 102(b), as enacted prior to the 2011 America Invents Act (AIA), includes a statutory bar that prevents a patent from being granted where the invention was "*on-sale* in this country, more than one year prior to the date of the application for patent in the United States."[1] The purpose of this requirement "stems from the undesirability of allowing an inventor to seek a patent long after sales of the invention have caused others to start making, using, or selling it in the belief that the invention was available to the public, free of restriction."[2] Called the *on-sale bar* (or on-sale activity), this limitation puts into force the law's "reluctance to allow an inventor to remove existing knowledge from public use."[3] The one-year grace period sets a clear time limit for an inventor to file an application after an offer for a sale begins.[4] The time limit pushes the inventor toward filing the patent application sooner, disclosing the details of the invention, and allowing the patent to expire earlier, than would be the case if no deadline were imposed. The inventor must file a patent application within the grace period or lose the ability to obtain the right entirely.[5]

---

[1] 35 U.S.C. § 102(b); *see generally* City of Elizabeth v. American Nicholson Pavement Co., 97 U.S. 126, 137 (1878) ("Any attempt to use [the invention] for a profit, and not by way of experiment, for a longer period than two years before the application, would deprive the inventor of his right to a patent.").

[2] Patrick J. Barrett, *New Guidelines for Applying the On-sale Bar to Patentability*, 24 Stan. L.R. 730, 733 (1972).

[3] Pfaff v. Wells Elec., Inc., 525 U.S. 55, 64 (1998).

[4] *Id.* at 65.

[5] General Elec. Co. v. U. S., 654 F.2d 55, 61 (C.C.P.A. 1981).

The on-sale bar also functions to prevent an inventor from extending the patent term. That is, as the first to develop an idea, the inventor is a first mover and typically enjoys market exclusivity before competitors emerge. A patentee who waits for several years to file a patent application might extend the inventor's effective period of exclusivity well beyond the statutory term. The pre-AIA on-sale bar minimizes this circumstance by limiting this exclusivity period to the patent term plus one year. In addition, this pre-AIA grace period is "inventor friendly" because it allows the inventor a limited time to test the market to see whether the expense of patent prosecution is warranted.[6] Although several of these policies focus on *inventor* activity, the on-sale bar applies with equal force to commercial activity by *third parties*.[7] An invention cannot be patented after a year has passed once any party has introduced the invention into the commercial sphere through on-sale activity.

The first on-sale bar appeared in the Patent Act of 1836, which authorized rejection of an application where the invention had been on-sale with the inventor's consent before the application was filed.[8] Subsequent amendments added a two-year grace period,[9] which was later shortened to the current one-year term. In time, further statutory amendments removed the requirement that sales activity occur with the inventor's knowledge or consent.[10] In so doing, Congress sought to "fix a period of limitation which should be certain, and require only a calculation of time, and should not depend upon the uncertain question of whether the applicant had consented to or allowed the sale or use."[11] In 1870, the Patent Act was again amended to add the geographic restriction to activity within the United States.[12] These principles were carried forward to the pre-AIA version of § 102, which limited sales activity to that which takes place in the U.S.

The 2011 AIA includes an analogous prior art provision in § 102(a)(1), which states that a patent will not be granted where the invention was "on-sale, or otherwise available to the public before the effective filing date of the claimed invention." Unlike the pre-AIA on-sale bar, the AIA includes no geographic restrictions. Sales anywhere in the world can be used as prior art. Following standard rules of statutory construction, it can be expected that the definition of

---

[6] *Id.; see also* Barrett, *supra* note 2, at 735.

[7] 35 U.S.C. § 102(b) (precluding the issuance of a patent where "the invention was . . . on-sale in this country, more than one year prior to the date of the application for patent in the United States"); General Elec. Co. v. U. S., 654 F.2d 55, 61-2 (C.C.P.A. 1981) ("It is well established that a placing of the invention 'on-sale' by an unrelated third party more than 1 year prior to the filing of an application for patent by another has the effect under § 102(b) of invalidating a patent directed to that invention.").

[8] Patent Act of 1836, Ch. 357, § 6, 5 Stat. 117 (July 4, 1836) (allowing patents where the invention was "not known or used by others before his or their discovery or invention thereof, and not, at the time of his application for a patent, in public use or *on-sale, with his consent or allowance*, as the inventor or discoverer") (emphasis added).

[9] Patent Act of 1839, Ch. 88, § 7, 5 Stat. 353-355 (March 3, 1839).

[10] The Driven-Well Cases, 123 U.S. 267 (1887).

[11] *Id.* at 274.

[12] Patent Act of 1870, Ch. 230, § 61,16 Stat. 198-217 (July 8, 1870). Unlike current 35 U.S.C. § 102, the 1870 Patent Act allowed consideration of foreign sales activity before the patent office. *See id.* at § 24.

"on-sale" — that is, a sale or an offer for sale — will largely be adopted by the courts construing the AIA.

As described in Chapter 12, the AIA formally eliminated the former statutory bars. Under the AIA, another's sale will prevent a later inventor from obtaining a claim that describes the same invention even if the patent application's effective filing date is a single day after the on-sale activity. However, as described in Chapter 12, § 12.04, the AIA has instituted a grace period. On-sale activity will not prevent a patent claim filed within one year of a public disclosure by the inventor or joint inventor, or if the invention was disclosed by another who obtained the subject matter from the inventor or joint inventor.[13] The AIA allows an inventor to engage in on-sale activity and file a patent application within one year. This has a similar effect to the grace period that existed under the pre-AIA § 102(b) statutory bar.[14]

As detailed in Chapter 12, § 12.04, it is not clear whether the AIA requires that the on-sale activity be *available to the public* to qualify as an invalidating event. Although precedent interpreting the phrase "on-sale" was satisfied with private offers and sales,[15] a colloquy on the Senate floor explained that under the AIA § 102(a)(1) the phrase "available to the public" acts as a modifier to the other categories of prior art.[16] As one of the AIA's sponsors proposed, the AIA "subsection 102(a) was drafted in part to do away with precedent under current law that private offers for sale . . . may be deemed patent-defeating prior art."[17] This statement continues, "the new paragraph 102(a)(1) imposes an overarching require-ment for availability to the public."[18] Whether the courts interpreting the on-sale provision of the AIA will follow this legislative history is likely to be determined in the coming years. At present, inventors who engage in offers to sell and sales should carefully weigh the timing of a decision to file for patent protection, with the potential for alternative constructions of the statute in mind.

§ 15.02   ON-SALE AND THE "READY FOR PATENTING" STANDARD

[A]   Introduction

To determine whether an invention is *on-sale* under patent law, the courts have long held that there must be either a *sale* or an *offer for sale*. The subject matter of the sale or offer must reflect a product or process that has strict identity with

---

[13] 35 U.S.C. § 102(b)(1).

[14] This interpretation is based on a colloquy between two of the Senate bill's sponsors, Senators Leahy and Hatch, which suggests that the prior art triggers of § 102(a)(1) are considered "disclosures" for purposes of the AIA § 102(b), which provide for a one-year grace period that inures to the benefit of the inventor. As with the other ambiguities identified in the AIA, judicial construction of these provisions is expected to resolve the issue in the coming years.

[15] *See* Crystal Semiconductor Corp. v. Tritech Microelectronics Intern., Inc., 246 F.3d 1336 (Fed. Cir. 2001).

[16] America Invents Act, 157 Cong. Rec. 1496.

[17] *Id.* (statement of Senator Leahy).

[18] *Id.*

the claim at issue. However, the offer for sale or sale is not required to specify each element of the claim sought to be patented in the offer or contract, so long as the evidence demonstrates that the invention was the subject of the transaction or offer.[19]

In some cases, an inventor may attempt to sell a product in an executory contract before the invention is complete. This raises the question of whether an idea that is not fully developed can constitute on-sale activity.[20] Historically, the precise stage of inventive development necessary to commence the one-year statutory period was the subject of conflict in the case law. Generally, there was agreement that "[i]f the inventor had merely a conception or was working towards development of that conception, it can be said there is not yet any 'invention' which could be placed on sale."[21] Prior to the Federal Circuit's formation in 1982, a number of the circuit courts had held that an invention must be reduced to practice.[22] Over time, the Federal Circuit rejected this standard and instead developed a *totality of the circumstances* test based on a fact-specific inquiry.[23] In 1998, the U.S. Supreme Court granted a writ of *certiorari* in *Pfaff v. Wells Electronics, Inc.* to consider whether the Federal Circuit's standard was correct.

[B]   The U.S. Supreme Court's *Pfaff v. Wells Electronics, Inc.*

The Supreme Court's *Pfaff v. Wells Electronics, Inc.*, considered on-sale activity for claims directed to a mechanical socket used for semiconductor devices.[24] In *Pfaff*, on March 17, 1981, the inventor showed some engineering drawings of the socket design to semiconductor manufacturer Texas Instruments. Several weeks later, on April 8, 1981, the inventor obtained a purchase order for 30,000 units. As of the date that the inventor received the purchase order, the inventor expected the invention to work for its intended purpose although the inventor did not reduce the invention to practice by creating a prototype. On April 19, 1982, the inventor filed a

---

[19] Scaltech Inc. v. Retec/Tetra, L.L.C., 178 F.3d 1378, 1383 (Fed. Cir. 1999); Sonoscan, Inc. v. Sonotek, Inc., 936 F.2d 1261, 1263-64 (Fed. Cir. 1991).

[20] Shatterproof Glass Corp. v. Libbey-Owens Ford Co., 758 F.2d 613, 622 (Fed. Cir. 1985) ("The clear weight of authority is that a bare offer to sell does not *ipso facto* satisfy the 'on-sale' bar, and that the surrounding circumstances must be considered.").

[21] UMC Elec. Co. v. U.S., 816 F.2d 647, 657 (Fed. Cir. 1987); *see also* David W. Carstens and Craig Allen Nard, *Conception and the 'On-sale' Bar*, 34 Wm. & Mary L. Rev. 393 (1993).

[22] *See, e.g.*, Timely Prod. Corp. v. Arron, 523 F.2d 288, 301 (2d Cir. 1975); Hobbs v. U.S., Atomic Energy Comm'n, 451 F.2d 849, 859 (5th Cir. 1971). Typically, reduction to practice exists when the patentee has an embodiment that meets every limitation and operates for its intended purpose — that is, the there is a demonstration of the workability or utility of the claimed invention. However, reduction to practice does not require an inventor to bring the invention to perfection or even commercial feasibility necessarily. *See* Fujikawa v. Wattanasin, 93 F.3d 1559, 1563 (Fed. Cir. 1996); Chapter 20.

[23] Western Marine Elec., Inc. v. Furuno Elec. Co., Ltd., 764 F.2d 840, 845 (Fed. Cir. 1985) (considering a number of factors, such as "the character and extent of commercial activities, the type of invention and its stage of development as evidenced by engineering models, prototypes, and production models, along with the character and extent of bona fide experimentation."). Under this test, reduction to practice was not required. *UMC Elec.*, 816 F.2d at 656 ("[W]e conclude that reduction to practice of the claimed invention has not been and should not be made an absolute requirement of the on-sale bar.")

[24] Pfaff v. Wells Electronics, Inc., 525 U.S. 55 (1998).

patent application claiming the socket. The relevant dates are summarized as follows:

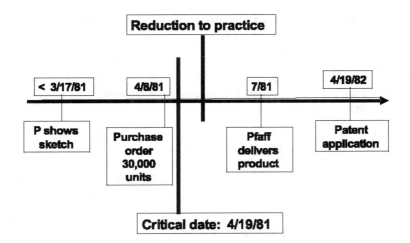

The issue presented to the Supreme Court in *Pfaff* was whether the Federal Circuit had properly held that the socket device was on-sale prior to the April 19, 1981, critical date. Certainly, the purchase order had been transmitted outside the grace period. Affirming invalidity, *Pfaff* held that a sale or an offer for sale, coupled with invention that is *ready for patenting*, triggers the one-year statutory grace period. *Pfaff* explained that the ready for patenting standard:

> . . . may be satisfied in at least two ways: by proof of reduction to practice before the critical date; or by proof that prior to the critical date the inventor had prepared drawings or other descriptions of the invention that were sufficiently specific to enable a person skilled in the art to practice the invention.[25]

Pfaff rejected the argument that full reduction to practice was required. In doing so, the Court reasoned that an invention could be "complete" before reduction to practice has been accomplished. Additionally, *Pfaff* rejected the Federal Circuit's totality of the circumstances test, explaining that the test was "unnecessarily vague" in a manner that "seriously undermines the patent system's interest in certainty."[26] In the final analysis, under *Pfaff*, two requirements must be met before the grace period is triggered. First, there must be a sale or an offer for sale. Second, the invention must be ready for patenting.

In result, *Pfaff* that the invention was ready for patenting based on the inventor's drawing that had been presented to Texas Instruments prior to the critical date.

_____

[25] *Id.*

[26] *Id.* at 66 and n.11.

The Court affirmed the finding that this diagram had sufficient detail to enable those of ordinary skill to produce the device. Further, *Pfaff* recognized that the inventor's acceptance of the purchase order demonstrated that an offer for sale had been made before the critical date. As the two requirements for on-sale were met, *Pfaff* affirmed the judgment of invalidity.

[C] Applying the Pfaff "Ready for Patenting" Standard

Pfaff's two required elements must be present prior to the patent's critical date. However, the *order* in which each occurs is not important. An invention does not need to be ready for patenting at the time of the offer or sale, so long as both events occur more than one year before the patent application is filed.[27] As the Federal Circuit explained:

> Completion of the invention prior to the critical date, pursuant to an offer to sell that invention, would validate what had been theretofore an inchoate, but not yet established, bar. It would validate it . . . as of the date of that completion, not the date of the original offer. Completion after the critical date, even if pursuant to the offer, would not create a bar.[28]

Moreover, ready for patenting is the *minimum* standard of inventive development that must be present to trigger the one-year grace period of § 102(b). Certainly, if the invention is *more* developed — i.e., reduced to practice or fully commercialized — the standard is met.

A comparison of *Pfaff's* "ready for patenting" standard with "conception" and "reduction to practice" is helpful. Specifically, conception is complete when the invention is "so clearly defined in the inventor's mind that only ordinary skill would be necessary to reduce the invention to practice, without extensive research or experimentation."[29] In other words, the inventor must have a clear idea of the entire invention in mind and include all elements of the invention.[30] Reduction to practice requires either actual reduction to practice, such as by the creation of a working prototype, or alternatively through the filing of a U.S. patent application that meets § 112's disclosure requirements.[31] *Pfaff's* ready for patenting standard sits between these two. Unlike conception, ready for patenting requires a reduction to some form of writing — that is, an enabling disclosure.[32] Unlike reduction to practice, the ready for patenting standard can be met without the creation of a working prototype or a U.S. patent filing. Recall that the *Pfaff* Court found an engineering

---

[27] Robotic Vision Sys., Inc. v. View Eng'g, Inc., 112 F.3d 1163 (Fed. Cir. 1997).

[28] *Id.* at 1168.

[29] Burroughs Wellcome Co. v. Barr Laboratories, Inc., 40 F.3d 1223, 1228 (Fed. Cir. 1994).

[30] Brown v. Barbacid, 276 F.3d 1327, 1336 (Fed. Cir. 2002).

[31] *See* Hybritech Inc. v. Monoclonal Antibodies, Inc., 802 F.2d 1367 (Fed. Cir. 1986); Mpep § 2138.05; Hyatt v. Boone, 146 F.3d 1348, 1352 (Fed. Cir. 1998) ("[T]he inventor need not provide evidence of either conception or actual reduction to practice when relying on the content of the patent application.").

[32] The cooberation rule typically requires one seeking to prove conception to provide some form of a writing. However, this is a rule that addresses an evidentiary requirement. In its purest form, conception is defined as a mental act. By contrast, ready for patenting requires an enabled disclosure as a substantive matter (rather than merely an evidentiary one).

diagram sufficient. This is not a working prototype or a U.S. patent application. In other words, an enabling disclosure may be less formal (and less expensive) than either a prototype or a filed U.S. patent application.

Since the time that the *Pfaff* case was decided, the Federal Circuit has provided additional guidance on the meaning of the phrase ready for patenting.[33] In cases that arise primarily in technological areas that are complex or uncertain, the Federal Circuit has reiterated the *Pfaff* rule that conception by itself is not sufficient. With respect to such inventions and where the inventor is unsure whether the invention will work, development and verification are necessary before on-sale activity is considered prior art.[34]

How does experimental use apply? It may be more accurate to say that the subject matter of the transaction that is a mere experiment is simply not ready for patenting. For example, in *EZ Dock, Inc. v. Schafer Systems, Inc.*, the court considered the patentee's sale of a floating dock device prior to the patent's critical date.[35] In response to an unsolicited inquiry, the patentee sold an item at a reduced rate, performed repairs at no charge, inspected the dock several times to monitor its durability and eventually modified the shape of the dock to improve its performance. *EZ Dock* explained a reasonable jury might find that the purpose of the sale was not commercial exploitation, but rather to determine whether the invention was "capable of performing its intended purpose in its intended environment" and remanded the case for trial.[36] As the *Pfaff* Court recognized, the law recognizes a "distinction between inventions put to experimental use and products sold commercially."[37] Where a product incorporates concepts that are still under development, the product cannot be said to incorporate the invention. In that case, the transaction does not involve a product that is "ready for patenting" under § 102.[38]

§ 15.03   DEFINING AN "OFFER FOR SALE" OR "SALE"

In *Pfaff*, the Supreme Court stated that "the product must be the subject of a commercial offer for sale" prior to the critical date.[39] To meet this prong of the test, an *offer* for sale is sufficient. The offeree does not need to accept the offer for on-sale activity to occur.[40]

---

[33] Space Systems/Loral, Inc. v. Lockheed Martin Corp., 271 F.3d 1076 (Fed. Cir. 2001).

[34] *Id.* at 1080 ("[W]hen development and verification are needed in order to prepare a patent application that complies with § 112, the invention is not yet ready for patenting.").

[35] EZ Dock, Inc. v. Schafer Systems, Inc., 276 F.3d 1347 (Fed. Cir. 2002).

[36] *Id.* at 1353 (citations omitted); *see also* Mas-Hamilton Group v. LaGard, Inc., 156 F.3d 1206 (Fed. Cir. 1998) (offer to provide patented devices for testing and display was not a commercial offer for sale).

[37] Pfaff v. Wells Electronics, Inc., 525 U.S. 55, 64 (1998).

[38] Atlanta Attachment Co. v. Leggett & Platt, Inc., 516 F.3d 1361, 1370 (Fed. Cir. 2008) ("a patentee may still avoid the on-sale or public use bars by proving that the 'invention' required additional experimentation, and was not in fact complete.").

[39] *Pfaff*, 525 U.S. at 67.

[40] Cargill, Inc. v. Canbra Foods, Ltd., 476 F.3d 1359, 1370 (Fed. Cir. 2007) ("[E]vidence of an offer to

The Federal Circuit has held that an offer for sale must constitute "an offer for sale in the contract sense, one that would be understood as such in the commercial community."[41] The court has rejected the notion that the contract law of any particular state controls this analysis, as that could lead to undesirable jurisdictional variations.[42] Instead, courts examine state and federal decisions applying the Uniform Commercial Code as the sources of law to determine whether an offer exists.[43]

As an example of the application of this standard, in *Linear Technology Corp. v. Micrel, Inc.*, the court examined whether the patentee had engaged in on-sale activity through a series of promotional activities for a newly developed silicon chip that incorporated patented circuitry.[44] The court applied the common law definition of an "offer," as "the manifestation of willingness to enter into a bargain, so made as to justify another person in understanding that his assent to that bargain is invited and will conclude it."[45] *Linear Technology* found that none of the patentee's promotional activity qualified. Specifically, the court found that intra-company communications could not constitute an offer because these purely internal statements were not communicated to any offeree. Likewise, the mere publication of preliminary data sheets and other promotional information were not offers because such activities only indicated preparation for upcoming sales, and not offers for an actual sale. The court held that the patentee's distribution of promotional materials to sales representatives and potential distributors was not an offer, although some orders did result afterwards. The *Linear Technology* court then faced the most difficult issue — that is, whether the third party offers created on-sale activity. Ultimately, the court found that these purchase orders were, in fact, third party offers to *buy*, rather than patentee offers to *sell*. In response, the patentee had entered these into the order system using the words "will advise," and then generated a form sent to customers that stated, among other things, "will advise," "new product/not booked/not released."[46] Emphasizing that acceptances must be objectively manifested to be effective under general principles of contract law, *Linear Technology* explained that no commercial offer for sale had occurred prior to the critical date:

> In the absence of a course of dealing or other evidence to the contrary, we think that a reasonable offeror in the distributors' position who received an acknowledgement that — unlike those for the unambiguously-accepted orders — explicitly states that the order . . . was "NOT BOOKED," would understand that [the sale] had not booked and therefore had not accepted the order.[47]

---

sell is sufficient to trigger the on-sale bar under 35 U.S.C. § 102(b). There is no requirement that the sale be completed.").

[41] Group One, Ltd. v. Hallmark Cards, Inc., 254 F.3d 1041, 1046 (Fed. Cir. 2001).

[42] *Id.* at 1047.

[43] Linear Technology Corp. v. Micrel, Inc., 275 F.3d 1040, 1048 (Fed. Cir. 2002).

[44] *Id.*

[45] *Id.* at 1050 (quoting Restatement (Second) of Contracts § 24 (1981)).

[46] *Id.* at 1045.

[47] *Id.* at 1053.

Linear Technology illustrates the application of the general rules of contract law that govern.

As described earlier, when the AIA becomes applicable, another layer of this analysis may be added. Prior precedents had allowed on-sale activity to act as an invalidating reference if based on a confidential sales agreement.[48] However, the AIA's legislative history states that the newly enacted section was intended to require that the offer or sale be publicly accessible. It is not clear whether the courts will follow the statements in the legislative history, given that Congress might have specified the "publicly on-sale," in the statute but did not do so. On the other hand, the courts may find the specific statements made on the Senate floor persuasive.[49]

§ 15.04   LICENSES AND ON-SALE ACTIVITY

On-sale activity occurs where parties engage in the sale or offer to sell a product — typically, a device or apparatus — that incorporates the claims at issue. In addition, the sale of a product made by a claimed process or method falls within the on-sale provision.[50] Likewise, a patentee's offer to perform a patented process for payment prior to the critical date has been held to constitute an on-sale bar.[51]

However, an offer or the assignment of patent rights does not.[52] Such acts are not considered as the type of commercialization that prevents patentability because of the "business realities" that such transactions might be necessary for funding to develop the invention and to prosecute the application, all of which are activities that further the goals of patent law.[53]

The distinction between a license and sale is not always clear, as demonstrated by the Federal Circuit's decision *In re Kollar.*[54] There, prior to the critical date, the patentee entered into an agreement with a company named Celanese to coordinate research efforts to build a commercial plaint to perform the claimed process. Under the agreement, Celanese obtained the right to commercialize the invention as well as necessary technical information from the patentee. In return, Celanse paid royalty payments. The *Kollar* court found that this agreement was not a sale of an invention under § 102(b), despite the fact that Celanese had obtained the right to

---

[48] Crystal Semiconductor Corp. v. Tritech Microelectronics Intern., Inc., 246 F.3d 1336 (Fed. Cir. 2001).

[49] *See* supra footnotes 17 and 18 and accompanying text.

[50] *In re* Kollar, 286 F.3d 1326, 1333 (Fed. Cir. 2002) ("Surely, a sale by the patentee or a licensee of the patent of a product made by the claimed process would constitute such a sale because that party is commercializing the patented process in the same sense as would occur when the sale of tangible patented item takes place.") (citation omitted).

[51] Scaltech, Inc. v. Retec/Tetra, L.L.C., 269 F.3d 1321, 1328 (Fed. Cir. 2001).

[52] Moleculon Research Corp. v. CBS, Inc., 793 F.2d 1261 (Fed. Cir. 1986).

[53] *See id.* at 1267 (stating that the rule "comports with the policies underlying the on-sale bar and with the business realities ordinarily surrounding a corporation's prosecution of patent applications for inventors.") (citation omitted); *see generally* Mas-Hamilton Group v. LaGard, Inc., 156 F.3d 1206 (Fed. Cir. 1998).

[54] *See Kollar*, 286 F.3d 1326.

sell the resultant product made by the claimed process. *Kollar* explained:

> Although the Celanese Agreement specifically contemplates that "resultant products" manufactured using the claimed process could *potentially* be sold, nowhere in the Celanese Agreement is there an indication that a product of the claimed process was actually offered for sale. Rather, that agreement constitutes a license to Celanese under any future patents relating to Kollar's invention. We have held that merely granting a license to an invention, without more, does not trigger the on-sale bar of § 102(b).[55]

Similarly, in *Elan Corp., PLC v. Andrx Pharmaceuticals, Inc.*,[56] the Federal Circuit held that a letter offering to license a patent and to become a partner in the clinical testing and the eventual marketing of pharmaceuticals made under the patent at some indefinite point in the future was not an offer to sell a commercial product.

Notwithstanding *Kollar* and *Elan*, the use of the term "license" does not render a transaction necessarily ineffective to create an on-sale bar. For example, in *Minton v. National Association of Securities Dealers, Inc.*,[57] the patentee licensed a software program used to execute stock trades prior to the critical date. *Minton* found the transaction triggered the one-year grace period of § 102(b), even though this transaction was labeled as a license rather than as a sale. In particular, the court was persuaded by the fact that as part of the transaction the patentee had transferred a fully operational computer program that implemented the claimed method as well as a warranty of workability. *Minton* distinguished *Kollar*, where further development was required before the claimed process could be performed, commercialized and sold.

Although a license to the future patent is not the sale of a product under § 102(b), some transactions are difficult to characterize. To qualify as an invalidating transaction as an on-sale bar, a license to the patent right that may result in future sales is not a commercial sale. On the other hand, a transaction that includes a transfer of a *product* within the scope of the claims at issue will be considered an on-sale bar, even if titled as a license. Thus, courts examine the substance of a transaction in light of the policies of § 102(b) to determine whether such agreements constitute a statutory bar.

§ 15.05   CONCLUSION

Under 35 U.S.C. § 102, an invention is not patentable if it was "on-sale in this country, more than one year prior to the date of the application for patent in the United States." Under the Supreme Court's *Pfaff* decision, a patent will not issue (or will be held invalid) if an inventor or third party offers to sell or sells a product that is considered ready for patenting more than one year prior to the patent application's filing date.

---

[55] *Id.* at 1330-31 (footnote omitted, italics in original).

[56] Elan Corp., PLC v. Andrx Pharm., Inc., 366 F.3d 1336 (Fed. Cir. 2004).

[57] Minton v. National Ass'n. of Sec. Dealers, Inc., 336 F.3d 1373 (Fed. Cir. 2003).

Pfaff's ready for patenting standard requires either reduction to practice or an enabling disclosure. The Federal Circuit has held that the determination of whether an offer for sale has occurred is based on general contractual principles as reflected in court interpretations of the Uniform Commercial Code. Together, these rules are designed to effectuate a number of policies, including the prompt disclosure of inventions and prohibiting inventors from obtaining a patent after a long period of obtaining the benefits of commercial sales.

For patents that will be evaluated under the AIA, it is likely that the courts will adopt the prior precedential interpretations of on-sale bar in the prior law. However, the courts may find that — based on the AIA's legislative history — confidential or private sales might no longer qualify. Although the PTO may promulgate some guidance to its examiners as the AIA is implemented into the examination process in early March 2013, it can be expected that definitive interpretations of the AIA are still some years away.

Chapter 16

ABANDONMENT AND THE PRE-AIA 35 U.S.C. § 102(c)

SYNOPSIS

§ 16.01 INTRODUCTION

§ 16.02 HISTORIC BACKGROUND OF ABANDONMENT

§ 16.03 PATENTEE DELAY

§ 16.04 ABANDONED INVENTION v. ABANDONED APPLICATION

§ 16.05 DISCLOSED BUT UNCLAIMED SUBJECT MATTER

§ 16.06 CONCLUSION

§ 16.01 INTRODUCTION

The pre-AIA 35 U.S.C. § 102(c) provides that "[a] person shall be entitled to a patent unless . . . he has *abandoned* the invention."[1] As one court explained, "[t]he concept of abandonment of an invention is not a simple one and the meaning of the phrase is not self-evident."[2] Fundamentally, this section refers to a patentee's intentional abandonment of the right to obtain a patent. Abandonment may be express, for example based on an inventor's statement that patent protection will not be sought or that the invention is available for public use.[3] Alternatively, the patentee's intent to abandon an invention may be implied from conduct.[4]

This version of § 102(c) was added to the Patent Act in 1952 founded on several earlier statutory provisions.[5] Because § 102(c) addresses an inventor's conduct after the invention date, it fits best within the category of a statutory bar.[6] That categorization is imperfect, because the section does not identify any critical date. Moreover, case law interpreting this provision is sparse. This may be because in many instances the grounds for abandonment overlap with other, more specific provisions of § 102, such as the statutory bars of the pre-AIA § 102(b). In those

---

[1] 35 U.S.C. § 102 (2002).

[2] *In re* Gibbs, 437 F.2d 486, 488 (C.C.P.A. 1971).

[3] *Id.* at 490.

[4] *Id.; see also* MPEP § 2134 ("Abandonment under 35 U.S.C. § 102(c) requires a deliberate, though not necessarily express, surrender to any rights to a patent").

[5] *See* H.R. REP. No. 82-1923, at 17 (1952) (accompanying H.R. 7794) (noting that § 102(c) derives from prior versions of the Patent Act).

[6] OddzOn Products, Inc. v. Just Toys, Inc., 122 F.3d 1396, 1402 (Fed. Cir. 1997) (referring to § 102(c) as a loss-of-right provision).

cases, it may be redundant to invoke § 102(c) as an additional ground where the other provisions more clearly control.[7]

The AIA omits any corollary to the 1952 version of § 102(c). This may be due to the elimination of the statutory bars from the AIA, as well as the shift to the effective filing date as the determinative critical date. Given that the pre-AIA § 102(c) appears to have been only rarely invoked, this deletion may have little practical impact on the patent system.

§ 16.02   HISTORIC BACKGROUND OF ABANDONMENT

Some very early cases considering abandonment provide insight into its under-lying policies. For example, in the 1813 decision *Whittemore v. Cutter*, Justice Story noted that particular features of an invention that had been in public use for an extended time period had fallen into the public domain.[8] Story framed invalidity of the patent in terms of abandonment, explaining that if an inventor of the disclosed features:

> . . . suffered them to be used freely and fully by the public at large for so many years . . . he must be deemed to have made a gift of them to the public, as much as a person, who voluntarily opens his land as a highway, and suffers it to remain for a length of time devoted to public use.[9]

Storey restated these same observations in 1829, this time writing for the U.S. Supreme Court in *Pennock v. Dialogue.*[10] There, the patentee had authorized the manufacture and sale of the invention for several years before applying for the patent. In assessing the propriety of a jury instruction on abandonment based on public use, Story wrote:

> . . . [it] cannot be denied, that an inventor may abandon his invention, and surrender or dedicate it to the public. This inchoate right, thus gone, cannot afterwards be resumed at his pleasure; for where gifts are once made to the public in this way, they become absolute.[11]

Today, the public use at issue in *Pennock* is typically determined based on the statutory bar of the pre-AIA § 102(b), rather than abandonment under § 102(c). Nonetheless, the *Pennock* opinion partially forms the foundation for the principle that an inventor's conduct can constitute an abandonment of the ability to obtain the patent.[12]

Abandonment is grounded on the principle that a patentee should not be permitted to profit by delay in seeking a patent. For example, in the 1917 decision *Macbeth-Evans Glass Co. v. General Electric Co.*, the circuit court affirmed a

---

[7] *Gibbs*, 437 F.2d at 906.

[8] Whittemore v. Cutter, 29 F. Cas. 1123, 1124 (C.C. Mass. 1813).

[9] *Id.*

[10] Pennock v. Dialogue, 27 U.S. 1 (1829).

[11] *Id.* at 16.

[12] *See generally* Invitrogen Corp. v. Biocrest Mfg., L.P., 424 F.3d 1374, 1381 (2005) (citing Pennock in assessing whether an inventor had engaged in public use of the invention).

finding of invalidity where the patentee used the claimed process in secret for years prior to filing the application.[13] This process was used to produce glass products that were sold to the public. The *Macbeth-Evans* court held that the patentee had abandoned the ability to patent by electing to rely on trade secret protection while profiting from the improvement. The court's invalidity ruling was based on the concern that a patentee should not unduly delay disclosure of an invention, "with an intent to expand the statutory period of monopoly and thereby reap additional profits."[14]

The abandonment doctrine recognizes that an inventor who elects to relinquish a right to obtain the patent is bound by that choice. This determination may be based on conduct inconsistent with a desire to patent, such as demonstrated by the public use at issue in the *Pennock* decision or reliance on trade secret protection to create a commercial product, as in the *Macbeth-Evans* case.

§ 16.03   PATENTEE DELAY

Interpreting the pre-AIA § 102(c), the U.S. PTO, has stated that a patentee's mere delay in seeking patent protection is not sufficient to support a finding of abandonment.[15] Synthesizing this rule with *Macbeth-Evans*, one who maintains an invention in secret would not abandon their invention so long as the patentee obtained no commercial benefit from doing so.[16] This is consistent with the U.S. Supreme Court's 1878 decision, *Bates v. Coe*, which held that "[i]nventors may, if they can, keep their invention secret; and if they do for any length of time, they do not forfeit their right to apply for a patent, unless another in the mean time has made the invention" and obtained the patent instead.[17]

This principle has some tangential support in the more recent Federal Circuit case *Moleculon Research Corp. v. CBS, Inc.*[18] There, the court held that an inventor who had maintained his invention in secret without any commercial activity for a number of years prior to seeking a patent did not lose the right to patent under the public use provision of § 102(b). Neither the U.S. Supreme Court nor the Federal Circuit has directly ruled on this issue under § 102(c).

Even where the patentee has engaged in some commercial activity, a patentee's delay of less than one year does not support a finding of abandonment. This principle was established in the Court of Custom and Patent Appeals' decision *In re*

---

[13] *See* Macbeth-Evans Glass Co. v. Gen. Elec. Co., 246 F. 695 (6th Cir. 1917).

[14] *Id.*

[15] *See* MPEP § 2134. This section of the MPEP cites conflicting district court authority for this proposition, and the Federal Circuit does not appear to have resolved this issue.

[16] *But see* Davis Harvester Co., Inc. v. Long Mfg. Co., 252 F. Supp. 989, 1010 (E.D.N.C. 1966) ("Mere delay will not amount to abandonment, but nonclaim for a period of time of considerable duration will result in abandonment due to the fact that the intention of the patent laws is defeated.").

[17] Bates v. Coe, 98 U.S. 31, 46 (1878).

[18] *See* Moleculon Research Corp. v. CBS, Inc., 793 F.2d 1261 (Fed. Cir. 1986) (considering validity under 35 U.S.C. § 102(b)).

Gibbs,[19] which held that it was of "no significance" "whether the duration of the hiatus was one or 364 days," so long as the filing occurred within the statutory grace period of § 102(b), the patentee had not abandoned the opportunity to obtain a patent.[20]

§ 16.04   ABANDONED INVENTION v. ABANDONED APPLICATION

The pre-AIA § 102(c) considers abandonment of an *invention* — that is, conduct that results in a permanent loss of the right to obtain a patent. By contrast, a patent applicant may abandon *an application* during prosecution, whether by filing a statement of abandonment by one authorized to do so or by some other conduct, such as failing to respond to a PTO Office Action.[21] Despite use of the term "abandonment" in both contexts, the abandonment of a patent application on file with the U.S. PTO is not necessarily an abandonment of an invention under the pre-AIA § 102(c).[22] For example, a patentee who files a subsequent application can negate the inference of an abandonment of the *invention* set forth in the prior application. In that instance, a patentee may have abandoned the patent application without abandoning the right to obtain a later patent.

§ 16.05   DISCLOSED BUT UNCLAIMED SUBJECT MATTER

Does a patentee invoke abandonment by failing to claim an invention that has been described in an earlier application? Some cases indicate that these circumstances raise an inference of abandonment. For example, in the 1931 case *Shipp v. Scott School Township*,[23] the court determined that a patentee who filed an application disclosing novel features of an invention that did not include claims corresponding to the disclosure raised the inference that "the inventor intended to waive his right to a patent monopoly upon the unclaimed novel feature of his invention."[24]

In 1971, the *Gibbs* court explained that a prima facie inference of abandonment of an invention can be rebutted in any of several different ways: 1) by a subsequent patent application claiming the invention filed within one year of the issuance of the initial application; 2) by a broadening reissue application filed in compliance with the two year limitation; or 3) by a co-pending application filed before the initial patent issues, "and possibly even thereafter."[25]

---

[19] *In re* Gibbs, 437 F.2d 486 (C.C.P.A. 1971).

[20] *Id.* at 489-90; *see also* MPEP § 2134 ("Any inference of abandonment (i.e., intent to dedicate to the public) of subject matter disclosed but not claimed in a previously issued patent is rebuttable by an application filed at any time before a statutory bar arises").

[21] *See* 37 C.F.R. §§ 1.135, 1.138 (2007); *see generally* MPEP § 711.

[22] *See* Marvin Glass & Assoc. v. Sears, Roebuck & Co., 318 F. Supp. 1089, 1101 (S.D. Tex. 1970) ("The abandonment of a patent application is not synonymous with abandonment of the invention.").

[23] Shipp v. Scott Sch. Twp., 54 F.2d 1019 (7th Cir. 1931).

[24] *Id.* at 1021.

[25] *In re* Gibbs, 437 F.2d 486, 494 (C.C.P.A. 1971).

Layered over this aspect of *Gibbs* is the American Inventor's Protection Act passed in 1999, which presumptively authorizes the publication of patent applications prior to issuance.[26] An inventor might be deemed to have dedicated an unclaimed invention to the public by the application of pre-AIA § 102(b)'s statutory bar that would consider a published U.S. patent as a printed publication. This result might be the same under the AIA § 102(a)(1), which holds that disclosures in a printed publication made after the effective filing date constitute prior art subject to the inventor grace period. Additionally, the AIA § 102(a)(2) establishes this same rule for U.S. patents and published U.S. applications. Under the new law, a disclosure in a patent or published application constitutes prior art.

As *Gibbs* suggests, the issue might be avoided through an appropriately filed continuation application through 35 U.S.C. § 120. If the patentee follows this procedure, the effective filing date of the inventor's second application is the same as the originally filed parent application and therefore no priority problem would arise.

§ 16.06 CONCLUSION

The pre-AIA version of § 102(c) provides that an inventor may intentionally abandon the right to obtain a patent. Although delay is not typically considered sufficient to demonstrate abandonment, other conduct, such as public use or an express disclaimer of intent to seek a patent may suffice. Abandonment is grounded on the principles that an inventor's voluntary relinquishment of an inchoate patent right should be deemed binding, causing the invention to become part of the public domain. Further, abandonment is invoked if an inventor seeks to artificially extend the patent term by profiting from the secret commercial use of an invention for a period of longer than one year. Because much of the conduct that was formerly encompassed within the abandonment doctrine has been subsumed in other provisions of the pre-AIA § 102, few cases have construed that subsection, and it appears to have been used infrequently.

The AIA does not include abandonment as an express ground for rejection or invalidation. Because the AIA has a very different structure and policy than the former law, each set of facts must be separately analyzed to determine the most likely result. Further, one who seeks to abandon an invention might do so by legal mechanisms outside of § 102, such as a contract not to sue or estoppel.

---

[26] American Inventor's Protection Act of 1999, Pub. L. No. 106-113, 113 Stat. 1501 (1999).

Chapter 17

PRIOR PATENTS

SYNOPSIS

§ 17.01 INTRODUCTION

§ 17.02 OPERATION OF THE PRE-AIA 35 U.S.C. § 102(d)

§ 17.03 IDENTIFYING PRIOR ART THAT IS "PATENTED"

§ 17.04 CLAIM SCOPE AND VALIDITY OF THE FOREIGN PATENT

§ 17.05 WHEN IS A FOREIGN INVENTION "PATENTED?"

§ 17.06 DISTINCTION BETWEEN § 102(d) AND THE "PATENTED" PROVISIONS OF §§ 102(a) & (b)

§ 17.07 CONCLUSION

§ 17.01 INTRODUCTION

The pre-AIA 35 U.S.C. § 102(d) provides that a patent will not be granted if the invention has been *previously patented* in a foreign country by the inventor more than twelve (12) months prior to the filing of an application for a U.S. patent.[1] As a doctrine that operates after invention and using the one year grace period, it operates as a statutory bar. The section was enacted to encourage patentees to file a U.S. application promptly after seeking and obtaining a foreign patent.[2]

The AIA presents a far more simplified approach toward that same goal. According to the new § 102(a)(1), the prior art includes a claimed invention that was "patented" prior to the effective filing date of the claim under examination. This section has no geographic restriction and applies to both inventors and third parties.[3] When read in connection with 35 U.S.C. § 119, the inventor can file a U.S. patent application within one year after the original foreign filing. Using this

---

[1] 35 U.S.C. § 102(d) (2000 & Supp. IV 2004). This pre-AIA version of this section states as follows:

A person shall be entitled to a patent unless —

d. the invention was first patented or caused to be patented, or was the subject of an inventor's certificate, by the applicant or his legal representatives or assigns in a foreign country prior to the date of the application for patent in this country on an application for patent or inventor's certificate filed more than twelve months before the filing of the application in the United States . . . .

[2] *In re* Kathawala, 9 F.3d 942, 946 (Fed. Cir. 1993).

[3] The section is subject to an exception for an inventor's disclosure during the one-year grace period. The AIA § 102(a)(2) is not analogous, given that the subsection requires that an application "names another inventor." In contrast, the pre-AIA § 102(d) considers a prior foreign application of the same inventor.

procedure, the effective filing date of the inventor's U.S. patent is the same as the original foreign filing date.[4] This mechanism allows the inventor to obtain a U.S. patent and rely on the date of the foreign filing to establish priority.

§ 17.02　OPERATION OF THE PRE-AIA 35 U.S.C. § 102(d)

The pre-AIA § 102(d) bars a patent where four requirements are met:

1. First, the patentee must file a patent application in a *foreign country*;

2. Subsequently, the patentee must file a U.S. patent application that claims the *same subject matter* as the previous foreign application;

3. The foreign patent *must issue before* the applicant files for a U.S. patent application; and

4. The filing date of the U.S. application must be *more than twelve (12) months* after the foreign application's filing date.[5]

This section operates as a statutory bar, in that it causes the inventor to the lose the right to patent despite the fact that she is the first to invent.

The following example illustrates how the rule operates.[6] Consider whether a U.S. patent application should issue in light of the inventor's prior patent application filed in Great Britain on July 21, 1970. The British application issued on April 11, 1973, two days before the applicant filed for patent protection for the same subject matter in the U.S.

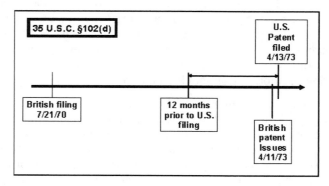

Under these facts, all conditions of the pre-AIA § 102(d) are met and the U.S. patent is barred. Specifically, the patentee has filed a patent application in a foreign country — here, Great Britain, on July 21, 1970. Second, the U.S. patent claimed the same subject matter as that disclosed in the British application. Third, the British patent issued *before* the patentee's U.S. filing. Finally, the patentee's U.S. patent

---

[4]　35 U.S.C. § 100(i)(1)(B).

[5]　*See* Bayer AG v. Schein Pharmaceuticals, Inc., 301 F.3d 1306, 1312 (Fed. Cir. 2002).

[6]　This hypothetical is based on *In re Monks*, 588 F.2d 308 (C.C.P.A. 1978), a case discussed later in this chapter.

application was filed more than twelve months after the foreign application's filing date.

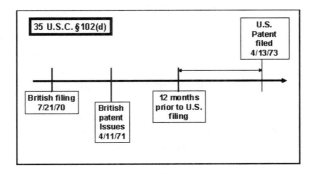

Notably, the pre-AIA § 102(d)'s requirements are met where the foreign patent issues *at any time* prior to the U.S. patent filing, whether or not the foreign patent issues before or after the twelve month window. Thus, if we modify the facts of our hypothetical so that the foreign patent issues on April 11, 1971, a date prior to the twelve month time period, the result is the same. That is, the bar arises and the U.S. patent cannot be granted.

§ 17.03   IDENTIFYING PRIOR ART THAT IS "PATENTED"

Both the pre-AIA and AIA versions of the statute use the term "patented." Does this only refer to utility patents, or are analogous intellectual property rights within that definition? Certainly, other countries grant intellectual property protection that is at variance with the substantive scope of U.S. law. Further, foreign systems do not always describe such protections using the same terminology and procedures used in U.S. law.

Courts construing the pre-AIA § 102(d) have concluded that a "patent" may include forms of protection that do not identically correspond with U.S. patent rights, "so long as such foreign rights are both *substantial* and *exclusive in nature*."[7] The historic origin of this standard is a 1967 case, *In re Weiss*, that examined a U.S. design patent application by an inventor who had previously filed for protection under a Geschmackmuster, a German registration system for the protection of industrial designs.[8] Noting that the German protection was somewhat akin to a U.S. copyright, the *Weiss* court explained that Germany's Geschmacks-muster system required the applicant to simply place a form on file at a local office along with a drawing or sample of the article to be protected. Unlike the U.S. design registration system, which requires individualized examination by the U.S. PTO, protection commences for a Geschmackmuster upon the filing of the registration

---

[7] *See In re* Carlson, 983 F.2d 1032, 1036 (Fed. Cir. 1992).

[8] *In re* Weiss, 159 U.S.P.Q. (BNA) 122 (Pat. Off. Bd. App. 1967); *see also, In re* Talbott, 443 F.2d 1397 (C.C.P.A. 1971) (finding that a German Geschmackmuster constituted a prior patent for purposes of 35 U.S.C. § 102(d)).

form. In a typical case, shortly after such filing, a list of registered designs is then published and distributed to the public.

In *Weiss*, the patentee argued that a prior German filing was not a prior "patent" for purposes of § 102(d), as the Geschmacksmuster protects only against actual copying by another.[9] Despite this disparity in protection, the *Weiss* court held that the Geschmackmuster qualified as a prior foreign patent under the pre-AIA § 102(d). *Weiss* explained that the German registration system provided for both "substantial and exclusive" rights precisely *because* rights under German law were similar to a U.S. copyright. Specifically, the court reasoned that such rights are "substantial otherwise, it could be argued that the rights under the United States copyright laws are not."[10] *Weiss* found that the Geschmackmuster provided for an exclusive right, just as copyrights provided for exclusivity that "may even be referred to as monopoly rights."[11]

A Court of Custom and Patent Appeals decision, *In re Talbott*, considered and determined that a disparity in the *nature* of the right granted by a foreign government does not eliminate the foreign filing as prior art under § 102(d).[12] In addressing a patentee's arguments, again concerning the German Geschmackmuster, *Talbott* explained:

> [The patentee] asserts that the provisions of section 102(d) may properly be applied, if at all, where the foreign rights differ from those to be obtained in the United States only in "scope" and not where, as here, they differ in their "nature". Recognizing that such a distinction may be made, we nevertheless believe it is not significant . . . . [I]t is sufficient if the inventor receives from the foreign country the exclusive privilege that its laws provide for.[13]

Thus, so long as the foreign right is both substantial and exclusive, the fact that a foreign right is in the nature of *copyright*, rather than *patent*, does not necessarily bar reliance on the prior foreign patent as prior art. Although it remains to be seen whether the AIA's definition of "patented" will rely on this same line of authorities, this interpretation is likely to be found relevant to the meaning of the term in the newly enacted statute.

§ 17.04   CLAIM SCOPE AND VALIDITY OF THE FOREIGN PATENT

How closely must the subject matter of the foreign filing match the U.S. patent to qualify as prior art under this section? The Federal Circuit has not required the *strict identity* standard applicable to other portions of § 102. This issue was

---

[9] This system stands in contrast to U.S. patent law, which grants a right to exclude others even where the infringing work is independently developed. *See* Kewanee Oil Co. v. Bicron Corp., 416 U.S. 470, 478 (1974) (patent right to exclude extends to works of independent creation).

[10] *Weiss*, 159 U.S.P.Q. at 124.

[11] *Id.*

[12] *In re* Talbott, 443 F.2d 1397 (C.C.P.A. 1971).

[13] *Id.* at 1399 (quotation and citation omitted).

explored in *In re Kathawala*, which considered whether a patentee could obtain a U.S. patent for a particular chemical compound used in pharmaceuticals.[14] The patentee's U.S. application was filed more than one year after patents in both Spain and Greece had been applied for and issued. In *Kathawala*, the applicant's Spanish patent was directed to a process for making a particular compound. According to the applicant, pharmaceutical compounds were not patentable under Spanish law and essentially the pursuit of such claims was futile. However, the patentee's U.S. patent included claims directed to the compounds.

Despite the lack of strict identity between the Spanish patent and the U.S. application, the Federal Circuit held the U.S. claims unpatentable. *Kathawala* explained that the futility of seeking protection for the compounds in Spain was not relevant, as "[w]hat is controlling is that the application that Kathawala filed in Spain disclosed and provided the opportunity to claim all aspects of his invention, including the compounds."[15] The *Kathawala* court emphasized that the purpose of the pre-AIA § 102(d) would be frustrated by permitting a patentee to pursue one type of claim in a foreign jurisdiction, only to later pursue a U.S. application beyond the statutory time period, explaining, "[a]n applicant cannot evade the statutory bar by citing alleged defects of foreign law concerning scope of patentable subject matter."[16]Here, the patentee's delay more than one year after the foreign filing date was fatal.

In re Kathawala stands for another important proposition. That is, a foreign patent may bar the issuance of a U.S. patent regardless of the foreign patent's validity. Specifically, Kathawala's Greek patent included claims for a chemical compound, composition and methods of use. The patentee argued that these claims were erroneously issued as invalid as non-statutory subject matter under Greek law, and that therefore such claims were not "patented" within the meaning of the pre-AIA § 102(d). The Federal Circuit held that the U.S. patent could not be granted regardless, explaining:

> Even assuming that Kathawala's compound, composition, and method of use claims are not enforceable in Greece . . . the controlling fact for purposes of section 102(d) is that the Greek patent issued containing claims directed to the same invention as that of the U.S. application. When a foreign patent issues with claims directed to the same invention as the U.S. application, the invention is "patented" within the meaning of section 102(d); validity of the foreign claims is irrelevant to the section 102(d) inquiry.[17]

In summary, under *Kathawala*, U.S. patent examiners and courts are not required to engage in an invalidity analysis under foreign law. Rather, the foreign jurisdiction's decision to issue protection can be accepted at face value in determining whether the U.S. patent is barred under the pre-AIA § 102(d). It is anticipated

---

[14] *In re* Kathawala, 9 F.3d 942 (Fed. Cir. 1993).

[15] *Id.* at 947.

[16] *Id.*

[17] *Id.* at 945.

that the definition of "patented" under the AIA § 102 is likely to follow these same principles.

§ 17.05 WHEN IS A FOREIGN INVENTION "PATENTED?"

Procedures for granting intellectual property protection vary from country to country. For example, a German Geschmackmuster becomes enforceable upon the filing of the registration form. However, a registrant may elect to keep the form secret until protection expires.[18] Does the foreign filing become "patented" for purposes of this subsection when the right becomes effective or when the foreign invention is disclosed to the public? Because invalidity under this section requires that the foreign patent actually issue prior to the applicant's U.S. application, the matter is important to determining the date that a foreign patent becomes "first patented . . . in a foreign country."[19]

In *In re Monks*, the Court of Customs and Patent Appeals determined that a foreign filing became patented for purposes of the pre-AIA § 102(d) at the time that the right is first *fixed, settled and enforceable.*[20] In *Monks*, the patentee had filed a British patent application which became publicly available on April 11, 1973. Several months later, in August, 1973, the British patent was "sealed." Under British law, a patent that is sealed can then be enforced, and a patentee is entitled to obtain damages back to the initial date of the patent's publication.[21]

Examining the legislative history of the section, *Monks* pointed out that the pre-AIA § 102(d) had been adopted as part of the 1952 amendments to the Patent Act, representing a change from the prior version of the statute. Specifically, in 1952, the enactment of § 102(d) added a requirement that the foreign patent be actually granted or issued to trigger applicability. *Monks* reasoned that this change demonstrated a Congressional intent to require "a formal bestowal of patent rights from the sovereign to the applicant such as that which occurs when a British patent is sealed."[22] Although the court acknowledged that damages became available retroactive to the date of the British publication, the court emphasized that such publication was "no certificate that a patent has been granted and no rights accrue to him as a patentee" as a result.[23] Under *Monks*, foreign protection becomes "first patented" when the right is fixed and enforceable, rather than at the commencement of the damages accrual period.

In the 1993 *Kathawala* decision, the Federal Circuit affirmed the continued viability of the *Monks* decision, finding that "an invention is 'patented' in a foreign country under § 102(d) when the patentee's rights under the patent become fixed."[24] In addition, *Kathawala* held that a patent need not be publicly available to

---

[18] *Weiss*, 159 U.S.P.Q. at 124.

[19] 35 U.S.C. § 102(d) (2000 & Supp. IV 2004).

[20] *In re* Monks, 588 F.2d 308 (C.C.P.A. 1978).

[21] *Id.* at 309.

[22] *Id.* at 310.

[23] *Id.* at 311.

[24] *In re* Kathawala, 9 F.3d 942, 946 (Fed. Cir. 1993).

constitute a patent under this section. Under these precedents, the enforceability — and not the public availability — of the foreign protection is dispositive of the time that the foreign right is "first patented."

Whether the AIA will follow all of these principles is open to question. As discussed in Chapter 12, it is not clear whether prior art under the AIA must be publicly accessible.[25] This is particularly problematic for the *Kathawala* interpretation, because the term "patented" in both the pre-AIA § 102(a) and (b) refer to publicly issued patents.[26] It can be expected that the courts will attempt to resolve this issue, although certainty on this point may be several years away.

§ 17.06   DISTINCTION BETWEEN § 102(d) AND THE "PATENTED" PROVISIONS OF §§ 102(a) & (b)

The AIA has incorporated the principles of several distinct subsections of the pre-AIA § 102(a)(1) into a single word — *patented.* In contrast, the pre-AIA version uses the term in several different subsections. For patents evaluated under the previous version, how are these subsections distinct?

Under the pre-AIA § 102(a) and (b), the provision is comparatively straightforward. A later patent will not be granted where the invention has already been patented.[27] Of course, the critical dates for each of these are different — the pre-AIA § 102(a) uses the date of first invention, while the pre-AIA § 102(b) uses the statutory bar date of one year prior to the application.

How is the pre-AIA § 102(d) different from (a) and (b)? Section 102(d) is both narrower and analytically distinct. For example, as a novelty provision, § 102(a) does not apply to an inventor's own work. In contrast, § 102(d) specifically targets prior patents of the same inventor. As a further dissimilarity, § 102(b)'s prohibition on prior patents includes filings by both inventors *and* third parties. Third party patents are not implicated by § 102(d). In addition, § 102(d) applies *solely* to prior foreign patents. Sections 102(a) and (b) apply to both U.S. and foreign patents. Furthermore, a prior patent for purposes of both sections (a) and (b) must be publicly available.[28] However, under § 102(d), a foreign patent that has been issued is sufficient even if that patent is kept in secret for some period of time after the patent has issued.[29]

§ 17.07   CONCLUSION

The pre-AIA § 102(d) bars a claim where the inventor has previously filed for a patent in a foreign country more than twelve (12) months prior to the filing of an application for a U.S. patent, where the foreign entity issues the patent before the patentee files for patent protection in the U.S. To qualify as an invalidating

---

[25] Chapter 12, section § 12.04.

[26] *In re* Carlson, 983 F.2d 1032 (Fed. Cir. 1992).

[27] 35 U.S.C. § 102(a), (b).

[28] *In re* Carlson, 983 F.2d 1032 (Fed. Cir. 1992).

[29] *See* MPEP §§ 2126, 2135.01; *see generally In re* Talbott, 443 F.2d 1397, 1398-99 (C.C.P.A. 1971).

reference, the patentee's foreign patent must be filed more than one year prior to the effective date of the U.S. patent application and claim approximately the same subject matter. Further, the foreign patent must issue before the U.S. patent application is filed. Although the definition of "patented" under § 102(d) authorities is expected to hold persuasive force under the AIA, this amendment had introduced some ambiguity. As one primary example, it is not clear whether non-public patents will constitute prior art under the newly enacted statute.

Chapter 18

EARLIER FILED PATENTS AND APPLICATIONS

SYNOPSIS

§ 18.01　INTRODUCTION

§ 18.02　U.S. PATENT APPLICATIONS

    [A]　Origins of U.S. Patents as Prior Art

    [B]　*In re Hilmer*: Prior U.S. Patents and Foreign Filings

§ 18.03　PATENT APPLICATIONS FILED UNDER THE PATENT COOPERATION TREATY

§ 18.04　PUBLISHED PATENT APPLICATIONS

§ 18.05　CONCLUSION

§ 18.01　INTRODUCTION

As discussed in Chapter 12, 35 U.S.C. § 102 of the Patent Act is in a time of transition. The version of § 102(e) that predates the American Invents Act (AIA),[1] includes within the prior art any reference that constitutes any of the following three categories:

- First, an issued *U.S. patent*.

- Second, a prior application that has been published by the U.S. PTO pursuant to the *American Inventors Protection Act of 1999* (the *AIPA*).

- Third, an international patent application filed under the *Patent Cooperation Treaty (PCT)* that designates the United States and has been published by the World Intellectual Property Organization (WIPO) in the English language.

Under this pre-AIA version of the Act, a prior art reference that falls into any of these three categories must pre-date the subject claim's date of invention and either expressly or inherently disclose all limitations of that subject claim.[2] Because this subsection specifies that the prior patent or application be "by another," an inventor's own prior work is excluded. As a general rule, the effective date of a U.S. patent or U.S. published patent application is the filing date. Reliance on foreign filings to establish priority is not permitted under the pre-AIA law. Consistent with the pre-AIA's first to invent system, an inventor can avoid references that pre-date

---

[1] The effective filing dates of each version of the statute are described in Chapter 12.

[2] SSIH Equipment S.A. v. U.S. Intern. Trade Com'n, 718 F.2d 365, 377 (Fed. Cir. 1983).

her application by establishing an earlier date of invention.

To a limited degree, the AIA incorporates some of these principles. Consistent with the prior authorities, the AIA § 102(a)(2) establishes that a U.S. patent and/or a published U.S. patent application that "names another inventor" constitutes prior art. Consistent with pre-AIA law, references must either expressly or inherently disclose all limitations of the subject claim. However, according to the AIA § 102(a)(2), the effective filing date of such references is the *earliest* of any of the following:

- The filing date of the first foreign application to which a later U.S. application establishes priority under § 119;

- The filing date of the first application to which a later continuation application has established priority under § 120;

- The filing date of the first U.S. application to which a later U.S. divisional application establishes priority under § 121;

- The filing date of the first PCT application to which a later U.S. application establishes priority under § 365(a, b);

- The filing date of the first PCT application to which a later U.S. continuation application establishes priority under § 365(c); or

- The application's actual filing date in the U.S. PTO.[3]

Unlike the pre-AIA law, the AIA does not permit the inventor to swear behind another's patent based on an earlier date of invention. Moreover, as the discussion in Chapter 12 details, the AIA § 102(b)(2) exempts from the prior art U.S. patents and published U.S. patent applications that disclose inventions that are obtained from an inventor or joint inventor, as well as those that are owned by the same person or are subject to a joint research agreement on the effective filing date.

§ 18.02   U.S. PATENT APPLICATIONS

[A]   Origins of U.S. Patents as Prior Art

The pre-AIA § 102(e) was initially added to the Patent Act in 1952 as the statutory embodiment of the U.S. Supreme Court's 1926 decision *Alexander Milburn Co. v. Davis-Bournonville Co.*[4] The *Milburn* opinion, drafted by Justice Holmes, considered the validity of the Whitford patent, which was directed to an improvement for a welding and cutting apparatus. In that case, the invalidity defense was based on a patent issued to Clifford from an application that had been filed prior to the Whitford application.

The presumed date of invention for the Whitford patent was the application date of March 4, 1911. The case was decided based on the then-current version of the

---

[3] 35 U.S.C. § 102(a)(2) & (d) (2011).

[4] Alexander Milburn Co. v. Davis-Bournonville Co., 270 U.S. 390 (1926); *see generally* Hazeltine Research, Inc. v. Brenner, 382 U.S. 252 (1965) (describing the legislative history of 35 U.S.C. § 102(e)).

Patent Act, which stated that an accused infringer could raise a defense that the patentee "was not the original and first inventor or discoverer of any material and substantial part of the thing patented."[5] The issue presented to the *Milburn* Court was whether this section provided grounds to invalidate Whitford based on the argument that the disclosure of the Clifford patent demonstrated that Whitford was not the "original and first inventor."

It was undisputed that Clifford described — but did not claim — the same invention claimed in Whitford. The relevant dates for the Whitford and Clifford patents are summarized in the chart, below:

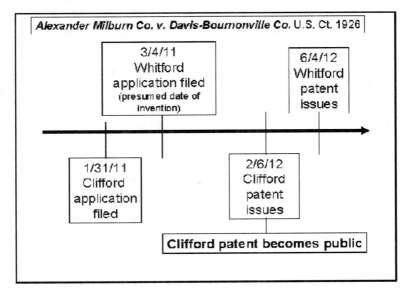

At the time that *Milburn* was decided, all U.S. patent applications remained inaccessible to the public until the Patent Office granted an application and issued the patent. Under that system, the Clifford application had remained a non-public document pending in the patent office until after Whitford's date of invention.

The *Milburn* Court considered whether the effective date of a prior patent reference was the date that the application for such a patent is *first filed* in the patent office or after such a patent *became public upon issuance*. The Court held that the former effective date was correct, and found that Clifford constituted an invalidating reference effective as of the date that the Clifford application was filed. Writing for the Court, Justice Holmes explained:

> Clifford had done all that he could do to make his description public. He had taken steps that would make it public as soon as the Patent Office did its work, although, of course, amendments might be required of him before the end could be reached. We see no reason in the words or policy of the law for

---

[5] *Alexander Milburn*, 270 U.S. at 399-400, *quoting* An Act to Revise, Consolidate, and Amend the Statutes Relating to Patents and Copyrights, ch. 230, § 61, 16 Stat. 198, 198 (1870).

allowing Whitford to profit by the delay and make himself out to be the first inventor when he was not so in fact . . .[6]

On that basis, the Court ruled the Whitford patent invalid. The *Milburn* rule was subsequently extended by the appellate courts to provide that properly supported continuation applications became part of the prior art on the date that the initial parent was filed.[7]

The *Milburn* decision is known for creating *secret prior art.* Although debated and somewhat controversial, the rule became accepted as a well established principle of patent law. As part of the 1952 amendments to the Patent Act, Congress codified this principle.[8] Specifically, in § 102(e)(2), a U.S. patent serves as a prior art reference that becomes effective on the initial filing date of the reference patent:

> A person shall be entitled to a patent unless . . . the invention was described in . . . a patent granted on an application for patent by another filed in the United States before the invention by the applicant for patent.[9]

In contrast, under the pre-AIA §§ 102(a) and (b), the term "patented" refers to all patents (domestic and foreign) that become part of the prior art when *issued.*

Modern law has adopted another aspect of the *Milburn* case. Specifically, the pre-AIA § 102(e) states that "the invention was described in" a prior U.S. patent or published U.S. application constitutes prior art. That phrase has been interpreted to mean that a prior patent need not claim, but only describe, the invention to constitute invalidating prior art consistent with the *Milburn* holding. Thus, an enabling description in another's earlier filed application which later matures into an issued patent is sufficient. This same phrase has been carried forward into the AIA § 102(a)(2) that states that an invention that "was described in" another's earlier U.S. patent or U.S. patent application constitutes prior art. As with the prior version of the statute, the Congressional choice to use the term "described in," rather than "claimed," signifies that an enabled disclosure is sufficient.[10]

Consistent with *Milburn,* the AIA establishes that another's U.S. patents and U.S. published patent applications constitute prior art as of the reference's filing

---

[6] *Id.* at 401.

[7] *In re* Klesper, 397 F.2d 882 (C.C.P.A. 1968), *but see In re* Wertheim, 646 F.2d 527 (C.C.P.A. 1981) (a reference continuation patent can become part of the prior art based on the filing date of the parent application only if the parent has a sufficient disclosure to support the later-filed reference patent).

[8] *See generally* S. Rep. No. 82-1979 (1952), *as reprinted in* 1952 U.S.C.C.A.N. 2394, 2410 ("Subsection (e) is new and enacts the rule of *Milburn v. Davis-Bournonville Co.*, 270 U.S. 390 (1926), by reason of which a United States patent disclosing an invention dates from the date of filing the application for the purpose of anticipating a subsequent inventor."); *see* Hazeltine Research, Inc. v. Brenner, 382 U.S. 252, 255 (1965) ("In its revision of the patent laws in 1952, Congress showed its approval of the holding in *Milburn* by adopting 35 U.S.C. § 102(e) (1964 ed.).").

[9] As originally enacted, Section 102(e) read "the invention described in a patent granted on an application for patent by another filed in the United States before the invention thereof by the applicant for patent." An Act to Revise and Codify the Laws Relating to Patents and the Patent Office, and to Enact Into Law Title 35 of the United States Code Entitled "Patents", ch. 950, 66 Stat. 797 (1952).

[10] Note that enablement for prior art references requires that one provide sufficient information to enable one of ordinary skill in the art to *make* the invention, but does not require one to enable one to *use* the invention. *See* Chapter 12, § 12.05.

date:

> 102(a) A person shall be entitled to a patent unless —
>
> . . . (2) the claimed invention was described in a patent issued under section 151,[11] or in an application for a patent published or deemed published under section 122(b),[12] in which the patent or application, as the case may be, names another inventor and was effectively filed before the effective filing date of the application.[13]

However, this AIA section, when read with the AIA § 102(d), provides that U.S. patents (and published U.S. patent applications) become part of the prior art on their *effective filing date*. The AIA enumerates the events that can establish the effective filing date, described in § 18.01 of this Chapter.

To apply the AIA to a hypothetical, assume that a continuation patent application was filed in the U.S. PTO on March 11, 2014, and is published on September 11, 2015. This application claimed priority to an earlier parent U.S. application filed on October 17, 2013. Can this application be used as a reference against another inventor's patent that is based on an application with an effective filing date of November 14, 2013? The answer is yes. Based on these dates, the AIA controls the inquiry. Although the application is not published until after the filing date of the other's patent, the reference has an effective filing date of October 17, 2013. Under the AIA, this published U.S. application can be used as a reference so long as other requirements, such as strict identity, have been met.

One final point should be observed. The *Milburn* Court held that the statute in force at the time of that decision required that the earlier inventor make the invention public before a reference could invalidate a later claim. As the Court explained, "it would have been no bar to Whitford's patent if Clifford had written out his prior description and kept it in his portfolio uncommunicated to anyone."[14] However, according to the pre-AIA § 102(g), some types of prior private uses of an invention might establish prior inventorship to invalidate a claim.[15] Section 102(g) was eliminated in the AIA, which appears to require a "public use," and/or information that is "otherwise available to the public."[16]

[B] *In re Hilmer*: Prior U.S. Patents and Foreign Filings

Many U.S. patentees file for patent protection in foreign jurisdictions. If a patentee files in foreign jurisdictions first, a patentee may then rely on the foreign filing as the priority date for the U.S. application where certain conditions are met. This rule dates back to 1903, when the Patent Act was modified in response to the

---

[11] 35 U.S.C. § 151 describes the issue of a U.S. patent.

[12] 35 U.S.C. § 122(b) describes that patent applications will be published 18 months after the filing date, absent certain exceptions apply.

[13] 35 U.S.C. § 102(a)(2) (2011) (emphasis added).

[14] *Id.* at 400.

[15] *See* Chapter 20; Thomson S.A. v. Quixote Corp., 166 F.3d 1172, 1175 n.3 (Fed. Cir. 1999).

[16] 35 U.S.C. § 102(a)(1) (2011).

Convention of Paris for the Protection of Intellectual Property of 20th March 1883 (also called the *Paris Convention*). Under its terms, an applicant from one member country may secure a priority date of an initial filing by filing a subsequent application in *any* member country within twelve months after the first application.[17]

After becoming a signatory to the Paris Convention, the U.S. adopted 35 U.S.C. § 119, "to provide for a right of priority in conformity with the International [Paris] Convention, for the benefit of United States citizens, by creating the necessary reciprocity with foreign members of the then Paris Union."[18] Under its terms:

> An application for patent for an invention filed in this country by any person who has . . . previously regularly filed an application for a patent for the same invention in a foreign country which affords similar privileges in the case of applications filed in the United States or to citizens of the United States, or in a WTO member country, *shall have the same effect* as the same application would have if filed in this country . . .[19]

This section allows U.S. patentees to obtain the benefit of the date of the foreign filing, so long as the inventor follows through with a U.S. patent application within one year.

Note that § 119 uses the phrase "shall have the same effect" as the foreign filing. Does this change the effective date of a U.S. patent that claims priority to a foreign counterpart under § 102(e) when the patent is used as a *reference*? In other words, under *Milburn*, the effective date of a U.S. patent is the application filing date. Where a foreign filing is made within twelve months of the U.S. application, does § 119 shift the *reference's* effective to its earlier foreign priority date? *In re Hilmer*[20] considered this question under the pre-AIA law for a U.S. application with a date of invention of July 31, 1957, the same date that the patentee Hilmer submitted a patent application in the German patent office. Nearly one year later, on July 25, 1958, Hilmer filed a U.S. application for the same invention.

---

[17] *See* Gerald J. Mossinghoff & Vivian S. Kuo, *World Patent System Circa 20XX, A.D.*, 80 J. PAT. & TRADEMARK OFF. SOC'Y 523, 526-27 (1998). For more information about the Paris Convention, *see infra* Chapter 42.

[18] *Hilmer*, 359 F.2d at 876.

[19] 35 U.S.C. § 119 (2000) (emphasis added).

[20] *See Hilmer*, 359 F.2d at 859.

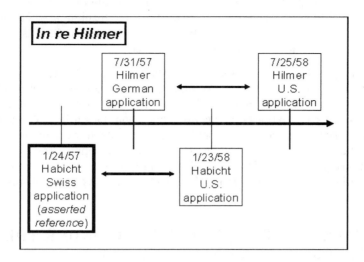

The *Hilmer* court reviewed the decision of the Board Patent Office Board of Appeals (the "Board"), which had rejected the Hilmer application based on an earlier-filed Swiss application by an inventor named Habicht. Although Habicht's U.S. application was filed *after* Hilmer's date of invention, the Board had reasoned that Habicht's U.S. application had the effective date of Habict's earlier Swiss filing. The *Hilmer* court held that § 119 does not extend the effective date of a U.S. patent reference to an earlier foreign filing date for purposes of § 102(e). Reluctant to expand the class of secret prior art, the court stated, "[s]ection 102(e) should be read to mean just what it says, 'filed in the United States.' "[21] *Hilmer* determined that the Board had erred in reading the pre-AIA § 102(e) and § 119 together, explaining that these two enactments were "totally different things, governing by different law, founded on different theories, and developed through different histories."[22] Specifically, *Hilmer* reasoned that § 119 was enacted to implement the Paris Convention, a distinct purpose from the novelty requirement of pre-AIA § 102(e).

Taking these rules together, the *Hilmer* court read § 119 as a "patent-obtaining" rule to establish foreign priority for a U.S. patent against another's prior art. However, under *Hilmer*, reliance on the pre-AIA § 119 as a "patent-defeating" rule was improper — that is, the *actual* U.S. filing date was found to be the effective date for the reference patent under the pre-AIA § 102(e), even if that reference claimed priority to a foreign application.

For patent applications filed on or after March 16, 2013, the AIA has eliminated the *Hilmer* rule. The AIA provides that U.S. patents, and published U.S. patent applications, used as references are keyed to their effective filing dates. Stated another way, the AIA provides that a U.S. patent or published U.S. patent

---

[21] *Id.* at 866.

[22] *Id.* at 863-864.

application, when used as a reference, becomes part of the prior art on its effective filing date, including one that claims priority to a foreign application.[23] This simplification can be viewed as a favorable modification to the law, as the *Hilmer* rule appeared to introduce unnecessary complexity.

Notably, the pre-AIA version of § 119(a) included a separate statutory bar based on pre-filing activity that occurred more than one year prior to the actual filing date of a U.S. patent application. Specifically, the pre-AIA § 119(a) prevented a U.S. patent from issuing where the same invention had been the subject of a prior patent, described in a printed publication, in public use or on sale, more than one year prior the actual filing date of the U.S. application. The AIA has eliminated this language, thereby simplifying the code. Under the AIA, § 119(a) can be read to implement the Paris Convention and nothing further. Its function as a type of statutory bar has been eliminated.

§ 18.03   PATENT APPLICATIONS FILED UNDER THE PATENT COOPERATION TREATY

Under the pre-AIA § 102(e)(2), a published PCT application[24] filed on or after November 29, 2000, constitutes prior art where the U.S. has been designated and the application has been published in the English language by WIPO. If these conditions are met, the PCT application can serve as a prior art reference. The effective date of such an application is the international filing date. Note that, according to the Manual of Patent Examining Procedure, a published PCT application may be entitled to a prior effective date if the PCT application relied on an earlier filing date of certain types of applications.[25]

Although the new provision has not been authoritatively construed, the AIA § 102(d) can be read to state that a U.S. patent (or a U.S. published patent application) is entitled to serve as a reference effective on the *earliest* of any foreign or international applications to a PCT application to which the U.S. establishes priority.[26] If that reading is adopted, the AIA will allow the filing date of a PCT application to which a U.S. patent (or published U.S. patent application) claims priority to establish the effective date for the reference, or alternatively a U.S. or foreign application to which the PCT application claims priority. Under the AIA, a PCT application that designates the U.S. will constitute prior art on its effective filing date even if its language has not yet been translated into English.

---

[23] 35 U.S.C. § 102(a)(2) & (d) (2011).

[24] For more about the Patent Cooperation Treaty, see § 2.06 and § 42.03 herein. *See also* MPEP § 706.02(f)(1).

[25] On this point, MPEP § 2136.03 states, "If such an international application properly claims benefit to an earlier-filed U.S. or international application, or priority to an earlier-filed U.S. provisional application, apply the reference under 35 U.S.C. 102(e) as of the earlier filing date, assuming all the conditions of 35 U.S.C. 102(e) and 35 U.S.C. 119(e), 120, or 365(c) are met."

[26] The AIA § 102(d) provides that a U.S. patent and published U.S. patent application can be used as prior art, with an effective date that claims priority to a PCT application under 35 U.S.C. § 365(a). That section, in turn, states that "a national application shall be entitled to the right of priority based on a prior filed international application which designated at least one country other than the United States."

§ 18.04 PUBLISHED PATENT APPLICATIONS

Justice Holmes' *Milburn* opinion was issued at a time when a patent application remained secret until the patent issued. During this period, an application that never issued as a patent and never became public was not available prior art.[27] Indeed, as originally passed in 1952, the pre-AIA § 102(e) specified that a patentee was entitled to a patent unless the invention was "described in a patent *granted* on an application . . . ."[28] The American Inventors Protection Act of 1999 (AIPA) subsequently modified the rule that U.S. patent applications remain confidential until issuance.[29] Currently, patent applications may be published eighteen (18) months after filing in the U.S. PTO, unless the patentee can demonstrate one of several reasons that the application should not be published.[30]

In 1999, § 102(e)(1) was amended to provide that a U.S. patent application published pursuant to the AIPA constitutes prior art. This section first opened up the class of prior art that was not possible under *Milburn* — that is, a published U.S. patent application. The effective date of such applications is the *filing* date of the published application.[31] Consistent with this rule, the AIA permits a published U.S. patent application to become part of the prior art on its effective filing date.[32]

These are earlier than the date of publication, at which point such applications can be considered "printed publications" for purposes of 35 U.S. § 102(a) and (b) because the U.S. PTO makes such documents available to the public (including on the agency's website) at that time.

§ 18.05 CONCLUSION

The pre-AIA § 102(e) encompasses three related categories of prior art. First, prior issued U.S. patents are references. Second, the prior art includes patent applications that are published pursuant to the AIPA under 35 U.S.C. § 122. Third, a PCT application qualifies only if it has been published by WIPO in English, designates the U.S., and has been filed on or after November 29, 2000. Each of these categories of prior art must disclose — but need not claim — all of the limitations of the claim that is the subject of a patentability analysis. For the U.S. references,

---

[27] *See In re* Lund, 376 F.2d 982, 991-92 (C.C.P.A. 1967).

[28] *Id.* at 988.

[29] 35 U.S.C. § 122 (2000).

[30] Specifically, 35 U.S.C. § 122(b)(2)(A) provides that "[a]n application shall not be published if that application is . . .

    (i) no longer pending;

    (ii) subject to a secrecy order under section 181 of this title;

    (iii) a provisional application filed under section 111(b) of this title; or

    (iv) an application for a design patent filed under chapter 16 of this title.

[31] Richard Neifeld, *Analysis of the New Patent Laws Enacted November 29, 1999*, 82 J. Pat. & Trademark Off. Soc'y 181, 186 (2000) (" 35 U.S.C. 102(e) is amended to provide prior art effect to a published application as of its filing date for . . . . a published U.S. national application . . . ."); Timothy R. Holbrook, *Territoriality Waning? Patent Infringement For Offering In The United States To Sell An Invention Abroad*, 37 U.C. Davis L. Rev. 701, 711 n.45 (2004).

[32] 35 U.S.C. § 102(a)(2) & (d) (2011).

the effective date is the date that the application is filed with the relevant agency. For PCT applications, the effective date is the international application's filing date or an earlier U.S. filing date to which priority has been established.

Under the AIA, the approach is simplified. U.S. patents and U.S. published patent applications constitutes prior art references effective as of their filing date, or the earliest priority date that can be established. Consistent with the *Milburn* decision, the AIA uses the terminology "described in," which connotes that the reference must describe — rather than claim — the invention to constitute prior art. The AIA has dropped the former prohibition, embodied in the *Hilmer* decision, which precluded reliance on foreign priority as a precondition as a reference. As described in Chapter 12, the AIA exempts from inventions that are obtained from an inventor, joint inventor, or were owned by the same person or subject to a joint research agreement.

Chapter 19

DERIVATION AND INVENTORSHIP

SYNOPSIS

§ 19.01 INTRODUCTION

§ 19.02 INVENTORSHIP

    [A] Who is an Inventor under the Patent Act?

    [B] Joint Inventors and Ownership

    [C] Filing a Patent Application: The Inventor's Oath

§ 19.03 WHAT IS "DERIVATION"?

    [A] The Legal Standard for Derivation

    [B] Application of § 102(f)'s Two-Prong Test

§ 19.04 DERIVATION ACTIONS UNDER THE AIA

§ 19.05 CORRECTION OF INVENTORSHIP

§ 19.06 CONCLUSION

§ 19.01 INTRODUCTION

The version of 35 U.S.C. § 102(f) enacted prior to the America Invents Act (AIA) specifies that a patent shall not be granted where the listed inventor "did not himself invent the subject matter sought to be patented."[1] This subsection enforces the principle that "one who did not himself invent the subject matter (*i.e.*, he did not originate it) has no right to a patent on it."[2] Under section 102(f), the central question is whether the listed inventor *derived* the subject matter of the application from another.[3] If so, this subsection prevents the claim.

Derivation is conceptually distinct from the pre-AIA § 102(g), which governs interference, considers *priority* of an invention among competing claims.[4] The interference proceeding determines which, usually among independent inventors, has a right to the patent under first-to-invent principles. Derivation considers whether the named inventor is the true inventor against a challenge that the invention was *obtained* from another.

---

[1] 35 U.S.C. § 102(f).

[2] *In re* Bass, 474 F.2d 1276, 1290 (C.C.P.A. 1973) (legislatively modified on other grounds).

[3] Lamb-Weston, Inc. v. McCain Foods, Ltd., 78 F.3d 540, 549 (Fed. Cir. 1996) (describing the purpose of § 102(f)) (Newman, J., dissenting).

[4] *See, e.g.*, Applegate v. Scherer, 332 F.2d 571, 573 n.1 (C.C.P.A. 1964).

There has been a recent significant shift in this area of patent law. The AIA eliminated derivation as a ground to reject or invalidate a claim, as well as interference practices, for patents with an effective filing date prior to March 16, 2013. Patent applications and issued claims subject to the AIA will not be subject to examination or invalidation on that ground. As an alternative, the AIA has created an entirely new action called a *derivation proceeding*.[5] Generally, this allows a true inventor to resolve inventorship of a claim that was obtained from the inventor. A true inventor who is a patent applicant can petition the PTO to resolve the inventorship of a claim against another who filed an earlier application that claims the same or similar subject matter. The petition must be supported by a showing that the subject matter of the claim in dispute was derived without authorization from the petitioner. Alternatively, for a patent that has issued, a true inventor may seek analogous relief in a U.S. District Court.[6]

Additional mechanisms exist. Pursuant to 35 U.S.C. § 256(a), parties may obtain a certificate correcting invention from the U.S. PTO if the matter is not contested. If the parties contest inventorship, a district court action can be filed to resolve the dispute. If the court finds that relief is warranted, an omitted inventor can be added, or alternatively, a wrongly listed inventor can be omitted. The result of such an action is a court order directing the PTO to change the patent's listed inventor consistent with the court's findings.

§ 19.02   INVENTORSHIP

[A]   Who is an Inventor under the Patent Act?

What type of activity qualifies as inventive activity? Under patent law an inventor is one who is responsible for the *conception* of the invention. Patent law defines conception as "the formation in the mind of the inventor, of a definite and permanent idea of the complete and operative invention, as it is hereafter to be applied in practice."[7] Conception requires that the inventor must have a "specific, settled idea, [of] a particular solution to the problem at hand, not just a general goal or research plan he hopes to pursue."[8]

The inventor's idea must be sufficiently detailed that the inventor could describe all of the elements of the invention in a manner that would permit one of ordinary skill to understand and then to reduce the invention to practice without undue experimentation. Conception does not require reduction to practice.[9] In most cases, an inventor's conception may be complete in the absence of confirmation that

---

[5] 35 U.S.C. § 135 (2011).

[6] 35 U.S.C. § 291 (2011).

[7] Hybritech, Inc. v. Monoclonal Antibodies, Inc., 802 F.2d 1367, 1376 (Fed. Cir. 1986) (citation omitted).

[8] Burroughs Wellcome Co. v. Barr Labs., Inc., 40 F.3d 1223, 1228 (Fed. Cir. 1994).

[9] As a general rule, conception does not require reduction to practice. However, there are instances of "simultaneous conception and reduction to practice," which may be applied to certain types of inventions in the unpredictable arts. *See* Mycogen Plant Science v. Monsanto Co., 243 F.3d 1316 (Fed. Cir. 2001).

an invention will work for its intended purpose.[10]

Many inventors rely on the assistance of others to realize the conception of their invention. Not all those who provide such assistance are considered inventors. For example, an inventor "may use the services, ideas, and aid of others in the process of perfecting his invention without losing his right to a patent."[11] In addition, one may rely on conversations with others to learn the relevant state of the art without naming the sources of such information as inventors.[12] As the U.S. Supreme Court observed long ago in assessing Samuel Morse's invention of the telegraph, "[n]either can the inquires [Morse] made, or the information or advice he received, from men of science in the course of his researches, impair his right to the character of an inventor."[13]

One useful example of a decision that analyzed inventorship is *Hess v. Advanced Cardiovascular Systems, Inc.*[14] Two physicians were working on an improved design for a balloon angioplasty catheter, a medical device used to clear the arteries in a patient's heart. The two physicians did extensive day-to-day research and development on the project. In the course of this work, these physicians spoke to Hess, a salesperson who suggested various materials and approaches for the device. Ultimately, none of Hess' suggested approaches proved feasible and the physicians patented an alternative that the two doctors subsequently developed. Hess sought recognition as an inventor of the patent.

The Federal Circuit concluded that Hess was not an inventor. The court found that Hess had merely discussed materials sold by his employer and explained principles to the doctors that were "well known and found in textbooks."[15] Contributions that amount to an explanation of the existing state of the art are not inventive activity. As the Federal Circuit has explained in another context, "[t]he basic exercise of the normal skill expected of one skilled in the art, without an inventive act, also does not make one a joint inventor."[16]

Likewise, acting as an inventor's assistant is not sufficient. For example, in *Acromed Corp. v. Sofamor Danek Group, Inc.*,[17] the court found that a machinist who had merely followed the inventor's directions for creating and setting connecting screws for a medical device was the work of an ordinary skilled

---

[10] The doctrine of simultaneous conception and reduction to practice is an exception to this statement. *See* Amgen, Inc. v. Chugai Pharm. Co., 927 F.2d 1200, 1206 (Fed. Cir. 1991) ("In some instances, an inventor is unable to establish a conception until he has reduced the invention to practice through a successful experiment. This situation results in a simultaneous conception and reduction to practice.").

[11] Shatterproof Glass Corp. v. Libbey-Owens Ford Co., 758 F.2d 613, 624 (Fed. Cir. 1985) (quotation and citation omitted).

[12] *See generally* Hess v. Advanced Cardiovascular Sys., Inc., 106 F.3d 976, 980-81 (Fed. Cir. 1997).

[13] O'Reilly v. Morse, 56 U.S. (15 How.) 62, 111 (1853).

[14] Hess v. Advanced Cardiovascular Sys., Inc., 106 F.3d 976 (Fed. Cir. 1997).

[15] *Id.* at 981.

[16] Fina Oil and Chemical Co. v. Ewen, 123 F.3d 1466, 1473 (Fed. Cir. 1997).

[17] Acromed Corp. v. Sofamor Danek Group, Inc., 253 F.3d 1371 (Fed. Cir. 2001) (machinist's contribution amounted to work of an ordinary skilled mechanic, and therefore was not an inventive contribution to conception).

mechanic and therefore not inventive. Likewise, one who performs testing to determine the operability of an already-conceived invention is not considered an inventor.[18] Thus, one who merely acts as "another pair of hands" to conduct routine experimentation to demonstrate utility has not contributed to conception, and therefore need not be listed as an inventor to the patent.[19]

[B] Joint Inventors and Ownership

Where more than one individual contributes to an invention, all inventors must jointly apply for a patent.[20] The principle of *joint inventorship* contemplates some form of collaboration or concerted effort between inventors, such as communications or other proximity of inventive efforts.[21] Nonetheless, joint inventors may apply for a single patent although: 1) the inventors did not physically work together in the same location or at the same time to conceive the invention; 2) each did not make the same type or amount of contribution the claims; and 3) each did not contribute to every claim of the patent.[22] A joint inventor must be listed as an inventor on a patent application even where the contribution is limited to a single claim.[23]

Each joint inventor "presumptively owns a *pro rata* undivided interest in the entire patent, no matter what their respective contributions."[24] As one court recognized, "[t]his interplay between inventorship and ownership creates the anomalous situation that a co-inventor of even a single claim can then assert a right of joint ownership over an entire patent with multiple claims."[25]

How much contribution is sufficient to render one a joint inventor? The Federal Circuit has stated that the contribution must be "not insignificant in quality, when that contribution is measured against the dimension of the full invention."[26] Work that contributes to a claim element is sufficient to meet this standard.[27] For example, in *Pannu v. Iolab Corp.,*[28] the Federal Circuit found that a *prima facie* case of joint inventorship existed where an individual demonstrated that he had contributed the concept of a "one-piece lens construction" for a medical device to be used in the human eye. Notably, the patent at issue in the *Pannu* case expressly relied on this one-piece construction feature as an element of the claims.

---

[18] *See, e.g.,* Burroughs Wellcome Co. v. Barr Labs., Inc., 40 F.3d 1223, 1230 (Fed. Cir. 1994) (individual who conducted post-conception testing of a compound for the treatment of HIV was not an inventor).

[19] Mattor v. Coolegem, 530 F.2d 1391, 1393 (C.C.P.A. 1976).

[20] 35 U.S.C. § 116 (2000).

[21] Eli Lilly and Co. v. Aradigm Corp., 376 F.3d 1352, 1359 (Fed. Cir. 2004).

[22] 35 U.S.C. § 116.

[23] Ethicon, Inc. v. U.S. Surgical Corp., 135 F.3d 1456, 1460 (Fed. Cir. 1998).

[24] *Id.* at 1465 (footnote omitted).

[25] Israel Bio-Engineering Project v. Amgen, Inc., 475 F.3d 1256, 1264 (Fed. Cir. 2007).

[26] Acromed Corp. v. Sofamor Danek Group, Inc., 253 F.3d 1371, 1379 (Fed. Cir. 2001).

[27] *See, e.g.,* Caterpillar Inc. v. Sturman Industries, Inc., 387 F.3d 1358, 1377 (Fed. Cir. 2004).

[28] *See* Pannu v. Iolab Corp., 155 F.3d 1344 (Fed. Cir. 1998).

[C] Filing a Patent Application: The Inventor's Oath

The Patent Act defines an inventor as one who has invented or discovered the subject matter of the invention.[29] A patent application must be accompanied by an inventor's oath, or, under the AIA, a substitute statement.[30] Among other things, the oath must state, "such individual believes himself or herself to be the original inventor or an original inventor of a claimed invention in the application."[31] The AIA allows a substitute statement to be filed in lieu of the inventor's oath where certain circumstances are present, such as if the inventor is deceased, under legal incapacity, cannot be found after a diligent effort, or refuses to make an oath and is under an obligation to assign the invention.

In addition, the AIA has added a newly amended provision to the law that permits the invention's assignee to file a patent application.[32] The former version required that patent applications be made, or authorized, by the inventor. This new section recognizes the modern reality that organizations employ inventors to accomplish a significant measure of research and development. Many employees have invention assignment obligations to their respective organizations, which have departments that oversee the filing and prosecution of the entity's inventions. AIA § 118 allows such an entity to file an application on behalf of the inventor to preserve the rights for the entity as the real party in interest.[33] Note that this section affects prosecution and ownership, but is not drafted to modify the substantive standards for inventorship.

§ 19.03 WHAT IS "DERIVATION"?

[A] The Legal Standard for Derivation

Long before § 102(f) was enacted, the U.S. Supreme Court recognized:

> Where [another's] suggestions [to the inventor] go to make up a complete and perfect machine, embracing the substance of all that is embodied in the patent subsequently issued to the party to whom the suggestion was made, the patent is invalid, because the real invention or discovery belonged to another.[34]

Section 102(f) was enacted based on the principle that a named inventor is not entitled to a patent if the person did not invent the subject matter of the claims, but

---

[29] 35 U.S.C. § 100 (2011).

[30] 35 U.S.C. § 115 (2011).

[31] *Id.* at § 115(b). This language is from the AIA version of § 115. A similar representation was required under the former version of the act, which stated "that the person making the oath or declaration believes the named inventor or inventors to be the original and first inventor or inventors of the subject matter which is claimed and for which a patent is sought."

[32] 35 U.S.C. § 118 (2011).

[33] The AIA sections that relate to the substitute statement and the assignee filing is one year after the AIA's enactment.

[34] Agawan Co. v. Jordan, 74 U.S. 583, 603 (1868).

rather derived the invention from another. The test for determining derivation is that the proponent of the defense must demonstrate two requirements — specifically, "a prior, complete *conception* of the claimed subject matter and *communication* of the complete conception to the party charged with derivation."[35]

The first requirement — proof of complete conception — cannot be established with the prior inventor's testimony alone, but rather requires corroborating evidence of prior conception. Adequate corroborative evidence includes "[p]hysical, documentary, or circumstantial evidence, or reliable testimony from individuals other than the alleged inventor or an interested party."[36]

The second prong requires that the true inventor communicate the invention to the patent applicant in a form that is enabled — that is, sufficient to enable one of ordinary skill in the art to construct and use the invention. A communication between a prior inventor and the applicant need not be available to the public. Thus, the requirements of the pre-AIA § 102(f) may be met where the applicant has gained access to a purely private document of the true inventor. Evidence that supports a showing of derivation need not occur within the U.S., but rather can be demonstrated by conception or a communication that takes place internationally.[37]

Unlike a number of other defenses based on § 102, there is no grace period or specified time restriction for the work of the true inventor. For example, in contrast to the statutory bars, derivation can be established by a prior conception and communication that takes place within one year of the application's filing date.

[B] Application of § 102(f)'s Two-Prong Test

Derivation was explored in the Federal Circuit's decision *Gambro Lundia AB v. Baxter Healthcare Corp.*[38] The invention in *Gambro* concerned an improvement for monitoring fluid flow within a dialysis machine, a device used to assist patients whose kidneys do not function properly. Such machines use sensors located at the machine's inflow and outflow to calculate the impurities removed from a patient's blood. As of the late 1970's, accurate outflow measurements were difficult to obtain because the outflow sensor might become clogged during operation, which caused the monitoring data from that source to drift off of an accurate reading.

In 1979, Whittingham, who at that time worked for a company named Repgreen, developed some improvements to the outflow sensor and discussed these ideas with the patentee Gambro on two occasions. In addition, Whittingham maintained a copy of a proposal that described his improvement in a file located at Repgreen. Subsequently, Gambro acquired Whittingham's files — including this proposal — during a corporate acquisition of Repgreen. Over the next few years, Gambro's own research team developed an improved dialysis monitoring system that Gambro subsequently patented. The patent's claims included a feature whereby the dialysis

---

[35] Hedgewick v. Akers, 497 F.2d 905, 908 (C.C.P.A. 1974) (emphasis added).

[36] Checkpoint Sys., Inc. v. All-Tag Sec. S.A., 412 F.3d 1331, 1339 (Fed. Cir. 2005).

[37] *Hedgewick*, 497 F.2d at 907-08; *see also* P.J. Federico, *Commentary on the New Patent Act*, 75 J. PAT. & TRADEMARK OFF. SOC'Y 161, 184-85 (1993).

[38] Gambro Lundia AB v. Baxter Healthcare Corp., 110 F.3d 1573 (Fed. Cir. 1997).

machine periodically recalibrated the machine's outflow monitor while dialysis was being performed, eliminating the drift.

After Gambro sued defendant Baxter for infringement, Baxter argued that Gambro's patent was invalid under the pre-AIA § 102(f), as derivative of Whittingham's work for Repgreen. The *Gambro* court reversed the trial court's finding of invalidity, finding that neither prong of the derivation defense had been established. First, *Gambro* noted that the defendant could not establish that a complete conception had been communicated to Gambro. Although Whittingham's testimony spoke to a complete prior conception, there was insufficient evidence of corroboration because the sole corroborating document — the proposal drafted by Whittingham — failed to describe the recalibration feature. This failure to provide sufficient corroborative evidence was deemed fatal.

Second, the court determined that the record failed to demonstrate that the named inventors of the Gambro patent had actually received an enabling description of the invention from Whittingham. As the *Gambro* court explained:

> During discovery, [Whittingham's] proposal appeared in the files of one of the named inventors. However, as discussed above, the proposal does not disclose recalibration during dialysis to one skilled in the art at the relevant time. If the proposal does not disclose recalibration during dialysis, it cannot serve as the basis for a communication of that idea.[39]

As neither prong of the derivation test was met, the Federal Circuit reversed a district court's finding that the § 102(f) defense had been established.

A district court decision, *Maxwell v. K Mart Corp.*,[40] stands in contrast to *Gambro*. There, the inventor Maxwell claimed that she had conceived of an invention for a fastening device used to keep pairs of shoes together for retail display. The asserted patent claimed the use of two tabs that extended from the area between the inner and outer sole of the shoe. A fastener was attached to these tabs, which kept both members of the pair together. This invention was an improvement over prior art fasteners, which relied on a filament that passed through holes punched directly into the shoe that left a permanent perforation.

The defendant argued that Maxwell had derived the invention from an employee of a Taiwanese company named Stepping Ahead. The defendant presented evidence that Maxwell learned of this feature after speaking with an intermediary shoe company working with Stepping Ahead. In addition, the evidence demonstrated that Stepping Ahead had sent Maxwell a prototype created in Taiwan that included the subject matter that was later claimed in Maxwell's patent.

The *Maxwell* court found that, although the evidence was in conflict, a jury could conclude that Stepping Ahead's employee had first conceived the invention. In contrast to *Gambro*, where there was a failure to corroborate the true inventor's testimony, the challenger in *Maxwell* presented a photograph of the Taiwanese prototype. The district court found this prototype sufficient to demonstrate

---

[39] *Id.*

[40] Maxwell v. K Mart Corp., 880 F. Supp. 1323 (D. Minn. 1995).

corroboration of the conception by Stepping Ahead. As this finding demonstrates, the corroborative prototype need not be created in the U.S., but may be established with evidence demonstrating conception in another country.

As to the second requirement for communication of the conception to the named inventor, the *Maxwell* court found that, "[a] reasonable jury could find that the tab connection system was created by Stepping Ahead without any input from Maxwell and that she derived the invention claimed in the [asserted] patent from the prototype she received."[41] Unlike the incomplete Whittingham memo at issue in *Gambro*, the *Maxwell* fastener prototype was a complete, enabled work that encompassed all of claim elements. In the final analysis, the *Maxwell* court found that the record had sufficient evidence of derivation to send the § 102(f) defense to trial.

Although patents that are subject to the AIA will not be invalidated (or barred) by derivation principles, it can be expected that these authorities will look to the existing precedent to establish the grounds for derivation actions.

The AIA's elimination of § 102(f) does not mean that non-inventors are entitled to patent another's invention. Recall that 35 U.S.C. § 101 of the Patent Act requires that a patent be granted to "Whoever invents or discovers. . .." This limits the ability to grant patent to those persons who have engaged in inventive activity with respect to the inventions claimed in the patent. Consistent with this statute, Article I, section 8 of the U.S. Constitution requires that the patent system grant patents to "Inventors." Furthermore, under § 115, an inventor must sign an "oath that he believes himself to be the original and first inventor" absent unusual circumstances. In addition to the AIA's new derivation proceedings, the law is clear that only true inventors are entitled to a patent.

§ 19.04 DERIVATION ACTIONS UNDER THE AIA

The U.S. Constitution, Article I, Section 8 provides, "To promote the Progress of Science and useful Arts, by securing for limited Times to Authors and Inventors the exclusive Right to their respective Writings and Discoveries." Under its terms, Congress is empowered to create a patent system consistent with this constitutional grant. How does the AIA approach inventorship consistent with this constitutional grant? An underlying principle the AIA's first to file system is that patents are awarded to a first *inventor* who files an application for a patent. A non-inventor who is the first to file is not entitled to a patent.

To enforce this rule, the AIA has created derivation proceedings to allow recourse against one who derived the subject matter of an earlier-filed patent from a true inventor. As the legislative history states:

> A new administrative proceeding — called a "derivation" proceeding — is created to ensure that the first person to file the application is actually a true inventor. This new proceeding will ensure that a person will not be able to obtain a patent for the invention that he did not actually invent.

---

[41] *Id.*

To commence a proceeding, a patent applicant may file a petition in the U.S. PTO, stating the grounds that justify relief.[42] Essentially, one seeking to establish grounds must demonstrate that an inventor named in an earlier application derived the claimed invention from the later filer, who is a true inventor. The time for filing a petition is limited to one year after the first publication of the claim that is the same (or substantially the same) as one in an earlier filed application.

Alternatively, the AIA provides for a civil action by "the owner of a patent" against someone who owns "another patent that claims the same invention" and has an earlier effective filing date.[43] These actions are limited to a one-year period from the issue date of a first patent that includes at least one derived claim. As previously stated, the application of standard rules of statutory construction supports the conclusion that the definition of derivation will track the previous law in the precedents.

§ 19.05   CORRECTION OF INVENTORSHIP

35 U.S.C. § 256 allows the correction of inventorship. If the request is properly supported, the U.S. PTO will issue a certificate correcting inventorship if the parties and the patent owner(s) agree to the change.[44]

If the matter is contested, a party may file a civil action in a federal district court.[45] Such an action will not affect the validity of a patent, as § 256(b) directs that "[t]he error of omitting inventors or naming persons who are not inventors shall not invalidate the patent in which such error occurred."[46] Generally, such actions are of two types. The first is *non-joinder* — that is, where an inventor has been omitted from the patent — under pre-AIA law, a court was authorized to add an inventor who lacked deceptive intent.[47] The second is *mis-joinder*, for cases in which an inventor has been erroneously added as an inventor on a patent.[48] The AIA has omitted the limitation on a court's ability to grant relief for non-joinder for an inventor who acts with deceptive intent. Therefore, under the AIA, a court may grant relief for both non-joinder and mis- joinder without considering the inventor's state of mind.

Note that those who submit false inventorship declarations to the U.S. PTO with deceptive intent might find that the patent is invalid based on inequitable conduct.[49]

---

[42] 35 U.S.C. § 135 (2011).

[43] 35 U.S.C. § 291 (2011).

[44] 35 U.S.C. §§ 116(c); 256(a) (2000); 37 C.F.R. § 1.324. For actions filed after September 16, 2012, § 256 has been amended to delete the statement "and such error arose without any deceptive intention on his part." As such actions were not contested, it is unlikely that this change will effect a significant change in the law.

[45] 35 U.S.C. § 256(b).

[46] 35 U.S.C. § 256 (2000).

[47] Stark v. Advanced Magnetics, Inc., 119 F.3d 1551, 1553 (Fed. Cir. 1997); *see also* 35 U.S.C. § 116(b) (allowing a patent application to be prosecuted by an inventor on behalf of an omitted inventor who cannot be located).

[48] *Stark*, 119 F.3d at 1555.

[49] For more information about inequitable conduct, *see* Chapter 36.

Under the theory that "[o]ne bad apple spoils the entire barrel," a patent tainted by inequitable conduct "may not enforced even by 'innocent' co-inventors."[50]

§ 19.06 CONCLUSION

The pre-AIA 35 U.S.C. § 102(f) provides that a patent will not be granted where the listed inventor "did not himself invent the subject matter sought to be patented."[51] To demonstrate derivation, one must show that another had a prior, complete conception of the invention that was communicated to the named inventor of the patent at issue. To demonstrate prior conception, one must submit corroborative evidence. Furthermore, the communication must be in a form that is sufficient to enable one of ordinary skill in the art to construct and use the invention.

The AIA has eliminated § 112(f) from the previous version of the Act. Therefore, for patents governed by the new act, derivation will not constitute grounds to invalidate a claim, or to bar a claim from issuing. However, a true inventor may seek recourse in the PTO or the district court to determine the correct inventor with respect to an earlier-filed claim was derived from him or her.

An alternative to invalidity is correction of inventorship under 35 U.S.C. § 256. Such correction can take place either in an administrative proceeding before the U.S. PTO or, if contested, in a district court proceeding.

---

[50] *Id.* at 1556.

[51] 35 U.S.C. § 102(f).

Chapter 20

THE FIRST TO INVENT SYSTEM

SYNOPSIS

§ 20.01   INTRODUCTION

§ 20.02   STRUCTURE AND OPERATION

§ 20.03   CONCEPTION AND REDUCTION TO PRACTICE

    [A]   Conception

        [1]   Complete Conception

        [2]   Conception: Inventor Recognition and Appreciation of the Invention

        [3]   Utility is Not Required to Establish Conception

        [4]   Conception's Corroboration Requirement

    [B]   Reduction to Practice

        [1]   Actual Reduction to Practice

        [2]   Reduction to Practice: All Elements Requirement

        [3]   Reduction to Practice: Demonstrating that the Invention Works for Its Intended Purpose

        [4]   Inventor's Appreciation and Recognition of the Invention's Utility

        [5]   Constructive Reduction to Practice

    [C]   Simultaneous Conception and Reduction to Practice

§ 20.04   PRIORITY RULES UNDER § 102(g)

    [A]   General Rule: The First to Reduce to Practice Has Priority

    [B]   Diligence and the First to Conceive

§ 20.05   "ABANDONED, SUPRESSED OR CONCEALED"

    [A]   Overview of the Doctrine and Policy

    [B]   Intentional Abandonment, Suppression or Concealment

    [C]   Patentee Delay and an Inference of Abandonment, Suppression or Concealment

    [D]   Patentee's Resumed Activity Negating a Finding of Abandonment, Suppression or Concealment

§ 20.06   CONCLUSION

§ 20.01 INTRODUCTION

Under the law that existed prior to the America Invents Act (AIA), the U.S. patent law was based a *first to invent* system. The governing rules are set forth in the pre-AIA 35 U.S.C. § 102(g), which describes *priority* of invention under circumstances where more than one person claims development of the same invention.[1] In addition, the subsection provides an independent ground to invalidate a patent where the proponent establishes that another has first invented the subject matter of the claim. This subsection was added as part of the 1952 amendments to the Patent Act, deriving from a prior subsection that served a similar function.[2]

An understanding of the pre-AIA § 102(g) will be vital to those practicing patent law over the coming years. As described in Chapter 14, the U.S. patent system is currently transitioning from a first to invent system to the AIA's first to file system. The transition will occur for patents with an effective filing date on or after March 16, 2013. Patents with an effective filing date prior to that time will be examined under the first to invent standard. The concept of inventorship has been a part of U.S. patent law for centuries, and it will remain relevant even under a pure first to file system. This system is based on Congress' expectation that a patent will issue to *an inventor* who is first to file or disclose. Further, there are other doctrines — such as nonobviousness — which are based on a shared background understanding of the process of invention. Although § 102(g) has been eliminated in the AIA, the principles that the subsection embodied are likely to carry forward in other areas of the law.

As background, the pre-AIA § 102(g)'s general rule of priority states that an inventor who is the *first to reduce the invention to practice* obtains the right to the patent. This rule implements the policy that one who can establish an operative version of the invention is entitled to the reward of the government granted right.[3] This general rule is subject to an important exception. Specifically, an inventor will prevail in a priority contest even if the second to reduce to practice where this inventor is the *first to conceive* and demonstrates *reasonable diligence to reduce the invention to practice from a time before the other's conception date.* This principle is consistent with "the spirit of indulgence that has always been manifested toward those who in good faith delay application for patent whilst engaged in a diligent effort to perfect their inventions."[4]

In addition, the subsection states that priority is not awarded to a first inventor who *abandons, suppresses or conceals* an invention. This rule favors inventors who seek a patent, publish a description of an invention, or publicly use or sell the invention to the public. Thus, one who provides the public with the benefit of an invention is favored over a first inventor who withholds or delays disclosure after invention is complete. Stated another way, priority is granted to the later inventor

---

[1] 35 U.S.C. § 102(g) (2000).

[2] *See, e.g.,* Paulik v. Rizkalla, 760 F.2d 1270, 1276-78 (Fed. Cir. 1985) (describing the history of § 102(g), stating, "[t]hese words were included in the section . . . to codify pre-existing case law pertaining to priority determinations in interference or infringement suits") (Rich, J., concurring).

[3] *See* Thomson v. Weston, 19 App. D.C. 373 (D.C. Cir. 1902).

[4] Mason v. Hepburn, 13 App. D.C. 86 (D.C. Cir. 1898).

where "all others have been led to believe has never been discovered, by reason of the indifference, supineness, or willful act of one who may, in fact, have discovered it long before."[5]

Underlying this subsection are two interrelated policies to be effectuated by these rules. First, under the first to invent system, the patent system favors the earlier inventor. Although the U.S. is moving toward a full system based on first to file, the former U.S. law encouraged the first and the diligent creator. Second, the pre-AIA § 102(g) indicates the patent law's preference to benefit the public by rewarding early disclosure of inventions.

§ 20.02   STRUCTURE AND OPERATION

Invention is part of incremental process of advancement. In any particular art, it is not uncommon for multiple inventors to reach the same solution nearly simultaneously. How does the patent system determine which among them is awarded a patent? Under the AIA, the answer is the first to file or disclose, assuming that the advance is nonobvious. The answer under the pre-AIA law is more complex. The governing section, under the pre-AIA § 102(g), states:

A person shall be entitled to a patent unless -

(g)(1) during the course of an interference conducted under section 135 or section 291, another inventor involved therein establishes, to the extent permitted in section 104, that before such person's invention thereof the invention was made by such other inventor and not abandoned, suppressed, or concealed, or

(2) before such person's invention thereof, the invention was made in this country by another inventor who had not abandoned, suppressed, or concealed it . . . .[6]

This pre-AIA subsection can be broken into two structural component parts. First, § 102(g)(1) governs priority of invention in *interference proceedings*, which is an action conducted before the U.S. PTO's Board of Patent Appeals and Interferences[7] to determine the priority of invention between a pending application and one or more pending applications and/or one or more unexpired patents.[8] An interference may be declared if the subject matter of at least one claim of a patentee would either anticipate or render obvious the subject matter of a claim of another.[9] In such proceedings, an administrative law judge decides which party is entitled to obtain patent coverage of the subject matter of the inference according to the priority rules.

---

[5] *Id.*

[6] 35 U.S.C. § 102(g).

[7] The AIA has created the Patent Trial and Appeal Board to supplant this board. 35 U.S.C. § 6 (2011).

[8] 35 U.S.C. § 102(g)(1) (". . . during the course of an interference conducted under section 135 or section 291 . . ."); *see also* 37 C.F.R. § 41.203 (2007); MPEP § 2301 (2001 & rev. 2007).

[9] 37 C.F.R. § 41.203.

Second, § 102(g)(2) applies outside the interference context. An inventor may file a declaratory judgment action in a U.S. District Court to determine inventorship under its standards. Additionally, an accused infringer can rely on this subsection as independent grounds to invalidate a patent that has been asserted in infringement litigation.[10]

Another important distinction between §§ 102(g)(1) and 102(g)(2) is that priority in interference proceedings includes inventions made in any NAFTA country or any country who is a member of the World Trade Organization (WTO).[11] Therefore, under § 102(g)(1), inventive activity that occurs in any of the over 150 nations that fit into these categories can be considered in interference proceedings before the Board. However, such foreign activity *cannot* be considered outside the interference context, as § 102(g)(2) applies only where "the invention was made *in this country*."[12]

§ 20.03   CONCEPTION AND REDUCTION TO PRACTICE

To apply the priority rules, some foundational understanding of the legal definitions of the terms *conception* and *reduction to practice* should be established. Both terms form crucial turning points in any priority dispute, according to the pre-AIA § 102(g), which states:

> In determining priority of invention under this subsection, there shall be considered not only the *respective dates of conception and reduction to practice of the invention*, but also the reasonable diligence of one who was first to conceive and last to reduce to practice, from a time prior to conception by the other.[13]

Both "conception" and "reduction to practice" represent legal conclusions based on consideration of the underlying facts and evidence, as detailed below.

[A]   Conception

In patent law, "[c]onception is the touchstone of inventorship."[14] That is, conception is the "formation in the mind of the inventor, of a definite and permanent idea of the complete and operative invention, as it is hereafter to be applied in practice."[15] Conception is the completion of all of the *mental* aspects of the creation of an invention.

---

[10] Thomson S.A. v. Quixote Corp., 166 F.3d 1172, 1175 n.3 (Fed. Cir. 1999).

[11] 35 U.S.C. § 102(g)(1); *see also* 35 U.S.C. § 104.

[12] 35 U.S.C. § 102(g)(2).

[13] 35 U.S.C. § 102(g)(2) (emphasis added).

[14] Burroughs Wellcome Co. v. Barr Labs., Inc., 40 F.3d 1223, 1227 (Fed. Cir. 1994).

[15] Invitrogen Corp. v. Clontech Lab, Inc., 429 F.3d 1052, 1063 (Fed. Cir. 2005).

[1]　Complete Conception

The inventor's conception must include the entire invention — that is, the inventor's idea must include *all claim limitations*.[16] Additionally, the inventor's idea must be *definite and permanent* — that is, the inventor must have a "specific, settled idea, a particular solution to the problem at hand, not just a general goal or research plan he hopes to pursue."[17] Conception is complete only where "the idea is so clearly defined in the inventor's mind that only ordinary skill would be necessary to reduce the invention to practice, without extensive research or experimentation."[18]

These standards were applied in *Hitzeman v. Rutter*.[19] There, the Federal Circuit assessed a claim of conception for an invention directed to a vaccine for hepatitis B, a medical condition transmitted by a virus. At the time of the asserted conception in 1981, the prior art described a vaccine made from a particular molecule, HBsAg. During the early 1980's, researchers attempted to derive HBsAg in a particulate of a specific size (22 nm). Hitzeman, the junior party in the interference, testified that during February 1981, he had "a hope" that HBsAg derived from yeast would succeed.[20]

The *Hitzeman* court held that the inventor's hope failed to constitute complete conception as of February 1981. Finding that particle size and sedimentation rate were "central to the patentability of the invention," the court determined that conception was not complete until Hitzeman demonstrated that "he had a definite and permanent understanding that the yeast would produce the 22 nm particles."[21] As *Hitzeman* illustrates, the inventor must demonstrate knowledge of all limitations of the invention, and not merely describe a research plan designed to reach the solution that has been claimed.

As the *Hitzeman* case suggests, chemical compounds may pose special problems. For example, the Federal Circuit has held that a description of a process for making a particular DNA was not sufficient to establish conception in the absence of conception of the structure, name, formula or the definitive chemical or physical properties of the resulting substance.[22] However, where an inherent property is redundant to other recited limitations, is not material to patentability and is recognizable to those of ordinary skill in the art, an inventor need not demonstrate

---

[16]　*See* Coleman v. Dines, 754 F.2d 353 (Fed. Cir. 1985).

[17]　*Burroughs Wellcome Co.*, 40 F.3d at 1228.

[18]　Stern v. Trustees of Columbia University, 434 F.3d 1375, 1378 (Fed. Cir. 2006) (citation omitted).

[19]　Hitzeman v. Rutter, 243 F.3d 1345 (Fed. Cir. 2001).

[20]　*Id.* at 1350.

[21]　*Id.* at 1356.

[22]　Fiers v. Revel, 984 F.2d 1164, 1169 (Fed. Cir. 1993). Although conception of the method of creating the substance alone would not suffice for a claim to a particular DNA, the *Fiers* court noted that conception of the method of preparing a particular form of DNA may suffice to establish a claim to the substance *as a process*. *Id.* ("conception only of a process for making a substance, without a conception of a structural or equivalent definition of that substance, can at most constitute a conception of the substance claimed as a process.").

specific conception of those features.[23]

[2]   Conception: Inventor Recognition and Appreciation of the Invention

Conception requires that the inventor *recognize* and *appreciate* the facts that comprise the claimed elements of the invention.[24] *Heard v. Burton* provides an example.[25] There, the court considered whether the inventor Heard had established conception for experiments that he conducted during the years 1949-1950.[26] During that time, Heard's experiments successfully used platinum as a catalyst for his chemical research relating to petroleum products. Heard's experiments were successful, however Heard conceded that he was unaware that the success of these experiments was due to the presence of a compound known as eta-alumina. Indeed, when Heard conducted these experiments, he was entirely unaware of the presence of this type of alumina in the tested compounds.

In 1952, Burton and others, all of whom were unaffiliated with Heard, filed a patent application claiming the use of eta-alumina as a catalyst. Later, in 1953, Heard's work was subjected to further analysis, and he then learned that the success of his earlier work was due to eta-alumina. On these facts, the court held that Heard could not demonstrate prior conception based on his earlier 1949-50 work. Although the court acknowledged that it was not necessary that Heard identify eta-alumina *by name* to demonstrate conception, the court explained:

> . . . we consider it fatal to [Heard]'s case that not until after appellees' filing date did Heard recognize that his "ammonia-aged" catalyst, as appellees put it, "contained any different form of alumina at all." . . . [T]he count calls for a particular form of alumina and we think that [Heard]'s failure to recognize that he had produced a new form, regardless of what he called it, is indicative that he never conceived the invention prior to appellees' filing date.[27]

Although an inventor must appreciate the facts underlying an invention, an inventor does *not* need to recognize that the invention is patentable as a matter of patent law.[28] For example, in *Dow Chemical Co. v. Astro-Valcour, Inc.*, the court considered whether conception had occurred on the date that certain employees had developed an improved blown insulation material.[29] The claimed subject matter was a plastic foam that was distinguished from the prior art by the use of a particular chemical, isobutene, as the blowing agent. In March, 1984, the patentee's employees practiced the invention using isobutene as the blowing agent successfully and

---

[23]   Hitzeman v. Rutter, 243 F.3d 1345, 1355 (Fed. Cir. 2001).

[24]   MPEP § 2138.04

[25]   *See* Heard v. Burton, 333 F.2d 239 (C.C.P.A. 1964).

[26]   *Id.* at 241.

[27]   *Id.* at 243; MPEP § 2138.04 ("There must be a contemporaneous recognition and appreciation of the invention for there to be conception.").

[28]   *See* Dow Chem. Co. v. Astro-Valcour, Inc., 267 F.3d 1334 (Fed. Cir. 2001).

[29]   *Id.*

several of them were "'surprised' and 'elated' at the ease of making the 'beautiful' and 'good' foam" on that date.[30] These employees further testified that they did not realize that their addition of isobutene was a patentable improvement under the law. The *Dow* court found that conception occurred in March 1984, when the patentee "clearly recognized and appreciated the existence of its new process and product."[31] As *Dow* explained, whether an inventor "understood that it had produced a legally patentable invention is immaterial for purposes of § 102(g)(2)."[32]

Where an invention has been reduced to practice, the inventor does not have to demonstrate appreciation of inherent elements of the claim. For example, in *Silvestri v. Grant,* the inventor prepared a new form of antibiotic and both recognized and appreciated that he had created a novel compound.[33] The court found that conception was complete even though the inventor did not know of the compound's specific properties, such as the molecular weight of the new substance, that were later detailed in the inventor's claim. The *Silvestri* court explained that the standard for conception does not require an inventor to "recognize[] the invention in the same terms as those recited in the count. The invention is not the language of the count but the subject matter thereby defined."[34]

[3]   Utility is Not Required to Establish Conception

An inventor does not need to know that the invention will actually work for the intended purpose to establish conception.[35] Furthermore, an inventor is not required to understand the precise underlying theoretical explanations for the invention's operation for conception to be complete.[36]

[4]   Conception's Corroboration Requirement

Courts require that one seeking to establish the subjective mental act of conception with inventor testimony must provide corroborating evidence to demonstrate credibility and alleviate the possibility of bias. Fundamentally, the corroboration requirement is intended to prevent fraud.[37] Thus, the "rule addresses the concern that a party claiming inventorship might be tempted to describe his actions in an unjustifiably self-serving manner in order to obtain a patent or to maintain an existing patent."[38]

---

[30] *Id.* at 1341.

[31] *Id.*

[32] *Id.*

[33] Silvestri v. Grant, 496 F.2d 593, 599 (C.C.P.A. 1974).

[34] *Id.*

[35] Burroughs Wellcome Co., v. Barr Labs., Inc., 40 F.3d 1223, 1228 (Fed. Cir. 1994) ("He need only show that he had the idea; the discovery that an invention actually works is part of its reduction to practice.").

[36] *See, e.g.*, Knorr v. Pearson, 671 F.2d 1368 (C.C.P.A. 1982).

[37] Kridl v. McCormick, 105 F.3d 1446, 1450 (Fed. Cir. 1997).

[38] Singh v. Brake, 317 F.3d 1334, 1341 (Fed. Cir. 2003).

Where corroborative evidence is required, its sufficiency is judged by the "rule of reason" — that is, the fact finder undertakes an analysis of all the evidence to assess its adequacy. Such evidence may take the form of writings in an inventor notebook, a patent application, or even informal evidence such as e-mails, business plans or other writings or testimony. Corroboration is *not* required where an inventor relies on a patent application's filing date to establish the date of conception.[39] Under those circumstances, the agency's filing date as reflected in the prosecution history of the application is sufficient.

[B]   Reduction to Practice

Reduction to practice can be established in either of two ways. An inventor may *actually* reduce the invention to practice, such as by assembling a working prototype of the invention.[40] Alternatively, an inventor may *constructively* reduce the invention to practice by filing a patent application that meets the U.S. standards for disclosure.[41] Both of these are explored in detail, below.

[1]   Actual Reduction to Practice

To establish actual reduction to practice, a party must establish both: (1) the construction of an embodiment or the performance of a process that meets every element of the claim, and (2) that the embodiment or process operates for its intended purpose.[42] Actual reduction to practice cannot be demonstrated solely by the inventor's testimony. As with proof of conception, corroboration of such testimony is required and assessed under the rule of reason.[43]

[2]   Reduction to Practice: All Elements Requirement

The *all elements* requirement is stringently applied to fixing the date of reduction to practice. For example, in *Evans v. Eaton*,[44] the Federal Circuit considered whether particular testing of an electronic memory cell established actual reduction to practice for purposes of an interference action. The claim required the use of a "sense amplifier" to respond to differences in voltage between two lines.[45] The PTO found that the inventor had reduced the invention to practice by testing a prototype — called the "TD01" — in December, 1986, although the testing relied on an oscilloscope rather than a sense amplifier. The Federal Circuit reversed the PTO's finding, despite the fact that the inventor had a reasonable expectation that the test device would operate for its intended purpose once a sense amplifier was installed. The *Eaton* court explained that testing that relied on a similar or equivalent component was not reduction to practice and that "the absence

---

[39] Hyatt v. Boone, 146 F.3d 1348, 1352 (Fed. Cir. 1998) ("[T]he inventor need not provide evidence of either conception or actual reduction to practice when relying on the content of the patent application.").

[40] *See* Hybritech, Inc. v. Monoclonal Antibodies, Inc., 802 F.2d 1367 (Fed. Cir. 1986); MPEP § 2138.05.

[41] *Hyatt*, 146 F.3d at 1352.

[42] Eaton v. Evans, 204 F.3d 1094, 1097 (Fed. Cir. 2000).

[43] Cooper v. Goldfarb, 154 F.3d 1321, 1330 (Fed. Cir. 1998).

[44] *Eaton*, 204 F.3d at 1097.

[45] *Id.* at 1096.

of a sense amplifier precludes a finding of an actual reduction to practice on December 1986 regardless of whether the TD01 testing was successful."[46]

As *Eaton* demonstrates, the actual reduction to practice must be complete in and of itself. The requirement that all claim elements be present cannot be met with evidence of the second requirement — that is, that the invention works for its intended purpose.

[3]   Reduction to Practice: Demonstrating that the Invention Works for Its Intended Purpose

Whether a patentee has sufficiently demonstrated that the invention works for its intended purpose is assessed on a reasonableness standard.[47] As one court described, "[t]esting need not show utility beyond a possibility of failure, but only utility beyond a probability of failure."[48] This standard varies from case to case, and thus the requisite level of the testing "varies with the character of the invention and the problem its solves."[49] Less complex inventions may not require anything more than assembly or performance of the claimed method to demonstrate workability.[50] By contrast, more complex inventions, or inventions in unpredictable arts, may require verification of the invention's utility by either laboratory or field testing.[51] However, "there is no requirement that the invention when tested be in a commercially satisfactory stage of development."[52] Instead, the invention need only be shown to be suitable for its intended purpose.

Taskett v. Dentlinger, illustrates the operation of these principles. There, the court considered whether reduction to practice had been shown for a process for the automated purchasing of prepaid telephone services.[53] The claim at issue required that the purchasing method obtain "financial authorization for said request by a central terminal."[54] In this priority dispute, the junior party, Dentlinger, demonstrated that he had reduced the invention to practice by setting up a system that obtained authorization from an internal computer located at Dentlinger's place of employment. The opposing party argued that such testing did not constitute reduction to practice on the ground that the term "financial authorization" required a showing of "communication and approval from an actual third-party financial institution holding actual money in an actual account."[55]

---

[46]   *Id.* at 1098 (citation omitted).

[47]   Scott v. Finney, 34 F.3d 1058 (Fed. Cir. 1994).

[48]   *Id.* at 1062.

[49]   *Id.*

[50]   King Instrument Corp. v. Otari Corp., 767 F.2d 853, 861 (Fed. Cir. 1985); E. Rotorcraft Corp. v. U.S., 384 F.2d 429, 431 (Ct. Cl. 1967) ("Some devices are so simple and their purpose and efficacy so obvious that their complete construction is sufficient to demonstrate their workability.").

[51]   *Scott*, 34 F.3d at 1062.

[52]   *King Instrument Corp.*, 767 F.2d at 861.

[53]   Taskett v. Dentlinger, 344 F.3d 1337, 1338-39 (Fed. Cir. 2003).

[54]   *Id.* at 1339, n.1.

[55]   *Id.* at 1340.

Rejecting this argument, the Federal Circuit found Dentlinger's testing sufficient to demonstrate that the invention worked for its intended purpose:

> That Dentlinger did not test this step of the count under conditions of actual use does not mean that he did not reduce it to practice. His test was sufficient to determine that the invention would work for its intended purpose . . . . To hold otherwise would be to require an inventor to have created a viable commercial embodiment before the Board or a court could find reduction to practice. This the law does not require.[56]

On this basis, the *Taskett* court affirmed a finding that Dentlinger was entitled to the patent.

Reduction to practice may exist even where substitute materials are used, so long as the requisite workability is shown. In *Mahurkar v. C.R. Bard, Inc.*, the court considered the date of invention for a device known as a double lumen catheter.[57] This device is a flexible surgical instrument which uses two separate channels, one to withdraw fluids and another to inject them, that is intended to maximize fluid flow while minimizing trauma to a patient's veins. Dr. Mahurkar asserted that he had reduced the invention to practice in late 1980 through 1981, in a series of tests performed in his kitchen using glycerine and a fragile polyethelene tubing, rather than actual blood and a more flexible tubing material that would be appropriate for use in humans.

The Federal Circuit held that Marhurker's experiments constituted reduction to practice, as these tests demonstrated the utility of the claimed invention. In particular, the court recognized that, "Dr. Mahurkar designed these tests to show the efficacy of his structure knowing that polyethelene tubing was too brittle for actual use with humans. But, he also knew his invention would become suitable for its intended purpose by simple substitution of a soft, biocompatible material."[58] As the *Mahurkar* case demonstrates, a simplified prototype that uses substitute materials may establish that the invention will work for its intended purpose.

[4]   Inventor's Appreciation and Recognition of the Invention's Utility

Where testing is required to demonstrate that an invention works for its intended purpose, the inventor must actually appreciate and recognize that the testing was successful for reduction to practice to occur. This issue was dispositive in *Estee Lauder Inc. v. L'Oreal, S.A.* In this case, the court considered a priority dispute for an invention concerning a copper compound used to increase the effectiveness of sunscreen.[59]

---

[56] *Id.* at 1342. The *Taskett* court further found that the claims themselves did not require actual authorization from an independent third-party financial institution therefore found that this testing encompassed all elements of the claim.

[57] Mahurkar v. C.R. Bard, Inc., 79 F.3d 1572 (Fed. Cir. 1996).

[58] *Id.*

[59] Estee Lauder Inc. v. L'Oreal, S.A., 129 F.3d 588, 590 (Fed. Cir. 1997).

The court found that L'Oreal's date of invention was April 13, 1987. Estee Lauder attempted to establish earlier invention by an asserted reduction to practice of testing by an independent laboratory that had successfully concluded on April 10, 1987. L'Oreal argued that Estee Lauder's reduction to practice was incomplete because no evidence established that the inventors of Estee Lauder's patent had received or analyzed test results until after L'Oreal's April 13th invention date. The Federal Circuit determined that "in addition to preparing a composition, an inventor must establish that he knew [the invention] would work" to demonstrate reduction to practice, and that such knowledge could not be applied retroactively:

> It is well-settled that conception and reduction to practice cannot be established *nunc pro tunc*. There must be contemporaneous recognition and appreciation of the invention represented by the counts.[60]

Estee Lauder determined that the requisite recognition and appreciation did not occur until Estee Lauder's inventor had received the test results from the third party laboratory and performed additional calculations to demonstrate successful utility. Because no evidence demonstrated this event had occurred before the critical date, the court found that L'Oreal was entitled to priority for the invention. Thus, under the *Estee Lauder* case, an inventor's subsequent recognition and appreciation that the invention worked cannot reach back in time to establish reduction to practice on an earlier testing date.

Does every inventor have to wait for testing results to be transmitted to demonstrate reduction to practice? A number of Federal Circuit decisions recognize that a testing agent's appreciation can inure to the benefit of the inventor under certain circumstances.[61] Specifically, a non-inventor's recognition can inure to the benefit of the inventor where at least the following facts have been demonstrated: (1) the inventor conceived of the invention; (2) the inventor had an expectation that the tested embodiment would work for the intended purpose; and (3) the inventor submitted the embodiment for testing for the intended purpose of the invention.[62] This standard contemplates that the inventor communicate sufficient information to the agent, such that the inventor's agent can be said to have recognized the workability of the invention if the requested testing is successful.[63]

[5]   Constructive Reduction to Practice

An inventor who does not wish to rely on actual reduction to practice can rely on constructive reduction to practice as the alternative. Constructive reduction to practice occurs with the filing of a patent application.[64] Foreign filings may constructively reduce an invention to practice for a U.S. patent,[65] so long as the application meets § 112, ¶ 1's requirements for enablement, written description and

---

[60]   *Id.* (quotation and citation omitted, emphasis omitted).

[61]   *See, e.g.,* Cooper v. Goldfarb, 240 F.3d 1378 (Fed. Cir. 2001); Genentech, Inc. v. Chiron Corp., 220 F.3d 1345, 1354 (Fed. Cir. 2000).

[62]   *Cooper,* 240 F.3d at 1384.

[63]   *Id.* at 1385 (inventor's failure to inform the testing agent of any information about conception).

[64]   Hybritech Inc. v. Monoclonal Antibodies, Inc., 802 F.2d 1367 (Fed. Cir. 1986).

[65]   35 U.S.C. § 119(a) (2000); *see* Scott v. Koyama, 281 F.3d 1243 (Fed. Cir. 2002).

best mode.[66] Thus, to demonstrate constructive reduction to practice, the application must "describe the claimed subject matter in terms that establish that [the applicant] was in possession of the claimed invention, including all of the elements and limitations."[67]

[C]   Simultaneous Conception and Reduction to Practice

In most cases, "[r]eduction to practice follows conception"[68] — that is, the inventor first conceives and subsequently actually or constructively reduces the invention to practice. However, there are some types of inventions that, as a practical matter, make conception impossible unless reduction to practice in a successful experiment has occurred. In such instances, *simultaneous conception and reduction to practice* may be required to establish a date of invention.

An example can be seen in *Amgen Inc. v. Chugai Pharmaceutical Co., Ltd.*[69] There, the Federal Circuit considered the dates of conception and reduction to practice for a particular purified and isolated DNA sequence used to produce a substance known as erythropoietin ("EPO"). The *Amgen* court recognized that a claim directed to the DNA sequence could not have been subject to a complete mental conception by the inventor until reduction to practice was complete. That is, an inventor cannot know the precise sequence of the DNA necessary to create EPO until the sequence was obtained, identified and characterized. As the *Amgen* court explained:

> [U]ntil [the inventor] had a complete mental conception of a purified and isolated DNA sequence encoding EPO and a method for its preparation, in which the precise identity of the sequence is envisioned, or in terms of other characteristics sufficient to distinguish it from other genes, all he had was an objective to make an invention which he could not then adequately describe or define.[70]

The *Amgen* court reasoned that conception would not be satisfied by a research plan to isolate the DNA sequence with the appropriate biological property, because conception of a chemical must identify its structure, method of preparation or the characteristics that define it. For a DNA sequence, "when an inventor is unable to envision the detailed constitution of a gene so as to distinguish it from other materials, as well as a method for obtaining it, conception has not been achieved until reduction to practice has occurred, i.e., until after the gene has been isolated."[71]

As the *Amgen* standard suggests, not all biotechnological inventions require simultaneous conception and reduction to practice. The Federal Circuit has suggested that conception may be established before reduction to practice where,

---

[66]   Fiers v. Revel, 984 F.2d 1164, 1169-71 (Fed. Cir. 1993).

[67]   Univ. Of Rochester v. G.D. Searle & Co., Inc., 358 F.3d 916, 926 (Fed. Cir. 2004) (citation omitted).

[68]   Mahurkar v. C.R. Bard, Inc., 79 F.3d 1572, 1578 (Fed. Cir. 1996).

[69]   Amgen Inc. v. Chugai Pharm. Co., 927 F.2d 1200 (Fed. Cir. 1991).

[70]   *Id.* at 1206.

[71]   *Id.*

for example, the process of creating the compound or its performance is "reasonably predictable."[72] In that instance, an inventor may be deemed to be in possession of the invention by conception alone.

§ 20.04　PRIORITY RULES UNDER § 102(g)

[A]　General Rule: The First to Reduce to Practice Has Priority

After the dates of conception and reduction to practice have been determined, the application of the priority rules of § 102(g) are relatively straightforward. As a general rule, *the patent is awarded to the first to reduce to practice.* This rule applies regardless of which inventor was first to conceive. This general rule is based on § 102(g)(2), which provides, "[i]n determining priority of invention under this subsection, there shall be considered . . . the respective dates of conception and reduction to practice of the invention."[73]

Assume that inventor A is both first to conceive and first to reduce to practice. Under this general rule, inventor A would be awarded the patent over inventor B based on inventor A's earlier reduction to practice. The result is the *same* if inventor A is the first to reduce to practice and the later to conceive. The pre-AIA § 102(g)'s general rule leads to the finding that, because A is the first to reduce to practice, A has priority even though A is the second to conceive.

[B]　Diligence and the First to Conceive

There is an important exception to the rule that the first to reduce to practice is entitled to the patent. One who is first to conceive and second to reduce to practice can establish priority with evidence of *diligence* that pre-dates other inventor's conception. Under this rule, the previously-described scenario obtains a different result if the first to conceive (here, inventor B) can demonstrate reasonable diligence from the time just prior to inventor A's date of conception up through inventor B's reduction to practice. In that instance, inventor B is awarded priority.[74] This rule allows the first to conceive to benefit from first conception where "the invention was not abandoned or unreasonably delayed by the first inventor during the period after the second inventor entered the field."[75] As with the other aspects of inventive activity, inventor testimony demonstrating diligence must be corroborated.[76]

---

[72] Hitzeman, v. Rutter, 243 F.3d 1345, 1357 (Fed. Cir. 2001).

[73] 35 U.S.C. § 102(g)(2).

[74] Brown v. Barbacid, 436 F.3d 1376, 1378 (Fed. Cir. 2006) ("The party that is first to conceive the invention in interference, if last to reduce the invention to practice, is entitled to the patent based on prior conception if, as first to conceive, he exercised reasonable diligence from a time before the other party's conception date to his own reduction to practice date.").

[75] *Id.* at 1379.

[76] *Id.* at 1380.

An inventor's diligence is *only* relevant where that inventor was first to conceive and second to reduce to practice.[77] In all other circumstances, there is no need to consider either inventor's diligence. The following illustrates the factual variation that assumes that B is the first to conceive but the second to reduce to practice. If B can demonstrate diligence from a time before A's conception continuously until B reduces the invention to practice, then B may establish priority:

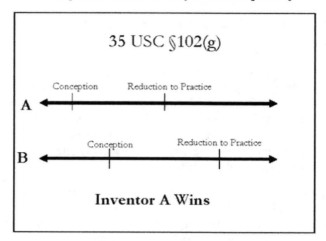

Diligence requires continuous progress toward reduction to practice performed without significant interruption and must be accomplished in a reasonably prompt manner in light of the circumstances. Different types of activity have been used to meet this standard, from formal laboratory work to a variety of other tasks needed to bring the invention into practice. For example, researchers who worked every day for a seven-month period, with the exception of six days spread throughout that time, were held to have demonstrated a sufficient record of reasonable diligence.[78] Likewise, an inventor's efforts to find a construction company to build a facility for the large-scale practice of a process invention was found to have demonstrated diligence.[79]

The diligence standard also applies in cases examining constructive reduction to practice. In *Bey v. Kollonitsch*, the court assessed whether reasonable diligence had been shown for a 41-day critical period prior to the filing of a patent application. There, a patent prosecutor was assigned to draft the application along with 22 other applications concerning closely related technology.[80] The *Bey* court acknowledged that "[c]learly, reasonable diligence can be shown if it is established that the attorney worked reasonably hard on the particular application in question during the continuous critical period."[81] Indeed, an attorney can demonstrate reasonable

---

[77] *Id.*, at 1379 ("diligence is only required for the party that is 'first to conceive.' ").

[78] *Brown*, 436 F.3d at 1380-82.

[79] Scott v. Koyama, 281 F.3d 1243, 1248 (Fed. Cir. 2002).

[80] Bey v. Kollonitsch, 806 F.2d 1024, 1026 (Fed. Cir. 1986).

[81] *Id.* at 1027.

diligence even where there is a reasonable backlog of work that is undertaken in chronological order and promptly completed.[82] In *Bey*, the court determined that the attorney was reasonably diligent in constructively reducing the subject application to practice. Specifically, *Bey* found that work on related cases can be "credited toward reasonable diligence if the work on the related case contributes substantially to the ultimate preparation of the involved application."[83] Further, the *Bey* court noted that the attorney's concurrent work on the 22 patent applications likely expedited the filing of all, serving the purpose of prompt public disclosure of all inventions.[84]

Activity evidencing continual progress to actual practice of the invention or constructive reduction by the filing of a patent application is typically considered sufficient to demonstrate diligence. However, the Federal Circuit has suggested that activity that relates solely to fundraising is insufficient.[85] For example, in *Griffith v. Kanamaru*,[86] the court found that diligence was lacking where a professor claimed that a delay was due to a need to comply with his university's policy to seek outside grant funding for the project. The *Griffith* court found that grant financing was "more in the nature of commercial development, not accepted as an excuse for delay," and that the university appeared to have "consciously chosen to assume the risk that priority in the invention might be lost to an outside inventor."[87]

An inventor is expected to make use of readily available resources. For example, in *Griffith*, the court noted that a professor's promise to a student to perform research that later led to inventive activity was not sufficient to demonstrate diligence, particularly in the absence of a showing that the student "was the only person capable of carrying on" with the experiment.[88] Nonetheless, the court will excuse an inventor's inability to move forward toward reduction to practice due to personal circumstances, such as for a vacation[89] or attending a full time job while undertaking reduction to practice after working hours.[90]

---

[82] *Id.* at 1028 (quoting Rines v. Morgan, 250 F.2d 365, 369 (C.C.P.A. 1957)).

[83] *Id.* at 1029.

[84] *Id.*

[85] Scott v. Koyama, 281 F.3d 1243, 1248 (Fed. Cir. 2002) ("Precedent illustrates the continuum between, on the one hand, ongoing laboratory experimentation, and on the other hand, pure money-raising activity that is entirely unrelated to practice of the process").

[86] Griffith v. Kanamaru, 816 F.2d 624 (Fed. Cir. 1987).

[87] *Id.* at 628. In *Griffith*, the evidence further demonstrated that the inventor had worked in unrelated research and another grant proposal during this time period.

[88] *Id.* at 627.

[89] *See, e.g.*, Reed v. Tornqvist, 436 F.2d 501 (C.C.P.A. 1971).

[90] Courson v. O'Connor, 227 F. 890, 894 (7th Cir. 1915) ("The exercise of reasonable diligence in preparing and filing his application does not require an inventor to devote his entire time thereto, or to abandon his ordinary means of livelihood.").

§ 20.05 "ABANDONED, SUPRESSED OR CONCEALED"

[A] Overview of the Doctrine and Policy

Under § 102(g), a first inventor cannot rely on a reduction to practice that has been *abandoned, suppressed, or concealed*.[91] One may abandon, suppress or conceal an invention by many different types of conduct, such as failing to file a patent application, failing to describe the invention in a public document or by failing to use the invention publicly within a reasonable time after reduction to practice has been completed.

The rule effectuates the policy favoring public benefit — that is, the patent is given to a later inventor who has taken steps to ensure that the public has obtained some advantage. As the Federal Circuit has explained, "the spirit and policy of the patent laws encourage an inventor to take steps to ensure that the public has gained knowledge of the invention which will insure its preservation in the public domain or else run the risk of being dominated by the patent of another."[92]

There are two distinct theories that can prevent a first inventor from establishing prior reduction to practice. First, an inventor may deliberately suppress or conceal an invention. Second, a decision-maker may infer that an inventor has engaged in suppression or concealment due to a long period of inactivity without any excuse or justification.

[B] Intentional Abandonment, Suppression or Concealment

As one court has explained, "[i]ntentional suppression refers to situations in which an inventor designedly, and with the view of applying it indefinitely and exclusively for his own profit, withholds his invention from the public."[93] For example, in *Lutzker v. Plet*,[94] the court considered an inventor's delay for over four years before filing a patent application for an improved canapé maker. After this delay, the inventor began showing a commercial version of the device and then four months later filed an application for a patent.

In *Lutzker*, the inventor attempted to justify the four year delay with evidence of various activities that he had undertaken, including making differently shaped molds to be used in the device, creating a recipe book to accompany the device when sold and work on packaging for the final product. The *Lutzker* court rejected these activities because this work was not directed to the invention as described in the patent, but rather was merely activity undertaken for commercialization. Moreover, *Lutzker* found that this activity demonstrated the inventor's intentional suppression or concealment under § 102(g), based on the inventor's "deliberate

---

[91] 35 U.S.C. §§ 102(g)(1), (2).

[92] Apotex USA, Inc. v. Merck & Co., 254 F.3d 1031, 1038 (Fed. Cir. 2001) (quotations and citations omitted).

[93] Fujikawa v. Wattanasin, 93 F.3d 1559, 1568 (Fed. Cir. 1996) (quotations and citations omitted).

[94] Lutzker v. Plet, 843 F.2d 1364 (Fed. Cir. 1988).

policy not to disclose his invention to the public until he is ready to go into commercial production."[95]

It has been said that the mere passage of time is not sufficient. At a minimum, one must establish that the patentee intentionally delayed filing to prolong the period during which the invention is maintained in secret.[96] However, as described in the next section, a very lengthy and unexcused delay can be used to demonstrate that the first inventor is not entitled to a patent.

[C]   Patentee Delay and an Inference of Abandonment, Suppression or Concealment

A lengthy and unexcused delay may create the inference of suppression or concealment. The courts have not set any "strict time limits regarding the minimum and maximum periods necessary to establish an inference of suppression or concealment."[97] Rather, each case must be decided on its facts based on the circumstances surrounding the first inventor's conduct.

As one example, in *Peeler v. Miller*, a patentee was found to have suppressed an invention by delaying the filing of a patent application for four years after reducing the invention to practice.[98] The *Peeler* court found the patentee's delay was unjustified because the delay was due to a several year backlog from the failure to adequately staff attorneys on prosecution matters.

The dispositive question is not the length of time, but what the inventor or patentee accomplished during that time. In contrast to *Peeler*, in *Checkpoint Systems, Inc. v. ITC*,[99] the court came to an opposite conclusion for the same period of time at issue in *Peeler* — four years between invention and disclosure. The *Checkpoint Systems* court affirmed a finding that throughout this time period, the inventor had diligently developed and commercialized a product incorporating an invention and the related components necessary for its implementation.[100] Because the inventor's activity during this time period was used to move the invention toward public disclosure in the form of a commercial product, the court found that the first inventor had not suppressed or concealed the invention.

---

[95] *Id.* at 1368.

[96] *Fujikawa*, 93 F.3d at 1567.

[97] *Lutzker*, 843 F.2d at 1368.

[98] Peeler v. Miller, 535 F.2d 647, 654 (C.C.P.A. 1976) (". . . a four-year delay from the time an inventor is satisfied with his invention and completes his work on it and the time his assignee-employer files a patent application is, prima facie, unreasonably long in an interference with a party who filed first").

[99] Checkpoint Sys., Inc. v. U.S. Int'l Trade Comm'n, 54 F.3d 756 (Fed. Cir. 1995).

[100] *Id.* at 762. *Checkpoint* distinguished the earlier-described *Lutzer* decision, where commercial activity had been found insufficient to demonstrate diligence. Specifically, the *Checkpoint* court noted that the *Lutzer* court had considered activity that brought the invention to the public in the form of a patent application. Regarding *Lutzer*, activity to commercialize an invention does not assist in the filing of a patent application that does not describe any of the inventor's commercialization efforts. By contrast, reliance on evidence of commercialization was appropriate because the manner of public disclosure at issue in *Checkpoint* was the commercial sale of items incorporating the invention and not the filing of a patent application.

A relatively brief period may be insufficient to result in a finding of suppression. Specifically, in *Fujikawa v. Wattanasin*, the court assessed a seventeen month delay between the invention's reduction to practice and the filing of the patent application.[101] During that time, the inventor was engaged in further work on the invention and the patent prosecutor in gathering information and preparing the application for filing. Despite a three-month gap of inactivity, the *Fujikawa* court found that the case was "squarely within the class of cases in which an inference of suppression or concealment is not warranted."[102] Given that the unexplained period was only three months, the court found that the first inventor was entitled to the patent based on the "complexity of the subject matter and our sense from the record as a whole that throughout the delay [the patentee] was moving, albeit slowly, toward filing an application."[103]

[D] Patentee's Resumed Activity Negating a Finding of Abandonment, Suppression or Concealment

What happens where an inventor initially delays after reducing an invention to practice but then resumes work at a later time? Can such work be considered to counter an inference of abandonment, suppression or concealment? In an *en banc* decision, the Federal Circuit held that a first inventor's resumption of work prior to the time that the second inventor enters the field can be considered as evidence that the first inventor has not abandoned, suppressed or concealed under the pre-AIA § 102(g).[104]

Why should an inventor who has delayed be permitted to show a renewed interest in moving the invention forward toward public disclosure? As an initial matter, such activity is consistent with the disclosure function of a first to invent system. An inventor who resumes activity prior to a second inventor's work is acting at an earlier time and, all other factors being equal, likely to bring the invention to the public first. Moreover, as the Federal Circuit has acknowledged, "[i]nvention is not a neat process."[105] A prior inventor may have undertaken "extensive and productive work done long before the newcomer entered the field" to reduce the invention to practice.[106] Such work should not become a first inventor's disadvantage against one who entered the field at a later time.

One example of this principle occurred in *Apotex U.S.A, Inc. v. Merck & Co., Inc.*[107] The prior inventor Merck created a compound that was used to treat high blood pressure. Although Merck had a patent to the *product* chemical compound, Merck had not pursued a patent for the *process* of making the drug. Merck began selling the drug in 1983. In 1988 and in the following years, Merck disclosed the drug's ingredients within a French pharmaceutical dictionary and a Canadian

---

[101] *Fujikawa*, 93 F.3d at 1568.

[102] *Id.* at 1568.

[103] *Id.* at 1569.

[104] Paulik v. Rizkalla, 760 F.2d 1270, 1272 (Fed. Cir. 1985).

[105] *Id.*

[106] *Id.*

[107] Apotex USA, Inc. v. Merck & Co., 254 F.3d 1031 (Fed. Cir. 2001).

publication. In 1994, Merck disclosed the entire manufacturing process during a trial which took place in Canada. Within days after this testimony was presented, a representative of Apotex claimed conception of a process for making enalapril that was the subject of a later Apotex patent. In response to Apotex's infringement suit, Merck raised § 102(g) as a defense to Apotex's assertion of the process claim.

The *Apotex* court found that Merck had not abandoned, suppressed or concealed the process for making the enalapril sodium compound, although Merck had done nothing to make process public during the five years from 1983 through 1988. The court found Merck's efforts to make its ingredients and process public from 1988 through 1994 sufficient. Specifically, the *Apotex* opinion explained that because Merck had resumed activity prior to Apotex's conception of the process, that Merck could not be found to have abandoned, suppressed or concealed under § 102(g).

However, the courts have viewed an inventor's resumed activity *simply because* a second inventor enters the field unfavorably. If an inventor is spurred into action by the appearance of a second inventor, a court might infer that "but for the efforts of the second inventor, the public would have never gained knowledge of the invention."[108] Thus, an inventor's resumption of activity after a second inventor begins pursuit of the invention may be insufficient to demonstrate a lack of abandonment, suppression or concealment.

§ 20.06 CONCLUSION

The pre-AIA § 102(g) implements the policy of U.S. patent law to award priority to the first inventor. According to the statute, the first to invent is the first to reduce the invention to practice. However, one who is first to conceive but the second to reduce to practice can establish priority with evidence of reasonable diligence to reduce the invention to practice from a time just before the other's conception date. However, no inventor can rely on a date of reduction to practice where that inventor has abandoned, suppressed or concealed an invention. Thus, one who had not made any efforts to patent, publish a description of an invention or publicly use or sell the invention may lose their right in favor of later inventor.

The AIA has eliminated § 102(g), as part of the shift to the first to file system. Although it can be expected that the concepts embedded into the patent system that rely on pre-existing definitions of inventorship will rely on the prior law, the AIA awards the patent to the one who is first to file or disclose. During the transition period, students and practitioners will be expected to understand and apply the law of both as appropriate under the circumstances.

---

[108] Fujikawa v. Wattanasin, 93 F.3d 1559, 1568 (Fed. Cir. 1996).

Chapter 21

NONOBVIOUSNESS

SYNOPSIS

§ 21.01 INTRODUCTION

§ 21.02 THE ORIGINS OF THE NONOBVIOUSNESS REQUIREMENT

    [A] Patentability Standards Prior to the Enactment of § 103

    [B] Origins of the Secondary Considerations of Nonobviousness

    [C] The Former "Flash of Creative Genius" Standard

§ 21.03 NONOBVIOUSNESS FRAMEFORK: *GRAHAM v. JOHN DEERE*

§ 21.04 HOW ANALYTICIS PRIOR ART USED UNDER § 103?

§ 21.05 BACKGROUND: COMBINING MULTIPLE REFERENCES

§ 21.06 CURRENT LAW: *KSR INT'L CO. v. TELEFLEX INC.*

§ 21.07 OBVIOUS TO TRY: *IN RE KUBIN*

§ 21.08 DETERMINING THE SCOPE AND CONTENT OF THE PRIOR ART

    [A] What is "Prior Art" Under § 103?

    [B] A Reference Must Constitute Analogous Art

§ 21.09 SECONDARY CONSIDERATIONS OF NONOBVIOUSNESS

§ 21.10 NONOBVIOUSNESS AND COMBINATION CLAIMS

§ 21.11 CONCLUSION

§ 21.01 INTRODUCTION

To obtain a patent, an applicant must meet the *nonobviousness* standard — that is, the application must claim an invention that represents more than an obvious advance to the existing state of the art.

The nonobviousness requirement has been referred to as "the heart of the patent system and the justification of patent grants."[1] Deriving from constitutional roots, the doctrine is based on the principle that "[i]nnovation, advancement, and things which add to the sum of useful knowledge are inherent requisites in a patent system which by constitutional command must 'promote the Progress of . . . useful Arts."[2] The nonobviousness requirement ensures that those constitutional goals are

---

[1] Hon. Giles S. Rich, *Laying The Ghost Of The 'Invention' Requirement*, 1 AIPLA Q.J. 26 (1972-1973).

[2] Graham v. John Deere Co., 383 U.S. 1, 6 (1966).

satisfied by reserving the patent grant only for those contributions that add to the sum of available knowledge and contribute more than would have been obvious to one of skill in the art.[3]

35 U.S.C. § 103(a) provides that a patent will not be granted "if the differences between the subject matter sought to be patented and the prior art are such that the subject matter as a whole would have been obvious" to the person of ordinary skill. For patent applications decided under the pre-AIA law, the time at which obviousness is assessed is the time of invention. For those examined under the AIA, the relevant time is the effective filing date of the patent at issue.

Section 103 is distinct from § 102's novelty requirement. Of the two, § 102 is more restrictive for two reasons. First, § 102 prior art is limited to consideration of a *single reference.* By contrast, a patent may be deemed obvious under § 103 using *multiple references* in addition to information that is in the state of the art. Second, § 102 novelty requires strict identity, such that each element of the claim must be found, either expressly or inherently, in the reference. Section 103 includes no such requirement, and instead inquires whether the state of knowledge and other drivers, such as market demand or design trends, would have rendered the invention obvious to one of ordinary skill. Because of § 102's additional require-ments, a claim may be novel under § 102 but obvious (and therefore invalid) under § 103. As another example, a single reference may not contain all claim elements and therefore present no impediment under § 102, but be deemed obvious if those elements appear in multiple references that would have been combined by the person of ordinary skill.

The nonobviousness analysis begins with a comparison between the patent claims and the existing state of the art. Once the distinctions are identified, the fundamental question is whether, given the state of knowledge existent at the time of invention, one of ordinary skill in the art would have been led from the prior art to the same solution set forth in the claim. In answering this question, the finder of fact can consider objective indicia of nonobviousness, called *secondary consider-ations,* that demonstrate that others in the art viewed the advance as significant. Some examples of secondary considerations are the commercial success of products incorporating the patent, licensing of the patent, whether the invention has been copied, a long-felt but unsolved need, the failure of others to solve the problem, and laudatory comments made by others in the field.

Nonobviousness is considered by the U.S. PTO in the examination process. If the situation warrants, one accused of infringement must prove nonobviousness in litigation by clear and convincing evidence. As this Chapter demonstrates, section 103 has been subject to an evolving series of case law interpretation.

---

[3] Rich, *supra* note 1, at 1; *see* Tyler T. Ochoa, *Origins and Meanings of the Public Domain,* 28 U. DAYTON L. REV. 215 (2002) (describing the history of the Statute of Monopolies).

§ 21.02   THE ORIGINS OF THE NONOBVIOUSNESS REQUIREMENT

[A]   Patentability Standards Prior to the Enactment of § 103

The nonobviousness requirement arose from the decisional law of the courts. The earliest patent statute, enacted in 1790, authorized a board comprised of the U.S. Secretary of State, the Secretary for the Department of War, and the Attorney General to issue a patent "if [they] shall deem the invention or discovery *sufficiently useful and important.*"[4] Very little was known about how this standard was applied. Although a draft of the later 1793 Act proposed a defense if the patented invention "is so unimportant and *obvious* that it ought not to be the subject of an exclusive right,"[5] that particular phrase was never enacted. For example, *Earle v. Sawyer*, decided in a Circuit Court under the 1793 Patent Act, rejected the defendant's argument that a patent "must be what would not occur to all persons skilled in the art."[6] Instead, this court found that the patentability requirements were limited to novelty and utility.[7]

In 1850, the U.S. Supreme Court established the nonobviousness doctrine in *Hotchkiss v. Greenwood.*[8] The Court considered a patent describing a doorknob made of clay that was attached to a shank and spindle. The clay knob had a dovetail cavity in the bottom of the knob. The art already included the use of a shank and spindle mechanism attached to metal and wood knobs. Further, the art already included knobs made of clay. As the court explained, ". . . the knob is not new, nor the metallic shank and spindle, nor the dovetail form of the cavity in the knob, nor the means by which the metallic shank is securely fastened therein."[9] The sole distinguishing feature of the *Hotchkiss* patent was the use of *clay* with the shank and spindle connection, which the patentee claimed was better and cheaper than using metal or wood.

---

[4] Butterworth v. U.S., 112 U.S. 50, 64 (1884); For one account of the history of the nonobviousness requirement, *see* George M. Sirilla & Honorable Giles S. Rich, *35 U.S.C. 103: From Hotchkiss to Hand to Rich, the Obvious Patent Law Hall of Famers*, 32 J. MARSHALL L. REV. 437 (1999).

[5] *See* Edward C. Walterscheid, *The Hotchkiss Unobviousness Standard: Early Judicial Activism In The Patent Law*, 13 J. INTELL. PROP. L. 103, 108 (2005) (describing 1793 legislative amendment process) (emphasis added).

[6] Earle v. Sawyer, 8 F. Cas. 254, 255 (D. Mass. 1825).

[7] *Id.* at 256.

[8] Hotchkiss v. Greenwood, 52 U.S. 248 (1851).

[9] Dundas v. Hitchcock, 53 U.S. 256, 265 (1852).

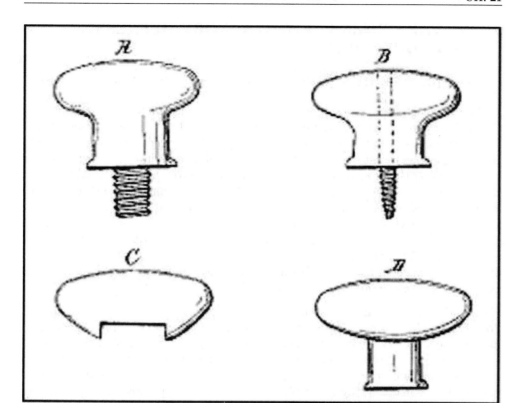

The trial court had given an instruction that if the jury found that it took "no more ingenuity or skill required to construct the knob in this way than that possessed by an ordinary mechanic acquainted with the business, the patent was invalid."[10] The Supreme Court affirmed the use of this instruction, explaining:

> . . . .unless more ingenuity and skill in applying the old method of fastening the shank and the knob were required in the application of it to the clay or porcelain knob than were possessed by an ordinary mechanic acquainted with the business, there was an absence of that degree of skill and ingenuity which constitute essential elements of every invention.[11]

Hotchkiss affirmed the jury's finding of invalidity under this standard, stating that the mere substitution of clay for wood or metal was "the work of the skilful mechanic, not that of the inventor."[12] Today, the *Hotchkiss* "ordinary mechanic acquainted with the business" standard is echoed in § 103, which defines nonobviousness as something obvious to "a person having ordinary skill in the art." The *Hotchkiss* test distinguishes between results delivered by a skilled worker from that delivered by an inventor. In later cases, this differentiation evolved into the a

---

[10] *Id.* at 265.

[11] *Id.* at 267.

[12] *Id.*

standard which became known as the *invention requirement*.[13]

[B] Origins of the Secondary Considerations of Nonobviousness

Twenty years after *Hotchkiss*, the Supreme Court added a layer to the nonobviousness standard by allowing the examination of certain factors grounded on objective evidence. In *Smith v. Goodyear Dental Vulcanite Co.*,[14] the Court considered a patent for dentures that relied on a vulcanized rubber insert to hold the teeth. At that time, various metals had been used, which were far more expensive and uncomfortably rigid. The defendant argued that the patent failed under *Hotchkiss*, asserting that the use of rubber could not constitute an invention because it represented the mere substitution of one substance (vulcanized rubber) for another (metal).

The *Smith* Court found that the patentee met the invention requirement, rejecting the argument that the patent claimed more than an insignificant substitution of materials. Finding that the device had "new uses and properties," the Court cited a number of objective facts that demonstrated that the patent advanced the art.[15] These included citation to writings that demonstrated that others had attempted to use vulcanized rubber and failed, a long-felt need for such a device, the fact that others had made laudatory comments about the patent as "the greatest improvement in dentistry" made in many years, and that the device had experienced widespread adoption in the field.[16] *Smith* used these facts to the support an inference that the patent included what "was, in truth, invention."[17]

Under current law, such facts are among the *secondary considerations* that are currently used to assess nonobviousness under modern standards. Today, these secondary considerations include commercial success of the patented invention, the failure of others to find the solution, a long felt need for the invention, copying, laudatory praise, and licensing by others.[18] This list is not exclusive. Rather, courts are willing to consider available evidence that demonstrates that unaffiliated parties within the market consider the advance significant.

[C] The Former "Flash of Creative Genius" Standard

In the hundred years that followed the *Hotchkiss* case, the courts and patent examiners failed to achieve uniformity in their application of the invention requirement. One decision that drew some of the most serious criticism was the

---

[13] *See, e.g.*, Reckendorfer v. Faber, 92 U.S. 347, 355 (1876) (determining patentability based on whether the asserted patent involved "an invention" or instead was merely "a product of mechanical skill").

[14] Smith v. Goodyear Dental Vulcanite Co., 93 U.S. 486 (1877).

[15] *Id.* at 494.

[16] *Id.* at 495.

[17] *Id.*

[18] *See generally* Robert P. Merges, *Commercial Success and Patent Standards: Economic Perspectives on Innovation*, 76 CAL. L. REV. 803 (1988).

Supreme Court's 1941 decision *Cuno Engineering Corp. v. Automatic Devices Corp.*[19] There, the Court considered the validity of a patent for an improved cigar lighter designed for use in an automobile. Unlike the prior art which required the user to monitor the heating cycle of the lighter, the patent at issue in *Cuno* used a sensor to turn off the heating element when it reached the proper temperature. According to the patentee, this improvement eliminated the need for the user to monitor the lighter's temperature.

In *Cuno*, the Supreme Court held that the patent was invalid for the failure to meet the invention requirement. *Cuno* is famous for requiring a "flash of creative genius" to meet this standard:

> That is to say the new device, however useful it may be, must reveal the flash of creative genius not merely the skill of the calling. If it fails, it has not established its right to a private grant on the public domain.[20]

In result, *Cuno* held that the patentee had "merely incorporated the well-known thermostat into the old 'wireless' lighter to produce a more efficient, useful and convenient article," and therefore did not meet "the level of inventive genius which the Constitution, Art. I, s 8, authorizes Congress to reward."[21] More broadly, *Cuno* was viewed by some as the culmination of a trend in the U.S. Supreme Court to introduce the inventor's subjective state of mind into the analysis and to raise the patentability standard. The *Cuno* opinion noted that a strict application of the patentability standard was necessary "lest in the constant demand for new appliances the heavy hand of tribute be laid on each slight technological advance in an art."[22] As Justice Learned Hand observed in 1942, "[w]e cannot . . . ignore the fact that the Supreme Court, whose word is final, has for a decade or more shown an increasing disposition to raise the standard of originality necessary for a patent."[23] Perhaps one of the sharpest criticisms was stated by U.S. Supreme Court Justice Jackson, in a dissent written in 1949, referring to the "strong passion in this Court for striking [patents] down so that the only patent that is valid is one which this Court has not been able to get its hands on."[24]

This is not to suggest that interpretations of *Cuno* were uniform, a circumstance that caused additional concerns.[25] For example, a National Patent Planning Commission appointed by President Roosevelt issued a report in 1943, stating, "[t]he most serious weakness in the present patent system is the lack of a uniform test or standard for determining whether the particular contribution of an invention merits the award of the patent grant."[26] Recognizing that patentability decisions

---

[19] Cuno Engineering Corp. v. Automatic Devices Corp., 314 U.S. 84 (1941).

[20] *Id.* at 91.

[21] *Id.*

[22] *Id.* at 92.

[23] Picard v. United Aircraft Corp., 128 F.2d 632, 636 (2d Cir. 1942).

[24] Jungersen v. Ostby & Barton Co., 335 U.S. 560, 572 (1949).

[25] *See*, Aram Boyajian, 25 J. Pat. Off. Soc'y 776 (1943) (describing differing reactions and interpretations of *Cuno*).

[26] National Patent Planning Commission, *The American Patent System, Report Of The National Patent Planning Commission, reprinted in*, 25 J. Pat. Off. Soc'y 455, 462 (1943).

were being made by patent examiners and courts at all levels, the report stated that "[t]here is an ever widening gulf between the decisions of the Patent Office in granting patents and decisions of the courts who pass on their validity."[27]

Giles Rich, a patent attorney who later served as a justice on the Federal Circuit, wrote of the patent system at this time that:

> . . . the requirement for "invention" became the plaything of the judiciary and many judges delighted in devising and expounding their own ideas of what it meant. This kind of mystical reasoning left the judiciary free to indulge their personal whims about patentability . . . . [W]e went through periods of too much leniency and too much strictness, depending primarily, just as now, on what judges thought and the mood of country.[28]

As Justice Learned Hand described of patent practice at this time, the invention standard had become "as fugitive, impalpable, wayward, and vague a phantom as exists in the whole paraphernalia of legal concepts."[29] As the National Patent Planning Commission stated, "[n]o other feature of our law is more destructive to the purpose of the patent system than this existing uncertainty as to the validity of a patent," and that a uniform legislative standard was necessary.[30] In an effort to stabilize the standard, the 1952 Patent Act was amended to add § 103. This provision shifted the terminology from the "invention requirement" to the term used today, "nonobviousness." As has been explained, the word "invention" was "in fact, carefully avoided with a view to making a fresh start, free of all the divergent court opinions about 'invention.' "[31]

§ 21.03　NONOBVIOUSNESS ANALYTIC FRAMEFORK: *GRAHAM v. JOHN DEERE*

The Supreme Court's first opportunity to construe § 103's nonobviousness requirement was in the 1966 case *Graham v. John Deere Co.*[32] Ultimately, this case became an important first step toward the creation of uniform standards for assessing obviousness. By the time *Graham* reached the Supreme Court, the Court's *Hotchkiss* decision from a century earlier had already laid some groundwork by articulating a standard for "invention" that required more ingenuity and skill than possessed by an ordinary mechanic. Some cases, including the Court's *Smith* decision, articulated objective criteria to assist in determining whether claims were patentable. Section 103 had been enacted among concerns that the invention requirement failed to provide meaningful guidance that could be consistently applied by the courts, the Patent Office, and patent practitioners.[33] As the

---

[27] *Id.*

[28] Rich, *supra* note 1, at 31.

[29] Harries v. Air King Products Co. 183 F.2d 158, 162 (2d Cir. 1950).

[30] National Patent Planning Commission, *supra* note 26, at 462-63.

[31] Rich, *supra* note 1, at 157.

[32] Graham v. John Deere Co., 383 U.S. 1, 6 (1966).

[33] *Id.* at 11-12 (". . . [invention] cannot be defined in such manner as to afford any substantial aid in determining whether a particular device involves an exercise of the inventive faculty or not.").

Graham Court acknowledged, the invention standard instead "brought about a large variety of opinions as to its meaning both in the Patent Office, in the courts, and at the bar."[34]

In the opinion, the *Graham* Court explicitly associated the nonobviousness requirement with the U.S. Constitution's grant of legislative power to create the patent system. The Court explained, "innovation, advancement, and things which add to the sum of useful knowledge are inherent requisites in a patent system which by constitutional command must 'promote the Progress of . . . useful Arts.' "[35] The *Graham* decision focused on the writings of Thomas Jefferson, whom the Court identified as an inventor, an early administrator of the patent system, and the author of the 1793 Patent Act. The Court noted that Jefferson had been adverse to monopolies, but had come to believe that a limited patent system should be enacted so that "ingenuity should receive a liberal encouragement."[36] The *Graham* Court summarized Jefferson's views on the patent system as follows:

> Only inventions and discoveries which furthered human knowledge, and were new and useful, justified the special inducement of a limited private monopoly. Jefferson did not believe in granting patents for small details, obvious improvements, or frivolous devices. His writings evidence his insistence upon a high level of patentability.[37]

Graham further observed that Jefferson had anticipated that the courts would develop patentability standards, and that the *Hotchkiss* case "laid the cornerstone of the judicial evolution" of such a standard.[38] Turning to the specific construction of § 103, the Court determined that the first sentence of the statute was "strongly reminiscent of the language in *Hotchkiss*"[39] and therefore represented a Congressional endorsement of this early decision. That is, under § 103, if "the difference between the subject matter sought to be patented and the prior art . . . is such that the subject matter as a whole would have been obvious at the time to a person skilled in the art, then the subject matter cannot be patented."[40]

Graham set forth an analytical framework for resolving the question of whether the nonobviousness requirement has been met:

- First, one must determine the scope and content of the prior art;

- Second, one compares the differences between the prior art and the claims at issue;

- Third, one determines the level of ordinary skill in the pertinent art; and

---

[34] *Id.* at 12.

[35] *Id.* at 6, *citing* U.S. Const., art. I, § 8, cl. 8.

[36] *Graham*, 383 U.S at 8, *quoting* Letter to Oliver Evans (May 1807), *in* V Writings of Thomas Jefferson at 75-76 (Washington ed.).

[37] *Graham*, 383 U.S. at 9.

[38] *Id.* at 11.

[39] *Id.* at 14.

[40] *Id.* at 15.

- Fourth, determine the ultimate question of whether the claims as a whole would have been obvious to one of ordinary skill at the time of the invention.

As to the ultimate issue of nonobviousness in the fourth step, the *Graham* Court explained that one may consult the secondary considerations in answering this inquiry. Additionally, the *Graham* Court examined the second sentence of § 103(a), which provides that "[p]atentability shall not be negatived by the manner in which the invention was made." This sentence, according to *Graham*, sought to abolish *Cuno's* "flash of creative genius" test.[41]

The *Graham* Court established a number of important principles for nonobviousness as a patentability standard. First, the Court placed this patentability requirement on constitutional foundations. Second, the Court articulated the analysis set forth in § 103 as an objective comparison of the claims with the existing state of the art. In doing so, *Graham* ensured that invention did not rest on any subjective criteria such as the inventor's state of mind. Third, the Court gave the analysis a four-part structure that currently holds today. Finally, *Graham's* interpretation of § 103, the relevant question is not whether the claim includes an *invention*, but rather whether the claim is patentable as *nonobvious*.

§ 21.04   HOW IS PRIOR ART USED UNDER § 103?

Unlike an analysis under § 102, which requires an element-by-element identity with the proposed claim, § 103 asks whether, based on a comparison of the claim and the state of the art, the invention would have been obvious to one of ordinary skill. How does one apply this standard as a practical matter? Certainly, simply isolating disparate elements that may be scattered throughout the prior art and adding them together is decidedly *not* correct. Such an analysis is contrary to the purpose of the statute — that is, the capabilities of the person of ordinary skill must be incorporated into the inquiry.

The Federal Circuit's *In re Winslow* provides some guidance.[42] There, an applicant appealed the rejection of claims directed to a packaging device that used a jet of air to open flexible plastic bags so that items could then be inserted. The apparatus shot the air into the uppermost of a horizontal stack of bags, which were held in place during the operation by the use of pins that punctured through the bag flaps. The Patent Office held the Winslow claims obvious over a number of references, including Hellman, which disclosed a machine for filling bags held vertically and held in place using a rod. The examiner also relied on another reference, known as Gerbe, which disclosed the same apparatus as the Winslow application with one exception. Instead of using pins to hold the bags in place, Gerbe had merely used a stop.

---

[41] *Id.* at 15. The *Graham* Court explained that *Cuno* had, in fact, been misunderstood to some degree. In particular, *Cuno* had "merely rhetorically restated the requirement that the subject matter sought to be patented must be beyond the skill of the calling" and not created any new patentability standard based on the state of mind of the inventor. *Id.* at n. 7.

[42] *See In re* Winslow, 365 F.2d 1017 (C.C.P.A. 1966).

The *Winslow* court affirmed rejection of the claims. In particular, *Winslow* found that Hellman's use of a "rod" was not distinguishable from the application's use of a pin to hold the bag in place. Additionally, *Winslow* found that Helman's use of vertical placement of the bags did not render the application's horizontal orientation of the bags nonobvious, as the "change requires only obvious mechanical adaptations such as substituting a spring to push up instead of a weight to slide down."[43]

In an often-quoted portion of the *Winslow* opinion, known as the "Winslow Tableau," the court described the proper mode of comparison between the prior art and the subject matter sought to be patented:

> We think the proper way to apply the 103 obviousness test to a case like this is to first picture the inventor as working in his shop with the prior art references-which he is presumed to know- hanging on the walls around him . . . . If there were any bag holding problem in the Gerbe machine when plastic bags were used, their flaps being gripped only by spring pressure between the top and bottom plates, Winslow would have said to himself, "Now what can I do to hold them more securely?" Looking around the walls, he would see Hellman's envelopes with holes in their flaps hung on a rod. He would then say to himself, "Ha. I can punch holes in my bags and put a little rod (pin) through the holes. That will hold them. After filling the bags, I'll pull them off the pins as does Hellman . . . ."[44]

Of course, the discussion of the inventive process in the *Winslow* decision is purely hypothetical. It is important to keep in mind that the nonobviousness inquiry is *objective* and based on the perspective of *one of ordinary skill in the art*. The inventor's subjective state of mind during the inventive process is not relevant. Rather, the nonobviousness analysis examines the differences between the prior art and the claim sought to be patented in light of the problem to be solved, and considers whether one of ordinary skill in the art would have been led to the result obtained in the claim under examination.

A critical aspect of *Winslow* is that the one of ordinary skill in the art is charged with knowledge of all of the relevant prior art. That is, the analysis of whether a claim is obvious to one of ordinary skill presumes that this hypothetical person has knowledge of all of the potentially invalidating references pertinent to the subject matter of the patent. Further, Winslow demonstrates that the person of ordinary skill can, if properly motivated, undertake some problem-solving abilities by piecing together already-existing information to arrive at a solution.

§ 21.05 BACKGROUND: COMBINING MULTIPLE REFERENCES

As previously stated, a nonobviousness analysis permits reliance on multiple references. As one example, in *Winslow*, the Supreme Court determined that the claims were obvious based on the combination of the rods from the Hellman reference with the apparatus of Gerbe. Prior to 2007, the Federal Circuit placed a

---

[43] *Id.* at 1577.

[44] *Id.* at 1578.

limitation on the use of multiple references known as the *teaching, suggestion or motivation to combine* test (sometimes called "the suggestion test" or the "TSM test"). This test was developed to avoid a problem known as *hindsight bias.*[45] During this time, the Court developed this test to address the statutory requirement that nonobviousness be assessed *"at the time the invention was made."*[46] As a practical matter, one assessing nonobviousness does so *after* the invention has been made with full knowledge of the patent that discloses the solution. These circumstances are said to give rise to hindsight bias. This phenomenon occurs when "[i]ndividuals routinely (and unconsciously) overestimate what would have been anticipated in foresight and tend to view what actually occurred as having been relatively inevitable and foreseeable."[47] The experience is akin to taking an exam when one already has seen the correct answer. At that point, solving the problem seems easy because one already knows both that the problem can be solved, and how to do so. When that occurs, "invention is often a combination of known elements which in hindsight seems preordained."[48]

To counter this bias, the Federal Circuit applied a test that required a *teaching, suggestion or motivation to combine* where multiple references are used.[49] Under this requirement, a court was required to examine whether one of ordinary skill in the art would have had some reason to combine the references which demonstrate nonobviousness. In doing so, a court could have considered a broader array of information than the references themselves. For example, the teaching, suggestion or motivation to combine might have been found in common knowledge, the prior art as a whole, or the nature of the problem to be solved.[50]

The Federal Circuit's *McGinley v. Franklin Sports, Inc.*, illustrates how this test was applied.[51] The patent was a standard baseball modified for pitching instruction through the addition of printed markings that included three sets of "finger placement indicia" to demonstrate how the baseball should be gripped for throwing three different types of pitches.[52] The ball had two different types of indicia, one for left-handed and another for right-handed pitchers. Additionally, the ball had an egg-shaped marking to orient the ball to the pitcher's palm. Although the McGinley patent did not include indicia for the thumb, the written description stated that the

---

[45] *See generally* Gregory N. Mandel, *Patently Non-Obvious: Empirical Demonstration that the Hindsight Bias Renders Patent Decisions Irrational*, 67 Ohio St. L.J. 1391, 1393 (2006) ("The core requirement for obtaining a patent is that the invention was not obvious at the time it was invented. . . . A proper non-obvious decision must not take into account the ex post fact that the invention was actually achieved."); and Orthopedic Equipment Co., Inc. v. U.S., 702 F.2d 1005, 1012 (Fed. Cir. 1983).

[46] 35 U.S.C. § 103(a) (emphasis added). Under the AIA, this has shifted to the effective filing date of the patent.

[47] *Orthopedic Equipment*, 702 F.2d. at 102.

[48] McGinley v. Franklin Sports, Inc., 262 F.3d 1339, 1351 (Fed. Cir. 2001).

[49] *Id., see also* MPEP § 2143.01 ("Obviousness can only be established by combining or modifying the teachings of the prior art to produce the claimed invention where there is some teaching, suggestion, or motivation to do so").

[50] DyStar Textilfarben GmbH & Co. Deutschland KG v. C.H. Patrick Co., 464 F.3d 1356, 1361 (Fed. Cir. 2006).

[51] *McGinley*, 262 F.3d at 1339.

[52] *Id.* at 1343.

thumb was to be positioned opposite the finger placement indicia.

One reference was Pratt, a prior art patent that disclosed markings on a standard baseball to teach the user three types of pitches. Pratt featured an equatorial band of complimentary colors that, when the ball was thrown with the correct spin, would visually blend into a single color to signify that the ball's rotation was proper. Unlike McGinley, Pratt did not include separate markings for left and right handed pitchers. Further, although Pratt described "phantom lines" for finger placement in the patent disclosure, Pratt did not describe these lines as actual markings on the baseball or any marking for the orientation of the pitcher's palm. Morgan, another asserted reference, used a lightweight, inexpensive replica rather than an actual baseball and a single set of markings for the forefinger, middle finger, and thumb.

Relevant here, *McGinley* considered the defendant's argument that McGinley was invalid as obvious in light of the combination of Pratt and Morgan. *McGinley* found that the then-required teaching, suggestion or motivation to combine was not present and therefore the patent was not rendered obvious. For Morgan, the court found that "none of the embodiments discuss or suggest using a conventional baseball as opposed to a hollow shell comprising two metallic or plastic hemispheres glued or otherwise bonded together."[53]

Significantly, the *McGinley* court observed that Pratt and Morgan *taught away* from McGinley. For Pratt, the court observed that "to combine the finger placements of Morgan onto the Pratt ball would also render the Pratt ball inoperable, by eliminating the multi-colored equatorial band, a claimed feature of the Pratt patent also required for successful operation of Pratt's invention."[54] On these basis, among others, the Federal Circuit affirmed the jury's validity finding.[55]

§ 21.06   CURRENT LAW: *KSR INT'L CO. v. TELEFLEX INC.*

Current law supports *McGinley's* holding that references that teach away from a claim are unlikely to render a claim obvious. Nonetheless, nonobviousness has undergone significant changes since *McGinley*. In particular, over the years a number of commentators criticized the Federal Circuit's application of the teaching, suggestion or motivation to combine test. For example, a 2004 report by the National Academy of Sciences states, "[s]ome critics have suggested that the standards of patentability — especially the non-obviousness standard — have

---

[53] *Id.* at 1354.

[54] *Id.*

[55] The Federal Circuit also found that Morgan's finger placement indicia were too large to be repeated three different times on a standard baseball, as required by the McGinley claims. Additionally, the Federal Circuit affirmed the jury's finding that Pratt alone did not render McGinley obvious. Specifically, *McGinley* noted that adding finger markings to the Pratt ball would have interfered with the multi-colored equatorial band such as to render Pratt inoperable. Further, *McGinley* noted that Pratt's disclosed phantom lines were so large that it would be impractical to reproduce them three times on a single ball as required by McGinley. *Id.*

become too lax as a result of court decisions."[56] During this same time period, the Federal Circuit held that nonobviousness could not be shown by demonstrating that the patented solution would be *obvious to try*.[57] Under these former authorities, an invalid claim must be obvious to one of ordinary skill; however, an invention that derived from a research plan that would have been merely obvious to try was nonobvious.[58]

In 2007, the U.S. Supreme Court reconsidered nonobviousness in *KSR Int'l Co. v. Teleflex Inc.*[59] In *KSR*, the patentee Teleflex asserted a patent (the "Engelgau patent"), which disclosed an automotive gas pedal that used an electronic sensor attached to the pivot point. When the pedal was either raised or lowered by the driver, the electronic sensor transmitted the pedal's position to a computer that controlled the throttle in the vehicle's engine.

The district court found the Engelgau patent obvious based on a number of references, some of which relied on mechanical sensing systems and others which included electronic sensors. Among other things, the district court found that these references, coupled with the industry's move toward using electronic controls, indicated that "the state of the industry would lead inevitably to combinations of electronic sensors and adjustable pedals."[60] The Federal Circuit reversed, finding that the district court had failed to properly apply the teaching, suggestion or motivation requirement by making appropriate specific findings demonstrating how the prior art solved the precise problem that the patentee was trying to solve such that one of ordinary skill would have been likely to consult those references. Further, the Federal Circuit found that the prior art did not render Engelgau obvious because the references merely rendered the solution described in Engelgau "obvious to try."[61]

---

[56] Nat'l Research Council, A PATENT SYSTEM FOR THE 21ST CENTURY 3 (Stephen A. Merrill et al. eds.) (2004).

[57] *In re* Deuel, 51 F.3d 1552, 1559 (Fed. Cir. 1995) *overruled in* KSR Int'l Co., v. Teleflex, Inc., 127 S. Ct. 1727 (2007); see also *In re* Kubin, 561 F.3d 1351 (Fed. Cir. 2009) (criticizing *Deuel* in light of the *KSR* decision).

[58] *See In re* Henderson, 348 F.2d 550 (C.C.P.A. 1965).

[59] KSR Int'l Co., v. Teleflex, Inc., 127 S. Ct. 1727 (2007).

[60] *Id.* at 1738.

[61] At the time that the Federal Circuit appellate panel decided *KSR*, their decisions held that a patent was not rendered obvious simply because the references rendered the invention obvious to try. *See, e.g., In re* Deuel, 51 F.3d 1552, 1559 (Fed Cir. 1995); and *In re* O'Farrell, 853 F.2d 894, 903 (Fed. Cir. 1988) (explaining the prohibition against a finding of obviousness based on references that rendered an invention obvious to try).

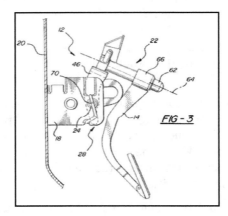

FIG - 3

Reversing the Federal Circuit, the Supreme Court's *KSR* opinion sought to return the obviousness inquiry to the fundamental question of "whether a patent claiming the combination of elements in the prior art is obvious."[62] To answer this question, *KSR* recognized that a finding of obviousness could be based on any number of different sources of information, such as "the interrelated teachings of multiple patents; the effects of demands known to the design community or present in the marketplace; and the background knowledge possessed by a person of ordinary skill in the art," and taking into account "the inferences and creative steps that a person of ordinary skill in the art would employ."[63]

In some cases, *KSR* recognized that it may be important to identify a *reason to combine* information available in disparate sources to avoid hindsight bias, language that appeared to allude to the teaching, suggestions or motivation test. However, *KSR* stated that a rigid and mandatory application of the teaching, suggestion or motivation test was inconsistent with the nonobviousness standard as set forth in the previous Supreme Court cases. Finding the Federal Circuit's approach erroneous, the Supreme Court instead endorsed a functional approach to the nonobviousness inquiry. Specifically, *KSR* promulgated a number of guidelines for nonobviousness, as follows:

- Information other than that specifically disclosed in cited prior art may bridge the gap between the prior art and the claim under examination. This may include market demand, forces or pressures, design trends or solutions that render the claim obvious to try. Further, "the combination of familiar elements according to known methods is likely to be obvious when it does no more than yield predictable results."[64]

- The prior art references themselves need not describe any specific teaching, suggestion or motivation to combine for the references to render

---

[62] *KSR*, 127 S. Ct. at 1740.

[63] *Id.* at 1740-41.

[64] *Id.* at 1739.

a claim obvious. Rather, a reason to combine may exist based on the inferences and creative steps that one of ordinary skill in the art would undertake.

• The Federal Circuit erred in looking only to the specific problem the patentee solved in determining whether a teaching, suggestion or motivation to combine existed. The *KSR* Court stated that instead, "*any* need or problem known in the field of endeavor at the time of invention and addressed by the patent can provide a reason for combining the elements in the manner claimed."[65]

• Available references should not be limited to those designed to solve the same problem as the patentee. The *KSR* Court said that "[a] person of ordinary skill is also a person of ordinary creativity, not an automaton" and may be assumed to use references that "may have obvious uses beyond their primary purposes."[66]

• A reference may be considered even if it renders the patented solution merely "obvious to try." As *KSR* explained, where there is "a design need or market pressure to solve a problem and there are a finite number of identified, predictable solutions, a person of ordinary skill has good reason to pursue the known options within his or her technical grasp."[67]

• The teaching, suggestions or motivation to combine standard should not be applied in a rigid manner simply to prevent hindsight bias. Rather, hindsight bias should be considered, but "preventative rules that deny fact finders recourse to common sense, however, are neither necessary under [the] case law nor consistent with it."[68]

In result, *KSR* found Engelgau obvious. The relevant inquiry, according to the Court, was "whether a pedal designer of ordinary skill, facing the wide range of needs created by developments in the field of endeavor" would have been led to upgrade the former mechanical implementations with an electronic sensor.[69] The Court found that, as cars transitioned toward reliance on computer-controlled components, one of ordinary skill in the art would have looked to the prior art solutions to arrive at a pedal with an electronic sensor on the pedal's pivot point as claimed in the patent at issue.

The Supreme Court's 2007 *KSR* opinion re-affirmed the fundamental principle — established in *Hotchkiss* — that a patent must provide more than can be readily developed by one of ordinary skill to obtain a patent. As part of this analysis, the Court recognized that forces beyond information contained in scientific literature or prior patents might render a patent obvious. Although *KSR* did not entirely eliminate the teaching, suggestion or motivation test, the Court rejected a formalistic application of the test. Additionally, *KSR* reconfirmed the *Graham*

---

[65] *Id.* at 1742 (emphasis added).

[66] *Id.*

[67] *Id.*

[68] *Id.* at 1742-43.

[69] *Id.* at 1744.

Court's analytic framework and the need for caution with respect to hindsight bias in performing this inquiry.

KSR offered a number of refinements to the nonobviousness analysis to implement these views. The *KSR* Court made clear that one of ordinary skill in the art is presumed to have some problem-solving capabilities. *KSR* rejected the notion that the teaching, suggestion or motivation to combine standard be subject to categorical rules, and that such motivation could be found in the fact that a design need or market pressure may lead one of ordinary skill to "to fit the teachings of multiple patents together like pieces of a puzzle."[70] It is evident that the *KSR* Court sought to allow findings of nonobviousness with greater frequency, as "the results of ordinary innovation are not the subject of exclusive rights under the patent laws."[71]

§ 21.07   OBVIOUS TO TRY: *IN RE KUBIN*

The Supreme Court's *KSR* decision has precipitated some lower court decisions that have important consequences. One of these is *In re Kubin,*[72] a post-*KSR* decision that analyzed nonobviousness for a claim to a combination of an identified isolated DNA fragment that could bind to a particular protein, known as CD48. According to the prior art, the isolated DNA fragment, known as NAIL, is a specific portion of a cell known as a "Natural Killer" cell. These Natural Killer cells had been shown to be capable of activating mechanisms within the body to kill toxic cells. NAIL is a specific receptor protein that played a role in activating Natural Killer cells.

The *Kubin* inventors claimed to have discovered a relationship between the NAIL sequence and CD48 that resulted in increased immune response. The claim at issue described a broader genus of the NAIL protein by including variants purportedly limited by the gene's propensity to bind with CD48:

> 73. An isolated nucleic acid molecule comprising a polynucleotide encoding a polypeptide at least 80% identical to amino acids 22–221 of SEQ ID NO:2, wherein the polypeptide binds CD48.

The *Kubin* opinion noted that a prior art reference — called "Valiante" — disclosed the NAIL protein, and that NAIL's specific sequence could be readily generated through conventional methodologies. Further, the record demonstrated that CD48 was the natural counter-structure to the NAIL protein — in other words, the two fit together like complimentary puzzle pieces. As the court stated, NAIL's ability to bind with CD48 was "not an additional requirement imposed by the claims on the NAIL protein, but rather a property necessarily present in NAIL."[73] Finding the claim obvious, the court explained:

---

[70] *Id.* at 1742.

[71] *Id.* at 1746.

[72] *In re* Kubin, 561 F.3d 1351 (Fed. Cir. 2009).

[73] *Id.* at 1357.

Valiante's p38 is the same protein as appellant's NAIL, Valiante's teaching to obtain cDNA encoding p38 also necessarily teaches one to obtain cDNA of NAIL that exhibits the CD48 binding property.[74]

As the *Kubin* court recognized, the discovery of an already existing attribute, such as the inherent binding relationship between NAIL and CD48, was not an invention.

In the course of the opinion, the *Kubin* court provided valuable guidance for the application of the "obvious to try" standard. Specifically, the *Kubin* court stated that an invention will not be obvious to try where one must undertake considerable exploratory effort among numerous possible choices. As the *Kubin* court explained, "[t]he inverse of this proposition is succinctly encapsulated by the Supreme Court's statement in *KSR* that where a skilled artisan merely pursues 'known options' from a 'finite number of indentified, predictable solutions,' obviousness under § 103 arises."[75] Second, a claim will not be obvious to try where one must explore a "new technology or general approach that seemed to be a promising field of experimentation," where the prior art gives "only general guidance as to the particular form of the claimed invention or how to achieve it."[76] Under this standard, a claim that operates with prior art that includes detailed enabling methodology and evidence suggesting success will likely be obvious to try.

§ 21.08   DETERMINING THE SCOPE AND CONTENT OF THE PRIOR ART

[A]   What is "Prior Art" Under § 103?

Section 103 determines nonobviousness by examining "the differences between the subject matter sought to be patented and *the prior art*." What does "prior art" mean under § 103? As a general rule, a reference must first qualify under § 102 before it can be used in determining nonobviousness under § 103, with the exception of the requirement for strict identity.[77] If strict identity exists, the claim will lack novelty, and no obviousness analysis is needed to render the claim invalid.

Certainly, public information such as a prior printed publication can be used to establish that a claim is obvious. Under pre-AIA law, such information must be part of the prior art prior to the date of invention. However, the AIA shifts the critical date from the date of invention to the application's effective filing date. For these new applications, it can be expected that courts will assess the knowledge of one of ordinary skill according to the effective filing date, rather than the date of invention as was done under pre-AIA law.

---

[74] *Id.*

[75] *Id.* at 1359.

[76] *Id.* (quoting *In re* O'Farrell, 853 F.2d 894, 903 (Fed. Cir. 1988)).

[77] MPEP § 2144.08 ("Each reference must qualify as prior art under 35 U.S.C. § 102 . . ." (citation omitted)); *see also* Panduit Corp. v. Dennison Mfg. Co., 810 F.2d 1561, 1568 (Fed. Cir. 1987) ("Before answering *Graham's* 'content' inquiry, it must be known whether a patent or publication is in the prior art under 35 U.S.C. § 102 . . . .").

Over the past several decades, courts have wrestled with the problem of whether non-public references can be used to demonstrate a claim as obvious. Such references are referred to as *secret prior art*. Such information is not known by one of ordinary skill, and therefore an argument can be made that it should not be considered. Yet in the 1965 decision, *Hazeltine Research, Inc. v. Brenner*,[78] the U.S. Supreme Court determined that a non-public patent application could be considered § 103 "prior art" as of the date that the application was filed even if the reference is not public as of that date. There, the patent at issue (the Regis patent) was filed December 23, 1957. A reference (the Wallace patent) contained sufficient information to render the Regis patent obvious. Wallace was filed in the patent office three years earlier, on March 24, 1954, but did not issue and did not become public until over one month *after* the Regis patent application had been filed.

The patentee argued that the Wallace patent should not be considered § 103 prior art, because such art should be limited to publicly known prior art. The *Hazeltine* Court rejected this position, relying primarily on the reasoning of *Alexander Milburn Co. v. Davis-Bournonville Co.*, which held that a filed, non-public patent application constituted prior art for purposes of § 102.[79] *Hazeltine* re-iterated the *Milburn* Court's statement, "[t]he delays of the patent office ought not to cut down the effect of what has been done."[80] *Hazeltine* found this logic applied with equal force to § 103, stating, "[w]e see no reason to read into § 103 a restricted definition of 'prior art' which would lower standards of patentability to such an extent that there might exist two patents where the Congress has plainly directed that there should be only one."[81] Thus, under *Hazeltine*, a prior art patent under 35 U.S.C. § 102(e) constitutes prior art for purposes of § 103.

Over the years, the courts have expanded the type of secret prior art that can be used to render a patent obvious. In addition to information disclosed in a previously filed patent under the pre-AIA § 102(e), inventions claimed under the pre-AIA § 102(f) and § 102(g) qualify.[82] These are subject to exceptions. In 1984, the Patent Act was amended to exempt the pre-AIA § 102(f) and § 102(g) prior art from rendering a patent obvious, where that prior art was owned by the applicant or by another in same *inventive entity* as the applicant. Under the inventive entity exception, researchers working together on a project are permitted to file patent applications that will not render later inventions in patents filed by others within the same team to be rendered obvious. According to the legislative history, "by disqualifying such background information from prior art, [it] will encourage communication among members of research teams, and patenting, and

---

[78] *See* Hazeltine Research, Inc. v. Brenner, 382 U.S. 252, 254 (1965).

[79] *See* Alexander Milburn Co. v. Davis-Bournonville Co., 270 U.S. 390 (1926). For more information about the *Alexander Milburn* decision and secret prior art, see Chapter 18.

[80] *Hazeltine*, 382 U.S. at 256.

[81] *Id.*

[82] *See* Oddzon Products, Inc. v. Just Toys, Inc., 122 F.3d 1396 (Fed. Cir. 1997) (§ 102(f) prior art can be considered to render a later patent obvious); *In re* Bass, 474 F.2d 1276 (C.C.P.A. 1973) (§ 102(g) prior art can be used to render a patent obvious); Kimberly-Clark Corp. v. Johnson & Johnson Co., 745 F.2d 1437 (Fed. Cir. 1984).

consequently public dissemination, of the results of 'team research.' "[83] The definition of inventive entity is sufficiently broad so as to include work undertaken by those working for the same company who are obliged to assign their inventions to their employers, as well as members of a joint research arrangement. In 1999, the Patent Act extended these exceptions to include the pre-AIA § 102(e) prior art.[84] At that point, the statute read:

> Subject matter developed by another person, which qualifies as prior art only under one or more of subsections (e), (f), and (g) of section 102 of this title, shall not preclude patentability under this section where the subject matter and the claimed invention were, at the time the claimed invention was made, owned by the same person or subject to an obligation of assignment to the same person.

The joint research concept has been carried forward into the AIA, together with other changes due to the Act's changed definitions of prior art.[85] Relevant to the joint research exception, the AIA § 102(c) provides that disclosures described in prior patent applications and patents are not considered prior art if the subject matter disclosed "were owned by the same person or subject to an obligation of assignment to the same person."[86] This definition includes parties to a joint research agreement.[87] The AIA expressly provides that this section is intended to promote joint research activities in the same manner as under the prior law.

The statutory bars presented special problems for nonobviousness determinations. Because under pre-AIA law the critical date under § 102(b) is one year prior to *filing*, this subsection created a conflict with the statutory language of § 103, which pins the nonobviousness inquiry to "the time the invention was made."[88] This point is illustrated in *In re Foster*, where the date of invention was established as December 26, 1952 but the patent application was not filed until August 21, 1956.[89] In the interim, in August 1954, a third party's article was published that rendered the invention obvious even though this 1954 reference did not exist as of the invention date for the Foster application. Notably, the 1954 article was within § 102(b)'s definition of a "printed publication" that had been published outside the grace period of the application's filing date.

---

[83] "Section-By-Section Analysis of H.R. 6286, Patent Law Amendments Act of 1984," Cong. Rec. H10525 (October 1, 1984).

[84] 35 U.S.C. § 103(c) provides that:

> Subject matter developed by another person, which qualifies as prior art only under one or more of subsections (e), (f), and (g) of section 102 of this title, shall not preclude patentability under this section where the subject matter and the claimed invention were, at the time the claimed invention was made, owned by the same person or subject to an obligation of assignment to the same person.

[85] Most notably, § 102(g) prior art has been eliminated. In addition, the former § 102(f), which governed derivation, has been modified by the AIA's definitional shift in that concept. For more information, see Chapter 19.

[86] 35 U.S.C. § 102(b)(2)(C) (2011).

[87] *Id.* at § 102(c) (2011).

[88] 35 U.S.C. § 103(a) (2000).

[89] *In re* Foster, 343 F.2d 980 (C.C.P.A. 1965).

Foster held that the 1954 article could be used as a reference under § 103, explaining:

> . . . since the purpose of the statute has always been to require filing of the application within the prescribed period after the time the public came into possession of the invention, we cannot see that it makes any difference how it came into such possession . . . . If the reference contains enough disclosure to make his invention obvious, the principle of the statute would seem to require denial of a patent to him.[90]

Under *Foster*, a § 102(b) reference can invalidate under § 103 even though that reference did not exist at "the time the invention was made" under § 103.

The AIA eliminates several of these concerns for future patent applications, because the time periods for the critical date are far more uniform. That is, prior art must be existent prior to the effective date of the filing of the application under examination. Thus, the issue illustrated in the *Foster* decision can be expected to diminish in significance as the number of patents assessed under the AIA's new standard increases.

The AIA does not entirely eliminate reliance on secret prior art for purposes of the nonobviousness inquiry. For example, the AIA appears to have adopted the holding of the *Hazeltine* decision in the AIA's § 102(a)(2), which provides that issued patents or published patent applications become part of the prior art as of their effective filing date (rather than their publication or issuance date). That is, between two published patent applications or issued patents, the one with the earlier effective filing date has priority even though patents are not publicly known on their effective filing date.

The extent of the availability of non-public information, such as a prior sale, of an invention will constitute prior art under the AIA's newly enacted § 102(a)(1).[91] Currently, the status of nonpublic information, such as a private contract for the sale of the invention, is unclear. It can be expected that judicial interpretation of the AIA will be key to understanding its applicability to the realm of nonobviousness.

[B]   A Reference Must Constitute Analogous Art

Unlike § 102, references used under § 103 must constitute *analogous art.* This means that for nonobviousness, "[i]n order to rely on a reference as a basis for rejection of an applicant's invention, the reference must either be in the field of applicant's endeavor or, if not, then be reasonably pertinent to the particular problem with which the inventor was concerned."[92] The definition of analogous art is framed in the disjunctive — that is, art may be analogous even though in a different field of endeavor if the subject matter is relevant to the problem that the inventor sought to solve, or the converse.

---

[90] *Id.* at 988.

[91] For more information on this issue, see Chapter 12.

[92] *In re* Oetiker, 977 F.2d 1443, 1447 (Fed. Cir. 1992).

In re Clay illustrates both prongs of an analogous art analysis.[93] The claims at issue described a process to maintain refined liquid hydrocarbon in a storage tank, which involved using a gel in the tank's dead volume. One of the asserted references, called Sydansk, used a gel to facilitate the forced extraction of crude petroleum from rock. Although both Clay and Sydansk were used in the petroleum industry, the *Clay* court found that Sydansk was not in the same field of endeavor as Clay. Specifically, the Federal Circuit determined that Clay field of endeavor was "the *storage* of refined liquid hydrocarbons," where as Sydansk's invention was "the *extraction* of crude petroleum."[94]

Clay then turned to examine the second prong of the analogous art test — that is, whether Sydansk was reasonably pertinent to the particular problem which Clay had attempted to solve. The court noted that "[a] reference is reasonably pertinent if, even though it may be in a different field from that of the inventor's endeavor, it is one which, because of the matter with which it deals, logically would have commended itself to an inventor's attention in considering his problem."[95] *Clay* found that this standard was not met, because Sydansk was directed to the problem of recovering oil from rock, but that Clay concerned preventing loss and contamination of stored liquid hydrocarbons. The court found that the structure and function of the two references rendered Sydansk non-analogous, as "the subterranean formation of Sydansk is not structurally similar to, does not operate under the same temperature and pressure as, and does not function like Clay's storage tanks."[96] Thus, *Clay* concluded that the examiner could not rely on Sydansk in assessing whether the claim in the Clay application met the nonobviousness requirement.

In re Paulsen, is a further illustration of the application of the "reasonably pertinent" criteria.[97] In *Paulsen,* the claims described a housing for a laptop computer that was connected with a hinge to the computer's midsection. When opened, the housing revealed the computer's keyboard and a display on the inside of the lid. Certain claims had been rejected over references outside the field of portable computing, including "hinges and latches as used in a desktop telephone directory, a piano lid, a kitchen cabinet, a washing machine cabinet, a wooden furniture cabinet, or a two-part housing for storing audio cassettes."[98]

The *Paulsen* court affirmed that the examiner's reliance on these references was appropriate. Although acknowledging that art such as a kitchen cabinet and furniture were not within the same field of endeavor as computers, *Paulsen* found that these were still "reasonably pertinent to the particular problem with which the inventor is involved."[99] Here, the court found that one of ordinary skill in the art would have been likely to have consulted to the mechanical arts generally to solve

---

[93] *In re* Clay, 966 F.2d 656 (Fed. Cir. 1992).

[94] *Id.* at 659 (emphasis in original).

[95] *Id.*

[96] *Id.* at 660.

[97] *In re* Paulsen, 30 F.3d 1475, 1482 (Fed. Cir. 1994).

[98] *Id.* at 1481.

[99] *Id.*

the problem of connecting and securing the laptop housing.

In re Klein[100] is a post-*KSR* decision that reconfirmed the analogous art standard. Like *Paulsen*, the *Klein* opinion analyzed whether references were reasonably pertinent to the problem to be solved. The claim at issue described a device for preparing nectar to feed different birds and insects. According to the patent, the device used a compartment with a sliding divider. The user could move the divider to facilitate the measurement of different ratios of sugar to water to accommodate the preferences of different insects and birds. After the divided compartments are filled, the user removed the divider so that the water and sugar would mix.

The *Klein* opinion emphasized that references outside the claim's field of endeavor must be directed to the same problem to be solved by the claim at issue. In this case, there were five references at issue. Three of the references — including a tool tray with movable dividers — were barred from consideration because they were directed to separating solid objects for storage, rather than measuring contents before mixing. The *Klein* court found that a person of ordinary skill would not have been motivated to consult these references, "particularly since none of these three references shows a partitioned container that is adapted to receive water or contain it long enough to be able to prepare different ratios in the different compartments." The remaining two references — which held two substances (including some liquids) in two separate compartments until ready for use — were deemed non-analogous because the dividers were not moveable such that they could be used to measure different ratios. *Klein* reiterated that references can be found "reasonably pertinent" where the reference "logically would have commended itself to an inventor's attention in considering his problem."[101] According to the court, this condition exists where the reference is directed to the same purpose as the one addressed by the claim.

§ 21.09 SECONDARY CONSIDERATIONS OF NONOBVIOUSNESS

Today's evaluation of the *secondary considerations* of nonobviousness derives from the 1876 case *Smith v. Goodyear*, described earlier in this Chapter.[102] In that case, the Supreme Court found a dental device nonobvious in part due to objective indicia such as the failure of others, long-felt need and laudatory comments of those in the field. Over time, the list of relevant secondary considerations has grown to include other considerations such as the commercial success of uses of the invention, copying and licensing activity.

Nearly a century after Smith, the Supreme Court indicated its continued approval of the use of such facts in *Graham v. John Deere. Graham* noted that such objective evidence is useful to counteract the hindsight bias — that is, if those in the art recognize the invention as a significant advance or otherwise solves a long-felt

---

[100] *In re* Klein, 647 F.3d 1343 (Fed. Cir. 2011).

[101] *Id.* at 1348.

[102] Smith v. Goodyear Dental Vulcanite Co., 93 U.S. 486 (1877).

but unmet need, the court should consider that one of ordinary skill may not find the invention obvious.

In *U.S. v. Adams*, a case decided the same day as *Graham*, the Supreme Court provided some insight into the proper use of secondary considerations.[103] The claims at issue described a lightweight battery that could be easily carried, and that became active after being filled with water. The prior art included all of the elements necessary to recreate the battery. Finding that the claims met the nonobviousness requirement, the Court noted that the invention delivered unexpected results and was a significant advance from the existing wet batteries. Critically, *Adams* observed that objective indicia weighed in favor of a finding of nonobviousness, including the recognition of experts in the field, the skepticism of experts that such a device would operate, and the ultimate success of the invention that overcame the doubt expressed by those in the field.

Although the Supreme Court has not phrased reliance on the secondary considerations as a mandatory consideration, the Federal Circuit has stated that these factors are "never of 'no moment,' [and] is always to be considered and accorded whatever weight it may have" in assessing nonobviousness.[104] Indeed, the Federal Circuit has stated that secondary considerations "may often be the most probative and cogent evidence in the record."[105]

There must be a nexus between the evidence of the secondary considerations and the technical or inventive aspects of the claimed invention.[106] This point was demonstrated in *Pentec, Inc. v. Graphic Controls Corp.*[107] There, the patent was directed to a device to attach a pen to an instrument arm for use in recording readouts on charts or graphs. The invention included an "integrally molded hinged member adapted to fold against a surface of the pen body" that locked against the pen when closed.[108]

---

[103] U.S. v. Adams, 383 U.S. 39 (1966).

[104] Simmons Fastener Corp. v. Illinois Tool Works, Inc., 739 F.2d 1573, 1575 (Fed. Cir. 1984) (citation omitted); *see also In re* Sullivan, 498 F.3d 1345 (Fed. Cir. 2007) (post-*KSR* decision, confirming that evidenced of secondary considerations must be weighed when such evidence is presented).

[105] *Simmons Fastener*, 739 F.2d at 1575 (citation omitted).

[106] *See* Merges, *supra* note 18.

[107] Pentec, Inc. v. Graphic Control, Corp., 776 F.2d 309 (Fed. Cir. 1985).

[108] *Id.* at 315.

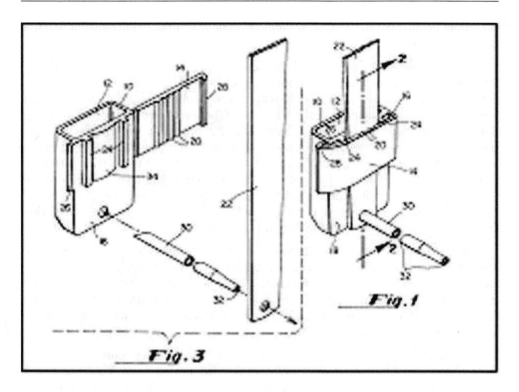

The *Pentec* court reviewed a district court finding that the invention was obvious, including considerations of the commercial success of the device that incorporated the invention. The defendant argued that part of the commercial success of the device was not due to the hinged member, but rather because the device was sold with a disposable pen, as, "[i]t was only when the plastic hinge was combined with disposable pens that that combination was received 'extremely warmly'" in the market.[109] In addition, the defendant proffered evidence that the popularity of the device was not due to the hinged locking mechanism, but rather to an extensive advertising campaign by the seller, who had been the market leader before the introduction of the patented device. *Pentec* found that this evidence broke the nexus between commercial success and the claimed invention. The court reasoned that sales due to advertising and the patentee's leading status demonstrated that the commercial success was due to "economic and commercial factors unrelated to the technical quality of the patented subject matter."[110]

Under *Graham* and the Federal Circuit's precedent, secondary considerations can play an important role in determining whether an invention meets the nonobviousness requirement and to prevent hindsight bias in the process. However, as the *Pentec* case demonstrates, to establish probative value, a nexus between these objective indicia and the invention must be established.[111]

---

[109] *Id.*

[110] *Id.*

[111] For a post-*KSR* decision analyzing secondary considerations, see Star Scientific, Inc. v. R.J.

§ 21.10   NONOBVIOUSNESS AND COMBINATION CLAIMS

Historically, the Supreme Court has provided specific instruction for assessing the nonobviousness of claims that are comprised of a combination of pre-existing elements. The test articulated by the Supreme Court in *Great Atlantic & Pac. Tea Co. v. Supermarket Equipment Corp.*, is that there must be some type of synergy — that is, "[t]he conjunction or concert of known elements must contribute something; only when the whole in some way exceeds the sum of its parts is the accumulation of old devices patentable."[112]

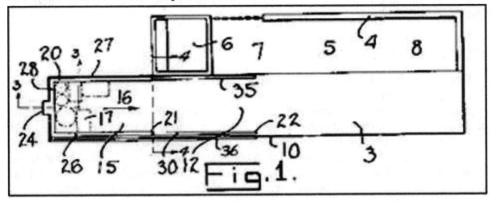

Fig. 1.

In the *Great Atlantic* case, the claim described a combination of parts used to form a cashier's counter for use in a grocery store. This included a counter and a three-sided frame used to push the groceries to be checked toward the clerk. The Court acknowledged that secondary considerations of commercial success and the filling of a long-felt need were present. Nonetheless, the Court found the claims nonobvious, finding that "[t]his case is wanting in any unusual or surprising consequences."[113] The *Great Atlantic* Court explained:

> Patents cannot be sustained when, on the contrary, their effect is to subtract from former resources freely available to skilled artisans. A patent for a combination which only unites old elements with no change in their respective functions . . . obviously withdraws what is already known into the field of its monopoly and diminishes the resources available to skillful men.[114]

Similarly, in 1976, the Supreme Court reaffirmed this principle in *Sakraida v. Ag Pro, Inc.*, in which the Court found a claim to a combination of already-existing elements nonobvious.[115] The *Sakraida* Court recognized that the combination produced a "desired result in a cheaper and faster way, and enjoying commercial

---

Reynolds Tobacco Co., 655 F.3d 1364 (Fed. Cir. 2011).

[112]   Great Atlantic & Pacific Tea Co. v. Supermarket Equipment Corp., 340 U.S. 147, 152 (1950).

[113]   *Id.*

[114]   *Id.* at 152-53.

[115]   Sakraida v. Ag Pro, Inc., 425 U.S. 273 (1976).

success," but nonetheless had failed to "produce a new or different function" and was therefore unpatentable.[116]

Despite these statements, in 1983 the Federal Circuit rejected that any synergy was required for combination claims.[117] However, these Federal Circuit authorities no longer retain viability under the Supreme Court's *KSR* decision, which holds that the "combination of familiar elements according to known methods is likely to be obvious when it does no more than yield predictable results."[118] This point has become a central principle of *KSR's* progeny.[119] Today, a combination claim that represents nothing more than the sum of its parts will likely be found predictable, and therefore obvious.

§ 21.11 CONCLUSION

Nonobviousness implicitly implements the policy concerns of the appropriate role of the patent system. Most recently, the Supreme Court's *KSR* opinion appeared concerned that "patents might stifle, rather than promote, the progress of useful arts."[120] Fundamentally, the question to be asked is whether the proposed claim would have been obvious to one of skill in the art at the time the invention was made (or for a patent controlled by the AIA, at the time of the effective filing date). If so, the nonobviousness requirement has not been met and the patent cannot be granted. This requirement derives from the principle that a patent should only be granted when the invention contributes more than ordinary innovation.

The *Graham* analytic framework controls the structure of the analysis. That is, first one must determine the scope and content of the prior art. "Prior art" must qualify under § 102 (except for the strict identity test), and must constitute analogous art. The Patent Act includes exceptions for certain types of prior art that are subject to a joint research program. Second, one compares the differences between the prior art and the claims at issue are identified. Unlike § 102, the nonobviousness requirement does not require element-by-element identity between the claim and the prior art. Rather, this step asks the decision maker to identify the distinctions between them. Third, one determines the level of ordinary skill in the pertinent art. It is presumed that one of ordinary skill has knowledge of the relevant art, and can exercise some measure of creativity in solving the problem at hand. Finally, one examines the ultimate question of whether the claims as a whole would have been obvious to one of ordinary skill at the time of the invention. In doing so, one examines the secondary considerations of nonobviousness as a guide. Furthermore, in applying this standard, the decision maker must guard against the possibility that a finding of obviousness may be based on hindsight bias.

---

[116] *Id.* at 282.

[117] Medtronic, Inc. v. Cardiac Pacemakers, Inc., 721 F.2d 1563, 1566 (Fed. Cir. 1983).

[118] KSR Int'l Co., v. Teleflex, Inc., 127 S. Ct. 1727, 1739 (2007).

[119] See, e.g., Dow Jones & Co., Inc. v. Ablaise Ltd., 606 F.3d 1338 (Fed. Cir. 2010); Ecolab, Inc. v. FMC Corp., 569 F.3d 1335 (Fed. Cir. 2009).

[120] *Id.* at 1746.

Chapter 22

UTILITY

SYNOPSIS

§ 22.01 INTRODUCTION

§ 22.02 OPERABLE UTILITY

§ 22.03 SPECIFIC OR PRACTICAL UTILITY

    [A] The Historical Context for the Modern Utility Standard

    [B] U.S. Supreme Court Sets § 101's Utility Standard: *Brenner v. Manson*

    [C] Subsequent Development of the *Brenner* Utility Standard

§ 22.04 MORAL UTILITY

§ 22.05 SOME ECONOMIC CONSIDERATIONS RELATING TO THE UTILITY REQUIREMENT

§ 22.06 CONCLUSION

§ 22.01 INTRODUCTION

The *utility* requirement ensures that patents are granted only for useful inventions.[1] The requirement can be traced to article I, section 8 of the U.S. Constitution, which grants Congress the power to "promote the Progress of . . . *useful* Arts."[2] In addition, § 101 of the Patent Act states, "Whoever invents or discovers any new and *useful* process, machine, manufacture, or composition of matter, or any new and *useful* improvement thereof, may obtain a patent therefor"[3] Each version of the Patent Act since 1790 has included the requirement that an invention's usefulness as a requirement of patentability.[4] As the U.S. Supreme Court has explained, "[t]he basic *quid pro quo* contemplated by the Constitution and the Congress for granting a patent monopoly is the benefit derived by the public from an invention with substantial utility."[5]

---

[1] Brenner v. Manson, 383 U.S. 519, 529 (1966) (defining utility, acknowledging, "[a]s is so often the case,. a simple everyday word can be pregnant with ambiguity when applied to the facts of life").

[2] U.S. Const. art. I, § 8 (emphasis added).

[3] 35 U.S.C. § 101 (1952) (emphasis added).

[4] *Brenner*, 383 U.S. at 529 & n.13 (reviewing statutes).

[5] *Id.* at 534-35.

Utility arises in different contexts.[6] The first is *operability* — that is, the patent claim must be for an invention that actually works. A patent will not be granted for an invention that is implausible or cannot be replicated by those of ordinary skill using currently available methods. Under this rule, an application for travel by a warp drive system was rejected for lack of utility as "incredible" and "theoretical in nature."[7]

The second, called *specific* or *practical utility*, requires a patentee to identify a practical or "real world" use for the invention.[8] For example, one who combines chemicals into a novel and nonobvious compound cannot obtain a patent unless the patentee can identify a specific and substantial utility in the compound's currently available form.[9] In other words, there must be a *use* for the compound; its mere existence is not sufficient. The application must disclose how one skilled in the art can use the invention to provide an immediate benefit to the public.[10]

Third, *moral utility* has its foundation in a landmark decision *Lowell v. Lewis*, decided in 1817, wherein Justice Story described the utility requirement as follows: "[t]he invention should not be frivolous or injurious to the well-being, good policy, or sound morals of society."[11] Although rejections for lack of moral utility were common at one time for such inventions as those used for gambling, the doctrine or moral utility "has not been applied broadly in recent years."[12]

The commercial success of an invention is not required for, or necessarily determinative of, a patent's utility.[13] A patentee's statement of utility in the application is presumed sufficient,[14] and the U.S. PTO has the burden to support the rejection of an application on any of these grounds.[15] Rejections might be made, for example, where the application fails to demonstrate operability because the specification does not conform to known scientific principles,[16] or the application fails to identify any specific and substantial utility. If the examiner meets this burden, the applicant must present evidence to support the invention's utility in rebuttal.[17] Alternatively, one may challenge an issued patent in court by demonstrating a lack of utility by clear and convincing evidence.[18]

---

[6] *See generally*, MPEP § 2107.01.

[7] Final Office Action on Application No. 10/182,373 (filed June 4, 2005).

[8] *See In re* Bremner, 182 F.2d 216, 217 (C.C.P.A. 1950) ("we feel certain that the law requires that there be in the application an assertion of utility and an indication of the use or uses intended).

[9] *See In re* Fisher, 421 F.3d 1365, 1370-71 (Fed. Cir. 2005).

[10] *Id.* at 1371.

[11] Lowell v. Lewis, 15 F. Cas. 1018, 1019 (D. Mass. 1817).

[12] Juicy Whip, Inc. v. Orange Bang, Inc., 185 F.3d 1364, 1366-67 (Fed. Cir. 1999).

[13] *See* Barmag Barmer Maschinenfabrik AG v. Murata Machinery, Ltd., 731 F.2d 831, 839 (Fed. Cir. 1984); *In re* Anthony, 414 F.2d 1383 (C.C.P.A. 1969).

[14] *In re* Swartz, 232 F.3d 862, 864 (Fed. Cir. 2000).

[15] *In re* Brana, 51 F.3d 1560, 1566 (Fed. Cir. 1995).

[16] *In re* Perrigo, 48 F.2d 965 (C.C.P.A. 1931).

[17] *Id.*

[18] 35 U.S.C. § 282 (2000); *see, e.g.*, Process Control Corp. v. HydReclaim Corp., 190 F.3d 1350 (Fed. Cir. 1999) (declaratory judgment action seeking an invalidity determination for lack of utility).

There is a relation between utility and the enablement requirement of § 112.[19] This is because enablement requires a patentee to disclose sufficient information about the claimed invention to enable one of ordinary skill in the art to make and *use* the invention.[20] Patent claims that fail operability or specific utility cannot meet the "how-to-use" portion of the enablement requirement because such devices cannot be used at all.[21] Therefore, "when a claim requires a means for accomplishing an unattainable result, the claimed invention must be considered inoperative as claimed and the claim must be held invalid under either § 101 or § 112 of 35 U.S.C."[22]

§ 22.02   OPERABLE UTILITY

For operable utility to be present, the subject matter of the patent claims must be capable for performing the utility described in the specification.[23] As one court explained, "[n]either the Constitution nor the statutes contemplate the granting of patents upon theories, nor giving a monopoly upon intellectual speculations embodied in devices incapable of scientific analysis."[24] One example of a rejection based on the operable utility requirement is the Federal Circuit's *Newman v. Quigg*, which considered a patent application for a perpetual motion machine.[25] The applicant argued that his prototype generated output energy greater than the input energy, a circumstance that would violate certain laws of thermodynamics. The district court ordered testing of the device by an independent laboratory, which confirmed that the device could not produce the claimed utility. On appeal, the Federal Circuit affirmed the district court's finding of invalidity because the independent testing of the device established that the invention "does not operate to produce what [the inventor] claims it does."[26]

Operable utility may be met by a description of the observable effects that demonstrate that the invention works, so long as these statements are not contrary to scientific norms, incapable of being reproduced or of a nature that would cause one of ordinary skill to doubt the asserted utility.[27] If this standard is met, an application's failure to disclose how, or why, an invention works does not render the

---

[19] *See* 35 U.S.C. § 112, ¶ 1 (2000); *see supra* Chapter 8.

[20] Monsanto Co. v. Syngenta Seeds, Inc., 503 F.3d 1352, 1360 (Fed. Cir. 2007) ("[T]o be enabling, the specification of the patent must teach those skilled in the art how to make and use the full scope of the claimed invention without undue experimentation.") (quotation and citation omitted).

[21] Process Control Corp. v. HydReclaim Corp., 190 F.3d 1350, 1358 (Fed. Cir. 1999).

[22] Raytheon Co. v. Roper Corp., 724 F.2d 951, 956 (Fed. Cir. 1983).

[23] Brooktree Corp. v. Advanced Micro Devices, Inc., 977 F.2d 1555, 1573 (Fed. Cir. 1992) (quoting jury instruction on utility).

[24] *In re* Perrigo, 48 F.2d 965, 966 (C.C.P.A. 1931).

[25] Newman v. Quigg, 877 F.2d 1575 (Fed. Cir. 1989).

[26] *Id.* at 1581.

[27] *In re* Swartz, 232 F.3d 862, 864 (Fed. Cir. 2000) (PTO properly rebutted the presumption of operability for a patent application that claimed an invention relating to cold fusion; examiner's reliance on articles that demonstrated that the patentee's results were irreproducible and that one of ordinary skill would doubt the invention's operability).

claims unpatentable.[28] Further, the law does not require that the inventor subjectively understand the scientific principles that underlie the operability of the claimed invention. So long as the invention is capable of operating to accomplish the asserted purpose, operable utility exists.

§ 22.03 SPECIFIC OR PRACTICAL UTILITY

Section 101 requires the disclosure of a specific, practical utility that demonstrates how the invention will be used in its "real world" application.[29] The essence of a utility application is that the claimed invention must confer a useful benefit existent on the filing date. The specific utility requirement prevents a patent from issuing to protect basic research or theories with only future possibilities after additional work has been performed. The doctrine of specific utility was comparatively dormant until the 1950's and 1960's, when the PTO began to rely on the doctrine to reject a number of patent applications in the chemical arts. Particularly since 1966, when the Supreme Court decided the foundational *Brenner v. Manson*,[30] utility has gained more importance in the chemical and biotechnological arts.

Generally, one specific utility is sufficient to support a patent.[31] Once this has been met for a combination or apparatus claim, the patentee can prevent others from using the claimed invention for *any* other purpose during the patent's term. For example, one who patents a chemical compound for use as a mouthwash can prevent others from using that same compound as a glass cleaner.[32] However, a later inventor who develops a new *use* for the chemical compound can obtain a *method* claim tailored to the new use.[33] There is an important caveat to this rule. That is, because the patent right confers only the right to exclude (and not the right to use), the later inventor must obtain a license to use the compound before this later inventor can practice the method that implements the new use.

[A] The Historical Context for the Modern Utility Standard

In the 1817 decision *Lowell v. Lewis*, Justice Story set the utility standard as a low bar, stating that "[a]ll that the law requires is, that the invention should not be frivolous or injurious to the well-being, good policy, or sound morals of society."[34] In the years immediately following the *Lowell* decision, the courts followed Story's rule and routinely held that any non-frivolous, non-injurious use, even solely for use

---

[28] *In re* Cortright, 165 F.3d 1353, 1359 (Fed. Cir. 1999).

[29] *See generally In re* Fisher, 421 F.3d 1365, 1371 (Fed. Cir. 2005).

[30] *See Brenner*, 383 U.S. 519.

[31] *See generally* U.S. P.T.O., Revised Interim Utility Guidelines, 66 Fed. Reg. 1092 (Jan. 5, 2001) (response to comments) (describing by way of example, "a patent granted on an isolated and purified DNA composition confers the right to exclude others from any method of using that DNA composition, for up to 20 years from the filing date" *Id.* at 1095.).

[32] *Id.* (emphasis added).

[33] *Id.* ("Where a new use is discovered for a patented DNA composition, that new use may qualify for its own process patent, notwithstanding that the DNA composition itself is patented.").

[34] Lowell v. Lewis, 15 F. Cas. 1018, 1019 (D. Mass. 1817).

in a laboratory, was sufficient to satisfy the utility requirement.[35] Any significant appreciation of the impact of upholding patents with dubious utility was not evident in these decisions. As *Lowell* explained, if an invention is "not extensively useful it will silently sink into contempt and disregard"[36] and striking down patents for lack of a specific utility was rare during this time frame.

In 1950, the Court of Customs and Patent Appeals decided *In re Bremner*, a case that considered whether an application directed to an identified chemical compound was useful.[37] The *Bremner* Court held the application deficient, based on the failure to comply with the requirement "that there be in the application an assertion of utility and an indication of the use or uses intended."[38] One source notes that, after *Bremner* was decided, the Patent Office relied on the case to reject a number of applications in the chemical arts that did not disclose an end use for the chemical along with a specific embodiment for the end use.[39] The Patent Office's practice represented a significant departure from the earlier *Lowell* standard, which merely required a description of any non-frivolous, non-injurious use.

Despite this shift in the Patent Office, a 1960 decision of the Court of Custom and Patent Appeals, *In re Nelson*,[40] maintained *Lowell's* minimal utility standard. *Nelson* evaluated an application directed to compounds used as intermediates for the preparation of certain steroids. The Patent Office had rejected the application, a decision affirmed by the Board of Patent Appeals, on the ground that the application failed to disclose that the claimed intermediaries could produce an end-product steroid that could be considered "useful" under § 101. On appeal from the Board's decision, the *Nelson* court reversed and found that the claimed intermediates met the utility requirement, explaining:

> Surely a new group of steroid intermediates is useful to chemists doing research on steroids, and in a "practical" sense too. Such intermediates are "useful" under section 101. They are often actually placed on the market before much, if anything, is known as to what they are "good" for, other than experimentation and the making of other compounds in the important field of research.[41]

Nelson observed that protecting intermediates was consistent with the disclosure function of patent law, based on the view that a contrary rule would discourage researchers from describing their work in a patent application. Under *Nelson*,

---

[35] Electro-Dynamic Co. v. U.S. Light & Heat Corp., 278 F. 80, 85 (2d Cir. 1921) ("The scheme might be called one of hope or aspiration; but the device will operate in a laboratory at least, and we do not think the patent can be struck down as inoperative in the sense of the patent law.").

[36] *Lowell*, 15 Cas. at 1042.

[37] *In re* Bremner, 182 F.2d 216, 217 (C.C.P.A. 1950).

[38] *Id.*

[39] Stanley H. Cohen and Charles H. Schwartz, *Do Chemical Intermediaries Have Patentable Utility?*, 43 J. Pat. Off. Soc'y 479, 486-89 (1961) (*quoting* Brief for the Am. Patent Law Ass'n as Amicus Curiae, pp. 2-3); see also *In re* Nelson, 280 F.2d 172 (C.C.P.A. 1960).

[40] *Id.*

[41] *Id.* at 180.

virtually *any* chemical intermediate meets the utility standard, because by defini-tion any "intermediate" is useful to make an end product of some kind. The *Nelson* opinion justified this relatively low standard by noting that "[t]he seemingly little advances are the bread and butter of progress and sometimes turn out to be of much greater importance than first thought."[42]

[B]   U.S. Supreme Court Sets § 101's Utility Standard: *Brenner v. Manson*

In *Brenner v. Manson*, the U.S. Supreme Court resolved the conflict that had developed between the Patent Office and the Court of Custom and Patent Appeals for the specific utility standard for chemical inventions.[43] In *Brenner*, the Court reviewed an interference decision in which Manson sought to establish inventorship for a chemical process for making steroids. The decisions below reflected the split that had developed between the Patent Office and the courts. Specifically, the examiner's rejection, upheld by the Board of Patent Appeals, was based on a finding that Manson's application failed to disclose any purpose for the steroid produced by his claimed process.[44] The Court of Custom and Patent Appeals reversed, applying *Nelson's* minimal utility standard. Specifically, the Court of Custom and Patent Appeals found that the fact that the process produced a steroid sufficient, stating that a process meets the utility requirement "if it operates as disclosed to produce its intended result or perform its intended function and if it is not, in operation or result, detrimental to the public interest."[45] The U.S. Supreme Court granted the Patent Office's request for review of this decision.

The Supreme Court's *Brenner* decision rejected the standard applied by the Court of Custom and Patent Appeals. Specifically, *Brenner* held that Manson's claimed process must produce *an end product that has been shown to be useful —* that is, where a "specific benefit exists in [the end product's] currently available form."[46] In doing so, the Court expressed concern that a low utility standard could harm development within the art for subsequent research and development:

> Until the process claim has been reduced to production of a product shown to be useful, the metes and bounds of [the patent] monopoly are not capable of precise delineation. It may engross a vast, unknown and perhaps unknowable area. Such a patent may confer power to block off whole areas of scientific development, without compensating benefit to the public.[47]

---

[42] *Id.* at 182 (observing that the patent system "is not like a system of military awards in which medals are given out by the people to their heroes as expressions of gratitude for their exceptional services." *Id.*).

[43] *See* Brenner v. Manson, 383 U.S. 519 (1966).

[44] In doing so, the Board stated, "It is our view that the statutory requirement of usefulness of a product cannot be presumed merely because it happens to be closely related to another compound which is known to be useful." *Id.* at 522 (quoting the Board's decision).

[45] *In re* Manson, 333 F.2d 234, 237-38 (C.C.P.A. 1964).

[46] *Brenner*, 383 U.S. at 534.

[47] *Id.* at 535.

Manson attempted to save his application by asserting that his process was useful because it yielded a steroid that was part of a class of steroids that was undergoing testing for anti-tumor effects. However, *Brenner* found that "use testing" of the end-product was not a sufficient use to meet § 101, explaining, "a patent is not a hunting license. It is not a reward for the search, but compensation for its successful conclusion."[48]

Further, the Court rejected Manson's argument that the end product was useful because a related steroid was shown to inhibit tumors in mice. *Brenner* explained that unpredictability in this art undercut any presumption that the steroid produced from Manson's process would perform similarly. *Brenner* expressly left open the question of whether a product used solely to inhibit the growth of tumors in lab animals is sufficient to meet the utility standard.

One year after the Supreme Court decided *Brenner v. Manson*, in *In re Kirk*, the Court of Customs and Patent Appeals expressly recognized that *Nelson* was no longer viable precedent.[49] In this same decision, *Kirk* expanded *Brenner's* holding to include claims for intermediate chemicals that are used to make an end product. Specifically, the court held, "[i]t seems clear that, if a process for producing a product of only conjectural use is not itself 'useful' within § 101, it cannot be said that the starting materials for such a process — i.e., the presently claimed intermediates — are 'useful.' "[50] Under *Kirk*, one who seeks to patent an intermediary must demonstrate more than that the end product possesses a high biological activity a general reaction. Under *Kirk*, such an assertion is too vague to establish a specific use for either the intermediate or the end product. Rather, *Kirk* requires that, at a minimum, the end product made by the intermediate chemical have an identified, specific benefit in its currently available form before a patent for the intermediate will be granted.

[C]   Subsequent Development of the *Brenner* Utility Standard

How is *Brenner* applied? Although the Federal Circuit has stated that *Brenner* applies "*in any scientific discipline*,"[51] the court has relied on this standard most visibly in cases involving the pharmaceutical and biotechnological arts.[52]

One example is the Federal Circuit's *In re Brana*, where the court evaluated the utility of chemical compounds that were asserted to have "a better action" as anti-tumor agents than previously existing compounds.[53] In *Brana*, one of the grounds for the examiner's rejection was a failure to demonstrate practical utility, in that

---

[48] *Id.* at 536

[49] *In re* Kirk, 376 F.2d 936, 946 (C.C.P.A. 1967) (expressly over-ruling *Nelson's* utility standard).

[50] *Id.* at 945.

[51] *In re* Fisher, 421 F.3d 1365, 1375 (Fed. Cir. 2005).

[52] *See* Dan L. Burk & Mark A. Lemley, *Biotechnology's Uncertainty Principle*, 54 Case W. Res. L. Rev. 691, 706 n.71 (2004) ("the court still requires more proof of experimentation in order to satisfy the utility requirement in biotechnology and pharmaceuticals than elsewhere.").

[53] *See In re* Brana, 51 F.3d 1560 (Fed. Cir. 1995).

the record failed to demonstrate tests that showed an anti-tumor activity in humans. On appeal to the Federal Circuit, the applicant submitted evidence demonstrating increased anti-tumor activity against a form of leukemia that occurred in mice upon injection with particular cell lines. The *Brana* court held that this evidence was sufficient to meet *Brenner's* practical utility standard, as sufficiently specific and useful in inhibiting tumors in mice and on human tissue tested in a lab.

The *Brana* court determined that testing in live human subjects, as required to obtain approval for a new drug application by the U.S. Food and Drug Administration ("FDA"), was not required to demonstrate utility for purposes of obtaining a patent:

> Usefulness in patent law, and in particular in the context of pharmaceutical inventions, necessarily includes the expectation of further research and development. The stage at which an invention in this field becomes useful is well before it is ready to be administered to humans. Were we to require [FDA] Phase II testing in order to prove utility, the associated costs would prevent many companies from obtaining patent protection on promising new inventions, thereby eliminating an incentive to pursue, through research and development, potential cures in many crucial areas such as the treatment of cancer.[54]

Brana represents the Federal Circuit's resolution of an issue left open by the Supreme Court in *Brenner* — that is, that practical utility may be established by showing the promise of the treatment of an identified disease through reactions in laboratory experiments. Testing in the human body is not required.

Ten years later, the Federal Circuit decided *In re Fisher*, in an opinion that considered utility for a patent application claiming an "expressed sequence tag," or "EST," which is a short, purified nucleotide sequence that represents a fragment of a DNA clone.[55] An EST may contain a known nucleotide sequence that can be introduced to sample mixtures of DNA material. If a known EST hybridizes, or binds, with a particular portion of DNA, then the sequence of the DNA sequence then can be identified. This event occurs because the four different nucleotides (adenine (or A), thymine (T), guanine (G), and cytosine (C)) that comprise each strand of DNA will only bind with its compliment. For example, adenine is the complement of, or will only pair with, thymine, and guanine will only pair with cytosine. When a known sequence in an EST binds with a portion of a strand of DNA, then that DNA portion can be identified through a comparison with the compliments of the known EST sequence. Thus, an EST with a sequence G-A-G-C-T-A can be used to identify a portion of a DNA sequence C-T-C-G-A-T.

The particular EST's at issue in *Fisher* were derived from maize plants. The applicant asserted that these EST's had several uses, such as serving as a molecular marker to map an entire maize genome, to provide information about gene expression more generally and to match, and therefore assist in the identification of,

---

[54] *Id.* at 1568.

[55] *See Fisher*, 421 F.3d 1365.

DNA sequences of other plants and organisms. During prosecution, the examiner rejected the *Fisher* application for lack of a specific utility by noting that these asserted utilities "were generally applicable to any EST," and that there was "no known use for the proteins produced as final products resulting from processes involving the claimed EST's."[56] On appeal to the Federal Circuit, the *Fisher* court agreed and affirmed the rejection.

Fisher relied, to some degree, on the U.S. PTO's Utility Application Guidelines,[57] which state that a polynucleotide that acts only as a gene probe or chromosome marker does not satisfy the specific utility requirement. As the Federal Circuit explained:

> . . . while Fisher's claimed ESTs may add a noteworthy contribution to biotechnology research, our precedent dictates that the '643 application does not meet the utility requirement of § 101 because Fisher does not identify the function for the underlying protein-encoding genes. Absent such identification, we hold that the claimed ESTs have not been researched and understood to the point of providing an immediate, well-defined, real world benefit to the public meriting the grant of a patent.[58]

Fisher further explained that the claimed EST's acted "as no more than research intermediates," and, as objects of use testing, lacked the specific and substantial utility required by *Brenner.*[59] Further, the court held that the EST's use as a research intermediate was not sufficient, because the record failed to demonstrate a specific and substantial utility for the genes that would be identified through the use of the claimed ESTs. As the *Fisher* court stated, a "substantial utility" is present where an invention "is useful to the public as disclosed in its current form, not that it may prove useful at some future date after further research."[60]

The U.S. PTO's guidelines, although not formally binding on the courts, provide some useful guidance.[61] The agency has summarized the relevant cases to seek a utility that is *specific, substantial, and credible* in patent applications. As the agency explains, "If the applicant has asserted that the claimed invention is useful for any particular practical purpose, (i.e., it has a "specific and substantial utility") and the assertion would be considered credible by a person of ordinary skill in the art, do not impose a rejection based on lack of utility."[62] This standard eliminates the possibility that patents will be granted on superficial or "throw-away" grounds, such as the use of a perpetual motion machine as a paperweight, or a newly developed chemical compound for filling a beaker.

---

[56] *Id.* at 1368.

[57] *See* Utility Examination Guidelines, 66 Fed. Reg. 1092 (Jan. 5, 2001) and Revised Interim Utility Guidelines Training Materials (1999); *see also* MPEP § 2101.01 (directing that "[o]ffice personnel must distinguish between inventions that have a specifically identified substantial utility and inventions whose asserted utility requires further research to identify or reasonably confirm.").

[58] *Id.* at 1376.

[59] *Fisher*, 421 F.3d at 1373.

[60] *Id.*

[61] *See* Utility Examination Guidelines, 66 Fed. Reg. 1092, 1098 (Jan. 5, 2001).

[62] *Id.*

According to PTO training materials, a utility is considered *credible* unless "the logic underlying the assertion is seriously flawed," or "the facts are inconsistent with the logic underlying the assertion."[63] To determine whether a utility is *specific*, the asserted use should not be "applicable to the broad class of invention,"[64] such as the gene probe at issue in *Fisher* or for "diagnosing an unspecified disease."[65] These materials explain that a utility is *substantial* where there is a real-world application of the invention. This excludes basic research, the diagnosis or treatment of an unspecified disease (for example, the issue confronted in *Kirk*), or methods for testing or making substances that have no identified specific, substantial, and credible utility. This interpretation can be a structured and helpful way to synthesize the current utility standard.

§ 22.04　MORAL UTILITY

The doctrine of *moral utility* derives from Justice Story's 1817 opinion *Lowell v. Lewis*, where the court considered a utility challenge to a patent for an improvement to the construction of a pump.[66] The accused infringer challenged the validity of the patent based on the argument that the patent must represent a superior solution to that existent in the art — that is, "a better pump than the common pump."[67] *Lowell* rejected this argument as "utterly without foundation" and contrary to the law, as Story explained, "The word "useful" . . . is incorporated into the act in contradistinction to mischievous or immoral. For instance, a new invention to poison people, or to promote debauchery, or to facilitate private assassination, is not a patentable invention."[68]

After *Lowell* was decided, some courts applied the doctrine of moral utility to invalidate patents relating to gambling. For example, in the 1889 decision *National Automatic Device Co. v. Lloyd*, the court invalidated a patent for a "Toy Automatic Race Horse" that was in use "in saloons, bar-rooms, and other drinking places, where the frequenters of such places make wagers as to which of the toy horses will stop first . . . . by dropping a nickel in the slot."[69] Although the court acknowledged that the device had other potential uses, such as a child's toy where no gambling was implicated, the court explained that "its use so far has been only pernicious and hurtful," and the court refused to issue an injunction to enforce its terms.[70]

Additionally, during the early 1900's, some cases invalidated patents that based utility on features that deceived the public. For example, in the 1900 case *Rickard v. Du Bon*, the Second Circuit invalidated a patent that claimed the use of chemicals

---

[63] Revised Interim Utility Guidelines Training Materials, 5 (1999).

[64] *Id.*

[65] *Id.*

[66] Lowell v. Lewis, 15 F. Cas. 1018 (D. Mass. 1817).

[67] *Id.* at 1019.

[68] *Id.*

[69] *See* National Automatic Device Co. v. Lloyd, 40 F. 89, 89-90 (N.D. Ill. 1889).

[70] *Id.* at 90; *see also* Reliance Novelty Co. v. Dworzek, 80 F. 902 (C.D. Cal. 1897) (similar, for a playing card machine used for gambling).

to artificially create a discolored spotting pattern on tobacco leaves that were used as cigar wrappers.[71] The claimed invention resulted in leaves that mimicked the more expensive and higher quality tobacco leaves, for which this spotting occurred naturally. Finding that the patent failed to meet the utility requirement, the court explained, "[C]ongress did not intend to extend protection to those which confer no other benefit upon the public than the opportunity of profiting by deception and fraud. To warrant a patent, the invention must be useful; that is, capable of some beneficial use as distinguished from a pernicious use."[72] Similarly, in the 1925 decision *Scott & Williams v. Aristo Hosiery Co.*,[73] the Second Circuit invalidated a patent for a stocking with a mock seam at the back of the leg, which imitated better quality and more expensive seamed stockings. The era of rejections for gambling devices and inventions for creating misimpressions appear to be over.

Currently, moral utility is rarely invoked in U.S. law. The reasons for this circumstance were explored in the 1999 Federal Circuit decision *Juicy Whip, Inc. v. Orange Bang, Inc.*[74] There, the court considered a utility challenge to a beverage dispenser in which syrup and water where mixed together immediately before the drink is poured. In addition, the patent claimed a reservoir bowl that stored pre-mixed beverage for display to consumers. The district court found that the purpose of the reservoir holding the pre-mixed beverage was "to increase sales by deception," as the purpose of the invention "is to create an illusion, whereby customers believe that the fluid contained in the bowl is the actual beverage that they are receiving, when of course it is not."[75]

On appeal, the Federal Circuit refused to follow the Second Circuit earlier opinions *Rickard* and *Aristo Hosiery*. Rather, *Juicy Whip* noted the lack of recent authority that invalidated patents on moral utility grounds and advised that the patent system was not a means to protect consumers from fraud or deception. Indeed, on the fact presented the *Juicy Whip* court found "[t]he fact that one product can be altered to make it look like another is in itself a specific benefit sufficient to satisfy the statutory requirement of utility."[76] *Juicy Whip* is characteristic of the modern rules that place little emphasis on moral utility as a basis to invalidate a patent.[77]

Advances in biotechnology have the potential to invoke the considerations that underlie moral utility. In the 1980 decision *Diamond v. Chakrabarty*, the Supreme Court held that patentable subject matter included living things while acknowledging that such inventions "may spread pollution and disease, that it may result in a loss of genetic diversity, and that its practice may tend to depreciate the value of

---

[71] Rickard v. Du Bon, 103 F. 868 (2d Cir. 1900).

[72] *Id.* at 873.

[73] Scott & Williams v. Aristo Hosiery Co., 7 F.2d 1003 (2d Cir. 1925).

[74] *See* Juicy Whip, Inc. v. Orange Bang, Inc., 185 F.3d 1364 (Fed. Cir. 1999).

[75] *Id.* at 1366.

[76] *Id.* at 1367.

[77] *But see* 42 U.S.C. § 2181 (2000) (providing that a patent cannot be granted for an atomic or nuclear weapon).

human life."[78] These concerns have not proven to pose onerous impediments to patents on life forms. For example, the U.S. PTO has issued a patent for the Harvard Mouse, a transgenic animal genetically altered to make it more susceptible to cancer[79]

However, in 1998, a biotechnological invention did raise moral utility concerns. In that instance, an inventor named Dr. Stuart Newman submitted some applications for a chimeric embryo from both a human and non-human.[80] Invoking *Lowell v. Lewis*, the PTO rejected one of Newman's applications and noted that humans are "not eligible for patents."[81] Further, this rejection recognized that "the exclusionary rights conveyed by a patent would be difficult to apply at best to humans in view of the constitutional rights of human persons."[82]Section 33(a) of the AIA now adds "Notwithstanding any other provision of law, no patent may issue on a claim directed to or encompassing a human organism." This exemption affects a broader range of inventions that the one at issue with respect to the Newman patent. Other than this extreme circumstance, rejections on the grounds of moral utility have not been plentiful in recent years.

§ 22.05 SOME ECONOMIC CONSIDERATIONS RELATING TO THE UTILITY REQUIREMENT

As with other patentability requirements, the application of the utility standard has the potential to encourage (or discourage) research and investment. The Supreme Court's *Brenner* decision recognized this to some degree in expressing concern that setting a low utility standard "may confer power to block off whole areas of scientific development."[83] As Professor Rebecca Eisenberg explains, the choice of setting a particular utility standard "makes a big difference to universities and some private firms that specialize in 'upstream' research that is removed from end product development."[84] The potential for broad patent protection may act as an incentive to engage in expensive or research-intensive science.

On the other hand, those wishing to build on early pioneering research may be precluded from engaging in development of technologies that has become subject to patents obtained by earlier researchers. This later circumstance, identified as a "tragedy of the anticommons," has particular significance for biotechnological and pharmaceutical inventions where the "proliferation of intellectual property rights upstream may be stifling life-saving innovations further downstream in the course

---

[78] Diamond v. Chakrabarty, 447 U.S. 303, 316 (1980).

[79] *See* U.S. Patent No. 4,736,866 (filed June 22, 1984).

[80] *See* Mark Dowie, *Gods and Monsters*, MOTHER JONES (January/ February 2004) (describing a press conference held by Hon. Bruce Lehman upon the filing of Newman's application, "stating that "[n]o half-human 'monsters' would be patented . . . or any other 'immoral inventions.' ").

[81] Office Action on U.S. Patent Application No. 08/993,564 (filed Dec. 03, 2002).

[82] *Id.* at 21.

[83] Brenner v. Manson, 383 U.S. 519, 535 (1966).

[84] Rebecca S. Eisenberg, *Analyze This: A Law And Economics Agenda for the Patent System*, 53 VAND. L. REV. 2081, 2088 (2000).

of research and product development."[85] In some cases, setting a high utility standard assists later researchers. As Professors Burk and Lemeley have stated, "[t]he utility and abstract ideas doctrines can restrict the anticommons problem in a few cases by preventing unnecessary upstream patents (for example on ESTs) that threaten to hold up downstream innovation."[86] Although the courts have not explicitly discussed the economic impact of the utility standard, those involved in research and development might be quite cognizant of its significance.

§ 22.06   CONCLUSION

The utility derives from the term "useful" used in both the U.S. Constitution and § 101 of the Patent Act. This requirement is grounded on the principle that basic research is not a proper subject matter for a patent, and that the public is entitled to a useful invention as part of the *quid pro quo* in exchange for a government grant of the patent right.

Utility arises in three circumstances. First, an invention must be operable. A patent will not be granted to inventions that are implausible or cannot be replicated by those of ordinary skill using currently available methods. Second, a patentee must identify a practical or "real world" use for the invention. A patentee must establish that one skilled in the art can use the invention to provide a specific and substantial utility that has an immediate benefit to the public. Finally, the very limited doctrine of moral utility can be used to ensure that patents will not be granted for inventions that are injurious to society.

---

[85] Michael A. Heller & Rebecca S. Eisenberg, *Can Patents Deter Innovation? The Anticommons in Biomedical Research*, 280 Science 698 (May 1998).

[86] Burk & Lemley, supra note 52, at 738. This article observes that broad protect for pioneers in biotechnology "raise[s] the specter of overlapping first-generation patents choking out innovation, particularly where those first-generation patents are granted on upstream research tools." *Id.* at 736.

Chapter 23

STATUTORY SUBJECT MATTER

SYNOPSIS

§ 23.01 INTRODUCTION

§ 23.02 PRODUCTS OF NATURE

    [A] History: Products of Nature and Natural Phenomenon

    [B] Products Made from Living Things: *Parke-Davis & Co. v. H.K. Mulford Co.*

    [C] Products of Nature v. Living Things: The Supreme Court's *Diamond v. Chakrabarty*

    [D] Claims Derived from Nature: *Mayo v. Prometheus*

    [E] Emerging Issues: The *Myriad* Case

§ 23.03 ABSTRACT SUBJECT MATTER, BUSINESS METHODS AND SOFTWARE

    [A] Introduction

    [B] *Gottschalk v. Benson*

    [C] *Parker v. Flook*

    [D] *Diamond v. Diehr*

    [E] Patentable Subject Matter at the Federal Circuit

    [F] The Federal Circuit's Restrictive Approach

§ 23.04 THE SUPREME COURT'S *BILSKI* OPINION

    [A] *Bilski* and the Prohibition on Abstract Subject Matter

    [B] *Bilski's* Progeny

§ 23.05 CONCLUSION

§ 23.01 INTRODUCTION

Utility patents must satisfy the *statutory subject matter requirement*, which is separate from and in addition to the novelty, non-obviousness, utility and disclosure obligations. In 35 U.S.C. § 101, Congress defined the scope of patentable subject matter as any *"process, machine, manufacture, or composition of matter"* or any improvement of any one of these. Many inventions fit easily within these terms. For example, mechanical and electronic apparatus can be included as a "machine" or article of "manufacture" under the statute. Pharmaceutical compounds may be considered a "composition of matter" or an article of "manufacture." A claim that describes a series of steps to create an apparatus or chemical compound is a "process."

However, there is another dimension to the patentable subject matter analysis that extends beyond the question of whether an invention fits within § 101's categorical terms. This presents the more difficult inquiry of whether a particular type of invention is within Congress' contemplation of the patent system. For example, a mathematical statement may literally constitute a "process," that demonstrates the equality of two different expressions. Nonetheless, that formula is not directed to the solution to any particular problem. As such, the formula may be of such universal application that granting a patent may constitute an abstract idea that is not patentable.[1] The U.S. Constitution contemplates that patents be granted only for inventions that are within the "useful arts." A law of nature or mathematical expression that represents a scientific fact or an abstract principle is viewed as outside of the reach of this purpose. As one Court has explained, "[a] principle, in the abstract, is a fundamental truth; an original cause; a motive; these cannot be patented, as no one can claim in either of them an exclusive right."[2] Other areas that constitute unpatentable subject matter include *physical phenomenon* and *mental steps*. As these examples demonstrate, policy considerations drive the inquiry of whether statutory subject matter is present, even for a claim that fits within an enumerated category of § 101.

The early U.S. patent system was developed at a time when the subject matters of many inventions were tangible — patents for equipment for the production of fabrics, steam engines, farm equipment and methods for tanning leather were common.[3] Over the years, the limits of patentable subject matter have been tested as newly inventive activity yields claims that do not fit harmoniously within the precedent of a previous era. Today, challenges are presented by patent applications for life forms, business methods, legal strategies and economic formulae. As a consequence, a number of decisions evidence the patent system's efforts to continue to reward inventive activity while maintaining the patent system's constitutional purpose.

§ 23.02 PRODUCTS OF NATURE

Significant scientific progress has been devoted to understanding the natural world, through the study of physics, medicine, and other disciplines. Although these fields make valuable contributions to the fund of human knowledge, not all of this information is considered patentable. Therefore, Einstein's theory of relativity, which transformed the fields of physics and astronomy, is not considered patentable because it captures a principle of nature. Patent law protects the *application* of a natural phenomenon (or its mathematical expression) to a real world problem. The articulation of natural principles is not.

---

[1] *See* Bilski v. Kappos, 130 S. Ct. 3218 (2010).

[2] Le Roy v. Tatham, 55 U.S. 156, 175 (1853).

[3] *See generally* Malla Pollack, *The Multiple Unconstitutionality of Business Method Patents: Common Sense, Congressional Consideration and Constitutional History*, 28 RUTGERS COMPUTER & TECH. L.J. 61, 108 (2002) (describing inventions during the origin of the patent system).

There are at least two reasons that support this exception. First, the discovery of a natural principle is not considered "inventive." Like "a new mineral discovered in the earth or a new plant found in the wild,"[4] man does not create nature, natural phenomena or products of nature. Second, granting such protection threatens to monopolize basic research and prevent both innovation and knowledge creation.[5] As the Supreme Court has explained, "Einstein . . . could not have patented his famous law by claiming a process consisting of simply telling linear accelerator operators to refer to the law to determine how much energy of mass has produced (or vice versa)."[6] To obtain patent protection for inventions that involve a principle of nature, the inventor must claim an application of the theory that adds an inventive component. How does one tell the difference? The courts have promulgated a series of cases that provide some guidance. Some questions have been settled for years. Yet as new fields of technologies arise, difficult questions of patentable subject matter continue to emerge. Presently, the Supreme Court appears more focused on articulating what invention is not, rather than defining what invention is. At times, one might regard the Court's patentable subject matter jurisprudence similar to the creation of an ice sculpture. That is, the Court has not provided a clear definition of invention. Rather, the Court's opinion chips away to eliminate protection for certain types of inventions. As the Court's decisions issue, a picture of patentable subject matter might begin to take shape.

[A] History: Products of Nature and Natural Phenomenon

The courts have long established that a *product of nature*, such as a chemical element or biological substances found in their natural state, is not patentable.[7] It seems intuitively sensible that patents cannot be granted for discoveries that have long existed in a state of nature. A person does not "invent" a rock or an insect. Granting a patent in favor of one who merely discovers — rather than invents — would permit an individual to obtain exclusivity without the countervailing benefit to the public that the patent system was intended to promote. Yet this simple proposition can be very difficult to apply to particular claims, particularly those that claim genetic material.

A corollary of this rule is that a patent will not issue to protect the discovery of *natural phenomena*. As the Supreme Court explained in 1852, the forces of nature — such as steam power — are not patentable, and that "[t]he same may be said of electricity, and of any other power in nature, which is alike open to all."[8] This principle was pivotal in the 1948 opinion *Funk Bros. Seed Co. v. Kalo Incolant Co.*,[9] where the Supreme Court considered the validity of a patent for a combination of a number of different bacterium used to infect the roots of several types of plants.

---

[4] Diamond v. Chakrabarty, 447 U.S. 303, 309 (1980).

[5] *See* Mayo Collaborative Services v. Prometheus Laboratories, Inc., 132 S. Ct. 1289, 182 L. Ed. 2d 321 (No. 10-1150 March 20, 2012).

[6] Id., Slip Op. at 9.

[7] General Electric Co. v. De Forest Radio Co., 28 F.2d 641, 642 (3d Cir. 1928).

[8] *Le Roy*, 55 U.S. 156, 175 (1853).

[9] *See* Funk Bros. Seed Co. v. Kalo Inoculant Co., 333 U.S. 127 (1948).

The *Funk Bros.* Court found that claims to the bacterium combination failed, because the patentee:

> . . . does not create state of inhibition or of non-inhibition of the bacteria. Their qualities are works of nature. Those qualities are of course not patentable. For patents cannot issue for the discovery of phenomena of nature.[10]

Nonetheless, *Funk Bros.* recognized that the patent system would allow a claim to issue for a machine, structure or process that *relies* on natural phenomena. Under this principle, although a force of nature — such as electricity — is not patentable, a patent can issue to protect a light bulb that relies on electricity to provide illumination via a filament within the bulb.

[B]　Products Made from Living Things: *Parke-Davis & Co. v. H.K. Mulford Co.*

Although products of nature cannot be patented, can a product *derived* from nature be patented? The 1911 appellate court opinion *Parke-Davis & Co. v. H.K. Mulford Co.*, demonstrates that such inventions are patentable where an inventor modifies such substances such that they are no longer in their natural state.[11] Specifically, the *Parke-Davis* court considered whether an inventor could obtain a patent to an isolated and purified substance made from the suprarenal glands of animals. The court found that this substance, which had medical uses, constituted a patentable "composition of matter," and was sufficiently distinct from an unpatentable product of nature because the inventor:

> . . . was the first to make it available for any use by removing it from the other gland-tissue in which it was found, and, while it is of course possible logically to call this a purification of the principle, *it became for every practical purpose a new thing commercially and therapeutically.* That was a good ground for a patent.[12]

The *Parke-Davis* opinion, which permitted the patent for a purified substance that evidenced properties beyond those existent in the material's natural state, has been recognized as laying the foundation for the patentability of the more complex biotechnological inventions developed today.[13] The *Parke-Davis* opinion demonstrates that a product derived from nature that evidences alternation from their natural origins constitutes patentable subject matter.

---

[10] *Id.* at 130. *But see* U.S. Patent No. 141,072 (filed May 9, 1873) (claim to "Yeast, free from organic germs of disease, as an article of manufacture", issued to Louis Pasteur).

[11] *See* Parke-Davis & Co. v. H. K. Mulford Co., 189 F. 95 (1911).

[12] *Id.* at 103 (emphasis added).

[13] *See* Robin Feldman, *Rethinking Rights in Biospace*, 79 S. CAL. L. REV. 1, 8 (2005).

[C] Products of Nature v. Living Things: The Supreme Court's *Diamond v. Chakrabarty*

In 1980, the U.S. Supreme Court's *Diamond v. Chakrabarty* considered whether human-made living material constituted statutory subject matter.[14] Specifically, the *Chakrabarty* Court considered claims for a genetically engineered bacterium that was capable of breaking down crude oil to perform spill cleanup.[15] The Court of Custom and Patent Appeals had found the claims to the bacterium patentable, and the PTO challenged this ruling.

The *Chakrabarty* Court affirmed the appellate ruling. In doing so, the Court addressed the PTO's argument that Congress had intended to exclude living things from the express categories of patentable subject matter in § 101, asserting that such subject matter was more appropriately governed by two federal statutes that authorized protection for plants, the 1930 Plant Patent Act and the 1970 Plant Variety Protection Act.[16] More specifically, the Commissioner argued that these two plant-specific statutes would be rendered unnecessary if § 101 authorized utility patent protection for living things.

Rejecting this argument, the *Chakrabarty* Court found that § 101 should be given broad construction to effectuate patent law's purposes. The Court relied on the writings of Thomas Jefferson in observing, "ingenuity should receive a liberal encouragement."[17] Further, *Chakrabarty* noted that the legislative history of § 101 demonstrated Congress' intent that statutory subject matter encompass "anything under the sun that is made by man."[18] Concerning the enactment of the 1930 Plant Patent Act and the 1970 Plant Variety Protection Act, the Court found nothing in the legislative history of either act that would preclude the application of § 101 to living things. In effect, the Court saw those statutes as potentially *alternative* forms of protection for living things, rather than a Congressional effort to preclude, or channel, protection toward those two statutes and *away* from the utility patent system. On these bases, the *Chakrabarty* Court rejected the argument that statutory subject matter was limited to the inanimate. Instead, *Chakrabarty* instructed that the proper analysis is between *products of nature* — which are unpatentable — and *human-made living things*, which are within the scope of § 101.

In addition, the Court addressed the PTO's argument that microorganisms cannot qualify as statutory subject matter protection because Congress had not expressly so authorized in the text of § 101. Invoking its power to construe

---

[14] *See* Diamond v. Chakrabarty, 447 U.S. 303 (1980).

[15] The U.S. PTO had issued claims for a process to create the bacterium, as well as the carrier material to enable the bacterium to float on water. The claims at issue before the *Chakrabarty* Court sought protection for the bacteria itself.

[16] For more information about these statutes, *see* Chapter 5 (describing statutory protection for plants).

[17] *Chakrabarty*, 447 U.S. at 308-09, *quoting* V WRITINGS OF THOMAS JEFFERSON 75-76 (Washington ed. 1871).

[18] *Id.* at 309, *quoting* S. REP. No. 1979, 82D CONG., 2D SESS., 5 (1952); H.R. REP. No. 1923, 82D CONG., 2D SESS., 6 (1952)).

statutory language, the *Chakrabarty* Court found that the section should be read broadly to reach inventions that could not have been anticipated in 1952 when the section was enacted. *Chakrabarty* explained, "the inventions most benefiting mankind are those that push back the frontiers of chemistry, physics and the like. Congress employed broad language in drafting § 101 precisely because such inventions are often unforeseeable."[19] The *Chakrabarty* Court declined to address the arguments by the PTO and *amicus* that presented a "gruesome parade of horribles" that "might pose a serious threat to the human race, or, at the very least, that the dangers are far too substantial to permit such research to proceed apace at this time."[20] Although *Chakrabarty* acknowledged the import of these concerns, the Court reasoned that considerable research had already been undertaken in the field and that, "[t]he grant or denial of patents on micro-organisms is not likely to put an end to genetic research or its attendant risks."[21] In addition, the Court stated that the matter was one of "high policy for resolution within the legislative process."[22]

Since the time that this opinion has issued, the U.S. PTO has stated that non-naturally occurring, non-human multi-cellular living organisms, including animals, are considered by the agency as patentable subject matter.[23] For example, in 1988, the U.S. PTO issued a patent for the "Harvard Mouse," which had claims directed to a genetically modified mammal.[24] It bears note that a least one block for protection on humans has been enacted. Section 33(a) of the AIA specifies that "Notwithstanding any other provision of law, no patent may issue on a claim directed to or encompassing a human organism." This limitation on the patentability of human life draws a statutory line that cannot be crossed. Further, the *Chakrabarty* opinion offers a useful summary of a number of well-established subject matters that are barred from patentability — specifically, patents cannot be granted for the *laws of nature, physical phenomena* and *abstract ideas.*[25] The Court explained that patents will not be granted for "a new mineral discovered in the earth or a new plant found in the wild."[26] As the Court further stated, "Einstein could not patent his celebrated law $E = mc^2$; nor could Newton have patented the law of gravity."[27] To some degree, such exclusions from statutory subject matter are based on the principle that "sometimes *too much* patent protection can impede rather than 'promote the Progress of Science and useful Arts,' the constitutional objective of patent and copyright protection."[28]

---

[19] *Id.* at 316 (quotation and citation omitted).

[20] *Id.*

[21] *Id.* at 317.

[22] *Id.*

[23] MPEP § 2105.

[24] U.S. Patent No. 4,736,866 (filed Jun. 22, 1984).

[25] The "mental steps" doctrine has been considered a subset of an abstract idea. *See* CyberSource Corp. v. Retail Decisions, Inc., 654 F.3d 1366 (Fed. Cir. 2011).

[26] *Chakrabarty*, 447 U.S. at 309.

[27] *Id.*

[28] Laboratory Corp. of America Holdings v. Metabolite Laboratories, Inc., 126 S. Ct. 2921, 2922 (2006)

[D]   Claims Derived from Nature: *Mayo v. Prometheus*

The patentability of natural phenomenon was raised — but not decided — in *Laboratory Corp. v. Metabolite Laboratories, Inc.*[29] The invention at issue was a Diagnostic claim that described a process for determining a vitamin deficiency. Specifically, the process consisted of using any type of test (whether patented or unpatented) to determine the level of a particular amino acid in the blood. Once that level was found, the process consisted of recognizing whether the level was elevated above normal. If it were, then a physician would understand that there was a likely deficiency of the two vitamins.[30] After holding oral argument, the Supreme Court dismissed the writ of certiorari as improvidently granted.[31] As is the practice of the Court, the reason for the dismissal was not revealed. Three justices joined in a dissent from the denial, and filed an opinion authored by Justice Breyer. This dissent stated that the Court should have reached the patentable subject matter issues raised by the petition because "those who engage in medical research, who practice medicine, and who as patients depend upon proper health care might well benefit from this Court's authoritative answer."[32]

Justice Breyer's dissent noted several important principles of the patentable subject matter doctrine. These stand in contrast to the *Chakrabarty's* broad view of patentable subject matter so that "ingenuity should receive a liberal encouragement."[33] Specifically, Breyer observed that:

> The problem arises from the fact that patents do not only encourage research by providing monetary incentives for invention. Sometimes their presence can discourage research by impeding the free exchange of information, for example by forcing researchers to avoid the use of potentially patented ideas, by leading them to conduct costly and time-consuming searches of existing or pending patents, by requiring complex licensing arrangements, and by raising the costs of using the patented information, sometimes prohibitively so.[34]

Breyer asserted that the limitations on patentable subject matter served an important function to strike an appropriate balance in this realm. Regarding the claims at issue, his dissent noted that the patentees "have simply described the

---

(Breyer, J., dissenting from dismissal of writ of certiorari as improvidently granted) (emphasis in original).

[29] Laboratory Corp. v. Metabolite Laboratories, Inc., 548 U.S. 124 (2006).

[30] Claim 13 of the patent in suit reads as follows:

A method for detecting a deficiency of cobalamin or folate in warm-blooded animals comprising the steps of:

    assaying a body fluid for an elevated level of total homocysteine; and

    correlating an elevated level of total homocysteine in said body fluid with a deficiency of cobalamin or folate.

[31] Laboratory Corp. of America Holdings v. Metabolite Laboratories, Inc., 548 U.S. 124 (2006).

[32] *Id.* at 126.

[33] *Chakrabarty*, 447 U.S. at 308-09, *quoting* V WRITINGS OF THOMAS JEFFERSON 75-76 (Washington ed. 1871).

[34] *Laboratory Corp.*, 548 U.S. at 126 (Breyer, J., dissenting).

natural law at issue in the abstract patent language of a 'process.' "[35] Although not precedential, this dissent raised important questions about the manner in which the patentable subject matter doctrine might moderate expansive claims to best serve the goals of the patent system.

In 2012, Justice Breyer authored a unanimous opinion, *Mayo v. Prometheus*,[36] that resolved some of the issues that had been left undecided in the dismissal of certiorari of the *Laboratory Corp.* case. The *Prometheus* case considered claims directed to processes that assisted doctors to determine whether patients with autoimmune disorders were receiving an appropriate dosage of a drug — called a thiopurine drug — designed to treat the condition. Generally, doctors have difficulty determining the amount of thiopurine drugs to prescribe, because different patients process the drug differently. Any patient who takes a thiopurine compound metabolizes the chemical in a measurable amount. The claims at issue in *Prometheus* depended on the measurement of the level of certain thiopurine metabolites, identified as 6-thioguanine and 6-methyl-mercaptopurine in the patient's bloodstream. The patents described that a measurement of the metabolite that was *above* an identified level indicated a dosage that was too high; a measurement *below* a different level indicated the dosage was too low.[37] The claims at issue had three components: First, an "administering" step that required a doctor to administer a thiopurine drug to a patient; second, a "determining" step that required measurement of the patient's metabolite levels, without specifying the manner in which the test should be undertaken; and third, a "wherein" step, which specified that a particular metabolite level suggested that an adjustment in dosage was required. As an example of this third step, the claim described that "wherein the level" of the patient's metabolites were greater (or less) than a specified amount, the dosage should be adjusted accordingly.

The *Prometheus* Court found that the claims represented unpatentable laws of nature.[38] Specifically, the opinion found that the relation between the ingestion of a thiopurine drug and metabolite levels in the body was the result of an entirely

---

[35] *Id.* at 137.

[36] Mayo Collaborative Services v. Prometheus Laboratories, Inc., 132 S. Ct. 1289, 182 L. Ed. 2d 321 (No. 10-1150 March 20, 2012).

[37] A representative claim of one of the patents at issue, U.S. Patent No. 6,355,623:

A method of optimizing therapeutic efficacy for treatment of an immune-mediated gastrointestinal disorder, comprising:

(a) administering a drug providing 6-thioguanine to a subject having said immune-mediated gastrointestinal disorder; and

(b) determining the level of 6-thioguanine in said subject having said immune-mediated gastrointestinal disorder, wherein the level of 6-thioguanine less than about 230 pmol per 8108 red blood cells indicates a need to increase the amount of said drug subsequently administered to said subject and wherein the level of 6-thioguanine greater than about 400 pmol per 8108 red blood cells indicates a need to decrease the amount of said drug subsequently administered to said subject.

[38] The Federal Circuit had found the claims patentable, determining that the claims involved a transformation within the human body and the blood and thereby satisfied the "machine or transformation" test. Further, the appellate court found that the claims did not pose a danger of preempting natural correlations. Prometheus Laboratories, Inc. v. Mayo Collaborative Services, 628 F.3d 1347 (Fed. Cir. 2010).

natural process, "[a]nd so a patent that simply describes that relation sets forth a natural law."[39] The Court found that the claim did nothing more than tell doctors about the natural correlation that the researchers had discovered:

> . . . the claims inform a relevant audience about certain laws of nature; any additional steps consist of well-understood, routine, conventional activity already engaged in by the scientific community; and those steps, when viewed as a whole, add nothing significant beyond the sum of their parts taken separately.[40]

The *Prometheus* opinion emphasized that the claim added "nothing specific to the laws of nature other than what is well-understood, routine, conventional activity, previously engaged in by those in the field."[41] Yet the Court made clear that its decision was firmly grounded on patentable subject matter under § 101 of the Patent Act, rather than under principles of novelty or nonobviousness.[42] The Court's primary concern was that the claims at issue added nothing to the laws of nature, and therefore failed to contribute any invention that warranted a patent. Further, the *Prometheus* decision observed that the claims' narrow field of application was insufficient to save their validity. The Court observed that the claims threatened to tie up future refinements and innovation despite the limited applicability of the claims. The Court stated:

> . . . the underlying functional concern here is a relative one: how much future innovation is foreclosed relative to the contribution of the inventor. A patent upon a narrow law of nature may not inhibit future research as seriously as would a patent upon Einstein's theory of relativity, but the creative value of the discovery is also considerably smaller.[43]

The Court acknowledged that prior precedents have not based patentability on a claim's narrowness. Rather, administrative concerns have established a bright-line prohibition on patents for laws of nature. In finding the claims at issue not patentable, the *Prometheus* opinion recognized that the determination involved a balance between appropriate incentives for creativity, invention, and research on one hand, and the burdens of search, licensing, and impeding the flow of information on the other.

[E]   Emerging Issues: The *Myriad* Case

For the past several years, the PTO had issued numerous patents directed to genetic sequences, finding that such material constituted patentable subject matter.[44] One recent decision, *Ass'n for Molecular Pathology v. U.S. Patent and Trademark Office*, also called the *Myriad* case, raises important questions

---

[39] Prometheus, ___U.S. at ___, Slip Op. at 8.

[40] *Id.*, Slip Op. at 11.

[41] *Id.*, Slip Op. at 13.

[42] *Id.*, Slip Op. at 22.

[43] *Id.*, Slip Op. at 20.

[44] U.S. Patent & Trademark Office, 2001 Utility Examination Guidelines, 66 Fed. Reg., No. 4, 1092, 1093 (Jan. 5, 2001) ("DNA compounds having naturally occurring sequences are eligible for patenting

concerning the patentability of modified genetic material.[45] The case was filed as a declaratory judgment action against the patentees University of Utah and Myriad Genetics, Inc. The challenge targeted the patentability of composition claims that cover two "isolated" human genes, BRCA1 and BRCA2 (as well as alterations and mutations of these genes), which are associated with a predisposition to breast and ovarian cancers, as well as diagnostic methods of identifying mutations in these sequences.

The most controversial aspect of the Federal Circuit's opinion focused on the product claims to the BRCA genes. The plaintiffs argued that claims to isolated DNA molecules fail to satisfy the patentable subject matter requirement because the claims to the BRCA genes were natural phenomena and products of nature. This argument asserted that a gene fragment must "have a distinctive name, character, and use, making it 'markedly different' from the natural product," and because "isolated DNAs retain the same nucleotide sequence as native DNAs, they do not have any 'markedly different' characteristics."[46] The PTO as amicus curie concurred with the plaintiffs, arguing to the Federal Circuit "if an imaginary microscope could focus in on the claimed DNA molecule as it exists in the human body, the claim covers unpatentable subject matter."[47]

The Federal Circuit found claims to the BRCA genes patentable. The court explained that the creation of a gene fragment included two steps — first, the naturally occurring DNA is transcribed into a complimentary RNA molecule, which has a chemically distinct sugar-phosphate backbone and uses a different nucleotide base.[48] As the second step, certain sequences (called "introns") are eliminated from the RNA to produce a messenger RNA (mRNA). This mRNA sequence is then translated into the encoded protein. The *Myriad* court stated that "the distinction . . . between a product of nature and a human-made invention for purposes of § 101 turns on a change in the claimed composition's identity compared with what exists in nature."[49] In its finding, the court distinguished the structure of naturally occurring DNA, which "exists in the body as one of forty-six large, contiguous DNA molecules."[50] The *Myriad* opinion explained that the BRCA genes at issue are structurally different:

> Isolated DNA has been cleaved (i.e., had covalent bonds in its backbone chemically severed) or synthesized to consist of just a fraction of a naturally occurring DNA molecule. For example, the BRCA1 gene in its native state resides on chromosome 17, a DNA molecule of around eighty million nucleotides. Similarly, BRCA2 in its native state is located on chromosome

---

when isolated from their natural state and purified, and when the application meets the statutory criteria for patentability.").

   [45] Ass'n for Molecular Pathology v. U.S. Patent and Trademark Office, 653 F.3d 1329 (Fed. Cir. 2011).

   [46] *Id.* at 1349.

   [47] *Id.* at 1350.

   [48] As the court explained, a DNA sequence uses a molecule made of adenine, thymine, cytosine, and guanine. In contrast, RNA uses uracil in the place of thymine. *Id.* at 1335-36.

   [49] *Id.* at 1351.

   [50] *Id.*

13, a DNA of approximately 114 million nucleotides. In contrast, isolated BRCA1 and BRCA2, with introns, each consists of just 80,000 or so nucleotides.[51]

Rejecting the government's magic microscope test, the court found that the informational similarities between the natural DNA and the claimed gene fragment were not relevant to determining patentable subject matter. Instead, the court focused on the DNA's structure, observing "when cleaved, an isolated DNA molecule is not a purified form of a natural material, but a distinct chemical entity."[52]

The *Myriad* case raises fascinating questions about the nature of patentable subject matter for biological material. The court's structural analysis represents one credible way to resolve the issue. As of this printing, the Supreme Court has asked the Federal Circuit to reconsider Myriad in light of Prometheus. The ultimate outcome of the Myriad case is expected to be significant.

§ 23.03   ABSTRACT SUBJECT MATTER, BUSINESS METHODS AND SOFTWARE

Over the past several decades, the courts have confronted challenges in applying the patentable subject matter doctrine to a variety of claims that had never been examined before. Unlike the patents from the Industrial Age, the inventions that arose from an emerging knowledge economy required the examination of numerous types of patent claims, including software, business methods, and processes that led to intangible results. Sorting through these subject matters has proven to be challenging, and the doctrine is still in its formative stages. To some degree, the courts have examined claims that are at the boundaries to determine whether the abstract idea exception to patentable subject matter should apply. In making this determination, the courts are attempting to determine whether granting patents to particular types of inventions will encourage inventive activity by "securing patents for valuable inventions without transgressing the public domain."[53]

[A]   Introduction

As computer software began to develop in importance and sophistication during the later half of the 20th century, the case law evidenced a consistent tension between several fundamental principles of patentability. A process is within the express terms of § 101.[54] A claim to software drafted as a series of commands may, therefore, fit within the literal meaning of the term "process." However, algorithms[55] by themselves can constitute a series of steps and yet are not

---

[51]   *Id.* at 1351-52.

[52]   *Id.* at 1352. In this vein, the court explained "We recognize that biologists may think of molecules in terms of their uses, but genes are in fact materials having a chemical nature and, as such, are best described in patents by their structures rather than their functions." *Id.*

[53]   *In re* Bilski, 130 S. Ct. 3218, 3227 (2010).

[54]   Diamond v. Diehr, 450 U.S. 175, 184 (1981).

[55]   In this context, an "algorithm" means a defined set of instructions for solving a mathematical

statutory subject matter because such formulas are considered expressions of scientific truths.[56] Thus, a claim to software that is comprised of what is essentially a series of calculations may amount to an unpatentable algorithm even where the claim may be considered a "process" under § 101. The question can become even more complex — for example, how does one assess the patentability of *software* — to the extent that software might be considered within the technological arts — with the function of performing a mathematical algorithm?

In 1968, the U.S. Patent & Trademark Office deemed computer programs that were directed to providing solely an *informational result*, such as a numerical or statistical calculation, as outside the scope of patentable subject matter.[57] At this time, only programs that were used to affect an appreciable change in *physical materials*, such as "in the knitting of a pattern or the shaping of a metal," were considered patentable.[58] Over the next several years, the U.S. Supreme Court considered three cases that attempted to sort through the patentability of software in *Gottschalk v. Benson* in 1972, *Parker v. Flook* in 1978, and *Diamond v. Diehr* in 1981.

[B] *Gottschalk v. Benson*

In *Gottschalk v. Benson*, the Supreme Court considered the patentability of a claim for a novel method to "convert binary coded decimal (BCD) numerals into pure binary numerals"[59] using software. *Benson* determined that the process claim at issue was not within the scope of patentable subject matter, reasoning that the claim amounted to a mathematical formula. In part, the *Benson* Court drew on a 1966 report of the President's Commission on the Patent System, which rejected the patentability of computer software by noting the difficulty of examining such applications and a lack of any substantial need for patent protection to grow the industry.[60] *Benson* explained:

> It is conceded that one may not patent an idea. But in practical effect that would be the result if the formula for converting BCD numerals to pure binary numerals were patented in this case. The mathematical formula involved here has no substantial practical application except in connection with a digital computer, which means that if the judgment below is affirmed, the patent would wholly pre-empt the mathematical formula and in practical effect would be a patent on the algorithm itself.[61]

---

problem. Algorithms might be performed in different ways, including by humans using a mental process or by a computer.

[56] *See* Mackay Radio & Telegraph Co. v. Radio Corp., 306 U.S. 86, 94 (1939).

[57] *See* Examination of Patent Applications on Computer Programs, 33 Fed. Reg. 15609-10 (October 22, 1968).

[58] *Id.* at 15610.

[59] Gottschalk v. Benson, 409 U.S. 63, 64 (1972).

[60] *Id.* at 72 (citing "To Promote the Progress of . . . Useful Arts," Report of the President's Commission on the Patent System (1966)).

[61] *Benson*, 409 U.S. at 71-72.

Despite this broad language, *Benson* left open the question of whether some types of software might constitute statutory subject matter in the context of a different type of claim.

Benson represents an early effort to frame the patentable subject matter requirement for intangibles. Notably, the *Benson* Court observed that "[t]ransformation and reduction of an article 'to a different state or thing' is the clue to the patentability of a process claim that does not include particular machines."[62] However, the Court refused to adopt this language as an absolute rule or exclusive test of patentable subject matter. Rather, the *Benson* Court rested on the fact that the claim might have preempted all uses of the algorithm, and therefore the claim was not patentable. As will be discussed in association with the upcoming analysis of the more recent cases, many of the principles discussed in the *Benson* opinion — such as the prohibition for patenting abstract mathematical formula and against preempting an entire field — remain viable today.

[C] *Parker v. Flook*

In the 1978 opinion *Parker v. Flook*, the U.S. Supreme Court considered whether a patent could be granted for a formula for calculating an alarm limit that signaled an abnormal or dangerous condition for a chemical reaction.[63] Critically, the claim included three steps: first, a step that measured a present value; second, a step that used a novel algorithm to calculate an updated alarm limit value; and third, which adjusted the actual alarm to the calculated value. The PTO had rejected the application, finding that a patent on the method would effectively be a patent on "the formula or mathematics itself," and therefore within the prohibition that prevents patenting of mathematical formulas.

To a significant degree, *Flook's* rejection of the claimed process rested on *Benson's* reasoning. The *Flook* applicant attempted to distinguish *Benson*, by arguing that the claimed subject matter was a patentable "process" rather than an unpatentable "abstract principle." Specifically, the patentee argued that the claim included a third step that demonstrated that the invention was directed to a practical effect in application — that is, an alarm adjustment made after the mathematical calculation was performed. The applicant's argument was that this so-called "post-solution" activity — the adjustment to the alarm limit — brought the claim from merely an abstract principle to a concrete (and therefore patentable) solution.

The *Flook* court rejected the applicant's argument, finding that the addition of post-solution activity was insufficient to save the claim. *Flook* held that "[t]he process itself, and not merely the mathematical algorithm, must be new and useful."[64] *Flook* found that the mathematical formulation could not be the subject matter of a patent unless there was some other inventive concept in the claim.[65] As

---

[62] *Id.* at 70.

[63] Parker v. Flook, 437 U.S. 584 (1978). The process at issue was used during the catalytic conversion of hydrocarbons, for example during petroleum refinement. *Id.* at 586.

[64] *Id.* at 591.

[65] *Id.* at 595.

the sole *novel* feature of the patent under examination involved the algorithm (the mathematical formula), and not the alarm adjustment (the practical effect asserted by the patentee), the claim failed. Indeed, *Flook* found that the novelty of the algorithm was irrelevant, as the algorithm was akin to an unpatentable "basic tool[] of scientific and technological work"[66] and therefore not a valid part of the statutory subject matter analysis.

In addition, *Flook* determined that the process was not the type of discovery that the patent laws were intended to protect. The Court noted that a claim that was "essentially to a method of calculating, using a mathematical formula" was not patentable subject matter.[67] As the Court explained its decision, "[d]ifficult questions of policy concerning the kinds of programs that may be appropriate for patent protection and the form and duration of such protection can be answered by Congress on the basis of current empirical data not equally available to this tribunal."[68]

[D]   *Diamond v. Diehr*

The final decision in the Supreme Court's software trilogy is the 1981 decision *Diamond v. Diehr*,[69] where the Court considered the patentability of a claim directed toward a novel process for molding uncured rubber into a final, cured product. The process claim at issue included multiple steps, including continuously measuring temperatures inside a mold, feeding the information into a computer that calculated the cure time and generating a signal for the time to open the press. Unlike the results in the earlier *Benson* and *Flook* cases, the *Diehr* Court found that the claim contained patentable subject matter, because it accomplished the transformation of an article into a different state or thing, noting that:

> . . . [the] claims involve the transformation of an article, in this case raw, uncured synthetic rubber, into a different state or thing cannot be disputed. The respondents' claims describe in detail a step-by-step method for accomplishing such, beginning with the loading of a mold with raw, uncured rubber and ending with the eventual opening of the press at the conclusion of the cure. Industrial processes such as this are the types which have historically been eligible to receive the protection of our patent laws.[70]

The fact that software was a part of the claimed process claim did not prevent *Diehr* from finding the claim constituted statutory subject matter. As the Court explained, ". . . that a claim drawn to [statutory] subject matter . . . does not become nonstatutory simply because it uses a mathematical formula, computer program or digital computer."[71] *Diehr* explained that the patentee was not attempting to patent a mathematical formula, but rather a process for curing synthetic rubber that

---

[66] *Id.* at 591 (citing Gottschalk v. Benson, 409 U.S. 63, 67 (1972)).

[67] *Id.* at 595.

[68] *Id.* at 595.

[69] *See* Diamond v. Diehr, 450 U.S. 175, 184 (1981).

[70] *Id.* at 183.

[71] *Id.* at 187.

employed a mathematical equation, and therefore was within the contemplation of protection under the patent system. *Diehr* represents a rule that software with a *practical and transformational effect on a tangible item* (there, turning uncured rubber into cured rubber) is sufficient.

[E] Patentable Subject Matter at the Federal Circuit

After this Supreme Court trilogy of cases, the Federal Circuit began to focus not on whether the software is "abstract" or "tangible" in an of itself, but rather whether the claim as drafted applied an abstract concept in a practical manner and produces a *useful, concrete, and tangible result*.[72] During the 1990's, the Federal Circuit took an expansive view of patentable subject matter. For example, the court routinely recognized software as subject matter.[73] In *In re Alappat*, the Federal Circuit provided this overview of the Supreme Court's analysis in the *Benson, Flook* and *Diehr* line of cases, as follows:

> [A]t the core of the Court's analysis in each of these cases lies an attempt by the Court to explain a rather straightforward concept, namely, that certain types of mathematical subject matter, standing alone, represent nothing more than *abstract ideas* until reduced to some type of practical application, and thus that subject matter is not, in and of itself, entitled to patent protection.[74]

Unlike the *Flook* Court, which had excluded a mathematical algorithm from its patentability analysis, the Federal Circuit had relied on *Diehr's* reasoning to direct that the appropriate inquiry examined the claimed subject matter *as a whole* inclusive of any algorithms or mathematical calculations performed. In result, *Alappat* held that a claim for circuitry that performed mathematical calculations used to create a waveform display qualified as patentable subject matter. *Alappat* explained, "[t]his is not a disembodied mathematical concept which may be characterized as an 'abstract idea' but rather a specific machine to produce a useful, concrete, and tangible result."[75] In 1999, the Federal Circuit held that a process claim for software that uses mathematics to calculate a value used to bill telephone customers met § 101 requirements.[76]

During this time, the Federal Circuit recognized that *business methods* constituted patentable subject matter. Before the Federal Circuit was formed in 1982, some courts had held that business methods were not considered patentable subject matter. As the First Circuit explained in a 1949 decision:

> . . . a system for the transaction of business, such, for example, as the cafeteria system for transacting the restaurant business, or similarly the

---

[72] AT&T Corp. v. Excel Communications, Inc., 172 F.3d 1352, 1358 (Fed. Cir. 1999).

[73] *See e.g., In re* Alappat, 33 F.3d 1526, 1545 (Fed. Cir. 1994) ("a computer operating pursuant to software may represent patentable subject matter, provided, of course, that the claimed subject matter meets all of the other requirements of Title 35.").

[74] *Id.* at 1543.

[75] *Id.* at 1544.

[76] *AT&T Corp.*, 172 F.3d 1358-59.

open-air drive-in system for conducting the motion picture theatre business, however novel, useful, or commercially successful is not patentable apart from the means for making the system practically useful, or carrying it out.[77]

In 1998, the Federal Circuit came to a contrary conclusion on this issue in *State Street Bank & Trust Co. v. Signature Financial Group, Inc.*[78] The court considered whether statutory subject matter was present for claims directed to financial services software that allowed several mutual funds. This system saved costs based on the administration consolidation and tax advantages. The *State Street* court considered whether the claims were patentable although they were "not applied to or limited by physical elements or process steps."[79] The Federal Circuit found that the transformation of *data* was patentable subject matter, "because it produces 'a useful, concrete, and tangible result' — a final share price momentarily fixed for recording and reporting purposes and even accepted and relied upon by regulatory authorities and in subsequent trades."[80] Under *State Street*, the presence or absence of a machine in the claim was not dispositive. Moreover, the *State Street* Court did not require the transformation of any physical or tangible substance — the informational output of the software was found sufficient.

Second, the *State Street* court examined the district court's decision to invalidate the claims based on a business methods exception to patentable subject matter. Reversing this finding, the Federal Circuit stated, "[w]e take this opportunity to lay this ill-conceived exception to rest."[81] The Federal Circuit's *State Street* opinion holds that business method claims are to be evaluated for conformance with the patentability requirements in the same manner as all other claims and that § 101 presents no *per se* bar to the patentability of business methods.

Although the *State Street* decision has drawn significant and influential criticism, this holding has not yet been explicitly overturned. Nonetheless, the *State Street* case must be read very carefully in light of the Supreme Court's 2010 *Bilski* opinion, discussed later herein. *State Street* can be seen as a low-water mark of patentable subject matter that might be open to question in light of the current trends in this area.

Part of the criticism of the *State Street* decision included the difficulty of searching for prior art, because "the most relevant prior art did not exist in the

---

[77] Lowe's Drive-In Theaters, Inc. v. Park-In Theaters, Inc., 174 F.2d 547, 552 (1st Cir. 1949).

[78] State Street Bank & Trust Co. v. Signature Financial Group, Inc., 149 F.3d 1368 (Fed. Cir. 1998).

[79] State Street Bank and Trust Co. v. Signature Financial Group, Inc., 927 F. Supp. 502, 510 (D. Mass. 1996), *rev'd*, 149 F.3d 1368 (Fed. Cir. 1998). In reaching this result, the district court relied on a test developed by the Court of Customs and Patent Appeals, known as the *Freeman-Walter-Abele* test. The line of cases in which this *Freeman-Walter-Abele* test was developed are *In re Freeman*, 573 F.2d 1237 (C.C.P.A. 1978); *In re* Walter, 618 F.2d 758 (C.C.P.A. 1980); and *In re* Abele, 684 F.2d 902 (C.C.P.A. 1982).

[80] *State Street Bank*, 149 F.3d at 1373. In addition, the Federal Circuit's *State Street* opinion rejected the *Freeman-Walter-Abele* test as inconsistent with the U.S. Supreme Court's *Diehr* and *Chakrabarty* decisions.

[81] *Id.* at 1375.

prior patent literature, which is a traditional source of relevant art."[82] In response, the PTO instituted a "second set of eyes" review for business method patent applications. Further, Congress reacted to the *State Street* decision by enacting § 273(b)(1), to enable an alleged infringer of a business method patent to assert a defense of prior use.[83] Perhaps most important, the reasoning of the *State Street* case has been constrained by later developments, most notably the Supreme Court's *Bilski* opinion.

[F]   The Federal Circuit's Restrictive Approach

Dating from around the time that Justice Breyer dissented from the denial of certiorari in the Supreme Court's *Laboratory Corp.*, the Federal Circuit began to restrict its approach to patentable subject matter. One example is the 2007 *In re Nuijten* decision.[84] This court considered the rejection of an application directed to an improved technique for manipulating a digital signal (such as an audio file) to include a "watermark" that would allow content providers to track unauthorized copying. The *Nuijten* court found that the claims at issue were not directed to any statutory subject matter for their failure to fit within any of the four statutory categories of § 101. For example, the *Nuijten* court found that claims to a signal were not directed to a "process," but rather to a thing — the signal itself. Yet the court determined that the intangible signal was not a patentable "composition of matter," because it was not a combination of two or more gases, fluids, powders or solids. As *Nuijten* explained, "[i]f a claim covers material not found in any of the four statutory categories, that claim falls outside the plainly expressed scope of § 101 even if the subject matter is otherwise new and useful."[85] Despite *Chakrabarty's* directive that § 101 is to be read broadly, the *Nuijten* court relied on § 101's enumerated categories as significant restrictions on the doctrine.

In 2007, the Federal Circuit decided *In re Comiskey*,[86] which *sua sponte* addressed the statutory subject matter requirement for a claims directed to methods for conducting mandatory arbitration. This case attempted to grapple with statutory subject matter under the *mental steps doctrine*. There were two different types of claims at issue in *Comiskey*. First, a number of independent claims did not require the use of a computer or other machine. Rather, as the *Comiskey* court described, these claims sought protection for "the mental process of resolving a legal dispute between two parties."[87] The court found these claims unpatentable, stating "mental processes — or processes of human thinking — standing alone are not patentable even if they have practical application."[88] *Comiskey* observed that mental processes that were not combined with another

---

[82] FEDERAL TRADE COMMISSION, TO PROMOTE INNOVATION: THE PROPER BALANCE OF COMPETITION AND PATENT LAW AND POLICY, 30 (2003).

[83] 35 U.S.C. § 273.

[84] *In re* Nuijten, 500 F.3d 1346 (Fed. Cir. 2007).

[85] *Id.* at 1354.

[86] *See In re* Comiskey, 499 F.3d 1365 (Fed. Cir. 2007).

[87] *Id.* at 1379.

[88] *Id.* at 1377.

category of statutory subject matter — such as a machine, manufacture, or composition of matter — were not within § 101 even where some useful result of that process had been claimed.

The second type of claims in *Cominsky* did require the use of a computer for the selection of an arbitrator and for the submission of an arbitration request. For these, the court found that these satisfied the statutory subject matter requirement, on the grounds that "[w]hen an unpatentable mental process is combined with a machine, the combination may produce patentable subject matter."[89]

In 2008, the Federal Circuit decided an appeal *In re Bilski*, which considered claims directed to a method for managing risk for commodities trading. Such trading is subject to volatile pricing dependant on supply and demand. The claim described a method for initiating a series of transactions that allowed a commodity provider to sell products at a fixed price, so that both buyers and sellers would be protected against spikes or drops in the market. The claim was not limited to actual commodities; it was sufficiently broad to encompass options. Relying on the Supreme Court's *Benson, Flook, Diehr* decisions, the Federal Circuit rejected the *Bilski* claims as unpatentable subject matter. The Federal Circuit construed these authorities as mandating a patentable subject matter test that requires that a claim be either 1) tied to a particular machine or apparatus; or 2) transform a particular article to a different state or thing. Called the *machine-or-transformation test*, the court found that it was the sole governing test for patentable subject matter. In adopting this as the exclusive test for patentability, the Federal Circuit essentially rejected the useful, concrete, and tangible result examination that had been previously used. As discussed in the next section, the Supreme Court granted certiorari to assess the Federal Circuit's holding.

§ 23.04   THE SUPREME COURT'S *BILSKI* OPINION

[A]   *Bilski* and the Prohibition on Abstract Subject Matter

Of the patentability exceptions, the Supreme Court's *Bilski v. Kappos* opinion examined the claims at issue in light of the prohibition against abstract subject matter.[90] The Court's opinion is fractured, with no single opinion capturing a majority of the votes. Generally, the *Bilski* opinion has been read to reject the machine-or-transformation test as *the sole and exclusive* test for patentable subject matter. Specifically, a majority of the Court rejected the Federal Circuit's reading of the prior Supreme Court precedents and explained, "this Court has not indicated that the existence of these well-established exceptions gives the Judiciary *carte blanche* to impose other limitations that are inconsistent with the text and the statute's purpose and design."[91]

---

[89]   *Id.* The *Comiskey* court remanded the case to the PTO to assess these claims for nonobviousness.

[90]   *In re* Bilski, 130 S. Ct. 3218 (2010).

[91]   *Id.* at 3226.

Although the *Bilski* Court rejected the machine-or-transformation test as the *exclusive* test for patentability, the Court found that the machine-or-transformation test "is a useful and important clue, an investigative tool, for determining whether some claimed inventions are processes under § 101."[92] The Court noted that the machine-or-transformation test was most useful for "processes similar to those in the Industrial Age — for example, inventions grounded in a physical or other tangible form."[93] As the *Bilski* opinion explained, "new technologies may call for new inquiries."[94]

In result, the majority of justices agreed that the claims were not patentable as an abstract idea, with reference to the *Benson, Flook,* and *Diehr* opinions. The most prominent concern, articulated in *Benson* and *Flook,* was that claims to abstract subject matter could *preempt entire fields* of related inquiry. As three justices of the *Bilski* Court stated, "the patent law faces a great challenge in striking the balance between protecting inventors and not granting monopolies over procedures that others would discover by independent, creative application of general principles."[95] The majority of the Court found the claims at issue were abstract, given that methods of hedging risk were a fundamental practice that had long been taught in economics and finance. Further, the claim would "pre-empt use of this approach in all fields, and would effectively grant a monopoly over an abstract idea."[96]

A plurality of the Court rejected that any particular category of invention — such as software or business methods — were always unpatentable. Rather, this portion of the opinion proposed that inventions should be assessed according to the traditional tests for determining whether a claim is patentable. These include whether the subject matter is an attempt to patent an abstract idea.

Justice Stevens authored a concurring opinion, joined by three other Justices, which agreed that the machine-or-transformation test was not the sole test for patentable subject matter.[97] This opinion proposed that the majority opinion should have held the claims at issue unpatentable because it described only a general method of doing business. Justices Breyer's separate concurrence agreed that business methods should not be patentable subject matter. In addition, Breyer's concurrence, joined by Justice Scalia, articulated the following points that appeared to be consistent with the majority opinion and consistent with prior Supreme Court precedent:

- Patentable subject matter does not include abstract subject matter that might preempt basic tools of scientific and technological work;

- The machine-or-transformation test can provide an important clue as to the patentability of a claimed process;

---

[92] *Id.* at 3227.

[93] *Id.*

[94] *Id.* at 3228.

[95] *Id.*

[96] *Id.* at 3231.

[97] *Id.* at 3232 (Stevens, J. concurring).

- However, the machine-or-transformation test is not the sole criteria for patentability. Rather, the key question is whether the claim, considered as a whole, "is performing a function which the patent laws were designed to protect;"[98]

- The former useful, concrete, and tangible result test used by the Federal Circuit has never been endorsed by the Supreme Court, and it may lead to results that are inconsistent with the Court's precedents.

The *Bilski* majority opinion relied on the abstract subject matter limitation as the foundation of its reasoning. Yet the opinion does not clearly delineate between claims that might be considered fatally abstract, from those that are not.[99] It can be expected that the machine-or-transformation test may remain an important consideration for whether a claim represents patentable subject matter. In addition, the preemptive reach of such claims is likely to remain an important determinant.

[B] *Bilski's* Progeny

Some examples of *Bilski's* implementation in the Federal Circuit are useful for understanding the current state of patentable subject matter law.

In *Cybersource Corp. v. Retail Decisions, Inc.*, the Federal Circuit examined two claims to methods for detecting fraud for credit card transactions over the Internet.[100] Relying on the Supreme Court's *Bilski* opinion, the *Cybersource* court considered a claim that described a method for obtaining information about the transaction, constructing "a map of credit card numbers," and then using this created map to determine whether the credit card is valid.[101] The *Cybersource* court held the claim invalid as abstract subject matter, unpatentable under the *mental steps* doctrine. Although the court framed the inquiry in terms of the machine-or-transformation test, the opinion viewed the claim analogous to the ones rejected in *Benson* and *Flook*. The *Cybersource* court found that the claim could be practiced entirely in the human mind, and was therefore an abstract idea. The court held that the mention of the Internet in the claim was insufficient to save it, because nothing in the claim *required* the use of the Internet to practice the steps. In other words, one could create a map simply by manually writing down a list of credit cards from a particular IP. As the court explained, "[t]he Internet is merely described as the source of the data. We have held that mere data-gathering steps cannot make an otherwise nonstatutory claim statutory."[102]

Another claim at issue in *Cybersource* was a so-called *Beauregard* claim,[103] which described the method in terms of storage on a computer readable medium that includes instructions for carrying out the method. Finding the claim invalid, the *Cybersource* opinion concluded that "simply reciting the use of a computer to

---

[98] *Id.* at 3258 (Breyer, J. concurring) (quoting Diamond v. Diehr, 450 U.S. 175, 192 (1981).

[99] *Id.* at 3225 (Stevens, J. concurring).

[100] Cybersource Corp. v. Retail Decisions, Inc., 654 F.3d 1366 (Fed. Cir. 2011).

[101] *Id.* at 1370 (quoting U.S. Pat. No. 6,029,154 (filed Jul. 28, 1997)).

[102] *Id.* at 1370 (quoting *In re* Grams, 888 F.2d 835, 840 (Fed. Cir. 1989)).

[103] *See In re* Beauregard, 53 F.3d 1583 (Fed. Cir. 1995).

execute an algorithm that can be performed entirely in the human mind" does not render a claim patentable.[104] Further, in contrast to the earlier *State Street* case, the court found that the transformation of data was insufficient to satisfy the "transformation" prong of the test. As the court explained, "the incidental use of a computer to perform the mental process of [the claim] does not impose a sufficiently meaningful limit on the court's claim scope."[105] Thus, *Cybersource* rejected the *Beauregard* claim as an unpatentable mental process.

Cybersource can be compared to *Sirf Technology, Inc. v. ITC*.[106] The *Sirf* court considered the patentability of claims to a method for calculating position using a global positioning system (GPS) receiver. The court found the claim met the patentable subject matter standard, as each claim required the use of a specific machine to perform the claimed method. The *Sirf* opinion note that the court was "not dealing with . . . a method that [could] be performed without a machine" and that there was "no evidence . . . that the calculations [could] be performed entirely in the human mind."[107] Significantly, the court noted that it was "clear that the methods at issue could not be performed without the use of a GPS receiver."[108] Unlike the claims at issue in *Cybersource*, reliance on GPS technology represented a meaningful limit on the claimed methods such that they could not be found abstract.

Bilski and its progeny suggest that the era of broad and vague process claims has drawn to a close. This line of cases demonstrates that indicia of patentability must include meaningful limits, with an emphasis on the application to a specific, contextualized problem. Alternatively, the process must transform a particular thing, such as an object or substance. Although the *Bilski* Court left the door open for alternative formulations for inventions in a new technological era, it is clear that a claim must provide a specific solution where the process is directed to the intangible. Some meaningful limits, such that the claim cannot be deemed to have preempted an entire field, are required.

§ 23.05 CONCLUSION

A statutory subject matter analysis starts by defining the invention at issue. Section 101 defines the scope of patentable subject matter as any "process, machine, manufacture, or composition of matter" or any improvement of thereof. According to *Diamond v. Chakrabarty*, this provision is broadly construed. Nonetheless, statutory subject matter does not encompass laws of nature, physical phenomena or abstract ideas. In *Bilski*, the Supreme Court made clear that the machine-or-transformation test is not the sole and exclusive test for statutory subject matter for process and method claims. However, the Court's opinion calls for some significant limit for process claims. Over the coming years, it can be expected that the courts will continue to refine the meaning of *Bilski* and *Prometheus*, including the

---

[104] *Cybersource*, 654 F.3d at 1375.

[105] *Id.* at 1375.

[106] Sirf Technology, Inc. v. ITC, 601 F.3d 1319 (Fed. Cir. 2010).

[107] *Id.* at 1333.

[108] *Id.* at 1332.

definition of the term "abstract" as used in those opinions.

Chapter 24

PROCEDURES FOR CLAIM CONSTRUCTION

SYNOPSIS

§ 24.01 INTRODUCTION

§ 24.02 COMPARISON: CLAIM INTERPRETATION AT THE U.S. PATENT & TRADEMARK OFFICE AND IN THE COURTS

§ 24.03 CLAIM INTERPRETATION IN THE COURTS

    [A] Former Law: Claim Construction Procedures

    [B] Current Law: *Markman v. Westview Instruments, Inc.*

        [1] *Markman's* Aftermath

§ 24.04 IMPLEMENTING *MARKMAN*

§ 24.05 CLAIM CONSTRUCTION AND THE ACCUSED DEVICE

§ 24.06 CONCLUSION

§ 24.01 INTRODUCTION

The primary task in claim interpretation — also called *claim construction* — is to determine the meaning and scope of a patent claim in light of the understanding of one of ordinary skill in the art. Claim construction serves an important role in supporting the public notice function of the patent system.[1] As the U.S. Supreme Court stated, "[a] patent holder should know what he owns, and the public should know what he does not."[2] Defining the boundaries of a patent's claims scope is important to promote invention, because without precise limits "a zone of uncertainty which enterprise and experimentation may enter only at the risk of infringement claims would discourage invention only a little less than unequivocal foreclosure of the field," and "[t]he public [would] be deprived of rights supposed to belong to it, without being clearly told what it is that limits these rights."[3]

Claim term meaning is integral to patent infringement, and, in turn, to the scope of a patentee's right to exclude. Claim construction is performed as the first step in a patent infringement analysis.[4] It is only after terms are interpreted that a finder of fact can compare the claim to the accused device, method or process.[5] There is

---

[1] *See e.g.*, Southwall Techs., Inc. v. Cardinal IG Co., 54 F.3d 1570, 1578 (Fed. Cir. 1995).

[2] Festo Corp. v. Shoketsu Kinzoku Kogyo Kabushiki Co., 535 U.S. 722, 731 (2002).

[3] Markman v. Westview Instruments, Inc., 517 U.S. 370, 391 (1996) (quotations and citations omitted).

[4] *See* Ultra-Tex Surfaces, Inc. v. Hill Bros. Chemical Co., 204 F.3d 1360, 1363 (Fed. Cir. 2000).

[5] *Id.*

logic in this two-tiered approach, as one must have an initial understanding of a claim's meaning before attempting to ascertain whether the claim reads on an accused device. In addition, claim construction may be necessary to determine whether a patent claim is valid and enforceable. This is because, as one example, one cannot establish whether the claim has strict identity[6] with a particular reference until one understands the claim under examination.

Claim construction requires more than simply reading a patent claim, even by those conversant with general principles of legal interpretation. Patent law imposes a number of interpretive rules that are unique to this field. For example, a claim term must be given its ordinary and customary meaning as understood by one of ordinary skill in the art as of the time of invention — typically, as of the effective filing date of the patent application.[7] Claim terms are read in the context of the entire patent including the written specification.[8] As will be explored in the next chapter, there are rules regarding the use of outside sources of information, such as expert testimony and dictionaries, to understand the words of a claim.

In addition, some terms may require construction because they have little meaning outside of an art and therefore may be difficult for lay jurors to understand. As some examples, terms such as "rotably,"[9] "possessing a 35 exonuclease activity,"[10] or "supply voltage Vddq during normal system operation using said ADC"[11] may require a court's interpretation before a juror can meaningfully apply the term. Further, open-ended or relative terms may lack clear boundaries, such as, "sufficiently charged state"[12] or "discrete, spaced-apart, approximately semi-spherically shaped depressions"[13] and benefit from a court's more complete explanation. Moreover, patent law has developed specific meanings for certain words or phrases. For example, the articles "a" and "the" typically mean "one or more" when used in a patent claim.[14] Certain types of claims — such as means-plus-function claims — require special rules of interpretation that are required by 35 U.S.C. § 112, ¶ 6.[15]

As a practical matter, jurors who are not versed in patent law lack an understanding of these principles. The procedural framework for claim construction is intended to ensure that the meaning of a patent claim allows fact finders to perform their tasks consistent with the policy of providing public notice of the claim. A court's claim interpretation order provides the definitions necessary to decide infringement.

---

[6] For more information about § 102's strict identity requirement, *see supra* Chapter 12.

[7] Phillips v. AWH Corp., 415 F.3d 1303, 1312-13 (Fed. Cir. 2005) (en banc).

[8] *Id.* at 1313.

[9] U.S. Patent No. 4,541,573 claim 1 (filed July 26, 1983).

[10] U.S. Patent No. 6,395,526 claim 2 (filed June 26, 1998).

[11] U.S. Patent No. 6,489,912 claim 1 (filed April 10, 2001).

[12] U.S. Patent No. 5,785,138 claim 8 (filed July 28, 1997).

[13] U.S. Patent No. 5,425,497 claim 1 (filed Nov. 9, 1993).

[14] Free Motion Fitness, Inc. v. Cybex Int'l, Inc., 423 F.3d 1343, 1349 n.5 (Fed. Cir. 2005).

[15] For more about the interpretation of means plus function claims, see Chapter 31.

Applying claim interpretation principles can be challenging. Part of the difficulty is, as the U.S. Supreme Court has explained, "the nature of language makes it impossible to capture the essence of a thing in a patent application."[16] A terse, single-sentence claim may not fully convey an invention in a manner that is useful to a finder of fact. Claim construction is performed by individual members of the judiciary, who through the use of judgment and experience, are an integral part of the claim construction process. Despite laudable goals to promote a stable claim construction process, there are indeterminacies associated with claim interpretation that can introduce uncertainty until resolved by an appellate court. Thus, although the process of claim construction has been refined over the past several years, complete clarity and precision are obtainable only after the court has ruled.

§ 24.02   COMPARISON: CLAIM INTERPRETATION AT THE U.S. PATENT & TRADEMARK OFFICE AND IN THE COURTS

Patent claims are interpreted by two distinct authorities. First, at the U.S. PTO, examiners construe patent claims to ascertain whether an application should be granted. Second, claims within issued patents are construed in the courts to resolve patent infringement and validity disputes. Although the goal for both is the same, the rules of interpretation vary.

The U.S. PTO gives claims in a patent application their *broadest* reasonable interpretation.[17] Giving claims a broad interpretation maximizes the potential for rejections, which in turn reduces "the possibility that claims, finally allowed, will be given broader scope than is justified."[18] According to the courts, a patentee is not prejudiced by this construction because claims can be readily amended during prosecution to overcome a rejection.[19] Indeed, a rejection based on broad interpretations of the proposed claims is said to be beneficial to the public, as this encourages interactions between the PTO and the applicant to "promote the development of the written record before the PTO that provides the requisite written notice to the public as to what the applicant claims as the invention."[20]

The "broadest reasonable interpretation" standard is not applied in infringement and validity litigation after a patent issues. Unlike examinations in the U.S. PTO, courts operate under a presumption that an issued patent is valid and claim amendments during litigation are not available. Therefore, courts endeavor to give claim terms their ordinary meeting as understood by those in the art.

---

[16] *Festo Corp.*, 535 U.S. at 731.

[17] MPEP § 2111; *see also* Phillips v. AWH Corp., 415 F.3d 1303, 1316 (Fed. Cir. 2005) (en banc).

[18] *In re* Yamamoto, 740 F.2d 1569, 1571 (Fed. Cir. 1984).

[19] *See In re* Hyatt, 211 F.3d 1367, 1372 (Fed. Cir. 2000).

[20] *In re* Morris, 127 F.3d 1048, 1054 (Fed. Cir. 1997) ("It would be inconsistent with the role assigned to the PTO in issuing a patent to require it to interpret claims in the same manner as judges who, post-issuance, operate under the assumption that patent is valid.").

§ 24.03 CLAIM INTERPRETATION IN THE COURTS

Over the past several decades, the courts have developed procedures for construing patent claims in litigation proceedings. These rules are based on an interpretation of the Seventh Amendment of the U.S. Constitution, and seek to negotiate the highly technical language in patents with the understanding of lay jurors who must decide factual issues in patent disputes.

Some background is necessary before a discussion of claim construction procedures can be understood. To interpret claim terms, there are two broad categories of potential sources of evidence. First, *intrinsic evidence* includes the four corners of the patent, including the claims and written specification, as well as the patent's prosecution history.[21] Second, *extrinsic evidence* is any other type of evidence, such as inventor or expert testimony, dictionaries, treatises and any other source of information.[22]

[A] Former Law: Claim Construction Procedures

The Patent Act does not expressly set forth any rules for the manner in which claim construction must be performed. Rather, the courts have been entirely responsible for the development of claim construction procedures. These rules have undergone a number of changes over the past several years.

The very earliest Federal Circuit cases held that claim construction was a matter of law to be performed by the court.[23] However, during the mid-1980's, some Federal Circuit cases recognized that underlying factual disputes might exist for the interpretations of some claim terms.[24] In a series of cases, the Federal Circuit found that a jury must resolve such factual conflicts where extrinsic evidence was necessary to determine the meaning of a disputed term. As one 1984 Federal Circuit decision explained:

> [i]f . . . the meaning of a term of art in the claims is disputed and extrinsic evidence is needed to explain the meaning, construction of the claims could be left to a jury. In the latter instance, the jury cannot be directed to the disputed meaning for the term of art.[25]

At that time, trial judges could determine the meaning of a disputed claim term only where that term's meaning could be resolved on intrinsic evidence alone.[26] Whenever extrinsic evidence was required, many trial courts asked juries to decide

---

[21] Vitronics Corp. v. Conceptronic, Inc., 90 F.3d 1576, 1582-83 (Fed. Cir. 1996).

[22] Phillips v. AWH Corp., 415 F.3d 1303, 1317 (Fed. Cir. 2005) (en banc).

[23] SSIH Equipment S.A. v. U.S. Int'l Trade Com'n, 718 F.2d 365, 376 (Fed. Cir. 1983); SRI Int'l v. Matsushita Elec. Corp. of America, 775 F.2d 1107, 1118 (Fed. Cir. 1985).

[24] McGill, Inc. v. John Zink Co., 736 F.2d 666, 672 (Fed. Cir. 1984) (citations omitted), *abrogated by* Markman v. Westview Instruments, Inc., 52 F.3d 967 (Fed. Cir. 1995), *aff'd*, 517 U.S. 370 (1996).

[25] *Id.; see also* Palumbo v. Don-Joy Co., 762 F.2d 969, 974 (Fed. Cir. 1985) (". . . when the meaning of a term in the claim is disputed and extrinsic evidence is necessary to explain that term, then an underlying factual questions arises, and construction of the claim should be left to the trier or jury under appropriate instruction.").

[26] Johnston v. IVAC Corp., 885 F.2d 1574, 1579-80 (Fed. Cir. 1989).

both claim construction and infringement in a single verdict.[27] In such cases, there was rarely any record of the manner in which the jury interpreted the claim. Further, the jury's claim construction was subject to a deferential standard of review on appeal, "[b]ecause of the respect due the constitutional right to a jury trial."[28] Thus, to succeed on appeal, an appellant had to demonstrate that no reasonable juror could have interpreted the claim in a manner that supported the infringement finding.[29]

[B] Current Law: *Markman v. Westview Instruments, Inc.*

In *Markman v. Westview Instruments, Inc.* the U.S. Supreme Court held that claim construction is a matter for the court.[30] The invention at issue concerned an inventory control and reporting system for dry cleaning stores. The patentee's asserted claim included the limitation "means to maintain an *inventory* total," as well as a limitation to "detect and localize spurious additions to *inventory*."[31] Throughout the litigation, the parties disputed the meaning of the claim term "inventory." The accused infringer Westview used a system that did not track any clothing, rather, the accused system tracked only invoices and cash totals. As might be expected, Westview argued that the meaning of the term "inventory" was limited to articles of clothing. The patentee argued that the term included other things such as "dollars," "cash" or "invoices."

The jury, which had been asked to construe the claims, found infringement. However, the trial court overturned the verdict by granting Westview's motion for judgment as a matter of law (JMOL). The trial court reasoned that the jury's construction of the term "inventory" was erroneous and that the term properly construed meant "articles of clothing" and not invoices or cash.

The Supreme Court's 1996 *Markman* opinion framed the issue of claim construction in light of the U.S. Constitution's Seventh Amendment right to a jury trial in civil cases, which states as follows:

> In Suits at common law, where the value in controversy shall exceed twenty dollars, the right of trial by jury *shall be preserved,* and no fact tried by a jury, shall be otherwise re-examined in any Court of the United States, than according to the rules of the common law.[32]

As this text states, the Seventh Amendment does not protect the right to a jury trial in *all* civil cases, but rather the right is *"preserved"* "according to the rules of the common law." As a general matter, this language is read to provide a right to a civil jury to the same extent as that which existed under the English common law in 1791 when the Seventh Amendment was adopted.[33]

---

[27] *See e.g.,* Senmed, Inc. v. Richard-Allan Medical Industries, Inc., 888 F.2d 815, 818 (Fed. Cir. 1989).

[28] Railroad Dynamics, Inc. v. A. Stucki Co., 727 F.2d 1506, 1513 (Fed. Cir. 1984).

[29] *McGill,* 736 F.2d at 672.

[30] Markman v. Westview Instruments, Inc., 517 U.S. 370 (1996).

[31] U.S Patent No. 4,550,246 claim 1 (filed April 13, 1984).

[32] U.S. Const. amend. VII (emphasis added).

[33] *Markman,* 517 U.S. at 376; *see also* Curtis v. Loether, 415 U.S. 189, 193 (1974) ("the thrust of the

Before the Supreme Court, the patentee argued that the district court's JMOL interfered with the Seventh Amendment right to have a jury determine infringement, which included a jury's ability to decide the meaning of claim terms. To answer the question of whether claim construction must be performed by juries as a matter of constitutional law, the *Markman* Court examined a two-part test set forth in an earlier Supreme Court opinion, *Granfinanciera, S.A. v. Nordberg.*[34] Under the first prong of the *Granfinanciera* test, the action must be compared to those brought in 18th-century English courts prior to the merger of the law and equity. In performing this comparison, a court decides whether the cause of action at issue (here, patent infringement) was tried formerly at law or equity. Under the second prong of *Granfinaciera*, if the action in question belongs in the law category, a court must examine whether the particular trial decision must fall to the jury in order to preserve the substance of the common law right as it existed in 1791.

Applying the *Granfinanciera* test, the *Markman* Court recognized that, as to the first prong, patent infringement actions had in fact been tried in the English law courts in the eighteenth century, and thus patent infringement actions were considered legal in nature.[35] The *Markman* Court then turned to examine the second prong of the test — that is, whether allowing juries to decide the claim construction issue was necessary to preserve the substance of the common law right. On this point, as the Court observed, there was little evidence that claims were a prevalent practice during that time period, and therefore there was "no direct antecedent of modern claim construction in the historical sources."[36] The record showed that the closest analogue — that of construing the specification to understand the invention — was discussed in only a few cases from which it appeared there was no established practice.

Finding little historic or precedential support for guidance to resolve this question, *Markman* next turned to examine a number of practical considerations to determine that judges — rather than juries — were the better choice for performing claim construction. To support this ruling, *Markman* examined various functional considerations unique to patent law. The *Markman* Court noted that judges are trained to provide proper interpretation to written instruments, such as patents, which may contain highly technical language. Further, the Court recognized that that judges were better positioned to evaluate live testimony while giving proper consideration to written patent documentation. Additionally, the Court emphasized that court-determined claim constructions better supported uniformity in the treatment of any particular patent:

> . . . we see the importance of uniformity in the treatment of a given patent as an independent reason to allocate all issues of construction to the court . . . [T]reating interpretive issues as purely legal will promote (though it

---

[Seventh] Amendment was to preserve the right to jury trial as it existed in 1791."); Baltimore & Carolina Line v. Redman, 295 U.S. 654 (1935) (explaining that under the Seventh Amendment, "The right of trial by jury thus preserved is the right which existed under the English common law when the amendment was adopted.").

[34] *See* Granfinanciera, S. A. v. Nordberg, 492 U.S. 33, 42 (1989).

[35] *Markman*, 517 U.S. at 377.

[36] *Id.* at 379.

will not guarantee) intrajurisdictional certainty through the application of *stare decisis* on those questions not yet subject to interjurisdictional uniformity under the authority of the single appeals court.[37]

On these bases, *Markman* unanimously held that no Seventh Amendment right to a jury trial exists to construe patent claims. In result, the Supreme Court affirmed the Federal Circuit's holding that the interpretation of the disputed claim term was a matter to be decided by a judge, and not a jury. In addition, the judgment of non-infringement based on the trial court's JMOL ruling concerning the term "inventory" was affirmed.

[1]　*Markman's* Aftermath

Although the *Markman* Court determined that claim construction is an issue for a judge to undertake, the Court did acknowledge that claim construction can be a "mongrel practice" — that is, that a claim construction can include *both* issues of law as well as issues of fact where disputed factual issues are necessary to define a claim's meaning.[38] The typical appellate standard of review for mixed questions of fact and law is "clear error," a standard that is deferential to the finder of fact in the court below.[39] However, after *Markman*, the Federal Circuit held in *Cybor Corp. v. FAS Technologies, Inc.*, that the standard of appellate review for a district court's claim construction is *de novo*, including for the review of any fact-based questions relating to claim construction.[38] This same standard of review applies to claim construction performed by the U.S. PTO.[40]

The Federal Circuit's *de novo* review standard for claim construction may have contributed to a relatively high reversal rate for issues that depend on claim meaning. Indeed, one study concluded that the Federal Circuit has held at least one term wrongly construed by a district court in 37.5% of all reviewed cases.[41] This study further concluded that, of those cases, the Federal Circuit has reversed or vacated the district court's judgment 29.7% of the time.[42] Another study found that these reversal rates held steady even for judges who handled a comparatively high number of patent cases, and who were therefore presumably most familiar with the

---

[37] *Id.* at 390.

[38] *Id.* at 377. (Such factual issues might arise in the form of conflicting evidence regarding who qualifies as one of ordinary skill in the art, the state of the art at the time of the invention or the scope of the pertinent art); *see also* Phillips v. AWH Corp., 415 F.3d 1303, 1332 (Fed. Cir. 2005) (en banc) (Mayer, J., dissenting).

[39] Saab Cars U.S.A, Inc. v. U.S., 434 F.3d 1359, 1371 (Fed. Cir. 2006) ("the appellate court should review the district court's legal conclusions de novo and review any factual inferences the district court made from the stipulated record as well as its application of the law to the facts for clear error") (citations and quotations omitted).

[38] *See* Cybor Corp. v. FAS Technologies, Inc., 138 F.3d 1448 (Fed. Cir. 1998).

[40] SRAM Corp. v. AD-II Engineering, Inc., 465 F.3d 1351, 1359 (Fed. Cir. 2006).

[41] Kimberly A. Moore, *Markman Eight Years Later: Is Claim Construction More Predictable?*, 9 LEWIS & CLARK L. REV. 231, 239 (2005).

[42] *Id.* For another study that provides results in approximately this same range, *see* David. L. Schwartz, *Practice Makes Perfect? An Empirical Study of Claim Construction Reversal Rates in Patent Cases*, 107 MICH. L. REV. 223 (2008).

legal standards for construing patent claims.[43]

The Federal Circuit rarely undertakes interlocutory review of claim construction.[44] In practice, this means that parties must wait until final judgment is entered before learning how the Federal Circuit will construe the claims. In most cases, this does not occur until after summary judgment or on a trial on the merits. As the Federal Circuit's Judge Rader observed, these circumstances add to the expense and delay of patent litigation:

> . . . To get a certain claim interpretation, parties must go past the district court's *Markman* proceeding, past the entirety of discovery, past the entire trial on the merits, past post trial motions, past briefing and argument to the Federal Circuit-indeed past every step in the entire course of federal litigation, except Supreme Court review. In implementation, a *de novo* review of claim interpretations has postponed the point of certainty to the end of the litigation process, at which point, of course, every outcome is certain anyway.[45]

In the final analysis, it may be that regardless of the neutrality of the procedures used, claim construction is difficult to predict. Therefore, parties who are seeking to ascertain the scope of any particular patent claim will not have certainty until a patent has been fully litigated through appeal.

§ 24.04 IMPLEMENTING *MARKMAN*

The case name "*Markman*" has become an adjective to refer to any number of procedural aspects of claim construction. For example, district courts sometimes hold "*Markman* hearings" to consider argument on disputed claim terms, after which the judge issues a "*Markman* order" that includes the court's construction of the terms at issue. In short, *Markman* has changed the conduct of patent litigation dramatically. The parties undertake considerable effort to present argument and, if permitted, evidence in support of a particular construction of an ambiguous or disputed claim term. In many courts, the district court's *Markman* order crystallizes the parties' strategy for remainder of the case. From that point forward, the parties tailor their cases based on the definitions set forth in the *Markman* order. Parties who do not dispute the operation of an accused device may pursue summary judgment. At trial, jurors are no longer asked to decide both claim construction and infringement in a single verdict. Rather, the district court's *Markman* order is provided to the jury to assess infringement and, if in dispute, validity and unenforceability of the asserted patent during deliberations.

---

[43] *Id.*

[44] Craig Allen Nard, *Process Considerations in the Age Of Markman and Mantras*, 2001 U. ILL. L. REV. 355, 372 (noting that "the Federal Circuit, without explanation, has thus far refused to exercise its discretion and grant an interlocutory appeal on the issue of claim interpretation.") (footnote omitted); but see Regents of University of Cal. v. Dako North America, Inc., 477 F.3d 1335 (Fed. Cir. 2007) (accepting an interlocutory appeal where the issue was already subject to a pending appeal of an order on a motion for a preliminary injunction).

[45] *Cybor*, 138 F.3d at 1476 (Rader, J. dissenting from the pronouncements on claim interpretation in the en banc opinion, concurring in the judgment, and joining part IV of the en banc opinion).

The U.S. Supreme Court's *Markman* case did not describe any specific rules that district courts must follow to fulfill their obligation to construe a patent's claims.[46] In practice, *Markman* procedures vary widely in both timing and structure. As stated by the MANUAL FOR COMPLEX LITIGATION (Fourth), "[t]here is no consistent approach among the courts as to the procedural boundaries of claim-construction proceedings."[47]

For the timing of claim construction, under *Markman*, a district court may construe the claims at issue at any time prior to submitting the case to the jury.[48] According to a survey conducted by the American Bar Association, most claim construction hearings (78%) occur after discovery but before trial.[49] Some claim constructions are performed prior to or during discovery. A few (6%) take place during the trial on the merits, whereupon the court's interpretation of the claims is given to the jury with the jury instructions after the close of evidence and before deliberations begin. Particularly where a large number of claims are asserted, a judge may bifurcate claim construction by interpreting some claims earlier in the case and then addressing the remaining claims later. Moreover, judges can — and do — change their *Markman* claim constructions as the case progresses.[50]

As for procedures to undertake claim construction, some courts will decide claim construction based solely on the parties' briefing coupled with a review of the patent and the prosecution history. Alternatively, a judge may elect to hold a *Markman* hearing in any variety of formats, ranging from a short hearing to consider the arguments of counsel, an evidentiary hearing, or a hearing consolidated with the trial on the merits.[51] At such hearings, judges may permit live testimony, including expert testimony, relevant to the technology, the understanding of one of ordinary skill in the relevant art, or a term's particular meaning in the pertinent field.[52] Also, a court may permit testimony by a sworn affidavit or declaration.

Parties advocate for the adoption of a construction to benefit their position in the litigation. For example, a patentee will argue for a construction that is broad enough to encompass the defendant's accused device or process, but narrow enough to avoid prior art that may invalidate the asserted claims. A court is free to adopt the claim

---

[46] *See generally* Sofamor Danek Group, Inc. v. DePuy-Motech, Inc., 74 F.3d 1216, 1221 (Fed. Cir. 1996) (". . . *Markman* does not obligate the trial judge to conclusively interpret claims at an early stage in a case. A trial court may exercise its discretion to interpret the claims at a time when the parties have presented a full picture of the claimed invention and prior art.").

[47] MANUAL FOR COMPLEX LITIGATION (Fourth) § 33.220 (2004).

[48] *See generally* ABA Committee No. 601- Federal Trial Practice and Procedure, *Claim Interpretation Proceedings and Appellate Review* 2002-2003, available at: http://www.abanet.org/intelprop/annualreport06/content/02-03/COMMITTEE%20NO%20601.pdf (last visited May 14, 2007).

[49] *Id.*

[50] *See e.g.*, Hon. Kathleen M. O'Malley, Hon. Patti Saris and Hon. Ronald H. Whyte, *A Panel Discussion: Claim Construction from the Perspective of the District Judge*, 54 CASE W. RES. L. REV. 671, 687-88 (2004).

[51] Federal Circuit Bar Ass'n Patent Litigation Committee Markman Project, *Guidelines For Patent Claim Construction: Post-Phillips-The Basics of a Markman Hearing*, 16 FED. CIR. B.J. 13, 23 (2006).

[52] Phillips v. AWH Corp., 415 F.3d 1303, 1318 (Fed. Cir. 2005) (en banc); *see also* ABA COMMITTEE NO. 601-FEDERAL TRIAL PRACTICE AND PROCEDURE 3 (Aug. 2001) ("For those courts that held hearings fifty percent (50%) permitted live testimony and fifty percent (50%) did not").

construction of either party, or alternatively to fashion its own. In some cases, a judge may appoint a neutral expert to assist the court's understanding of the technology or of the meaning of the claim terms. On occasion, district courts delegate the task of making an initial effort at claim construction to a special master.[53]

The end result of a district court's claim construction is an order defining claim terms. As one example, in *In re Dippin' Dots Patent Litigation*, a case concerning flash-frozen beads of ice cream, the district court construed the claim term "dripping" in a claim directed to making the ice cream beads to mean "letting fall in drops."[54] As another example, in *Nikon Corp. v. ASM Lithography B.V.*, a case concerning semiconductor manufacturing, the term "pattern" in a claim describing a method of making a semiconductor means "a design or series of marks in a semiconductor integrated circuit that is to be transferred to a photoresist layer of a substrate."[55] At trial, these constructions are given to the jury to consider when determining infringement. Alternatively, such constructions can be used as a foundation for a motion for summary judgment.

A number of federal districts have created uniform rules to govern procedure in all patent cases pending within those districts.[56] Local patent rules supplement the case management and discovery obligations set forth in the Federal Rules of Civil Procedure. These district-wide patent rules are intended to facilitate case management, focus discovery, and establish a full record for the claim construction ruling, which may be issued as early as one year after the case is commenced.[57]

§ 24.05 CLAIM CONSTRUCTION AND THE ACCUSED DEVICE

As previously stated, patent infringement requires a two-step analysis. First, under *Markman*, the claims must be construed by the court to determine their scope and meaning.[58] Second, the claim as construed is compared to the accused device or process by the finder of fact to determine if infringement exists.[59]

The Federal Circuit has emphasized that these two steps should be undertaken separately and in the prescribed order. The district court's claim construction inquiry must not include any analysis of whether the claim terms will encompass (or

---

[53] *See generally* FED. R. CIV. PROC. 53.

[54] *In re* Dippin' Dots Patent Litigation, 249 F. Supp. 2d 1346, 1366 (N.D. Ga. 2003).

[55] Nikon Corp. v. ASM Lithography B.V., 308 F. Supp. 2d 1039, 1058 (N.D. Cal. 2004).

[56] Federal Circuit Bar Ass'n Patent Litigation Committee Markman Project, *supra* note 51, at 30 (Appendix A) (citing local patent rules for seven U.S. District Courts).

[57] *See e.g.*, Integrated Circuit Systems, Inc. v. Realtek Semiconductor Co., 308 F. Supp. 2d 1106, 1107 (N.D. Cal. 2004) (describing one purpose of the Northern District of California's Local Patent Rules as ". . . plac[ing] the parties on an orderly pretrial track which will produce a ruling on claim construction approximately a year after the complaint is filed.").

[58] Applied Med. Ress. Corp. v. U.S. Surgical Corp., 448 F.3d 1324, 1332 (Fed. Cir. 2006).

[59] *Id.*

not encompass) the accused product.[60] Because of the strong public notice requirement of patent claims, it is not appropriate for a court to construe claims to drive an infringement result in any particular case. Thus, "[i]t is only after the claims have been construed without reference to the accused device that the claims, as so construed, are applied to the accused device to determine infringement."[61]

Nonetheless, the court may consider the accused product to narrow or limit the parties' dispute about the number or type of claim terms that must be interpreted.[62] Furthermore, a district court's knowledge of the accused product can be used to provide some context for the claim construction.[63]

§ 24.06 CONCLUSION

Claim construction represents a critical phase of infringement litigation, as the claims are the definitional focus of the patentee's right to exclude. The procedures for determining the meaning of the patent claims are set forth in the U.S. Supreme Court's *Markman* decision as implemented by the courts. *Markman* requires the court to construe the patent claims in the first instance, prior to a comparison of the claims to the accused product. In doing so, *Markman* overturned prior law that permitted juries to make decisions about the meaning of patent claims.

Since the time that *Markman* was decided, district court judges have exercised their discretion to create procedures to carry out their claim construction obligations. Generally, district court judges must issue an order setting forth the meaning of the terms of the asserted claims to assist the jury in rendering their infringement verdict, as well deciding invalidity or unenforceability defenses. Alternatively, the court's claim construction may form the basis of a motion for summary judgment. On appeal, both the PTO's and the district court's claim construction is examined under a *de novo* standard of review.

---

[60] SRI Intern. v. Matsushita Elec. Corp. of America, 775 F.2d 1107, 1118 (Fed. Cir. 1985) ("[C]laims are not construed 'to cover' or 'not to cover' the accused device.").

[61] *Id.*

[62] Aero Products Intern., Inc. v. Intex Recreation Corp., 466 F.3d 1000, 1012 n.6 (Fed. Cir. 2006) (". . . it is efficient to focus on the construction of only the disputed elements or limitations of the claims.").

[63] *Id.*

Chapter 25

HOW TO INTERPRET PATENT CLAIM TERMS

SYNOPSIS

§ 25.01 INTRODUCTION

§ 25.02 HISTORY: FORMER APPROACHES TO CLAIM CONSTRUCTION

§ 25.03 THE CURRENT APPROACH: THE FEDERAL CIRCUIT'S EN BANC DECISION IN *PHILLIPS v. AWH CORP*

  [A] The *Phillips* Claim Construction Methodology

  [B] Application of the *Phillips* Claim Construction Methodology

§ 25.04 A CLOSER LOOK AT THE INTERACTION OF THE SPECIFICATION AND CLAIM TERMS

  [A] Putting a Claim Construction Analysis Together

  [B] The Patentee as Lexicographer: *SciMed*

§ 25.05 CLAIM CONSTRUCTION AND VALIDITY

§ 25.06 CANONS OF CLAIM CONSTRUCTION

  [A] The Doctrine of Claim Differentiation

  [B] Construction of Terms in the Preamble

  [C] Additional Canons of Claim Construction

§ 25.07 CONCLUSION

§ 25.01 INTRODUCTION

Patent claims are read according to the understanding of one of ordinary skill in the art at the time of invention.[1] The claim is read within the context of the entire patent, including the other claims, the specification, and the prosecution history.

Although easily stated, the application of these rules to a particular claim can be remarkably complicated. In part, this is due to a fundamental tension between the policies of promoting the public notice policy of the patent system against the need for flexible standards to accommodate entirely new inventions in a wide range of subject matters. The courts have developed a body of case law and interpretative principles to assist. Nonetheless, it should be appreciated that these rules cannot entirely resolve this tension to a point of objective certainty. Claim construction is not amenable to absolutes and claim construction has been acknowledged to lead to

---

[1] Ortho-McNeil Pharm., Inc. v. Caraco Pharm. Lab., Ltd., 476 F.3d 1321, 1326 (Fed. Cir. 2007).

interpretations upon which "[r]easonable people can differ."[2]

A brief example illustrates that claim construction requires more than a good command of language. Interpreting a claim term requires, at least to some degree, understanding the technological context in which the term is used. Consider, for example, a claim that uses the word *charge*. Depending on the term's context, the word *charge* might refer to a demand for payment, a property that causes electrical particles to attract or repel, a quantity of explosive, or the replenishment of supply (such as to *charge* a battery). Interchanging any of these definitions out of context leads to absurdity. Adding information from the specification and prosecution history complicates the analysis further. For example, if the claim concerns an improved rechargeable battery, does the term "charge" refer to the electrical particles or to the battery's ability to renew its power?

Since the *Markman* case was decided, the Federal Circuit has attempted to formulate a claim construction methodology to balance the goal of clarity with the need for extrinsic evidence to explain the understanding of one of ordinary skill in the art. These efforts have resulted in rules that place primary emphasis on the intrinsic record — that is, the claims, the written specification, and the prosecution file history. In addition, the courts have promulgated interpretative guidance, sometimes referred to as the *canons of claim construction*, that incorporate standards that can be used to understand claim meaning when it is appropriate to use them.

§ 25.02 HISTORY: FORMER APPROACHES TO CLAIM CONSTRUCTION

A few months after the U.S. Supreme Court decided the *Markman* case[3] in 1996, the courts began to explore the type of information that can provide the proper interpretative context to understand claims, as well as the weight that such information should be given. The intrinsic evidence, consisting of the claims, the patent's written specification and its prosecution history, represents the most important source of information from which claim terms can be defined. Relying on intrinsic sources has been said to further the goal of certainty and the public notice policy of the patent system, as these sources are both finite and static.

However, the controlling legal standard requires construction of claim terms from the perspective of one of ordinary skill in the art. Information about the relevant term might be available from a number of extrinsic sources, such as learned treatises, experts, employees working in the art at the time that the invention was made, industry reports, documentation from organizations in the field and perhaps even the patent's inventor. Expanding claim construction to include extrinsic sources of information provides valuable background information about the understanding of one of ordinary skill that may not be available from the intrinsic sources alone. However, there is a significant downside to reliance on

---

[2] Phillips v. AWH Corp., 415 F.3d 1303, 1329 (Fed. Cir. 2005) (en banc).

[3] This refers to Markman v. Westview Instruments, Inc., 517 U.S. 370 (1996). For a full explanation of the *Markman* decision, see Chapter 24.

extrinsic information. That is, using extrinsic sources interferes with the certainty and public notice policies of the patent system.[4] This is because one trying to understand the patent cannot know how an expert will testify or which sources of documentation a court will find persuasive at a later infringement trial.

One early leading case was the Federal Circuit's 1996 *Vitronics v. Conceptronic, Inc.*[5] This case described a structured methodology that prioritized reliance on the intrinsic record, stating that the patent and the prosecution history is "the most significant source of the legally operative meaning of disputed claim language."[6] *Vitronics* emphasized that the first and primary focus should be on the claims themselves, followed by the specification as a highly relevant source of information about the claim's meaning. Further, the *Vitronics* court allowed consideration of the patent's prosecution history as a third source to be consulted.[7] Under *Vitronics*, a court was permitted to rely on extrinsic evidence only if the intrinsic record could not resolve a genuine ambiguity. *Vitronics* explained that "[t]he claims, specification and file history, rather than the extrinsic evidence constitute the public record of the patentee's claim, [and is] a record on which the public is entitled to rely."[8]

Decided in 2002, eight years after the *Vitronics* case, a three-judge panel of the Federal Circuit issued an conflicting opinion in *Texas Digital Systems, Inc. v. Telegenix, Inc.*[9] *Texas Digital* emphasized the use of dictionaries, encyclopedias, and treatises as the primary interpretive sources in order to give "a claim term the full range of its ordinary meaning as understood by persons skilled in the relevant art."[10] Specifically, the *Texas Digital* court instructed that sources such as dictionaries and treatises were presumed as the *primary* source of information to determine a claim term's meaning, which could only be overcome where: 1) the patentee "has clearly set forth an explicit definition of the term different from its ordinary meaning;"[11] or 2) the inventor used "words or expressions of manifest exclusion or restriction, representing a clear disavowal of claim scope."[12] The *Texas Digital* court explained that dictionaries, encyclopedias, and treatises were most indicative of meaning understood by those of skill in the art, as follows:

> Such references are unbiased reflections of common understanding not influenced by expert testimony or events subsequent to the fixing of the intrinsic record by the grant of the patent, not colored by the motives of the parties, and not inspired by litigation. Indeed, these materials may be the

---

[4] For a full discussion of these policy concerns, *see* Craig Allen Nard, *A Theory of Claim Interpretation*, 14 HARV. J.L. & TECH. 1 (2000).

[5] Vitronics Corp. v. Conceptronic, Inc., 90 F.3d 1576 (Fed. Cir. 1996).

[6] *Id.* at 1582.

[7] *Id.* at 1582.

[8] *Id.*

[9] Texas Digital Systems, Inc. v. Telegenix, Inc., 308 F.3d 1193 (Fed. Cir. 2002), *abrogated by* Phillips v. AWH Corp., 415 F.3d 1303, 1329 (Fed. Cir. 2005) (en banc).

[10] *Texas Digital*, 308 F.3d at 1202.

[11] *Id.* at 1204.

[12] *Id.*

most meaningful sources of information to aid judges in better understanding both the technology and the terminology used by those skilled in the art to describe the technology.[13]

Texas Digital's preference toward the understanding of one of ordinary skill was at odds with the *Vitronics* court's emphasis on the intrinsic record to describe the patentee's definition of the invention. Resolution of this conflict was both necessary and inevitable.

§ 25.03   THE CURRENT APPROACH: THE FEDERAL CIRCUIT'S EN BANC DECISION IN *PHILLIPS v. AWH CORP*

In 2005, the Federal Circuit issued its opinion in *Phillips v. AWH*,[14] an en banc decision that represents the current methodology for the interpretation of patent claims. In *Phillips*, the Federal Circuit resolved the theoretical disparity between *Vitronics* and *Texas Digital*. The patent at issue was directed to vandalism-resistant modular wall panels. The dispute centered on the claim term "baffle," which referred to a panel that formed a barrier. The district court had relied on the written specification to conclude that a "baffle" required placement at angles other than 90° — in other words, placement at either oblique or acute angles. On appeal, the patentee argued that the district court had erroneously limited the analysis to the embodiment described in the patent specification. The Federal Circuit granted en banc review to consider whether "the public notice function of patent claims better served by referencing primarily to technical and general purpose dictionaries and similar sources to interpret a claim term or by looking primarily to the patentee's use of the term in the specification?"

Ultimately, the en banc *Phillips* decision returned the law of claim interpretation to the *Vitronics* view that favors reliance on the intrinsic record. Because claim construction is of central importance to defining the right to exclude, the *Phillips* en banc decision warrants careful attention.

[A]   The *Phillips* Claim Construction Methodology

Phillips established a hierarchy of sources of interpretative information, assigning different weights to each. A summary chart of these sources is below, followed by a more complete explanation of the rules of the *Phillips* case:

---

[13] *Id.* at 1202-03.

[14] Phillips v. AWH Corp., 415 F.3d 1303 (Fed. Cir. 2005) (en banc).

Phillips v. Awh: Hierarchy of Interpretive Sources

Intrinsic evidence (primary importance)
  1. Patent claims
  2. Specification
  3. Prosecution history

Extrinsic evidence (secondary importance)
  • Expert & inventor testimony
  • Dictionaries and treatises

Consistent with well-established law, *Phillips* reiterated that claim terms must be given their ordinary and customary meaning as understood by one of ordinary skill in the art at the time of invention. The court promulgated the following steps to construe patent claims:

Common words or phrases can be readily understood by the fact finder and do not require additional analysis. The *Phillips* court acknowledged that some widely understood claim terms must be construed according to their plain meaning. Thus, a non-specialized or commonly used term such as the word "or" can be readily comprehended by a lay jury or judge without resorting to sources of information outside the claim.[15] In such cases, claim construction of the term "involves little more than the application of the widely accepted meaning of commonly understood words."[16] However, specialized or ambiguous terms require further examination.

An analysis of an ambiguous or disputed claim term begins with the words of the claim in which the term is used. The *Phillips* court unequivocally established that the starting point for a claim construction analysis is the claim language in which the term appears. The court pointed that a patentee is statutorily obligated to particularly point out and distinctly claim the subject matter that the applicant regards as his invention. Further, the public has a right to rely on the claim language to understand the patent's scope. Thus, the *Phillips* holding directs courts to *first* examine the claim in which the term appears to provide context and, in some cases, the definition of an ambiguous or a disputed claim term. As the *Phillips* court stated, "the context in which a term is used in the asserted claim can

---

[15] *Id.* (citing Brown v. 3M, 265 F.3d 1349, 1352 (Fed. Cir. 2001)) (claim term "or" is "not technical terms of art, and do[es] not require elaborate interpretation.").

[16] Phillips v. AWH Corp., 415 F.3d 1303, 1314 (Fed. Cir. 2005) (en banc).

be highly instructive."[17]

The court may examine other claims within the patent to assist in construing the relevant term. Other claims that contain the same, or similar, terms may be "valuable sources of enlightenment" as to the meaning of a claim term.[18] Further, the *Phillips* opinion acknowledged that *differences* between various claims could help define a particular claim term. For example, if a dependent claim had specified that a "baffle" included a structure which projected at any angle *other than* 90°, then the word "baffle" in an independent claim without a similar limitation could be construed to encompass a baffle that *does* project at 90°.

The court must examine the specification of the patent of which the claim is a part. One of ordinary skill in the art is presumed to read the claims in the context of the entire patent, including its specification. As the *Phillips* opinion pointed out, § 112 of the Patent Act requires a patentee to include significant descriptive information about the invention in the written specification. In a claim construction analysis, this same information is an ideal source from which one can learn the meaning of claim terms. As *Phillips* explained, the specification is usually dispositive on interpretive questions, as "the single best guide to the meaning of a disputed term."[19] For these reasons, the *Phillips* court instructed courts to review the written specification to construe an ambiguous or disputed claim term, stating, "[t]he construction that stays true to the claim language and most naturally aligns with the patent's description of the invention will be, in the end, the correct construction."[20]

A patent's written description becomes particularly important where a patentee specifically defines a claim term in a way that might differ from common usage. This is because a patentee can "act as his own lexicographer to specifically define terms of a claim contrary to their ordinary meaning."[21] Additionally, a patentee may intentionally limit the scope of the claims by disavowing particular subject matter. Under either of those circumstances, a court's consultation of the patent's specification is crucial to understand the claim terms.

The prosecution history may be relevant in construing a claim term. Although the *Phillips* decision placed the heaviest priority on the claims and the written specification for interpretation, a court must also consult the patent's prosecution history. However, the *Phillips* court noted that the prosecution history can be entitled to less weight that the other intrinsic evidence, because the prosecution file "often lacks the clarity of the specification and is therefore less useful for claim construction purposes."[22] Yet the *Phillips* opinion recognized that communications between the patentee and the U.S. PTO may provide valuable information concerning the manner in which the patentee and the examiner

---

[17] *Id.*

[18] *Id.*

[19] *Id.* at 1315.

[20] *Id.* at 1316, *quoting* Renishaw PLC v. Marposs Societa' per Azioni, 158 F.3d 1243, 1250 (Fed. Cir. 1998).

[21] *See* Chef Am., Inc. v. Lamb-Weston, Inc., 358 F.3d 1371, 1374 (Fed. Cir. 2004).

[22] Phillips v. AWH Corp., 415 F.3d 1303, 1317 (Fed. Cir. 2005) (en banc).

understood the invention. Such information can be particularly relevant where the prosecution history contains a statement defining the invention or where the patentee expressly limits the invention's scope. *Phillips* underscored that the clarity of such statements in the file history is important, and cautions that an ambiguous statement in the prosecution file will not be considered controlling over a clear meaning set forth in the patent itself.

A court has discretion to consider extrinsic evidence, although such evidence may be less reliable than intrinsic sources. The *Phillips* court authorized district courts to consider extrinsic sources of evidence, such as expert and inventor testimony, dictionaries and learned treatise, but warns that such evidence is "less significant than the intrinsic record in determining the legally operative meaning of claim language."[23] *Phillips* expressly cautioned that reliance on extrinsic evidence "is unlikely to result in a reliable interpretation of patent claim scope unless considered in the context of the intrinsic evidence."[24] Specifically, *Phillips* noted that extrinsic evidence is not part of the patent prosecution and therefore not optimal to explain the patent's scope and meaning, nor does such evidence necessarily include an accurate reflection of the understanding of those skilled in the art.

Additionally, the *Phillips* court recognized that expert reports and testimony, which are created for the litigation, can suffer from bias. The court admonished that, "[i]n the course of litigation, each party will naturally choose the pieces of extrinsic evidence most favorable to its causes."[25] Beyond these practical considerations, the court observed that reliance on extrinsic evidence inconsistent with the public notice function of claims:

> . . . undue reliance on extrinsic evidence poses the risk that it will be used to change the meaning of claims in derogation of the indisputable public records consisting of the claims, the specification and the prosecution history, thereby undermining the public notice function of patents.[26]

Phillips' emphasis on the intrinsic record clearly favors the *Vitronics* approach. Expressly disapproving *Texas Digital's* preference for dictionary definitions over intrinsic evidence, *Phillips* acknowledged that courts do have some discretion to consult dictionaries to gain an understanding of commonly known words or to learn the underlying technology, "so long as the dictionary definition does not contradict any definition found in or ascertained by a reading of the patent documents."[27]

---

[23] *Id.*

[24] *Id.* at 1319.

[25] *Id.*

[26] *Id.* at 1319 (internal quotation and citation omitted).

[27] *Id.* at 1322-23.

[B] Application of the *Phillips* Claim Construction Methodology

The *Phillips* court applied these principles to consider whether the term "baffle" in the patent's claim 1 includes an embodiment that would protrude at a 90° right angle. First, *Phillips* examined claim 1 and found no language limiting the term in that manner. The court examined the term's use within the claim — that is, the phrase "further means disposed inside the shell for increasing its load bearing capacity comprising internal steel baffles extending inwardly from the steel shell walls."[28] Based on this context, the court concluded that "baffle" had three requirements — that is, it must be made of steel, serve a load-bearing function, and point inward from the walls. The court found no claim language limited the orientation of a "baffle" to obtuse or acute angles.

Second, the court examined other claims, finding that these expressly included limits on a baffle's angular orientation. This suggested that the term "baffle" standing alone in claim 1 should be read *without* any orientation limitation. Examining the specification, *Phillips* then found that one of ordinary skill in the art would not find the term "baffle" limited to obtuse or acute angles, and on these bases reversed the district court's claim construction.

Significantly, the *Phillips* court resolved claim construction without examining *any* extrinsic evidence at all. Yet the decision allows some latitude in how the terms of any particular patent will be construed. As *Phillips* states, "there is no magic formula or catechism for conducting claim construction."[29] The *Phillips* court cautioned that reliance on extrinsic evidence must be considered in the context of the intrinsic evidence, and such evidence should not be used if unreliable, biased, or inconsistent with the intrinsic record. Further, *Phillips* rejected *Texas Digital's* preference for dictionaries. The *Phillips* court's claim construction of the term "baffle" illustrates that claim construction can be performed through reliance on the intrinsic record alone.

§ 25.04 A CLOSER LOOK AT THE INTERACTION OF THE SPECIFICATION AND CLAIM TERMS

[A] Putting a Claim Construction Analysis Together

The Federal Circuit's claim construction jurisprudence teaches that claims *must be read in light of the specification* of which they are a part. In application, this principle raise an interpretative tension with another principle of claim construction — that is, *claims are not limited to the description set forth in the specification* and are given their full breadth as drafted.[30] This tension is not easily resolved. Indeed, court decisions "recognize that there is sometimes a fine line

---

[28] *Id., quoting* U.S. Patent No. 4,677,798 (filed Apr 14, 1986).

[29] Phillips v. AWH Corp., 415 F.3d 1303, 1324 (Fed. Cir. 2005) (en banc).

[30] Sjolund v. Musland, 847 F.2d 1573, 1581 (Fed. Cir. 1988) ("If everything in the specification were required to be read into the claims, or if structural claims were to be limited to devices operated precisely as a specification-described embodiment is operated, there would be no need for claims."); *see also*

between reading a claim in light of the specification, and reading a limitation into the claim from the specification."[31]

For example, assume that a patent specification describes and enables a wall-mounted wine rack that holds up to six bottles. Further assume that the body of the claim broadly states that the invention has "vertically placed support members configured to hold a multiplicity of bottles." Although the specification describes an embodiment that supports a specific number of bottles (here, six), the claim as drafted is not so limited (because the claim uses the term "multiplicity of bottles" rather than a specific number). Additionally, the specification describes the invention's use for a particular type of bottle (here, wine bottles), but the claim is drafted broadly to include *all* types of bottles (by using the broad term "bottles" without qualification). Does an accused device that is otherwise similar but designed to hold *twelve plastic water bottles* within the literal claim scope?

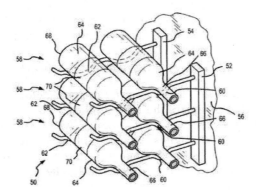

To resolve the question, one might reference some claim construction principles. First, a claim is given the ordinary meaning as understood by one of ordinary skill in the art. As a general rule, the embodiments and examples in a patent's specification will not limit a claim's breadth so long as § 112's disclosure obligations are met.[32] The right to exclude is defined by the patent's claims, not by the specification. Thus, a specification's description of a single embodiment typically does not limit otherwise broad claim language.[33] This is because one of ordinary skill in the art would rarely restrict their understanding of a particular term to the disclosed embodiments.[34] Indeed, a patentee may disclose only a single embodiment in the specification and still obtain a wide claim scope to cover varied embodiments, so long as the claim is fully enabled and the other disclosure

Gemstar-TV Guide Int'l, Inc. v. Int'l Trade Comm'n, 383 F.3d 1352 (Fed. Cir. 2004).

[31] Comark Communs., Inc. v. Harris Corp., 156 F.3d 1182, 1186 (Fed. Cir. 1998).

[32] Constant v. Advanced Micro-Devices, Inc., 848 F.2d 1560, 1571 (Fed. Cir. 1988).

[33] *Comark*, 156 F.3d at 1187.

[34] *Id.; see also* Phillips v. AWH Corp., 415 F.3d 1303, 1323 (Fed. Cir. 2005) (en banc) ("persons of ordinary skill in the art rarely would confine their definitions of terms to the exact representations depicted in the embodiments").

requirements have been met. In that case, the application of these general rules likely means that the claim should encompass a holder designed for twelve plastic water bottles.

There are exceptions to this general rule. A patentee can act as a lexicographer by specially defining a claim term in the specification.[35] Under those circumstances, a patentee's own definition in the specification will be imported into the claim to define the relevant term. Thus, if the specification had defined the word "multiplicity" as "six," or clearly stated that the term "bottles" referred to "wine bottles only," then the accused device for holding twelve water bottles is likely to be construed to fall outside the claim scope.

Another question is whether the patentee's specification expressly limited, disclaimed or disavowed the particular subject matter. If so, the inventor's intent to limit the scope of the claim will control the claim term's meaning. Therefore, if the patentee had included a statement in the specification that expressly excluded embodiments for bottles other than wine bottles, or for devices holding more than six bottles, the device that holds twelve water bottles would not infringe.

[B] The Patentee as Lexicographer: *SciMed*

SciMed Life Systems Inc. v. Advanced Cardiovascular Systems Inc.[36] is a widely cited decision that considers the effect of the specification on claim meaning. The patent at issue concerned a type of catheter, which is a tube device used in medical procedures to allow fluids to flow or to open a passageway. The specification described that "all embodiments" of the invention used a "coaxial" catheter — that is, a configuration whereby the smaller of the catheter tube fits within a larger tube. An illustration from one of the *SciMed* patents shows this configuration, with the smaller tube 52 within the larger tube 63, as follows:[37]

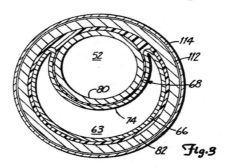

Significantly, the *SciMed* patent specifically distinguished prior art dual catheters that used a side-by-side configuration whereby two tubes were placed in parallel to each other.

---

[35] *Id.* at 1316.

[36] SciMed Life Sys., Inc. v. Advanced Cardiovascular Systems Inc., 242 F.3d 1337 (Fed. Cir. 2001).

[37] U.S. Patent No. 5,156,594 (filed Aug 28, 1990).

The *SciMed* court interpreted the claims using the term "catheters" to exclude side-by-side dual catheter configurations, stating, "[i]t is difficult to imagine how the patents could have been clearer in making the point that the coaxial lumen configuration was a necessary element of every variant of the claimed invention."[38] The *SciMed* case illustrates the principle that if the specification clearly defines the invention, that meaning will control even if the claim language uses broad terminology.[39]

§ 25.05   CLAIM CONSTRUCTION AND VALIDITY

A court's claim construction is constant for all purposes — that is, the same claim construction governs for both validity and infringement.[40] Thus, a claim that is interpreted broadly may be invalid because the broader construction encompasses the prior art. Alternatively, a claim might be construed in a manner that renders the claim unsupported by the written specification that is in violation of the disclosure requirements of § 112.

The courts have developed an axiom that claims should be construed, if possible, to preserve their validity.[41] This principle has deep roots in the U.S. Supreme Court's 1863 decision *Turrill v. Michigan Southern & N.I.R. Co.*, which stated that patents should "if practicable, to be so interpreted as to uphold and not to destroy the right of the inventor."[42] In the en banc *Phillips* opinion, the Federal Circuit noted that this rule currently has limited applicability.[43] Specifically, *Phillips* determined that courts should *not* perform a validity analysis as a routine part of claim construction.[44] Rather, the *Phillips* court stated that a court's efforts to construe a claim to preserve its validity should be undertaken *only* if the claim is still ambiguous after *all* of the available tools of claim construction have been exhausted. According to other Federal Circuit precedent, a court cannot rewrite unambiguous claim terms to maintain the validity of a claim.[45] There are times when, as the courts have found, "the claim is simply invalid."[46]

For example, in *Rhine v. Casio*, the Federal Circuit considered a district court's claim construction for a patent directed to a watch with an illuminated face that included "at least one light source."[47] The district court had construed the claim to require at least *two* light sources in order to avoid prior art. The Federal Circuit reversed, finding that the district court had improperly contradicted the ordinary

---

[38] *SciMed*, 242 F.3d at 1344.

[39] *Id.* at 1341.

[40] *See* Yoon Ja Kim v. Conagra Foods, Inc., 465 F.3d 1312 (Fed. Cir. 2006).

[41] Rhine v. Casio, Inc., 183 F.3d 1342, 1344 (Fed. Cir. 1999).

[42] Turrill v. Mich. S. & N.I.R.R. Co., 68 U.S. 491, 510 (1863).

[43] Phillips v. AWH Corp., 415 F.3d 1303, 1327-28 (Fed. Cir. 2005) (en banc).

[44] *Id.* at 1327 ("we have certainly not endorsed a regime in which validity analysis is a regular component of claim construction.").

[45] Nazomi Communs. Inc. v. Arm Holdings, PLC, 403 F.3d 1364, 1368 (Fed. Cir. 2005).

[46] *Rhine*, 183 F.3d at 1345.

[47] *Id.* at 1344.

meaning of the claim language "at least one," which the appellate court stated, "means that there could be only one or more than one."[48] Thus, a court's attempt to sustain validity of the claim cannot overcome an unambiguous meaning of a claim term.

§ 25.06 CANONS OF CLAIM CONSTRUCTION

The courts have developed some guidelines that are referred to as *canons of claim construction* to assist with recurring issues in claim interpretation. The courts have developed in the course of interpreting patent claims. Generally, these canons should be considered to be recommendations and not unqualified rules of law. As one opinion cautioned, "no canon of claim construction is absolute."[49] These principles are merely tools to assist in the interpretation of the words used by the patentee to define the invention. In the final analysis, the application of any canon cannot control over the intrinsic evidence and the understanding of one of ordinary skill in the art.

[A] The Doctrine of Claim Differentiation

Claim differentiation can be a useful canon of construction to determine claim meaning. This doctrine rests on the assumption that separate claims are presumed to have a different meaning and scope.[50] For example, an independent claim will not be construed to encompass a dependent claim that contains a limitation that the independent claim lacks.[51] This doctrine can be overcome by contrary evidence in the intrinsic record. Thus, "the written description and prosecution history overcome any presumption arising from the doctrine of claim differentiation."[52]

[B] Construction of Terms in the Preamble

A claim's preamble typically designates a *use* for invention rather than an element such as structure, a portion of a composition or a step within a process.[53] Should a preamble be considered a limitation? An example demonstrates the circumstances under which this question arises. Assume that a claim preamble identifies an "apparatus for use as a *wine rack*," where the body includes the language "vertically placed support members configured to hold a multiplicity of bottles." Does a rack with vertical support members used to hold *water bottles* infringe? If the preamble is construed as a limitation, then the answer to that question is "no." In that event, the accused device must be used as a wine rack to establish infringement.

---

[48] *Id.*

[49] Renishaw PLC v. Marposs Societa' per Azioni, 158 F.3d 1243, 1248 (Fed. Cir. 1998).

[50] Andersen Corp. v. Fiber Composites, LLC, 474 F.3d 1361, 1369 (Fed. Cir. 2007).

[51] D.M.I., Inc. v. Deere & Co., 755 F.2d 1570, 1574 (Fed. Cir. 1985).

[52] *Andersen Corp.*, 474 F.3d at 1370.

[53] *See In re* Neugebauer, 330 F.2d 353, 356 (C.C.P.A. 1964).

How does one tell whether a claim preamble constitutes a limitation? As a general rule, where a patentee defines a complete invention in the claim body, the language in the preamble is not considered a claim limitation.[54] For example, where a claim recites an entire and complete structure consistent with the written description, the preamble is considered superfluous and its terms are not operative limitations. However, where the preamble is "necessary to give life, meaning and vitality" to the claim, the preamble will be found to include a limitation.[55] The distinction is made by examining "the entire[ ] . . . patent to gain an understanding of what the inventors actually invented and intended to encompass by the claim."[56]

This standard was applied in *Pitney Bowes, Inc. v. Hewlett-Packard Co.*[57] The claims at issue were directed to an apparatus and method for laser printing. As background, a laser printed character is made from hundreds, or perhaps thousands, of small dots of toner particles. In brief, this process relies on the use of a laser that strikes a drum (called a "photoreceptor drum") and creates a small discharge. To create a final image, this discharged area attracts charged toner ink, which is transferred from the drum onto paper. The *Pitney Bowes* patent taught an improvement that used different sized toner dots that resulted in more legible characters with smoother edges. To vary the toner dot size, the specification taught a method of practicing the invention by varying both the intensity of the beam of light and the length of time that the light remained in contact with the photoreceptor.

In *Pitney Bowes*, the parties disputed whether the phrase for an apparatus or method for "producing on a photoreceptor an image of *generated shapes* made of *spots*," that appeared in two claim preambles constituted a claim limitation.[58] Significantly, the body of these claims included the words "*spots*" and the clause "whereby the appearance of smoothed edges are given to the *generated shapes*."[59] The *Pitney Bowes* court held that the preamble phrase was a limitation. In part, the court relied on the fact that the preamble provided the *antecedent basis*[60] for the use of the words "spots" and "generated shapes" that were both used in the body of the two claims at issue. The court explained that the use of these same terms could only be understood with reference to the statement in the preamble, which provided the necessary explanation that the "spots" and "generated shapes" were each created on a photoreceptor drum. Under these circumstances, the *Pitney Bowes* court found it "essential that the court charged with claim construction construe the preamble and the remainder of the claim . . . as one

---

[54] Rowe v. Dror, 112 F.3d 473, 478 (Fed. Cir. 1997).

[55] Pitney Bowes, Inc. v. Hewlett-Packard Co., 182 F.3d 1298, 1305 (Fed. Cir. 1999).

[56] Catalina Marketing Int'l, Inc. v. Coolsavings.com, Inc., 289 F.3d 801, 808 (Fed. Cir. 2002).

[57] *Pitney Bowes*, 182 F.3d at 1298.

[58] *Id.* at 1302, *quoting* U.S. Patent No. 4,386,272 (filed Jun 22, 1982).

[59] *Pitney Bowes*, 182 F.3d at 1302 (emphasis added).

[60] The antecedent basis of a claim term refers to the first time that an identified word or phrase is used in a claim, which typically provides a foundation for the use of that same term later in the same claim.

unified and internally consistent recitation of the claimed invention."[61] Under this construction, a photoreceptor in the accused device and method is necessary for a finding of infringement.

In *Catalina Marketing International, Inc. v. Coolsavings.com, Inc.*,[62] the court gave some examples of circumstances under which a preamble might be construed as a limitation, such as: 1) the use of a term in the preamble as the antecedent basis for a term used in the body of a claim (as in *Pitney Bowes*); 2) use of preamble terms was essential to understand a term in the claim body;[63] 3) the structure in the preamble was acknowledged as important in the written specification; 4) there was clear reliance on the preamble during the patent's prosecution to distinguish the prior art from the claimed invention; and 5) Jepson claims.[64]

These rules do not easily lead to predictable outcomes. As the Federal Circuit has stated, "[n]o litmus test defines when a preamble limits claim scope."[65] Preamble construction is heavily context-dependent and may include the use of both intrinsic and extrinsic evidence. Fundamentally, the issue is whether the body of the claim fully describes the invention or whether the preamble language is necessary to fully define the invention.

[C] Additional Canons of Claim Construction

Additional common canons of claim construction include the following:

- The word "about" does not have a strict numerical boundary, but rather should be read in light of the intrinsic and technological context.[66]

- General descriptive terms will ordinarily be given their full meaning; modifiers will not be added to broad terms standing alone.[67]

- A claim construction that would exclude the preferred embodiment "is rarely, if ever, correct and would require highly persuasive evidentiary support."[68]

---

[61] *Id.* at 1306.

[62] Catalina Marketing Int'l, Inc. v. Coolsavings.com, Inc., 289 F.3d 801 (Fed. Cir. 2002).

[63] In *In re Kropa*, 187 F.2d 150, 152 (C.C.P.A. 1951), the court considered a claim to a composition of chemical elements. The *Kropa* court held that a preamble term "an abrasive article" was a limitation, reasoning that the term was necessary to explain terms "abrasive grains" and a "binder" used later in the claim. *Kropa* explained that the phrase "an abrasive article" was necessary to give "life, meaning and vitality to the claims or counts" because "it is only by that phrase that it can be known that the subject matter defined by the claims is comprised as an abrasive article." *Id.* at 152.

[64] Jepson claims are discussed *supra*, in Chapter 4.

[65] *Id.* at 809.

[66] Ortho-McNeil Pharmaceutical, Inc. v. Caraco Pharmaceutical Laboratories, Ltd., 476 F.3d 1321, 1326 (Fed. Cir. 2007).

[67] Johnson Worldwide Assoc., Inc. v. Zebco Corp., 175 F.3d 985, 989 (Fed. Cir. 1999).

[68] Rexnord Corp. v. Laitram Corp., 274 F.3d 1336, 1342 (Fed. Cir. 2001).

- A single claim term should be given the same meaning throughout an entire patent, or in any related patents.[69]

The foregoing list is not exhaustive and are not relevant in every case. Rather, these principles act to assist courts in applying *Philips* to derive an articulation of the invention.

§ 25.07 CONCLUSION

In *Markman*, the Supreme Court left the precise methodology for the interpretation of patent claims to the Federal Circuit.[70] Patent claims are read according to the understanding of one of ordinary skill in the art at the time of invention, read in the context of the patent and its prosecution history.[71] In the en banc *Phillips* opinion, the Federal Circuit held that a court performing claim construction first must look to the intrinsic record.

Specifically, the *Phillips* inquiry begins with an examination of the claims, which may provide context and meaning that can be used in interpreting the meaning of ambiguous or disputed terms. For example, under the doctrine of claim differentiation, different claim terms used in separate claims are presumed to indicate a different meaning. Second, the claim must be examined and read in light of the specification. A patentee's description may provide the best evidence of the claim's meaning. However, the court must not import limitations from the specification into the claims. As the courts have recognized, reconciling these principles of claim construction may be difficult in individual cases.

Under *Phillips*, the patent's prosecution history should be examined as part of the claim construction inquiry. Although *Phillips* considered the prosecution history less useful that the four corners of the patent itself, *Phillips* recognized that the prosecution history could contain important information concerning the patentee's definition of the invention.

To the extent that the patent's intrinsic sources do not resolve an ambiguity, *Phillips* authorizes consideration of extrinsic evidence such as expert testimony, dictionaries, and learned treatises. Further, *Phillips* permits consideration of such extrinsic sources to provide background information about the technology that is the subject matter of the patent. However, *Phillips* expressly disapproved of the claim construction practice that placed primary emphasis on dictionaries, as exemplified by the *Texas Digital* court. Furthermore, although claim terms should be construed to preserve their validity, a validity analysis should not be undertaken as a regular part of claim construction. Rather, this maxim should only be undertaken when other methods of claim construction fail. Further, a preamble should not be construed as a limitation where the body of the claim defines a complete invention. However, where terms in the preamble are necessary to give life, meaning and vitality to the claim body, a term in a preamble may constitute operative limitations of the claim.

---

[69] CVI/Beta Ventures, Inc. v. Tura LP, 112 F.3d 1146, 1159 (Fed. Cir. 1997).

[70] *See* Markman v. Westview, 52 F.3d 967 (Fed. Cir. 1995).

[71] Phillips v. AWH Corp., 415 F.3d 1303, 1313 (Fed. Cir. 2005) (en banc).

Chapter 26

AN INTRODUCTION TO PATENT INFRINGEMENT

SYNOPSIS

§ 26.01   INTRODUCTION

§ 26.02   VIOLATION OF THE PROVISIONAL RIGHT

§ 26.03   OVERVIEW OF INFRINGEMENT THEORIES

   [A]   Direct and Indirect Infringement

   [B]   Literal Infringement and Infringement under the Doctrine of Equivalents

§ 26.04   CONCLUSION

§ 26.01   INTRODUCTION

A patentee's exercise of the right to exclude requires a showing that another *infringes* at least one valid and enforceable claim. The Patent Act defines the patentee's right to exclude in 35 U.S.C. § 154:

> Every patent shall . . . grant to the patentee . . . the right to exclude others from *making, using, offering for sale,* or *selling* the invention throughout the United States or *importing* the invention into the United States . . . .[1]

A patentee enforces the patent right by filing a civil action under one or more subsections of § 271. As a primary example, § 271(a) governs direct infringement. That section mirrors § 154 by enumerating that one engages in an infringing activity when one "makes, uses, offers to sell or sells" or "imports" a patented invention:

> [W]hoever without authority *makes, uses, offers to sell,* or *sells* any patented invention, within the United States or *imports* into the United States any patented invention during the term of the patent therefore, infringes the patent.[2]

Notably, § 271(a)'s prohibited acts are limited to those that take place "within the United States" or constitute importation "into the United States." One does not

---

[1] 35 U.S.C. § 154(a)(1) (emphasis added). For process claims, section 154(a)(1) grants the patentee "the right to exclude others from using, offering for sale or selling throughout the United States, or importing into the United States, products made by that process, referring to the specification for the particulars thereof."

[2] 35 U.S.C. § 271(a).

infringe a patent under this particular subsection by practicing a claim entirely outside U.S. borders. However, as will be explored in a later chapter, there are other subsections that permit limited extraterritorial reach of a U.S. patent under certain circumstances.[3] Acts must occur during the patent's effective term to constitute infringement.[4] There is no infringement if the patent is invalid or unenforceable.

§ 26.02   VIOLATION OF THE PROVISIONAL RIGHT

In addition to providing relief for infringing acts within the patent's term, the Patent Act grants a patentee a *provisional right* to relief for infringing acts that occur before a patent is issued in particular circumstances.[5] This relief is confined to infringement that is in a patent that derives from a published application eighteen (18) months after filing under § 122(b)(1).[6]

This provisional right allows a patentee to recover a reasonable royalty as compensation for infringement of a published patent application only if all three of the following conditions are satisfied: 1) the infringer has actual notice of the patent application; 2) the infringed claim is issued in a substantially identical form to the claim as published in the application; and 3) the patentee files suit within six (6) years after the patent is issued.[7] The provisional right does not mature until the patent issues.[8] After that time, a patentee can assert a claim for infringement of the provisional right based on activity that occurred after the infringer gained actual notice of the published application and before the date that the patent issued.

The statute requires *"actual* notice of the published patent application."[9] Constructive notice is not sufficient.[10] Actual notice does not require any affirmative act of the patentee, rather the standard can be met if the infringer learns of the published patent application from any source.[11] Further, the statute's requirement is directed to notice of the patent *application*, in contrast to notice of *infringement*. Thus, one court has held that the statute does not require the defendant to become apprised of any specific charge of infringement that is directed to a particularly defined product, process or device.[12]

---

[3] For a discussion of whether an activity may be considered within or outside U.S. borders, see Chapter 35.

[4] *See* Joy Technologies, Inc. v. Flakt, Inc., 6 F.3d 770, 773 (Fed. Cir. 1993). For more about the effective life of a patent, see Chapter 2.

[5] 35 U.S.C. § 154(d).

[6] For more information about the publication of patent applications, see Chapter 2.

[7] 35 U.S.C. § 154(d). *See* Stephens v. Tech Int'l., Inc., 393 F.3d 1269, 1275-76 (Fed. Cir. 2004).

[8] *See* Classen Immunotherapies, Inc. v. King Pharm., Inc., 403 F. Supp. 2d 451, 457 (D. Md. 2005).

[9] 35 U.S.C. § 154(d)(1)(B).

[10] Arendi Holding Ltd. v. Microsoft Corp., 2010 U.S. Dist. LEXIS 27020 (D. Del. Mar. 22, 2010).

[11] K-TEC, Inc. v. Vita-Mix Corp., 2010 U.S. Dist. LEXIS 51858 (D. Utah May 24, 2010) (evidence that the infringer had monitored the progress of the patent application was sufficient to demonstrate "actual notice" prior to the patent's grant).

[12] *See* The First Years, Inc. v. Munchkin, Inc., 2008 U.S. Dist. LEXIS 70482 (W.D. Wis. Sept. 17, 2008).

When is a claim in a "substantially identical form to the claim as published in the application"? There are few cases considering this question, although one district court has applied the standard used to assess the significance of a claim amendment for a reissued or reexamined claim.[13] Another has noted that an amendment made to overcome a rejection will rarely meet this standard.[14]

§ 26.03 OVERVIEW OF INFRINGEMENT THEORIES

As the portion of the patent that defines the right to exclude, the patent claim is the center of a patent infringement analysis. As patent jurist Giles S. Rich once stated, "[t]he name of the game is the claim."[15] The patentee's commercial embodiment is not relevant to determine infringement. Indeed, "it is error for a court to compare in its infringement analysis the accused product or process with the patentee's commercial embodiment or other version of the product or process; the only proper comparison is with the claims of the patent."[16]

The first step in an infringement analysis requires the court to interpret the claim to ascertain its scope and meaning.[17] After a court has defined the invention, a finder of fact must determine whether a particular defendant's conduct is infringing.[18]

[A]   Direct and Indirect Infringement

Direct infringement is governed by § 271(a), which provides that "whoever . . . makes, uses, offers to sell, or sells any patented invention, within the United States or imports into the United States any patented invention . . ." infringes. The term "patented invention" in the statute refers to the invention as embodied in an accused device or process. Where another has engaged in at least one of the enumerated acts without the patentee's permission, a patentee establishes direct infringement by proving a one-to-one correspondence between all limitations of the claim (as interpreted by the court) and the accused device or process.[19] A patentee is not required to demonstrate that the accused infringer was aware of the patent, because "there is no intent element to direct infringement."[20] Rather, infringement

---

[13] *Cf.* Prestige Pet Products, Inc. v. Pingyang Huaxing Leather & Plastic Co., 767 F. Supp. 2d 806, 812-13 (E.D. Mich. 2011), citing Laitram Corp. v. NEC Corp., 163 F.3d 1342 (Fed. Cir. 1998). For more about the modification of claims after a patent issues and the doctrine of intervening rights, see Chapter 3.

[14] *See* Pandora Jewelry, LLC v. Chamilia, LLC, 2008 U.S. Dist. LEXIS 61064 (D. Md. Aug. 8, 2008).

[15] *In re* Hiniker Co., 150 F.3d 1362, 1369 (Fed. Cir. 1998) (quoting Giles Sutherland Rich, *Extent of Protection and Interpretation of Claims-American Perspectives*, 21 INT'L REV. INDUS. PROP. & COPYRIGHT L. 497, 499 (1990)).

[16] Zenith Laboratories, Inc. v. Bristol-Myers Squibb Co., 19 F.3d 1418, 1423 (Fed. Cir. 1994).

[17] Cybor Corp. v. FAS Technologies, Inc., 138 F.3d 1448, 1454 (Fed. Cir. 1998). Claim interpretation is discussed in Chapters 24 and 25.

[18] *See Cybor Corp.*, 138 F.3d at 1457-58.

[19] *See* Bayer AG v. Elan Pharm. Research Corp., 212 F.3d 1241, 1247 (Fed. Cir. 2000).

[20] Intel Corp. v. U.S. Int'l Trade Comm'n, 946 F.2d 821, 832 (Fed. Cir. 1991) (emphasis omitted); *see also* Warner-Jenkinson Co., Inc. v. Hilton Davis Chemical Co., 520 U.S. 17, 35 (1997) ("Application of the

exists if the accused product or process is within the scope of the patentee's claims. One may infringe a patent even where one *independently develops* the accused product or process with no knowledge of, or access to, the patented claim.[21]

For example, to demonstrate direct infringement of an apparatus claim, a patentee must show that a defendant has made, used, offered to sell, or sold any patented invention within the U.S., or imported into the U.S., a device that meets all of the structural limitations of the claim.[22] To demonstrate direct infringement of a process claim, a patentee must show that the defendant performed all of the steps enumerated in the claim — that is, "[t]o be direct infringers, the defendants must have used the plaintiff's process."[23] Alternatively, a patentee may demonstrate that a defendant has infringed a process claim where the defendant has used, sold or imported into the U.S. a product that has been made by the claimed process.[24]

Indirect infringement is governed by §§ 271(b) and (c). Under these sections, an indirect infringer is one who either actively induces or contributes to the infringing activities of another. An indirect infringer need not practice the claims him or herself to be liable. Rather, an indirect infringer can be secondarily liable for the infringing conduct of another. For example, a defendant may be liable for indirect infringement by attempting to circumvent a patent through selling components with instructions that inform purchasers how to create an infringing device from those components. As a predicate to indirect infringement liability, the patentee must demonstrate that at least one person or entity has engaged in direct infringement.[25]

[B] Literal Infringement and Infringement under the Doctrine of Equivalents

A person who is engaging in direct, indirect or joint infringement can do so either *literally* or under the *doctrine of equivalents*.

Literal infringement means that the accused item or process is met by a one-to-one correspondence with the literal terms of the claims. In other words, there must be a one-to-one correspondence between the elements in the patent claim and the limitations found in the accused product, process or method. Under this standard,

---

doctrine of equivalents, therefore, is akin to determining literal infringement, and neither requires proof of intent.").

[21] *See e.g.*, Hilton Davis Chem. Co. v. Warner-Jenkinson Co., 62 F.3d 1512, 1520 (Fed. Cir. 1995), *rev'd on other grounds*, 520 U.S. 17 (1997).

[22] *See* Cross Med. Prods., Inc. v. Medtronic Sofamor Danek, Inc., 424 F.3d 1293, 1311 (Fed. Cir. 2005).

[23] Canton Bio Med. v. Integrated Liner Tech., Inc., 216 F.3d 1367, 1370 (Fed. Cir. 2000); Joy Technologies, Inc. v. Flakt, Inc., 6 F.3d 770, 773 (Fed. Cir. 1993) (quoting B. B. Chem. Co. v. Ellis, 117 F.2d 829, 833 (1st Cir. 1941)).

[24] 35 U.S.C. § 271(g) ("Whoever without authority imports into the United States or offers to sell, sells, or uses within the United States a product which is made by a process patented in the United States shall be liable as an infringer, if the importation, offer to sell, sale, or use of the product occurs during the term of such process patent.").

[25] Dynacore Holdings Corp. v. U.S. Philips Corp., 363 F.3d 1263, 1272 (Fed. Cir. 2004). Chapters 33 and 34 provide a detailed look at indirect infringement.

a claim comprised of chemicals A, B, and C together in equal proportions is infringed by a compound that includes a combination of these same elements A, B, and C combined in equal proportions. As the U.S. Supreme Court has stated, "[i]f accused matter falls clearly within the claim, infringement is made out and that is the end of it."[26] If any single claim element is not literally met, then there is no literal infringement.[27]

Infringement under the *doctrine of equivalents* does not require this same one-to-one correspondence. Rather, infringement under the doctrine of equivalents may exist where an accused device or process includes every claim limitation *or its equivalent*.[28] Under this doctrine, a claim limitation may be met by an element of an accused device or process that is insubstantially different from the claim's literal limitation. When applied, "[t]he scope of a patent is not limited to its literal terms but instead embraces all equivalents to the claims described."[29]

The U.S. Supreme Court has explained the underlying justification for the doctrine of equivalents as a way to preserve incentives to disclose an invention without concern that others will copy the invention by making an insubstantial change:

> The language in the patent claims may not capture every nuance of the invention or describe with complete precision the range of its novelty. If patents were always interpreted by their literal terms, their value would be greatly diminished. Unimportant and insubstantial substitutes for certain elements could defeat the patent, and its value to inventors could be destroyed by simple acts of copying.[30]

As an example of the application of these principles, a claim to an ice cream server with a round scoop is not literally infringed by a server with an oval-shaped scoop. However, the accused server may infringe under the doctrine of equivalents if the finder of fact finds that an oval-shaped scoop represents an insubstantial difference from the claimed round scoop.

§ 26.04 CONCLUSION

The Patent Act provides that the patent right is the right to exclude others from making, using, selling, offering to sell within the U.S., or importing into the U.S., that which falls within the scope of a claim either literally or under the doctrine of equivalents. In addition, the Patent Act includes certain provisional remedies for those who knowingly engage in patent infringement of claims in a published patent application that are issued in substantially similar form. One may infringe a patent claim directly by practicing the claim, or indirectly by actively inducing or contributing to the infringement of another.

---

[26] Graver Tank & Mfg. Co. v. Linde Air Prods. Co., 339 U.S. 605, 607 (1950).

[27] *Bayer AG*, 212 F.3d at 1247.

[28] *See e.g., Warner-Jenkinson Co. v. Hilton Davis Chem. Co., 520 U.S. 17, 18-19 (1997)*.

[29] Festo Corp. v. Shoketsu Kinzoku Kogyo Kabushiki Co., 535 U.S. 722, 731 (2002).

[30] *Id.*

Chapter 27

DIRECT INFRINGEMENT

SYNOPSIS

§ 27.01   INTRODUCTION

§ 27.02   TYPES OF CLAIMS AND DIRECT INFRINGEMENT

    [A]   Product, Device and Apparatus Claims

    [B]   Process and Method Claims

§ 27.03   ACTS THAT CONSTITUTE INFRINGEMENT UNDER § 271(a)

    [A]   "Makes"

    [B]   "Uses"

    [C]   "Offers to Sell"

    [D]   "Sells"

    [E]   "Imports into the U.S."

§ 27.04   MULTIPLE INFRINGERS: DIVIDED INFRINGEMENT

§ 27.05   CONCLUSION

§ 27.01   INTRODUCTION

A utility patent grants the patentee the right to exclude others from practicing the invention in the U.S. during the patent term.[1] A violation of that right by another who acts without authorization is *direct infringement*.

The Patent Act's section § 271(a) defines the predicate acts of a direct infringer as one who ". . . without authority makes, uses, offers to sell, or sells any patented invention, within the United States, or imports into the United States any patented invention during the term of the patent therefor, infringes the patent."[2] Each is a stand-alone basis for infringement. Therefore, one who "sells" a patented invention infringes even if that same person does not "make" or "use" the patented invention.

Where an operative act is established, the direct infringement analysis turns to whether the act has been undertaken with respect to the patentee's invention. Answering this question involves two steps. First, the asserted claim must be

---

[1]   35 U.S.C. § 154.

[2]   35 U.S.C. § 271(a). See Paper Converting Mach. Co. v. Magna-Graphics Corp., 745 F.2d 11, 16 (Fed. Cir. 1984) ("[B]y the terms of the patent grant, no activity other than the unauthorized making, using, or selling of the claimed invention can constitute direct infringement of a patent, no matter how great the adverse impact of that activity on the economic value of a patent.").

construed by the court[3] under the *Markman* decision.[4] Second, a finder of fact compares the claim with the accused product, to determine whether all of the limitations of the claim are present either literally or under the doctrine of equivalents.[5] The patentee bears this burden by a preponderance of the evidence. It is critical to understand that direct infringement of the "patented invention" must include each and every claim limitation.[6]

Section 271(a) specifies that infringement occurs by conduct undertaken "without authority" of the patentee. A license or permission to use the patent is a complete defense to a claim for patent infringement. The accused infringer bears the burden of demonstrating that either an express or implied license precludes a finding of infringement.[7] Moreover, § 271(a) specifies that an infringer's acts must take place either "within the United States" or must constitute an importation "into the United States."[8]

§ 27.02   TYPES OF CLAIMS AND DIRECT INFRINGEMENT

The central focus of an infringement analysis is the patent claim. Although *patent* infringement is a frequently used term, in fact, an infringement analysis focuses on a particular *claim* and not the patent as a whole. Stated another way, infringement of a single claim is sufficient to demonstrate the right to relief. The infringer's state of mind is not relevant, as there is no intent element to a claim for direct infringement.[9] Likewise, a defendant's awareness of the patent is not relevant, although such knowledge may increase the measure of damages if the patentee demonstrates that the defendant has willfully infringed.

[A]   Product, Device and Apparatus Claims

A claim directed to a product, device or apparatus protects a device's structure as described in the claim.[10] Infringement of these claims depends on whether the accused device incorporates the claim's structural limitations.[11] An example of an apparatus claim for a chair follows:

An apparatus for sitting, comprising:

---

[3] Cybor Corp. v. FAS Techs., Inc., 138 F.3d 1448, 1454 (Fed. Cir. 1998).

[4] For more on claim construction, see *supra*, Chapters 24 through 27.

[5] Cross Medical Products, Inc. v. Medtronic Sofamor Danek, Inc., 424 F.3d 1293, 1310 (Fed. Cir. 2005).

[6] Warner-Jenkinson Co., Inc. v. Hilton Davis Chemical Co., 520 U.S. 17, 29 (1997) ("[e]ach element contained in a patent claim is deemed material to defining the scope of the patented invention").

[7] *See generally* Air Prods. and Chems., Inc. v. Reichhold Chems., Inc., 755 F.2d 1559, 1563-64 (Fed. Cir. 1985).

[8] Extraterritorial conduct is examined in Chapter 35.

[9] Intel Corp. v. U.S. Int'l Trade Comm'n, 946 F.2d 821, 832 (Fed. Cir. 1991).

[10] *See generally* Cross Medical Products, Inc. v. Medtronic Sofamor Danek, Inc., 424 F.3d 1293, 1311-12 (Fed. Cir. 2005) ("To infringe an apparatus claim, the device must meet all of the structural limitations.").

[11] *See* Hewlett-Packard Co. v. Bausch & Lomb, Inc., 909 F.2d 1464, 1468 (Fed. Cir. 1990) ("[A]pparatus claims cover what a device is, not what a device does.").

a substantially flat horizontal surface;

a vertical back portion attached to the top of said horizontal surface using two-penny nails;

at least three elongated support members connected to the bottom of said horizontal portion using two-penny nails.

Here, this claimed combination essentially includes the seat portion, a back support and at least three legs. If the accused thing has all three features in the same relational position described in the claim, direct infringement will be found. Because of the open-ended transition word "comprising," additional features on accused chair (for example, arm rests) will not bring the accused device outside the claim scope.

However, the omission of a single claim element means that the accused product or device does not infringe.[12] For example, if the accused product is a stool that lacks any back rest, a claim element is missing and there is no direct infringement. A device need not be in optimal working order for infringement to be found. As the Federal Circuit has advised, "imperfect practice of an invention does not avoid infringement," so long as all of the claim elements are present.[13] Thus, if the accused chair is assembled with all elements attached in the manner described in the claim, the chair is infringing even though the chair may be a bit wobbly.

Some devices can be configured in a number of different ways. For these products, infringement may be found if the device is reasonably capable of satisfying the claim limitations in some configurations, even though the product is also capable of non-infringing arrangements.[14] To some degree, whether infringement exists for multi-configuration products depends on the claim language. As one example, in *Intel Corporation v. U.S. International Trade Commission*,[15] the court considered a configurable computer semiconductor device. The claim limitation at issue required a "programmable selection means." The court found that the accused chip could be converted to perform the selection means. The accused infringer argued that no customer had been told how to accomplish the conversion, or even that the conversion was possible.[16] The *Intel* court rejected that these circumstances could avoid a finding of infringing, stating, "[b]ecause the language of claim 1 refers to 'programmable selection means' the accused device, to be infringing, need only be capable of operating" in the mode described in the patent claim.[17] Based on the claim language, the device's capability brought the accused element within the language of the claim.

---

[12] Paper Converting Mach. Co. v. Magna-Graphics Corp., 745 F.2d 11 (Fed. Cir. 1984).

[13] *Id.* at 20.

[14] Hilgraeve Corp. v. Symantec Corp., 265 F.3d 1336, 1343 (Fed. Cir. 2001).

[15] Intel Corp. v. U.S. Int'l Trade Comm'n, 946 F.2d 821 (Fed. Cir. 1991).

[16] *Id.* at 832.

[17] *Id.; see also* Fantasy Sports Props., Inc. v. Sportsline.com, Inc., 287 F.3d 1108, 1119 (Fed. Cir. 2002) (finding that software met a limitation "[a] computer for playing football," because "no reasonable juror could find that the [accused] product is not software installed on a 'computer for playing football' that may directly infringe the patent").

In contrast to the *Intel* decision, the Federal Circuit came to the opposite conclusion in *High Tech Medical Instrumentation v. New Image Industries, Inc.*[18] There, the patent described a small video camera within a thin, tube-shaped device designed to be placed inside a dental patient's mouth. The asserted claim required that the camera be "rotably coupled" within the tube housing — that is, according to the claim, the camera could rotate within the camera housing tube. The *High Tech* court reviewed a preliminary injunction that had been granted for a camera that was fixed within its housing by two set screws that prohibited the camera from rotating.

The *High Tech* court found that the patentee had not demonstrated a likelihood of success for infringement based on the claim's "rotably coupled" limitation. The appellate court based this decision of the fact that the camera did not rotate unless the set screws were loosened. *High Tech* distinguished the *Intel* case based on the differences in the claim language — that is, *High Tech* drew a distinction between the term "rotably coupled" as requiring a *current and specific* configuration and the term "programmable" at issue in *Intel*, which encompassed capabilities beyond product's present configuration. Further, the *High Tech* court rejected the patentee's argument that a device infringed merely because it could be altered to operate in an infringing manner. According to the *High Tech* court, the relevant question for multi-configuration products is whether the device actually operates in the manner stated in the asserted claim. The court noted that the accused device was not designed or advertised to rotate, was not anticipated to rotate, and was not operated by users in that manner, and therefore did not likely infringe.

Whether a configurable device infringes depends on whether the words of the asserted claim encompass reasonable product alternations. *Intel* shows that a claim term phrased as a capability (there, the term "programmable") may be infringed by modifiable product where the claimed capability reasonably exists in the accused product. However, *High Tech* shows that an accused product will not infringe if the apparatus must be altered or assembled in a manner that is unusual for the product's design and use, particularly where the claim language is directed to a fixed, present configuration.

[B] Process and Method Claims

Process and method claims (for simplicity, "process claims" hereinafter) consists of one or more acts or steps.[19] Process claims consist of "of doing something, and therefore has to be carried out or performed."[20] For example, consider the following variation on the chair claim:

> A process for making a chair, comprising:
>
> sanding wood into a substantially flat horizontal surface;
>
> attaching a vertical back portion to the top of said horizontal wood surface with two-penny nails;

---

[18] *High Tech Medical Instrumentation v. New Image Industries, Inc.*, 49 F.3d 1551 (Fed. Cir. 1995).

[19] *In re* Kollar, 286 F.3d 1326, 1332 (Fed. Cir. 2002).

[20] *Id.*

attaching at least three elongated support members to the bottom of said horizontal portion with two-penny nails.

Note that each sub-part of the claim describes an act or step — here, "sanding" and "attaching." Process claims are directly infringed where one performs each and every one of the steps recited in the claim.[21] One who performs less than all of the claimed steps is not a direct infringer.[22] For example, one who creates a stool by omitting the second step of attaching a vertical back portion to the seat does not infringe the claim. Additionally, the claim must be practiced as specifically described. One does not literally infringe this example claim where one makes a chair using glue to attach the component parts rather than the two-penny nails as specified in the claim.

Process claims require that the infringer *perform* the acts specified in the claim. Therefore, one does not infringe this claim by *using* a chair that has been made under the claimed process, because such use does not practice each step set forth in the claim.

Further, a patentee must prove direct infringement of a process claim by showing that the defendant itself engaged in the acts described in the claim. For example, in *Warner-Lambert Co. v. Apotex Corp.*,[23] the court considered whether a pharmaceutical manufacturer directly infringed a method claim for treating certain diseases by administering particular compounds. The *Warner-Lambert* court held that no direct infringement had been shown as the pharmaceutical maker did not actually perform the steps of treating any patient.[24] Because the defendant manufacturer had never, and likely would never, itself actually practice the claimed method, the Federal Circuit ruled that summary judgment on the patentee's direct infringement claim was proper.

Where a process or method claim includes multiple steps, one question that arises is whether the limitations must be performed in the same order as those steps appear in the claim. Using our chair claim as an example, the steps are listed in the following order: First, sanding the wood to form a seat; second, attaching a back support to the top of the seat; and third, attaching the legs to the bottom of the seat.

One consideration is whether one who attaches the supporting legs *before* attaching the back support avoids infringement. As a general rule, the answer to this question is "no." However, that result may be different where the claim is drafted in a manner which demonstrates the order of the steps acts as a limitation. In *Altiris, Inc. v. Symantec Corp.*,[25] the court first examined "the claim language to determine if, as a matter of logic or grammar, they must be performed in the order

---

[21] *See e.g.*, NTP, Inc. v. Research In Motion, Ltd., 418 F.3d 1282, 1318 (Fed. Cir. 2005); Joy Technologies, Inc. v. Flakt, Inc., 6 F.3d 770, 775 (Fed. Cir. 1993).

[22] *Id.* at 1321.

[23] Warner-Lambert Co. v. Apotex Corp., 316 F.3d 1348 (Fed. Cir. 2003).

[24] *Id.* at 1363 n.7. *Warner-Lambert* noted that this finding "is hardly surprising-pharmaceutical companies do not generally treat diseases; rather, they sell drugs to wholesalers or pharmacists, who in turn sell the drugs to patients possessing prescriptions from physicians." *Id.*

[25] Altiris, Inc. v. Symantec Corp., 318 F.3d 1363 (Fed. Cir. 2003).

written."[26] Here, the court examines whether the claim uses any language, such as using the terms "first" and "second," that demonstrates that order is a requirement of the invention. Further, the order of performance may be implicitly stated, for example where a later step indicates that an earlier step has already been completed.[27] Second, if the answer cannot be derived from the claim language, the court next examines the specification and prosecution history.[28] Unless this exception applies, the order in which the steps appear in a method claim do not act as a requirement to finding infringement.

§ 27.03 ACTS THAT CONSTITUTE INFRINGEMENT UNDER § 271(a)

Section 271 states that "whoever without authority makes, uses, offers to sell, or sells any patented invention, within the United States, or imports into the United States any patented invention" during the patent's term is an infringer. There are a few notable aspects to this definition. First, one who engages in *any* of the infringing acts during the term of the patent infringes. Second, these acts must occur "within the United States," except for importation which must be "into the United States."[29]

[A] "Makes"

To *make* a device means to fabricate, assemble, combine or otherwise create a thing that includes each element of an identified claim.[30] Under § 271(a), a defendant who makes such a device directly infringes the claim, even if the device is never used, sold or offered for sale. Designing an infringing device or even partial construction is not sufficient, rather the infringing device must be actually made such that all elements of the claim are present.[31]

A defendant who is not responsible for making an entire device that encompasses all elements of the claim does not infringe.[32] For example, in *Cross Medical Products, Inc. v. Medtronic Sofamor Danek, Inc.*,[33] the court considered

---

[26] *Id.* at 1369-70.

[27] *Id.* at 1370 (*citing* Loral Fairchild Corp. v. Sony Elecs. Corp., 181 F.3d 1313, 1321 (Fed. Cir. 1999)).

[28] *Altiris*, 318 F.3d at 1370-71 (noting the absence of "any statement that this order is important, any disclaimer of any other order of steps, or any prosecution history indicating a surrender of any other order of steps" and finding that the written order of steps was not required for a finding of infringement).

[29] Because the territorial aspects of this provision are arising with more frequency in recent years, a more detailed discussion of cross-border activity has been included in Chapter 35.

[30] *See generally* Bauer & Cie v. O'Donnell, 229 U.S. 1, 10 (1913) ("The right to make can scarcely be made plainer by definition, and embraces the construction of the thing invented").

[31] *See generally* Laitram Corp. v. Cambridge Wire Cloth Co., 919 F.2d 1579, 1582 (Fed. Cir. 1990) *superseded by statute on other grounds by* 35 U.S.C. § 271(a) (2000) (product that had been designed by not made could not be the basis of an infringement action prior to statutory amendment authorizing infringement action based on offers for sale).

[32] An emerging theory of joint infringement may prove to become an exception to this rule. A discussion of this theory is later in this Chapter.

[33] Cross Medical Products, Inc. v. Medtronic Sofamor Danek, Inc., 424 F.3d 1293 (Fed. Cir. 2005).

allegations of direct infringement against a medical device maker. There, the invention concerned a surgical implant used to stabilize and align the bones of a patient's spine. The asserted claim included a limitation requiring an interface that was "operatively joined" to the patient's bone. The Federal Circuit found that the medical device manufacturer did not directly infringe the claim because surgeons — and not the device maker — "operatively joined" the interface to the spinal bone and therefore the device manufacturer did not "make" a device that met this limitation of the claim.[34]

Typically, § 271(a)'s "makes" provision may be incapable of supporting a finding of direct infringement for a method claim. Certainly, making an apparatus that performs a claimed process is distinct from actually undertaking to perform the claimed process steps oneself.[35] Although the courts have not entirely foreclosed the possibility, there is an admitted conceptual difficulty attempting to demonstrate that one can "make" the performance of an act or step.

[B] "Uses"

Section 271(a)'s term *uses* is given a broad interpretation that encompasses any conduct that puts the invention into action or service.[36] For example, establishing a use of a claimed apparatus requires the infringer to have operated the all of the claim elements in the infringing item. Operations of only a portion of the claimed components results in a finding of no infringement.[37]

Notably, direct infringement of a claim to an entire system warrants separate attention. This issue arises for patents directed to network-based inventions. In one decision, *Centillion Data Systems LLC v. Qwest Communications*, the court analyzed an invention claiming a system for collecting, processing, and delivering information from a service provider (such as a telephone company) to customers by computer.[38] The accused system included a "back-end," which was maintained by the telephone company and was responsible for processing and transferring billing data. In addition, the system included a "front-end," which is software downloaded on the customer's computer when the customer subscribed to the service. The front-end allowed the customer to download the data, as well as to request additional data on an on-demand basis. The district court found no infringement because no single party engaged in the "use" all of the elements of the claimed system within the meaning of § 271(a).

On appeal, the Federal Circuit reversed, finding that the statute did not require practice of every element by a single person. Distinguishing method claims, the court determined that infringement of a system claim occurs where any party has

---

[34] *Id.* at 1310.

[35] 35 U.S.C. § 271(a) (2000). *See generally* Harris Corp. v. Ericsson Inc., 417 F.3d 1241, 1256 (Fed. Cir. 2005) (noting that a claim to a method "of using a communication system," can "be directly infringed only by one who uses the system, not by one who makes or sells the components of the system.").

[36] NTP, Inc. v. Research In Motion, Ltd., 418 F.3d 1282, 1316-17 (Fed. Cir. 2005).

[37] Waymark Corp. v. Porta Systems Corp., 245 F.3d 1364, 1366-67 (Fed. Cir. 2001).

[38] Centillion Data Systems, LLC v. Qwest Communications International, Inc., 631 F.3d 1279 (Fed. Cir. 2011).

"put the invention into service, i.e., control the system as a whole and obtain benefit from it."[39] In this case, the court determined that the customers used the system by subscribing to the service to receiving billing data, or by generating on-demand requests. As the court explained, "it is the customer initiated demand for the service which causes the back-end system to generate the requisite reports. This is 'use' because, but for the customer's actions, the entire system would never have been put into service."[40]

To demonstrate direct infringement based on the "use" of a method claim, a patentee must show that the defendant actually carried out each and every step of the claim.[41] Indeed, the primary means of proving direct infringement of a process or method claim is through § 271(a)'s "use" provision.

[C] "Offers to Sell"

The *offers to sell* portion of § 271(a) was added to the Patent Act in 1994, in response to the U.S. adoption of the GATT Uruguay Round Trade Related Aspects of Intellectual Property ("TRIPS") agreement.[42] Prior to adoption into law, § 271(a) only prohibited "making, using or selling" a patented invention. One purpose of this addition is to prohibit others from "generating interest in a potential infringing product to the commercial detriment of the rightful patentee."[43]

Section 271(i) defines an "offer to sell" as an offer "in which the sale will occur before the expiration of the term of the patent." The courts have indicated that whether particular conduct constitutes an "offer to sell" is governed by traditional contract law principles.[44] Generally, this requires a defendant to communicate "a manifestation of willingness to enter into a bargain, so made as to justify another person in understanding that his assent to that bargain is invited and will conclude it."[45] The Federal Circuit has indicated that this standard may be met where letters describing the allegedly infringing merchandise, along with a price at which the products could be purchased.[46] Further, to meet the "offer for sale"

---

[39] *Id.* at 1284 (citing NTP Inc. v. Research in Motion, Ltd., 418 F.3d 1282, 1317 (Fed. Cir. 2005).

[40] *Id.* at 1285.

[41] *Harris Corp.*, 417 F.3d at 1256 (to demonstrate direct infringement of a method claim directed to a cellular telephone system, the patentee failed to demonstrate patent infringement where the manufacturer may have simulated, rather than actually carried out, each limitation of the claim); see also Rotec Industries, Inc. v. Mitsubishi Corp., 215 F.3d 1246 (Fed. Cir. 2000) (describing the history of the statutory amendment).

[42] As a result of the U.S. negotiations on the TRIPS agreements, § 271(a) was amended effective January 1, 1996. For more information about the implications of the TRIPS Agreement to U.S. patent law, *see infra*, Chapter 42.

[43] 3D Sys., Inc. v. Aarotech Labs., Inc., 160 F.3d 1373, 1379 (Fed. Cir. 1998).

[44] Fieldturf Int'l, Inc. v. Sprinturf, Inc., 433 F.3d 1366, 1369-70 (Fed. Cir. 2006).

[45] MEMC Elec. Materials, Inc. v. Mitsubishi Materials Silicon Corp., 420 F.3d 1369, 1376 (Fed. Cir. 2005); *quoting* Restatement (Second) of Contracts, § 24 (1979)).

[46] *3D Sys.*, 160 F.3d at 1377 (determining issue on appeal from an order dismissing the defendants for lack of personal jurisdiction).

requirement, the offer must be concern a product or process that meets all limitations of the patent claim.[47]

[D] "Sells"

Selling an infringing device is a stand-alone act of infringement. Section 271(a) prohibits the sale of an infringing product to "secure[s] to the inventor the exclusive right to transfer the title for a consideration to others."[48] For example, retailers may be sued for patent infringement even though the retailer has no notice of the asserted patent and did not make the device.[49]

A "sale" can be established through evidence of a binding contract where the clear object of the contract is the accused implementation.[50] For example, in *Transocean Offshore Deepwater Drilling, Inc. v. Maersk Contractors U.S.A, Inc.,* the Federal Circuit held that a signed contract between two parties and an accompanying schematic of the accused device was sufficient to show a sale of the patentable invention.[51] There, the *Transocean* court came to this conclusion even though the device was not yet constructed or ready for use. Notably, the rig that was ultimately built was modified from the original design. Underscoring the principle that the infringing *sale* constitutes the infringing act, the *Transocean* court found that "[t]he potentially infringing article is the rig sold in the contract, not the altered rig that [was] delivered."[52]

Regarding sales for method claims, the Federal Circuit has held that selling a product that performs a claimed method is not direct infringement of a method claim within the meaning of § 271(a).[53] Thus, selling a product that is made by a process that is the subject of a patent claim is *not* a "sale" for purposes of § 271(a).[54] For example, a pharmacy that sells a pharmaceutical made by a patented process does not infringe § 271(a). However, the pharmaceutical manufacturer who performed the infringing process to make the product may be found to have infringed under the "use" provision of the statute.[55]

---

[47] *Id.* (proposal for sale of product that failed to meet claim limitations was not an 'offer for sale' that constitutes infringement under § 271(a).).

[48] Bauer & Cie v. O'Donnell, 229 U.S. 1, 11 (1913).

[49] *See e.g.*, Golight, Inc. v. Wal-Mart Stores, Inc., 355 F.3d 1327 (Fed. Cir. 2004) (suit for patent infringement against retail seller of infringing goods).

[50] Transocean Offshore Deepwater Drilling, Inc. v. Maersk Contractors USA, Inc., 617 F.3d 1296 (Fed. Cir. 2010).

[51] *Id.* at 1311.

[52] *Id.*

[53] Moba, B.V. v. Diamond Automation, Inc., 325 F.3d 1306, 1313 (Fed. Cir. 2003).

[54] U.S. v. Studiengesellschaft Kohle, m.b.H., 670 F.2d 1122, 1128 (Fed. Cir. 1981).

[55] Nonetheless, the pharmacy may be liable under § 271(g), which prohibits the sale of products made using infringing process. *See* 35 U.S.C. § 271(g) (providing that "[w]hoever without authority imports into the United States or offers to sell, sells, or uses within the United States a product which is made by a process patented in the United States shall be liable as an infringer . . . ."); *see also infra*, Chapter 35.

[E]   "Imports into the U.S."

To be liable for an *importation* under § 271(a), one must bring an infringing product into the U.S. Once imported, the patentee must demonstrate that the product as configured while present in the United States is within the scope of the patent claim.[56] One imports by providing the infringing items to the U.S., even where one is physically located outside the U.S. when doing so.[57]

As a comparatively new provision in the Patent Act, there is little authoritative case law on this provision.[58] Some district court opinions suggest that one who imports a product that will not be used in an infringing manner has a valid defense to liability.[59] However, a contrary district court opinion rejected this approach and restricted the infringement inquiry to the act of importation. The court found examination of any subsequent uses of the accused article within the U.S. irrelevant. As this court explained, "to directly infringe under § 271(a), an importation of an infringing product need not include, nor be followed by, a sale, offer to sell, or any other particular course of action; the infringing activity is the unauthorized importation of an infringing product itself."[60] As of this printing, this issue has not yet been presented to the higher courts for resolution.

§ 27.04   MULTIPLE INFRINGERS: DIVIDED INFRINGEMENT

An infringement analysis can be complicated where two or more unaffiliated parties are accused of practicing separate limitations of a single method claim. Under these circumstances, the traditional test for direct infringement fails because neither actor practices each and every limitation of the claim. Indirect infringement may be difficult to prove in these circumstances for at least two reasons. First, no single party may be directly infringing the claim and, in that circumstance, the necessary predicate for indirect liability is lacking. Second, if both parties are acting independently neither may be actively inducing or contributing to the other's infringement.[61] To demonstrate a right to relief in such cases, the patentee must demonstrate a theory of *divided infringement*, which is sometimes called *joint infringement*. Over the past several years, the standards for doing so have been in

---

[56] Biotec Biologische Naturverpackungen GmbH & Co. KG v. Biocorp, Inc., 249 F.3d 1341, 1350 (Fed. Cir. 2001) ("Infringement of product claims by an imported product requires that the product be viewed in the form in which it is present within the United States").

[57] Nuance Communications Inc. v. Abbyy Software House, 626 F.3d 1222, 1233 (Fed. Cir. 2010).

[58] The "import" provision was added to this subsection as part of the U.S. agreement to TRIPS, and became effective January 1, 1996.

[59] *See* Medtronic Vascular, Inc. v. Boston Scientific Corp., 348 F. Supp. 2d 316 (D. Del. 2004) (shipping medical devices that are subject to an experimental use exemption from infringement is not infringement); Creo Products, Inc. v. Presstek, Inc., 166 F. Supp. 2d 944, 976 (D. Del. 2001) (importation without an intent to sell the product is not actionable; bringing products into the U.S. solely for use at a trade show was not sufficient to demonstrate direct infringement).

[60] Fellowes, Inc. v. Michilin Prosperity Co., Ltd., 491 F. Supp. 2d 571, 583 (E.D. Va. 2007).

[61] In addition, a claim for indirect infringement in the absence of a showing of direct infringement by at least one person or entity.

transition. As of this writing, the Federal Circuit is considering a case, *Akamai Technologies, Inc. v. Limelight Networks, Inc.*, in an en banc rehearing that is expected to clarify the requirements to demonstrate a right to relief in these circumstances.[62]

This situation arises for method claims. One case that considered a claim for divided infringement is *BMC Resources, Inc. v. Paymentech, L.P.*[63] There, the patent described a method for processing bank payments for a customer debit account via voice without the need for the customer to enter a personal identification number (PIN). The claims described steps that required interaction with a customer that were performed by the accused infringer Paymentech, as well as steps that related to the payment processing that were performed by independent financial institutions. Because Paymentech did not perform all steps of the method claims, it could not be held liable under the general rule that "[i]nfringement requires . . . a showing that a defendant has practiced each and every element of the claimed invention."[64] The court explained that the divided infringement theory of recovery exists to prevent a party from escaping liability where that party directs or controls others to participate in the infringement. In assessing the patentee's theory of divided infringement for the claims at issue, the court found that Paymentech could not be liable. Here, the facts demonstrated that the financial institutions operated independently of Paymentech, and that therefore direction and control were lacking.

In the case that will be decided by the Federal Circuit en banc, *Akamai Technologies, Inc. v. Limelight Networks, Inc.*, the patent described a system that allowed webpage creators to store objects (such as an image or sound) on an outsourced server.[65] These objects were replicated, updated and then combined with the user's webpage when the viewer went to the content creator's webpage. Essentially, the system was designed to minimize the expense and maximize the performance for websites that experienced periods of very heavy traffic by "flash crowds" of viewers.

The *Akamai* patent's method claims included several steps performed by the accused infringer Limelight. In addition, the claims included steps that required the "tagging" of an embedded object, and "serving" the content for delivery to viewers. Webpage creators performed the tagging and serving steps; Limelight did not. However, it was undisputed that Limelight instructed webpage creators how to tag objects and use the service. In addition, Limelight provided step-by-step instructions, offered technical assistance and contractually obligated users to perform the tagging step if they wished to use Limelight's outsourced servers.

---

[62] Akamai Technologies, Inc. & MIT v. Limelight Networks, Inc., 419 Fed. Appx. 989 (Fed. Cir. 2011). In the order, the court requested that the parties brief the following issue: "If separate entities each perform separate steps of a method claim, under what circumstances would that claim be directly infringed and to what extent would each of the parties be liable?"

[63] BMC Resources, Inc. v. Paymentech, L.P., 498 F.3d 1373 (Fed. Cir. 2007).

[64] *Id.* at 1380.

[65] Akamai Technologies, Inc. v. Limelight Networks, Inc., 629 F.3d 1311 (Fed. Cir. 2010).

The *Akamai* panel held that a claim for divided infringement could not succeed. The panel reiterated the rule that a claim for divided infringement can be established against one who controls or directs another to practice one or more steps of a claim. Regarding the facts of this case, the panel held that Limelight's instructions to, contracts with, and assistance for its customers did not suffice to meet this standard. The court held that liability for divided infringement could be established only where "there is an agency relationship between the parties who perform the method steps or when one party is contractually obligated to the other to perform the steps."[66] *Akamai* noted that an arms-length transaction would rarely be sufficient to meet the divided infringement standard. The panel found that the webpage creators were not performing the tagging step as agents for Limelight, and therefore the customer's conduct was not properly attributable to Limelight. Further, the court determined that Limelight's customers were not contractually obligated to performing the tagging and serving steps on behalf of Limelight. Rather, the website creators could choose to do so if they wished to take advantage of Limelight's servers.

In April 2011, the Federal Circuit granted en banc rehearing of the *Akamai* case. As of this writing, oral argument has been conducted. Once issued, the final decision is expected to clarify the appropriate standard for divided infringement.

To maximize the potential for an enforceable claim, those who draft patents must consider whether the elements of such claims are likely to be practiced by a single person. As the courts have observed, some of the issues can be avoided by rephrasing the claim in a manner that allows practice by a single entity.[67]

§ 27.05   CONCLUSION

In order to demonstrate direct infringement under § 271(a), a patentee must demonstrate by a preponderance of the evidence that the defendant has made, used, offered for sale or sold within the U.S., or imported into the U.S., a patented invention. The patentee must further demonstrate that the defendant's actions occurred during the patent's effective term. Each of the enumerated actions (making, using, offering for sale, selling or importing into the U.S.) constitute stand-alone grounds for demonstrating liability. Unless the defendant engaged in at least one of the enumerated actions, no direct infringement under § 271(a) can be found.

The courts have left open the possibility that one may be liable under a theory of divided infringement under certain circumstances. The contours of the doctrine will likely be determined by the upcoming *Akami* decision.

---

[66] *Id.* at 1320.

[67] BMC Resources, Inc. v. Paymentech, L.P., 498 F.3d 1373, 1381 (Fed. Cir. 2007), citing Mark A. Lemley et al., *Divided Infringement Claims*, 33 AIPLA Q. J. 255 (2005).

Chapter 28

PRIOR USE RIGHTS

SYNOPSIS

§ 28.01 INTRODUCTION
§ 28.02 IMPLEMENTING THE PRIOR USE RIGHTS UNDER THE AIA
    [A] Prior Law
    [B] Prior use Rights Under the AIA
        [1] Subject Matter Scope
        [2] Who is a Prior User?
        [3] Effect of the Defense
        [4] The University Exclusion
§ 28.03 CONCLUSION

§ 28.01 INTRODUCTION

Instances of multiple, near-simultaneous discovery have long been observed in the sciences.[1] As Justice Frankfurter stated, "the history of thought records striking coincidental discoveries — showing that the new insight first declared to the world by a particular individual was 'in the air' and ripe for discovery and disclosure."[2] Although some multiple, near-simultaneous discoveries may manifest in interference proceedings or priority contests, some exist without any formal record. As one example, one entity might practice a novel, nonobvious manufacturing process and hold the information as a trade secret rather than to pursue patent protection. Because this practice is secret, a competitor might independently develop the same practice unaware that anyone else has been using the same method. Ultimately, every company must, as a matter of individual judgment, decide which inventions warrant the cost and potential value of patent protection. For any particular invention, it would not be unusual for one company to pursue patent protection, while another would not.

Certainly, a patentee can establish a prima facie case of infringement against one who practices the patentee's claimed invention even if the invention was independently created by the infringer. What happens if the defendant has been practicing the patent long before the patentee? Under former law, the defendant's best option

---

[1] Amy L. Landers, *Ordinary Creativity: The Artist Inside the Scientist*, 75 MISSOURI L. REV. 1, 63 (2010) (citing sources).

[2] Marconi Wireless Telegraph Co. of America v. United States, 320 U.S. 1 (1943) (Frankfurther, J. dissenting).

was to establish that the claim was invalid for lack of novelty, statutory bar, or obviousness. In many cases the defendant might do so for private uses, because section 102(g) and section 103 allow secret prior art to invalidate a claim.

The answer might have been far more difficult under the new first to file system of the America Invents Act. The former section 102(g) has been eliminated. The revised section 102 authorizes the use of prior art that has been made "available to the public" to invalidate a claim. Depending on future judicial interpretations of this provision, private uses might be unavailable to establish invalidity. If so, under the first to file system the entity that chooses to file a patent application can enforce it against an independent prior creator, even if the other actually invented first. In these circumstances, those who choose trade secret protection over patenting are at a decided disadvantage. As a U.S. PTO report explained, "[w]ithout a prior use defense, the risk of going down the trade secret path is that a competitor who independently arrives at the same invention may obtain a patent and sue for infringement even though the prior user invented the enhancements and has been using it commercially for a long time."[3]

The prior use right resolves this issue to a significant degree. The defense shields one who independently developed the invention and has been using it commercially before another's patent filing. Unlike the "all or nothing" approach of the former first to invent system, the prior use right allows the first developer to benefit from the earlier investment, yet still upholds the validity of the patent so that it can be enforced against others who subsequently infringe.[4]

§ 28.02   IMPLEMENTING THE PRIOR USE RIGHTS UNDER THE AIA

[A]   Prior Law

The AIA's prior use right is not the first time that such a right has been enacted in U.S. patent law. In 1999, Congress created a limited prior use right that applied solely to business method patents.[5] This was just one year after the Federal Circuit held business methods as patentable subject matter in *State Street Bank & Trust Co. v. Signature Financial Group, Inc.*[6] This defense, enacted into the Patent Act's section 273, provided a personal defense to a claim of patent infringement to a person who, acting in good faith, "actually reduced the subject matter to practice at least 1 year before the effective filing date of such patent, and commercially used the subject matter before the effective filing date of such

---

[3] United States Patent and Trademark Office, Report to Congress: Report on the Prior User Defense, 7 (2012) (hereinafter "U.S. PTO Prior User Report").

[4] Gary L. Griswold & F. Andrew Ubel, *Prior User Rights — A Necessary Part of a First-to-File System*, 26 John Marshall L. Rev. 567, 573 (1993).

[5] 35 U.S.C. § 273 (2001).

[6] American Inventors Protection Act of 1999, 106 Cong. 1st Sess., H.R. Rep. No. 106- 287, 45 (1999); State Street Bank & Trust Co. v. Signature Financial Group, Inc., 149 F.3d 1368 (Fed. Cir. 1998).

patent."[7] The statute expressly limited its applicability to "a method of doing or conducting business."[8]

The relevant House Report stated that the defense was needed to prevent prejudice to users of business methods who might be sued by those filing new patent applications just after *State Street Bank* was decided:

> Thousands of "back office" processes are now being patented. In the past, many businesses that developed and used such processes thought secrecy was the only protection available. Under established law, these pre-existing processes do not now qualify for patent protection because they have been in commercial use.

As this history explains, this defense allowed these prior users "to continue their bona fide commercial operations without interference from a subsequent inventor who obtains a patent claiming common subject matter as her invention."[9]

It appears that this defense was not widely used and therefore few judicial interpretations of the section can be found.[10] Therefore, the AIA's prior use right currently has little, if any, judicial interpretative guidance that can be drawn from the prior provision.

[B] Prior use Rights Under the AIA

In 2011, the AIA was enacted with a prior use right applicable to all patents. By adopting this right, the U.S. implemented a practice that is widespread in nations that have long-established first to file patent systems.[11] Unlike the earlier prior user right for business method patents, the AIA provides that a prior use defense can be asserted against a claim of patent infringement if the prior user has commercially used the subject matter *at least one (1) year before* either 1) the effective filing date of the patent; or 2) the invention was disclosed to the public by the patent's inventor or joint inventor under the new section 102(b).

Subject to certain exclusions discussed herein, the prior use defense applies to patents issued on or after September 16, 2011, the AIA's first date of enactment. The accused infringer must demonstrate the defense by clear and convincing evidence.

[1] Subject Matter Scope

The AIA's new section 273 provides that the prior use defense is available to all classes of technology — specifically, "subject matter consisting of a process, or consisting of a machine, manufacture, or composition of matter used in a manufac-

---

[7] 35 U.S.C. § 273(b)(1).

[8] *Id.* at § 273(a)(3).

[9] *Id.* at 47.

[10] *See* PB Farradyne, Inc. v. Peterson, 2006 WL 132182 (N.D.Cal. 2006) (noting the lack of interpretative authority).

[11] Griswold and Ubel, *supra* note 4, at 573 (noting that many nations with first to file systems have adopted a first to file system).

turing or other commercial process."[12] This language roughly tracks section 101's "process, machine, manufacture, or composition of matter." It can be expected that the subject matter of the prior use defense will cover the full range of patentable subject matter.[13]

Mere possession of information is not sufficient. Rather, the prior user must reduce the invention to practice and *commercially use* the invention to qualify. Therefore, one who has independently developed, but never commercially implemented, the subject matter of the asserted claim will not be protected by the defense. Commercial use includes internal commercial uses, arm's length sales, and other commercial transfers. The statute includes two additional specific examples of commercial uses. First, a prior use includes premarket regulatory review for testing required by regulatory agencies, such as the U.S. Food and Drug Administration.[14] As a second example, the AIA provides that commercial use includes nonprofit uses in research laboratories, universities, and hospitals. Thus, "commercial use" appears to be broadly defined to preserve an entity's investment against a patentee who later files a patent application on the same subject matter.

The AIA provides that the prior commercial use must occur within the U.S.

[2]   Who is a Prior User?

The AIA's prior user is specified as a person, including entities engaged in prior commercial use, and is not restricted to prior inventors. The language is sufficiently broad to encompass one who performed the work, directed the work to be performed, and "an entity that controls, is controlled by, or is under common control with such person."[15] By extending protection in this manner, the act covers businesses, universities, and organizations that are the most likely targets of infringement allegations.

The proponent of the defense must have acted in good faith during the period of commercial use. Further, the defense is not available to anyone who derived the invention from the patentee, or from a person in privity with the patentee. If the commercial use is abandoned, the section prevents activity prior to the abandonment to establish the defense. Presumably, this exception would support the defense for abandoned activity if such activity is resumed more than one year prior to the patentee's effective filing date or disclosure.

The right is personal to the prior user, and cannot be transferred except to the patent owner or to a successor as part of the transfer of an entire business unit. In the later event, the prior use right is restricted to the same geographic site in use prior the patent's effective filing date or the date of transfer (whichever is later).

---

[12] 35 U.S.C. § 273(a).

[13] *See* U.S. PTO Prior User Report, *supra* note 3, at 1 ("the AIA . . . extends the prior user rights defense to patents covering all technologies").

[14] 35 U.S.C § 273(b)(1) states that "Subject matter for which commercial marketing or use is subject to a premarket regulatory review period during which the safety or efficacy of the subject matter is established." Although this section appears targeted toward regulatory review by the FDA, the language might be broad enough to encompass other types of products subject to premarket testing.

[15] 35 U.S.C.§ 273(e)(1).

[3] Effect of the Defense

When established, the prior commercial use defense bars liability. Furthermore, a patentee is not entitled to pursue relief against purchasers of the product made under a prior use right. Thus, the prior user's sale of a good that is subject to a prior commercial use exhausts the patentee's right with respect to that item.

Notably, the AIA provides that establishing the prior use defense does not necessarily result in a finding that a patent is invalid. Moreover, the statute provides that the prior use right is "not a general license under all claims of the patent," but rather is limited to the subject matter that has actually been practiced by the prior user.[16]

[4] The University Exclusion

The AIA bars the prior use defense against a patent that is owned, or subject to an obligation of assignment, to an institution of higher education, or an affiliated technology transfer organization that commercializes its technology.[17] This section benefits universities, which are thereby authorized to assert patents without confronting a prior use defense by businesses and, presumably, other universities.

§ 28.03 CONCLUSION

The prior use defense, codified at 35 U.S.C. § 273, is a new provision in U.S. law that includes many features common to foreign first to file systems. The defense permits one who practices an independently developed invention to continue its commercial use, if that use has been continuous from at least one year prior to either the patent application's effective filing date or the date of the inventor's disclosure. This section is intended to ensure that one who has invested in commercial uses is not prejudiced by a later-filed patent that claims the same subject matter.

---

[16] 35 U.S.C. § 273(e)(3).

[17] The AIA provides that the section does not apply to research for which Federal funding is not available.

Chapter 29

INFRINGEMENT UNDER THE DOCTRINE OF EQUIVALENTS

SYNOPSIS

§ 29.01   INTRODUCTION

§ 29.02   *WINANS v. DENMEAD*: THE HISTORIC FOUNDATIONS OF THE DOCTRINE OF EQUIVALENTS

§ 29.03   THE DEVELOPMENT OF THE CURRENT DOCTRINE OF EQUIVALENTS: *GRAVER TANK & MFG. CO. v. LINDE AIR PRODUCTS CO*

§ 29.04   THE U.S. SUPREME COURT'S REFINEMENT OF THE DOCTRINE OF EQUIVALENTS: *WARNER-JENKINSON CO. v. HILTON DAVIS CHEMICAL CO*

   [A]   Factual Background of the *Warner-Jenkinson* Opinion

   [B]   *Warner-Jenkinson's* Affirmation of the Doctrine of Equivalents

   [C]   *Warner-Jenskinson* and the Principle Prosecution History Estoppel

   [D]   The Doctrine of Equivalents and After-Arising Technology

§ 29.05   TESTS FOR INFRINGEMENT IN A POST-*WARNER-JENKINSON* ERA

§ 29.06   PUTTING THE DOCTRINE TOGETHER: AN EXAMPLE OF THE APPLICATION OF THE *WARNER-JENKINSON* STANDARD

§ 29.07   THE REVERSE DOCTRINE OF EQUIVALENTS

§ 29.08   CONCLUSION

§ 29.01   INTRODUCTION

The *doctrine of equivalents* extends a patentee's right to exclude beyond the patent claim's literal scope. When the doctrine is applied, a product or process will be found to infringe if there is an insubstantial difference ("equivalence") between an element of the accused product or process and the claim limitation under examination.[1]

As an example, assume that a claim to a chair states as follows:

An apparatus for sitting, comprising:

---

[1]   Warner-Jenkinson Co., Inc. v. Hilton Davis Chem. Co., 520 U.S. 17, 21 (1997).

a substantially flat horizontal surface;

a vertical back portion attached to the top of said horizontal surface *using two-penny nails*;

at least three elongated support members connected to the bottom of said horizontal portion *using two-penny nails.*

For literal infringement to exist, the claim requires that the back support and legs attach to the horizontal seat *"using two-penny nails."* If the accused device uses *four-penny nails* to attach the back and seat, a jury may find infringement under the doctrine of equivalents if the jury decides that four-penny nails used in the accused device represent an *equivalent* of the two-penny nail limitation set forth in the claim. This is so even though a literal element of the claim ("two-penny nails") is missing from the accused device.

Courts have articulated various reasons supporting the doctrine of equivalents. The U.S. Supreme Court has explained that the doctrine is needed because the textual expression in a patent claim may be inadequate to capture "every nuance of the invention or describe with complete precision the range of its novelty."[2] Under such circumstances, if courts adhered to the literal text of a claim, then "[u]nimportant and insubstantial substitutes for certain elements could defeat the patent, and its value to inventors could be destroyed by simple acts of copying."[3] The doctrine of equivalents has been described as preserving the incentive to patent, because allowing others to recreate the invention with only insubstantial variations "would foster concealment rather than disclosure of inventions, which is one of the primary purposes of the patent system."[4] Further, the doctrine of equivalents is said to preserve the patentee's right against infringement relying on technology developed in the future that represent "unanticipated equivalents"[5] that may be developed over a patent's effective life.

Despite these advantages, the doctrine of equivalents can conflict with the certainty and public notice goals of the patent system.[6] The Supreme Court has recognized that clear delineation of claim scope is "essential to promote progress, because it enables efficient investment in innovation."[7] Unambiguous claim boundaries provide parties with certainty for purposes of licensing or assigning patent rights. Certainty allows patentees an increased assurance of success when asserting their rights against others. Competitors seeking to enter a field can design around existing patents with some confidence. As the Supreme Court has stated, "[a] patent

---

[2] Festo Corp. v. Shoketsu Kinzoku Kogyo Kabushiki Co., Ltd., 535 U.S. 722, 731 (2002).

[3] *Id.*

[4] Graver Tank & Mfg. Co. v. Linde Air Prods. Co., 339 U.S. 605, 607 (1950).

[5] Kinzenbaw v. Deere & Co., 741 F.2d 383, 389 (Fed. Cir. 1984); *See also* Michael J. Meurer & Craig Allen Nard, *Invention, Refinement And Patent Claim Scope: A New Perspective On The Doctrine Of Equivalents*, 93 Geo. L.J. 1947 (2005).

[6] *Festo*, 535 U.S. at 732 ("It may be difficult to determine what is, or is not, an equivalent to a particular element of an invention.").

[7] *Id.*, at 730-31.

holder should know what he owns, and the public should know what he does not."[8]

Another relevant consideration is § 112's requirement that a patentee conclude the patent with a claim "particularly pointing out and distinctly claiming the subject matter which the applicant regards as his invention."[9] As a practical matter, the application of the doctrine of equivalents allows patentees to establish infringement despite this statutory obligation. For these and other reasons, the doctrine has received some criticism. For example, some scholars have argued that the doctrine of equivalents has introduced ambiguity into the patent system by the doctrine is unnecessary, in part because patent prosecutors have a variety of tools to ensure that an invention is clearly and accurately described when an application is drafted.[10]

The development of the doctrine of equivalents over the past several decades has attempted to negotiate a balance between these considerations. From these efforts, a rather complex set of rules and exceptions has emerged as described in this Chapter and in the following Chapter 30.

§ 29.02   *WINANS v. DENMEAD*: THE HISTORIC FOUNDATIONS OF THE DOCTRINE OF EQUIVALENTS

The 1854 case *Winans v. Denmead* was the first U.S. Supreme Court case to discuss the doctrine of equivalents.[11] The *Winans* Court considered a patent directed to an improvement for railroad cars for transporting coal. The patent described a car with a rectangular top and a bottom portion that formed a "frustum of a cone" with a hinged base. This design allowed for more even distribution of weight when compared with the existing art, a lower center of gravity and more efficient discharge of the coal when the hinged base was opened.

The defendant's accused railroad car used an octagonal shaped bottom, rather than a shape resembling the "frustum of a cone." The patentee asked for a jury instruction which permitted a finding of infringement without meeting the patent's literal terms if the jury found that the accused car accomplished the substantially the same result, with substantially the same principle and in the same mode of operation as that described in the patent.[12] The district court refused the patentee's request and, based on the patent's literal terms, a verdict of non-infringement was entered.

---

[8] *Id.*

[9] 35 U.S.C. § 112, ¶ 2 (2000).

[10] *See* Meurer & Nard, *supra* note 5, at 1975 ("Patent prosecutors have access to a range of claim-drafting techniques that mitigate problems with language and later-developed technology.").

[11] Winans v. Denmead, 56 U.S. 330, 344 (1854). At the time that *Winans* was decided, some earlier lower court cases had recognized that substantially similar embodiments could be deemed infringing. *See e.g.*, Odiorne v. Winkley, 18 F. Cas. 581 (C.C. D. Mass 1814) and Gray v. James, 10 F. Cas. 1015, 1016 (C.C. D. Pa. 1817).

[12] *Winans*, 56 U.S. at 334.

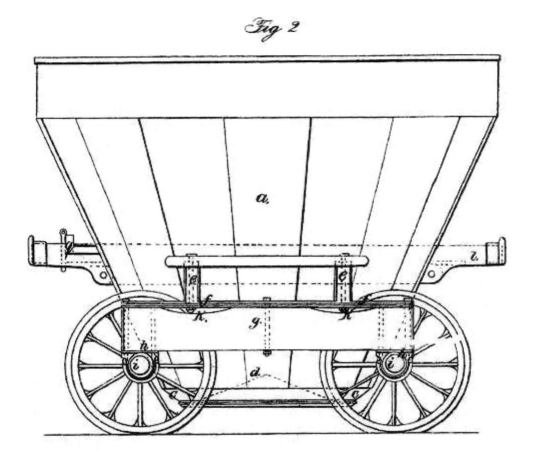

Fig. 2

The *Winans* Court reversed, finding that the trial court had erred in limiting the jury's infringement consideration to the conical shape described in the patent. *Winans* explained that a jury might find that the octagonal bottom of the accused device might be "so near to a true circle as substantially to embody the patentee's mode of operation" and therefore infringing.[13] The *Winans* court emphasized that patents "are to be construed liberally," and noted that "the exclusive right to the thing patented is not secured, if the public are at liberty to make substantial copies of it, varying its form or proportions."[14]

Four justices dissented from the *Winans* majority, in part based on the view that the majority's ruling contravened the statutory requirement that patentees specify and point out their invention. Further, the dissenters predicted that the uncertainty introduced by the majority would bring troubling developments, noting that nothing in patent law "will be more mischievous, more productive of oppressive and costly litigation, of exorbitant and unjust pretension and vexatious demands, more

---

[13] *Id.* at 343.

[14] *Id.* at 341.

injurious to labor, than a relaxation of these wise and salutary requisitions of the act of Congress."[15]

The contrasting views of the *Winans* majority and dissent illustrate the tension between allowing for flexibility in the application of claim scope and the goal of clear claim definition that continue to reverberate today. These same tensions continued to shape the doctrine of equivalents as later courts have attempted to create rules that accommodate these sharply competing concerns.

§ 29.03 THE DEVELOPMENT OF THE CURRENT DOCTRINE OF EQUIVALENTS: *GRAVER TANK & MFG. CO. v. LINDE AIR PRODUCTS CO*

In 1950, the U.S. Supreme Court again considered the doctrine of equivalents in *Graver Tank Mfg. v. Linde Air Products Co.*[16] Shifts in the law had occurred in the century since *Winans* was decided. First, patent practice had moved from peripheral claiming to central claiming, which more readily fixed the outer boundaries of the definition of the invention.[17] Also since *Winans*, courts had applied the doctrine of equivalents where an "infringing device embodies the substance of the invention and accomplishes the objects of the invention in substantially the same way and by substantially the same or equivalent means."[18]

The invention at issue in *Graver Tank* concerned the use a composition (called "flux") for electronic arc welding, whereby one joins two pieces of steel together with a molten metal heated by electricity generated from electrodes.[19] A flux is typically used to protect an electronic arc weld. The patent described a welding method that used a particular flux composition, claimed as an "alkaline earth metal silicate," as the intermediary between the electrode of the arc welder and the metals to be welded. Literal infringement could not be shown because the accused device used silicates of calcium and manganese, which are not alkaline earth metals.

Graver Tank reaffirmed the *Winans* Court's holding that insubstantial changes between the composition described in the claim and that used in the accused methods were merely differences in "name, form or shape" that did not avoid infringement.[20] *Graver Tank* explained that the question of infringement under the doctrine is a question of fact, based on "the context of the patent, the prior art, and

---

[15] *Id.* at 347.

[16] Graver Tank & Mfg. Co. v. Linde Air Prods. Co., 339 U.S. 605, 607 (1950).

[17] *See supra* Chapter 4.

[18] Nachman Spring-Filled Corporation v. Spring Products Corporation, 68 F.2d 829, 831 (2d Cir. 1934); *see also* Schiebel Toy & Novelty Co. v. Clark, 217 F. 760, 770 (6th Cir. 1914) finding infringement based on a finding that between the patent and the accused device, "there is substantial identity between them in essence of elements and combination and in principle of operation; and they are the same in results attained.").

[19] Linde Air Prods. Co. v. Graver Tank & Mfg. Co., 167 F.2d 531, 532 (7th Cir. 1948), *rev'd* 339 U.S. 605 (1950). For additional information about the *Graver Tank* decision, see Paul M. Janicke, *Heat of Passion: What Really Happened in Graver Tank*, 24 AIPLA Q. J. 1 (Winter, 1996).

[20] *Id.* at 608.

the particular circumstances of the case."[21] The Court referred to the doctrine as a necessary protection against the "the unscrupulous copyist"[22] who deprives the patentee of the benefits of an invention.

In result, The *Graver Tank* Court affirmed the trial court's infringement finding, deferring to the findings of fact that demonstrated that the accused flux was substantially similar in many respects to the alkaline earth metal stated in the claim. These findings were based on evidence that those in the art recognized that a silicate of manganese was a reasonable substitute for a silicate of alkaline earth metals in flux compositions, and that the two substances were "substantially identical in operation and in result."[23]

Justice Black's dissent criticized the majority's ruling as inconsistent with the statutory claim requirements that a patentee "particularly point out and distinctly claim" the invention.[24] Black's dissent expressed the view that "it is unjust to the public, as well as an evasion of the law, to construe it in a manner different from the plain import of its terms."[25] As in the *Winans* case that preceded it a century before, the majority and dissenting views of the *Graver Tank* decision mirror disagreement about the proper balance between flexibility and certainty in the administration of the patent right.

§ 29.04   THE U.S. SUPREME COURT'S REFINEMENT OF THE DOCTRINE OF EQUIVALENTS: *WARNER-JENKINSON CO. v. HILTON DAVIS CHEMICAL CO*

Two years after *Graver Tank* was decided, the 1952 amendments to the Patent Act became effective. The impact of these amendments on the doctrine of equivalents was considered in 1997 by the Supreme Court in *Warner-Jenkinson Co. v. Hilton Davis Chemical Co.*[26] This case added several significant refinements to the law governing liability under the doctrine of equivalents.

[A]   Factual Background of the *Warner-Jenkinson* Opinion

In *Warner-Jenkinson*, the court considered a jury finding of infringement under the doctrine of equivalents based on a method claim for "ultrafiltration," a process for removing impurities from dyes that are used in foods and drugs. The ultrafiltration process allows an impure dye to pass through a filter membrane, subject to certain variables such as filter pressure, pH levels,[27] and pore diameters

---

[21] *Id.* at 609.

[22] *Id.* at 607.

[23] *Id.* at 611.

[24] *Graver Tank*, 339 U.S. at 613 (Black, J. dissenting) (quoting R.S. § 4888, as amended 35 U.S.C. § 112 (2004)).

[25] *Id.* at 614.

[26] Warner-Jenkinson Co. v. Hilton Davis Chem. Co., 520 U.S. 17 (1997).

[27] As the *Warner-Jenkinson* Court explained, the pH "of a solution is a measure of its acidity or alkalinity." *Id.* at 22, n.1.

of the membrane to ensure that the dye is highly purified to meet governmental requirements for human consumption.

The focus of the *Warner-Jenkinson* Court's analysis was on the following claim to a specific ultrafiltration process, as follows:

> In a process for the purification of a dye . . . the improvement which comprises: subjecting an aqueous solution . . . to ultrafiltration through a membrane having a nominal pore diameter of 5-15 Angstroms under a hydrostatic pressure of approximately 200 to 400 p.s.i.g., *at a pH from approximately 6.0 to 9.0*, to thereby cause separation of said impurities from said dye . . . .[28]

Notably, the phrase "at a pH from approximately 6.0 to 9.0" had been added to the claim during patent prosecution to avoid prior art that claimed ultrafiltration at a pH level above 9.0.[29] The record did not disclose the reason that the lower pH range of 6.0 had been chosen. The accused process operated at a pH of 5.0 and therefore did not literally infringe the claim. The jury's infringement finding could be sustained, if at all, based on infringement under the doctrine of equivalents.

[B]   *Warner-Jenkinson's* Affirmation of the Doctrine of Equivalents

As an initial matter, in *Warner-Jenkinson*, the defendant argued that the doctrine of equivalents as set forth in *Graver Tank* was inconsistent with — and therefore did not survive — the 1952 amendments to the Patent Act. In particular, the defendant stated that the doctrine was inconsistent with the requirement for a claim set forth in § 112, ¶ 2,[30] the reissue process,[31] and the PTO's role in defining claim scope during prosecution. The *Warner-Jenkinson* Court rejected these arguments, reasoning that such changes were not materially different than the patent law in effect two years earlier when *Graver Tank* was decided.[32]

The *Warner-Jenkinson* Court acknowledged that one significant change since *Graver Tank* was the enactment of 35 U.S.C. § 112, ¶ 6, which allows for claims written in a means-plus-function format.[33] Section 112, ¶ 6 provides that such claims "shall be construed to cover the corresponding structure, material, or acts described in the specification and *equivalents* thereof." The statute's use of the term "equivalent" was the basis of the defendant's argument that Congress disapproved of any *other* type of "equivalents," such as the doctrine of equivalents to demonstrate infringement. *Warner-Jenkinson* rejected this argument, reasoning that § 112, ¶ 6 could not have been enacted to overturn the doctrine's

---

[28] *Id.* at 22 (quoting United States Patent No. 4,560,746 (filed Nov 30, 1984) (emphasis added)).

[29] *Id.* at 22.

[30] For more about this subsection, which govern means plus function claims, see Chapter 10.

[31] For more about reissue see Chapter 3.

[32] *Warner-Jenkinson*, 520 U.S. at 26 ("Such minor differences as exist between those provisions in the 1870 and the 1952 Acts have no bearing on the result reached in *Graver Tank*, and thus provide no basis for our overruling it.").

[33] For detailed information about means-plus-function claims, *see supra* Chapters 4 and 26.

lengthy history. Specifically, the Court noted that means-plus-function claiming had been statutorily enacted in response to an earlier Supreme Court decision, *Halliburton Oil Well Cementing Co. v. Walker*,[34] which had rejected the use of functional claiming. Based on this narrow purpose of § 112, ¶ 6, *Warner-Jenkinson* stated that "such limited congressional action should not be overread for negative implications. Congress in 1952 could easily have responded to *Graver Tank* as it did to the *Halliburton* decision. But it did not."[35]

In addition to reaffirming the existence of the doctrine of equivalents, *Warner-Jenkinson* observed that the then-current application of the doctrine of equivalents had "taken on a life of its own, unbounded by the patent claims" that had the potential to conflict with the policy of public notice.[36] To address this, *Warner-Jenkinson* held that the doctrine of equivalents "be applied to *individual limitations* of a claim, not to a claim as a whole."[37] Additionally, the *Warner-Jenkinson* court articulated an important corollary to this rule — that is, the doctrine of equivalents cannot be applied in a manner that completely *eliminates* an entire claim element.[38]

The *Warner-Jenkinson* Court declined a request to require consideration of the equities in determining infringement under the doctrine of equivalents, such as where one has knowingly infringed. Rather that adopting *Graver Tank's* concerns about "the unscrupulous copyist" into a rule of law, *Warner-Jenkinson* confirmed that infringement under the doctrine of equivalents is determined on an objective basis by comparing the accused device with the claim language.[39] Therefore, under *Warner-Jenkinson*, neither copying nor intent to infringe must be found before the doctrine of equivalents can be applied.

[C]   *Warner-Jenskinson* and the Principle Prosecution History Estoppel

The *Warner-Jenkinson* Court considered a further limitation to the doctrine of equivalents — that is, the effect of *prosecution history estoppel.* Generally, prosecution history estoppel prevents a patentee from relying on the doctrine of equivalents to recapture claimed subject matter that had been surrendered by a claim amendment made during prosecution.

In *Warner-Jenkinson*, the petitioner argued that prosecution history estoppel barred the range of equivalents beyond that disclosed in the limitation "at a pH from approximately 6.0 to 9.0" added during prosecution. The *Warner-Jenkinson* Court accepted the principle that prosecution history estoppel acted as a limitation on the application of the doctrine of equivalents. Significantly, the Court held that

---

[34]   Halliburton Oil Well Cementing Co. v. Walker, 329 U.S. 1, 8 (1946).

[35]   *Warner-Jenkinson*, 520 U.S. at 28.

[36]   *Id.*, at 28-29.

[37]   *Id.* at 29.

[38]   *Id.* ("It is important to ensure that the application of the doctrine, even as to an individual element, is not allowed such broad play as to effectively eliminate that element in its entirety.").

[39]   Warner-Jenkinson Co. v. Hilton Davis Chem. Co., 520 U.S. 17, 35-36 (1997).

the *reasons* for the claim amendment must be considered, explaining:

> . . . if the PTO has been requesting changes in claim language without the intent to limit equivalents or, indeed, with the expectation that language it required would in many cases allow for a range of equivalents, we should be extremely reluctant to upset the basic assumptions of the PTO without substantial reason for doing so. Our prior cases have consistently applied prosecution history estoppel only where claims have been amended for a limited set of reasons, and we see no substantial cause for requiring a more rigid rule invoking an estoppel regardless of the reasons for a change.[40]

Warner-Jenkinson held that the patentee bears the burden of establishing the reason for the amendment. If the patentee proffers a reason, the court should decide whether that reason is sufficient to overcome prosecution history estoppel. If the patentee cannot establish any reason for the claim amendment, the court is to presume that the patent applicant had a substantial reason related to patentability and prosecution history estoppel would bar the application of the doctrine of equivalents for that element.[41] Here, to determine the result with respect to the claim limitation "at a pH from approximately 6.0 to 9.0," which had been amended, *Warner-Jenkinson* remanded the case so that the lower court could determine the reason that the lower pH limit of 6.0 had been added.

It is important to note that the doctrine of prosecution history estoppel has been modified and refined since *Warner-Jenkinson* was decided. In particular, in 2002, the Supreme Court decided *Festo Corp. v. Shoketsu Kinzoku Kogyo Kabushiki Co., Ltd.*,[42] which must be considered when performing any prosecution history estoppel analysis today.[43] A full discussion of these standards is in Chapter 30.

[D]   The Doctrine of Equivalents and After-Arising Technology

The petitioner in the *Warner-Jenkinson* argued that the doctrine of equivalents should be limited to either the equivalents disclosed in the patent, or in the alternative to those equivalents known at the time the patent issued. The Court disagreed, finding that the appropriate time for determining whether an accused element is equivalent to a claimed element is *at the time of infringement.*[44] Thus, infringement under the doctrine of equivalents can reach forward in time to encompass later-developed technology that is within the scope of the patent claims. This aspect of *Warner-Jenkinson* allows patents to encompass implementations that have been neither described nor enabled in the written description. This is because § 112's disclosure requirements are assessed for sufficiency as of the date

---

[40] *Id.* at 32.

[41] *Id.* at 33 ("If no explanation is established, however, the court should presume that the patent applicant had a substantial reason related to patentability for including the limiting element added by amendment. In those circumstances, prosecution history estoppel would bar the application of the doctrine of equivalents as to that element.").

[42] *Festo Corp. v. Shoketsu Kinzoku Kogyo Kabushiki Co.*, 535 U.S. 722 (2002).

[43] The current standards are detailed *supra* in Chapter 31.

[44] *Id.* at 37.

that the application is *filed.*[45] Technology developed in the years since the patent issued may be deemed an equivalent even if based on improvements that did not exist until years after.

One frequently-cited example of this principle is *Hughes Aircraft Co. v. U.S.*, a Federal Circuit opinion which considered the application of the doctrine of equivalents of a patent directed to a communications satellite.[46] The asserted patent disclosed a system for controlling the satellite's orientation relative to the earth. In general terms, the specification described the use of onboard sensors to collect data about the spin angle of the satellite at a particular point in time. This information was transmitted to earth, where the data was analyzed by a ground crew who sent a radio signal command back to the satellite. This command prompted the satellite to fire a jet that caused the satellite to shift orientation to its proper position.

In *Hughes*, the government argued that its system did not infringe under the doctrine of equivalents, based on the fact that the government's device used an on-board computer to orient the satellite, rather than relying on communications with a ground crew as disclosed in the patent. Underscoring that the proper time to assess infringement is at the time of infringement, the Federal Circuit rejected the government's argument. Finding that the differences noted by the government were the "result in an advance in technology"[47] in the years since the original patent filing, the court affirmed a finding that the government's system infringed under the doctrine of equivalents.

§ 29.05   TESTS FOR INFRINGEMENT IN A POST-*WARNER-JENKINSON* ERA

Having affirmed the continued viability of the doctrine of equivalents as a theory under which infringement can be established, the *Warner-Jenkinson* Court declined to mandate any precise formulation of how "equivalence" should be determined. Rather, the Court asked the Federal Circuit to refine the standard. The Supreme Court provided the guidance that any applicable test must satisfy the essential inquiry of whether "the accused product or process contain[s] elements identical or equivalent to each claimed element of the patented invention."[48] As the Court directed, "what constitutes equivalency must be determined against the context of the patent, the prior art, and the particular circumstances of the case."[49] In practice, then, it is well to bear in mind the Supreme Court's guidance that equivalence "is not the prisoner of a formula and is not an absolute to be considered in a vacuum."[50]

---

[45] *See* W.L. Gore & Assocs., Inc. v. Garlock, Inc., 721 F.2d 1540, 1556-57 (Fed. Cir. 1983) (stating rule).

[46] Hughes Aircraft Co. v. U.S., 140 F.3d 1470 (Fed. Cir. 1998).

[47] *Id.* at 1475.

[48] Warner-Jenkinson Co. v. Hilton Davis Chem. Co., 520 U.S. 17, 40 (1997).

[49] Graver Tank & Mfg. Co. v. Linde Air Products Co., 339 U.S. 605, 609 (1950).

[50] *Id.*

Warner-Jenkinson did refer to two tests in the opinion. First, the Court referred to the *triple identity test* (which is also called the *function-way-result* test. This test asks whether the element of the accused device at issue performs *substantially the same function*, in *substantially the same way*, to achieve *substantially the same result*, as the limitation at issue in the claim.[51] All three must be present for equivalence to exist. Second, *Warner-Jenkinson* referred to another test that examines whether there are *insubstantial differences* between the claim limitation and the accused element.

The Federal Circuit has considered cases under both standards, favoring the function-way-result test for inventions that are comprised of structural or mechanical components. An example of the application of the function-way-result test in the Federal Circuit is *Engel Industries, Inc. v. The Lockformer Co.*, which considered infringement of a patent directed to a method and apparatus for connecting ducts used in the heating and ventilation industry.[52] The asserted claims included a corner connector that required the installer to crimp the materials together to hold the piece in place. In addition, the patent described this connector as having an outwardly rolled flange. By contrast, the accused system used a spring force to hold the corner piece in place (rather than manual crimping as described in the claims), and relied on an inwardly rolled flange. The *Engel Industries* court recognized that although both systems performed substantially the same function (both were used to connect duct sections without rivets or welds) and achieved substantially the same result (attaching the corner pieces in an efficient manner), the systems did so in different ways. Specifically, *Engel Industries* stated that the accused "flange is constructed differently (it is rolled to the inside . . .) and performs differently (it acts as a spring seat for the corner connectors)" rather than requiring an installer to crimp the material in place.[53] On these bases, the patentee's efforts to establish equivalents failed.

In contrast, the Federal Circuit affirmed a finding of infringement under the doctrine of equivalents in *Voda v. Cordis Corp.*[54] The invention was a cardiac guide catheter that included a long thin flexible tube that a surgeon inserted into an artery. The guide is led through the aorta of the heart and then into the coronary artery. Once in place, a balloon on the end of the catheter is inflated so that blockage in the coronary artery is cleared. According to the asserted patent, a portion of the device rested against the opposing wall of the aorta in an area called a "contact portion." This contact portion was intended to provide stability and backup when the balloon is opened. According to the claim, this contact was made between the wall of the aorta and a "second straight portion" of the device.

---

[51] Dawn Equipment Co. v. Kentucky Farms Inc., 140 F.3d 1009, 1016 (Fed. Cir. 1998).

[52] Engel Industries, Inc. v. The Lockformer Co., 96 F.3d 1398 (Fed. Cir. 1996).

[53] *Id.* at 1407.

[54] Voda v. Cordis Corp., 536 F.3d 1311 (Fed. Cir. 2008).

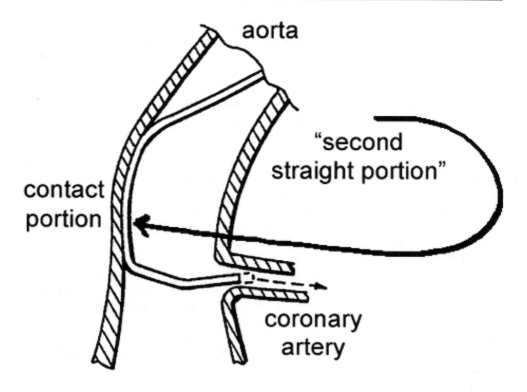

The accused device did not have a "second straight portion"; rather, the portion of the device that contacted the wall of the aorta was curved. Applying the triple identity test, the *Voda* court found sufficient evidence to support a finding of infringement under the doctrine of equivalents. Specifically, this evidence showed:

- First, the accused curve portion performed the same *function* as "second straight portion" of the claim. Specifically, both rested on the wall of the aorta and steadied the device while in use;

- Second, the curved portion accomplished this function in a substantially similar way as the claimed "second straight portion." Essentially, the curved portion achieved back up stability by resting on the wall of the aorta during use; and

- Third, the accused curve achieved the same result. Essentially, both the accused curve and the patented "second straight portion" achieved stability for the device while in use.

In addition, the *Voda* court cited testimony that cardiologists would have a difficult time distinguishing the accused device from the claimed device in use. Based on evidence of these similarities, the *Voda* court affirmed the infringement finding based on the doctrine of equivalents.

§ 29.06 PUTTING THE DOCTRINE TOGETHER: AN EXAMPLE OF THE APPLICATION OF THE *WARNER-JENKINSON* STANDARD

What follows is a simplified example of an application of the *Warner-Jenkinson* standard. Assume that the analysis centers on the chair claim recited at the beginning of this chapter:

> An apparatus for sitting, comprising:
>
> a substantially flat horizontal surface;
>
> a vertical back portion attached to the top of said horizontal surface *using two-penny nails*;
>
> at least three elongated support members connected to the bottom of said horizontal portion *using two-penny nails.*

As before, assume that literal infringement cannot be met because the accused device uses four-penny nails.

The starting point is to *identify the limitation* for which the doctrine will be applied. The courts have not articulated a rule for determining the parts of the claim that constitute a single limitation.[55] Most courts have focused on a series of words or phrases, typically less than the total number of words in the asserted claim.[56] For example, in *Warner-Jenkinson*, the Supreme Court selected the limitation "at a pH from approximately 6.0 to 9.0" as the focus of the equivalents analysis. In this case, we will use the limitation "using two-penny nails."

Once this term is chosen, one should determine whether there are any restrictions on the doctrine of equivalents which would bar its application, as described in the next Chapter. For example, if a claim has been amended while the application was pending, the doctrine of prosecution history estoppel may limit the potentially applicable equivalents. As a further example, as established in *Warner-Jenkinson* one cannot use the doctrine of equivalents to eliminate a claim limitation entirely. Applying this rule using the chair claim example, a chair which was carved entirely from a single block of wood could not infringe under the doctrine of equivalents because that result would eliminate the attachment element ("attached to the top of said horizontal surface using a two-penny nail") from the claim.

The next relevant question is whether the limitation "using two-penny nails" is an equivalent of the four-penny nails used in the accused chair. As an apparatus claim made of structural elements, one is likely to rely on the function/way/result test to determine equivalence, as follows:

---

[55] Dan L. Burk & Mark A. Lemley, *Quantum Patent Mechanics*, 9 Lewis & Clark L. Rev. 29, 41 (2005).

[56] *Id.* at 45-46; *see also* Matthew C. Phillips, *Taking a Step Beyond Maxwell to Tame the Doctrine of Equivalents*, 11 Fordham Intell. Prop. Media & Ent. L.J. 155, 162 (2000) ("Presently, an element seems to be more than just a single word, but potentially less than an entire step in a method or an entire constituent part of an apparatus (as is typically demarcated by semicolons).").

	"using two-penny nails" limitation	Accused device attaches using four-penny nails
Function	Attaching legs and back to the chair seat	Attaching legs and back to the chair seat
Way	A rigid metal rod with a flattened end and a pointed end, hammered through one piece of wood to hold another.	A *larger*, rigid metal rod with a flattened end and a pointed end, hammered through one piece of wood to hold another.
Result	Nail holds the chair pieces to the seat	Nail holds the chair pieces to the seat

Here, the "function" and "result" are identical. However, a finder of fact may be required to decide whether the use of a four-penny nail represents a substantially different "way" of attachment from a "two-penny nail" recited in the claim limitation under examination. If the fact finder determines that using a four-penny nail is substantially similar, and if all other limitations of the claim are literally present in the accused chair, then the accused chair infringes the claim under the doctrine of equivalents.

§ 29.07   THE REVERSE DOCTRINE OF EQUIVALENTS

The doctrine of equivalents establishes infringement even where the literal terms of the claim are not met. However, where literal infringement has been established, can non-infringement be found where there is little resemblance between the accused device and the patented invention in fact? Stated another way, should a patent claim scope encompass all literal elements, even those well outside the original inventor's contemplation? An 1898 Supreme Court decision acknowledges that patent law may find no infringement under these circumstances under the *reverse doctrine of equivalents*:

> The patentee may bring the defendant within the letter of his claims, but if the letter has so far changed the principle of the device that the claims of the patent, literally construed, have ceased to represent his actual invention, he is as little subject to be adjudged an infringer as one who has violated the letter of statute has to be convicted, but has done nothing in conflict with its letter or spirit.[57]

Likewise, the *Graver Tank* Court acknowledged the reverse doctrine of equivalents in dicta, stating that, "where a device is so far changed in principle from a patented article that it performs the same or a similar function in a substantially different way, but nevertheless falls within the literal words of the claim, the doctrine of equivalents may be used to restrict the claim and defeat the patentee's

---

[57] Boyden Power-Brake Co. v. Westinghouse, 170 U.S. 537, 568 (1898).

action for infringement."[58] The principle supporting the doctrine is to prevent a patentee from extending the patent far beyond that which has been invented.[59]

Today, the principle is rarely invoked by the courts. This may be because other doctrines — such as written description, definiteness and enablement — have been more frequently used to tether the scope of a patentee's claims to that disclosed in the specification.[60] Using those principles, a court may find that a claim scope is invalid or worthy of a narrowed construction if the claim's breadth exceeds that which has been invented in fact.

Nonetheless, there may be instances where the application of the reverse doctrine of equivalents is appropriate. For example, in *Scripps Clinic & Research Foundation v. Genentech, Inc.*, the Federal Circuit considered the application of this doctrine to a patent describing a blood clotting agent made for medical uses.[61] In *Scripps*, the patent described an agent that had been purified and derived from human plasma. In contrast, the accused product was produced from recombinant human cells. The patentee argued that the reverse doctrine of equivalents prevented a finding of literal infringement, asserting that its accused product was far superior in its purity and activity level to the technology claimed in the asserted claims. The Federal Circuit acknowledged that such facts "if found to be correct could provide–depending on the specific facts of the similarities and differences — sufficient ground for invoking the reverse doctrine."[62] On that basis, the *Scripps* court found summary judgment inappropriate and remanded the case for trial. The Federal Circuit's suggestion that the law supports a finding based on the described facts demonstrates that the reverse doctrine of equivalents retains some vitality despite the availability of alternative doctrines.

§ 29.08   CONCLUSION

Under the doctrine of equivalents, a product or process that fails to meet the literal limitations of a claim may infringe if there is an insubstantial difference between an element of an accused product or process and a limitation of a patent claim. The foundational concepts of the doctrine of equivalents established in *Winans* and *Graver Tank* cases were affirmed and modified in the Supreme Court's *Warner-Jenkinson Co. v. Hilton Davis Chemical Co.*

Under *Warner-Jenkinson*, one must first isolate the claim limitation that is not met literally and for which the doctrine of equivalents must be applied. Once identified, a finder of fact should determine whether there are insubstantial differences between the identified claim limitation and an identified element in the accused product or process. Under *Warner-Jenkinson*, the doctrine of equivalents

---

[58] *Graver Tank*, 339 U.S. at 608-09.

[59] *See generally* Scripps Clinic & Research Foundation v. Genentech, Inc., 927 F.2d 1565, 1581 (Fed. Cir. 1991).

[60] *See* Tate Access Floors, Inc. v. Interface Architectural Res., Inc., 279 F.3d 1357, 1368 (Fed. Cir. 2002).

[61] *See Scripps*, 927 F.2d at 1568-69.

[62] *Id.* at 1581.

is examined by comparing the accused device to the claim limitation without regard to the accused infringer's state of mind. Further, whether equivalents exist is assessed according to the state of the art at the time of infringement. Therefore, the doctrine of equivalents can be applied to establish infringement against after-arising technology.

Warner-Jenkinson noted that prosecution history estoppel is a further limitation to the doctrine of equivalents. Under this rule, the doctrine of equivalents cannot be used to reclaim subject matter that was lost where a claim has been amended for reasons related to patentability during the patent's prosecution. The doctrine of prosecution history estoppel was to be further refined in the U.S. Supreme Court's *Festo* decision, discussed in the next Chapter.

Chapter 30

RESTRICTIONS ON THE DOCTRINE OF EQUIVALENTS

SYNOPSIS

§ 30.01　INTRODUCTION

§ 30.02　PROSECUTION HISTORY ESTOPPEL: THE *FESTO* CASES

    [A]　Overview of the Doctrine of Prosecution History Estoppel

    [B]　*Festo*: The Ground Rules of Prosecution History Estoppel

    [C]　*Festo*: The Federal Circuit's Refinement

    [D]　Putting the *Festo* Analysis Together: Application of the Doctrine of Prosecution History Estoppel

§ 30.03　ADDITIONAL RESTRICTION ON THE DOCTRINE OF EQUIVALENTS: AN EQUIVALENT CANNOT ENCOMPASS THE PRIOR ART

§ 30.04　THE PUBLIC DEDICATION RULE

§ 30.05　THE DOCTRINE OF EQUIVALENTS CANNOT VITIATE AN ENTIRE CLAIM ELEMENT

§ 30.06　CONCLUSION

§ 30.01　INTRODUCTION

As discussed in the previous chapter, the doctrine of equivalents permits a finding of infringement outside a claim's literal scope. This chapter will explore the four major limitations on the doctrine of equivalents. First, the doctrine of amendment-based prosecution history estoppel limits a patentee from relying on the doctrine of equivalents where that patentee has surrendered the subject matter at issue during prosecution.[1] Second, an element cannot be established as an equivalent that is already in the prior art, or an obvious variant of the equivalent. Third, under the public dedication rule, a patentee cannot obtain infringement by equivalents on subject matter that has been disclosed but not claimed by the patentee. Fourth, the doctrine of equivalents cannot be applied in a manner that vitiates an entire claim limitation.

Each restriction on the doctrine of equivalents is independent of the others. If one applies, then the patentee cannot rely on the doctrine of equivalents.

---

[1] K2 Corp. v. Salomon S.A., 191 F.3d 1356, 1367 (Fed. Cir. 1999).

§ 30.02   PROSECUTION HISTORY ESTOPPEL: THE *FESTO* CASES

[A]   Overview of the Doctrine of Prosecution History Estoppel

Amendment-based *prosecution history estoppel* is perhaps the most complex limitation on the doctrine of equivalents. A patentee has long been estopped from recapturing claim scope in an infringement suit after surrendering that same subject matter via a claim amendment before the PTO.[2] In the 1997 decision *Warner-Jenkinson Co. v. Hilton Davis Chemical Co.*,[3] the U.S. Supreme Court reaffirmed the use of prosecution history estoppel to bar the doctrine of equivalents from encompassing subject matter that the patentee had relinquished during claim amendment. In the years following *Warner-Jenkinson*, the courts developed a number of dramatic and complex changes to prosecution history estoppel in a series of opinions titled *Festo Corp. v. Shoketsu Kinzoku Kogyo Kabushiki Co., Ltd.*[4] These changes evidence the turbulence that occurred as the courts attempted to reconcile a need for certain and clear claim scope with a desire to ensure incentives for invention.

As the Supreme Court noted in *Graver Tank & Mfg. Co. v. Linde Air Products Co.*, "to permit imitation of a patented invention which does not copy every literal detail would be to convert the protection of the patent grant into a hollow and useless thing."[5] At the same time, courts have recognized that the flexibility inherent in applying the doctrine of equivalents interferes with certainty, which is a valuable attribute to those operating within the patent system. Public notice serves an important function for a patent, which is a right that is, in theory, enforceable against all. As a 1991 Federal Circuit opinion, *London v. Carson Pirie Scott & Co.*, discusses:

> Application of the doctrine of equivalents is the exception, however, not the rule, for if the public comes to believe (or fear) that the language of patent claims can never be relied on, and that the doctrine of equivalents is simply the second prong of every infringement charge, regularly available to extend protection beyond the scope of the claims, then claims will cease to

---

[2] Shepard v. Carrigan, 116 U.S. 593, 597 (1886) ("Where an applicant for a patent to cover a new combination is compelled by the rejection of his application by the patent-office to narrow his claim by the introduction of a new element, he cannot after the issue of the patent broaden his claim by dropping the element which he was compelled to include in order to secure his patent.").

[3] Warner-Jenkinson Co., Inc. v. Hilton Davis Chemical Co., 520 U.S. 17, 33 (1997) ("Where the reason for the change was not related to avoiding the prior art, the change may introduce a new element, but it does not necessarily preclude infringement by equivalents of that element.").

[4] Festo Corp. v. Shoketsu Kinzoku Kogyo Kabushiki Co., Ltd., 234 F.3d 558 (Fed. Cir. 2000), *vacated*, 535 U.S. 722 (2002); Festo Corp. v. Shoketsu Kinzoku Kogyo Kabushiki Co., Ltd., 535 U.S. 722, 728 (2002); Festo Corp. v. Shoketsu Kinzoku Kogyo Kabushiki Co., Ltd., 344 F.3d 1359 (Fed. Cir. 2003); and Festo Corp. v. Shoketsu Kinzoku Kogyo Kabushiki Co., Ltd., 493 F.3d 1368 (Fed. Cir. 2007).

[5] Graver Tank & Mfg. Co. v. Linde Air Prods. Co., 339 U.S. 605, 607 (1950).

serve their intended purpose. Competitors will never know whether their actions infringe a granted patent.[6]

Moreover, under the definiteness requirement of § 112, ¶ 6, a patentee is charged with drafting a claim by "particularly pointing out and distinctly claiming the subject matter which the applicant regards as his invention." The doctrine of equivalents allows a patentee to cover implementations despite this statutory directive. In some respects, prosecution history estoppel is an effort to reconcile these competing concerns.

Prosecution history estoppel represents a conclusion that a patentee has surrendered subject matter while the application is pending in order to obtain the right. When such circumstances exist, the policy supporting flexible claim scope diminishes. Stated another way, efforts to preserve the patentee's rights through the doctrine of equivalents become far less compelling where the patentee has decided to narrow the scope of the claim in a manner that excludes an equivalent to obtain the patent. The *Festo* cases, discussed in detail below, provide a structured analysis for determining when, on balance, a patentee's conduct warrants a finding that this surrender has occurred.

[B]   *Festo*: The Ground Rules of Prosecution History Estoppel

As factual background to the *Festo* decisions, patent holder Festo held two patents — the "Carroll patent,"[7] and the "Stoll Patent."[8] Both patents concerned magnetically coupled rodless cylinders. The cylinders house a piston that is driven back and forth by a fluid under pressure. The piston contains magnets, which are coupled to a sleeve that also contains magnets and operates on the outside of the cylinder. As the piston moves inside the cylinder, the magnetic coupling causes the sleeve outside the cylinder to move in tandem. As the driver sleeve moves, the sleeve carries a load. According to the prior art, the cylinders must be twice as long as a stroke length for this design to operate. According to the Carroll and Stoll patents, the rodless cylinder needed to be only as long as a piston stroke.

The Carroll patent had undergone amendment during reexamination, and the Stoll patent had been amended during prosecution. Both patents had added a limitation for *a pair of sealing rings* with a lip on one side to prevent impurities from invading the piston assembly.[9] Defendant SMC's accused device did not literally infringe, as SMC's cylinder used a *single* sealing ring with a two-way lip rather than using two one-way sealing rings as required by the asserted claims.[10]

---

[6]   London v. Carson Pirie Scott & Co., 946 F.2d 1534, 1538 (Fed. Cir. 1991).

[7]   U.S. Patent No. 3,779,401 (filed Feb. 17, 1972).

[8]   U.S. Patent No. 4,354,125 (filed May 28, 1980).

[9]   *See* Festo Corp. v. Shoketsu Kinzoku Kogyo Kabushiki Co., Ltd., 535 U.S. 722, 728 (2002). For example, the Carroll amendment added the following language, "*a pair of resilient sealing rings* situated near opposite axial ends of the central mounting member and engaging the cylinder to effect a fluid-tight seal therewith." Festo Corp. v. Shoketsu Kinzoku Kogyo Kabushiki Co., Ltd., 234 F.3d 558, 584 (Fed. Cir. 2000), *vacated*, 535 U.S. 722 (2002).

[10]   Festo Corp. v. Shoketsu Kinzoku Kogyo Kabushiki Co., Ltd., 535 U.S. 722, 728-29 (2002). Generally,

The patentee asserted infringement based on the doctrine of equivalents.

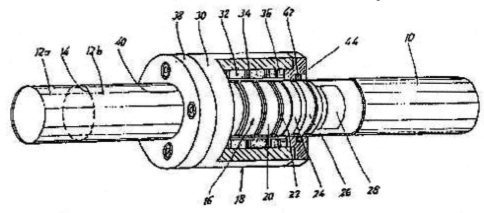

The U.S. Supreme Court's *Festo* opinion directly confronted the tension between the policies that favor flexible claim scope and the need for certainty in patent law. On one hand, *Festo* recognized that § 112, ¶ 2, requires a patentee to describe an invention in "full, clear, concise and exact terms," and that the uncertainty that results from the doctrine of equivalents may deter others from pursuing "innovations, creations, and new ideas beyond the inventor's exclusive rights."[11] As the *Festo* Court noted that "if competitors cannot be certain about a patent's extent, they may be deterred from engaging in legitimate manufactures outside its limits, or they may invest by mistake in competing products that the patent secures."[12]

On the other hand, the Court acknowledged that historically the doctrine of equivalents had been adopted despite these difficulties as "the price of ensuring the appropriate incentives for innovation."[13] In connection with this point, *Festo* expressed concern that patentees may be unable to adequately describe an invention using textual claim communication, explaining:

> The language in the patent claims may not capture every nuance of the invention or describe with complete precision the range of its novelty. If patents were always interpreted by their literal terms, their value would be greatly diminished. Unimportant and insubstantial substitutes for certain elements could defeat the patent, and its value to inventors could be destroyed by simple acts of copying.[14]

The Court noted that concerns about incentives might be secondary where a patentee "knew the words for both the broader and narrower claim, and affirma-

---

a sealing ring with a one-way sealing lip seals against fluid flow on that side, and a two-way sealing ring has a lip on both sides of the ring that allows both sides to seal against fluid flow.

[11] *Id.* at 731.

[12] *Id.* at 732.

[13] *Id.* at 732.

[14] *Id.* at 731.

tively chose the latter".[15] In such circumstances, estoppel is justified. Where broader claim language had, in fact, been drafted to encompass an equivalent prior to the amendment, the Court noted, "the patentee cannot assert that he lacked the words to describe the subject matter in question."[16]

The *Festo* Court held that a narrowing amendment that has been made to satisfy *any* requirement of the Patent Act may gives rise to a presumption that prosecution history estoppel bars the application of the doctrine of equivalents as to the amended claim element. These include amendments that have been made to: 1) overcome the prior art, 2) bring the claim within the patentable subject matter requirement; 3) satisfy the nonobviousness requirement; 4) meet the utility requirement; or 4) to provide sufficient disclosure gives rise to a presumption that prosecution history estoppel applies.

How can the presumption be rebutted? *Festo* explains that the patentee must demonstrate that "at the time of the amendment one skilled in the art could not reasonably be expected to have drafted a claim that would have literally encompassed the alleged equivalent."[17] A patentee can do so by demonstrating any of the following:

- The equivalent was *unforeseeable* at the time of the patent application;

- The reason for the amendment bears only a *tangential relation* to the equivalent in question; or

- Some *other reason* suggesting the patentee could not reasonably have been expected to describe the equivalent in question.

Notably, the application of the doctrine of prosecution history estoppel does not bar the ability to reach *all* equivalents. In other words, the narrowed element is not limited to its strict literal terms. As the *Festo* court explained, "A patentee's decision to narrow his claims through amendment may be presumed to be a general disclaimer of the territory between the original claim and the amended claim."[18] As an example, assume that the original claim is a combination of A + B. During prosecution, the patentee adds an additional element "C" for a reason relating to patentability, which narrows the original claim to "A + B + C." This amendment gives rise to a presumption that prosecution history applies. If that presumption is not rebutted by the patentee, then the patentee may be precluded from relying on the doctrine of equivalents as to the subject matter difference between "A + B" and "A + B + C" in a later infringement case.

To dispose of the *Festo* case, the Supreme Court recognized that the patentee had added the "sealing ring" limitation to avoid the prior art, thereby raising the presumption that prosecution history estoppel barred reliance on the doctrine of equivalents. The Supreme Court remanded the case for a determination of whether the patentee could bear the burden of rebutting this presumption by demonstrating

---

[15] *Id.* at 734-35.

[16] *Id.*

[17] *Id.* at 741.

[18] *Id.* at 740.

that the sealing ring equivalent had not been surrendered.

[C] *Festo*: The Federal Circuit's Refinement

On remand from the U.S. Supreme Court, the Federal Circuit's subsequent *Festo* opinions[19] provided additional guidance for the implementation of the Supreme Court's *Festo* rulings. The remanded *Festo* cases held that if the record fails to reveal any reason for a narrowing claim amendment, the court will presume that the amendment was made to satisfy a patentability requirement and a presumption of prosecution history estoppel will arise. Additionally, the Federal Circuit confirmed that whether prosecution history estoppel applies, including whether the presumption has been rebutted by the patentee, is a question of law for the court.

Further, the court determined that voluntary claim amendments give rise to prosecution history estoppel. Thus, the doctrine is not limited to those amendments that are made in response to an examiner's rejection.

The Federal Circuit's *Festo* opinions provide some guidance for determining whether a patentee has successfully rebutted the presumption under the Supreme Court's rule. The Federal Circuit stated that whether an equivalent is *unforeseeable* at the time of an amendment must be judged by objective standards according to one of skill in the art. Thus, a patentee's subjective ability to foresee an equivalent is not controlling, rather an equivalent cannot be deemed unforeseeable where "a reasonable applicant at the time of the amendment would have been aware of the equivalent as an alternative under the broader claim before the amendment" was made.[20] On the other hand, "if the alleged equivalent represents later-developed technology (*e.g.*, transistors in relation to vacuum tubes, or Velcro® in relation to fasteners) or technology that was not known in the relevant art, then it would not have been foreseeable."[21]

Concerning whether a claim amendment may be deemed *tangential* to the equivalent, the Federal Circuit noted that this criterion focuses on whether a patentee can be said to have rebutted a presumption of surrender because the *reason* for the claim amendment bears little relevance to the equivalent under examination. Certainly, where the amendment has been made to avoid prior art that describes the equivalent, the amendment cannot be said to be tangential to the equivalent.[22] However, some amendments do not bear a close relation to equivalent sought. This concept was explored in *Instituform Technologies, Inc. v. CAT Contracting, Inc.*, where the claim at issue concerned a method for repairing underground pipe by installing a resin-filled liner within a broken pipe section.[23] During prosecution, the patentee amended the claim to avoid a prior art reference that used a large compressor to create a vacuum at the far end of the tube. In

---

[19] Festo Corp. v. Shoketsu Kinzoku Kogyo Kabushiki Co., Ltd., 344 F.3d 1359 (Fed. Cir. 2003); Festo Corp. v. Shoketsu Kinzoku Kogyo Kabushiki Co., Ltd., 493 F.3d 1368 (Fed. Cir. 2007).

[20] *Id.* at 1381.

[21] *Festo Corp.*, 344 F.3d at 1369.

[22] *See* Chimie v. PPG Industries, Inc., 402 F.3d 1371, 1383 (Fed. Cir. 2005).

[23] Instituform Technologies, Inc. v. CAT Contracting, Inc., 385 F.3d 1360 (Fed. Cir. 2004).

doing so, the patentee narrowed the claim to add a limitation that required the use of a small vacuum source connected to the liner with "a cup" in a location much closer to the resin. The accused product differed from the claim in that it relied on *multiple* cups (rather than "a cup" as recited in the claim) and therefore did not literally infringe. After reviewing the prosecution history, the *Insituform Technologies* court held that the patentee had successfully rebutted the presumption because this record demonstrated that the patentee's narrowing amendment bore only a tangential relationship to the "multiple cups" as equivalents. As the *Insituform* court explained, "there is no indication in the prosecution history of any relationship between the narrowing amendment and a multiple cup process, which is the alleged equivalent in this case."[24] Similar to the unforeseeable exception, determining whether the reason for an amendment is tangential is assessed on an objective basis grounded on evidence "discernible from the prosecution history record, if the public notice function of a patent and its prosecution history is to have significance."[25]

In *Festo*, the Supreme Court left open the possibility that a patentee could overcome the presumption with a catch-all exception — that is, "some *other reason* suggesting that the patentee could not reasonably be expected to have described the insubstantial substitute in question."[26] According to the Federal Circuit on remand, this category is "a narrow one" that is reserved for situations such as where "there was some reason, such as the shortcomings of language, why the patentee was prevented from describing the alleged equivalent when it narrowed the claim."[27] Thus, one cannot rely on this reason where one is actually aware of — but simply fails to claim — the equivalent at issue.[28]

[D] Putting the *Festo* Analysis Together: Application of the Doctrine of Prosecution History Estoppel

Taking all of these rules in total, an analysis for the application of prosecution history estoppel can be summarized as follows:

1. *Is the amendment narrowing?* If not, then prosecution history estoppel does not apply and infringement under the doctrine of equivalents can be asserted by the patentee. If the amendment is narrowing, proceed to question #2.

2. *Does the prosecution history file reveal the reason for the amendment?* If not, then the court presumes that prosecution history estoppel applies

---

[24] *Id.* at 1370.

[25] *Festo*, 344 F.3d at 1369.

[26] Festo Corp. v. Shoketsu Kinzoku Kogyo Kabushiki Co., Ltd., 535 U.S. 722, 741 (2002) (emphasis added).

[27] Festo Corp. v. Shoketsu Kinzoku Kogyo Kabushiki Co., Ltd., 344 F.3d 1359, 1370 (Fed. Cir. 2003).

[28] *See* Amgen Inc. v. Hoechst Marion Roussel, Inc., 457 F.3d 1293, 1316 (Fed. Cir. 2006) (finding that the presumption was not rebutted where no linguistic barrier existed, and where the patentee "knew about the 165-amino acid sequence at the time of the amendment, but still chose to claim the incorrect 166-amino acid sequence.").

and one must proceed to question #4. If the record does reveal a reason, proceed next to question #3.

3. *Does the reason for the claim amendment relate to any of the patentability requirements?* If not, then the doctrine of prosecution history estoppel does not apply and the patentee can rely on the doctrine of equivalents. If yes, then a rebuttable presumption arises that prosecution history estoppel applies. To determine whether the patentee may rebut this presumption, proceed to question #4.

4. *Can the patentee establish that at the time of the amendment one skilled in the art could not reasonably be expected to have drafted a claim that would have literally encompassed the alleged equivalent by any of the following: a) the equivalent was unforeseeable at the time of the patent application; b) the rationale underlying the amendment bears only a tangential relation to the equivalent in question; or c) there is some other reason suggesting the patentee could not reasonably have been expected to describe the equivalent in question?* If yes, then prosecution history estoppel does not bar the doctrine of equivalents. If not, then prosecution history estoppel applies and proceed to question #5.

5. *What is the scope of the surrendered subject matter?* If the accused element falls in the territory between the original claim and the amended claim, then the doctrine of equivalents cannot be used. If the accused element is outside the scope of the surrendered subject matter, then a finder of fact should determine whether the element represents an equivalent to the amended limitation.

When applying this framework, the policies that underlie the doctrine of equivalents should be considered. These include the incentive policy, the need for clarity and certainty in patent law, and the nature of estoppel as articulated in the *Festo* cases.

§ 30.03 ADDITIONAL RESTRICTION ON THE DOCTRINE OF EQUIVALENTS: AN EQUIVALENT CANNOT ENCOMPASS THE PRIOR ART

In addition to prosecution history estoppel, the courts have developed a number of additional and separate bars to the doctrine of equivalents. For example, the doctrine of equivalents cannot be used to encompass subject matter encompassed by the *prior art* or an *obvious variation* of the existing art.[29]

For example, in *K-2 Corp. v. Salomon S.A.*, the court considered infringement under the doctrine of equivalents for a claim directed to an in-line roller skate with a boot portion "permanently affixed" to the skate at the heel and toe area.[30] The accused in-line skate used a *removable* screw in the heel area, and was therefore

---

[29] K-2 Corp. v. Salomon S.A., 191 F.3d 1356, 1366-67 (Fed. Cir. 1999).

[30] The relevant claim language read, ". . . said non-rigid shoe portion being *permanently affixed* to said base portion at least at said toe area and said heel area . . . ." *Id.* at 1360 (quoting U.S. Patent No. 5,437,466 cl. 1 (filed Jul. 19, 1993)) (emphasis added).

outside the literal scope of the "permanently affixed" limitation.[31] Two pieces of prior art demonstrated in-line skates with detachable boots, one of which showed removable screw attachments at the toe and heel. The *K-2 Corp.* held that the patentee could not rely on the doctrine of equivalents to demonstrate infringement, because the claim could not be used to cover an obvious variation of the two asserted pieces of prior art using a detachable boot.[32] As the court explained, the doctrine of equivalents could not be used "to cover subject matter that could not have been legally patented in the first instance."[33]

§ 30.04   THE PUBLIC DEDICATION RULE

In *Johnson & Johnstone Assoc., Inc.*,[34] the Federal Circuit ruled *en banc* that under the *public dedication rule* the doctrine of equivalents cannot be used to encompass subject matter that is disclosed but not claimed in a patent. In *Johnson*, the court considered an invention that relates to the manufacture of printed circuit boards. Typically, very thin sheets of copper foil are used to join sheets of resin together to create a board. These sheets of copper foil are fragile, and easily damaged. The invention at issue in *Johnson* used a substrate sheet to strengthen the copper foil. The specification expressly disclosed the use of *stainless steel* to form the substrate sheet, however the claims were directed solely to the use of *aluminum* to make the substrate.

In the trial court, a jury found that an accused device relying on steel as substrate material infringed under the doctrine of equivalents. The Federal Circuit's *en banc* court reversed, on the grounds that the doctrine of equivalents could not be used to cover an implementation that was disclosed but not claimed in the patent. The *Johnson* court explained that the failure to claim disclosed subject matter operates to "dedicate[ ] that unclaimed subject matter to the public."[35] The court stressed that "[a]pplication of the doctrine of equivalents to recapture subject matter deliberately left unclaimed would conflict with the primacy of the claims in defining the scope of the patentee's exclusive rights."[36]

Further, *Johnson* pointed out that a contrary result would allow a patentee to disclose broadly and claim narrowly in order to obtain a patent from the PTO, and thereby avoid agency examination of the broader claim scope. Here, the court found that the patent could not cover the disclosed but unclaimed steel substrate and therefore the jury's verdict could not stand as a matter of law.

Subject matter is considered "disclosed" in the specification for purposes of the public dedication rule even if the description does not meet the disclosure

---

[31] *K- 2 Corp.*, 191 F.3d at 1361.

[32] *Id.* As an alternative ground, the *K-2 Corp.* court found that the patentee had made statements in the prosecution history that relinquished subject matter for the equivalent. *Id.* at 1369.

[33] *Id.* at 1368.

[34] Johnson & Johnstone Assoc., Inc., 285 F.3d 1046 (Fed. Cir. 2002).

[35] *Id.* at 1054.

[36] *Id.* (quotation and citation omitted).

requirements of § 112, ¶ 1.[37] For example, a disclosure does not need to enable the subject matter for dedication to the public to occur. As long as "one of ordinary skill in the art can understand the unclaimed disclosed teaching upon reading the written description," the subject matter is considered disclosed has been dedicated to the public if not claimed.[38] Further, whether the prior art bars the use of the doctrine of equivalents is a purely objective inquiry based on the patent and its prosecution history. A patentee's inadvertence in failing to claim a particular subject matter is insufficient — and indeed irrelevant — as to whether equivalence is barred.[39]

§ 30.05   THE DOCTRINE OF EQUIVALENTS CANNOT VITIATE AN ENTIRE CLAIM ELEMENT

According to the *all elements rule*, every limitation of a claim is material. In *Warner-Jenkinson Co. v. Hilton Davis Chemical Co.*,[40] the Supreme Court held that the doctrine of equivalents cannot be applied in a manner that completely eliminates an entire claim element.[41]

An illustration of this rule is found in *Sage Products, Inc. v. Devon Industries, Inc.*[42] There, the asserted patent described a container for disposing hazardous medical waste, such as syringes. The asserted claim included a limitation for "an elongated slot at the top of the container body" and another which stated that the slot was placed below a first barrier, stated as "a first constriction extending over said slot."[43] The accused medical waste container included an elongated slot that was placed *inside* the container body (rather than at the top of the container, as stated in the claim) and underneath *two* barriers (and not a single barrier as described in the claim).

The *Sage Products* court held that the patentee could not establish infringement under the doctrine of equivalents. Specifically, the court found that a finding of equivalence would entirely eliminate both the "top of the container" and "over said slot" limitations in the claim. *Sage Products* noted that the claim described a relatively simple structure that was specifically and narrowly drafted, and that the variations at issue were foreseeable at the time the patent application was filed.[44] Further, *Sage Products* explained "as between the patentee who had a clear opportunity to negotiate broader claims but did not do so, and the public at large, it is the patentee who must bear the cost of its failure to seek protection for this

---

[37] The Toro Co. v. White Consol. Indus., Inc., 383 F.3d 1326 (Fed. Cir. 2004).

[38] *Id.* (quoting PSC Computer Prods., Inc. v. Foxconn Int'l, Inc., 355 F.3d 1353, 1360 (Fed. Cir. 2004)).

[39] The Toro Co., 383 F.3d at 1332-33.

[40] Warner-Jenkinson Co. v. Hilton Davis Chem. Co., 520 U.S. 17 (1997).

[41] *Id.* at 29 ("It is important to ensure that the application of the doctrine, even as to an individual element, is not allowed such broad play as to effectively eliminate that element in its entirety.").

[42] Sage Prods., Inc. v. Devon Indus., Inc., 126 F.3d 1420 (Fed. Cir. 1997).

[43] *Id.* at 1422.

[44] *Id.* at 1425.

foreseeable alteration of its claimed structure."[45]

Similarly, in *Bicon, Inc. v. The Straumann Co.*,[46] the Federal Circuit determined that the doctrine of equivalents could not be used to cover subject matter that was "clearly contrary to and thus excluded by" structural claim language. There, the invention was directed to a dental device, a part of which was described as having a frusto-*spherical* basal surface and a *convex* neck portion of the device. The accused device had a corresponding portions with "opposite shapes,"[47] — that is, a frusto-*conical* surface and a *concave* neck portion. The *Bicon* court held that infringement under the doctrine of equivalents was not available to the patentee because the claim's recitation of the specific frustro-spherical surface and the convex structure could not encompass an equivalent that was an entirely the reverse.

Under these authorities, the all elements rule prevents the doctrine of equivalents from being applied in a manner that eliminates an entire limitation.

§ 30.06 CONCLUSION

The doctrine of equivalents is grounded on the view that patentees should not be deprived of the benefits of their invention by the limitations of capturing the invention in textual expression. Nonetheless, a number of independent reasons exist to restrict patentees to their literal terms. The doctrine of prosecution history estoppel limits a patentee from relying on the doctrine of equivalents where that patentee has surrendered subject matter during prosecution to obtain the patent. The doctrine of equivalents cannot be used to encompass elements that already exist in the prior art. Infringement by equivalents cannot be used to capture subject matter that is disclosed but not claimed by the patentee. Further, the doctrine of equivalents cannot be applied in a manner that eliminates an entire claim limitation.

---

[45] *Id.*

[46] Bicon, Inc. v. The Straumann Co., 441 F.3d 945, 956 (Fed. Cir. 2006).

[47] *Id.* at 955.

Chapter 31

CLAIM CONSTRUCTION OF MEAN PLUS FUNCTION CLAIM TERMS

SYNOPSIS

§ 31.01 INTRODUCTION

§ 31.02 IDENTIFYING A "MEANS PLUS FUNCTION" CLAIM TERM

§ 31.03 EXAMPLE: CLAIM CONSTRUCTION UNDER § 112, ¶ 6

§ 31.04 LITERAL INFRINGEMENT ANALYSIS FOR MEANS PLUS FUNCTION CLAIMS

  [A] Literal Infringement of Claims Governed by § 112, ¶ 6

  [B] Literal Infringement and After-Arising Technologies

  [C] Application of the Literal Infringement Standard for Claims Governed by § 112, ¶ 6 Governing Rules: *Al-Site Corp. v. VSI Int'l, Inc.*

§ 31.05 INFRINGEMENT OF A MEANS PLUS FUNCTION CLAIM UNDER THE DOCTRINE OF EQUIVALENTS

  [A] Doctrine of Equivalents and Functional Claims

  [B] A Comparison of "Equivalent Structure" for § 112, ¶ 6 Limitations: Literal and Doctrine of Equivalents Infringement

§ 31.06 CONCLUSION

§ 31.01 INTRODUCTION

To fully understand *means plus function* claiming, some background about standard claiming should be considered. A typical utility claim for an apparatus describes the *structure* of the invention. Its limitations include the individual parts, their locations relative to each other and how these individual limitations operate in relation to the invention as a whole.[1] Consider this example claim to a chair:

An apparatus for sitting, comprising:

a substantially flat horizontal surface;

a vertical back portion attached to the top of said horizontal surface using two-penny nails;

---

[1] *See* Robert C. Faber, *The Winning Mechanical Claim*, 884 PLI/Pat 49, 66 (2006).

at least three elongated support members connected to the bottom of said horizontal portion using two-penny nails.

This claim describes the invention by its particular structural elements — here, the chair, the back of the chair, and the legs. Also, the terms indicate how these structural element relate to each other — that is, the back is attached to the top of the seat, and the legs to the bottom of the seat, and both are attached by the use of two-penny nails. Together, these structural descriptions depict an invention in a standard claim format.

Alternatively, the Patent Act authorizes claims to use *functional* language rather than a structural description. Specifically, 35 U.S.C. § 112, ¶ 6, states that "[a]n element in a claim for a combination may be expressed as a means or step for performing a specified function without the recital of structure, material, or acts in support thereof . . . ."[2] Claims that rely on this provision use a *means plus function* format. To see how such a claim reads, consider that an applicant seeking to claim the chair described, above, may use a term such as a "fastening means" to describe the function of attaching the back and legs to the chair seat, rather than the specific structure "two-penny nails."[3] A revised chair claim using means plus function as authorized by § 112, ¶ 6 reads as follows:

An apparatus for sitting, comprising:

a substantially flat horizontal surface;

a vertical back portion attached to the top of said horizontal surface using *a fastening means*;

at least three elongated support members connected to the bottom of said horizontal portion using *a fastening means*.

In this example, the functional language "fastening means" was substituted for the more specific, structural term "two-penny nails."

As will be examined later in this Chapter, this claiming practice allows patentees an alternative that may provide some advantages. This ability was added to the Patent Act in 1952 in response to a 1946 U.S. Supreme Court case, *Halliburton Oil Well Cementing Co. v. Walker*.[4] In *Halliburton*, the Supreme Court had prohibited use of functional language to describe the "most crucial element" of a combination claim.[5] The *Halliburton* Court expressed concern that claims stated in functional terms threatened to be both overbroad and ambiguous.[6] When section 112, ¶ 6 was enacted, Congress responded to these concerns by limiting the construction of

---

[2] 35 U.S.C. § 112.

[3] Warner-Jenkinson Co., Inc. v. Hilton Davis Chem. Co., 520 U.S. 17, 27 (1997).

[4] *See* Halliburton Oil Well Cementing Co. v. Walker, 329 U.S. 1 (1946); *see also*, 35 U.S.C. § 112.

[5] *Halliburton*, 329 U.S. at 9 ("The language of the claim thus describes this most crucial element in the "new" combination in terms of what it will do rather than in terms of its own physical characteristics or its arrangement in the new combination apparatus. We have held that a claim with such a description of a product is invalid as a violation of [the patent statute].").

[6] *Id.* at 12.

means plus function claims to the equivalent structure described by the patentee.[7]

How does this section apply to a means plus function claim limitation? First, one must identify the *function*. The answer to that question appears in the claim. In the previous chair claim using the phrase "fastening means," the stated function of this means plus function limitation is "fastening."

However, read literally, a "fastening means" might encompass almost anything that fastens — taken to absurd extremes, a "fastening means" might encompass staples, cellophane tape or even ribbon. Section 112, ¶ 6 confines an expansive construction of means plus function claim terms by imposing the requirement that functional terms "shall be construed to cover the corresponding structure, material, or acts described in the specification and equivalents thereof."[8] This information appears in the patent's written specification. Applying this rule, our "fastening means" example is limited to the disclosed structure and any equivalents set forth in the patent's written description. If the specification discloses only a two-penny nail to attach the back and legs to the seat, then the term "fastening means" can only be literally infringed by a device using either two-penny nails or their equivalents. All things being equal, a patentee who discloses a greater number of alternative fastening means in the written description will have a broader § 112, ¶ 6 claim scope that one who limits the disclosure to a single structure.

§ 31.02   IDENTIFYING A "MEANS PLUS FUNCTION" CLAIM TERM

A series of rules define the identification means plus function limitations. Specifically, a phrase that uses the word "means" invokes a rebuttable presumption that it is a means plus function limitation.[9] Indeed, those who draft patent claims use the terms "means" or "step" as a convention to signal the invocation of § 112, ¶ 6.[10] Using our chair claim example, a court will presume that the limitation "fastening means" is a means plus function limitation because the word "means" has been expressly used. In contrast, a claim term that does *not* use "means" will trigger a rebuttable presumption that the limitation is *not* a means plus function limitation.[11]

The presumption that the words "means" or "step" invoke means plus function treatment may be rebutted in at least two ways. First, the presumption will be rebutted if the claim does not specify any corresponding function. For example, in *York Products, Inc. v. Central Tractor Farm & Family Center*, the court considered the claim limitation "means formed on the . . . sidewall portions including . . .

---

[7] For additional information about the enactment of 35 U.S.C. § 112, ¶ 6 and the *Halliburton* case, see Paul M. Janicke, *The Crisis In Patent Coverage: Defining Scope Of An Invention By Function*, 8 HARV. J.L. & TECH. 155 (1994).

[8] 35 U.S.C. § 112.

[9] CCS Fitness, Inc. v. Brunswick Corp., 288 F.3d 1359, 1369 (Fed. Cir. 2002).

[10] Greenberg v. Ethicon Endo-Surgery, Inc., 91 F.3d 1580, 1583 (Fed. Cir. 1996).

[11] *Id.*

ridge members."[12] *York Products* held that this limitation was not a means plus function limitation although the claim included the word "means" because the limitation described no function and only recited structure — there, the ridge members.[13]

Second, the presumption can be rebutted where the claim itself includes sufficient structure to perform the recited function entirely.[14] For example, in *Cole v. Kimberly-Clark Corp.*, the court considered a patent directed to disposable training briefs for toddlers.[15] *Cole* examined whether the claim language "perforation means" constituted a means plus function limitation in the context of the following claim:

> . . . *perforation means* extending from the leg band means to the waist band means through the outer impermeable layer means *for tearing* the outer impermeable layer means for removing the training brief in case of an accident by the user.[16]

Cole found the presumption rebutted because the claimed function (here, "tearing") could be entirely accomplished by the structure disclosed in the claim — here, the use of perforations. Additionally, the *Cole* court noted that the claim described the location of the perforation structure (extending from the leg band to the waist band) and the extent of the perforation (extending through the outer impermeable layer). The court explained, "[a]n element with such a detailed recitation of its structure, as opposed to its function, cannot meet the requirements of the [§ 112, ¶ 6]."[17]

§ 31.03   EXAMPLE: CLAIM CONSTRUCTION UNDER § 112, ¶ 6

A claim construction analysis for a mean plus function claim can be broken into three parts:

- First, one must determine whether the limitation that is the subject of the analysis is, in fact, a means plus function limitation and therefore subject to § 112, ¶ 6.

- If the answer to the first question is "yes," then one should identify the limitation's *function*. This function is found in the *claim itself*.

---

[12] *See* York Products, Inc. v. Central Tractor Farm & Family Center, 99 F.3d 1568 (Fed. Cir. 1996) (quoting U.S. Patent 4,958,876) (filed Sep. 25, 1990)).

[13] *Id.* at 1574 ("The claim language, however, does not link the term 'means' to a function . . . . Instead, the claim recites structure. Without a 'means' sufficiently connected to a recited function, the presumption in use of the word "means" does not operate.").

[14] Sage Prods., Inc. v. Devon Indus., Inc., 126 F.3d 1420, 1427-28 (Fed. Cir. 1997).

[15] Cole v. Kimberly-Clark Corp., 102 F.3d 524, 531 (Fed. Cir. 1996) (quoting U.S. Patent 4,743,239 ('239 Patent) cl. 1 (filed Nov. 7, 1986)).

[16] *Id.* at 530 (quoting '239 Patent, cl. 1) (emphasis added).

[17] *Id.*

- Third, one must identify the *structure* that accomplishes the claim limitation's stated function. The structure can be found in the *written description* portion of the patent or application.

An example illustrates the operation of these steps. Assume that a patent covers a system for connecting two shoes to ensure that the shoes will not be separated from their mate while on display in a retail store.[18] The invention has a tab attached into each shoe, as pictured below, between the inner and outer sole. These tabs are then connected using a filament, which keeps the mated shoes together.

Claim 1 of the patent states as follows:

A system for attaching together mated pairs of shoes, which comprises in combination:

a pair of shoes, each of which has an inner sole and an outer sole, each shoe also having a shoe upper with an inside surface and a top edge, each of said shoes further having a fastening tab and *means for securing said tab between said inner and outer soles;* . . . .[19]

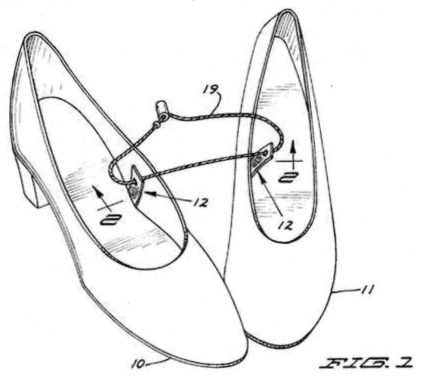

FIG. 2

---

[18] *See generally* U.S. Patent No. 4,624,060 (" '060 Patent"), cl. 1 (filed May 8, 1985); *see generally* Maxwell v. J. Baker, Inc., 86 F.3d 1098 (Fed. Cir. 1996) (construing the '060 Patent).

[19] '060 Patent, cl. 1 (emphasis added).

The first step is to determine whether the "means for securing" limitation is a means plus function term. As set forth in the claim, the word "means" triggers a presumption that the "means for securing" term is a means plus function limitation and therefore subject to § 112, ¶ 6.

This presumption is not likely to be rebutted by either of the two exceptions. This is because the claim specifically identifies the limitation's function as "securing [the] tab between said inner and outer soles."[20] Further, the claim itself does not appear to describe any structure to accomplish this purpose. Therefore, the "means for securing" limitation is likely to be construed as a means plus function limitation.

The second step is identifying the claimed *function*. Here, the claim identifies "securing [the] tab between said inner and outer soles" within the shoe as the function.[21]

The third step requires identification of the claimed physical *structure* by examining the written specification. At column 2, the patentee describes the structure that performs the securing function by the use of either "adhesive, stitching, staples or some combination of these,"[22] or "stitched into a lining seam of the shoes as the sides or back of the shoes."[23]

In summary, the "means for securing" limitation can be construed as follows: First, the term is governed by § 112, ¶ 6, because use of the word "means" triggers a presumption that is not rebutted by either exception. Second, the stated function is to secure the tabs in each shoe between the inner and outer sole. Third, the identified structure to perform this identified function is found in the written description, by the use of adhesive, stitching or staples (or some combination of these) or further, stitching the tab into the lining seam at the sides or back of the shoes. Under § 112, ¶ 6, the claim will be construed to encompass a device element that uses the identical function and the identical structures or their equivalents.

§ 31.04 LITERAL INFRINGEMENT ANALYSIS FOR MEANS PLUS FUNCTION CLAIMS

Literal infringement of a standard utility claim requires a one-to-one correspondence between the elements in the patent claim and the limitations found in the accused product.[24] That is, each and every limitation of the claim must be present in the identical form and in the same manner as stated in the patent claim. For example, a claim stating that the invention is comprised of chemicals A, B and C together in equal portions will be found infringed by a compound that includes a combination of these same compounds (A, B and C) combined in equal portions. If one limitation of a standard utility claim is missing in the accused compound — such as the absence of compound C — then there is no literal infringement.

---

[20] *Id.*

[21] *Id.*

[22] *Id.* at col. 2 l.31-32.

[23] *Id.* at col. 2 l.41-43.

[24] Graver Tank & Mfg. Co. v. Linde Air Prod. Co., 339 U.S. 605, 607 (1950); *see also* Chapter 28 (explaining the standards for direct infringement).

In contrast, the rules governing literal infringement of a § 112, ¶ 6 limitation varies from those governing standard patent claims, as explored in the following section.

[A]   Literal Infringement of Claims Governed by § 112, ¶ 6

The test for determining whether literal infringement of a mean plus function limitation exists depends on whether an element within an accused device performs the *identical function* recited in the claim and has the *identical or equivalent structure* that accomplishes the identified function.[25] Both are required. For example, if the accused device does not have functional identity, there is no literal infringement regardless of whether structural identity or equivalence exists.

An *identical function* is present where the accused element performs the precise function identified in the claim.[26] To use the shoe pairing hypothetical, a device that includes an element that secures a tab between the shoe's inner and outer sole performs the identical function identified in the claim as the "means for securing said tab between said inner and outer soles."[27]

An *identical structure* must have a one-to-one correspondence with the structure identified in the written specification. For example, an accused device that secures a tab using adhesive, stitching or staples has structural identity with the structure identified in the written description of the patent. By contrast, an *equivalent structure* does not require this same one-for-one correspondence. Whether structural equivalence exists depends on a test similar to that used to determine infringement under the doctrine of equivalents[28] — that is, whether the accused device has insubstantial differences from that disclosed in the specification.[29] Generally a difference is insubstantial under § 112, ¶ 6 when it "adds nothing of significance to the structure, material, or acts disclosed in the patent specification."[30]

Other aspects of the *doctrine of equivalents* and *structural equivalents* should be compared. Specifically, the most widely-used test for analyzing insubstantial differences for doctrine of equivalents infringement is the *function-way-result test.*[31] When applied to decide infringement under the doctrine of equivalents, the function-way-result test asks whether the element of the accused device at issue performs *substantially the same function*, in *substantially the same way*, to

---

[25] Odetics, Inc. v. Storage Tech. Corp., 185 F.3d 1259, 1267 (Fed. Cir. 1999) (emphasis added).

[26] Applied Med. Res. Corp. v. U.S. Surgical Corp., 448 F.3d 1324, 1334-35 (Fed. Cir. 2006).

[27] U.S. Patent 4,624,060, cl. 1 (filed May 8, 1985).

[28] Infringement under the doctrine of equivalents may exist where an accused device or process includes every claim limitation *or its equivalent.* Under this doctrine, a claim limitation may be met by an element of an accused device or process that is insubstantially different from the claim's literal limitation. *See e.g.*, Warner-Jenkinson Co., Inc. v. Hilton Davis Chem. Co., 520 U.S. 17 (1997), and Chapter 29 (explaining infringement standards under the doctrine of equivalents).

[29] Chiuminatta Concrete Concepts, Inc. v. Cardinal Indus., Inc., 145 F.3d 1303, 1309 (Fed. Cir. 1998).

[30] *Id.* (quoting Valmont Indus., Inc. v. Reinke Mfg. Co., 983 F.2d 1039, 1043 (Fed. Cir. 1993) (citation omitted)).

[31] Kemco Sales v. Control Papers Co., 208 F.3d 1352, 1364 (Fed. Cir. 2000).

achieve *substantially the same result*, as the limitation at issue in the claim.[32] However, the function-way-result test is narrower when used to determine structural equivalence for a § 112, ¶ 6 limitation. This is because under § 112, ¶ 6, a *function* must be *identical* to establish literal infringement.[33] If an accused element has been found to have an identical function, further analysis of function is unnecessary. Thus, to determine structural equivalence of a means plus function claim, one examines only the "way" and "result" portions of the function-way-result test.

Infringement under the doctrine of equivalents	Literal infringement-means plus function element
function	function
way	equivalent structure
result	

Under these rules, the prevalent test for *equivalent structure* is whether the "way" and "result" of the accused element are substantially similar to the corresponding structure disclosed in the written specification.

In summary, a literal infringement analysis of a means plus function limitation is: 1) identical function; 2) either identical structure or an equivalent structure. Equivalent structure is based on an examination of whether the "way" that accused structure performs the claimed function, and the "result" of that performance, are substantially similar to the "way" and the "result" of the corresponding structure described in the specification.

One additional point should be made with respect to the structural equivalence analysis of a means plus function limitation. Under the doctrine of equivalents, an infringement analysis is performed on a limitation-by-limitation basis. However, the description of the corresponding structure in the written description is not the same as a claim limitation. Thus, the "way" and "result" prongs of the structural equivalence test rest on an examination of the *overall structure* described in the written specification.[34] For this reason, "structures with different numbers of parts may still be equivalent under § 112, ¶ 6, thereby meeting the claim limitation."[35]

---

[32] Dawn Equip. Co. v. Kentucky Farms Inc., 140 F.3d 1009, 1016 (Fed. Cir. 1998).

[33] Odetics, Inc. v. Storage Tech. Corp., 185 F.3d 1259, 1267 (Fed. Cir. 1999).

[34] *Id.*

[35] *Id.*

[B]   Literal Infringement and After-Arising Technologies

Literal infringement of a means plus function claim has a temporal dimension. As the Federal Circuit has explained, "An equivalent structure or act under section 112 cannot embrace technology developed after the issuance of the patent because the literal meaning of a claim is fixed upon its issuance."[36] Thus, a structural equivalent that appears in an accused device must have been available at the time that the patent claim issued in order for literal infringement to be found.[37] Under this rule, a variant developed after the patent issues cannot infringe even if the variant is insubstantially different from the structure disclosed in the patent. To use the mated shoe pair patent as an example, an infringing device relying on a newly-developed equivalent for securing tabs that was not existent at the time the application was filed cannot infringe.

[C]   Application of the Literal Infringement Standard for Claims Governed by § 112, ¶ 6 Governing Rules: *Al-Site Corp. v. VSI Int'l, Inc.*

Al-Site Corp. v. VSI Int'l, Inc. provides an example of a literal infringement analysis for a means plus function element in a patent directed to an invention for a display hanger for eyeglasses.[38] The invention included a "hanging member" that attaches to glasses to allow them to hang from a display rack. The means plus function limitation at issue was a "means for securing a portion of said frame of said eyeglasses to said hanger member."[39] In the trial court, a jury found that the defendant's product infringed.

After finding that this "means for securing" limitation was governed by § 112, ¶ 6, the Federal Circuit considered the jury's infringement finding. *Al-Site* found that the accused device performed the identical function of the "means for securing" limitation, because the accused hanger tag secured a portion of the eyeglasses frame to the hanger member.

Turning to the structural analysis, the *Al-Site* court noted that the specification disclosed that the structure for the "means for securing" limitation was a "a mechanically fastened loop that . . . can be formed from a separate extension or integral extension and includes either the rivet fastener or the button and hole fastener."[40] The accused hanger tag, which used holes rather than a mechanically fastened loop, was not *structurally identical* to the mechanically fastened loop structure described in the written specification. Nonetheless, the court found that that the accused hanger tag was *structurally equivalent* to the mechanically fastened loop and affirmed a jury's finding of infringement of the "means for securing" limitation of the claim.[41] The court determined that the jury's verdict

---

[36]   Al-Site Corp. v. VSI Intern., Inc., 174 F.3d 1308, 1319 (Fed. Cir. 1999).

[37]   Chiuminatta Concrete Concepts, Inc. v. Cardinal Indus., Inc., 145 F.3d 1303, 1310 (Fed. Cir. 1998).

[38]   *See Al-Site Corp.*, 174 F.3d 1308.

[39]   *Id.* (quoting U.S. Patent 5,144,345 (filed Oct. 31, 1990)).

[40]   *Id.*

[41]   *Id.* at 1323. Although the jury had found infringement under the doctrine of equivalents, the

reflected insubstantial differences between the patented structure and the infringing structure.

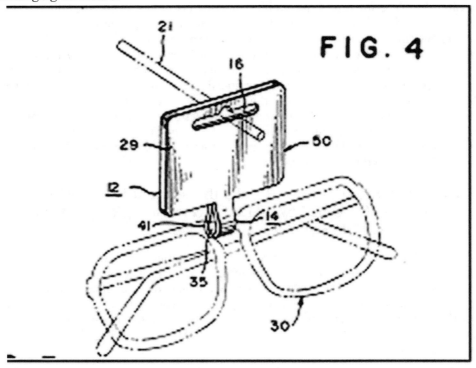

§ 31.05 INFRINGEMENT OF A MEANS PLUS FUNCTION CLAIM UNDER THE DOCTRINE OF EQUIVALENTS

[A] Doctrine of Equivalents and Functional Claims

As with any doctrine of equivalents analysis, the test for infringement under § 112, ¶ 6 is whether the accused element represents an *insubstantial difference* from the claim limitation.[42] If the function-way-result test is used to examine the substantiality of the differences, the accused element must, at a minimum, perform a substantially similar function, using a structure that performs in a substantially similar way and delivers a substantially similar result to that described in the patent. Note that one primary difference between literal infringement and infringement under the doctrine of equivalents for a § 112, ¶ 6 limitation is that for the latter, a patentee need only show performance of a *substantially similar function*, and not an *identical function* as is required for a literal infringement analysis.

Federal Circuit found that the verdict could be sustained under a theory of literal infringement as a matter of law and thus affirmed the verdict. *Id.*

[42] Kemco Sales v. Control Papers Co., 208 F.3d 1352, 1364 (Fed. Cir. 2000).

An example of the distinction between literal infringement and infringement under the doctrine of equivalents can be seen in *WMS Gaming Inc. v. International Game Tech.*[43] In that case, the Federal Circuit considered infringement of a patent for a slot machine that relied on circuitry to decrease the probability of winning when compared with mechanical slot machines. The patent described that when the machine is operated, the circuitry selects a random number from a range greater than the number of stop positions on the mechanical reel. The circuitry can be programmed to assign these random numbers to favor certain reel stop positions, so that the probability of winning can be adjusted. For example, in a slot machine with 20 stop positions, the circuitry can select a number between 1 and 40, and then assign more of these numbers to certain stop positions so that these preferred stop positions come up more frequently than others.

By contrast, the accused device used a system that first calculates the payoff before selecting the reel's stop positions. The accused device selected two random numbers, and then mapped those numbers to payoff numbers, which calculated the payoff amount. The accused machine then selected reel stops that corresponded to the payoff amount that had been calculated.

The *WMS Gaming* court considered infringement of two means plus function elements. The first was a "means for assigning a plurality of numbers representing said angular positions of said reel, said plurality of numbers exceeding said predetermined number of radial positions such that some rotational positions are represented by a plurality of numbers."[44] The court identified the function of this limitation as "assigning a plurality of numbers to stop positions, where the plurality of numbers exceeds the number of stop positions and some stop positions are represented by more than one number."[45] The second limitation considered by the *WMS Gaming* court was "means for randomly selecting one of said plurality of assigned numbers."[46] The court construed the function of this limitation as "randomly selecting one of the numbers that was assigned to reel stop positions by the 'means for assigning' limitation."[47] *WMG Gaming* stated that together, that the function of these two limitations "is assigning and selecting *single numbers.*"[48]

WMS Gaming held that the accused device did not literally infringe because the accused device assigned and selected *combinations* of numbers, rather than a *single* number as required by the two limitations, and therefore the function was not identical. Nonetheless, *WMS Gaming* affirmed a finding of infringement under the doctrine of equivalents, noting that "the doctrine [of equivalents] only requires substantially the same function, not identity as in § 112, ¶ 6."[49] Stated summarily, under *WMS Gaming*, the function-way-result test permits a finding of infringement of a means plus function claim where there are insubstantial

---

[43] WMS Gaming Inc. v. Int'l Game Tech., 184 F.3d 1339 (Fed. Cir. 1999).

[44] *Id.* at 1347 (quoting U.S. Patent 4,448,419 (filed Feb. 24, 1984)).

[45] *Id.*

[46] *Id.* at 1349.

[47] *Id.*

[48] *Id.* at 1352 (emphasis added).

[49] *Id.* at 1353.

differences in the identified functionality of the means plus function limitation.

[B]   A Comparison of "Equivalent Structure" for § 112, ¶ 6 Limitations: Literal and Doctrine of Equivalents Infringement

The tests for *equivalent structure* for both literal infringement and infringement under the doctrine of equivalents are similar. For both types of infringement, one looks for insubstantial differences between the structure disclosed in the patent and the accused element. If relying on the "function-way-result" test, one examines whether the accused element performs the identified function in a substantially similar "way" and delivers a substantially similar "result."

Because the tests for equivalent structure appear to be similar, if a structure is not equivalent for literal infringement then it may be logical to conclude that structural equivalence does not exist under the doctrine of equivalents either.[50] However, this is not true in all cases. This is because there is a fundamental temporal difference between the two.

§ 112, ¶ 6 Function–Way–Result

Literal infringement:

- **Identical function**
- **Identical or substantially equivalent structure**
- **Structure exists at time patent issues**

Doctrine of Equivalent Infringement

- **Substantially equivalent function**
- **Substantially equivalent structure**
- **Can cover later-developed solutions**

For literal infringement, a structural equivalent that appears in an accused device must have been available at the time that the patent claim issued. In contrast, infringement under the doctrine of equivalents can encompass *after-arising tech-nology*. Therefore, even if an element is not literally infringed because the accused structure was not available at the time that the patent issued, a device may still under the doctrine of equivalents where the after-arising technology is insubstantially different from the structure disclosed in the patent.

---

[50] Chiuminatta Concrete Concepts, Inc. v. Cardinal Indus., Inc., 145 F.3d 1303, 1310 (Fed. Cir. 1998).

§ 31.06 CONCLUSION

Under 35 U.S.C. § 112, ¶ 6, a patentee may claim an apparatus or combination by using functional language, supported by a description of the structure which supports the described structure in the patent's written specification. Such claims are construed by reference to the specified function and the disclosed structure.

Literal infringement of § 112, ¶ 6 limitations must have an identical function, plus either an identical or equivalent structure. An equivalent structure exists where the "way" that an accused structure performs the claimed function, and the "result" of that performance, are substantially similar to the "way" and the "result" of the corresponding structure described in the specification. However, an accused element developed after the patent issues cannot infringe even where the test for an equivalent structure has been met.

For infringement of a § 112, ¶ 6 limitation, an accused element must, at a minimum, perform a substantially similar function, using a structure that performs in a substantially similar way and delivers a substantially similar result to that described in the patent. Unlike literal infringement, the doctrine of equivalents may encompass after-arising technologies as equivalent structure.

Chapter 32

EXPERIMENTAL USE

SYNOPSIS

§ 32.01 INTRODUCTION

§ 32.02 COMMON LAW EXPERIMENTAL USE

    [A] The Origins of Common Law Experimental Use

    [B] Current Standards: Common Law Experimental Use

§ 32.03 STATUTORY EXPERIMENTAL USE: 35 U.S.C. § 271(e)

    [A] The Background and Structure of Statutory Experimental Use

    [B] Statutory Experimental Use and the FDA Approval Process

    [C] The Supreme Court's Construction of Statutory Experimental Use: *Merck KGaA v. Integra Lifesciences I, Ltd.*

§ 32.04 CONCLUSION

§ 32.01 INTRODUCTION

The patent system exempts activity from infringement liability where the actor is held to have engaged in an experimental use. There are two types — one based in common law and the other enacted by statute. Despite the similarity in their names, the operation and applicability of each are quite different.

Common law experimental use has been applied for a very narrow class of non-commercial activity, such as where one practices a patent out of idle curiosity. This doctrine has not been successfully asserted in the courts for decades. Common law experimental use was developed in the courts in the early 19th century, and even then failed to gain recognition in all jurisdictions deciding patent cases during that time. More recently, the Federal Circuit has acknowledged the existence of common law experimental use but has cautioned that the doctrine's applicability is limited. Indeed, one member of the court has stated that this doctrine should be eliminated entirely as inconsistent with modern patent law.

Statutory experimental use arises from 35 U.S.C. § 271(e)(1), which exempts activity from patent infringement where the accused conduct is "reasonably related to the development and submission of information" to the Food and Drug Administration ("FDA") for approval for either pharmaceuticals or medical devices. Under this section, experimental use applies where there is a reasonable basis that information generated from the accused activity may be submitted to the FDA.

§ 32.02 COMMON LAW EXPERIMENTAL USE

[A] The Origins of Common Law Experimental Use

The beginnings of the common law experimental use exception can be traced to language in an opinion by Justice Story in the 1813 decision *Whittemore v. Cutter.*[1] There, the defendant's appeal was based on a jury instruction that directed a finding of infringement if the jury found the defendant had made a machine with intent to profit. The defendant's appeal centered on the argument that the making of a *machine* should not constitute infringement, but rather infringement for "making" under the then-enacted Patent Act should be limited to making *compositions of matter.*

The *Whittemore* court rejected this argument, finding the instruction proper. In the course of examining the particular instruction, Justice Story appeared to focus on the concept that infringement was limited to activity undertaken for profit. During the course of this discussion, Justice Story observed, "it could never have been the intention of the legislature to punish a man, who constructed such a machine merely for philosophical experiments, or for the purpose of ascertaining the sufficiency of the machine to produce its described effects."[2] Underscoring the point, Justice Story repeated this principle in a subsequent opinion, *Sawin v. Guild.*[3]

Justice Story's statements in both *Whittemore* and *Sawin* were dicta, and neither case cited any authority for the rule. With respect to this rather unusual origin of common law experimental use, one commentator concluded:

> The only explanation for the experimental use exception which seems to make any sense is that Justice Story, after a brief reflection on the matter, simply felt that the plain language of the statute could not have really been intended to cover the case of a man sitting at home in his parlor or basement workshop and tinkering around with a piece of apparatus as a "philosophical experiment"[4]

A number of subsequent courts applied common law experimental use based on Story's statements. Primarily, this exemption was applied where the accused infringer had not attempted to obtain any commercial gain or profit from the accused activity.

For example, in *Standard Measuring Machine Co. v. Teague*, the court held that a single machine made solely for display at an exhibition was not infringing, noting

---

[1] Whittemore v. Cutter, 29 F. Cas. 1120 (C.C.D. Mass. 1813) (No. 17,600).

[2] *Id.*

[3] Sawin v. Guild, 21 F. Cas. 554, 555 (C.C.D. Mass 1813) (No. 12,391) ("[T]he making of a patented machine to be an offence within the purview of it, must be the making with an intent to use for profit, and not for the mere purpose of philosophical experiment, or to ascertain the verity and exactness of the specification.").

[4] Richard E. Bee, *Experimental Use as an Act of Patent Infringement*, 39 J. Pat. Off. Soc'y 357, 367 (1957).

that the defendant had not attempted to sell the accused device.[5] Similarly, in *Kaz Manufacturing Co. v. Chesebrough-Ponds, Inc.*, the court held that a defendant's assembly and use of a device shown in a short portion of a television commercial were non-infringing.[6] As the *Standard Measuring* court had done, *Kaz Manufacturing* noted that the defendant was not seeking to market the accused device but was only using the accused device for demonstration. *Kaz Manufacturing* explained, "[t]he use of the patented machine for experiments for the sole purpose of gratifying a philosophical taste or curiosity or for instruction and amusement does not constitute an infringing use."[7] Likewise, in *Chesterfield v. United States*, in an action against the government, the Court of Claims held that the government's use of a patented alloy "for testing and for experimental purposes" was not an infringement.[8]

Since the time that Justice Story articulated the doctrine of experimental use through the formation of the Federal Circuit in 1982, the contours of the common law experimental use were not consistently defined. Most courts focused on *Whittemore's* language, finding experimental use applicable where the accused's conduct was purely non-commercial in character. Other courts indicated that the exemption applied if the activity was undertaken to test the sufficiency of the patent's specification. However, some courts refused to recognize the common law experimental use at all.[9]

[B]   Current Standards: Common Law Experimental Use

Under the current standard in the Federal Circuit, the application of experimental use is quite limited.

Soon after the court was formed, the Federal Circuit addressed the common law experimental use exception in the 1984 decision *Roche Products, Inc. v. Bolar Pharmaceutical Co.*[10] The patentee, a pharmaceutical company, asserted a patent to a compound for a prescription sleeping pill called "Dalmane." About a year before the patent to Dalmane was due to expire, the defendant Bolar, a generic drug company, developed a compound with the same properties as Dalmane. Without waiting for the patent to expire, the accused infringer Bolar began to prepare an application to approve its generic version of Dalmane for the FDA. In connection with this work, Bolar made caplets of the patented compound and began to perform tests necessary to obtain data for the FDA application. If successful, Bolar would have used the generic to compete directly with Roche's

---

[5]   Standard Measuring Mach. Co. v. Teague, 15 F. 390 (C.C.D. Mass. 1883).

[6]   Kaz Mfg. Co. v. Chesebrough-Ponds, Inc., 317 F.2d 679, 680-81 (2d Cir. 1963).

[7]   *Id.* at 680 (quoting Ruth v. Stearns-Roger Mfg. Co., 13 F. Supp. 697, 713 (D. Colo. 1935), *rev'd on other grounds*, 87 F.2d 35 (10th Cir. 1936)).

[8]   Chesterfield v. U.S., 159 F. Supp. 371, 375-76 (Ct. Cl. 1958).

[9]   *See e.g.*, Albright v. Celluloid Harness Trimming Co., 1 F. Cas. 320, 323 (C.C.D.N.J. 1877) (No. 147) (finding that defendant's experimentation with the plaintiff's invention was a "technical infringement" and imposing an injunction against future use); Bee, *supra* note 4, at 369.

[10]   Roche Products, Inc. v. Bolar Pharmaceutical Co., Inc., 733 F.2d 858 (Fed. Cir. 1984).

Dalmane once Roche's patent expired and FDA approval for Bolar's generic was obtained.

The court rejected Bolar's reliance on common law experimental use, holding "the experimental use exception to be truly narrow."[11] The *Bolar* court pointed out that the drug preparation activity was outside experimental use, which the court instructed is reserved for "gratifying a philosophical taste, or curiosity, or for mere amusement."[12] The *Bolar* opinion explained that the infringer Bolar's uses were performed with a "definite, cognizable, and not insubstantial commercial purposes" — here, the infringing activity was performed in preparation to sell a generic drug to compete with the patentee's product. On this basis, the Federal Circuit held that experimental use did not apply. Today, *Bolar* is no longer precedent for the pharmaceutical industry, based on the Congressional enactment of statutory experimental use set forth in 35 U.S.C. § 271(e)(1), a section examined in more detail later in this chapter. Nonetheless, the *Bolar* case remains good law for the proposition that, outside the pharmaceutical context, common law experimental does not shield pre-sale practice of an invention.

This point was underscored in the 2000 decision, *Embrex, Inc. v. Service Engineering Corp.*[13] In *Embrex*, the defendant practiced a patented method in order to design around the patentee's claims. The court rejected the defendant's argument that this exploratory work was subject to an experimental use exception, reiterating the *Bolar* standard that the doctrine does not apply where there are "definite, cognizable, and not insubstantial commercial purposes."[14] In *Embrex*, the defendant's efforts to develop machines to perform the method were deemed to be commercial in nature and therefore outside the scope of experimental use.

Embrex creates significant practical difficulties for those who wish to design around patents, because under this decision one cannot "make" or "use" a claimed invention as the basis for study to invent an alternative to it in a commercial context. Under such circumstances, obtaining a license to design around another's patent is unlikely because few patentees wish to share the market with a competitor. Taking these circumstances together, the practical impact of *Embrex* appears to conflict with the Federal Circuit's acknowledgement that "[d]esigning around patents is, in fact, one of the ways in which the patent system works to the advantage of the public in promoting progress in the useful arts, its constitutional purpose."[15]

---

[11] *Id.* at 863.

[12] *Id.* at 862 (quoting Peppenhausen v. Falke, 19 F. Cas. 1048, 1049 (C.C.S.D.N.Y. 1861) (No. 11,279)).

[13] Embrex, Inc. v. Service Engineering Corp., 216 F.3d 1343 (Fed. Cir. 2000).

[14] *Id.* at 1349 (quoting *Bolar*, 733 F.2d at 862).

[15] Slimfold Mfg. Co. v. Kinkead Indus., Inc., 932 F.2d 1453, 1457 (Fed. Cir. 1991). Designing around is viewed favorably in many contexts because such activity may yield alternatives that are more efficient or more effective. Indeed, one famous example of a design around is Xerox's photocopying technology which was designed to accomplish duplication while avoiding Kodak's photography patents. FED. TRADE COMM'N, TO PROMOTE INNOVATION: THE PROPER BALANCE OF COMPETITION AND PATENT LAW AND POLICY ch. 2, at 21 (2003), *available at* http://www.ftc.gov/os/2003/10/innovationrpt.pdf. An additional example in this report is the drug Zantac, which was a design around of another successful drug Tagamet. *Id.*

In a concurring opinion to the *Embrex* decision, Judge Rader indicated that he would have gone further. Specifically, Judge Rader wrote that common law experimental use should be eliminated entirely as inconsistent with the current Patent Act. Judge Rader pointed out that the defendant's intent to practice another's invention is legally irrelevant to determining infringement and therefore "neither the statute nor any past Supreme Court precedent gives any reason to excuse infringement because it was committed with a particular purpose or intent, such as for scientific experimentation or idle curiosity."[16]

In 2002, the Federal Circuit reconfirmed that experimental use should be narrowly construed in *Madey v. Duke University*,[17] the court's most recent decision in this area. There, the patent holder, Madey, was a research professor hired by the defendant Duke University from his former position at Stanford University. When Madey joined Duke, he brought from Stanford a free electron laser that had been installed there. Throughout this time, Madey held two patents for some of that equipment. Some years later, Madey left Duke amidst a dispute and left the laser equipment behind. After Madey left, Duke continued to use the equipment encompassed by Madey's patents, and Madey sued Duke for infringement.

In response, Duke raised common law experimental use, a position that was accepted by the district court based on the university's stated purpose that Duke was "dedicated to teaching, research, and the expansion of knowledge."[18] The Federal Circuit reversed, finding that Duke's non-profit, educational status was not determinative of whether Duke's conduct was subject to the experimental use exception. Stating that any activity that is performed within the scope of the defendant's legitimate business is not immunized, the Federal Circuit explained as follows:

> [R]egardless of whether a particular institution or entity is engaged in an endeavor for commercial gain, so long as the act is in furtherance of the alleged infringer's legitimate business and is not solely for amusement, to satisfy idle curiosity, or for strictly philosophical inquiry, the act does not qualify for the very narrow and strictly limited experimental use defense.[19]

The *Madey* court observed that, as a general matter, university research may be akin to commercial activity given that some projects serve "to increase the status of the institution and lure lucrative research grants, students and faculty."[20] The court remanded the case for factual findings on whether Duke's use of Madey's invention was within the scope of its legitimate business, which the court identified as "educating and enlightening students and faculty participating in these projects."[21] If the accused uses of the invention were related to Duke's legitimate business as so

---

[16] *Id.* at 1353 (Rader, J. concurring).

[17] Madey v. Duke University, 307 F.3d 1351 (Fed. Cir. 2002).

[18] *Id.* at 1356.

[19] *Id.* at 1362.

[20] *Id.*

[21] *Id.*

defined, the Federal Circuit indicated that experimental use did not bar a finding of infringement.

The *Madey* court's narrow view of experimental use raises an important question — that is, whether common law experimental use continues to exist as a practical matter for the types of inventions that are likely to be subject to litigation. Virtually all uses within the business realm are likely to be found commercial in nature, and therefore outside the experimental use exemption. For inventions used in research institutions, such as universities, *Madey* narrows experimental use almost to a vanishing point. To use the *Madey* case as an example, few could be expected to undertake a purely philosophical inquiry with a university's free electron laser without *some* relation to the school's educational or research mission. As one article notes, experimental use "may have been largely obliterated by recent Federal Circuit decisions."[22]

Perhaps unsurprisingly, the district court that considered *Madey* on remand ruled that Duke could not establish experimental use, given concessions in the record that Duke had undertaken at least some of this activity "in furtherance of the school's educational purpose."[23] Professor Katherine Strandburg explains that the result in the *Madey* decision may have been driven by the nature of the patented invention.[24] Specifically, the *Madey* patents were directed to equipment used for the type of basic research typically performed by universities. Strandburg writes, "[b]ecause this type of research was the primary intended use of the patented equipment, a judicial exemption of such research as noncommercial experimental use would have gutted the core grant of exclusivity supposedly provided by the patent."[25]

Nonetheless, under the Federal Circuit's precedent of the common law research exemption as discussed in *Bolar, Embrex*, and *Madey*, there appears to be scant space to practice inventions under common law experimental use.

§ 32.03 STATUTORY EXPERIMENTAL USE: 35 U.S.C. § 271(e)

[A] The Background and Structure of Statutory Experimental Use

35 U.S.C. § 271(e)(1) is the statutory experimental use provision, which excludes from patent infringement activity undertaken to develop information for submission to the FDA for the approval of prescription drugs and medical devices.[26] It was passed as legislative change in light of the *Bolar* decision,

---

[22] Dan L. Burk & Brett H. McDonnell, *The Goldilocks Hypothesis: Balancing Intellectual Property Rights at the Boundary of the Firm*, 2007 U. ILL. L. REV. 575, 604 n.194 (2007).

[23] Madey v. Duke Univ., 336 F. Supp. 2d 583, 592 (M.D.N.C. 2004).

[24] *See* Katherine J. Strandburg, *What Does the Public Get? Experimental Use and the Patent Bargain*, 2004 WIS. L. REV. 81, 84-85 (2004).

[25] *Id.*

[26] *See* Eli Lilly & Co. v. Medtronic, Inc., 496 U.S. 661, 673-74 (1990).

discussed earlier. Under *Bolar*, a generic drug company had to wait until a drug development company's patent expired before gathering necessary data for FDA approval for the sale of the generic to the public. The FDA submission and approval process for a generic drug may take several years. As the Supreme Court has explained, "[s]ince that activity could not be commenced by those who planned to compete with the patentee until expiration of the entire patent term, the patentee's *de facto* monopoly would continue for an often substantial period until regulatory approval was obtained."[27]

Section 271(e)(1) resolves this concern. Under this section, acts that are reasonably related to the development and submission of information to the FDA for regulatory approval are exempted from infringement.[28] Thus, a company wishing to gain FDA approval of a generic may begin testing and compiling information at any time prior to the patent's expiration and these acts will not constitute infringement.

In a companion provision passed with this subsection, Congress enacted a subsection that assists companies that patent products subject to FDA approval.[29] Specifically, Congress amended the Patent Act to add a term extension to restore some of the time lost on patent's life while those patented products are awaiting approval from the FDA.[30]

[B] Statutory Experimental Use and the FDA Approval Process

In *Merck KGaA v. Integra Lifesciences I, Ltd.*,[31] the Supreme Court considered the breadth of the statutory language of § 271(e), which states that activity is not infringement where it is "solely for uses reasonably related to the development and submission of information" to the FDA.[32] Before examining the *Merck* decision, some insight into the FDA's approval process for pharmaceuticals is helpful.

Typically, the development of a new drug begins with exploration. At this stage, the drug maker may perform basic research in a laboratory environment that examines the disease of interest or the interaction of particular compounds with substances found in the human body. The drug maker then begins a testing stage, which is frequently a process of trial and error, to identify particular drug candidates. Sometimes hundreds or even thousands of substances may be studied for favorable effects before one is identified. Various substances are considered as additional developments and insights are gained. At this juncture, a drug developer

---

[27] *Id.*

[28] 35 U.S.C. § 271(e)(1) (2000) ("It shall not be an act of infringement to make . . . a patented invention . . . solely for uses reasonably related to the development and submission of information under a Federal law which regulates the manufacture, use, or sale of drugs or veterinary biological products.").

[29] *See Eli Lilly*, 496 U.S. at 671-73.

[30] 35 U.S.C. § 156(a) (2000); *see generally* Pfizer Inc. v. Dr. Reddy's Labs., Ltd., 359 F.3d 1361 (Fed. Cir. 2004).

[31] Merck KGaA v. Integra Lifesciences I, Ltd., 545 U.S. 193 (2005).

[32] 35 U.S.C. § 271(e).

may perform all of the research without administering any substances to human subjects.

Once the most promising drug candidate is determined, the pharmaceutical company approaches the FDA to begin the regulatory process. This phase can be broken down into two steps. First, one must file an "investigational new drug application" (IND) to gain the FDA's approval to test the identified drug in humans. An IND must demonstrate that the compound has active properties and is reasonably safe for exposure to human subjects. At this stage, the FDA requires the drug maker to submit data from preclinical tests, including tests on animals, in support of the IND.

If the applicant's IND is approved, the drug maker moves to the second stage of the FDA approval process. This phase includes obtaining data necessary to support the drug company's new drug application ("NDA"). As part of the NDA stage, the drug company must conduct a series of three separate phases of clinical trials to test the proposed pharmaceutical's effectiveness and risks in human subjects. The clinical studies are overseen by the FDA, and determinations are made at each phase to determine whether the clinical trials should continue. The number of study subjects increases from phase to phase. These clinical trials are the fundamental pre-market testing ground for the proposed drug. Once completed, an NDA must include data on the drug's efficacy, toxicity and pharmacological properties learned during the clinical and preclinical studies. The applicant also submits other information concerning the drug's method of manufacture and proposed labeling. Overall, the FDA estimates that it takes approximately eight and one half years to test a new drug before it can be sold to the public.

[C] The Supreme Court's Construction of Statutory Experimental Use: *Merck KGaA v. Integra Lifesciences I, Ltd.*

In *Merck*, the patentees Integra Lifesciences I, Ltd. and the Burnham Institute (together, "Integra"), owned five patents related to the "RGD peptide," and recognized that this knowledge could be used to promote the adhering capability of cells both in the body and in cell cultures. With the use of better adherence, wounds could be induced to heal faster, and artificial prosthetic devices could be more quickly integrated when implanted into the body.

Beginning in 1988, the accused infringers, Dr. David Cheresh and Scripps Research Institute ("Scripps") independently discovered, through the performance of experiments, a number of the same properties of the RGB peptides that were also the subject matter of Integra's patents. From 1995 through 1998, Scripps performed a number of tests using RGB peptides. During this time, Scripps identified one of the RGB peptides as the most promising candidate for submission for regulatory approval to the FDA, later shifting focus to another. Also during this time, Scripps used RGB peptides as a control for basic research to determine whether other substances had similar properties.

In response to Integra's infringement suit, Scripps raised § 271(e)(1). On writ of *certiorari*, the Supreme Court considered the extent to which Scripps conduct could be deemed "for uses *reasonably related* to the development and submission of information" to the FDA under that subsection.[33] Integra argued that only conduct associated with *testing in humans* should be immunized from infringement.

The Supreme Court rejected Integra's argument, finding that § 271(e)(1) immunizes conduct necessary to develop all preclinical and clinical studies of the compound, including testing necessary to support an IND. The *Merck* Court went further, stating that this safe harbor applies to the trial and error process of drug candidate identification so long as the drug maker has a reasonable basis to believe that a particular compound may work and, if the testing is successful, would be included in a submission to the FDA. *Merck* noted that "reasonably related" standard might encompass experimentation on drugs that are not ultimately the subject of an FDA submission and data that is not ultimately submitted to the FDA.

However, *Merck* noted that § 271(e)(1) does not encompass "[b]asic scientific research on a particular compound, performed without the intent to develop a particular drug or a reasonable belief that the compound will cause the sort of physiological effect the researcher intends to induce."[34] After providing this guidance, the Supreme Court remanded the case for reconsideration of the facts under these standards.

In sum, unlike the common law experimental use exception, section 271(e)(1) has given a broad construction to immunize a drug maker from infringement liability. Under *Merck*, such conduct is not subject to suit so long as the proponent has a reasonable basis to believe that the information gathered from testing may be included in a submission to the FDA if the testing is successful. A drug maker is not required to actually submit the information in a regulatory filing to successfully assert rely on statutory experimental use.

§ 32.04 CONCLUSION

Although both common law experimental use and statutory experimental use share a common name, these exceptions are quite different in operation. Under recent Federal Circuit decisions, common law experimental use has been recognized but narrowed to arise only if the accused's conduct is for "gratifying a philosophical taste, or curiosity, or for mere amusement."[35] If the defendant acts with a commercial purpose or performs infringing activity within the legitimate scope of the defendant's business, the common law experimental use exception is not available. As a practical matter, the Federal Circuit has not affirmed the use of this defense since the court was first formed in 1982.

Statutory experimental use, codified at 35 U.S.C. § 271(e)(1), applies to activity that is "reasonably related to the development and submission of information" to

---

[33] *See id.* at 202.

[34] *Id.* at 205-06.

[35] Roche Prods., Inc. v. Bolar Pharm. Co., 733 F.2d 858, 862 (Fed. Cir. 1984) (quoting Poppenhusen v. Falke, 19 F. Cas. 1048, 1049 (C.C.S.D.N.Y. 1861) (No. 11,279)).

the FDA for approval of either pharmaceuticals or medical devices. The Supreme Court has given this provision a broad construction, permitting immunity from suit for conduct undertaken for testing where the drug maker has a reasonable basis to believe that a particular compound may work and, if the testing is successful, would be included in a submission to the FDA. However, a drug maker's engagement in basic research is not within the safe harbor of § 271(e).

Chapter 33

CONTRIBUTORY INFRINGEMENT

SYNOPSIS

§ 33.01   INTRODUCTION

§ 33.02   POLICY ISSUES RELATING TO CONTRIBUTORY
INFRINGEMENT

§ 33.03   "A MATERIAL PART OF THE INVENTION"

§ 33.04   KNOWLEDGE OF USE FOR INFRINGEMENT

§ 33.05   SUBSTANTIAL NONINFRINGING USES

§ 33.06   DIRECT INFRINGEMENT

§ 33.07   CONCLUSION

§ 33.01   INTRODUCTION

The doctrine of *contributory infringement* imposes liability on one who sells, offers to sell or imports a component which is a material part of another's invention knowing that the component is designed for a product that infringes another's patent. Like active inducement,[1] contributory infringement is a theory of *indirect infringement*, whereby one is liable if one has contributed to, and thereby aided and abetted, another's infringement.

Historically, indirect infringement developed from an analogy to joint liability for those who aid or participate in the commission of a tort.[2] Courts applied this principle to impose liability for patent infringement "against those who, by furnishing the parts which distinguish the combination, make it possible for others to assemble and use the combination."[3] Contributory infringement and active inducement initially arose from a common body of case law.[4] Today, the doctrines have been separated into individual subsections of Patent Act.[5] Under current law, a party who provides a component with knowledge that it is especially designed for use in an infringing device or system may be liable as a contributory infringer so

---

[1] For information about active inducement, *see infra* Chapter 34.

[2] *See, e.g.*, Thomson-Houston Electric Co. v. Ohio Brass Co., 80 F. 712, 721 (6th Cir. 1897) ("An infringement of a patent is a tort analogous to trespass or trespass on the case.").

[3] *Id.*

[4] *See* Mark A. Lemley, *Inducing Patent Infringement*, 39 U.C. Davis L. Rev. 225, 227 (2005).

[5] 35 U.S.C. § 271(b) & (c).

long as the component is not a staple item of commerce with substantial nonin-fringing uses.[6]

The 1871 *Wallace v. Holmes* is a paradigm case for the doctrine as it existed in earlier years that exemplifies principles consistent with current law.[7] In that case, the asserted patent claimed an oil burning lamp with a novel burner as the key feature of invention. Significantly, the patent claimed both the burner and a standard glass chimney to surround the burner's flame. The defendant made and sold only the burner alone, expecting that purchasers would add an off-the-shelf-chimney. Because the claimed combination included both the novel burner and a standard chimney, the defendant argued that an infringement finding was errone-ous because the defendant only made and sold a portion of the claimed device.

The court rejected this argument, finding infringement based on the fact that "the defendants have manufactured and sold extensively the burner, leaving the purchasers to supply the chimney, without which the burner is useless."[8] The court noted that the defendant had demonstrated the device assembled with a standard chimney to prospective customers.[9] The *Wallace* Court found that the defendant's conduct had "the express purpose of assisting, and making a profit by assisting, in a gross infringement of the complainant's patent."[10] *Wallace* illustrates the funda-mental principles of contributory infringement — that is, a manufacturer or distributor is held responsible for providing a material component to another with the knowledge that it will be used to directly infringe.

The current statute governing contributory infringement is 35 U.S.C. § 271(c), which states:

> Whoever offers to sell or sells within the United States or imports into the United States a component of a patented machine, manufacture, combina-tion, or composition, or a material or apparatus for use in practicing a patented process, constituting a material part of the invention, knowing the same to be especially made or especially adapted for use in an infringement of such patent, and not a staple article or commodity of commerce suitable for substantial noninfringing use, shall be liable as a contributory infringer.

Under this statute, one may hold a component supplier liable for contributory infringement where:

• the product's use constituted "a material part of the invention";

• the supplier knew its product was "especially made or especially adapted for use in an infringement" of the patent;

• the product is not a staple article or commodity of commerce suitable for substantial noninfringing use; and

---

[6] Wordtech Systems, Inc v. Integrated Networks Solutions, Inc., 609 F.3d 1308, 1316 (Fed. Cir. 2010).

[7] Wallace v. Holmes, 29 F. Cas. 74 (Conn. Cir. Ct. 1871).

[8] *Id.* at 79-80.

[9] *Id.* at 80.

[10] *Id.* at 80.

   • the supplier's product was used to commit acts of direct infringement.[11]

In addition, the defendant's conduct must occur within the United States.[12]

§ 33.02   POLICY ISSUES RELATING TO CONTRIBUTORY INFRINGEMENT

Some contributory infringement cases raise difficult policy considerations. Generally, restrictions on the sale of goods are disfavored because such limits tend to restrict consumer choice.[13] The patent system's incentive structure is thought to justify variation from this general rule where a product or process infringes a patent claim.

However, liability for contributory infringement is imposed for providing a component of an invention that, because it represents only a portion of an infringement device, does not itself meet all the limitations of a claim.[14] Indeed, the component that gives rise to contributory infringement liability may not meet the patentability requirements, and may be part of the prior art. The component may have valuable uses that might assist other inventive or innovative activity. As the Supreme Court has noted, "[w]hen a charge of contributory infringement is predicated entirely on the sale of an article of commerce that is used by the purchaser to infringe a patent, the public interest in access to that article of commerce is necessarily implicated."[15] Further, imposing liability for the sale or importation of a device that does not meet all of the claim limitations may increase the patentee's right beyond that which the patentee has invented.

As one example, consider a supplier who mines and sells a naturally-occurring chemical. By itself, the chemical is a product of nature and, therefore, not patentable. Assume that this supplier sells the product knowing that its sole use is as a crucial component of a patented drug. Such conduct can lead to liability for contributory infringement. Yet imposing liability on the supplier would be very different if there were thousands of other uses for the naturally occurring chemical, and it was only an incidental part of the patented compound. To distinguish these scenarios, section 271(c)'s has been crafted with a number of these policy considerations that limit liability to those instances to those most closely connected to facilitating infringement. These limits are explored below.

---

[11] Arris Group, Inc. v. British Telecommunications PLC, 639 F.3d 1368 (Fed. Cir. 2011).

[12] 35 U.S.C. § 271(c) (2000) (". . . offers to sell or sells *within the United States* or imports *into the United States* a component of a patented machine, manufacture, combination . . .") (emphasis added).

[13] *See generally* Giles S. Rich, *Contributory Infringement*, J. Pat. Off. Soc'y 449 (1949) (reprinted in 14 Fed. Cir. B. J. 99 (2004)).

[14] This circumstance could arise if the accused component is not novel, or the right to patent had been relinquished due to a statutory bar. *See, e.g.*, 35 U.S.C. § 102. Such a component may, nonetheless, constitute a material part of an entire combination where the combination as a whole meets all patentability requirements.

[15] Sony Corp. of America v. Universal City Studios, Inc., 464 U.S. 417, 440 (1984).

§ 33.03   "A MATERIAL PART OF THE INVENTION"

One important limitation to the doctrine of contributory infringement is that the component, material or apparatus that is produced by the infringer must constitute a *material part of the invention*. This requirement ensures that there is a strong connection between the defendant's conduct and infringement of the patent claim.

Whether a component is material is determined with reference to the claim. As an example, in *Arris Group, Inc. v. British Telecommunications PLC*, the court considered patent claims to a system for transmitting telephone calls over the Internet. The patentee asserted infringement against a voice over the internet telephone system that relied, in part, on components provided by the defendant Arris.[16] According to the patentee, Arris' components "satisf[ied] at least one essential element or method step for every asserted claim."[17] This was sufficient to demonstrate that Arris' components were a material part of the invention.

On the other hand, components that are outside the claim scope are very unlikely to lead to liability. For example, one decision considered claims to an invention that described a system that broke data into segments before transmittal — a process called "fragmenting."[18] The claims described identifiers placed on each data segment. However, the devices made by the accused contributory infringer were receivers that re-assembled fragmented messages — which is called "defragmenting." The patent did not disclose defragmenting. The court held that an accused device that *defragmented* data was not a material part of an invention directed solely to *fragmenting* data. Although the court acknowledged that these features were related, the court determined that "a product that only defragments cannot constitute a 'material part' of a claimed invention drawn solely to fragmentation."[19]

The requirement that a contributory infringer provide a component that is a material part of the invention requires a close relation between the claimed invention and the accused component. This is an important limitation on the doctrine that associates liability with the claim scope. As one jurist describes, "to give the inventor of a patented teapot the exclusive right to sell the tea used in it is essentially very different from giving him the right to enjoin others from making a novel part of the pot itself."[20]

§ 33.04   KNOWLEDGE OF USE FOR INFRINGEMENT

Section 271(c) provides that liability depends on whether the component was provided while the defendant was "knowing the same to be especially made or especially adapted for use in an infringement of such patent." Does this language mean that a contributory infringer must have knowledge that the device is

---

[16] Arris Group, Inc. v. British Telecommunications PLC, 639 F.3d 1368 (Fed. Cir. 2011).

[17] *Id.* at 1378.

[18] Fujitsu Ltd. v. NETGEAR INC., 620 F.3d 1321 (Fed. Cir. 2010).

[19] *Id.* at 1331.

[20] *See* Rich, *supra* note 13, at 449.

especially designed for a particular device that happens to infringe? Or does it additionally require that the defendant possess the specific knowledge that the component is designed for a device that infringes an identified patent?

In *Aro Mfg. Co. v. Convertible Top Replacement Co.*,[21] a majority of the Supreme Court held the later of these two standards was required. Although the *Aro* opinion is fractured, five justices agreed that section 271(c) required specific knowledge of the patent and the infringing nature of the conduct. One of the opinions provided this summary of the statute's legislative history:

> The House Committee . . . attempted to make clear that innocent persons, who acted without any knowledge that the goods they sold were adapted for use in the infringement of a patent which they knew about, could not be held liable as contributory infringers. It is hard to believe that Congress intended to hold persons liable for acts which they had no reason to suspect where unlawful . . . .[22]

In the *Aro* case, the Court found that the contributory infringer had the requisite knowledge for many of the allegedly infringing sales, based on a letter sent by the patentee that informed the defendant of the patent and pointed out that the component provided by the defendant to the direct infringers made it "guilty of contributory infringement of said patent."[23] This letter placed the contributory infringement on notice of both the asserted patent and the allegations of infringement.

In summary, to meet § 271(c)'s "knowing" requirement, the patentee must show that the accused contributory infringer knew that the component was especially designed for an infringing use, knows of the patent, and knows that the use of the accused product is infringing.[24]

§ 33.05   SUBSTANTIAL NONINFRINGING USES

According to 35 U.S.C. § 271(c), contributory infringement cannot be established unless the product is "not a staple article or commodity of commerce suitable for substantial noninfringing use." This requirement limits the applicability of contributory infringement to sales of items that have a strong logical connection to infringement. If a product has no substantial use other than for infringement, then there is "no legitimate public interest in its unlicensed availability."[25] To state the converse, infringement cannot be presumed from sales of products with substantial noninfringing uses. As a policy matter, the need for "breathing room for innovation and a vigorous commerce"[26] warrants permitting sales of devices with substantial

---

[21]   Aro Manufacturing Co. v. Convertible Top Replacement Co., 377 U.S. 476 (1964).

[22]   *Id.* at 527 (Black, J., dissenting). This view was held by five justices. The four dissenting justices believed that the statute required only knowledge that the component was especially designed for use in an infringing combination, and not knowledge of the patent or assertion of infingement.

[23]   *Id.* at 490.

[24]   *See also* Trell v. Marlee Electronics Corp., 912 F.2d 1443, 1447-48 (Fed. Cir. 1990).

[25]   Metro-Goldwyn-Mayer Studios Inc. v. Grokster, Ltd., 545 U.S. 913, 932 (2005).

[26]   *Id.* at 933.

noninfringing uses to continue without restraint.

In *C.R. Bard, Inc. v. Advanced Cardiovascular Systems*,[27] the court considered the "substantial noninfringing use" requirement to assess the alleged infringement of a claim for a method of performing a heart procedure. There, the patentee alleged that defendant ACS contributorily infringed by selling a catheter[28] that could be used by surgeons who performed angioplasty treatments as described in the asserted claim. Generally, angioplasty treatments open blockage within the coronary arteries, which are the arteries that branch off into the heart from the aorta.[29] Coronary arteries provide blood to the heart muscle, and in some patients have become narrowed by plaque that forms along the artery walls. Where plaque has built up in the artery over time, the artery fails to provide sufficient blood flow to the heart muscle. An angioplasty procedure opens the coronary artery by the insertion of a catheter with a balloon on its end into the artery's interior. As the balloon is placed into the coronary artery and then inflated, the pressure from the balloon causes the plaque to be pushed back against the artery wall and allows blood to flow more freely throughout the artery.

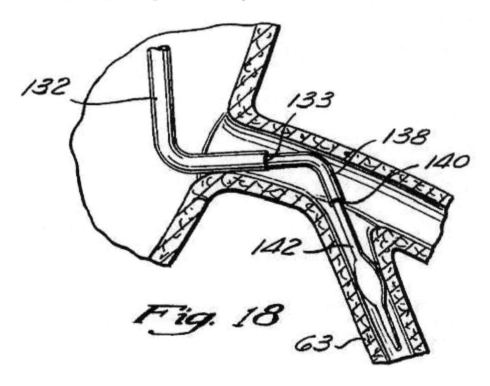

Fig. 18

---

[27] C.R. Bard, Inc. v. Advanced Cardiovascular Systems, 911 F.2d 670, 673 (Fed. Cir. 1990).

[28] A "catheter" is a "tubular, flexible, surgical instrument that is inserted into a cavity of the body to withdraw or introduce fluid." Dorlands Illustrated Medical Dictionary 308 (30th ed. 2003).

[29] *See C.R. Bard*, 911 F.2d at 671 (describing an angioplasty procedure).

The asserted claim required the insertion of the catheter into a coronary artery to a point where the catheter opening could draw blood. ACS' accused balloon dilation catheter had a series of side openings in the tube at the proximal end through which the drawn blood could flow.[30] The *C.R. Bard* court found that ACS' catheter could be used to infringe under the asserted claim, by placing the device into the coronary artery in a manner which allowed the side openings to draw blood from that area. However, the court further found that the catheter could accomplish the angioplasty procedure if the doctor held the ACS catheter such that the side openings remained in the aorta and entirely outside the coronary artery.[31] This second manner of use did not infringe the asserted method claim. The *C.R. Bard* court found that the patentee's motion for summary judgment of infringement was not proper. A jury was needed to determine whether this second manner of operation was a noninfringing use of the ACS catheter could be considered "substantial" under § 271(c).

Noninfringing uses are considered substantial when they are "not unusual, far-fetched, illusory, impractical, occasional, aberrant, or experimental."[32] One decision considered this standard for a patent that claimed a method of preventing the formation of air pockets around the blades of a food blender.[33] The patent was clearly directed to ensuring that no air bubbles formed inside the mixer. The prosecution history disclaimed any attempt to protect any stirring operation that broke up air pockets after formation. The accused blenders came supplied with a stir stick that could be gripped by the user. The stir stick could be used in either of two ways. First, if this stir stick were inserted during operation without being touched by the user, no air pockets formed and the accused blender directly infringed. Second, if instead the user inserted the stir stick after blending was complete, the user would be able to use the stir stick to break up air pockets that had been formed during the operation of the blender. This second mode of operation did not infringe. The court found that liability for contributory infringement could not be imposed as a matter of law, due to the presence of substantial noninfringing uses. The court found that use of the stir stick to break up existing air bubbles after blending was complete was a "common use that neither infringes nor requires infringement."[34]

Whether a noninfringing use is substantial focuses on uses of the accused features of a device, rather than the device as a whole. Therefore, one cannot escape liability for contributory infringement by bundling a noninfringing alternative for sale with an infringing product.[35] The Federal Circuit has observed that, if the rule were otherwise, evading liability for contributory infringement "would become rather easy."[36]

---

[30] According to the *C.R. Bard* court, "The proximal end of the catheter refers to that end which is nearest the doctor during use, i.e., the end remaining outside the patient." *Id.* at 672 n.1.

[31] *Id.* at 674.

[32] Vita-Mix Corp. v. Basic Holding, Inc., 581 F.3d 1317, 1326 (Fed. Cir. 2009).

[33] *Id.* at 1321.

[34] *Id.* at 1329 n.1.

[35] Ricoh Co., Ltd. v. Quanta Computer Inc., 550 F.3d 1325, 1337 (Fed. Cir. 2008).

[36] *Id.*

§ 33.06   DIRECT INFRINGEMENT

Liability for contributory infringement depends on a showing of direct infringement.[37] Typically, this showing is based on practice by someone other than the contributory infringer.[38] This showing can be made with direct evidence that the accused component has been incorporated into a device or system that has been used to infringe, or with circumstantial evidence that the device or system will necessarily infringe under certain circumstances.[39] This showing parallels the direct infringement analysis under section 271(a).[40]

Two opinions issued by the U.S. Supreme Court, *Aro Mfg. Co. v. Convertible Top Replacement Co.*,[41] show how contributory infringement operates for products that may be subject to the *first sale doctrine*.[42] Essentially, the first sale doctrine permits purchasers of a product incorporating a patented invention to use the item and to keep the item fit for the purpose for which it was sold. Both *Aro* cases considered liability for infringement of a combination patent concerning a fabric and metal roof covering for a convertible car. The patentee filed suit against two car makers — General Motors and Ford Motor Co. ("Ford") — as well as against Aro Manufacturing Co., Inc. ("Aro"), who produced a specially tailored fabric that customers used to replace the original cloth in the convertible top after the fabric became worn after a period of years. General Motors had a license to the asserted patent throughout the entire sales period. Ford did not have a license during a two-year sales period, 1952 through 1954, although Ford subsequently obtained one. Aro did not have a license at any time.

In the first of these, *Aro I*, the Court held that customer replacement of the fabric tops constituted a permissible repair within the scope of the first sale doctrine.[43] In *Aro I*, the Court held that, because General Motors had a license to the patent throughout the entire sales period, customers who replaced the fabric tops did not directly infringe because their repair was authorized by an implied license to repair.[44] As the *Aro I* Court explained "it is settled that if there is no direct infringement of a patent there can be no contributory infringement."[45]

In contrast, in *Aro II*, the Court found that the first sale doctrine did not bar a finding that Ford customers had directly infringed during the time period that Ford lacked a license. Based on the existence of customer's direct infringement for Ford cars sold during those years, *Aro II* found direct infringement as the necessary

---

[37] Dynacore Holdings Corp. v. U.S. Philips Corp., 363 F.3d 1263, 1272 (Fed. Cir. 2004).

[38] *Id.*

[39] Vita-Mix Corp. v. Basic Holding, Inc., 581 F.3d 1317, 1326 (Fed. Cir. 2009).

[40] Direct patent infringement is analyzed in Chapters 27 and 28.

[41] Aro Mfg. Co. v. Convertible Top Replacement Co., 365 U.S. 336, 341-42 (1961) ("*Aro I*") *and* Aro Mfg. Co. v. Convertible Top Replacement Co., 377 U.S. 476, 488-91 (1964) ("*Aro II*"). For more information about the Aro decisions and their relationship to the first sale doctrine, *see infra*, Chapter 39.

[42] For more about the first sale doctrine, see Chapter 39.

[43] *Aro I*, 365 U.S. at 369.

[44] *Aro II*, 377 U.S. at 480.

[45] *Id.* at 483, (quoting *Aro I*, 365 U.S. at 341-42).

predicate for holding defendant Aro as a contributory infringer. The *Aro* cases illustrate how authorization for direct uses of the patented invention can operate to vitiate liability for activity that is otherwise subject to the doctrine of contributory infringement. Like the tort principles from which the doctrine derived, contributory infringement is a form of derivative liability that depends on a showing of direct infringement by another.

§ 33.07 CONCLUSION

Contributory infringement is a type of indirect infringement, whereby liability is imposed on one who offers to sell, sells or imports a device that the defendant knows is used to infringe. A patentee relying on this theory must demonstrate that the accused product is a material part of the claimed invention, that the product is especially made or adapted for an infringing use, that the product has no substantially noninfringing uses and that this conduct has led to direct infringement by another. In addition, the patentee must show that the contributory infringer acted with the requisite knowledge, including the knowledge that the use was both patented and infringing. The patentee must also show that the defendant's conduct occurred in the United States.

Chapter 34

ACTIVE INDUCEMENT

SYNOPSIS

§ 34.01   **INTRODUCTION**

§ 34.02   **INTENT TO INDUCE INFRINGEMENT**

§ 34.03   **CONDUCT THAT INDUCES INFRINGEMENT**

§ 34.04   **DIRECT INFRINGEMENT BY ANOTHER**

§ 34.05   **CONCLUSION**

§ 34.01   INTRODUCTION

The Patent Act allows patentees to obtain relief from one who does not directly infringe, but rather who *actively induces* another's infringement. The current statutory basis is 35 U.S.C. § 271(b), which states "[w]hoever actively induces infringement of a patent shall be liable as an infringer."[1] To demonstrate active inducement, the patentee bears the burden to show these three elements by a preponderance of the evidence: 1) the requisite level of *specific intent* to cause infringement; 2) *conduct* that actively induces another to infringe; and 3) *direct infringement* by the one who has been actively induced.[2]

Active inducement may be asserted against one who supplies a product to consumers who directly infringe the patent claim. For example, assume that a defendant manufacturer sells software that, when used as the manufacturer instructs, is directly infringed by end-users who load and implement the software on their home computers. Asserting direct infringement against thousands, if not millions, of individual home computer users is prohibitively expensive and extremely difficult to prove. A patentee would expend more financial resources identifying, serving, and individually proving infringement against each direct infringer than could be expected to be recovered in the lawsuits. By comparison, suing a single software manufacturer in one lawsuit under the theory of active inducement is less expensive and poses far fewer practical problems. Moreover, a case against a single manufacture is more likely to result in an enforceable judgment.

As another example, a patentee might assert active inducement against one who supplies a product to another who offers to sell (or sells) the invention.[3] In addition,

---

[1] Minnesota Min. & Mfg. Co. v. Chemque, Inc., 303 F.3d 1294, 1304 (Fed. Cir. 2002).

[2] *Id.* at 1304-05.

[3] *See* Global-Tech Applicances, Inc. v. SEB S.A., 131 S. Ct. 2060 (2011).

asserting active inducement can be useful to enforce certain types of method claims.[4] For example, consider a claim to a method for a nonobvious method for applying a pesticide compound to kill weeds. The formulator who *makes* the pesticide does not directly infringe this method claim because it does not apply pesticide.[5] However, the formulator who sells the pesticide with instructions to perform the patented method may be liable if farmers who purchase the pesticide follow such instructions and, thereby, directly infringe.

Active inducement was developed through the common law.[6] As with contributory infringement, a defendant's liability for active inducement does not rest on her own practice of the claim. Rather, the earliest cases were based on tort concepts asserted against those "who instigated others to infringe, the planners and promoters of infringement."[7] As one foundational case explained:

> An infringement of a patent is a tort analogous to trespass or trespass on the case. From the earliest times, all who take part in a trespass, either by actual participation therein or by aiding and abetting it, have been held to be jointly and severally liable for the injury inflicted.[8]

Active inducement and contributory infringement arise from a series of cases that considered both. In fact, the early patent cases used active inducement to support liability for contributory infringement.[9]

After several decades of development in the courts, active inducement was codified in 1952.[10] Unlike the former cases, the statute cleanly separated contributory infringement and active inducement into separate subparagraphs of section 271. Today, each is an independent basis to establish liability. Certainly, the statutory enactment of these standards did not create an entirely clean break from the past. Rather, section 271(b), which governs active inducement liability, is interpreted against the common law background from which it derived.[11]

---

[4] *See* Joy Technologies, Inc. v. Flakt, Inc., 6 F.3d 770, 774 (Fed. Cir. 1993) ("Although not direct infringement under section 271(a), a party's acts in connection with selling equipment may, however, constitute active inducement of infringement or contributory infringement of a method claim under 35 U.S.C. § 271(b) and (c).").

[5] *Cf.* Harris Corp. v. Ericsson Inc., 417 F.3d 1241, 1256 (Fed. Cir. 2005) (noting that a claim to a method "of using a communication system," can "be directly infringed only by one who uses the system, not by one who makes or sells the components of the system.").

[6] Giles S. Rich, *Infringement under Section 271 of the Patent Act*, 21 GEO. WASH. L. R. 521 (1953) (describing the history of the section).

[7] *Id.* at 537; *see also* Hewlett-Packard Co. v. Bausch & Lomb Inc., 909 F.2d 1464, 1468-69 (Fed. Cir. 1990).

[8] Thomson-Houston Electric Co. v. Ohio Brass Co., 80 F. 712, 721 (6th Cir. 1897)).

[9] See, e.g., B. B. Chemical Co. v. Ellis, 117 F.2d 829, 834 (1st Cir. 1941) aff'd 314 U.S. 495 (1942) (finding that the defendants "induce their customers to infringe" and therefore "are contributory infringers"); Individual Drinking Cup Co. v. Errett, 297 F. 733, 739-40 (2d Cir. 1924) (referring to one who "assists the infringer by active participation" or "inducing a person to use an infringing device" as liable for "contributory infringement"); Global-Tech Applicances, Inc. v. SEB S.A., 131 S. Ct. 2060, 2067 (2011) (noting that the early courts deciding patent cases treated active inducement "as evidence of 'contributory infringement' ").

[10] Rich, *supra* note 6, at 522.

[11] *See* Rich, *supra* note 6, at 537-38; *Global-Tech*, 131 S. Ct. at 2067.

§ 34.02 INTENT TO INDUCE INFRINGEMENT

The statute that authorizes liability for active inducement states that "[w]hoever actively induces infringement of a patent shall be liable as an infringer."[12] In the 2011 *Global-Tech Applicances, Inc. v. SEB S.A.*, the U.S. Supreme Court considered whether this subsection required that the defendant act with intent. There, the patentee asserted a patent for an improved deep fryer that sold well in the U.S. market. The accused infringer, Pentalpha, had copied the functional features of the patentee's deep fryer and sold these copies through a U.S. distributor, Sunbeam. The patentee asserted that Pentalpha induced Sunbeam to infringe the deep fryer patent by encouraging Sunbeam to sell infringing devices.

The *Global-Tech* Court noted that the terms "knowledge" and "intent" are not stated in the relevant code subsection. Nonetheless, because the nature of inducement suggests that the defendant will lead or persuade another to engage in infringing activity, the court reasoned that the term "induce" implies "that at least some intent is required."[13] The *Global-Tech* Court recognized two possible iterations of intent. Under the first, the defendant might intentionally induce another to engage in conduct that just so happens to infringe another's patent. In this second interpretation, the defendant acts with specific intent to encourage another to undertake behavior that the inducer *knows infringes another's patent*. The *Global-Tech* Court adopted the second of these, primarily to ensure a parallel construction with the intent requirement that applies for contributory infringement.[14] To some degree, this holding recognizes the common historical link between active inducement and contributory infringement.

Nonetheless, *Global-Tech* stopped short of requiring that the inducer act with actual knowledge of the asserted patent before liability could be imposed. Instead, the *Global-Tech* Court held that to demonstrate active inducement, a patentee must show that the inducer had *either* actual knowledge that the induced activity will infringe another's patent *or* is willfully blind to such facts. To demonstrate the second of these, willful blindness, the patentee must show both that: 1) the defendant subjectively believed that there is a high probability that the invention is patented and 2) the inducer took deliberate actions to avoid learning those facts.

The following chart summarizes the *Global-Tech* Court's rules regarding the requisite intent for an active inducement cause of action:

---

[12] 35 U.S.C. § 271(b).

[13] *Global-Tech*, 131 S.Ct. at 2065.

[14] For more information about the intent requirement for contributory infringement, see Chapter 33.

Intent for Active Inducement
Global-Tech

Must show either:

Actual knowledge that the induced conduct infringes a known patent

or

Willful blindness including 1) the inducer subjectively believes there is a high probability the invention is patented and 2) the inducer takes deliberate actions to avoid learning those facts.

In result, the *Global Tech* Court found sufficient evidence of intent. The record contained no evidence that the inducer had actual knowledge of the asserted patent. However, the Court found sufficient evidence that the inducer had acted with willful blindness that its conduct induced Sunbeam to sell Pentalpha's infringing fryers in the U.S. Specifically, Pentalpha had performed extensive market research in the U.S., and thereby learned that the patentee's fryer had growing sales in the U.S. The Court noted that the inducer would have reason to believe that the product included advanced technological features that were valuable in that market. In fact, the defendant had copied all of the product's functional features. The device that the defendant chose to copy was made for a foreign market (purchased in Hong Kong). As is typical of items made for non-U.S. markets, the item was not marked with any U.S. patent number. Further, the defendant engaged an attorney to conduct a right-to-use study for their derivative design, but refrained from informing the attorney that the device had been copied from the patentee. Taken together, the Court held that this evidence demonstrated that the defendant "subjectively believed that there was a high probability that [the patentee]'s fryer was patented, that Pentapha took deliberate steps to avoid knowing that fact, and that it therefore willfully blinded itself to the infringing nature of Sunbeam's sales."[15]

---

[15] *Id.* at 2071.

§ 34.03   CONDUCT THAT INDUCES INFRINGEMENT

Mere intent to induce infringement is not sufficient to establish infringement, rather the defendant must engage in some affirmative *conduct* that induces another to infringe. Such conduct may be advertising infringing uses, demonstrations, training, articles, instructions, or labeling that demonstrates how the product may be used to infringe.[16] As an additional example, the Federal Circuit found that evidence of continued technical support that enables another to purchase and use an infringing product is sufficient conduct to sustain liability for inducement.[17]

Such precedents should be considered illustrative rather than exclusive. Essentially, so long as the defendant takes any "active steps" to encourage or foster infringement, this aspect of a claim for active inducement is met.[18]

§ 34.04   DIRECT INFRINGEMENT BY ANOTHER

Liability for active inducement of infringement depends on the existence of direct infringement by another.[19] An example of this rule in application is *Moleculon Research Corp. v. CBS, Inc.*[20] There, the asserted claim was directed to a method of playing a puzzle cube game with movable rotating parts. The patentee sued a manufacturer of a competing puzzle cube, asserting that the manufacturer's extensive puzzle sales and dissemination of an instruction sheet teaching the accused method of playing with the device constituted active inducement of infringement.[21]

The *Moleculon Research* court found that the end users did not infringe the asserted method claim, because these users did not practice the claim limitations directed to "engaging eight cube pieces as a composite cube" and "rotating . . . four cubes" either literally or under the doctrine of equivalents by using the defendant's product.[22] Because the end users did not directly infringe, the *Moleculon Research* court held that the defendant manufacturer could not be held liable for active inducement.[23] *Moleculon Research* underscores that derivative liability cannot be imposed absent direct infringement by at least one other person.

---

[16] Charles W. Adams, *A Brief History of Indirect Liability for Patent Infringement*, 22 Santa Clara Computer & High Tech L.J. 369, 389-90 (2006); MEMC Electronic Materials, Inc. v. Mitsubishi Materials Silicon Corp., 420 F.3d 1369, 1379 (Fed. Cir. 2005).

[17] *Id.* at 1380.

[18] DSU Medical Corp. v. JMS Co., Ltd., 471 F.3d 1293 (Fed. Cir. 2006) (quoting Metro-Goldwyn-Mayer Studios Inc. v. Grokster, Ltd., 545 U.S. 913, 936 (2005)).

[19] Joy Technologies, Inc. v. Flakt, Inc., 6 F.3d 770, 774 (Fed. Cir. 1993).

[20] Moleculon Research Corp. v. CBS, Inc., 872 F.2d 407 (Fed. Cir. 1989).

[21] *See, e.g.*, Moleculon Research Corp. v. CBS, Inc., 793 F.2d 1261, 1272 (Fed. Cir. 1986) (describing patentee's theory of infringement).

[22] *Id.* at 409.

[23] *Id.* at 410.

§ 34.05   CONCLUSION

Active inducement is a form of indirect infringement, whereby the defendant is found to have intentionally aided and abetted another's infringement. Under 35 U.S.C. § 271(b), such defendants can be held liable to the same extent as a direct infringer. To establish liability, the patentee must demonstrate that the defendant: 1) had the requisite *specific intent* to encourage another to infringe; 2) undertook *conduct* that actively induces another to infringe; and 3) *direct infringement* by the one who has been actively induced to infringe.

Chapter 35

EXTRATERRITORIAL ACTIVITY AND PATENT INFRINGEMENT

SYNOPSIS

§ 35.01   INTRODUCTION

§ 35.02   SECTION 271(a) AND EXTRATERRITORIAL ACTIVITY

[A]   Infringing Uses: *NTP, Inc. v. Research in Motion, Ltd.*

[B]   The Locus of an Infringing Offer to Sell and Infringing Sales

[1]   Offers for Sale and Sales Outside the U.S.

[2]   Extra-Territorial Activity Directed toward the U.S.

§ 35.03   EXPORTING COMPONENTS FROM THE U.S.

[A]   "Makes" and Extraterritorial Activity: *Deepsouth Packing Co. v. Laitram Corp.*

[B]   The Enactment of Section 271(f): Closing the *Deepsouth* Loophole

[C]   Interpretation of Section 271(f): What is a "Component of a Patented Invention"?

[1]   Designs and Plans

[2]   Tangible Items and Section 271(f): Software

[3]   Method Claims and Section 271(f)

§ 35.04   SECTION 271(G) AND THE IMPORTATION OF PRODUCTS INCORPORATING U.S. PATENTED INVENTIONS

[A]   The Enactment of Section 271(g)

[B]   The Operation of Section 271(g)

§ 35.05   INFRINGEMENT ACTIONS BEFORE THE U.S. INTERNATIONAL TRADE COMMISSION

[A]   The Jurisdiction of the International Trade Commission

[B]   The International Trade Commission Process

[C]   Section 271(g) and Patent Infringement in the International Trade Commission

§ 35.06   CONCLUSION

§ 35.01   INTRODUCTION

U.S. patent law is territorial to those events that occur within the U.S. and to importations into this country. Activities that have no contact with this country cannot infringe a U.S. patent, even if that same activity would be considered infringing if within the U.S.[1] This rule is consistent with the canon of statutory construction that "legislation of Congress, unless a contrary intent appears, is meant to apply only within the territorial jurisdiction of the United States."[2] The presumption that federal statutes apply solely to U.S.-based activity "serves to protect against unintended clashes between our laws and those of other nations which could result in international discord."[3] In the Patent Act, Congress specifically limited the reach of inventor's rights to activities *"throughout the United States"* or importation *"into the United States."*[4]

In an 1856 decision *Brown v. Duchesne*,[5] decided in a far simpler technological era, the U.S. Supreme Court examined the policies underlying the territorial limits of U.S. patent law. There, the Court considered whether a patent infringement claim could be brought against a French citizen who had sailed a French ship into the port at Boston, Massachusetts. The ship had been previously equipped with an improved sail that was alleged to infringe a U.S. patent.

In *Duchesne*, the Supreme Court held that the patentee's action failed, finding that the Congress should not be presumed to have enacted patent legislation to operate beyond U.S. shores. *Duchesne* recognized that the patent right granted a patentee "a right of private property, which would in effect enable him to exercise political power" if the patentee were permitted to seek revenue from a foreign ship that had already paid port charges negotiated under an international treaty.[6] Further, *Duchesne* rejected the notion that Congress would have granted an individual property right that might be used to "embarrass the treaty-making power in its negotiations with foreign nations, and also to interfere with the legislation of Congress when exercising its constitutional power to regulate commerce."[7]

Some of the considerations expressed by the *Duchesne* Court are relevant today. Comity considerations militate in favor of each country's ability to set intellectual property policy that suits the economic, cultural and political interests of that country. Permitting U.S. patentees to assert rights outside this country interferes with other nations' interests without support in the Patent Act. Those who wish to

---

[1] *See, e.g.*, Dowagiac Mfg. Co. v. Minnesota Moline Plow Co., 235 U.S. 641, 650 (1915) ("The right conferred by a patent under our laws is confined to the United States and its territories, and infringement of this right cannot be predicated of acts wholly done in a foreign country.") (citation omitted).

[2] E.E.O.C v. Arabian Am. Oil Co., 499 U.S. 244, 248 (1991) (internal quotation marks omitted) (holding that employment laws did not apply outside the U.S.).

[3] *Id.*

[4] 35 U.S.C. § 154(a) (2000) (emphasis added).

[5] Brown v. Duchesne, 60 U.S. (19 How.) 183 (1857).

[6] *Id.* at 198.

[7] *Id.* at 197.

obtain patent protection outside the U.S. have the ability to apply for patent protection in the relevant foreign jurisdiction, which will assess the application according to its own standards.

Nonetheless, the question addressed by the *Duchesne* Court is more difficult to answer today. Although the patent laws are "domestic in character, and necessarily confined within the limits of the United States,"[8] as a practical matter the line between domestic and extra-territorial activity can be difficult to draw in individual cases. Increasing globalization, greater technological complexity of patented inventions, and a broader scope of patentable subject matter have made the determination of the precise location of activity more challenging to ascertain. Although the Patent Act has been amended to address some of these concerns, the case law remains in a state of continual development. Generally, answers to questions of territoriality require attention to the precise scope of the asserted claim, the geography of the allegedly infringing conduct and the specific subsection of the Patent Act that is alleged to have been violated.[9]

§ 35.02   SECTION 271(a) AND EXTRATERRITORIAL ACTIVITY

35 U.S.C. § 271(a) defines that an infringer is one who "makes, uses, offers to sell, or sells any patented invention, *within the United States*," or "imports *into the United States*" a patented invention.[10] Infringement of this subsection cannot be based on acts done entirely outside the U.S.[11]

[A]   Infringing Uses: *NTP, Inc. v. Research in Motion, Ltd.*

Difficult questions arise where the defendant's conduct occurs *both* inside and outside the U.S. This can be particularly problematic where practice of a single claim is accomplished by multiple parties in both U.S. and foreign jurisdictions. In *NTP, Inc. v. Research in Motion, Ltd.*,[12] the Federal Circuit considered a jury finding of infringement of claims relating to the transmission of email over a wireless communication network. The accused infringer, Research in Motion ("RIM"), maintained a wireless data transmission system to receive and send email through the Blackberry, a wireless handheld device sold by RIM to U.S. customers. Although RIM's customers used the Blackberry device throughout the U.S., RIM's wireless system controlled data transmissions to RIM's Blackberry devices through a relay located in Canada. RIM's Canadian relay was alleged to meet either the "interface" or "interface switch" limitations which were present in several of the asserted claims.

---

[8] *Id.* at 195.

[9] In analyzing the problem of the territorial scope of a U.S. patent, the patentee's citizenship is not considered. Indeed, there is no citizenship requirement for obtaining or enforcing a U.S. patent

[10] 35 U.S.C. § 271(a) (2000).

[11] Dowagiac Mfg. Co. v. Minn. Moline Plow Co., 235 U.S. 641, 650 (1915).

[12] NTP Inc. v. Research in Motion, Ltd., 418 F.3d 1282 (Fed. Cir. 2005).

On appeal, RIM argued that the jury's verdict was erroneous because the evidence did not sustain a finding that direct infringement had occurred "within the United States" as required by § 271(a). To establish direct infringement under the "all limitations rule," each limitation of the claim must be met by an accused system. RIM argued that because the "interface" and "interface switch" limitations could only be met by RIM's relay located in Canada, the system did not infringe.

To analyze these arguments, the Federal Circuit approached the territoriality analysis separately for apparatus claims and method claims. For the apparatus claims, the *NTP* court found that direct infringement under § 271(a) was not barred by virtue of the defendant's location of the relay in Canada. Rather, the court found that RIM's system could be found to have been "used" within the United States for purposes of § 271(a) for an apparatus claim so long as *control of the system is exercised and beneficial use of the system is obtained in the U.S.*[13]

The *NTP* court relied by analogy on a 1975 case, *Decca Ltd. v. U.S.*[14] There, the court considered the territoriality of an accused navigation system that relied on transmission stations to send radio signals to ships or aircraft. Two stations were located in the U.S., and a third station in Norway. One of the asserted claims required three transmitting stations. The court found that the "master" station, located in Washington D.C., monitored and controlled all the other stations. On this basis, the *Decca* court found that the system was located in the United States for purposes of a direct infringement analysis, pointing out "the ownership of the equipment by the United States, the control of the equipment from the United States and the actual beneficial use of the system within the United States."[15] The *NTP* court adopted *Decca's* test, holding that the place of infringement of an apparatus claim depends on where the control of the system is exercised and the beneficial use of the system is obtained. Affirming the jury's verdict that RIM's customers directly infringed, the *NTP* court found determinative that "RIM's customers located within the United States controlled the transmission of the originated information and also benefited from such an exchange of information."[16]

For the *method* claims at issue, the *NTP* court held that direct infringement did not exist unless *each one of the steps is performed within the United States.* The court reasoned that because a method claim cannot be infringed unless one performs each step of the recited limitations, the performance of even one step outside the U.S. results in a finding of no direct infringement. On this basis, the *NTP* court reversed the jury's verdict on method claims that included use of the "interface" or "interface switch" limitations, as those steps could not be performed by RIM's relay located in Canada.

From a patent prosecution perspective, those drafting patents are likely to prefer apparatus claims for system, rather than method claims, because the "control and beneficial use" test encompasses the broader range of infringing conduct. Beyond this, it can be anticipated that the case law in this area will

---

[13] *Id.* at 1317 & n.13.

[14] Decca Ltd. v. U.S., 544 F.2d 1070 (Ct. Cl. 1976).

[15] *Id.* at 1083.

[16] *Id.*

continue to bring additional developments.

[B] The Locus of an Infringing Offer to Sell and Infringing Sales

[1] Offers for Sale and Sales Outside the U.S.

Increasingly, business is being conducted on a global stage. The Patent Act provides that one who "sells" or "offers to sell" must be within the United States. How does one determine whether a sale is considered to have occurred within the U.S., and when is one considered extraterritorial? The cases that endeavor to answer that question demonstrate that this area of the law is in the evolutionary stages.

As a starting point, *MEMC Electronic Materials, Inc. v. Mitsubishi Materials Silicon Corp.*, considered the potential liability of the Japanese silicon wafer manufacturer SUMCO.[17] The patentee MEMC alleged that defendant SUMCO had engaged in infringing offers to sell and sales to Samsung Austin, which was located in Texas. SUMCO, who manufactured the accused devices in Japan, defended on the grounds that the "offer for sale" and "sale" were formed entirely outside the U.S. In fact, SUMCO's contract for sale was with Samsung Japan.

MEMC argued that Samsung Japan was a "mere conduit" for the goods to reach the U.S., and that Samsung Austin was the "true customer" for the infringing devices.[18] In support, MEMC presented email communications between SUMCO and Samsung Austin, which demonstrated that SUMCO presented test data for approval or modification by Samsung Austin as a precondition to shipment. After receiving approval, SUMCO packaged the wafers labeled for shipment to Samsung Austin.

Despite these facts, the *MEMC* court held that SUMCO did not infringe as a matter of law based on the territorial limits of U.S. patent law. The court found that the record established that both the offers for sale and sales occurred outside the U.S. For the offers to sell, the *MEMC* court found that the relevant inquiry focused on "the norms of traditional contractual analysis," and that no negotiations had occurred between SUMCO and Samsung Austin.[19] Further, the opinion held that all communications between SUMCO and Samsung Austin did not constitute "offers," as they did not discuss price or other contractual terms. As the court observed, such communications could not be "an 'offer' which Samsung Austin could make into a binding contract by simple acceptance."[20] With respect to the locus of the sales, the court noted that all relevant activities had occurred in Japan — that is, Samsung Japan was responsible for sending purchase orders, arranged for packaging and labeling, and paid for the accused wafers. The court noted that the loss that

---

[17] MEMC Electronic Materials, Inc. v. Mitsubishi Materials Silicon Corp., 420 F.3d 1369 (Fed. Cir. 2005).

[18] *Id.* at 1372.

[19] *Id.* at 1376, quoting Rotec Indus. v. Mitsubishi Corp., 215 F.3d 1246, 1255 (Fed. Cir. 2000).

[20] *MEMC*, 420 F.3d at 1376.

impacted the patentee — that is, the place where the patentee lost business — all occurred in Japan. As the *MEMC* court explained, "[m]ere knowledge that a product sold overseas will ultimately be imported in the United States is insufficient to establish liability under section 271(a)."[21] In result, the court found that no offers for sales or sales occurred within the U.S.

[2]   Extra-Territorial Activity Directed toward the U.S.

The Federal Circuit has found that certain sales activities that take place partially outside the U.S. are within the reach of U.S. patent laws. As one example, an entity could be liable under U.S. patent law for shipping the allegedly infringing product from a foreign jurisdiction directly to U.S. customers.[22]

In another decision, *Transocean Offshore Deepwater Drilling, Inc. v. Maersk Contractors U.S.A, Inc.*, the Federal Circuit held that a contract negotiated abroad between a Danish company and a Norwegian company was an "offer for sale" within the meaning of U.S. patent law.[23] Ultimately, the contract was signed in Norway by the negotiating parties' U.S. affiliates. Further, the object of the agreement was an oil rig that was targeted for installation in U.S. waters in the Gulf of Mexico. Rejecting the argument that the place of contract execution controlled the inquiry, the *Transocean* court explained, "[t]he focus should not be on the location of the offer, but rather the location of the future sale that would occur pursuant to the offer."[24] For the same reasons, the *Transocean* court determined that these facts demonstrated that the parties' contract constituted a sale within the U.S. as a matter of law. Noting that the parties' contract concerned the accused product, the opinion focused on the U.S. as the place of performance — here, delivery of the accused rig.

Together, cases analyzing whether extra-territorial activity constitutes an "offer for sale" or "sale" under U.S. patent law analyze the totality of the circumstances. As more international activity becomes the subject of U.S. patent litigation, cases litigating the locus of offers to sell and sales can be expected to become more common.

§ 35.03   EXPORTING COMPONENTS FROM THE U.S.

[A]   "Makes" and Extraterritorial Activity: *Deepsouth Packing Co. v. Laitram Corp.*

Exporting products raise additional infringement concerns. Section 271(a), the primary statute governing direct infringement, does not enumerate "export" as an infringing act. Absent some other provision that captures this activity, a copyist

---

[21] *Id.* at 1377.

[22] Litecubes, LLC v. Northern Lights Products Inc., 523 F.3d 1353 (Fed. Cir. 2008) (sales of product shipped from Canada to U.S. customers were within the reach of U.S. patent law).

[23] Transocean Offshore Deepwater Drilling, Inc. v. Maersk Contractors U.S.A, Inc., 617 F.3d 1296 (Fed. Cir. 2010).

[24] *Id.* at 1309.

who wishes to profit from another's invention might use the absence of such language to evade liability. To appreciate this problem, assume that another's U.S. patent claims a novel combination of an insulated travel mug together with a spill-proof lid, as follows:

> A travel mug for transporting and drinking liquids comprising:
>
> a dual-walled container containing an insulation material;
>
> said container having threads around the top interior of said container;
>
> a cover with threads around the circumference of the top that meets the threaded portion of said container; and
>
> said cover having a small opening for drinking.

To directly infringe this apparatus claim under § 271(a), one must make, use, offer to sell, sell or import a single product that incorporates all of the limitations of the claim. Assume that one wishes to export and sell the product for sale abroad but does not wish to pay the patentee for a license. Can one circumvent U.S. patent laws by making and exporting the individual parts of the mug and cover separately, leaving it to purchasers in foreign countries to combine the two? Note the product does not meet all limitations of the claim until the individual mug and lid have been combined and that combination does not occur within the U.S.

In 1984, Congress amended the Patent Act by adding § 271(f) in an effort to reach such activity. The U.S. Supreme Court's 1972 decision *Deepsouth Packing Co. v. Laitram Corp.*,[25] provides some historic background to this amendment. The invention at issue in *Deepsouth* was a device for deveining shrimp. The asserted combination claim included a number of elements that were not novel by themselves, as all were commonly known and used in the industry. The claim at issue based its novelty on the combination of these pre-existing parts — that is, the patentee had developed a patentable combination by inventing "a novel union of old means [that] was designed to achieve new ends."[26]

Defendant Deepsouth sought a judicial declaration to authorize the manufacture of the individual parts of the patented deveining machine, shipped in "to foreign customers in three separate boxes, each containing only parts of the machine, yet the whole assemblable in less that one hour" by the end users outside the U.S.[27] The Supreme Court granted this relief, finding that the practice was not an infringement under the patent law in force at the time. The *Deepsouth* Court determined that the defendant did not "make" the patented combination in the U.S., because to "make" something under the patent law required that manufacture of "the operable assembly as a whole and not the manufacture of its parts."[28] The Court explained:

> The relationship is the essence of the patent . . . no wrong is done the patentee until the combination is formed. His monopoly does not cover the

---

[25] Deepsouth Packing Co. v. Laitram Corp., 406 U.S. 518 (1972).

[26] *Id.* at 521.

[27] *Id.* at 524.

[28] *Id.* at 528.

manufacture or sale of separate elements capable of being, but never actually, associated to form the invention. Only when such association is made is there a direct infringement of his monopoly, and not even then if it is done outside the territory for which the monopoly was granted.[29]

Noting that Congress had specifically defined the territorial reach of the patent right in § 271(a) with reliance on U.S.-based conduct, the *Deepsouth* Court refused to grant the patentee broader protection in the form of "the bonus of a favored position as a flagship company free of American competition in international commerce."[30]

The Court further found that defendant Deepsouth's practice did not contribute to infringement under § 271(c), reasoning that "there can be no contributory infringement in the absence of direct infringement."[31] Reasoning that Deepsouth's customers did not directly infringe because all assembly and use occurred outside the U.S., the Court found § 271(c) inapplicable.

The *Deepsouth* decision laid bare a loophole in U.S. patent law for infringement of combination claims. Under the statute as it existed in 1972, a competitor could have copied a U.S. patent and avoided infringement by supplying components of a patented product from the United States and assembling those components abroad. For example, applying *Deepsouth* to the claim for the travel mug claim set forth earlier, under pre-1984 law, one could have circumvented U.S. patent laws by making and exporting the individual parts of the mug and cover separately. A manufacturer that combined the two parts itself abroad, or left it to purchasers in foreign countries to combine the two, did not infringe because the separate components would not meet the claim limitation "a cover *that is attached to* said container" during the time that those components were present in the U.S.

[B]   The Enactment of Section 271(f): Closing the *Deepsouth* Loophole

In 1984, Congress amended the Patent Act in a direct response to the *Deepsouth* decision. In order to "prevent copiers from avoiding U.S. patents by supplying components of a patented product in this country so that the assembly of the components may be completed abroad," the legislature passed 35 U.S.C. § 271(f) to reach export as infringing conduct.[32]

Section 271(f) is divided into two subsections. The first of these, § 271(f)(1), parallels the standard for active inducement.[33] This subsection imposes infringement liability on one who exports "all or a substantial portion of the components of a patented invention, in such manner as to actively induce the combination of such components outside of the United States in a manner that

---

[29] *Id.* at 529 (quoting Radio Corp. of America v. Andrea, 79 F.2d 626, 628 (2d Cir. 1935)).

[30] *Deepsouth Packing*, 406 U.S. at 523.

[31] *Id.* at 526.

[32] *See* 35 U.S.C. § 271(f) (2000).

[33] For more about active inducement, see Chapter 34.

would infringe the patent if such combination occurred within the United States."[34] To apply § 271(f)(1) to the travel mug invention, one is liable for the exportation of the mug and cover separately if the exporter actively induces purchasers outside the U.S. to combine the two such that the limitation "a cover that is attached to said container" has been met.

The second subsection is § 271(f)(2), which parallels the standard for contributory infringement.[35] This imposes liability for infringement where one who exports "any component of a patented invention that is especially made or especially adapted for use in the invention and not a staple article or commodity of commerce suitable for substantial noninfringing use" where the exporter knows "that such component is so made or adapted and intending that such component will be combined outside of the United States in a manner that would infringe the patent if such combination occurred within the United States."[36] Unlike § 271(f)(1), under this subsection the patentee does not have to demonstrate that the exported components actively induced the infringement. However, the patentee must demonstrate that the components that have been shipped are nonstaple articles that are "especially made or especially adapted" for the infringing combination, and that the exporter had knowledge of this circumstance.

Some qualifications to these principles should be considered. First, Congress' 1984 amendments adding § 271(f) to the Patent Act did not overrule *Deepsouth's* holding that one does not infringe a patent under § 271(a) for "making" or "selling" less than an entire invention.[37] Second, reliance on § 271(f) is not necessary to demonstrate infringement by one who "makes" an entire product within the U.S. that incorporates a patented invention because direct infringement for this activity exists under § 271(a).[38] Section 271(f) typically comes into play where a direct infringement theory under § 271(a) fails.

[C] Interpretation of Section 271(f): What is a "Component of a Patented Invention"?

A body of case law has been developed that considers infringement under § 271(f). Unlike patents of past centuries which largely claimed inventions in the mechanical or electronic arts, the current scope of patentable subject matter embraces increasingly intangible subject matter such as information and software. Moreover, manufacturing models are shifting toward offshore activity. These changes have uncertain application to the language and purpose of § 271(f). For example, can "data" be exported? Should one who designs an infringing device in the U.S. and manufactures offshore be deemed to have exported an infringing product? Over the past few years, the courts have attempted to discern answers to

---

[34] 35 U.S.C. § 271(f)(1).

[35] For more about contributory infringement, see Chapter 33.

[36] 35 U.S.C. § 271(f)(2).

[37] *See, e.g.,* Rotec Industries, Inc. v. Mitsubishi Corp., 215 F.3d 1246, 1252 n.2 (Fed. Cir. 2000) (noting *Deepsouth's* continued viability for this rule).

[38] 35 U.S.C. § 271(a) (defining "makes" as a stand-alone act of infringement).

such questions in a number of cases from both the Federal Circuit and the U.S. Supreme Court.

[1] Designs and Plans

In *Pellegrini v. Analog Devices, Inc.*, the Federal Circuit considered whether § 271(f) imposes liability against one who designed and instructed a foreign manufacturing facility to make a product that was within the claim scope of a U.S. patent.[39] There, the patentee claimed a semiconductor circuit used to control a particular type of motor. The defendant Analog Devices, Inc. ("Analog"), which had its headquarters in the U.S., sought summary judgment of non-infringement based on accused devices that were manufactured abroad. Analog's motion was limited to those devices that had been sold and shipped to customers outside the U.S.

The patentee argued that summary judgment was not proper, contending that Analog had designed and directed the foreign manufacture of devices from the U.S., and therefore met § 271(f)(1)'s requirement that Analog "supplie[d] or causes to be supplied in or from the United States" information that led to the design and manufacture of infringing devices. Rejecting this argument, the Federal Circuit held that summary judgment of noninfringement was proper, explaining:

> "[S]uppl[ying] or caus[ing] to be supplied" in § 271(f)(1) clearly refers to physical supply of components, not simply to the supply of instructions or corporate oversight. In other words, although Analog may be giving instructions from the United States that cause the components of the patented invention to be supplied, it is undisputed that those components are not being supplied in or from the United States.[40]

Under *Pellegrini*, U.S. companies that establish or contract with manufacturers outside the U.S. are insulated from liability for all foreign sales. Liability does not exist under § 271(f), because no sale or export of a "component" occurs from the U.S. Further, such activity does not directly infringe under § 271(a), because such companies do not make, use, offer to sell or sell infringing products within the U.S. or import any infringing products into the U.S.

[2] Tangible Items and Section 271(f): Software

In the 2005 case *Eolas Technologies Inc. v. Microsoft Corp.*,[41] the Federal Circuit attempted to distinguish *Pellegrini*, finding that the defendant's transfer of software outside the U.S. for foreign sale constituted a "component[] of a patented invention" under § 271(f)(1). In *Eolas*, the Federal Circuit rejected the argument that the *Pellegrini* case required that a "component" be a tangible item, explaining "*Pellegrini* requires only that components are physically *supplied* from the United States, *Pellegrini* does not impose on section 271(f) a tangibility requirement that does not appear anywhere in the language of that section."[42]

---

[39] Pelligrini v. Analog Devices, Inc., 375 F.3d 1113 (Fed. Cir. 2004).

[40] *Id.* at 1118.

[41] Eolas Techs., Inc. v. Microsoft Corp., 399 F.3d 1325 (Fed. Cir. 2005).

[42] *Id.* at 1341.

However, since the time that *Eolas* was decided, the U.S. Supreme Court has weighed in on § 271(f)'s applicability to software in *Microsoft Corp. v. AT&T Corp.*[43] There, AT&T asserted a patent directed to technology for digitally encoding and compressing recorded speech. AT&T accused Microsoft's Windows software of infringement under § 271(f)(1), on the ground that a computer loaded with the accused software actively induced end-users outside the U.S. to directly infringe by using the accused speech processing feature.

In order to fully understand the holding of the *Microsoft* case, some background understanding of the creation and distribution of the accused software is necessary. Windows software is designed and created by Microsoft in the U.S. However, for sales of Windows outside the country, Microsoft transmitted a master copy of Windows on either an disk or by an encrypted electronic transmission to replicators located throughout the world. Once a foreign replicator received a copy of Windows from Microsoft, the replicator used the master copy to generate the actual copies sold to users abroad.[44] The parties agreed that AT&T's patent was not practiced until an end user loaded Windows onto a computer and the software then became capable of performing the claimed digital speech features. The issue presented to the Court was: "[d]oes Microsoft's liability extend to computers made in another country when loaded with Windows software copied abroad from a master disk or electronic transmission dispatched by Microsoft from the United States?"[45]

The Supreme Court agreed with Microsoft that the software transmitted from the U.S. was not a "component" of an invention "supplie[d]. . . from the United States" under § 271(f). The Court conceptualized Windows as existent in two different forms — first, the Court viewed Windows as *an abstract set of instructions* and secondly as software code (in the form of object code) that was *placed onto a medium* such as a CD-ROM disc. The Court reasoned that the first of these concepts — Windows as an abstract set of instructions — was not a "component" within the meaning of § 271(f) because these instructions were merely abstract information. The *Microsoft* court reasoned that only the second of these — Windows as placed on media such as a CD-ROM — could be considered a component, explaining, "[w]hat retailers sell, and consumers buy, are *copies* of software."[46] Under this reasoning, the Court ruled that Windows was not a "component" until the software was in the form that was capable of interfacing with the customer's computer, in this case burned onto a CD-ROM by the foreign replicator or otherwise loadable onto the end user's hard drive.

In addition, the Supreme Court found that because software installed on the foreign computers were *copies* that been created overseas, Windows sold outside the U.S. had not "supplie[d] . . . from the United States" under § 271(f). The *Microsoft* Court invoked the presumption against extraterritoriality, indicating that respect for foreign law was particularly appropriate in the patent field, because other countries' laws "may embody different policy judgments about the relative

[43] Microsoft Corp. v. AT&T, 127 S. Ct. 1746 (2007).

[44] *Id.* at 1753.

[45] *Id.* at 1750-51.

[46] *Id.*

rights of inventors, competitors, and the public in patented inventions."[47] In the final analysis, the Court found that AT&T could not recover for copies of Windows distributed outside the U.S. created from defendant Microsoft's golden master disks.

The rule promulgated in *Microsoft* case should be understood in the context of the facts upon which the case was decided. In order to determine whether software is a "component" that is "supplie[d] . . . from the United States" under *Microsoft*, one must determine whether the software is infringing according to the claim language at the time of the supply. In close cases, the *Microsoft* Court counsels that doubts should be resolved by finding against extraterritorial rights of a U.S. patentee. AT&T's patent required the use of software *on a computer* and therefore the result might have been different if the claim language did not do so.[48] In all, the *Microsoft* Court's analysis represents a far more complex and nuanced inquiry than the Federal Circuit's resolution of the issue in the *Eolas* case.

[3] Method Claims and Section 271(f)

Method and process claims are a series of acts or steps. Can one who supplies components that are used to infringe a method claim outside the U.S. be liable for infringement? As an example, assume that a distributor ships a medical device overseas that enables the practice of a method claiming a medical procedure. Further assume that this medical procedure, if practiced by a doctor within the U.S., would constitute practice of the patentee's method claim. Can the distributor be liable for foreign uses of the device under § 271(f)?

As previously noted, § 271(f) provides that one who "supplies or causes to be supplied in or from the United States all or a substantial portion of the components of a patented invention" may be liable for infringement.[49] In *Cardiac Pacemakers, Inc. v. St. Jude Medical, Inc.*, the Federal Circuit held that this subsection can not create liability for infringement of a method claim.[50] The *Cardiac Pacemakers* court found that a "component" of a method or process "is a step in that method or process," rather than a tangible item.[51] Noting that § 271(f) requires that a component be "supplied" in or from the United States, the *Cardiac Pacemakers* court found that the term "supplied," implies "the transfer of a physical object."[52] Because supplying an intangible step is "a physical impossibility," the court held that § 271(f) cannot reach the infringement of a method claim.[53]

---

[47] *Id.* at 1758.

[48] *Id.* at 1756 n.13 ("We need not address whether software in the abstract, or any other intangible, can *ever* be a component under § 271(f). If an intangible method or process, for instance, qualifies as a "patented invention" under § 271(f) (a question as to which we express no opinion), the combinable components of that invention might be intangible as well.").

[49] *See, e.g.*, NTP Inc. v. Research in Motion, Ltd., 418 F.3d 1282, 1318 (Fed. Cir. 2005); Joy Tech., Inc. v. Flakt, Inc., 6 F.3d 770, 775 (Fed. Cir. 1993).

[50] Cardiac Pacemakers, Inc. v. St. Jude Medical, Inc., 576 F.3d 1348 (Fed. Cir. 2009) (en banc).

[51] *Id.* at 1362.

[52] *Id.* at 1364.

[53] *Id.*

§ 35.04   SECTION 271(G) AND THE IMPORTATION OF PRODUCTS INCORPORATING U.S. PATENTED INVENTIONS

[A]   The Enactment of Section 271(g)

In 1988, Congress enacted the Process Patent Amendments Act, codified at 35 U.S.C. § 271(g).[54] This provision was intended to preserve the value of U.S. process claims, and to address a disparity between those practicing patents domestically and abroad. Before this amendment, a patentee could file a court action *only* against those who practiced the claim domestically. At this time, a competitor could perform the patentee's process overseas to create products that were imported, sold and used in the U.S. all without violating the Patent Act.

The former law created an affirmative disadvantage for inventors who disclosed a process in a U.S. patent.[55] Once a patentee's enabling disclosure was published, a competitor abroad could simply copy the claimed process in an offshore location to make products that were then imported and sold in competition with the patentee's own products within the U.S.[56] As one Senator described at the time, "[t]here, of course, is something very inherently unfair about U.S. research-based industries pouring resources into a product or a process patent and then having that product or process pirated abroad and shipped back into this country for sale."[57]

Before § 271(g) was added to the Patent Act in 1988, a patentee's sole available form of relief was to file an action before the administrative courts of the International Trade Commission ("ITC") under 19 U.S.C. § 1337.[58] However, ITC actions were seen as limited and inadequate to protect process patent holders. For example, although the ITC may issue an order barring the importation of products made under the claimed process, the ITC lacks authority to award monetary damages for infringement that was not discovered by the patentee until after the products entered the U.S. Further, a patentee cannot file an ITC action unless the patentee can demonstrate injury to existing or soon-to-be established domestic

---

[54] 35 U.S.C. § 271(g) (2000) provides:

> Whoever without authority imports into the United States or offers to sell, sells, or uses within the United States a product which is made by a process patented in the United States shall be liable as an infringer, if the importation, offer to sell, sale, or use of the product occurs during the term of such process patent . . . . A product which is made by a patented process will, for purposes of this title, not be considered to be so made after-
>
> (1) it is materially changed by subsequent processes; or
>
> (2) it becomes a trivial and nonessential component of another product.

[55] Glenn Law, Note, *Liability Under the Process Patent Amendments Act of 1988 for the Use of a Patented Process Outside the U.S.*, 60 Geo. Wash. L. Rev. 245, 246-47 (1991).

[56] *Id.* at 247.

[57] *Id.* (*quoting* Senator Charles Grassley of the Senate Judiciary Subcommittee on Patents, Copyrights and Trademarks).

[58] *See, e.g.*, 19 U.S.C. § 1337(a)(1)(B) (2000) (declaring as "unlawful" the importation of those articles that "are made, produced, processed, or mined under, or by means of, a process covered by the claims of a valid and enforceable United States patent.").

industry.[59] These impediments do not exist for patent infringement actions filed in a U.S. District Court. After several years of consideration, Congress enacted § 271(g) to provide adequate remedies that would fully protect the owners of process patents by authorizing infringement suits in court.[60]

[B]   The Operation of Section 271(g)

Under the 1988 Process Patent Amendments Act, the law remains that one may practice a claimed process abroad without infringing a U.S. patent.[61] Instead, Section 271(g) imposes liability for *importing* into the U.S., or *offering to sell, selling* or *using* a product made by the claimed products within the U.S. during the patent's term.

A "product" under § 271(g) must be a physical good produced by a manufacturing process.[62] An intangible such as information learned from the performance of a process is not an infringement under this provision. One can transfer into the U.S. all of the knowledge gained from the offshore practice of a U.S. process claim.[63] Likewise, the Federal Circuit has held that wireless data transmission of email is not a "product" for purposes of § 271(g).[64]

The application of § 271(g) is relatively straightforward where a tangible product has been made by the patented process and then imported into the U.S. in a direct and unchanged state. Thus, the performance of a claimed process to make Chemical ABC would lead to infringement liability if a foreign manufacturer performed that claimed process and then imported Chemical ABC into the U.S.[65]

However, in some cases, the patented process is one of several steps performed to create an imported product. The legislative history of the statute evidences a concern that patentees might use the provision to overreach by preventing the importation of products which incorporate an immaterial or trivial part of a U.S. process claim.[66] For example, assume that a foreign manufacturer uses the patented process to create Chemical ABC but then adds significant improvements to this compound to create a new generation product, Chemical XYZ. Under what circumstances should the manufacturer be barred from importing Chemical XYZ

---

[59] *See* 19 U.S.C. § 1337(a)(2) (providing that relief can be granted for articles "an industry in the United States, relating to the articles protected by the patent . . . "). The ITC's "domestic industry" requirement is discussed in more detail later in this chapter.

[60] Bayer AG v. Housey Pharm., Inc., 340 F.3d 1367, 1373-74 (Fed. Cir. 2003).

[61] Bio-Technology General Corp. v. Genetech, 80 F.3d 1553, 1560 (Fed. Cir. 1996) ("Infringement under § 271(g) does not consist of the making of a product by a process patented in the United States . . .").

[62] *Bayer AG*, 340 F.3d at 1372-73.

[63] *Id.* at 1376.

[64] *See* NTP Inc. v. Research in Motion, Ltd., 418 F.3d 1282 (Fed. Cir. 2005).

[65] Eli Lilly and Co. v. American Cyanamid Co., 82 F.3d 1568, 1575 (Fed. Cir. 1996) (quoting H.R. Rep. No. 99-807 (1986)).

[66] *Id.* at 1572 ("A concern raised during Congress's consideration of the process patent legislation was . . . whether the new statute would apply when a product was produced abroad by a patented process but then modified or incorporated into other products before being imported into this country.").

into the U.S.? To address these concerns, Congress included express limits on § 271(g)'s coverage to exclude from liability those circumstances where the product "is materially changed by subsequent processes;" or "it becomes a trivial and nonessential component of another product."[67]

Section 271(g)'s exclusions were examined by the Federal Circuit in *Eli Lilly and Co. v. American Cyanamid Co.*,[68] on an appeal from a district court's denial of a motion for preliminary injunction. In that case, Lilly was the maker of the antibiotic compound cefaclor. At the time that the case was decided, many of Lilly's product patents on cefaclor had expired. Two competitors, American Cyanamid and Zenith Laboratories, began to import a generic version of cefaclor that had been manufactured in Italy. Presumably to protect its U.S. market for cefaclor, Lilly purchased the '085 patent, which was directed to a method for producing an intermediate product that was used to make cefaclor and its generic equivalent. Lilly asserted this patent in U.S. District Court against American Cyanamid and Zenith Laboratories, asserting that the defendants' importation of the generic cefaclor infringed Lilly's patent to the process for making the intermediary.

Lilly asserted that the defendant's generic was a product "made by a process" covered by Lilly's '085 patent in violation of § 271(g). The defendants argued that the asserted claim was directed to an *intermediary*, and that the imported generic was "materially changed by subsequent processes" and therefore within an exemption from infringement. To counter this argument, Lilly asserted that § 271(g) should apply wherever the defendant's use undercuts the commercial value of a U.S. process patent, pointing to the underlying purposes of the Process Patent Amendments Act to preserve the value of U.S. process claims.

The *Eli Lilly* court rejected the patentee's argument. Although the court recognized the appeal of this argument in light of the statute's purpose, ultimately the Federal Circuit found that this proposed approach was inconsistent with the legislative history, which placed the emphasis for analysis on changes to the *product* rather than on commercial circumstances.To decide whether the imported generic had been "materially changed by subsequent processes" from the intermediate derived from the claimed process, the *Eli Lilly* court relied on portions of the legislative history that described a two-part test for determining whether a chemical intermediary would be deemed "materially changed" under this exception to § 271(g), as follows:

- First, a product is made by the patented process if it would not be possible or commercially viable to make that product but for the use of the patented process; and

- Second, a minor change in the physical or chemical properties of a product, even though minor, may be "material" if the change relates to a physical or chemical property which is an important feature of the product produced by the patented process. However, additional steps which are not covered by the patent and do not change the physical or chemical

---

[67] 35 U.S.C. § 271(g) (2000).

[68] *See Eli Lilly*, 82 F.3d at 1568.

properties of the product in a manner which changes the basic utility of the product are not considered "material."[69]

Applying this test to the facts presented, the *Eli Lilly* court recognized that for the first part of the test at least one other commercially feasible method of performing the intermediary step existed. The court found that the legislative history indicated that the existence of such an alternative — even if that alternative is *not actually used* — would be "enough to defeat the claim of infringement."[70] The court then examined the second part of the legislature's test, finding that three structural changes between the intermediate compound created by the patented process and the cefaclor generic impacted the final product's effectiveness as an antibiotic drug. Based on this reading of the legislative history, the *Eli Lilly* court found that the imported generic was "materially changed" from the claimed intermediary and that therefore Lilly would not be able to establish a likelihood of demonstrating infringement. More broadly, the *Eli Lilly* court's reasoning has troubling implications for inventors whose work focuses on intermediary processes. As the *Eli Lilly* concurring opinion recognizes, under these tests section 271(g) does not offer protection unless the claimed process cannot be performed in any other commercially viable way.[71]

Bio-Technology General Corp. v. Genentech,[72] presents a factual contrast to the *Eli Lilly* case. In *Bio-Technology*, the patentee Genetech claimed a method for constructing a plasmid, which is an intermediary gene used in cloning. The defendant, who was headquartered in Israel, practiced Genetech's method claim there by creating a plasmid that the defendant used to manufacture a human growth hormone for importation into the United States. The *Bio-Technology* court found that the plasmid and the growth hormone were "entirely different materials."[73] However, the court found that the entry of a preliminary injunction under § 271(g) was proper. Unlike the *Eli Lilly* case in which alternative processes were available to be used, *Bio-Technology* found that the plasmid was "an *essential* part" of the overall process for creating the hormone.[74]

Section 271(g) seeks to prevent manufacturers from circumventing U.S. patent rights by practicing inventions abroad. Although the statute seeks to preserve appropriate rewards for patenting, the statute also attempts to guard against patentees who may seek to obtain broader relief than their inventions warrant. The two-part test set forth in *Eli Lilly* draws the line between cases in which importations are infringing and those that are not.

---

[69] *Id.* at 1576-77.

[70] *Id.* at 1577.

[71] *Id.* at 1581 ("This decision denies protection to a patented process anytime it is not the only way to make an intermediate, even if it is the most economically efficient way to produce the intermediate.") (Radar, J., concurring). Whether a change is material is a question of fact for the jury. Amgen Inc. v. F. Hoffman-LA Roche Ltd., 580 F.3d 1340, 1379 (Fed. Cir. 2009).

[72] Bio-Technology Gen. Corp. v. Genentech, 80 F.3d 1553 (Fed. Cir. 1996).

[73] *Id.* at 1561.

[74] *Id.* (emphasis added).

§ 35.05   INFRINGEMENT ACTIONS BEFORE THE U.S. INTERNATIONAL TRADE COMMISSION

[A]   The Jurisdiction of the International Trade Commission

The International Trade Commission ("ITC") provides an administrative forum to prevent the importation of products that infringe a U.S. patent. The statutory basis of these actions is 19 U.S.C. § 1337(a), which prohibits the unlawful importation of certain articles, including those that "infringe a valid and enforceable United States patent" or that "are made, produced, processed, or mined under, or by means of, a process covered by the claims of a valid and enforceable United States patent."[75]

If successful, the primary relief available in such actions is an *exclusion order* that prevents such products from entry into the U.S., unless there are public policy reasons not to do so.[76] In addition, the ITC can issue a *cease and desist order* to prevent a party from engaging in unfair acts of competition within the U.S. For example, a cease and desist order may order one from continuing to sell infringing products in the U.S. that have been imported prior to the entry of the ITC's exclusion order. As stated earlier, the ITC does not have the authority to award monetary relief for past infringement.

Although the patent holder need not demonstrate U.S. citizenship to initiate an action in the ITC, the patentee must demonstrate a U.S.-based *domestic industry* that may be harmed by the infringement. This domestic industry is commercial activity related to the asserted patent and must concern: a) significant investment in plant and equipment; b) significant employment of labor or capital; or c) substantial investment in its exploitation, including engineering, research and development, or licensing.[77] The domestic industry requirement reflects the congressional purpose in enacting 19 U.S.C. § 1337, which is intended to provide "an adequate remedy for domestic industries against unfair practices beginning abroad and culminating in importation."[78]

[B]   The International Trade Commission Process

ITC proceedings have a number of similarities to proceedings in a U.S. District Court. For example, ITC proceedings commence with the filing of a complaint. The rules allow the parties to take discovery of fact and expert witnesses under the rules that are very similar to the Federal Rules of Civil Procedure and include an evidentiary trial on the merits before an administrative law judge. Additionally,

---

[75] 19 U.S.C. § 1337(d) (2000 & Supp. IV 2004).

[76] *Id.* (providing that an exclusion order may be entered "unless there are after considering the effect of such exclusion upon the public health and welfare, competitive conditions in the United States economy, the production of like or directly competitive articles in the United States, and United States consumers, it finds that such articles should not be excluded from entry.").

[77] 19 U.S.C. § 1337(a)(3) (2000); Schaper Mfg. Co. v. U.S. Int'l Trade Comm'n, 717 F.2d 1368, 1371 (Fed. Cir. 1983); *see also,* In the Matter of Certain Airtight Cast-Iron Stoves, U.S.ITC Inv. No. 337-TA-69 (U.S.I.T.C 1981).

[78] Akzo N.V. v. U.S. Int'l Trade Comm'n, 808 F.2d 1471, 1488 (Fed. Cir. 1986).

there is a right of appeal to the Federal Circuit.

There are a number of dissimilarities. Unlike a district court action, a government agency known as the Office of Unfair Import Investigations is a party to the suit to protect the public interest throughout the proceedings. An ITC proceeding concerning the unfair importation of a product that infringes a U.S. patent "is not purely private litigation 'between the parties' but rather is an 'investigation' by the Government into unfair methods of competition or unfair acts in the importation of articles into the United States."[79] Complaints submitted to the ITC, which must meet fact pleading standards, are reviewed by the Office of Import Investigations and the ITC's Commissioners for approval before the case commences and notice is served on the respondent. Moreover, ITC actions proceed on an extremely fast track, typically reaching trial within a year after an action is instituted. Generally, an ITC action proceeds as follows:

Complaint: A complainant (typically, the patent holder), files a detailed complaint with the ITC, along with all required documentation. In patent cases, this includes copies of the patent, a certified copy of the prosecution history, license agreements that pertain to the patent and other related documentation.

Upon receipt, the Office of Unfair Import Investigations reviews the documentation and makes a recommendation concerning the propriety of institution of an action to the ITC Commissioners. The Commission, in turn, then decides whether an action should be instituted. If the Commission decides to do so, notice of the action is published in the Federal Register, and serves notice on all respondents. This initial review period is typically no longer than 35 days. The case is then assigned to an administrative law judge, and the respondents are required to file an answer.

Discovery: The parties conduct fact and expert discovery. Unlike district court actions in which the discovery period can last well over a year or more, discovery in ITC actions typically last only about five to seven months. This time period includes both fact and expert discovery, including the production of expert reports.

Trial: Approximately six to nine months after the complaint has been served, the administrative law judge assigned to the case presides over an evidentiary hearing on the merits. Afterwards, the parties submit papers addressing the issues raised and proposing their findings of fact and conclusions of law.

Administrative Law Judge's Initial Determination/ Commission Review: Approximately forty-five days after the trial has ended, the Administrative Law Judge issues a decision in the form of an Initial Determination. This document makes factual findings and legal conclusions as to the recommended outcome of the investigation. The losing party may file a petition for review before the Commission.

---

[79] Young Engineers, Inc. v. U.S. Int'l Trade Comm'n, 721 F.2d 1305, 1315 (Fed. Cir. 1983).

The Commission has discretion as to whether to grant a party's request for review. If the Commission does grant review, the Commission may issue its own decision on the merits. Any Initial Determinations that the Commission declines to review become the final decision of the Commission. If the Commission determines that no relief should be granted, the order becomes final and can be appealed.

Presidential Review Period: If the Commission's report finds that relief is appropriate, the report is submitted for presidential review. The President has sixty (60) days to veto an ITC determination based on policy considerations. Historically, presidential actions on these orders have been rare. If the President does not disapprove the Commission's decision, the order becomes final and can be appealed.

Appeal: After the Commission's decision becomes final, any adversely affected party may appeal the decision to the U.S. Court of Appeals for the Federal Circuit.

A patentee may file a concurrent action in U.S. District Court to preserve access to monetary relief and forms of injunctive relief that may not be available from the ITC. A parallel district court actions is typically stayed pending the outcome of the ITC proceeding.[80]

[C]   Section 271(g) and Patent Infringement in the International Trade Commission

Patent owners have long been able to obtain relief before the ITC to prevent the importation of products that are made by a patented process. As discussed earlier in this chapter, in 1988, Congress enacted § 271(g) to allow such patent holders analogous relief in court proceedings. In doing so:

> Congress recognized the availability of redress from the ITC, but noted that the remedies available thereunder were insufficient to fully protect the owners of process patents . . . [T]he legislative history suggests that section 271(g) was intended to address the same "articles" as were addressed by section 1337, but to add additional rights against importers of such "articles."[81]

The additional rights referred to in this quotation are § 271(g)'s exclusions, which exempt products from liability if they are "materially changed by subsequent processes;" or have become "trivial and nonessential component(s) of another product."[82]

After § 271(g) was enacted, it was argued that § 271(g)'s exclusions should apply to assist respondents in ITC proceedings. In *Kinik Co. v. International Trade Commission*,[83] the Federal Circuit rejected this argument, finding that these

---

[80]   28 U.S.C. § 1659 (2000).

[81]   Bayer AG v. Housey Pharmaceuticals, Inc., 340 F.3d 1367, 1373-74 (Fed. Cir. 2003).

[82]   35 U.S.C. § 271(g) (2000).

[83]   Kinik Co. v. Int'l Trade Comm'n, 362 F.3d 1359 (Fed. Cir. 2004).

defenses could *not* be relied upon in actions adjudicated in the ITC based on § 271(g). In doing so, the Court relief on both the Commission's interpretation of § 271(g) and the legislative history of this subsection, stating:

> Although [the defendant] argues that it is anomalous to create a legislative distinction in the defenses available in different tribunals, before this enactment there was an even greater distinction, for overseas manufacture could not be reached at all in the district courts.[84]

Under the *Kinick* case, respondents accused of infringing a process claim abroad under § 271(g) are unable to defend by arguing that the process added an immaterial change or that the process represented a trivial and nonessential contribution to the imported product. Those defenses are available only to defendants in an analogous position sued under § 271(g) in federal court.

§ 35.06   CONCLUSION

As a general rule, conduct that is entirely outside the U.S. cannot support a finding of patent infringement, even if such conduct would fall within a U.S. Patent's claim scope if that activity took place domestically. The more difficult questions arise where the conduct partially occurs on U.S. territory, or raises the problem of importing or exporting goods that have been made with a patented invention.

One gating inquiry is to determine the type and scope of the U.S. patent claim. Apparatus, compound or system claims raise issues of direct infringement under § 271(a) if such activities occur entirely or partially in the U.S. These system types of claims implicate § 271(f) if the defendant exports all or a part of a patented invention, with a view that such products will be used to infringe abroad.

For process and method claims, one should examine potential liability under § 271(a) under direct infringement principles. If the process is practiced abroad, then § 271(g) may provide the patentee with grounds for relief. For any important claim, the ITC might be an alternative forum for the adjudication of such dispute.

---

[84] *Id.* at 1363.

Chapter 36

INEQUITABLE CONDUCT AND THE DUTY TO DISCLOSE

SYNOPSIS

§ 36.01   INTRODUCTION

§ 36.02   INEQUITABLE CONDUCT: HISTORY AND POLICY

    [A]   Origins in Equity

    [B]   Development of Inequitable Conduct

§ 36.03   THE CURRENT STANDARD FOR INEQUITABLE CONDUCT

    [A]   *Therasense*: Intent to Deceive

    [B]   A Closer Examination of the Materiality Standard

    [C]   Application of the *Therasense* Standard

§ 36.04   REGULATION OF ATTORNEY CONDUCT BY THE U.S. PATENT & TRADEMARK OFFICE

§ 36.05   SUPPLEMENTAL EXAMINATION AND INEQUITABLE CONDUCT

§ 36.06   CONCLUSION

§ 36.01   INTRODUCTION

A patent operates as a powerful privately enforceable right. Applicants and their attorneys seek claims with the broadest possible coverage. Some of a patentee's most significant interactions with the U.S. PTO are ex parte. During prosecution and post-issuance procedures, a patentee is trusted to make accurate representations to the agency. Not all applicants do so with the candor that is necessary to a well-functioning patent system. For example, an applicant who files a response to an agency rejection might submit false evidence about the state of the art. Alternatively, a patentee may decide to withhold known evidence that might be detrimental to an application. Patent examiners may not have sufficient time or resources to investigate whether the patentee's statements represent full disclosures, that all known material information has been submitted, and that all factual assertions are well grounded.

Congress has granted the U.S. PTO authority to govern practice before the agency.[1] Since the beginning of the 20th century, the U.S. PTO has exercised this

---

[1]   *See, e.g.*, 35 U.S.C. § 2(b) (providing that the U.S. PTO "may establish regulations, not inconsistent

authority to refuse to issue a patent affected by fraud.[2] Patentees have a duty of candor and good faith, including a duty to disclose known information that is material to patentability.[3] The agency may impose one or more sanctions for fraudulent or intentional violations of these duties, including denying the affected patent application.

What happens if the PTO does not discover a patentee's misconduct? If a fraudulently obtained patent is asserted against another in litigation, the accused infringer may raise an unenforceability defense under the doctrine of *inequitable conduct*. This defense has undergone dramatic changes over the past several decades and continues to evolve today. Under current law, the doctrine has two independent requirements. First, the patentee must act with *intent to deceive* the PTO. Second, the information that is the subject of the charge must be *material*. If an accused infringer establishes these elements through clear and convincing evidence with respect to a single claim, the court will find the entire patent unenforceable.

Certainly, other alternatives might address patentee misconduct. If the fraudulently obtained patent is asserted against another, that party may seek relief under antitrust and/or unfair competition laws, or may seek to have the infringement action dismissed under the doctrine of unclean hands. This Chapter will primarily focus on inequitable conduct, one of the most prevalent mechanisms for the enforcement of the patentee's duty to disclose, as well as the doctrine of unclean hands.

§ 36.02   INEQUITABLE CONDUCT: HISTORY AND POLICY

[A]   Origins in Equity

Inequitable conduct derives from the court's exercise of its equitable power. The earliest patent statutes, the Patent Acts of 1790 and 1793, did not include an inequitable conduct defense. Rather, these statutes provided that a court could repeal a patent that "was obtained surreptitiously by, or upon false suggestion."[4] Congress eliminated these provisions in the 1836 version of the Patent Act, leading the Supreme Court to conclude in 1869 that one could not challenge a patent based on fraud at all in the courts of equity. According to the Court's ruling at that time, "[t]he law made it the duty of the commissioner to examine and decide" whether a patent should issue and that there was "[n]o provision is made for appeal or

---

with law, which . . . shall govern the conduct of proceedings in the Office"); *see also*, 35 U.S.C. §§ 3, 131, *and* 132.

[2] Norton v. Curtiss, 433 F.2d 779, 792 (C.C.P.A. 1971) (noting that at least since 1911, the patent commission could refuse to grant a patent if "an application or applications are so permeated with fraud as to justify the opinion that any patent or patents granted on those applications, whether amended or not, would be annulled or set aside by a court of equity on petition of the United States through the Attorney-General") (quoting *In re* Heany, 1911 C.D. 139, 154 (1911)).

[3] 37 C.F.R. § 1.56.

[4] Act of Apr. 10, 1790, ch. 7, 1 Stat. 109, § 5 (1790) *and* Act of Feb. 21, 1793, ch. 11, 1 Stat. 318, § 10 (1793); *see generally* Robert J. Goldman, *Evolution of the Inequitable Conduct Defense in Patent Litigation*, 7 Harv. L. J. & Tech. 37 (1993) (detailing the history of the doctrine of inequitable conduct).

review" in the court system for patentee conduct relating to patent prosecution.[5]

This shifted in 1888 when the U.S. Supreme Court decided *U.S. v. American Bell Tel. Co.*[6] This case was filed by a government agency, not a private litigant. The *Bell* opinion held that a court sitting in equity possessed the power to invalidate a fraudulently procured patent. In this decision, the Court identified the patentee's wrong as a fraud against the government and the patent office as the party "imposed upon and deceived."[7] The *Bell* Court explained that this remedy operated to vindicate the interests of the agency, and that "the government, authorized both by the constitution and the statutes to bring suits at law and in equity, should find it to be its duty to correct this evil, to recall these patents, to get a remedy for this fraud, is so clear that it needs no argument . . ."[8]

After *Bell*, the Supreme Court decided three major cases-- *Keystone Driller*, *Hazel-Atlas*, and *Precision Instrument Mfg.* — that found that private litigants could obtain dismissal of an infringement case where the patentee had engaged in fraud through the doctrine of unclean hands. In the earliest of these, the 1933 *Keystone Driller Co. v. General Excavator Co.* the Supreme Court affirmed dismissal of an action based on a patentee's suppression of evidence before the agency and in court.[9] There, the plaintiff had obtained a patent and a prior court judgment after paying the patent's inventor to suppress evidence of prior use. In a subsequent action against other accused infringers, the patentee submitted the fraudulently obtained judgment as evidence of the patent's validity. The defendant in the second action discovered the fraud, and submitted evidence in that proceeding that "furnish[ed] the details of the corrupt transaction."[10] The Supreme Court affirmed dismissal of the second action as the proper remedy for the patentee's unclean hands.

In 1944, the Supreme Court decided *Hazel-Atlas Glass Co. v. Hartford-Empire Co.*[11] The asserted patent's file history included an article submitted by Hartford, the patentee, and "signed by an ostensibly disinterested expert" that described the invention as "a remarkable advance in the art."[12] The article was not considered by the district court, which dismissed the case. However, the article was presented to the Circuit Court, which relied on the article in directing the lower court to find the patent valid and infringed. After the Circuit Court ruled, the defendant's investigators uncovered the fact that the article had been written by the patentee

---

[5] Rubber Co. v. Goodyear, 76 U.S. 788, 798 (1869).

[6] U.S. v. American Bell Tel. Co., 128 U.S. 315 (1888); *see also* Hazel-Atlas Glass Co. v. Hartford-Empire Co., 322 U.S. 238, 251(1944) (recognizing that a patent obtained by fraud could be vacated in a proceeding brought by the government).

[7] *See Bell*, 128 U.S. at 357. *Bell* further acknowledged that the public was the party ultimately harmed by a patentee who had obtained a patent through fraud. *See, e.g., id.* (explaining that a patentees who obtain patents by fraud "perpetrate a grievous wrong upon the general public, upon the United States, and upon its representatives.").

[8] *Id.* at 370.

[9] Keystone Driller co. v. General Excavator Co., 290 U.S. 240 (1933).

[10] *Id.* at 244.

[11] Hazel-Atlas Glass Co. v. Hartford-Empire Co., 322 U.S. 238 (1944).

[12] *Id.* at 240.

and its attorneys, who had paid an expert to list himself as author. By this point, the fraud had affected *both* the patent prosecution and the proceedings before the Circuit Court. In the Supreme Court, *Hazel-Atlas* expressly authorized courts to exercise their power in equity to set aside infringement judgments based on a fraudulently obtained patent. The *Hazel-Atlas* Court required that the patentee's misrepresentation must be *material*.[13] In contradistinction to the earlier *Bell* decision finding that fraud in prosecution primarily affected the government, the *Hazel-Atlas* Court emphasized instead that such fraud affects the public, explaining, "This matter does not concern only private parties . . . . It is a wrong against the institutions set up to protect and safeguard the public, institutions in which fraud cannot be completely tolerated consistently with the good order of society."[14]

Soon after the *Hazel-Atlas* case was decided, the Supreme Court fully crystalized the unclean hands defense in the 1945 decision *Precision Instrument Mfg. v. Automotive Maintenance Machinery Co.*[15] There, the PTO granted a patent based on a fraudulent declaration of inventorship and falsified dates of conception and reduction to practice submitted by the applicant. These misrepresentations were made to gain ownership and priority over the true inventor from whom the idea had been taken. The patentee Automotive learned of the fraud and acquired the tainted application nonetheless. While this application was still pending, Automotive did not inform the agency that the declaration was fraudulent. After the PTO approved the patent application, Automotive asserted the patent against a third party, Precision Instrument. The Supreme Court held that the trial court had properly dismissed Automotive's patent case, holding that "[t]hose who have applications pending with the Patent Office or who are parties to Patent Office proceedings have an uncompromising duty to report to it all facts concerning possible fraud or inequitableness underlying the applications in issue."[16] According to *Precision Instrument*, a court may dismiss a case where the patentee acted "with inequitableness or bad faith relative to the matter in which he seeks relief."[17] The *Precision Instrument* Court explained, "[t]he far-reaching social and economic consequences of a patent . . . give the public a paramount interest in seeing that patent monopolies spring from backgrounds free from fraud or other inequitable conduct and that such monopolies are kept within their legitimate scope."[18]

These three major unclean hands cases — *Keystone Driller, Hazel-Atlas,* and *Precision Instrument Mfg.* — all authorized dismissal of an action as the appropriate remedy for a patentee's fraud. Today, these cases retain their relevance because the doctrine of unclean hands remains a viable defense separate

---

[13] *Id.* at 241.

[14] *Id.* at 246.

[15] Precision Instrument Mfg. v. Automotive Maintenance Machinery Co., 324 U.S. 806 (1945).

[16] *Id.* at 818.

[17] *Id.* at 814.

[18] *Id.* at 816.

from inequitable conduct.[19] Notably, the remedies for each are distinct. The precedents held that unclean hands resulted in the dismissal of a single case in which the defense was litigated. In contrast, the inequitable conduct defense results in a finding of unenforceability of the patent for all purposes. Thus, although there is an historical and theoretical connection between the two doctrines, inequitable conduct has led to the more powerful remedy.

[B] Development of Inequitable Conduct

Soon after *Precision Instrument*, the U.S. PTO first promulgated a rule governing the patentee's duty of candor and good faith.[20] This version, and its current version, are set forth in the Code of Federal Regulations at 37 C.F.R. § 1.56, commonly referred to as *Rule 56*.[21] If the PTO finds a violation of Rule 56, the PTO may direct that the application be withdrawn.[22] In theory, the PTO may also take disciplinary action against an attorney responsible for such actions, although such actions rarely occur. More commonly, the agency will rely on Rule 56 to refuse to grant a patent where the patentee has engaged in or attempted fraud on the U.S. PTO, or where the patentee has acted with bad faith or has acted intentionally in violating the duty of disclosure.[23] Affirming the agency's authority to sanction fraudulent conduct, a decision of the Court of Customs and Patent Appeals explained that the ex parte nature of prosecution, coupled with the limited resources of the agency, required "[t]he highest standards of honesty and candor on the part of applicants" when presenting facts to the agency.[24] In reviewing the decision, this court considered the PTO's fact-finding in light of the requirements to show common law fraud — specifically: intent, materiality, reliance and harm.

In parallel, the courts developed the doctrine of inequitable conduct to render defective patents unenforceable during infringement litigation. One early leading decision was the Federal Circuit's 1988 *Kingsdown Medical Consultants, Ltd. v. Hollister, Inc.*[25] There, the court articulated the legal standard for inequitable conduct as a failure to disclose information, or the submission of false information, to the PTO with the intent to deceive. If a single claim of a patent meets this standard, the entire patent is rendered unenforceable.[26] Thus, unlike unclean

---

[19] Thereasense, Inc. v. Becton, Dickinson and Co., 649 F.3d 1276, 1287 (Fed. Cir. 2011).

[20] Digital Equip. Corp. v. Diamond, 653 F.2d 701 (Fed. Cir. 1981) (citing 37 C.F.R. § 1.56 (1951)) (emphasis added).

[21] Note that the PTO has promulgated numerous iterations of Rule 56 in the interim. To the extent that Rule 56 relates to an issue raised in litigation, a court will typically apply the version of the rule that was in effect at the time that the patent at issue was filed. *See, e.g.*, Purdue Pharma L.P. v. Endo Pharmaceuticals Inc., 438 F.3d 1123, 1129 (Fed. Cir. 2006).

[22] *See* 35 U.S.C. § 32 (authorizing the PTO to suspend or exclude for intentional deception); 37 C.F.R. § 1.313(b)(2) (providing that an application may be withdrawn for a violation of Rule 1.56 or illegality).

[23] 37 C.F.R. § 1.56(a) ("no patent will be granted on an application in connection with which fraud on the Office was practiced or attempted or the duty of disclosure was violated through bad faith or intentional misconduct").

[24] Norton v. Curtiss, 433 F.2d 779, 794 (C.C.A.P. 1970).

[25] Kingsdown Medical Consultants, Ltd. v. Hollister, Inc., 863 F.2d 867 (Fed. Cir. 1988).

[26] *Id.* at 877; Monsanto Co. v. Bayer Bioscience N.V., 514 F.3d 1229, 1243 (Fed. Cir. 2008).

hands, which results in the dismissal of an infringement case, a finding of inequitable conduct prevents the patent from being enforced in all contexts. Inequitable conduct is an equitable defense that is decided by the court.

§ 36.03   THE CURRENT STANDARD FOR INEQUITABLE CONDUCT

Although developed for important reasons, inequitable conduct became regarded as a doctrine that created numerous adverse consequences. The Federal Circuit stated in 1988, "the habit of charging inequitable conduct in almost every major patent case has become an absolute plague."[27] Some opinions drew concurring or dissenting opinions that remarked that the doctrine was too lenient and thereby encouraged aggressive assertion by accused infringers.[28] Further, a report issued by the ABA Section of Intellectual Property Law reported that prosecutors who feared being accused of inequitable conduct overwhelmed the PTO with irrelevant references, stating that "patent examiners must devote a large percentage of the time allowed for examination of an application to dealing with mountains of references, many of which may have little to do with the patentability of the claimed subject matter."[29] One concurring opinion in a court decision observed that a patent in suit had been subject to inequitable conduct charges multiple times despite the submission of hundreds of references to the PTO.[30]

The standard governing inequitable conduct was not stable. Although *Kingsdown* established that both intent and materiality are required, the standard drifted when applied in subsequent decisions. Some Federal Circuit decisions applied a sliding scale which balanced intent and materiality — that is, a very low evidentiary level of intent could be remedied by a showing of a high level of materiality and vice versa.[31] In addition, the standard for intent shifted unpredictably. In 1988, the en banc portion of the *Kingsdown* opinion held that gross negligence was not sufficient to demonstrate intent.[32] In contrast, the 1997 *Critikon* opinion applied a lesser

---

[27] Burlington Industries, Inc. v. Dayco Corp., 849 F.2d 1418, 1422 (Fed. Cir.1988).

[28] Larson Mfg. Co. of South Dakota, Inc. v. Aluminart Products Ltd., 559 F.3d 1317, 1343 (Fed. Cir. 2009) ("The ease with which inequitable conduct can be pled, but not dismissed, is a problem of our own making") (Linn, J., concurring); Aventis Pharma S.A. v. Amphastar Pharmaceuticals, Inc., 525 F.3d 1334, 1350 (Fed. Cir. 2008) ("Although designed to facilitate U.S. PTO examination, inequitable conduct has taken on a new life as a litigation tactic") (Radar, J., dissenting); McKesson Information Solutions, Inc. v. Bridge Medical, Inc., 487 F.3d 897, 926-27 (Fed. Cir. 2007) (Newman, J., dissenting) ("a low standard for inequitable conduct results in "encouraging unwarranted charges of inequitable conduct, spawning the opportunistic litigation that here succeeded despite consistently contrary precedent.").

[29] ABA Section of Intellectual Property Law, A Section White Paper: Agenda for 21st Century Patent Reform, 13 (2009).

[30] Larson Mfg. Co. of South Dakota, Inc. v. Aluminart Products Ltd., 559 F.3d 1317, 1342-43 (Fed. Cir. 2009) (Linn, J., concurring);

[31] *See* Critikon, Inc. v. Becton Dickinson Vascular Access., Inc. 120 F.3d 1253 (Fed. Cir. 1997); LaBounty Mfg., Inc. v. U.S. Intern. Trade Com'n, 958 F.2d 1066, 1076 (Fed. Cir. 1992); Monsanto Co. v. Bayer Bioscience N.V., 514 F.3d 1229, 1241 (Fed. Cir. 2008).

[32] Kingsdown Medical Consultants, Ltd. v. Hollister, Inc., 863 F.2d 867, 876 (Fed. Cir. 1988) (en banc).

"should have known" standard.[33] In the 2006 *Ferring B.V. v. Barr Laboratories, Inc.*,[34] the court lowered the standard more by stating that "in the absence of a credible explanation, intent to deceive is *generally inferred* from the facts and circumstances surrounding a knowing failure to disclose material information."[35] Dissenting in the *Ferring* case, Justice Newman criticized the majority for "reviving the culture of attack on inventor rights and attorney reputations based on inference and innuendo."[36]

In the 2011 *Therasense, Inc. v. Becton, Dickinson and Co.*, the Federal Circuit issued an en banc opinion that reconsidered the substantive standards for inequitable conduct.[37] In this decision, the court re-affirmed that inequitable conduct must be established with a showing of both intent to deceive and materiality. However, the court expressed concern that inequitable conduct had become the "atomic bomb" of patent litigation," citing a study that found that the defense appeared in 80% of all infringement cases.[38] The *Therasense* court noted that "[w]ith inequitable conduct casting the shadow of a hangman's noose, it is unsurprising that patent prosecutors regularly bury PTO examiners with a deluge of prior art references, most of which have marginal value."[39] Although recognizing that applicants have a duty of honesty and good faith to the PTO, the *Therasense* court tightened the standard for inequitable conduct. In doing so, the court attempted to minimize the adverse consequences of the doctrine, including the increased cost and complexity of litigation, the burden of over-disclosure on the PTO, and the reduced likelihood of litigation settlement.

[A] *Therasense*: Intent to Deceive

The Federal Circuit's 2011 en banc *Therasense* opinion recalibrated the inequitable conduct intent standard back to that required by *Kingsdown*. Rejecting cases that had found gross negligence adequate, the Federal Circuit held that the accused infringer must show that the applicant acted with the *specific intent to deceive the PTO*. Where the conduct involves nondisclosure, the proponent must demonstrate that the patentee made a deliberate decision to withhold a known material reference.

The *Therasense* court confirmed that both intent and materiality are separately required. In a departure from the earlier panel decisions, the en banc *Therasense* court rejected that these two elements are subject to a sliding scale. The court underscored that a strong showing of one element cannot satisfy a weak showing of the other. Following this rule, the court held that a court is not permitted to infer intent to deceive solely from a strong showing of materiality. As the opinion

---

[33] Critikon, Inc. v. Becton Dickinson Vascular Access, Inc., 120 F.3d 1253, 1256 (Fed. Cir. 1997).

[34] Ferring B.V. v. Barr Laboratories, Inc., 437 F.3d 1181 (Fed. Cir. 2006).

[35] *Id.* at 1191 (emphasis added).

[36] *Id.* at 1195 (Newman, J., dissenting).

[37] Therasense, Inc. v. Becton, Dickinson and Co.,649 F.3d 1276 (Fed. Cir. 2011).

[38] *Id.* at 1288, citing Christian Mammen, *Controlling the "Plague": Reforming the Doctrine of Inequitable Conduct*, 24 BERKELEY TECH. L.J. 1329 (2009).

[39] *Therasense*, 649 F.3d at 1289.

explained, "[p]roving that the applicant knew of the reference, should have known of its materiality, and decided not to submit it to the PTO does not prove specific intent to deceive."[40] Where indirect or circumstantial evidence is used to demonstrate intent, the proponent must demonstrate that specific intent to deceive is "the single most reasonable inference available to be drawn from the evidence."[41]

[B]   A Closer Examination of the Materiality Standard

How does a patentee know whether information can be considered material, and therefore must be submitted to the agency? Formerly, the minimum threshold level was met where a reasonable examiner may have considered the information to be important — but not necessarily determinative — to the patentability decision.[42] This standard created an incentive for patentees to submit a broad range of information relevant to patentability to avoid the risk of a later finding of unenforceability.

Recall that *Therasense* expressed concern that PTO examiners were buried "with a deluge of prior art references, most of which have marginal value."[43] To address this problem, the *Therasense* court narrowed the scope of materiality significantly. Specifically, the court held that the standard is *but for materiality* — that is, the proponent of the inequitable conduct defense must demonstrate that, but for the submission of false information, the patent application would have been denied. For information that has been withheld, the court must find that the PTO would have refused the claim if the omitted information had been submitted. Under *Therasense*, this standard requires applicants to submit only information that is outcome determinative of patentability.

The but for standard clearly overlaps with the patentability standards. Of course, this overlap is not complete. It is possible that a district court might hold a patent valid against a challenge, and still find inequitable conduct. As one example, this can occur where a district court finds that a reference does not render a claim unenforceable under the clear and convincing evidence standard applied to the inequitable conduct defense in court. In that case, a district court could still find that the accused infringer had shown that the PTO would have refused to issue the claim under the lower standard of proof that applies to patent examination.[44]

[C]   Application of the *Therasense* Standard

In *Therasense*, the patentee Abbott asserted infringement based on a patent (the "'551 patent") that was directed to an improved test strip for determining the glucose levels of diabetes patients. The asserted point of novelty was the invention's

---

[40] *Id.* at 1290.

[41] *Id.* at 1290.

[42] Digital Control Inc. v. The Charles Machine Works, 437 F.3d 1309 1315-16 (Fed. Cir. 2006) (citing cases).

[43] *Therasense*, 649 F.3d at 1289.

[44] MPEP §§ 706 (preponderance of the evidence); 2111 (claims are given their broadest reasonable construction).

ability to test a patient's "whole blood" (meaning all parts of the blood, including red blood cells) without a protective membrane over an electrode that functioned as the strip's sensitized area. According to the record, some prior art test strips used a protective membrane over the electrode to control the flow of glucose to prevent the sensitized area from being overwhelmed. Other prior art test strips used a protective membrane to filter out red blood cells that might block glucose from reaching the electrode and thereby interfering with an inaccurate read.

Originally, the PTO rejected Abbott's application for the '551 patent based on an earlier Abbott patent (the " '382 patent"). The specification of this '382 patent, which described an electronic sensor for glucose testing, stated that "[o]ptionally, but preferably" a protective membrane would be used to test whole blood.[45] By using the terms "optionally," and "preferably," this specification suggested that successful testing could be performed without a protective membrane. However, in support of its application for the '551 patent, Abbott submitted a declaration that disclaimed this qualification, stating, "one skilled in the art would not read [the '382 patent] to teach that the use of a protective membrane with a whole blood sample is optionally or merely preferred."[46] After Abbott filed this declaration, the PTO issued the '551 patent.

Unknown to the PTO, Abbott had submitted a contrary representation to the EPO to obtain protection for the European counterpart to Abbot's '382 patent. Specifically, to avoid a German reference that required a protective membrane, Abbott's declaration to the EPO represented that the term "optionally, but preferably," in the specification of the European counterpart meant that the invention did not require a protective membrane.[47]

On appeal, the Federal Circuit remanded *Therasense* for the court to assess whether these facts constituted inequitable conduct. This result follows logically from the premise that the district court's findings had been made under the former, more lenient standard. Moreover, it is plausible that the omitted declaration was relevant to the patentee's credibility rather than the merits of the patentability question. On the other hand, the applicant's representation to the EPO might be held as a binding admission that the state of the art encompassed the invention described in the '551 patent and prevented its issuance. On remand, the Federal Circuit asked the district court to make the final determination on the inequitable conduct defense using the newly modified standard.

§ 36.04 REGULATION OF ATTORNEY CONDUCT BY THE U.S. PATENT & TRADEMARK OFFICE

The PTO has independent authority to regulate the conduct of those who practice before the agency.[48] As described earlier in this Chapter, the PTO has promulgated Rule 56 to govern the patentee's duty of disclosure to the agency. The

---

[45] *Therasense*, 649 F.3d at 1283, citing U.S. Patent No. 4,545,382 (filed Oct. 22, 1982).

[46] *Id.* at 1283.

[47] *Id.* at 1283-84.

[48] 35 U.S.C. § 2(b)(2)(D).

current version of Rule 56 applies to those "individuals associated with the filing or prosecution of a patent application," including the named inventors, the attorney or patent agent and any other person who is "substantively involved" in preparing or filing the application.[49] This language would seem to exclude those whose assistance is merely ministerial, such as a clerk or typist.[50] Additionally, Rule 56's use of the term "individuals" does not appear to include organizations, such as a corporation to whom the application is assigned.[51]

Although the doctrine of inequitable conduct and Rule 56 are both focused on a patentee's wrongful conduct in the procurement of a patent, they remain separate doctrines that rest on separate lines of authority.[52] The Supreme Court's unclean hands cases provide the derivation of the exercise of equity to support the inequitable conduct defense.[53] Under the court-created defense of inequitable conduct, a patent (or a family of patents) is found unenforceable although the invention may meet all of the requirements of patentability. In this context, inequitable conduct is raised by one accused of infringement as an affirmative defense that must be proven by clear and convincing evidence.

In contrast, Rule 56 is a rule promulgated by the PTO pursuant to the agency's authority under the Patent Act.[54] The substance of this standard has varied over time, particularly with respect to the standard of materiality. For example, when *Therasense* was decided, Rule 56 required the disclosure of all information that established "a prima facie case of unpatentability of a claim," or "refutes, or is inconsistent with, a position the applicant takes" before the agency regarding the patentability of an application.[55] This encompasses all information that *might have* influenced an examiner during the course of prosecution. In contrast, *Therasense's* but for standard requires an outcome determinative level of relevance — that is, only information that *would have* influenced the agency's decision is considered material.

In July 2011, the U.S. PTO issued a proposed rule to align Rule 56 with *Therasense's* but for materiality standard.[56] Harmonizing Rule 56's materiality standard with *Theresense* can be expected to simplify prosecution. This operates to reduce the incentives for patentees to submit marginally relevant information to the PTO. Those engaged in patent practice and students should consult the PTO to

---

[49] MPEP § 2001.01 (noting that the rule "would apply to individuals within the corporation or institution who were substantively involved in the preparation or prosecution of the application, and actions by such individuals may affect the rights of the corporation or institution.").

[50] *Id.*

[51] *Id.* (". . . the duty applies only to individuals, not to organizations. For instance, the duty of disclosure would not apply to a corporation or institution as such.").

[52] *See generally* R. Carl Moy, *The Effect of New Rule 56 on the Law of Inequitable Conduct*, 74 J. Pat. & Trademark Off. Soc'y 257, 259 (1992).

[53] Digital Control Inc. v. The Charles Machine Works, 437 F.3d 1309, 1315 (Fed. Cir. 2006).

[54] 35 U.S.C. §§ 2, 3, 131, *and* 132.

[55] 37 C.F.R. § 1.56.

[56] Revision of the Materiality Standard to Patentability Standard for the Duty to Disclose Information in Patent Applications, 140 Fed. Reg. 43631 (July 21, 2011).

determine whether this proposed rule has been adopted, and to determine the amended rule's final form.

§ 36.05 SUPPLEMENTAL EXAMINATION AND INEQUITABLE CONDUCT

As detailed in Chapter 3, the AIA has introduced Supplemental Examination to enable patentees to submit information to the PTO in connection with an issued patent.[57] This procedure acts as an amnesty program for those who realize that material information was omitted from the agency's consideration of the patentability of a claim. The information considered in a supplemental examination cannot later be used to hold the patent unenforceable on the grounds that the patentee has engaged in inequitable conduct. If the agency finds that the information submitted during supplemental examination is material, it will conduct a reexamination of all claims that are the subject of the request.

Supplemental examination does not entirely remove all potential for inequitable conduct claims to be brought. If the defense has already been properly asserted in litigation before the request for a supplemental examination has been filed, filing a request for a supplemental examination will not prevent the defense from being litigated.[58] Further, the exemption does not apply for section 337 actions filed in the International Trade Commission, unless the supplemental examination has been completed before the action is filed.[59]

§ 36.06 CONCLUSION

A patentee has a duty of candor and good faith toward the PTO. The inequitable conduct defense renders all of the claims of a patent unenforceable. In order to demonstrate inequitable conduct, one accused of infringement must demonstrate by clear and convincing evidence that a threshold level of both materiality and intent are present.

The precise contours of the materiality and intent standard continue to evolve in the courts. Under current law, a proponent of the defense must demonstrate a specific intent to deceive the agency or a deliberate decision to withhold a known material reference. Information is considered material if it would have caused the PTO to deny the patent. Inequitable conduct was developed by the courts to invalidate a patent if a patentee has made "an affirmative misrepresentation of a material fact, failed to disclose material information, or submitted false material

---

[57] *See* Chapter 3, § 3.09; 35 U.S.C. § 257.

[58] 35 U.S.C. § 257(c)(2)(a) (stating that the immunity afforded by supplemental examination is not applicable where the allegation has already been pled with particularity in a court action or under 21 U.S.C. § 355(j)(2)(B)(iv)(II) (a notice of opinion that a patent is invalid, unenforceable or not infringed under the Federal Food, Drug and Cosmetic Act).

[59] For more information about patent infringement actions based on section 337 and filed in the International Trade Commission, see Chapter 6, section 6.04.

information to the U.S. PTO, when coupled with intent to deceive."[60] If the defendant proves by clear and convincing evidence that the patentee engaged in inequitable conduct, the court may find *all* of the patent's claims are unenforceable.

The U.S. PTO has promulgated Rule 56 to govern proceedings before the agency. Currently, the PTO's standard of materiality is broader than that used by the courts to find inequitable conduct. However, the PTO has issued a proposed rule that aligns with *Therasense's* but for standard.

---

[60] Pharmacia Corp. v. Par Pharm., Inc., 417 F.3d 1369, 1373 (Fed.Cir. 2005) (citing Molins PLC v. Textron, Inc., 48 F.3d 1172, 1178 (Fed.Cir. 1995).

Chapter 37

PATENT MISUSE

SYNOPSIS

§ 37.01 INTRODUCTION

§ 37.02 THE ORIGINS OF THE PATENT MISUSE DOCTRINE

    [A] Early Common Law Roots

    [B] The *Mercoid* Cases: Patent Misuse and Contributory Infringement

§ 37.03 THE 1952 PATENT ACT: *DAWSON CHEMICAL v. ROHM & HAAS*

§ 37.04 THE 1988 AMENDMENTS TO THE PATENT ACT: REFUSALS TO
        LICENSE AND MARKET POWER

§ 37.05 INCREASING THE TEMPORAL SCOPE OF A PATENT LICENSE

§ 37.06 TYING AND PATENT POOLS

§ 37.07 CONCLUSION

§ 37.01 INTRODUCTION

The patent right to exclude is a patentee's reward for an invention and may be exercised lawfully despite an adverse impact on competition. As one court recognized, "[b]y their nature, patents create an environment of exclusion, and consequently, cripple competition. The anticompetitive effect is already present."[1] Characteristically, the patent right includes the ability to control prices, including charging higher prices for patented advances that represent a unique advance, or requiring licensees to pay a royalty which is typically passed on to consumers. Patentees have a legal right to restrict output where an injunction has been granted to prevent others from practicing the invention. Because of the public benefits that they offer, patents are considered "a limited exception to the general federal policy favoring free competition."[2]

However, a patentee who acts *beyond* the legitimate scope of the patent right may be found to have engaged in *patent misuse.*[3] The courts established this equitable defense to prevent patentees from using a patent to obtain advantages

---

[1] Schering-Plough Corp. v. Fed. Trade Comm'n, 402 F.3d 1056, 1065-66 (11th Cir. 2005).

[2] Lear, Inc. v. Adkins, 395 U.S. 653, 663 (1969).

[3] Windsurfing Int'l, Inc. v. AMF, Inc., 782 F.2d 995, 1001 (Fed. Cir. 1986) (recognizing that patent misuse may be found where "the alleged infringer show[s] that the patentee has impermissibly broadened the 'physical or temporal scope' of the patent grant with anticompetitive effect" (quoting Blonder-Tongue Labs., Inc. v. Univ. of Ill. Found., 402 U.S. 313, 343 (1971))).

beyond those inherent in the patent grant.[4] To determine whether conduct constitutes patent misuse, "[t]he key inquiry is whether, by imposing conditions that derive their force from the patent, the patentee has impermissibly broadened the scope of the patent grant with anticompetitive effect."[5]

Historically, patent misuse originated from cases decided under the equitable doctrine of unclean hands.[6] Through statutory amendment and changes in the decisional law, patent misuse has come to track antitrust law in many respects.[7] The terminology and some of the principles between these two bodies of law frequently intersect.[8] Yet the Federal Circuit has described patent misuse as a "broader wrong" than an antitrust violation, as a misuse may be found even if all of the requirements of an antitrust claim are not met.[9]

Unlike an affirmative claim for violation of the antitrust laws, patent misuse operates as an affirmative defense that renders a patent unenforceable. The unenforceability only lasts as long as the improper conduct. If the patentee ceases the misuse, then the misuse is considered "purged" and the patent can be found to be enforceable once again. Unlike an antitrust claim, one who establishes patent misuse cannot obtain damages or other relief from the violator.[10]

§ 37.02 THE ORIGINS OF THE PATENT MISUSE DOCTRINE

[A] Early Common Law Roots

In the late nineteenth and early twentieth centuries, the courts were protective of patentee rights.[11] One example is the Supreme Court decision *Henry v. A.B. Dick Co.*,[12] decided in 1912. There, a patent holder made copy machines that incorporated its patented invention. The patentee sold these machines subject to an express restriction that purchasers could use the machines only with the unpatented paper, ink, and other supplies made by the patentee. The patentee sued an ink seller for *contributory infringement*,[13] asserting that the defendant's sale of

---

[4] *See* C.R. Bard, Inc. v. M3 Systems, Inc., 157 F.3d 1340, 1372 (Fed. Cir. 1998).

[5] *Id.*

[6] *Id.*

[7] U.S. Philips Corp. v. Int'l Trade Comm'n, 424 F.3d 1179, 1185 (Fed. Cir. 2005). For more information on patents and antitrust law, see *infra*, Chapter 38.

[8] Students who have very little familiarity with antitrust law should read this chapter together with Chapter 38, Patents and Antitrust, herein.

[9] *C.R. Bard*, 157 F.3d at 1372.

[10] *See* B. Braun Medical, Inc. v. Abbott Laboratories, 124 F.3d 1419, 1427 (Fed. Cir. 1997) (patent misuse acts as a defense that "results in rendering the patent unenforceable until the misuse is purged. It does not, however, result in an award of damages to the accused infringer").

[11] For a comprehensive history of the origins of patent misuse, see Robin C. Feldman, *The Insufficiency of Antitrust Analysis for Patent Misuse*, 55 Hastings L.J. 399 (2003).

[12] Henry v. A.B. Dick Co., 224 U.S. 1 (1912).

[13] *Contributory infringement* supports liability on one who provides a material part of an invention

ink contributed to customers' direct infringement through uses of the copy machine in violation of the restriction.

The defendant challenged the patentee's restriction as unlawful, arguing that the patentee had used a patent right to restrict competition in a second market for unpatented ink. Such an allegation parallels a claim for *tying* under antitrust law.[14] The *Henry* Court rejected this theory, reasoning that the patentee's restriction amounted to a lawful effort to reap the benefit of the reward inherent in the patent grant. The Supreme Court explained that the patentee "had the exclusive right to keep all others from using [the invention] during the life of the patent. This larger right embraces the lesser of permitting others to use upon such terms as the patentee chooses to prescribe."[15]

Five years after *Henry v. A.B. Dick* was decided, it was expressly overruled by the Supreme Court in *Motion Picture Patents Co. v. Universal Film Mfg. Co.*[16] There, the Court considered a patent directed to a part used in the patentee's film projectors. These projectors were sold with a restriction that the machine could only be used with film made by the patentee. A previously issued patent on the film had expired, thus competition in the market for the film should have been unrestricted.

The patentee sued the defendant for contributory infringement, based on the defendant's sale of film to those who used the patentee's projectors. The defendant argued that the restriction was invalid because, in the absence of the patentee's restriction, those who purchased the patentee's film projectors would have enjoyed an implied license under the first sale doctrine[17] to use the projector with any manufacturer's film. The Supreme Court agreed with the defendant, explaining:

> [W]e are convinced that the exclusive right granted in every patent must be limited to the invention described in the claims of the patent, and that it is not competent for the owner of a patent, by notice attached to its machine, to, in effect, extend the scope of its patent monopoly by restricting the use of it to materials necessary in its operation, but which are no part of the patented invention . . . .[18]

In *Motion Picture Patents*, the patentee attempted to impose restrictions on sales and uses on the film used with the project, which was not part of the patent's claim scope. The Court invalidated the patentee's restriction as an attempt "to continue the patent monopoly in this particular character of film after it has expired, and because to enforce it would be to create a monopoly in the manufacture and use

---

which has no substantial non-infringing uses. For more information about contributory infringement, *see* *supra*, Chapter 33.

[14] Generally, *tying* may exist where a party agrees to sell a product (the tying product) but only on a condition that a buyer purchases a different (or tied) product, or otherwise agrees not purchase that product from any other supplier. In most instances, the seller has market power in the tying product. For more information about tying claims, *see* *infra*, Chapter 38.

[15] *Henry*, 224 U.S. at 35.

[16] Motion Picture Patents Co. v. Universal Film Mfg. Co., 243 U.S. 502 (1917).

[17] For more about the first sale doctrine, *see* *infra* Chapter 39.

[18] *Id.* at 516.

of moving picture films, wholly outside of the patent in suit and of the patent law as we have interpreted it."[19] This holding is based on tying in the patent misuse context — that is, the patent holder had attempted to use the patent right in the projector part to restrain competition in a second market for its film.

[B] The *Mercoid* Cases: Patent Misuse and Contributory Infringement

In a series of cases decided after *Motion Picture Patents*, the Supreme Court continued to invalidate restrictions that attempted to expand the patent right beyond its scope.[20] This trend reached its peak in two controversial decisions known as the "*Mercoid* cases" decided by the Court in 1944: *Mercoid Corp. v. Mid-Continent Investment Co.*,[21] and *Mercoid Corp. v. Minneapolis-Honeywell Regulator Co.*[22]

In the *Mercoid* cases, the patentee Mid-Continent owned a patent (the "Cross patent") that claimed a combination of elements for a furnace. Mid-Continent licensed the Cross patent to Minneapolis-Honeywell, who made and sold stoker switches that were specifically designed to be used with the patented system.[23] Minneapolis-Honeywell sold these switches to customers who manufactured furnaces under a license to the Cross patent subject to a restriction that stoker switches must be purchased from Minneapolis-Honeywell. Mercoid sold a competing stoker switch designed to be used in the patented combination. Critically, there was *no* use for Mercoid's stoker switches other than in a Cross furnace system. The patentee and licensee sued Mercoid for contributory infringement. In response, Mercoid raised the defense of patent misuse based on the license restriction. In a ruling later subject to legislative reversal, the Supreme Court accepted Mercoid's defense, finding that the licensing restriction operated as an unwarranted attempt to expand the Cross patent beyond the subject matter of the claims to restrict competition for the manufacture and sale for the stoker switch.

The rulings in the *Mercoid* cases were troublesome because their holdings encroached on the doctrine of *contributory infringement*. As more fully described in Chapter 33, a seller engages in contributory infringement when it supplies a material *non-staple article* component that the actor knows is used for infringement.[24] Contributory infringement presumes that such products enable others to directly infringe. Here, the stoker switch was a non-staple material component, as the switch was designed specifically for use in the patented combination and there were no material non-infringing uses. In essence, *Mercoid's*

---

[19] *Id.* at 518.

[20] *See, e.g.*, Carbice Corp. of Am. v. Am. Patents Dev. Corp., 283 U.S. 27 (1931); Leitch Mfg. Co. v. Barber Co., 302 U.S. 458 (1938); Morton Salt Co. v. G.S. Suppiger Co., 314 U.S. 488 (1942).

[21] Mercoid Corp. v. Mid-Continent Investment Co., 320 U.S. 661 (1944).

[22] Mercoid Corp. v. Minneapolis-Honeywell Regulator Co., 320 U.S. 680 (1944).

[23] *Id.* at 663. A "stoker switch" responds to a low temperature in the furnace by causing a stoker to fuel the furnace's fire. *Id.* at 664.

[24] *See, e.g.*, Dawson Chem. Co. v. Rohm & Haas Co., 448 U.S. 176, 218-19 (1980).

rulings deprived the patentee of a cause of action for contributory infringement. As the *Mercoid* Court acknowledged, "[t]he result of this decision, together with those which have preceded it, is to limit substantially the doctrine of contributory infringement."[25] The *Mercoid* cases were destined to be overturned, and they were several years later.

§ 37.03 THE 1952 PATENT ACT: *DAWSON CHEMICAL v. ROHM & HAAS*

The *Mercoid* decisions prompted the addition of subsections to § 271, wherein Congress undertook to resolve the "the wavering line between legitimate protection against contributory infringement and illegitimate patent misuse."[26]

As a structural matter, § 271(c) defines contributory infringement[27] and § 271(d) exempts certain conduct from the doctrine of patent misuse. Thus, while § 271(c) contains a definition of what contributory infringement affirmatively *is*, § 271(d) only defines what patent misuse *is not*. As the section contains no stated definition of misuse, § 271(d) must be read in connection with the decisional law of the courts to obtain a complete picture of the current application of the patent misuse defense.

The 1952 amendments added the following subsections, at § 271(d), which created safe harbors for patentees who seek to engage in certain acts such as the practice, licensing or assertion of rights relating to contributory infringement:

> (d) No patent owner otherwise entitled to relief for infringement or contributory infringement of a patent shall be denied relief or deemed guilty of misuse or illegal extension of the patent right by reason of his having done one or more of the following:
>
>> (1) derived revenue from acts which if performed by another without his consent would constitute contributory infringement of the patent;
>>
>> (2) licensed or authorized another to perform acts which if performed without his consent would constitute contributory infringement of the patent;
>>
>> (3) sought to enforce his patent rights against infringement or contributory infringement.

The application of § 271(c) and (d) was explored in the Supreme Court's 1980 decision *Dawson Chemical Co. v. Rohm & Haas Co.*[28] There, the Court found that

---

[25] *Mercoid*, 320 U.S. at 669.

[26] *Dawson*, 448 U.S. at 199.

[27] 35 U.S.C. § 271(c) states as follows:

> Whoever offers to sell or sells within the United States or imports into the United States a component of a patented machine, manufacture, combination, or composition, or a material or apparatus for use in practicing a patented process, constituting a material part of the invention, knowing the same to be especially made or especially adapted for use in an infringement of such patent, and not a staple article or commodity of commerce suitable for substantial noninfringing use, shall be liable as a contributory infringer.

[28] Dawson Chemical Co. v. Rohm & Haas Co, 448 U.S. 176 (1980).

the addition of these subsections to the Patent Act was designed to reverse the effects of the *Mercoid* decisions by allowing patentees to assert contributory infringement claims against sellers of material, non-staple goods used to directly infringe the patent without concern that such conduct constitutes patent misuse.

In *Dawson Chemical*, the patent holder Rohm & Haas owned a patent on a process for the use of a chemical herbicide known as "propanil." Propanil was not patented; rather, Rohm & Haas' patent claimed a *process* for applying propanil in particular quantities to eliminate weeds from rice fields. Rohm & Haas filed suit for contributory infringement and inducement to infringe against Dawson Chemical, a manufacturer that made and sold propanil marketed in containers that instructed users to apply propanil in the same way described in the patentee's claims. Dawson Chemical raised the defense of patent misuse, arguing that Rohm & Haas was tying the use of its process patent to restrict competitor's sales of unpatented propanil.

After an exhaustive review of § 271's legislative history, the Supreme Court concluded that Congress had intended to grant "to patent holders a statutory right to control nonstaple goods that are capable only of infringing use in a patented invention."[29] Here, because propanil was a non-staple, material component neces-sary to the practice of Rohm & Haas' claim, the Court found no patent misuse. Stated another way, Rohm & Haas' assertion of a claim for contributory infringe-ment of its process patent claim was a legitimate exercise of its patent right to prevent sales of a non-staple, material component of the process claims. The defendant's sales of unpatented propanil constituted contributory infringement of the Rohm & Haas process claims based on end users' application of propanil as directly infringers.

Dawson Chemical demonstrates that under § 271(d) a patentee's efforts to assert a valid patent right under a contributory infringement theory, as was at issue in that case, does not constitute misuse. A patentee's conduct that restricts material, non-staple items unsuitable for substantial, non-infringing uses will find that such conduct has a safe harbor in one of the subsections of 271(d).

§ 37.04 THE 1988 AMENDMENTS TO THE PATENT ACT: REFUSALS TO LICENSE AND MARKET POWER

In 1988, the Legislature added two more subsections to the patent misuse statute. The first of these, at § 271(d)(4), exempts a patentee from patent misuse where the patentee has "refused to license or use any rights to the patent." It is a long-standing principle of patent law that a patentee retains the full scope of the patent right even if the patentee does not practice or license the patent.[30] Section 271(d)(4) confirms that a patentee's refusal to license or use the patent is a legitimate exercise of the right and does not constitute patent misuse.

---

[29] *Id.* at 214.

[30] *See* Cont'l Paper Bag Co. v. Eastern Paper Bag Co., 210 U.S. 405, 429 (1908) (the patentee's right to exclude "may be said to have been of the very essence of the right conferred by the patent, as it is the privilege of any owner of property to use or not use it, without question of motive.").

In addition, the 1988 amendments added § 271(d)(5), which exempts conduct from patent misuse that:

> (5) conditioned the license of any rights to the patent or the sale of the patented product on the acquisition of a license to rights in another patent or purchase of a separate product, unless, in view of the circumstances, the patent owner has market power in the relevant market for the patent or patented product on which the license or sale is conditioned.

Section 271(d)(5) exempts certain types of tying conduct from patent misuse, particularly where the patentee lacks *market power* either in the relevant market for the patent or the patented product.[31] Generally, market power is the ability to control prices or to restrict output in a relevant market.[32] For example, a patentee that owned several key patents concerning CD-ROM technology during a time when the discs were considered "unique products [with] no close practice substitutes" was found to possess market power.[33] Although patents are sometimes referred to as "monopolies," there is no presumption that a patent confers market power on a patentee.[34] Indeed, some posit that *most* patents confer *no* market power.[35]

If a court determines that a patentee *does* have market power, § 271(d)(5)'s safe harbor does not apply. However, this does not mean that such a patent owner has engaged in patent misuse in all cases. Rather, this means that the conduct must be examined to determine whether the patentee has impermissibly broadened the scope of the patent such that unenforceability should result.

Although this subsection appears to apply to patent licenses that tie to the purchase of a separate product or patent ("tie-in"), one district court has held that the section encompasses situations where the license prevents the licensee from purchasing or using a separate product ("tie-out").[36] Additionally, some courts suggest that the subdivision applies to package licensing as well.[37]

The legislative history of § 271(d) suggests that the use of the phrase "under the circumstances" in this subsection was intended to eliminate per se misuse where the

---

[31] U.S. Philips Corp. v. Int'l Trade Comm'n, 424 F.3d 1179, 1186 (Fed. Cir. 2005) ("To establish the defense of patent misuse, the accused infringer must show that the patentee has power in the market for the tying product.").

[32] *See* U.S. v. E.I. du Pont de Nemours & Co., 351 U.S. 377, 391-92 (1956); Fortner Enters., Inc. v. U.S. Steel Corp., 394 U.S. 495, 503-04 (1969). Monopoly power can be inferred from one entity's "possession of a predominant share of the market." Eastman Kodak Co. v. Image Technical Servs., Inc., 504 U.S. 451, 464 (1992).

[33] *U.S. Philips Corp.*, 424 F.3d at 1186.

[34] Ill. Tool Works Inc. v. Indep. Ink, Inc., 547 U.S. 28, 31 (2006).

[35] *See* William M. Landes & Richard A. Ponser, The Economic Structure of Intellectual Property Law 374-75 (2003); Feldman, *supra* note 10, at 437 & nn.172-73.

[36] *In re* Recombinant DNA Tech. Patent & Contract Litig., 850 F. Supp. 769, 776-77 (S.D. Ind. 1994); *see also* Va. Panel Corp. v. MAC Panel Co., 133 F.3d 860, 869 (Fed. Cir. 1997) ("A 1988 amendment to § 271(d) provides that, *inter alia*, in the absence of market power, even a tying arrangement does not constitute patent misuse.").

[37] *See, e.g.*, Scheiber v. Dolby Labs., Inc., 293 F.3d 1014, 1020 (7th Cir. 2002); U.S. Philips Corp. v. International Trade Comm'n, 424 F.3d 1179, 1186 (Fed. Cir. 2005).

subsection applies.[38] Notably, in the en banc *Princo Corp. v. ITC*, suggests that this interpretation is correct and that this amendment "makes clear that Congress intended to limit patent misuse to practices having anticompetitive effects."[39]

§ 37.05 INCREASING THE TEMPORAL SCOPE OF A PATENT LICENSE

A patentee who acts outside the patent's *temporal* scope may be found to have engaged in patent misuse. This issue was explored in the Supreme Court's 1964 decision *Brulotte v. Thys Co.*[40] Although all patents relevant to the machine had expired by the end of 1957, the patentee continued to charge the royalty annually beyond that date. The Supreme Court found the *Brulotte* licenses unenforceable, explaining:

> A patent empowers the owner to exact royalties as high as he can negotiate with the leverage of that monopoly. But to use that leverage to project those royalty payments beyond the life of the patent is analogous to an effort to enlarge the monopoly of the patent by tying the sale or use of the patented article to the purchase or use of unpatented ones.[41]

The *Brulotte* Court noted a significant exception to the rule, however, such as where payments beyond the patent term were based on a continuing use or in place to accommodate a deferred purchase price.[42]

Justice Harlan dissented from the *Brulotte* majority on a number of grounds. Harlan pointed out that a number of analogous situations presented no legal impediments, such as extending credit terms beyond patent expiration or selling unpatented machines for a flexible price based on use. Harlan concluded the dissent by noting that "[i]f indeed the impact of the opinion is that Thys must redraft its contracts to achieve the same economic results, the decision is not only wrong, but conspicuously ineffectual."[43]

In 1979, the Supreme Court examined a related principle in *Aronson v. Quick Point Pencil Co.*[44] There, Aronson filed a patent application for an improved keyholder, and entered into a contract granting Quick Point an exclusive right to make and sell the keyholder. Among other things, the contract provided that Quick

---

[38] *See* 134 CONG. REC. 32,294-95 (1988) (statement of Rep. Kastenmeier); *id.* at 32,471 (statement of Sen. DeConcini); *id.* at 32,471-72 (statement of Sen. Leahy) ("Through the use of the phrase 'in view of the circumstances,' Congress is making clear that courts are never automatically to conclude that a tie-in constitutes misuse, even where market power is present, unless the court has considered and assessed all of the circumstances surrounding, the justifications for, and the impact of, the tie-in in the marketplace."). For a discussion of per se liability under antitrust law, *see infra* Chapter 38.

[39] Princo Corp. v. ITC, 616 F.3d 1318 (Fed. Cir. 2010) (en banc).

[40] Brulotte v. Thys Co., 379 U.S. 29 (1964).

[41] *Id.* at 33.

[42] *Id.* at 32 ("The sale or lease or unpatented machines on long-term payments based on a deferred purchase price or on use would present wholly different considerations.").

[43] *Id.* at 39 (Harlan, J. dissenting).

[44] Aronson v. Quick Point Pencil Co., 440 U.S. 257 (1979).

Point would pay Aronson a 5 percent royalty for all sales. However, the parties further agreed that this royalty would be reduced to 2½ percent if Aronson's patent application was not allowed within five years.

Aronson's patent application was ultimately rejected by the Patent Office, and therefore did not issue within the five years as set forth in the Quick Point contract. For a number of years after the PTO rejection, Quick Point continued to pay the 2 ½ percent royalty according to the parties' agreement. However, because Aronson's keyholder was not subject to patent protection, Quick Point's competitors began to make the keyholders without incurring any royalty expenses. Thereafter, Quick Point filed suit seeking a declaration that the agreement with Aronson was unenforceable. Despite the fact that the royalty was not supported by an issued patent, the Supreme Court rejected Quick Point's challenge. The *Aronson* Court explained that its ruling was not inconsistent with *Brulotte*, as follows:

> The principle underlying [*Brulotte*] . . . was simply that the monopoly granted under a patent cannot lawfully be used to "negotiate with the leverage of that monopoly." The [*Brulotte*] Court emphasized that to "use that leverage to project those royalty payments beyond the life of the patent is analogous to an effort to enlarge the monopoly of the patent . . . ." Here the reduced royalty which is challenged, far from being negotiated "with the leverage" of a patent, rested on the contingency that no patent would issue within five years.[45]

The impact of *Aronson* on *Brulotte* is unclear. Some scholarly criticism posits that *Aronson* overrules or limits *Brulotte's* holding "to cases in which the patent expires rather than fails to issue."[46] Others observe that, despite the Court's effort to distinguish *Brulotte*, the *Aronson* Court violated *Brulotte's* policy of preventing contractual extensions of the patent right beyond the scope of a valid and issued claim.[47]

Brulotte has been criticized by the lower courts. For example, in *Scheiber v. Dolby Laboratories, Inc.* Justice Posner describes Brulotte's foundation as "a free-floating product of a misplaced fear of monopoly."[48] *Scheiber* questioned whether post-expiration royalties represented an extension of the patent term at all, because "[a]fter the patent expires, anyone can make the patented process or product without being guilty of patent infringement. The patent can no longer be used to exclude anybody from such production. Expiration thus accomplishes what it is supposed to accomplish."[49] In addition, *Scheiber* reasoned that courts should not relieve licensees from obligations to pay post-expiration royalty payments, as such payments should logically be presumed to be deferred payments. As the court

---

[45] *Id.* at 265 (quoting Brulotte v. Thys Co., 379 U.S. 29, 33 (1964)).

[46] Rochelle Cooper Dreyfuss, *Dethroning Lear: Licensee Estoppel and the Incentive to Innovate*, 72 Va. L. Rev. 677, 709 (1986).

[47] *See* Harold See & Frank M. Caprio, *The Trouble with Brulotte: The Patent Royalty Term and Patent Monopoly Extension*, 1990 Utah L. Rev. 813, 841 (1990) ("*Aronson* yields a result inconsistent with the anti-patent extension policy of *Brulotte*.").

[48] Scheiber v. Dolby Labs., Inc., 293 F.3d 1014, 1018 (7th Cir. 2002).

[49] *Id.* at 1017.

explained, "[t]he duration of the patent fixes the limit of the patentee's power to extract royalties; it is a detail whether he extracts them at a higher rate over a shorter period of time or a lower rate over a longer period of time."[50]

Despite these criticisms, the *Scheiber* court reluctantly followed *Brulotte*, noting that "we have no authority to overrule a Supreme Court decision no mater how dubious its reasoning strikes us, or even how out of touch with the Supreme Court's current thinking the decision seems."[51] The Supreme Court has not revisited the issues presented in *Brulotte* and the decision remains as binding precedent.

§ 37.06   TYING AND PATENT POOLS

Those engaged in parallel research and innovation in a single industry may create a patent pool to facilitate a market. This aggregation of rights is akin to multi-party cross licensing arrangement set up within an administrative structure, such as a joint venture. In a typical arrangement, a covenant not to sue allows the pool's participants to practice the patents in exchange for a royalty. Patent pools have been used at least since 1856, when the Sewing Machine Combination was formed to resolve patent litigation and provide industry participants with the necessary rights to make and sell machines.[52]

Generally, patent pools can create a clearinghouse for patent rights. Their potential advantages include increased legal certainty, access to patents that might otherwise block improvements, and reduced licensing transaction costs. Some pools are comprised of complimentary patents, such as those used to practice the MPEG-2 file compression standard. However, some patent pools include competing technological solutions, which allow participants to engage in experimentation toward the best solution from an array of possibilities.[53] However, improperly administered, patent pools can pose risks to competition by facilitating collusion. Some adverse effects might include price fixing, reduced incentives to challenge invalid patents, and the enforcement of technological preferences that can suppress more viable solutions.

In *Princo Corp. v. ITC*, the Federal Circuit issued an en banc opinion that considered a patent misuse allegation for conduct relating to a patent pool.[54] There, the allegations focused on patents that were a patent pool formed by Sony and Philips. These two disc drive companies had formed the pool to ensure industry wide compatibility for recordable and rewritable compact discs. Before the patent pool was formed, Sony and Philips had discussed which of two competing technological solutions would ensure proper positioning of a CD in a consumer's reader/writer. Rejecting Sony's approach claimed in the "Lagadec patent," the

---

[50] *Id.*

[51] *Id.*

[52] *See* Adam Mossoff, *The Rise and Fall of the First American Patent Thicket: The Sewing Machine War of the 1850s*, 53 ARIZ. L. REV. 165 (2011).

[53] See Roger B. Andewelt, *Analysis of Patent Pools Under the Antitrust Laws*, 53 ANTITRUST. L.J. 611 (1984).

[54] Princo Corp. v. ITC, 616 F.3d 1318 (Fed. Cir. 2010).

Philips solution embodied in the "Raaymakers patents" prevailed. This agreement was memorialized in specifications called the Orange Book standard. To facilitate commercialization of the standard, Philips and Sony created a package license that included both the Lagadec and Raaymakers patents. This pool included a field of use restriction that extended only to patents that complied with the Orange Book standard. Because the Raaymakers patents were essential to practicing the Orange Book standard, industry participants who joined the pool would not have had the rights to use the positioning method claimed in the Lagadec patent.

Although Princo initially took a license to the pool, it soon stopped paying fees. In response, Philips filed an ITC complaint against Princo alleging patent infringement. In response, Princo asserted that the asserted patents were unenforceable based on patent misuse.

Princo relied primarily on two theories to support its patent misuse defense. First, Princo asserted that the patent pool constituted illegal tying, because access to the essential Raaymakers patent required a license to inessential Lagadec patent.[55] This contention, which had been extensively addressed in an earlier panel decision, was rejected. The court found that pooling inessential patents together with essential patents was a matter of convenience rather than leveraging. As the court explained, this conduct was "the functional equivalent of promising not to sue licensees on any of the patents in the group, which had the advantages of minimizing transaction costs and ensuring against the risk of post-agreement disputes as to whether those additional patents were required to practice the patented technology."[56]

Second, Princo alleged that the patent pool operated to suppress other technological solutions in favor of the Orange Book standard. According to this theory, conditioning access to the key patents in the pool deterred the development of competing alternatives — in this case, the solution claimed in the Lagadec patent. Princo argued that this circumstance allowed both Sony and Philips to collect royalties on their respective patents, rather than permitting the market to decide the superiority of each technology. The Federal Circuit rejected this theory as insufficient to demonstrate patent misuse, in part because this conduct did not allege a broadening of the Raaymaker's patent scope. The court stated that no physically or temporally restrictive conditions had been placed on the license, and certainly none that had any anticompetitive effect. Further, the court reasoned that any agreement between Sony and Phillips to suppress technology, if it existed, was not the type of agreement that patent misuse was designed to prevent. As the court explained, "the assertion of patent misuse arises not from the terms of the license itself but rather from an alleged collateral agreement between Sony and Philips."[57]

In the course of the decision, the *Princo* court suggested that patent misuse applies only to particular types of conduct — most typically to those that directly

---

[55] Although Philips did not assert the Lagadec patent against Princo, Philips later contended that one of the claims of the Lagadec patent was sufficiently broad to read on the Orange Book standard. Princo contested this point and argued that Lagadec was not an essential patent.

[56] *Id.* at 1324.

[57] *Id.* at 1334.

relate to the patent in suit. Nonetheless, two separate opinions — one concurring in part and another dissenting — suggest that some theoretical inconsistencies exist among members of the court. These inconsistencies might lead to shifts in the doctrine in future cases.

§ 37.07   CONCLUSION

Patent misuse is an affirmative defense that results in the unenforceability of the patent during the period of misuse. The patentee's conduct is assessed to determine whether there has been an impermissible broadening of the patent's subject matter or temporal scope. Conduct that constitutes the legitimate exercise of the patent right does not constitute misuse. Although this defense is rooted in the equitable doctrine of unclean hands, the defense has developed through statutory amendment and decisional law to parallel, and in some instances merge, with antitrust principles. As with many doctrines that implicate the proper role of patent policy within the larger context of commercial activity and competition, the law of patent misuse has experienced some turbulent shifts in both the courts and the legislature. Although statutory definitions have attempted to reign in some uncertainty, the doctrine remains in a state of fluctuation, and close attention should be paid to recent authorities that continue to shape the doctrine.

Chapter 38

PATENTS AND ANTITRUST LAW

SYNOPSIS

§ 38.01 INTRODUCTION

§ 38.02 TYING CLAIMS

   [A] Defining the Relevant Terminology: Tying, Per Se Illegality and the Rule of Reason

   [B] The Evolving Jurisprudence of Patent Tying Cases

§ 38.03 UNILATERAL REFUSALS TO LICENSE A PATENT

§ 38.04 SETTLEMENTS AND REVERSE PAYMENTS

§ 38.05 PATENT INFRINGEMENT LITIGATION AND THE SHAM EXCEPTION

   [A] Background: Anticompetitive Patent Infringement Litigation: *Handgards, Inc. v. Ethicon, Inc.*

   [B] The First Amendment and *Noerr-Pennington* Immunity

   [C] The Sham Exception to *Noerr-Pennington* Immunity

§ 38.06 FRAUDULENT PROCUREMENT OF A PATENT: *WALKER PROCESS* CLAIMS

§ 38.07 CONCLUSION

§ 38.01 INTRODUCTION

Antitrust law is intended to perfect the operation of competitive markets.[1] What impact does this principle have on the patent system? The pragmatic answer is that claimants may raise an antitrust counterclaim or defense where one uses a patent illegally or as a defense to invalidate the patent in suit. As one example, antitrust allegations may arise where a fraudulently obtained patent has been asserted in an anticompetitive manner. As another example, a patentee who files a series of baseless patent lawsuits with a subjective intent to halt competition may become the subject of antitrust allegations.

---

[1] Frank H. Easterbrook, *The Limits of Antitrust*, 63 Tex. L. Rev. 1 (1984). Antitrust analysis requires consideration of a relevant market, subject to certain exceptions. *See* Fed. Trade Comm'n v. Indiana Fed'n of Dentists, 476 U.S. 447 (1986) and Walker Process Equip, Inc. v. Food Mach. & Chem. Corp., 382 U.S. 172, 177 (1965) (noting the necessity to define a relevant product market in order to assess a patent holders potential liability under Section 2 of the Sherman Act).

There are differences between the goals of antitrust and patent law.[2] Unlike antitrust law's concern with competitive markets, the patent system represents a "carefully crafted bargain for encouraging the creation and disclosure of new, useful and nonobvious advances in technology and design in return for the exclusive right to practice the invention."[3] The *valid* exercise of a patent right can "create an environment for exclusion, and consequently, cripple competition."[4] Under patent law, the right to exclude competitors is inherent in the right. Striking a balance between these disparate goals present courts with difficult policy choices.

Despite language in some cases referencing patents as "monopolies,"[5] the patent right to exclude and antitrust monopoly are notably distinct concepts.[6] Generally, the antitrust definition of the exercise of *monopoly power* is the ability to control prices or to restrict output in a relevant market.[7] By contrast, the patent *right to exclude* exists regardless of a patentee's ability to exercise monopoly power.[8]

There is no presumption that a patent has monopoly power.[9] As a practical matter, many patent claims may have little or no impact in any commercial market in fact.[10] Although a patent may allow an entity to enjoy a high market share or exclusive right to sell a unique product, a patent holder has no market power[11] if

---

[2] For a more comprehensive examination of the patent and antitrust law interface, as well as additional examples, see H. HOVENKAMP, M. D. JANIS & MARK A. LEMLEY, IP AND ANTITRUST (2002). Another useful source of information is the U.S. Department of Justice and Federal Trade Commission, Antitrust Guidelines for the Licensing of Intellectual Property, http://www.usdoj.gov/atr/public/guidelines/0558.htm (last visited Feb. 1, 2008).

[3] Bonito Boats, Inc. v. Thunder Craft Boats, Inc., 489 U.S. 141, 150-51 (1989).

[4] Schering-Plough Corp. v. Fed. Trade Comm'n, 402 F.3d 1056, 1065-66 (11th Cir. 2005) (determining that neither the per se nor rule of reason analysis was appropriate for a case analyzing the competitive effects of a patent settlement).

[5] *See, e.g.*, Festo Corp. v. Shoketsu Kinzoku Kogyo Kabushiki Co., Ltd., 535 U.S. 722, 726 (2002) ("[B]y extending protection beyond the literal terms in a patent the doctrine of equivalents can create substantial uncertainty about where the patent monopoly ends."); Brenner v. Manson, 383 U.S. 519, 534 (1966) (discussing "[t]he basic *quid pro quo* contemplated by the Constitution and the Congress for granting a patent monopoly . . . ."); Graham v. John Deere Co., 383 U.S. 1, 9 (1966) ("The patent monopoly was not designed to secure to the inventor his natural right in his discoveries. Rather, it was a reward, an inducement, to bring forth new knowledge."); and Henry v. A. B. Dick Co., 224 U.S. 1, 27 (1912) (referring to the patent statute as "a statute creating and protecting a monopoly. It is a true monopoly, one having its origin in the ultimate authority, the Constitution.").

[6] *See* WILLIAM M. LANDES & RICHARD A. POSNER, THE ECONOMIC STRUCTURE OF INTELLECTUAL PROPERTY LAW 374 (2003).

[7] U. S. v. E. I. du Pont de Nemours & Co., 351 U.S. 377, 391-92 (1956) ("Monopoly power is the power to control prices or exclude competition."); Fortner Enterprises, Inc. v. U.S. Steel Corp., 394 U.S. 495, 503-04 (1969). Monopoly power can be inferred from one entity's possession of a predominant share of the market. Eastman Kodak Co. v. Image Technical Services, Inc., 504 U.S. 451, 464 (1992).

[8] 35 U.S.C. § 271 (Supp. IV 2004).

[9] Ill. Tool Works Inc. v. Indep. Ink, Inc., 547 U.S. 28 (2006).

[10] Peter M. Boyle, Penelope M. Lister & J. Clayton Everett, Jr., *Antitrust Law at the Federal Circuit: Red Light or Green Light at the IP-Antitrust Intersection?*, 69 ANTITRUST L.J. 739, 754 (2002).

[11] The term "market power" is an ability to raise prices without losing significant sales or to restrict output. Eastman Kodak Co. v. Image Technical Services, Inc., 504 U.S. 451, 464 (1992) (stating that market power "has been defined as "the ability of a single seller to raise price and restrict output.") (citation omitted); *see also* William M. Landes & Richard A. Posner, *Market Power in Antitrust Cases*,

there is a *close substitute*.[12] For example, a patent for a mousetrap will not enjoy monopoly power if there is a different, but equally effective, close substitute in the form of an alternative mousetrap that consumers can readily purchase for a comparable price.

The vast majority of patent transactions amount to the lawful exercise of the patent right and pose no antitrust concerns. Nonetheless, some patent practices can implicate violations of the antitrust law. As a cautionary note, the relevant legal standards have undergone dramatic shifts over the years and are likely to continue to do so in the future. Therefore, precedent must be read as part of the trend in which any particular case has been decided.

§ 38.02 TYING CLAIMS

Antitrust concerns may arise if a patentee seeks to *expand* the scope of the patent right in an anti-competitive manner. Thus, "a patent owner may not take the property right granted by a patent and use it to extend his power in the marketplace improperly, *i.e.* beyond the limits of what Congress intended to give in the patent laws."[13] As the Supreme Court has described, "power gained through some natural and legal advantage such as a patent, . . . can give rise to liability if a seller exploits his dominant position in one market to expand his empire into the next."[14]

A line of antitrust authority "reflect[s] a hostility to use of the statutorily granted patent monopoly to extend the patentee's economic control to unpatented products."[15] Under these cases, "the patentee is protected as to his invention, but may not use his patent rights to exact tribute for other articles."[16]

[A] Defining the Relevant Terminology: Tying, Per Se Illegality and the Rule of Reason

Under Section 1 of the Sherman Act, *tying* may exist where a party agrees to sell a product (the tying product) but only on a condition that a buyer purchases a different (or tied) product, or otherwise agrees not purchase that product from any

---

94 HARV. L. REV. 937 (1981). *Market power* is related to the concept of *monopoly power*, although the terms may be used in different contexts. *See* PHILLIP E. AREEDA & HERBERT HOVENKAMP, ANTITRUST LAW, ¶ 801 (Aspen 2002) (discussing monopoly power under the Sherman Act, § 2 as "'substantial' market power"); *see also* Reazin v. Blue Cross and Blue Shield of Kansas, Inc., 899 F.2d 951 (10th Cir. 1990) ("Market and monopoly power only differ in degree-monopoly power is commonly thought of as 'substantial' market power."); see also, Eastman Kodak Co., 504 U.S. at 461-62 (considering market power in assessing whether a defendant engaged in tying).

[12] Jefferson Parish Hosp. Dist. No. 2 v. Hyde, 466 U.S. 2, 37 n.7 (1984) (O'Connor, J., concurring).

[13] *In re* Independent Service Organizations Antitrust Litigation, 203 F.3d 1322, 1327 (Fed. Cir. 2000) (quoting Atari Games Corp. v. Nintendo of Am., Inc., 897 F.2d 1572, 1576 (Fed. Cir. 1990)).

[14] Eastman Kodak Co. v. Image Technical Services, Inc., 504 U.S. 451, 479 n.29 (1992).

[15] *See* U.S. v. Loew's, Inc., 371 U.S. 38, 46 (1962).

[16] *Id.*

other supplier.[17] Tying may violate antitrust law where the seller has market power in the tying product market and if the arrangement affects a substantial volume of commerce in the tied market.[18]

The market power that must be exercised in the tying market is power "to force a purchaser to do something that he would not do in a competitive market."[19] As the Supreme Court has explained, "the essential characteristic of an invalid tying arrangement lies in the seller's exploitation of its control over the tying product to force the buyer into the purchase of a tied product that the buyer either did not want at all, or might have preferred to purchase elsewhere on different terms."[20] As one example of how patent-related tying can occur, a patentee may condition the lease of a patented film projector (the tying product) on the licensee's agreement to use the projector only with film supplied by the patentee (the tied product).[21]

Antitrust law has undergone a series of changes in the jurisprudence that considers tying activity in the context of patent licenses or in association with patented products. As one example, courts have wrestled with whether such conduct should be assessed under the *rule of reason* or be determined a *per se* violation of antitrust law. Under the rule of reason, a finder of fact must examine whether the challenged conduct imposes an unreasonable restraint on competition.[22] Where the rule of reason applies, an antitrust plaintiff "must demonstrate that a particular contract or combination is in fact unreasonable and anticompetitive before it will be found unlawful."[23] In *Chicago Board of Trade v. United States*,[24] Justice Brandeis, writing for the U.S. Supreme Court, explained the application of the rule of reason as determining whether the restraint promotes or restricts competition, as follows:

> [T]he court must ordinarily consider the facts peculiar to the business to which the restraint is applied; its condition before and after the restraint was imposed; the nature of the restraint and its effect, actual or probable. The history of the restraint, the evil believed to exist, the reason for

---

[17] *Eastman Kodak Co.*, 504 U.S. at, 461-62 (citing Northern Pacific R. Co. v. U.S., 356 U.S. 1, 5-6 (1958)).

[18] *Id.* at 462.

[19] *Id.* at 464 (quoting Jefferson Parish Hosp. Dist. No. 2 v. Hyde, 466 U.S. 2, 14 (1984)).

[20] Jefferson Parish Hosp. Dist. No. 2 v. Hyde, 466 U.S. 2, 12 (1984). Patent cases have examined two distinct types of tying arrangements. A *tie in* is the conditioning of a patent license on the agreement to use some specific unpatented product. Eastman Kodak Co. v. Image Technical Services, Inc., 504 U.S. 451, 461 (1992) (stating, "[a] 'tying arrangement' is where a seller agrees to sell one product (the tying product), but only on the condition that the buyer also purchase a different (or tied) product"); *see also In re* Recombinant DNA Technology, 850 F. Supp. 769, 776 (S.D. Ind. 1994). A *tie out* occurs where a patent license is conditioned on a licensee's promise *not* to use the products or devices of another — most typically, the patentee's competitor. *See id.* In either event, the patent owner must possess market power in the tying market.

[21] This example is loosely based on Motion Picture Patents Co. v. Universal Film Mfg. Co., 243 U.S. 502 (1917), a case considering similar facts based on the patent misuse defense.

[22] Leegin Creative Leather Products, Inc. v. PSKS, Inc., 127 S. Ct. 2705, 2713 (2007).

[23] Texaco Inc. v. Dagher, 547 U.S. 1, 5 (2006).

[24] Chicago Bd. of Trade v. United States, 246 U.S. 231 (1918).

adopting the particular remedy, the purpose or end sought to be attained, are all relevant facts. This is not because a good intention will save an otherwise objectionable regulation or the reverse; but because knowledge of intent may help the court to interpret facts and to predict consequences.[25]

By contrast, a per se rule "treat[s] categories of restraints as necessarily illegal, eliminates the need to study the reasonableness of an individual restraint in light of the real market forces at work."[26] Generally, assessment under the per se rule is waning. Under current standards, "[p]er se liability is reserved for only those agreements that are 'so plainly anticompetitive that no elaborate study of the industry is needed to establish their illegality'."[27]

[B] The Evolving Jurisprudence of Patent Tying Cases

The Supreme Court has varied the legal standards for patent-related tying over the past several decades. The U.S. Supreme Court's 1947 *International Salt Co. v. U.S.*,[28] represents the approach under former law. There, defendant International Salt licensed its patented machines to process salt products. The U.S. brought an antitrust action to prevent enforcement of a tie-in provision stated in these licenses that required licensors to purchase all unpatented salt and salt tablets exclusively from International Salt.

The Supreme Court's opinion found that this licensing arrangement was an illegal tie under antitrust law applying a per se analysis, explaining that "[n]ot only is price-fixing unreasonable, per se, but also it is unreasonable, per se, to foreclose competitors from any substantial market."[29] In addition, the *International Salt* Court presumed that the patents conferred market power, noting that "[t]he appellant's patents confer a limited monopoly of the invention they reward."[30] *International Salt* recognized that the challenged conduct reached more than the right to exclude permitted under the patent law, stating, "[b]y contracting to close this market for salt against competition, International has engaged in a restraint of trade for which its patents afford no immunity from the anti-trust laws."[31]

At the time that *International Salt* was decided, a series of patent misuse cases applied this presumption of market power to a patent or a patented product, a concept that "migrated from patent law to antitrust law.[32] To some degree, the

---

[25] *Id.* at 238.

[26] *Leegin Creative Leather Products*, 127 S. Ct. at 2713 (citing Business Electronics Corp. v. Sharp Electronics Corp., 485 U.S. 717, 723 (1988)).

[27] *Texaco*, 547 U.S. at 4 (quoting Nat'l Soc. of Prof'l Engineers v. United States, 435 U.S. 679, 692 (1978)).

[28] Int'l Salt Co. v. U.S., 332 U.S. 392 (1947).

[29] *Id.* at 396 (citations omitted).

[30] *Id.* at 395.

[31] *Id.* at 396.

[32] Ill. Tool Works, Inc. v. Indep. Ink, 547 U.S. 28, 38-39 (2006) (reviewing history). The misuse decisions presumed "[t]he requisite market power" over the tying product such that the patentee could "extend [its] economic control to unpatented products." *Id.* at 37 (quoting United States v. Loew's Inc,

presumption arose from the view that the patent right to exclude permits a patentee to exercise market power in that the "patentee may sell a nonstaple article himself while enjoining others from marketing that same good without his authorization. By doing so, he is able to eliminate competitors and thereby to control the market for that product."[33] The presumption became evident in the antitrust jurisprudence.[34] As the Court stated in the 1984 antitrust decision *Jefferson Parish Hospital District No. 2 v. Hyde,* "if the government has granted the seller a patent or similar monopoly over a product, it is fair to presume that the inability to buy the product elsewhere gives the seller market power."[35]

Criticisms of this presumption quickly emerged. Indeed, Justice O'Connor's concurring opinion in *Jefferson Parish* noted that it was a "common misconception" that patents confer market power, as "a patent holder has no market power in any relevant sense if there are close substitutes for the patented product."[36] As one later work describes:

> The average patent . . . confers too little monopoly power on the patentee in a meaningful economic sense to interest a rational antitrust enforcer, and sometimes it confers no monopoly power at all — think of defensive patents, and of the many patents that are never licensed or if licensed never produce royalties for the license.[37]

In 1988, Congress amended the Patent Act to modify the doctrine of *patent misuse.* In doing so, the legislature added section 35 U.S.C. § 271(d)(5), which eliminated the defense for tying conduct unless the plaintiff affirmatively demonstrates that the patentee possesses market power, as follows:

> No patent owner . . . shall be denied relief or deemed guilty of misuse or illegal extension of the patent right by reason of his having done one or more of the following . . . (5) conditioned the license of any rights to the patent or the sale of the patented product on the acquisition of a license to rights in another patent or purchase of a separate product, unless, in view of the circumstances, *the patent owner has* market power *in the relevant*

---

371 U.S. 38, 45-46 (1962)). For more about patent misuse, see Chapter 37.

[33] Dawson Chem. Co. v. Rohm and Haas Co., 448 U.S. 176, 201 (1980).

[34] *Loew's,* 371 U.S. at 45-46 ("Since one of the objectives of the patent laws is to reward uniqueness, the principle of these [misuse] cases was carried over into antitrust law on the theory that the existence of a valid patent on the tying product, without more, establishes a distinctiveness sufficient to conclude that any tying arrangement involving the patented product would have anticompetitive consequences.") *Id.* at 46.

[35] Jefferson Parish Hosp. Dist. No. 2 v. Hyde, 466 U.S. 2, 16 (1984).

[36] *Id.* at 38 n.7.

[37] Landes & Posner, *supra* note 6 at 375; *see also* Donald F. Turner, *The Validity of Tying Arrangements Under the Antitrust Laws,* 72 Harv. L. Rev. 50, 53 (1958) (distinguishing between dominance required to demonstrate market power from the distinctiveness necessary to obtain a patent, stating "[d]ominance means market power - power over price and power to exclude competition. But distinctiveness, though likely to confer some slight power to vary price within narrow limits, may confer no power at all. A product's unique element may be wholly offset by other attractions of competing commodities.").

market for the patent or patented product on which the license or sale is conditioned.[38]

By requiring that those relying on a patent misuse defense to affirmatively establish market power, Congress eliminated the presumption of market power that derives from a patent or patented product for purposes of the patent misuse defense.[39]

This 1988 amendment to the Patent Act has now influenced changes to *antitrust* law's presumption of market power for patents. Specifically, in the Supreme Court's 2006 decision *Illinois Tool Works, Inc. v. Independent Ink*, the Court eliminated the *Jefferson Parish* presumption that a patented product confers market power in antitrust cases, noting that "it would be anomalous to preserve this presumption in antitrust after Congress has eliminated its foundation"[40] for patent misuse. In addition, the *Illinois Tool Works* Court relied on "the vast majority of academic literature [that] recognizes that a patent does not necessarily confer market power."[41] As *Illinois Tool Works* points out, "[m]any tying arrangements, even those involving patents and requirements ties, are fully consistent with a free, competitive market."[42]

§ 38.03   UNILATERAL REFUSALS TO LICENSE A PATENT

The question of whether a patentee's *refusal to license* constitutes an antitrust violation is controversial. On one hand, a fundamental attribute of the patent right is the right to exclude others from practicing the invention.[43] "This includes the right to suppress the invention while continuing to prevent all others from using it . . . to license others, or to refuse to license, and to charge such royalty as the leverage of the patent monopoly permits."[44] These rights are granted as part of the patent system's incentive system, which "confer[s] on the authors of useful inventions an exclusive right in their inventions for the time mentioned in their patent. It is the reward stipulated for the advantages derived by the public for the exertions of the individual, and is intended as a stimulus to those exertions."[45] Imposing antitrust liability for a patentee's exercise of the right to prevent others from practicing the invention may be thought to encroach on the value of the reward that the patent system is intended to provide.

On the other hand, patentees may possess significant power that derives from a key patent for which no design around exists. One can imagine that, if one patented

---

[38] 35 U.S.C. § 271(d)(5) (2000) (emphasis added).

[39] Va. Panel Corp. v. MAC Panel Co., 133 F.3d 860, 869 (Fed. Cir. 1997).

[40] Ill. Tool Works, Inc. v. Indep. Ink, 547 U.S. 28, 42 (2006).

[41] *Id.* at 44.

[42] *Id.* at 45.

[43] Zenith Radio Corp. v. Hazeltine Research, Inc., 395 U.S. 100, 135 (1969) ("The heart of his legal monopoly is the right to invoke the State's power to prevent others from utilizing his discovery without his consent.").

[44] U.S. v. Studiengesellschaft Kohle, mbH., 670 F.2d 1122, 1127 (D.C. Cir. 1981) (citation omitted).

[45] U. S. v. Line Material Co., 333 U.S. 287, 340 n.13 (1948) (quoting Grant v. Raymond, 31 U.S. 218, 241-2 (1832)).

a critical feature of telephone or email communications and foreclosed competition in either of those communication markets, the public would suffer detriment from a lack of competition. Moreover, under antitrust law outside the patent context, a monopolist's refusal to deal with competitors in a manner that harms the competitive process may be subject to liability under Section 2 of the Sherman Act.[46] This is because a refusal to deal can take on "exclusionary connotations when practiced by a monopolist."[47] Given that non-patent exclusionary conduct is subject to antitrust scrutiny, the question is whether patent rights merit special treatment.

In the 1997 decision *Image Technical Services, Inc. v. Eastman Kodak Co.*,[48] the Ninth Circuit attempted to set up a legal structure to provide an answer. There, the court considered the antitrust liability of Kodak relevant to the company's sales of photocopiers and micrographics equipment. Kodak and others provided repair and maintenance service for these machines. Kodak owned over 200 patents that covered 65 of its thousands of replacement parts that were needed to service this equipment. Although initially Kodak allowed independent service operators ("ISO's") to purchase these parts to service Kodak machines, during the 1980's Kodak stopped all part sales to ISO's. Further, during this time Kodak obtained contracts with manufacturers that prevented any sales of these parts to the ISO's. The ISO's asserted a claim under Section 2 of the Sherman Act against Kodak, claiming exclusionary conduct in that the ISO's were unable to compete in the market for service for Kodak machines without ready access to Kodak parts.

A jury found against Kodak, awarding $71.8 million in damages in favor of the ISO's. Kodak's appeal to the Ninth Circuit was premised on a jury instruction, which stated "the fact that some of the replacement parts are patented or copyrighted does not provide Kodak with a defense against any of those antitrust claims."[49] The Ninth Circuit acknowledged the "obvious tension between the patent and antitrust laws: one body of law creates and protects monopoly power while the other seeks to proscribe it."[50] The *Kodak* court attempted to resolve this tension by permitting a patentee with a legitimate justification defense, holding that "while exclusionary conduct can include a monopolist's unilateral refusal to license a patent . . . or to sell its patented . . . work, a monopolist's desire to exclude others from its protected work is a *presumptively valid business justification* for any immediate harm to consumers."[51] Thus, the Ninth Circuit's *Kodak* decision affords patentees who are seeking to stand on their intellectual property rights with a presumptively valid defense to Section 2 liability, which may be rebutted with evidence that this justification is *pretextual*.

---

[46] *See, e.g.*, Data General Corp. v. Grumman Systems Support Corp., 36 F.3d 1147, 1183 (1st Cir. 1994) (considering whether a copyright holder's refusal to license constitutes exclusionary conduct under antitrust law).

[47] Eastman Kodak Co. v. Image Technical Services, Inc., 504 U.S. 451, 488 (1992).

[48] Image Technical Services, Inc. v. Eastman Kodak Co., 125 F.3d 1195 (9th Cir. 1997).

[49] *Id.* at 1214.

[50] *Id.* at 1215 (internal quotations and citation omitted).

[51] *Id.* at 1218 (internal quotations and brackets omitted).

In result, despite the error in the trial court's jury instruction, the *Kodak* court affirmed the verdict based on a finding that the error was harmless. Specifically, the Ninth Circuit found sufficient evidence to demonstrate that defendant Kodak's asserted justification was a pretext to mask anticompetitive conduct. Among other things, the court found that Kodak's blanket refusal to supply *any* of its thousands of parts to the ISO's — of which only 65 were protected by Kodak's patents — demonstrated that Kodak was not actually motivated by a desire to protect its intellectual property rights in cutting off sales of all replacement parts to the ISO's.

In 2000, the Federal Circuit stated a view contrary to the Ninth Circuit's *Kodak* rule in *In re Independent Service Organization Antitrust Litigation* ("ISO"),[52] on facts that are remarkably similar to those considered by the Ninth Circuit in *Kodak*. Specifically, the Federal Circuit's *ISO* case examined antitrust claims against Xerox, who manufactures, sells and services high-volume copiers. In 1984, Xerox implemented a policy to refuse to sell replacement parts to ISO's who sought to compete with Xerox's service business for this line of copiers. The ISO's antitrust claim alleged that Xerox's policy effectively eliminated ISO's as competitors in the market for servicing affected Xerox products. In defense, Xerox asserted patent rights on the parts that were the subject of the ISO's antitrust claims.

The Federal Circuit's opinion affirmed the district court grant of summary judgment, dismissing the ISO's antitrust claims against Xerox. Unlike the Ninth Circuit's *Kodak* decision, the Federal Circuit's *ISO* opinion rejected the antitrust claim based on "the right of the patentee to refuse to sell or license in markets within the scope of the statutory patent grant."[53] The *ISO* court expressly rejected the Ninth Circuit's *Kodak* presumption and instead foreclosed *any* inquiry into Kodak's intent:

> We decline to follow *Image Technical Services* [*v. Kodak*] . . . . In the absence of any indication of illegal tying, fraud in the Patent and Trademark Office, or sham litigation, the patent holder may enforce the statutory right to exclude others from making, using, or selling the claimed invention free from liability under the antitrust laws. We therefore will not inquire into his subjective motivation for exerting his statutory rights, even though his refusal to sell or license his patented invention may have an anticompetitive effect, so long as that anticompetitive effect is not illegally extended beyond the statutory patent grant.[54]

Furthermore, the *ISO* court underscored that "absent exceptional circumstances, a patent may confer the right to exclude competition altogether in more than one antitrust market."[55] In the final analysis, the Federal Circuit's *ISO* opinion appears to entirely block any antitrust inquiry into a patentee's unilateral refusal to deal.[56]

---

[52] *In re* Independent Service Organization Antitrust Litigation, 203 F.3d 1322 (Fed. Cir. 2000).

[53] *Id.* at 1327.

[54] *Id.* at 1327-28.

[55] *Id.* at 1327.

[56] A number of decisions support the view that a patentee's right to refuse to license does not give rise to antitrust liability. *See, e.g.,* SCM Corp. v. Xerox Corp., 645 F.2d 1195, 1206 (2d Cir. 1981) ("we hold that where a patent has been lawfully acquired, subsequent conduct permissible under the patent laws cannot

§ 38.04   SETTLEMENTS AND REVERSE PAYMENTS

In the vast majority of circumstances, settlement is a favored and efficient way to resolve disputes. Despite this, some patent settlements in the pharmaceutical field have been subject to antitrust allegations.[57] These issues arise where the parties engage in an agreement that serves their individual interests but harm competition. Some challenges have been brought under section 1 of the Sherman Act, which prohibits agreements that unreasonably restrain of trade.

As background, in a typical case the pharmaceutical innovator has obtained a patent and FDA approval. The cost to develop and test a drug is quite significant, although estimates for the industry average vary.[58] Because the patent gives the patentee market exclusivity, the drug can be priced above competitive levels. This illustrates the value of patenting to the pharmaceutical industry — that is, the high cost of drug development can be recouped during the patent term and used for research and development in exploring new pharmaceutical solutions going forward. Once the patent expires, generic entrants can sell competing formulations. Some informal estimates suggest that an initial inventor's drug prices can fall between 10% and 80% during this post patent expiration period.[59] These lower prices are beneficial for consumers and the organizations that pay for health care.

Generic entrants are able to offer lower prices because such entities do not incur the high cost and risk of drug development. In addition, under the 1984 Drug Price Competition and Patent Term Restoration Act (also called the "Hatch–Waxman Act"),[60] generic manufacturers may obtain FDA approval by submitting an Abbreviated New Drug Application ("ANDA"), which is far less costly to prepare compared with the cost of testing and data development necessary for an initial New Drug Application ("NDA"). This is because an ANDA may rely on the FDA's prior determination for safety and efficacy made in the course of approving an earlier "pioneer" drug.

---

trigger any liability under the antitrust laws."); Miller Insituform, Inc. v. Insituform of North America, Inc., 830 F.2d 606, 609 (6th Cir. 1987) ("A patent holder who lawfully acquires a patent cannot be held liable under Section 2 of the Sherman Act for maintaining the monopoly power he lawfully acquired by refusing to license the patent to others."); U.S. v. Westinghouse Elec. Corp., 648 F.2d 642, 647 (9th Cir. 1981) ("The right to license that patent, exclusively or otherwise, or to refuse to license at all, is 'the untrammeled right' of the patentee.") (citation omitted).

[57] For more information about the antitrust implications for intellectual property litigation, see Herbert Hovenkamp, et al., *Anticompetitive Settlements of Intellectual Property Disputes*, 87 MINN. L. REV. 1719 (2003)

[58] See Joseph A. DiMasi, Ronald W. Hansen, Henry G. Grabowski, *The Price of Innovation: New Estimates of Drug Development Costs*, 22 J. HEALTH ECON. 151 (2002) (estimating that the cost of developing a new drug through the approval process is $802 million); but see Donald W. Light and Rebecca Warburton, *Demythologizing the High Costs of Pharmaceutical Research*, BIOSOCIETIES 1 (2001) (criticizing estimates).

[59] Jonathan D. Rockoff, *Helping Lipitor Live Longer*, WALL STREET JOURNAL ONLINE (Nov. 22, 2011) (citing DRX Inc., a health-care data provider, as the source of this figure) available at http://online.wsj.com/article/SB10001424052970203710704577052350701638614.html.

[60] The Hatch-Waxman Act was an amendment to Federal Food, Drug, and Cosmetic Act. 21 U.S.C. §§ 301–399.

However, this fast track through the FDA does not remove the patents owned by the company that first created the drug. When the FDA grants an NDA, the drug is listed in the Approved Drug Products with Therapeutic Equivalence Evaluations, commonly known as the Orange Book, together with any relevant patents that would be infringed by another's reproduction of the formulation.

Hatch-Waxman includes a structure that is intended to preserve the initial developer's patent rights. Specifically, when a generic drug maker wishes to file an ANDA, it must include a "certification that, in the opinion of the applicant and to the best of his knowledge, the proposed generic drug does not infringe any patent listed" in the Orange Book.[61] That certification can take several forms, including that a patent application has never been filed or that all relevant patents have expired. Another, called a "paragraph IV certification," allows the generic applicant to represent that any relevant patent list in the Orange Book "is invalid or will not be infringed by the manufacture, use, or sale of the new drug for which the application is submitted."[62] An applicant filing a paragraph IV certification must give notice to the patentee. This certification establishes a technical act of infringement even where the generic company has not yet made or sold any product. The patentee then has forty-five days to file a patent infringement action against the ANDA applicant. If the patentee files suit, a thirty-month stay goes into effect, which means that the FDA cannot approve the generic drug before the expiration of that thirty-month period. To provide generic entrants with an incentive to challenge patents and compensate for the thirty-month delay, the Hatch-Waxman Act provides that the first generic manufacturer that submits an ANDA with a paragraph IV certification receives a 180–day period of exclusive marketing rights against all other generic companies. This 180–day period begins the earlier of either (1) when the first ANDA applicant begins commercial marketing of its generic drug or (2) when a court finds that the patent is either invalid or not infringed.

When an ANDA has been filed, the inventing company and the ANDA filer become engaged in patent litigation in which the patent is challenged. Some pharmaceutical patent disputes settle, and sometimes on terms that appear counterintuitive. Although other settlements might require the accused infringer to pay the patentee, some pharmaceutical patent cases are resolved in reverse. That is, some settlements require the patentee to make payments to the generic drug company in exchange for an agreement to refrain from entering the market for a specified period of time. Because the patentee is paying the infringer, rather than the other way around, such settlements have been said to include "reverse payments." In these cases, the patentee is able to continue to enjoy patent ownership, market exclusivity, and presumably pre-litigation price levels. In return, the generic company obtains a significant payment without selling a single pill.

The appellate courts have approached antitrust analysis of reverse payments inconsistently. In the Eleventh Circuit's *In re Cardizem CD Antitrust Litigation*, the court examined a litigation settlement agreement in which the generic delayed

---

[61]　*Id.* § 355(j)(2)(A)(vii).

[62]　*Id.* § 355(j)(2)(A)(vii)(IV).

entry for an equivalent formulation of the patentee's heart medication Cardizen CD. As part of the settlement, the patentee paid the generic manufacturer $89 million dollars and the delay amounted to an 11 month period.[63] Because the generic had filed a paragraph IV certification, this had the effect of delaying other generic entrants for an additional 180-day period. The Court explained, "There is simply no escaping the conclusion that the Agreement . . . was, at its core, a horizontal agreement to eliminate competition in the market for Cardizen CD throughout the United States, a classic example of a *per se* illegal restraint of trade."[64]

One example of the contrary approach is the Second Circuit's *In re Tamoxifen Citrate Antitrust Litigation.*[65] Rejecting an antitrust challenge to the reverse payment settlement agreement, the *Tamoxifen* court found that this scenario was an expected result from the dynamic of Hatch-Waxman litigation as it affected patent settlements. The court observed that, unlike typical patent infringement litigation, generics have not yet invested in manufacturing and distribution prior to suit. According to the court, "[t]he prospective generic manufacturer therefore has relatively little to lose in litigation precipitated by paragraph IV certification beyond litigation costs and the opportunity for future profits."[66] On the other hand, "[t]he patent holder's risk if it loses the resulting patent suit is correspondingly large: It will be stripped of its patent monopoly."[67] In addition to the general policy favoring of settlements, the *Tamoxifen* court concluded that "[w]hatever damage is done to competition by settlement is done pursuant to the monopoly extended to the patent holder by patent law."[68]

The Supreme Court has not yet accepted certiorari to consider how reverse payment settlements should be assessed, although petitions have been filed. Legislation was introduced after the Federal Trade Commission recommended, "that Congress should pass legislation to protect consumers from such anticompetitive agreements."[69] This recommendation is accompanied by a study that estimates that consumer harm from such settlements is $35 billion over the next ten years.[70] As of this writing the legislation has not been enacted. However, because the issues raised by these settlements are pressing and complex, the practice is likely to remain controversial over the coming years.[71]

---

[63] In re Cardizem CD Antitrust Litigation, 332 F.3d 896 (11th Cir. 2003).

[64] *Id.* at 908 (emphasis in original); *see also* Valley Drug Co. v. Geneva Pharmaceuticals, Inc. 344 F.3d 1294 (11th Cir. 2003).

[65] In re Tamoxifen Citrate Antitrust Litigation, 466 F.3d 187 (2nd Cir. 2006).

[66] *Id.* at 206-07.

[67] *Id.* at 207.

[68] *Id.* at 213.

[69] See Federal Trade Comm'n, Pay-for-day: How Drug Company Pay-Offs Cost Consumers Billions: an Ftc Staff Study, 2 (2010), available at http://www.ftc.gov/os/2010/01/100112payfordelayrpt.pdf; see also the Preserve Access to Affordable Generics Act (S.27) (Jan. 5, 2011).

[70] *Id.* at 6.

[71] For a more detailed analysis, see Herbert J. Hovenkamp, *Antitrust and Patent Law Analysis of Pharmaceutical Reverse Payment Settlements* (January 15, 2011), available at http://ssrn.com/abstract=1741162.

§ 38.05   PATENT INFRINGEMENT LITIGATION AND THE SHAM EXCEPTION

[A]   Background: Anticompetitive Patent Infringement Litigation: *Handgards, Inc. v. Ethicon, Inc.*

Some accused infringers have asserted antitrust claims against a patent holder based on the allegation that the infringement lawsuit is an illegitimate tool to suppress competition. As Judge Posner has described:

> Suppose a monopolist brought a tort action against its single, tiny competitor; the action had a colorable basis in law; but in fact the monopolist would never have brought the suit-its chances of winning, or the damages it could hope to get if it did win, were too small compared to what it would have to spend on the litigation-except that it wanted to use pretrial discovery to discover its competitor's trade secrets; or hoped that the competitor would be required to make public disclosure of its potential liability in the suit and that this disclosure would increase the interest rate that the competitor had to pay for bank financing; or just wanted to impose heavy legal costs on the competitor in the hope of deterring entry by other firms. In these examples the plaintiff wants to hurt a competitor not by getting a judgment against him, which would be a proper objective, but just by the maintenance of the suit, regardless of its outcome.[72]

As this paragraph suggests, patent litigation can impose serious costs on competitors. However, only a narrow class of such cases can give rise to an antitrust claim.

One viable theory for establishing an antitrust violation is based on the filing and maintenance of a series of "ill-founded patent infringement actions, [brought] in bad faith" with the intent to monopolize an industry.[73] This principle was explored in the 1979 decision *Handgards, Inc. v. Ethicon, Inc.*,[74] in which the Ninth Circuit considered the conduct of a patentee who had acquired two patents relating to disposable plastic gloves made by heat-sealing. The alleged infringers asserted that the patentees had sought to monopolize the market for heat-sealed plastic gloves by prosecuting a patent infringement lawsuit with the intent to exclude Handgards, a competitor, from the market.

The *Handgards* court recognized that Section 2 of the Sherman Act might be violated where the patentee files and prosecutes a series of patent infringement actions in bad faith and the patentee has exclusionary power in the relevant market.[75] At the same time, the *Handgards* court cautioned that not all claims brought under this theory will be successful. As the court explained, legitimate efforts to assert patent rights might be chilled if every unsuccessful patent case was subject to the threat of antitrust enforcement and remedies, including treble

---

[72] Grip-Pak, Inc. v. Ill. Tool Works, Inc., 694 F.2d 466, 472 (7th Cir. 1982).

[73] *See* Handgards, Inc. v. Ethicon, Inc., 601 F.2d 986, 990 (9th Cir. 1979).

[74] *Id.* at 995-96.

[75] *Id.* at 993.

damages. For this reason, there are a number of protections in place that must be overcome for one to establish a *Handgards* claim. First, the *Handgards* case requires that a patent infringement suit is presumed to be brought in good faith. Therefore, one seeking to establish a *Handgards* claim must rebut this presumption by demonstrating a patentee's subjective bad faith by clear and convincing evidence. Second, as discussed in the following section, one must also overcome constitutional immunity.

[B]   The First Amendment and *Noerr-Pennington* Immunity

The First Amendment protects a citizen's right to petition the government under a doctrine known as the *Noerr-Pennington doctrine*, named after two foundational U.S. Supreme Court decisions.[76] Under the 1961 *Eastern Railroad Presidents Conference v. Noerr Motor Freight* ("*Noerr*"), this protection is based on the policy that "the whole concept of representation depends on the ability of the people to make their wishes known to their representatives."[77] *Noerr* held that the First Amendment insulated an association's efforts to influence government action from liability from suit based on the Sherman Act.[78] In the 1965 *Pennington* decision, the Court reaffirmed that "a concerted effort to influence public officials" was immune from antitrust liability even if competition is eliminated as a result of that conduct.[79]

Over the years, *Noerr-Pennington* immunity has been expanded to encompass access to the courts.[80] Under this protection, one is immune from antitrust law when one files a court action to obtain redress for the violation of a legal right. Thus, absent an applicable exception, claims brought under a *Handgards* theory confront the impediment that a patentee's ability to file suit against infringers is a constitutionally protected right that may be insulated from antitrust scrutiny.

[C]   The Sham Exception to *Noerr-Pennington* Immunity

In *Noerr*, the Supreme Court recognized that antitrust immunity does not apply where the activity "is a mere *sham* to cover what is actually nothing more than an attempt to interfere directly with the business relationships of a competitor."[81] In 1993, the Court elaborated on the applicability of *Noerr's* sham exception in *Professional Real Estate Investors, Inc. v. Columbia Pictures, Inc.* ("*PRE*").[82] The *PRE* Court examined litigation filed by a copyright holder, Columbia Pictures, who asserted infringement against various entities for circulating videodiscs for use in hotel rooms. Columbia's suit claimed that such use facilitated the public performance of its films in violation of the copyright laws. The defendants

---

[76] Eastern Railroad Presidents Conference v. Noerr Motor Freight, Inc., 365 U.S. 127 (1961) and United Mine Workers v. Pennington, 381 U.S. 657 (1965).

[77] *Noerr*, 365 U.S. at 137.

[78] Cal. Motor Transp. Co. v. Trucking Unlimited, 404 U.S. 508 (1972).

[79] *Pennington*, 381 U.S. at 670.

[80] *Cal. Motor Transp. Co.*, 404 U.S. at 510.

[81] *Noerr*, 365 U.S. at 144.

[82] Prof'l Real Estate Investors, Inc. v. Columbia Pictures, Inc., 508 U.S. 49 (1993).

successfully blocked the copyright holder's action by demonstrating to the court that the rental of the discs for in-room use was a private, rather than public, performance. On this ground, Columbia's copyright action against the defendants failed.

In response, Professional Real Estate Investors, who owned a hotel and had been named in Columbia's copyright suit, counterclaimed based on §§ 1 and 2 of the Sherman Act and state antitrust law. Specifically, the antitrust suit alleged that Columbia's copyright action was filed to monopolize and restrain trade in the market for content on videodiscs.

The *PRE* Court focused on whether the lawsuit filed and maintained by Columbia was subject to the sham exception to the *Noerr-Pennington* doctrine. To decide the issue, the Court formulated a two-part test. The first prong of this test requires that the lawsuit be shown to be *objectively baseless* — that is, "[i]f an objective litigant could conclude that the suit is reasonably calculated to elicit a favorable outcome, the suit is immunized under *Noerr*."[83] This first prong of the *PRE* standard requires an antitrust plaintiff to demonstrate that the patentee lacked *probable cause* to bring the suit. *PRE* defined "probable cause" as an objectively "reasonable belief that there is a chance that a claim may be held valid upon adjudication."[84] Unless the first prong of the *PRE* test is met, the patentee has an absolute defense to the antitrust claim.

The second prong of the *PRE* test, which is examined only if the challenged litigation is held as objectively baseless under the first prong, queries whether the lawsuit is based on a *subjective motivation* to "interfere *directly* with the business relationship of a competitor through the use of a governmental *process* — as opposed to the *outcome* of that process — as an anticompetitive weapon."[85] Unless these two elements are met, *Handgards* actions are immune under the *Noerr-Pennington* doctrine as constitutionally protected activity.

An additional point about the *PRE* test should be observed — that is, if both prongs of *PRE* are met, then the sham exception to *Noerr* immunity is invoked. At that juncture, the antitrust plaintiff must then demonstrate a violation of antitrust laws. As explained by the Supreme Court, "[p]roof of a sham merely deprives the defendant of immunity; it does not relieve the plaintiff of the obligation to establish all other elements of his [antitrust] claim."[86]

The Federal Circuit has considered the application of the *PRE* test to patent litigation.[87] In *C.R. Bard, Inc. v. M3 Systems, Inc.*, the court recognized that an antitrust violation might exist where a patentee files suit for an anticompetitive

---

[83] *Id.* at 60.

[84] *Id.* at 62-63 (quoting Hubbard v. Beatty & Hyde, Inc., 178 N.E.2d 485, 488 (1961)).

[85] *Id.* at 60-61. (emphasis in original) (citation and quotations omitted).

[86] *Prof'l Real Estate Investors, Inc.*, 508 U.S. at 61; *see also Handgards*, 601 F.2d at 993 n.11 (stating, "It is worth emphasizing that the absence of immunity does not create an antitrust offense. The fact that defendant's conduct is not immune from antitrust scrutiny does not satisfy the plaintiff's burden of proving the usual elements of an antitrust offense . . . .").

[87] C.R. Bard, Inc. v. M3 Systems, Inc., 157 F.3d 1340, 1368 (Fed. Cir. 1998).

purpose with knowledge that the patent is invalid or not infringed.[88] *C.R. Bard* held that patentees are entitled to a presumption that the patentee's right of enforcement is made in good faith, based on the patent's systems incentive function to provide inventors with a right of enforcement.[89] Finding that *Noerr-Pennington* protected the patentees' conduct on the facts presented, the *C.R. Bard* court cautioned that an unsuccessful verdict is insufficient to demonstrate an antitrust violation. Rather, both elements of the *PRE* test be met and "affirmative evidence of bad faith" is required.[90] The *C.R. Bard* court explained, "Since a principal purpose of the patent system is to provide innovators with a property right upon which investment and other commercial commitments can be made, absent the *PRE* criteria the patentee must have the right of enforcement of a duly granted patent, unencumbered by punitive consequences should the patent's validity or infringement not survive litigation."[91]

§ 38.06   FRAUDULENT PROCUREMENT OF A PATENT: *WALKER PROCESS* CLAIMS

In 1965, the U.S. Supreme Court decided *Walker Process Equipment, Inc. v. Food Machinery & Chemical Corp.*,[92] which established that an antitrust violation might be based on one's assertion of a patent that was knowingly and willfully obtained by fraud. In that case, the patentee had submitted a false declaration to the Patent Office, asserting that the invention claimed in the patentee's application was novel, when, in fact, the invention was in public use outside the grace period.

To establish an antitrust claim for Section 2 of the Sherman Act under *Walker Process*, one must affirmatively demonstrate that the patentee has market power[93] in the relevant product market. In addition, a claimant must show fraud: (1) the patentee used a patent acquired by deliberate and willful fraud to restrain competition in that market,[94] (2) a false representation or deliberate omission of a fact material to patentability, (3) intent to deceive the patent examiner, (4) the examiner's justifiable reliance on the misrepresentation or omission in granting the patent, and (5) a causal connection between the misrepresentation or omission and the granting of the patent. *Walker Process* has been construed in the Federal Circuit to require a more stringent showing than that required to demonstrate inequitable conduct; rather, one must demonstrate "clear, convincing proof of intentional fraud involving affirmative dishonesty, a deliberately planned and

---

[88] *Id.* at 1368.

[89] *Id.* at 1369.

[90] *Id.* ("Neither the bringing of an unsuccessful suit to enforce patent rights, nor the effort to enforce a patent that falls to invalidity, subjects the suitor to antitrust liability.").

[91] *Id.*

[92] Walker Process Equip., Inc. v. Food Mach. & Chem. Corp., 382 U.S. 172 (1965).

[93] *See supra* footnote 11 (defining market power).

[94] *See* C.R. Bard, Inc. v. M3 Systems, Inc., 157 F.3d 1340, 1367 (Fed. Cir. 1998) (describing the elements of a *Walker Process* claim under Section 2 of the Sherman Act). In *C.R. Bard*, the Federal Circuit recognized that the regional circuits may impose additional requirements, such as specific intent to monopolize, anticompetitive conduct and a dangerous probability of success. *Id.* at 1368.

carefully executed scheme to defraud the Patent Office."[95]

How does the *Noerr-Pennington* doctrine, and the *PRE* test for the sham exception, affect claims for fraudulent procurement under *Walker Process*? In *PRE*, the Supreme Court expressly disclaimed any effort to reach a decision on this issue.[96] The appellate courts are split on the question. The Ninth Circuit has indicated its willingness to apply the *PRE* two-part test to *Walker Process* claims.[97]

However, the Federal Circuit came to the opposite conclusion in *Nobelpharma AB v. Implant Innovations, Inc.*[98] In *Nobelpharma*, the jury found in favor of the accused infringer on an antitrust counterclaim based on findings that the inventors had obtained the asserted patent through knowing and willful fraud. In particular, in 1977, one of the named inventors authored and published a book that described critical portions of an invention for improved dental implants. These implants relied on a particular size and spacing for small indentations, called "micropits," which permitted the implants to securely connect to the patient's bone tissue. A later-prepared draft Swedish patent application referenced the inventor's 1977 book. However, the patentee's final patent applications filed in both Sweden in 1979 and in the U.S. in 1980 contained no references to the inventor's 1977 book.

According to *Nobelpharma*, "*PRE* and *Walker Process* provide alternative legal grounds on which a patentee may be stripped of its immunity from the antitrust laws; both legal theories may be applied to the same conduct."[99] As a corollary, *Nobelpharma* determined that the *PRE* test for a sham inquiry was not necessary to proving a *Walker Process* fraudulent procurement claim. As the court explained, "*Walker Process* antitrust liability is based on the knowing assertion of a patent procured by fraud on the PTO, very specific conduct that is clearly reprehensible."[100] Finding *Handgards* and *Walker Process* antitrust theories as analytically distinct, the Federal Circuit stated that the court "need not find a way to merge these decisions."[101] Rather, "[e]ach provides its own basis for depriving a patent owner of immunity from the antitrust laws; either or both may be applicable to a particular party's conduct in obtaining and enforcing a patent."[102]

---

[95] *C.R. Bard*, 157 F.3d at 1364 (Fed. Cir. 1998) (citation and quotation omitted). For more information about the standards governing inequitable conduct, *see supra* Chapter 36.

[96] Prof'l Real Estate Investors v. Columbia Pictures, Inc., 508 U.S. 49, 61 n.6 (1993) (stating, "[w]e need not decide here whether and, if so, to what extent *Noerr* permits the imposition of antitrust liability for a litigants fraud or other misrepresentations.").

[97] Liberty Lake Investments, Inc. v. Magnuson, 12 F.3d 155, 159 (9th Cir. 1993) ("Read in context with the entire *Professional Real Estate Investors* opinion, footnote 6 does not obviate application of the Court's two-part test for determining sham litigation in the absence of proof that a party's knowing fraud upon, or its intentional misrepresentations to, the court deprive the litigation of its legitimacy"); *see also* Hydranautics v. Filmtec Corp., 70 F.3d 533, 538 (9th Cir. 1995) (requiring a showing of intentional fraud to avoid application of *Noerr* immunity).

[98] Nobelpharma AB v. Implant Innovations, Inc., 141 F.3d 1059 (Fed. Cir. 1998).

[99] *Id.* at 1071.

[100] *Id.*

[101] *Id.*

[102] *Id.*

In result, the *Nobelpharma* court affirmed the jury's verdict on the accused infringer's *Walker Process* fraud theory. Specifically, *Nobelpharma* found sufficient evidence demonstrating the inventor's intent to withhold the 1977 book from the U.S. filing in order to defraud the U.S. PTO. The court noted that, "[i]mportantly, the 1977 book was thought by at least one inventor to be relevant, as evidenced by the initial disclosure to the patent agent, but it was inexplicably not later disclosed to the PTO."[103] Further, *Nobelpharma* found the inventor's book was material because the use of the micropits would have anticipated the U.S. patent. Additionally, the court found that the patent's assignee was aware of the applicant's fraud when bringing suit, based on a legal opinion that "if we were to sue anyone on the patent we would lose in the first round . . . . [T]here was prior art, not the least of which was . . . [the 1977 Book] that would invalidate the patent."[104] *Nobelpharma* found that these circumstances were sufficient to strip the patentee of antitrust immunity without requiring the application of the *PRE* test to asserted *Walker Process* claims. In addition, the *Nobelpharma* court affirmed that the record contained sufficient evidence to demonstrate that a *Walker Process* claim had been established.

§ 38.07   CONCLUSION

An exploration of the considerations of asserting antitrust against patent related conduct demonstrates a difficulty inherent in preserving the right to exclude under the patent law with antitrust law's concern with ensuring competitive markets. A number of examples where these concerns exist include a patentee's filing and maintenance of baseless and anticompetitive infringement actions, the assertion of a fraudulently procured patent, a unilateral refusal to license a patent, reverse payment settlements, and tying. In each, Congress and the courts endeavor to preserve the patentee's right to exclude as the reward for the invention. Nonetheless, a particular abuse or extension of this right may give rise to antitrust liability where the applicable standards have been met.

---

[103] *Id.* at 1072.

[104] *Id.* at 1073.

Chapter 39

EXHAUSTION AND THE FIRST SALE DOCTRINE

SYNOPSIS

§ 39.01   INTRODUCTION

§ 39.02   FIRST SALE AND EXHAUSTION

§ 39.03   EXHAUSTION: UNAUTHORIZED AND FOREIGN SALES

§ 39.04   POST SALE RESTRICTIONS

§ 39.05   THE DOCTRINE OF REPAIR/RECONSTRUCTION

    [A]   The Analytic Framework

    [B]   The Sequential Replacement of Parts

§ 39.06   REPLACEMENTS THAT ARE "AKIN TO REPAIR": *HUSKY INJECTION MOLDING SYSTEMS, LTD. v. R & D TOOL ENGINEERING CO*

§ 39.07   CONCLUSION

§ 39.01   INTRODUCTION

Under the *first sale* doctrine and the doctrine of *patent exhaustion*, a patentee who unconditionally sells a product that incorporates the patented invention exhausts all rights to control the product.[1] This allows a purchaser of a device that includes a patented invention to enjoy the right to use, repair, modify, discard or resell the item.[2] In other words, a device that includes a patented invention becomes the private property of the purchaser. The first sale doctrine ensures that the purchaser has the full right to use the device free from the patentee's ability to seek a license or sue the purchaser for infringement. Consumers have an intuitive understanding of this rule. For example, those who buy a computer can use the computer maker's patented technology in the device and such activity is not considered an infringing "use" under section 271(a). However, this authorization does not allow a purchaser to construct a completely new device based on the original.

First sale is implied in law, and is distinct from the doctrine of *implied license.* An implied license is formed by a patentee's words or conduct from which another

---

[1] *See* Mitchell v. Hawley, 83 U.S. (16 Wall.) 544, 547 (1872) ("[T]he patentee must be understood to have parted to that extent with all his exclusive right, and that he ceases to have any interest whatever in the patented machine so sold and delivered or authorized to be constructed and operated.").

[2] Jazz Photo Corp. v. Int'l Trade Comm'n, 264 F.3d 1094, 1102 (Fed. Cir. 2001).

"may properly infer that the owner consents to his use of the patent in making or using it, or selling it, upon which the other acts, constitutes a license . . . ."[3] An implied license is based on the principle that a patent license can be created without an express agreement of the parties, but rather inferred from circumstances or a course of conduct that demonstrates a patentee's consent, waiver or estoppel that the patent be practiced by another.[4] For example, a license to make products under the patent may be implied if the patentee misleadingly suggests to another that the patent will not be enforced.[5] By comparison, the first sale doctrine is narrow — for example, the first sale doctrine does not authorize the purchaser to construct an entirely new device using the originally purchased product as a template. In contrast, an implied license can allow another to reproduce another's invention.

This Chapter considers the central principles and limits of first sale and patent exhaustion. Both have become significant in recent years as patentees have sought to impose licensing terms on subsequent purchasers of patented products.

§ 39.02   FIRST SALE AND EXHAUSTION

The terms first sale and patent exhaustion have been used interchangeably. Essentially, both refer to the effect of an unconditional sale of a patented device, which ends the patentee's rights over the item. Each unrestricted sale of a patented device is made with an understanding, implied in law, that the parties have bargained for a price that includes the entire value of the goods, including any patent rights necessary to use and maintain the particular item. This leaves the patentee no additional rights or recourse with respect to that item.[6]

Patent exhaustion can preclude a patentee's ability to enforce the patent against downstream purchasers, even when the first sale of the patented device is unfinished at the time of sale. One early decision on this point is *U.S. v. Univis Lens Co.*, decided by the U.S. Supreme Court in 1942. In that case, the patentee owned several patents that claimed various aspects of the shape, size, and composition of finished prescription eyeglass lenses. The patentee commissioned a company to create "lens blanks," which are rough opaque pieces of glass that could be used to make the patented lenses. In addition, the patentee issued three classes of licenses: 1) to wholesalers, who ground and polished the lens blanks into prescription quality lenses; 2) to finishing retailers, who ground and polished the lenses into finished pairs of glasses; and 3) prescription retailers, who prescribed and adjusted glasses for customers. Unlike wholesalers and finishing retailers, prescription retailers did not have the capacity to grind or finish lens blanks. Rather, prescription retailers purchased finished lenses from wholesalers.

In *Univis Lens*, the patentee required all licensees to maintain a rigid pricing schedule for the lenses. The Court held that the patentee had exhausted its patent rights on the first sale of the lens blank to the wholesalers and finishing retailers.

---

[3] De Forest Radio Tel. & Tel. Co. v. U.S., 273 U.S. 236, 242 (1927).

[4] Wang Labs., Inc. v. Mitsubishi Elecs. Am., Inc., 103 F.3d 1571, 1580-81 (Fed. Cir. 1997).

[5] *Id.* at 1581.

[6] Keeler v. Standard Folding Bed Co., 157 U.S. 659 (1895).

Finding that the price maintenance schedule constituted an antitrust violation, the *Univis Lens* Court explained:

> The first vending of any article manufactured under a patent puts the article beyond the reach of the monopoly which that patent confers. Whether the licensee sells the patented article in its completed form or sells it before completion for the purpose of enabling the buyer to finish and sell it, he has equally parted with the article, and made it the vehicle for transferring to the buyer ownership of the invention with respect to that article. To that extent he has parted with his patent monopoly in either case, and has received in the purchase price every benefit of that monopoly which the patent law secures to him.[7]

The Court reached this result even though the patent claims required finished lenses but the lens blanks were not infringing when sold. This result was justified by two critical conclusions: 1) the *only reasonable and intended use* of the lens blanks was in the alleged infringing glasses; and 2) each blank embodied *essential features* of the patented product, that had no use until it was made into the finished, patented lenses. On this basis, the Court found that "[s]ale of a lens blank by the patentee or by his licensee is thus in itself both a complete transfer of ownership of the blank, which is within the protection of the patent law, and a license to practice the final stage of the patent procedure."[8]

The most recent decision analyzing patent exhaustion is the Supreme Court's 2008 decision *Quanta Computer, Inc. v. LG Electronics*, a modern application of *Univis Lens*.[9] The *Quanta* Court considered patent exhaustion for Intel microprocessors and chipsets, designed for use in a computer, made under a patent license to electronics maker LG. The LG patents claimed methods to ensure timely and shared access to active computer memory. The parties' agreement expressly stated that no third party rights were created under the contract. However, the license stated, "nothing herein shall in any way limit or alter the effect of patent exhaustion."[10] LG asserted these method claims against computer manufacturers, including Quanta, who had incorporated Intel's microprocessors and chipsets into computers.

The *Quanta* Court concluded that patent exhaustion applied to method claims. The opinion rejected the patentee's argument that "because method patents are linked not to a tangible article but to a process, they can never be exhausted through a sale."[11] The Court reasoned that a method could be embodied in a product in much the same manner as an apparatus claim. Further, the court explained that eliminating exhaustion for method claims would "seriously undermine the exhaustion doctrine" given that patentees might simply attempt to avoid the defense by redrafting their claims in a method format.[12] This point is illustrated by the claims

---

[7] *Univis Lens Co.*, at 252.

[8] *Id.* at 249.

[9] Quanta Computer, Inc. v. LG Electronics, 553 U.S. 617 (2008).

[10] *Id.* at 623.

[11] *Id.* at 628.

[12] *Id.* at 629.

at issue here — that is, the claims to the use of computer memory might easily have been drafted in either an apparatus or a method format.

Next, *Quanta* considered whether the sale of Intel's microprocessors and components exhausted LG's claims against the computer manufacturers. The patentee argued that exhaustion was inapplicable, because Intel's components required additional physical components — a computer environment into which Intel's components were placed — before the patents were infringed. Further, LG argued that the Intel components did not precisely correspond to the patented claim scope, and therefore "allowing sale of these components to exhaust the patent would impermissibly ascribe to one element of the patented combination the status of the patented invention in itself."[13]

Rejecting these arguments, the *Quanta* Court applied a two-part test based on *Univis Lens*. First, the *only reasonable and intended use* of the Intel components was within the allegedly infringing computers. As the Court explained, "[a] microprocessor or chipset cannot function until it is connected to buses and memory."[14] Second, the Intel products incorporated the *essential features* of the claims. Specifically, the Court found that the inventive aspects of the claims were embodied in the microprocessors and chipsets sold by Intel to Quanta. The *Quanta* opinion reasoned that the work performed by the computer makers, including incorporating Intel's components into standard computers, represented the mere addition of standard prior art components. Thus, "Quanta was not required to make any creative or inventive decision when it added those parts," and that "Intel all but practiced the patent itself by designing its products to practice the patent, lacking only the addition of standard parts."[15]

Finally, the *Quanta* Court examined whether Intel's sales exhausted LG's rights within the context of the Intel license. In particular, the Court focused on two provisions. First, the LG-Intel Agreement provided that "no license is granted by either party hereto . . . to any third party," which cut off the possibility that computer makers acquired an implied right to use Intel's products. However, the Court found this term irrelevant, carefully distinguishing the doctrine of implied license from patent exhaustion. As the Court explained, "exhaustion turns only on Intel's own license to sell products practicing the LGE patents."[16] Further, despite the various limitations in the LGE-Intel contract, the Court found that the sale of the Intel components was unrestricted. In other words, "[n]o conditions limited Intel's authority to sell products substantially embodying the patents."[17] In result, the Court found that this unrestricted sale of the essential features of the patented invention exhausted LG's ability to pursue a license or sue the computer makers.

---

[13] *Id.* at 631.

[14] *Id.* at 632.

[15] *Id.* at 634.

[16] *Id.* at 637.

[17] *Id.*

§ 39.03   EXHAUSTION: UNAUTHORIZED AND FOREIGN SALES

For the first sale doctrine to apply, the patent holder must *authorize* the sale.[18] For example, in *Quanta*, the Supreme Court examined sales authorized by the patent holder LG to Intel in finding that patent exhaustion barred suit against the computer makers as subsequent purchasers of the Intel components. A patentee cannot exhaust a right that the patentee did not approve. Thus, the purchase of a computer does not exhaust the rights of a third party patent holder who did not authorize the use of its patented inventions within that computer. It follows that a third party patentee might assert infringement against both the computer maker for making and selling the computer that incorporates such inventions and the purchaser who uses the technology claimed by the third party.[19]

Does patent exhaustion apply if the sales are made outside the U.S.? After the *Quanta* case was decided, the Federal Circuit determined that foreign sales do not trigger patent exhaustion for U.S. patents.[20] According to this authority, exhaustion applies only to patented products that are sold in the U.S.

§ 39.04   POST SALE RESTRICTIONS

The first sale doctrine is a default rule that operates in the absence of notice by the patentee to the contrary. However, the Federal Circuit has held that a patentee's express contractual restriction made with purchasers can limit or prevent the operation of the doctrine. Whether these authorities are viable after the Supreme Court's *Quanta* decision has not yet been resolved.[21] Until the issue is authoritatively decided, an examination of the Federal Circuit's cases on post-sale restrictions is warranted.

Specifically, in *Mallinckrodt, Inc. v. Medipart, Inc.*, the Federal Circuit examined a post-sale restriction on a medical device known as a "nebulizer" — that is, a machine that pumps air through a liquid which is changed into vapor to be inhaled by a patient.[22] Once inhaled, the vapor is absorbed into the patient's lungs. The patented device at issue in the *Mallinckrodt* case was designed to deliver either a prescribed drug or a radioactive material used for image scanning for diagnosis of lung conditions.

The patentee Mallickrodt sold these devices to hospitals with a package insert that stated that each unit is a "For Single Patient Use Only" and required that, after use, the unit be discarded as biohazardous waste. According to Mallickrodt,

---

[18] *See* Honeywell Int'l v. U.S., 609 F.3d 1292 (Fed. Cir. 2010).

[19] In all likelihood, the third party would follow the more efficient approach and sue the computer maker for both direct infringement for making and selling, and the third party would add a claim for indirect infringement against the computer maker to capture relief for the end user's direct uses.

[20] Fujifilm Corp. v. Benun, 605 F.3d 1366 (Fed. Cir. 2010).

[21] *See* Static Control Components, Inc. v. Lexmark Intern., Inc., 615 F. Supp. 2d 575, 585-86 (E.D.Ky. 2009) (suggesting that the Federal Circuit's cases have been over-ruled, citing conflicting scholarly literature).

[22] Mallinckrodt, Inc. v. Medipart, Inc., 976 F.2d 700 (Fed. Cir. 1992).

this restriction was supported by reasons of health, safety, efficacy, and a concern about incurring liability from subsequent patient contact with used, contaminated units. Rather than honoring this restriction, certain hospitals sent their used nebulizers to defendant Medipart, who sterilized the devices and returned them to the hospitals for re-use.

The *Mallinckrodt* court reversed a district court ruling that found the restriction unenforceable, finding that a patentee could limit the first sale doctrine by a contract made with notice. The *Mallinckrodt* court explained, "[u]nless the condition violates some other law or policy (in the patent field, notably the misuse or antitrust law), private parties retain the freedom to contract concerning conditions of sale."[23] Here, the Federal Circuit remanded the case asking the district court to determine if the one time use restriction was reasonably within the scope of the patent grant and, if so, to uphold the restriction. Finding that the limitation did not implicate antitrust or per se misuse, the Federal Circuit instructed the district court that, if deemed outside the scope of the patent right, that the restriction should be invalidated as patent misuse only for failure to withstand a "rule of reason" analysis.

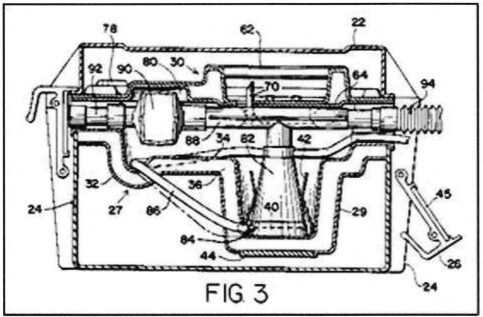

FIG. 3

The *Mallinckrodt* case illustrates that an express contractual limitation might control over the first sale rights that are implied in law. Specifically, the court explained that the defendant's violation of the patentee's "one use only" sales term — by itself — was sufficient to support a finding that the patent had been infringed. In that decision, the Federal Circuit instructed the lower court that if the restriction was upheld as valid, the hospital's violation of the defined permissible use of the

---

[23] *Id.* at 708.

nebulizer meant that there was no need to examine the repair-reconstruction distinction on remand.

Note that the Federal Circuit's *Mallinckrodt* was decided before the U.S. Supreme Court's *Quanta* decision. The *Quanta* Court did not expressly reach a conditional sale, and therefore did not expressly overrule this earlier precedent.

§ 39.05   THE DOCTRINE OF REPAIR/RECONSTRUCTION

[A]   The Analytic Framework

The first sale doctrine authorizes the patent owner the right to maintain the device in good working order. However, it does not transfer the patentee's right to exclude others from *reproducing* the invention by creating a duplicate product using the original as a template.[24] However, a consumer may preserve the life of a patented product by repairing the item or replacing spent or worn parts that were originally present in the item when sold.

As a practical matter, the line between a permissible "repair" and an unauthorized "reproduction" is not always easy to draw. At one end of the spectrum, a purchaser who reconstructs an *entire* patented item at a single point in time is typically found to engage in an infringing reconstruction. For example, in *American Cotton-Tie Co. v. Simmons*, the invention was a simple metallic band and a buckle used to tie cotton bales.[25] These ties were stamped with the notice "Licensed to use once only." When bales reached their destination, these ties are cut and then sold as scrap iron. The defendants purchased these scrap ties and re-created the ties by re-using the buckle and piecing several bands together. The Court found that the defendant's activities infringed, as the re-creation of the band constituted an infringing reconstruction of the tie.

At the other end of the spectrum, a repair to *less* than the entire device to extend the life of a patented item may fall within the first sale doctrine. For example, if a patent claims an entire automobile, a purchaser's replacement of a minor component, such as the windshield wiper blades, would undoubtedly constitute a permissible repair. However, many cases are not always so clear. As the Federal Circuit has explained, "there is a continuum between these concepts; precedent demonstrates that litigated cases rarely reside at the poles wherein 'repair' is readily distinguished from 'reconstruction.' "[26]

The foundational principles used to distinguish between permissible repair and infringing reconstruction were examined in a set of U.S. Supreme Court cases, both named, *Aro Mfg. Co. v. Convertible Top Replacement Co.*[27] Both cases considered liability for infringement of combination claims for a folding fabric and

---

[24]   *See generally* Monsanto Co. v. Bowman, 657 F.3d 1341 (Fed. Cir. 2011).

[25]   American Cotton-Tie Co. v. Simmons, 106 U.S. 89 (1882).

[26]   Jazz Photo Corp. v. International Trade Com'n, 264 F.3d 1094, 1102 (Fed. Cir. 2001).

[27]   Aro Mfg. Co. v. Convertible Top Replacement Co., 365 U.S. 336 (1964) ("Aro I"); and Aro Mfg. Co. v. Convertible Top Replacement Co., 377 U.S. 476 (1964) ("Aro II").

metal roof structure used on convertible cars. These tops were installed in cars sold by two defendants, General Motors and Ford. Although the metal structure of these tops was meant to last as long as the car, the fabric portion typically wore out after about three years. A third defendant, Aro Manufacturing Co., Inc. ("Aro"), made and sold fabric to replace the worn cloth tops. As the *Aro* cases describe, the patentee had granted General Motors a license to the patent. Ford was unlicensed from 1952 through 1954, after which time Ford took a license. Defendant Aro was not licensed at any time.

In the first *Aro* case ("*Aro I*"), the Court considered the question of whether replacement of the fabric constituted a permissible repair under the first sale doctrine or was an infringing reconstruction.[28] The *Aro I* Court confirmed that the first sale doctrine permits a purchaser to "preserve [a patented product's] fitness for use so far as it may be affected by wear or breakage."[29] Reversing the lower court's finding, the *Aro I* Court promulgated a bright line test, holding that replacing a worn part of a combination claim that is not separately patented is a non-infringing repair and not an impermissible reconstruction. Under *Aro I*, the replacement of a single element that was not individually patented may be replaced "no matter how essential it may be to the patented combination and no matter how costly or difficult replacement may be."[30]

The second *Aro* case, ("*Aro II*"), illustrates an important permutation to the first sale doctrine. Specifically, in *Aro II*, the Court considered liability for cars sold by Ford during the two-year period that Ford was not a licensee to the asserted patent. *Aro II* held that customers who had purchased cars from Ford during the unlicensed time period did not have any rights under the first sale doctrine. The *Aro II* Court reasoned that because Ford had no authority to make and sell the original convertible top during those years, Ford could not grant purchasers a license to replace the fabric under the first sale doctrine. Thus, customers who had replaced the fabric on cars made or sold by Ford when Ford lacked a license had directly infringed. However, those customers who had purchased their cars from General Motors (who was fully licensed) or Ford during the license period were entitled to purchase and install replacement fabric without infringing.

[B]   The Sequential Replacement of Parts

In *dicta*, *Aro I* considered the issue of the sequential replacement of worn parts, stating, "[m]ere replacement of individual unpatented parts, one at a time, whether of the same part repeatedly or different parts successively, is no more than the lawful right of the owner to repair his property."[31] In *FMC Corp. v. Up-Right, Inc.*,[32] the Federal Circuit considered the *Aro I* Court's statement in examining infringement of claims directed to an improved grape harvester. There, defendant Up-Right sold replacement parts for these grape harvesters, particularly for worn

---

[28] *Aro I*, 365 U.S. at 336.

[29] *Id.* at 345 (quoting Leeds & Catlin Co. v. Victor Talking Machine Co., 213 U.S. 325, 336 (1909)).

[30] *Aro I*, 365 U.S. at 345.

[31] *Aro I*, 365 U.S. at 346.

[32] FMC Corp. v. Up-Right, Inc., 21 F.3d 1073 (Fed. Cir. 1994).

out or broken parts for the picking heads, which were known to fail with some frequency. The patentee argued that most of the claimed combination had been replaced in most or all of the picking heads that had been sold, and that such sequential replacement would, at some point in time, amount to a substantial reconstruction of these heads and therefore infringement.

The Federal Circuit rejected this argument, relying on the Court's pronouncement in *Aro I*, stating:

> . . . mere replacement of broken or worn-out parts, one at a time, whether of the same part repeatedly or of different parts successively, is no more than the lawful right of the owner to repair his property, so long as any single instance of repair does not in and of itself constitute reconstruction.[33]

The *FMC* court explained that a contrary rule was "unworkable," reasoning that those who supply parts or repair could not be expected to undertake the burdensome process of tracking old parts against new parts each time a repair is requested or made.[34] If the rule of the *FMC* case is applied literally, the first sale doctrine might permit a purchaser to replace each part of a device piece by piece over time until the device is comprised entirely of new parts without infringing.

§ 39.06   REPLACEMENTS THAT ARE "AKIN TO REPAIR": *HUSKY INJECTION MOLDING SYSTEMS, LTD. v. R & D TOOL ENGINEERING CO*

A purchaser may wish to replace portions of a patented device before the parts are worn or spent, whether out of precaution or where a user wishes the device to perform an alternative function. Can such activity be considered a "repair" under the first sale doctrine?

The Federal Circuit considered this issue in *Husky Injection Molding Systems Ltd. v. R & D Tool Engineering Co.*[35] There, patentee Husky made and sold a patented machine for making objects using molten plastic. According to the patent, the objects were formed when the machine injected the molds with heated plastic. The formed object was then held in a carrier plate to cool in order to preserve the object's shape until the plastic completely hardened.

In addition to selling the machine, Husky sold substitute molds and carrier plates that were purchased by customers who wished to change the design of the objects that the machine created. Customers typically purchased substitute molds and carrier plate every three to five years. The accused contributory infringer, R & D, also made substitute molds and carrier plates designed to be used with Husky's machine. R & D defended the case arguing that a customer's use was not direct infringement because the use of R & D's molds and carrier plates was permitted under the first sale doctrine.

---

[33] *Id.* (quoting *Aro I*).

[34] *Id.* at 1078 n.7.

[35] Husky Injection Molding Systems Ltd. v. R & D Tool Engineering Co., 291 F.3d 780 (Fed. Cir. 2002).

The Federal Circuit held that the use of new molds and carrier plates was permissible as "akin to repair" although used as replacements for parts that were neither worn nor spent. In finding that customers did not directly infringe by using R & D's parts and, in turn, that R & D was not a contributory infringer, the *Husky* court relied on facts demonstrating that purchasers were within their first sale rights by using substitutes for components that were *readily replaceable*. These included that the design of the machine allowed such replacement; customers routinely used these items to change designs and the patentee Husky separately priced and sold these carrier plates and molds.

As *Husky* demonstrates, purchasers may replace parts of a patented item for reasons other than wear or breakage.[36] Thus, the first sale doctrine includes those actions which are *akin to repair* — that is, "an owner may use, repair, and modify the device as long as there is not reconstruction of the entity as to in fact make a new article."[37] This rule derives from the underlying policy that a patentee exhausts the right to control the use of the patented device once the device passes into the hands of the purchaser. Under *Husky*, purchasers may make changes to a device not only to preserve the item, but also to increase the item's versatility. Indeed, the Federal Circuit has upheld a customer's right to replace parts for other reasons, such as substituting a part that has features that increase safety.[38] However, because the patentee retains the right to *make* the patented device, the limits of this principle are exceeded when a purchaser makes substantial changes that amount to reconstruction.

§ 39.07 CONCLUSION

Under the first sale doctrine, a purchaser of a patented item has the right to use, repair, modify, discard or resell the item subject to any express conditions imposed on the sale. Once the item has been sold, the patentee's ability to sue for the use or maintenance of the item has been exhausted. Thus, a patentee has no rights against a purchaser, or any subsequent purchaser, as a default rule.

Minor replacements or modifications of readily replaceable components to expand the item's functionality or for other reasons are permissible. However, where the patented device is substantially re-created, such conduct might be deemed an impermissible reconstruction and therefore infringing.

Post-*Quanta*, the law concerning post-sale restrictions is not clear. The prior Federal Circuit law held that a valid, express contract could limit the first sale doctrine. Under these authorities, a patentee can limit the purchaser's ability to modify or replace components of a device so long as the limitation does not violate other provisions of law, such as antitrust or patent misuse. Over the coming years, it can be expected that more authoritative rules applying *Quanta* to post-sale restrictions will be issued.

---

[36] *See also* Surfco Hawaii v. Fin Control Systems Pty, Ltd., 264 F.3d 1062, 1066 (Fed. Cir. 2001) (". . . the right to replace or modify a part of a patented device does not require that the part be spent or broken").

[37] *Husky*, 291 F.3d at 787-88.

[38] *Id.* at 786.

Chapter 40

PROSECUTION LACHES

SYNOPSIS

§ 40.01   INTRODUCTION
§ 40.02   THE HISTORIC FOUNDATIONS OF PROSECUTION LACHES
§ 40.03   THE CURRENT STANDARD
   [A]   Delay
   [B]   Prejudice
§ 40.04   CONCLUSION

§ 40.01   INTRODUCTION

One might assume that all patentees file a patent application at the earliest opportunity and move the prosecution forward expeditiously to more quickly secure the benefits of the patent right. The sooner a patent is obtained, the sooner the patentee can exploit the right through licensing fees or assert the patent to prevent others from selling products that incorporate the patentee's invention. Moreover, the patent system benefits from early disclosures and an earlier expiration of patents, because after a patent expires, the invention passes into the public domain and can be used by all.

However, as one article has identified, some patentees use any number of procedures to keep claims pending before the patent office for years.[1] For example, in *In re Bogese*,[2] the patentee established a pattern of filing continuation applications based on claims that had already been rejected by the U.S. PTO and affirmed as unpatentable by the Federal Circuit. Despite these continued rejections, the *Bogese* patentee continued to re-file these same rejected claims in continuation applications eight (8) times between 1989 and 1994. This conduct eventually led the Board of Patent Appeals and Interferences to reject the last application on the grounds that the patentee's actions to "retain the benefit of the filing date of June 14, 1978 while at the same time delaying prosecution of the applications, is so egregious in defeating the policy of the patent laws of promoting science and the useful arts as to be presumed unreasonable."[3]

---

[1] *See generally* Mark A. Lemley & Kimberly A. Moore, *Ending Abuse of Patent Continuations*, 84 B.U. L. Rev. 63 (2004) (stating that a significant number of patents are delayed by means such as filing continuations, modifying claims, and issuing "submarine patents").

[2] *In re* Bogese, 303 F.3d 1362 (Fed. Cir. 2002).

[3] *Id.* at 1366.

According to a recent study by the U.S. PTO, on average a patent application remains pending before the agency less than 32 months.[4] Nonetheless, some patentees take actions to delay a patent's issuance for several years or even decades. Courts have developed the doctrine of *prosecution laches* to render the patent unenforceable where patentee delays constitute an abuse of the patent system.

Why would a rational patentee wish to delay? There are at least two possible reasons. A patentee may have an invention that is truly "ahead of its time." As a practical matter, a patentee with an invention relevant only in a nascent market may find no interested licensees until the industry begins to design and sell the product. In that instance, an issued patent has no real value to the patentee until that market develops.

This is illustrated in Scenario 1, below, where the patent term begins well before the market. A patentee wishing to optimize the strategic or financial advantages of the patent may wish to push the effective term back to capture more years of licensing revenue over the patent's effective life. As shown under Scenario 2, delaying a patent's effective term reaches much further into the years in which the market is active.

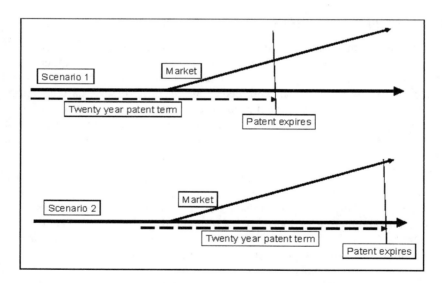

One may also attempt to strategically delay finalizing the claim language in a pending application so that they can be tailored to encompass a competitor's products. The Federal Circuit approved this practice in *Kingsdown Medical Consultants, Ltd. v. Hollister Inc.*:[5]

---

[4] U.S. Pat. & Trademark Office, Performance and Accountability Report Fiscal Year 2006 (2006), http://www.uspto.gov/web/offices/com/annual/2006/3020100_patentperfrm.html.

[5] Kingsdown Medical Consultants, Ltd. v. Hollister Inc., 863 F.2d 867 (Fed. Cir. 1988).

It should be made clear at the outset of the present discussion that there is nothing improper, illegal or inequitable in filing a patent application for the purpose of obtaining a right to exclude a known competitor's product from the market; nor is it in any manner improper to amend or insert claims intended to cover a competitor's product the applicant's attorney has learned about during the prosecution of a patent application.[6]

Some patentees rely on continuation or divisional applications to delay prosecution without incurring any loss in priority.[7] This has the effect of re-starting the prosecution process for the newly-filed application even where the second application is based on the same invention as the first.

Under former law, the incentive to delay prosecution was greater because the patent term was seventeen years after the patent issued, and one who delayed issuance also delayed the expiration date of the patent.[8] Now, for patent applications filed on or after June 8, 1995, the patent term is twenty years from the date of the *filing* of the patent application.[9] The current term reduces a patentee's incentive to delay prosecution because more time in prosecution reduces the overall patent term. Although this might appear to have eviscerated the problem, there are still some patents in the pipeline filed under the former law. Therefore, the issue has not disappeared entirely.

Moreover, some patentees are likely to continue the practice and forego some years of protection to gain the benefit of claims crafted to encompass implementations adopted by competitors.[10] Indeed, in some industries the *useful* life of a patent is far less than seventeen years, so losing some years of patent life is not of concern. For example, a software patent may claim technology that is rapidly replaced and may be meaningful for only a few years.[11] Such a patentee does not expect to rely on the same patent for more than a few years, and may wish to delay prosecution to mold claim amendments toward recent technological trends while maintaining the priority date from the original application. Thus, prosecution laches is likely to remain a viable defense despite the statutory change in the patent term.

---

[6] *Id.* at 874.

[7] *See* 35 U.S.C. § 120 (providing that a continuation "shall have the same effect, as to such invention, as though filed on the date of the prior application"); 35 U.S.C. § 121 (providing that a divisional application that complies with § 120 is also "entitled to the benefit of the filing date of the original application").

[8] *See* Merck & Co., Inc. v. Hi-Tech Pharmacal Co., Inc., 482 F.3d 1317, 1319 (Fed. Cir. 2007) (discussing the patent term under former law).

[9] 35 U.S.C. § 154(a)(2). Patent terms may be limited or extended for certain reasons. For example, a patent term may be shorter if the patentee relies on a priority date from an earlier U.S. patent application. *Id.* As a further example, a patent term may be extended when the U.S. PTO fails to issue the patent in three (3) years. 35 U.S.C. § 154(b).

[10] Lemley & Moore, *supra* note 1, at 86 (observing that for some patentees, "it may be worth forgoing some years of royalties if they can coerce licensing payments from companies who have already made asset-specific investments in the technology that is ultimately patented.").

[11] Paul J. Heald, *Mowing The Playing Field: Addressing Information Distortion And Asymmetry In The TRIPS Game*, 88 Minn. L. Rev. 249, 288 (2003) (estimating that the useful life of a software patent may be from "nine months to two years").

§ 40.02 THE HISTORIC FOUNDATIONS OF PROSECUTION LACHES

Two U.S. Supreme Court cases form the foundation of the prosecution laches defense in U.S. patent law: *Woodbridge v. U.S.*,[12] and *Webster Electric Co. v. Splitdorf Electrical Co.*[13] Both were decided in the early 1920's when patent applications were not publicly accessible, and the patent term was calculated from the date that the patent issued.

The first case, *Woodbridge*, considered the enforceability of a patent application that had been granted but not yet issued for a new type of cannon.[14] The patentee filed a request that the patent office delay issuance for one year pursuant to a provision of the patent act in effect at the time that authorized such requests. The PTO agreed. In fact, neither the patentee nor the PTO took any action for over nine (9) years. After that time had passed, the patentee wrote to the PTO requesting that the agency issue the patent, hoping to capitalize on the fact that the Civil War had begun and the United States had allegedly begun widespread infringement by using the improved cannon in the war. Indeed, the patentee admitted that he delayed any further requests for issuance because "he thought that course best fitted to enable him to avail himself of the value of the patent."[15] The PTO denied the patentee's request to issue the patent after this long delay.

Affirming the patent office's actions, the Supreme Court found that the patentee had forfeited any rights to the patent. The *Woodbridge* Court noted that others had obtained patents for the same invention in the interim without any awareness of Woodbridge's patent application. Additionally, the Court noted that the patentee had failed to offer an acceptable reason for delay, stating "he deliberately and without excuse postpone[d] beyond the date of the actual invention, the beginning of the term of his monopoly, and thus put[ ] off the free public enjoyment of the useful invention, [which] is an evasion of the statute and defeats its benevolent aim."[16]

One year later, the Supreme Court reaffirmed the doctrine of prosecution laches in *Webster Electric*. The patentee attempted to add two broad claims to an application that had been pending before the patent office for eight (8) years.[17] During that time, the subject matter of the broadened claims had become widely used. The Court noted that the patentee's attempts to broaden the patent were not based on newly developed inventive activity, but were an attempt to capitalize on market adoption that had occurred while the patentee had "simply stood by and awaited developments."[18] *Webster Electric* applied the doctrine of prosecution

---

[12] Woodbridge v. U.S., 263 U.S. 50 (1923).

[13] Webster Elec. Co. v. Splitdorf Elec. Co., 264 U.S. 463 (1924).

[14] *Woodbridge*, 263 U.S. at 52.

[15] *Id.* at 53.

[16] *Id.* at 56.

[17] Webster Elec. Co. v. Splitdorf Elec. Co., 264 U.S. 463, 465 (1924).

[18] *Id.*

laches in finding that the patentee had forfeited any rights to add the broader claims to the application.

§ 40.03 THE CURRENT STANDARD

[A] Delay

The first requirement of a prosecution laches defense is *unreasonable and unexplained delay.* The Federal Circuit considered this issue in *Symbol Technologies, Inc. v. Lemelson Medical.*[19] The patents at issue were directed to electronic scanning technology. In 1998, Lemelson sent letters asserting infringement of these patents to a number of companies that were involved in the design, manufacture, and sale of bar code scanning devices and machine vision technology. In response, a number of companies filed suit for declaratory relief against Lemelson asserting, among other things, that many of the asserted patents were unenforceable due to prosecution laches.

The patents that were the subject of the prosecution laches defense had a remarkably long and complex prosecution history. The prosecution spanned over forty (40) years, from the filing of the first application in 1954 to after the last application was filed in 1993. During this time, some of the applications issued as patents even as the inventor sought to file more. As the district court described, some of the claims filed by Lemelson "w[ould] not expire until 2011, fifty-five years after the 1956 application was filed and forty-eight years after the application issued as a patent."[20]

During this extensive period of time, the industry, including "many who had never heard of the Lemelson patents,"[21] developed machine vision and bar code technologies such as those devices commonly used in retail stores to register price and product sales. In an early proceeding in the case, the district court dismissed the laches defense, ruling that it was "improper to introduce the equitable doctrine of laches into the statutory scheme of continuation practice."[22] However, the Federal Circuit relied on *Woodbridge* and *Webster Electric* as precedent and found that the prosecution laches defense was viable based on the long-established equitable practice.[23] The *Symbol* court reasoned that this power survived the 1952 amendments to the Patent Act.[24] However, the *Symbol* court provided little guidance as to the factual circumstances when this defense might apply. Rather,

---

[19] Symbol Techs., Inc. v. Lemelson Med., Educ. & Research Found., LP, 422 F.3d 1378 (Fed. Cir. 2005) amended by 429 F.3d 1051 (Fed. Cir. 2005).

[20] Symbol Techs., Inc. v. Lemelson Med. Educ.& Research Found., LP, 301 F. Supp. 2d 1147, 1156 (D. Nev. 2004).

[21] *Id.* at 1156.

[22] Symbol Techs., Inc. v. Lemelson Med., Educ. & Research Found., LP, No. 99CV0397, 2000 U.S. Dist. LEXIS 21863, at *18 (D. Nev. Mar. 21, 2000).

[23] *See* Symbol Techs., Inc. v. Lemelson Med., 277 F.3d 1361, 1364 (Fed. Cir. 2002).

[24] *Id.* at 1364, 1366. The patentee's argument relied on 35 U.S.C. § 120 (governing continuation practice) and § 121 (governing divisional applications). The Symbol court reasoned that the addition of unenforceability as an equitable defense in 35 U.S.C. § 282 warranted this inference.

the court remanded the case to the district court for further proceedings.

On remand of the *Symbol* case, the district court found that fourteen of the asserted patents were unenforceable due to prosecution laches.[25] In its opinion, the district court explained that "unreasonable delay alone is sufficient to apply prosecution laches without the requirement that Lemelson intended to gain some advantage by the delay."[26] The court found that Lemelson's delay "amount[ed] to culpable neglect as he ignored the duty to claim his invention promptly."[27] Further, the district court found that a showing of intent to delay "is not required to support the defense of prosecution laches."[28] Lemelson appealed this ruling, again bringing prosecution history estoppel to the Federal Circuit.

On appeal from this decision, the Federal Circuit affirmed the district court's application of the prosecution laches defense to bar enforceability of the claims.[29] The court emphasized that this equitable doctrine was not amenable to bright line rules:

> [T]here are no strict time limitations for determining whether continued refiling of patent applications is a legitimate utilization of statutory provisions or an abuse of those provisions. The matter is to be decided as a matter of equity, subject to the discretion of a district court before which the issue is raised.[30]

The Federal Circuit advised that prosecution laches is a doctrine that "should be used sparingly lest statutory provisions be unjustifiably vitiated" and "only in egregious cases of misuse of the statutory patent system."[31] The court explained that a prosecution history that contained multiple examples of repetitive re-filings may support a finding that the patent should not be enforced. Further, the Federal Circuit found that the district court had not abused its discretion, emphasizing that this extraordinary pattern of delay rendered this an "exceptional case" and that "prejudice to the public as a whole has been shown here in the long period of time during which parties, including the plaintiffs, have invested in the technology described in the delayed patents."[32]

In this second appeal, the *Symbol* court listed a number of circumstances where prosecution laches should *not* be applied, explaining that one may re-file a patent application so long as "such refiling is not unduly successive or repetitive."[33] For example, the court stated that re-filing an application that contained previously rejected claims "to present evidence of unexpected advantages of an invention when that evidence may not have existed at the time of an original rejection" or to "add

---

[25] *Symbol*, 301 F. Supp. 2d at 1155.

[26] *Id.* at 1156.

[27] *Id.*

[28] *Id.*

[29] *Symbol*, 422 F.3d at 1386.

[30] *Id.* at 1385.

[31] *Id.*

[32] *Id.*

[33] *Id.* at 1385.

subject matter in order to attempt to support broader claims as the development of an invention progresses" does not warrant a finding of prosecution laches.[56] Although the principle that prosecution laches exists only in egregious cases, the court found that the conduct at issue was sufficient to render the patents unenforceable based on the record.[57][58]

[B]　Prejudice

In addition to unreasonable and unexplained delay, a recent decision has held that the proponent of a prosecution laches defense must show *prejudice*. This includes evidence of an *intervening right* — that is, that either the accused infringer or another worked on, invested in, or used the technology during the period of delay. This principle was established in *Cancer Research Tech. Ltd. v. Barr Laboratories, Inc.*, which considered a patent application filed in 1982 for the use of a chemical compound, temozolomide, to treat leukemia.[34] The PTO initially rejected the application for lack of operable utility. Rather than respond, the applicant withdrew the application and re-filed identical continuation applications nine subsequent times. Finally, a further continuation was supported with data demonstrating successful results by using the compound to treat leukemia in animals. More than ten years after the initial application was filed, the PTO granted Cancer Research the patent and the company began to sell a pharmaceutical formulation based on the claims.

Subsequently, Cancer Research asserted the patent against an infringer, Barr, who sought to make a generic version of the drug. Barr asserted that the patent was unenforceable based on prosecution laches. In addition to the evidence of delay, Barr argued that no showing of prejudice was necessary. Further, Barr asserted that such delay was inherently prejudicial to the public. The Federal Circuit rejected this position explaining that, "[a]n inventor is not obligated to develop its product at any particular time prior to issuance or within the patent's terms."[35] In the absence of evidence that Barr or others had either developed or invested in the patented solution during the period of delay, the *Cancer Research* court held that prosecution laches could not be shown.

The facts of the *Cancer Research* case can be distinguished from *Symbol*, where an industry had developed numerous scanning products while the Lemelson applications were pending. Nonetheless, five justices dissented from a denial to rehear the *Cancer Research* case en banc.[36] These justices indicated that the strict prejudice requirement of the earlier panel decision improperly weakened the doctrine. Given this disagreement among the Federal Circuit's jurists, this area

---

[56] *Id.*

[57] *See Symbol*, 422 F.3d at 1385; *see also* Kothmann Enters., Inc. v. Trinity Indus., Inc., 455 F. Supp. 2d 608, 646 (S.D. Tex. 2006) (stating that "[t]he standard of proof and type of evidence necessary to establish prosecution laches are unclear").

[58] *Symbol*, 301 F. Supp. 2d at 1156.

[34] Cancer Research Tech. Ltd. v. Barr Laboratories, Inc., 625 F.3d 724 (Fed. Cir. 2010).

[35] *Id.* at 731.

[36] Cancer Research Tech. Ltd. v. Barr Laboratories, Inc., 637 F.3d 1293 (Fed. Cir. 2011).

may be the subject of doctrinal change in the coming years.

§ 40.04   CONCLUSION

The doctrine of prosecution laches was developed by the courts to address a patentee's unreasonable delays in the patent application process. If successful, this defense renders the patent unenforceable, even in the absence of a showing of patentee intent to delay. The defense is equitable in nature, and may be applied even where a patentee's acts comply with the rules of practice before the agency. However, the Federal Circuit has cautioned that the defense is reserved for the most egregious cases of delay or misuse.

Under current law, the defense requires that the proponent demonstrate both unreasonable and unexplained delay and prejudice. Where these elements are shown, the patent is rendered unenforceable.

Chapter 41

REMEDIES FOR PATENT INFRINGEMENT

SYNOPSIS

§ 41.01 INTRODUCTION

§ 41.02 INJUNCTIVE RELIEF

    [A] Permanent Injunctive Relief

        [1] Statutory Basis and Former Law

        [2] The Current Standard: *eBay v. MercExchange*

        [3] Application of the *eBay* Standard

        [5] Compensation for Ongoing Infringement

    [B] Preliminary Injunctions

§ 41.03 MONETARY RELIEF: STATUTORY BACKGROUND

§ 41.04 MONETARY RELIEF: LOST PROFITS

    [A] The *Panduit* Test: Proof of a Causal Relationship to Infringement

    [B] Spotlight on the Second *Panduit* Factor: Availability of Non-Infringing Alternatives

    [C] Lost Profits: Price Erosion

    [D] Market Share Calculation of Lost Profits

§ 41.05 MONETARY RELIEF: REASONABLE ROYALTY

    [A] Established Royalty

    [B] The Analytic Approach

    [C] The Reasonable Royalty Based on a Hypothetical Negotiation

§ 41.06 MONETARY RELIEF: ADDITIONAL CONSIDERATIONS

    [A] The Entire Market Value Rule

    [B] Patentee Delay and the Ability to Recover Monetary Relief

    [C] Actual and Constructive Notice/Marking

§ 41.07 WILLFUL INFRINGEMENT AND EXCEPTIONAL CASES

§ 41.08 PREJUDGEMENT INTEREST

§ 41.09 CONCLUSION

§ 41.01 INTRODUCTION

The Patent Act provides a range of remedies for patent infringement. These include preliminary and permanent injunctive relief to prevent future uses of the invention, and monetary relief for past infringement. If the defendant has acted willfully, the compensatory award might be trebled. In exceptional cases, the defendant may be required to pay the plaintiff's attorney fees. Most recently, the Federal Circuit has held that a defendant may be ordered to pay for post-trial use of an invention where no permanent injunction has been entered.

Who is entitled to obtain relief? As a foundational matter, there is *no* requirement that one asserting the patent actually practice the invention in order to enforce the right.[1] The Patent Act allows the *patent's owner* to sue for infringement.[2] Under this standard, an inventor who retains ownership of the patent may sue, or a patent owner to whom the inventor has assigned the patent can bring an enforcement action.[3] In addition, an *exclusive licensee* can sue if the patent owner is joined in the suit, whether voluntarily or involuntarily.[4] It should be noted that a *nonexclusive* licensee cannot sue to enforce a patent.[5]

To compliment a discussion of available relief for patent infringement, a few words about the cost of patent litigation is warranted. Patent suits are among the most complex, uncertain and expensive types of litigation, and such cases are said to have earned the title of "the sport of kings."[6] A recent survey placed the average cost to litigate a patent dispute at between $650,000 for less than $1 million at issue to an average of $5 million for cases in which over $25 million is at stake.[7] These figures are solely litigation fees and costs and do not include any monetary damages. If a patentee successfully obtains a permanent injunction, a defendant may be forced to either design around the patent or abandon the accused product line entirely — a circumstance that may have a significant economic impact, depending on the nature of the invention at issue. Thus, patent litigation costs and

---

[1] Continental Paper Bag Co. v. Eastern Paper Bag Co., 210 U.S. 405, 424-30 (1908); Rite-Hite Corp. v. Kelley Co., Inc., 56 F.3d 1538, 1547-48 (Fed. Cir. 1995).

[2] 35 U.S.C. § 281 (2000).

[3] 35 U.S.C. § 100(d) (defining "patentee" as to include "not only the patentee to whom the patent was issued but also the successors in title to the patentee"); *see generally* Intellectual Property Development, Inc. v. TCI Cablevision of California, Inc., 248 F.3d 1333 (Fed. Cir. 2001) (explaining standing for assignees/transferees).

[4] *Id.* at 1347-48 ("[u]nlike an assignee that may sue in its own name, an exclusive licensee having fewer than all substantial patent rights (that is not subject to an exception) that seeks to enforce its rights in a patent generally must sue jointly with the patent owner."). To simplify the discussion, the term *patentee* will be used throughout this chapter to refer to both patent owners and exclusive licensees.

[5] Ortho Pharmaceutical Corp. v. Genetics Institute, Inc., 52 F.3d 1026, 1031 (Fed. Cir. 1995) ("A holder of such a nonexclusive license suffers no legal injury from infringement and, thus, has no standing to bring suit or even join in a suit with the patentee."); A.L. Smith Iron Co. v. Dickson, 141 F.2d 3, 6 (2d Cir. 1944) (explaining that licensees are not granted standing to sue for patent infringement to spare the infringer the threat of multiple suits and to preserve the patentee's ability to choose the forum for the litigation).

[6] James Bessen & Michael J. Meurer, *Lessons For Patent Policy from Empirical Research on Patent Litigation*, 9 Lewis & Clark L. Rev. 1, 2 (2005).

[7] Am. Intellectual Prop. Law Assoc., Report of the Economic Survey 2011, at 35 (2011).

the attendant consequences of a judgment are beyond those evident through a calculation of the remedies formally authorized by statute.

§ 41.02 INJUNCTIVE RELIEF

[A] Permanent Injunctive Relief

[1] Statutory Basis and Former Law

Injunctions are governed by 35 U.S.C. § 283, which states:

> The several courts having jurisdiction of cases under this title may grant injunctions in accordance with the principles of equity to prevent the violation of any right secured by patent, on such terms as the court deems reasonable.

Consistent with the premise that a patent represents a form of property,[8] courts have viewed the imposition of an injunction favorably for patentees who establish infringement of a valid patent. Before 2006, the Federal Circuit had implemented an automatic injunction rule, based on the theory that, "[i]nfringement having been established, it is contrary to the laws of property, of which the patent law partakes, to deny the patentee's right to exclude others from use of his property."[9] Denials of permanent injunctions were reserved for "rare instances," such as where necessary to protect the public health.[10]

Under this standard, accused infringers faced a near-certainty of a permanent injunction after an adverse verdict. Some concluded that this circumstance facilitated unreasonably high settlements, particularly where the infringer had invested in designing a product, noting, "the threat of an injunction can enable a patent holder to negotiate royalties far in excess of the patent holder's true economic contribution."[11]

---

[8] Connell v. Sears, Roebuck & Co., 722 F.2d 1542, 1548 (Fed. Cir. 1983) ("the right to exclude recognized in a patent is but the essence of the concept of property."); 35 U.S.C. § 261; *see also* Carl Schenck, A.G. v. Nortron Corp., 713 F.2d 782, 784 (Fed. Cir. 1983) ("Patents and licenses are exemplifications of property rights."); see also Guido Calabresi & A. Douglas Melamed, *Property Rules, Liability Rules, and Inalienability: One View of the Cathedral*, 85 Harv. L. Rev. 1089, 1115-16 (1972) (explaining the general rule that property rules are remedied by injunction and liability rules by monetary relief).

[9] Richardson v. Suzuki Motor Co., Ltd., 868 F.2d 1226, 1246-47 (Fed. Cir. 1989) *overruled by* eBay Inc. v. MercExchange, L.L.C., 126 S.Ct. 1837 (2006).

[10] Rite-Hite Corp. v. Kelley Co., Inc., 56 F.3d 1538, 1547-48 (Fed. Cir. 1995) ("courts have in *rare instances* exercised their discretion to deny injunctive relief in order to protect the public interest.") (emphasis added).

[11] *See* Mark A. Lemley & Carl Shapiro, *Patent Holdup and Royalty Stacking*, 85 Tex. L. Rev. 1991, 1993 (2007); *but see* J. Gregory Sidak, Holdup, Royalty Stacking, and the Presumption of Injunctive Relief for Patent Infringement: A Reply to Lemley and Shapiro, 92 Minn. L. Rev. 714 (2008).

[2] The Current Standard: *eBay v. MercExchange*

In the 2006 decision *eBay v. MercExchange*,[12] the Supreme Court considered the standard for granting permanent injunctive relief in patent cases. As background, the patentee MercExchange, asserted claims directed to a business method for selling goods on an electronic network including the Internet. MercExchange, who did not practice its patents and earned revenue solely by licensing the patents to others, brought the case against eBay and Half.com, two online companies that were held to infringe the patents.

After trial, the district court denied MercExchange's motion for a permanent injunction. In its opinion, the district relied in part on the fact that MercExchange licensed — and had never practiced — the patent. Further, the district court noted that the fact that "the patent holder is willing to license his patent rights suggests that any injury suffered by [the patent holder] would be compensable in damages assessed as part of the final judgment in the case."[13]

On appeal, the Federal Circuit reversed, based on the automatic injunction rule.[14] The court noted that the record failed to disclose any reason "sufficiently exceptional to justify the denial of a permanent injunction."[15] Further, the Federal Circuit found that the district court's reliance on MercExchange's licensing practices to deny injunctive relief improper, explaining, "[i]f the injunction gives the patentee additional leverage in licensing, that is a natural consequence of the right to exclude and not an inappropriate reward to a party that does not intend to compete in the marketplace with potential infringers.[16]

The Supreme Court's *eBay* decision[17] reversed the Federal Circuit, finding that the automatic injunction rule was unsupported by the Patent Act, which specified that injunctions be granted "in accordance with the principles of equity."[18] The *eBay* Court held that the traditional four-factor test in equity must be examined to determine whether a permanent injunction should be entered in a patent case, as follows:

- First, that the plaintiff has suffered an irreparable injury;

- Second, that remedies available at law, such as monetary damages, are inadequate to compensate for that injury;

- Third, consider the balance of hardships between the plaintiff and defendant; and

- Fourth, consider whether the public interest would be served by a permanent injunction.

---

[12] eBay Inc. v. MercExchange, L.L.C., 126 S.Ct. 1837 (2006).

[13] MercExchange, LLC v. eBay, Inc., 275 F. Supp. 2d 695, 713 (E.D. Va. 2003).

[14] *See* MercExchange, LLC v. eBay, Inc., 401 F.3d 1323, 1338 (Fed. Cir. 2005).

[15] *Id* at 1339.

[16] *Id.*

[17] eBay Inc,. v. MercExchange, L.L.C., 126 S. Ct. 1837 (2006).

[18] 35 U.S.C. § 283.

Additionally, the *eBay* Court rejected any categorical application of these standards, observing that a licensing entity might obtain a permanent injunction even if the patentee does not practice the invention.[19] Most significantly, the Court rejected the Federal Circuit's presumption favoring injunctive relief, explaining, "the creation of a right is distinct from the provision of remedies for violations of that right."[20]

The *eBay* opinion is brief, although there are two significant concurring opinions. In one, Justice Roberts advised that, based on historical practice, injunctions were properly given in most patent cases, "given the difficulty of protecting a right to exclude through monetary remedies that allow an infringer to use an invention against the patentee's wishes-a difficulty that often implicates the first two factors of the traditional four-factor test."[21] In a separately concurring opinion, Justice Kennedy expressed concerns that district courts remain sensitive to a licensing industry that "has developed in which firms use patents not as a basis for producing and selling goods but, instead, primarily for obtaining licensing fees."[22] Kennedy stated that injunctions for such entities "can be employed as a bargaining tool to charge exorbitant fees to companies that seek to buy licenses to practice the patent."[23] Further, Kennedy suggested that injunctions should not typically be granted for business method patents, as the "potential vagueness and suspect validity of some of these patents may affect the calculus under the four-factor test."[24] Both of these concurring opinions have been cited by the lower courts to suggest the manner in which the *eBay* standard should be applied.

[3] Application of the *eBay* Standard

Prior to the Supreme Court's *eBay* decision, the automatic injunction rule permitted patentees to rely on a presumption of irreparable harm.[25] Since then, *eBay* has been interpreted to remove this presumption, placing the burden on the patentee to affirmatively demonstrate all four *eBay* factors, including irreparable injury.[26] Although the Court rejected the use of categorical rules, some patterns have emerged. That is, some opinions have observed that permanent injunctions are more likely to be granted in cases involving infringement by a competitor of the patentee, and less likely where the patentee is a non-competing licensor.[27]

---

[19] *eBay*, 126 S. Ct. at 1840 (explaining that "some patent holders, such as university researchers or self-made inventors, might reasonably prefer to license their patents, rather than undertake efforts to secure the financing necessary to bring their works to market themselves. Such patent holders may be able to satisfy the traditional four-factor test, and we see no basis for categorically denying them the opportunity to do so.").

[20] *Id.*

[21] *Id.* at 1841 (Roberts, J. concurring).

[22] *Id.* at 1842 (Kennedy, J. concurring).

[23] *Id.*

[24] *Id.*

[25] *See, e.g.,*

[26] Robert Bosch LLC v. Pylon Manufacturing Corp., 659 F.3d 1142, 1149 (Fed. Cir. 2011).

[27] *Id.* at 1150; *see also* CSIRO v. Buffalo Technology, Inc., 492 F. Supp. 2d 600, 603 (E.D. Tex. 2007) (citing cases).

In *Robert Bosch LLC v. Pylon Manufacturing Corp.*, the Federal Circuit considered a permanent injunction in an action between competitors.[28] The court held that it was an abuse of discretion for a district court to deny permanent relief to a patentee who had presented evidence of lost market share, lost access to customers, direct competition between the parties, and the infringer's inability to satisfy a money judgment.[29] Relying on the concurrence in *eBay*, the *Robert Bosch* court stated that, despite *eBay's* rejection of the automatic injunction rule, "it does not follow that courts should entirely ignore the fundamental nature of patents as property rights granting the owner the right to exclude."[30] The court found that a denial of a permanent injunction under these circumstances was error. In essence, the *Robert Bosch* court appeared to reinforce the pre-*eBay* practice to allow an injunction in a case between competitors, where the patentee was suffering ongoing harm in the market from a competitor's infringement.

An example of a suit between competitors in the pharmaceutical field is the district court opinion in *Sanofi-Synthelabo v. Apotex Inc.*[31] The patentee was a pharmaceutical manufacturer who had developed and patented Plavix, a drug used to reduce heart attacks and strokes. The infringer made a generic version of the drug. The court found that the patentee had suffered irreparable harm in the form of "price erosion, loss of goodwill, and a negative impact on the amount of research devoted to developing other medical uses for" the patented drug.[32] The court balanced "the public interest in having access to generic drugs at reduced prices with the significant public interest in encouraging the massive investment in research and development that is required before a new drug can be developed and brought to market."[33] Finding that the public interest was either even or slightly favored the patentee, the court entered the permanent injunction enjoining further sales of the generic.

One interesting district court opinion demonstrates that permanent injunctions are not reserved for suits between competitors. Specifically, in *CSIRO v. Buffalo Technology, Inc.*,[34] the court considered a motion for a permanent injunction brought by a patentee that was the principle scientific research organization of the Australian Federal Government. Granting the permanent injunction, the district court noted that the patentee's primary source of research funding derived from patent licensing. The court explained:

> CSIRO has shown that its harm is not merely financial. While CSIRO does not compete with Buffalo for market share, CSIRO does compete internationally with other research groups-such as universities-for resources, ideas, and the best scientific minds to transform those ideas into realities. CSIRO's reputation is an important element in recruiting the top scientists

---

[28] *Robert Bosch*, 659 F.3d at 1145.

[29] *Id.* at 1150.

[30] *Id.* at 1149.

[31] Sanofi-Synthelabo v. Apotex Inc., 492 F. Supp. 2d 353 (S.D.N.Y. 2007).

[32] *Id.* at 397.

[33] *Id.* (citation and quotation omitted).

[34] CSIRO v. Buffalo Technology, Inc., 492 F. Supp. 2d 600 (E.D. Tex. 2007).

in the world. Having its patents challenged via the courts not only impugns CSIRO's reputation as a leading scientific research entity but forces it to divert millions of dollars away from research and into litigation costs . . . . [T]he harm of lost [research] opportunities is irreparable. They cannot be regained with future money because the opportunity that was lost already belongs to someone else.[35]

Relating to the fourth *eBay* factor, the *CSIRO* court found that the public interest favored enforcement of patent rights by injunction, and emphasized that "because the work of research institutions such as CSIRO is often fundamental to scientific advancement, it merits strong patent protection."[36]

[5]　Compensation for Ongoing Infringement

When a court denies a preliminary injunction, no court order prevents the infringer from continuing the activity that was adjudged infringing. In that event, the patentee's invention is used by the infringer without the patentee's consent. Should the patentee be compensated for continued use of the invention after an adverse infringement judgment at trial?

In *Paice LLC v. Toyota Motor Corp.*, the Federal Circuit recognized that a district court possesses authority to enter an order for ongoing payments where necessary to provide for an effective remedy for continued use of the patented technology.[37] The *Pace* court noted that a district court "may wish to allow the parties to negotiate a license amongst themselves," and impose the royalty only if such negotiations failed.[38] Further, the Federal Circuit held that ongoing payments were not damages that required consideration by a jury under the Seventh Amendment of the U.S. Constitution.[39] This ongoing royalty allows the patentee to receive compensation for use of the invention after the litigation is terminated, so long as the infringer's conduct continues or the patent expires.

[B]　Preliminary Injunctions

A court may enter a preliminary injunction to prevent ongoing injury to the patentee while the litigation is pending. A patentee who moves for a preliminary injunction must prove: (1) a reasonable likelihood of success on the merits; (2) irreparable harm if an injunction is not granted; (3) a balance of hardships tipping in its favor; and (4) the injunction's favorable impact on the public interest.[40]

---

[35] *Id.* at 604.

[36] *Id.* at 607.

[37] Paice LLC v. Toyota Motor Corp., 504 F.3d 1293 (Fed. Cir. 2007); *see also* Innogenetics, N.V v. Abbott Laboratories, 512 F.3d 1363 (Fed. Cir. 2008).

[38] *Paice*, 504 F.3d at 1315; *see also* Telcordia Tech., Inc. v. Cisco Systems, 612 F.3d 1365 (Fed. Cir. 2010).

[39] For more information about the Seventh Amendment right to jury trial in patent cases, *see supra* Chapter 24.

[40] Amazon.com, Inc. v. Barnesandnoble.com, Inc., 239 F.3d 1343, 1350 (Fed. Cir. 2001).

A patentee demonstrates the first factor by demonstrating the likelihood that the defendant is infringing. If the accused infringer raises a substantial question of patent validity, the patentee has the opportunity to counter this showing by demonstrating that the defense lacks substantial merit.[41] In assessing the totality of the evidence, the court takes into account the presumptions and burdens that would be applied to such evidence at trial. Nonetheless, at this stage the court is merely estimating the likelihood of success and its findings are not binding on the ultimate outcome of the litigation. As the Federal Circuit has explained, rulings on a motion for preliminary injunction are "often made on an incomplete record and are inherently tentative in nature."[42] Where the patentee demonstrates a *clear* showing of validity and infringement, the Federal Circuit had formerly recognized a rebuttable presumption of irreparable harm.[43] However, some opinions have questioned whether this presumption is consistent with the Supreme Court's 2006 *eBay* decision.[44]

It should be noted that a patentee's failure to seek a preliminary injunction may adversely affect the ability to obtain a permanent injunction[45] and monetary relief for willful infringement for conduct that occurs after a complaint is filed.[46]

§ 41.03 MONETARY RELIEF: STATUTORY BACKGROUND

35 U.S.C. § 284 governs the right to monetary relief, permitting the primary forms of monetary awards of *lost profits* and a *reasonable royalty*:

> Upon finding for the claimant the court shall award the claimant damages adequate to compensate for the infringement but in no event less that a reasonable royalty for the use made of the invention by the infringer, together with interest and costs as fixed by the court.

This section establishes that the proper measure of damages is an amount which will compensate the patent owner for pecuniary losses sustained because of the infringement.[47] A patentee may pursue a lost profits theory of recovery for sales lost due to infringement, a reasonable royalty for use of the patented invention, or

---

[41] Titan Tire Corp. v. Case New Holland, Inc., 566 F.3d 1372 (Fed. Cir. 2009).

[42] Abbott Laboratories v. Andrx Pharmaceuticals, Inc., 473 F.3d 1196, 1205 (Fed. Cir. 2007).

[43] Bell & Howell Document Mgmt. Prods. Co. v. Altek Sys., 132 F.3d 701, 708 (Fed. Cir. 1997).

[44] *See* Kimberly-Clark Worldwide, Inc. v. First Quality Baby Products, LLC, 660 F.3d 1293, 1299 (Fed. Cir. 2011) (Newman, J.) (dissenting from denial of the petition for rehearing en banc); *see also* Canon Inc. v. GCC Intern. Ltd., 450 F. Supp. 2d 243, 251-52 (S.D.N.Y. 2006); Torspo Hockey Intern., Inc. v. Kor Hockey Ltd., 491 F. Supp. 2d 871, (D. Minn. 2007); *but see* Christiana Industries v. Empire Electronics, Inc., 443 F. Supp. 2d 870, 884 (E.D. Mich. 2006) (finding that the *eBay* decision did not affect the presumption of irreparable harm).

[45] *See generally* MercExchange, L.L.C. v. eBay, Inc., 500 F. Supp. 2d 556, 573 (E.D. Va. 2007) (stating that a patentee's failure to seek preliminary injunctive relief may be considered in assessing whether the patentee has been irreparably harmed, although not dispositive of the issue).

[46] *In re* Seagate Technology, LLC, 497 F.3d 1360, 1374 (Fed. Cir. 2007) ("A patentee who does not attempt to stop an accused infringer's activities [by seeking preliminary relief] . . . should not be allowed to accrue enhanced damages based solely on the infringer's post-filing conduct.").

[47] *See generally* General Motors Corp. v. Devex Corp., 461 U.S. 648, 654 (1983).

both if necessary to achieve full compensation.[48] In addition, this section grants the district court discretion to award prejudgment interest.

Recovery for violation of the patent right is limited by the doctrine of proximate cause.[49] Under this principle, harms caused by the infringement are recoverable so long as they are not remote or unforeseeable. "For example, remote consequences, such as a heart attack of the inventor or loss in value of shares of common stock of a patentee corporation caused indirectly by infringement are not compensable."[50] Generally, items of compensable harms are sought for lost sales, price erosion, a reasonable royalty for use of the patented invention during the period of infringement, prejudgment interest and, in exceptional cases, the patentee's attorney fees.

§ 41.04 MONETARY RELIEF: LOST PROFITS

[A] The *Panduit* Test: Proof of a Causal Relationship to Infringement

To recover lost profits, the patentee must demonstrate a reasonable probability that the patentee would have made particular sales but for the infringement. To do so, a patentee may present direct evidence of lost sales — for example, testimony of particular customers who state that they would have purchased the patentee's device but for the availability of the infringing device. Frequently, such evidence is very difficult to obtain and can become prohibitively expensive to gather particularly for products that are mass-marketed to consumers.

Alternatively, the patentee may rely on a four-factor test, referred to as the *Panduit* test, named for the case from which the test derives.[51] Under *Panduit*, a patentee can demonstrate lost profits by presenting evidence supporting each of these four factors:

(1) demand for the patented product;

(2) the absence of acceptable noninfringing substitutes;

(3) the patentee's capacity to exploit the demand; and

(4) the volume of profits lost due to the infringement.

The *Panduit* test is based on a series of inferences that customers would have purchased the patentee's products rather than the infringer's, and therefore demonstrates a "but for" causal link between the patentee's lost sales and the infringement. Where all four factors are met, *Panduit* demonstrates that if there is consumer demand for the patented product and consumers have no meaningful

---

[48] *See* State Industries, Inc. v. Mor-Flo Industries, Inc., 883 F.2d 1573, 1577 (Fed. Cir. 1989) (affirming that lost profits can be awarded for sales of certain infringing products, and a reasonable royalty as to the remaining infringing products, stating "the award may be split between lost profits as actual damages to the extent they are proven and a reasonable royalty for the remainder.").

[49] Rite-Hite Corp. v. Kelley Co., Inc., 56 F.3d 1538, 1546 (Fed. Cir. 1995).

[50] *Id.*

[51] *See* Panduit Corp. v. Stahlin Bros. Fibre Works, Inc., 575 F.2d 1152, 1156 (6th Cir. 1978).

non-infringing alternatives to fill that demand, then the patentee would have likely made the sales that the infringer actually made so long as the patentee had capacity to meet demand.

Panduit is the predominant test for proving lost profits, although the Federal Circuit has stated that other economically sufficient methods might be used to do so.[52] Moreover, the *Panduit* test must be applied with attention to the underlying purpose of demonstrating but for causation. Thus, *Panduit* "operates under an inherent assumption . . . [that] the patent owner and the infringer sell products sufficiently similar to compete against each other in the same market segment."[53]

This principle was examined in *BIC Leisure Products, Inc. v. Windsurfing Intern., Inc.*, where the court considered a patentee's claim for lost profits based on the defendant's sale of a sailboard sold in a significantly less expensive price category. The defendant's entry level sailboards were made with a lower priced process, and it was shown that the price-sensitive purchasers of the defendant's products were unlikely to pay for the higher priced boards sold by the patentee. The *BIC Leisuretime* court found that the patentee could not rely on the *Panduit* test, because "[i]f the patentee's and the infringer's products are not substitutes in a competitive market, *Panduit's* first two factors do not meet the 'but for' test — a prerequisite for lost profits."[54]

The *Panduit* test may be used to establish lost profits even where the patentee's products do not incorporate the patented invention. This rule assists patentees whose products *compete* with the infringing device even where such products implement a different technological solution than that set forth in the patent. This principle was explored in an *en banc* decision of the Federal Circuit in *Rite-Hite Corp. v. Kelley Co., Inc.*[55] The *Rite-Hite* opinion reviewed an infringement action based on a patent directed to a device designed to securely hold a vehicle against a loading dock to prevent movement that might injure those working nearby. The patentee sought lost profits for two different dock-levelers made of different designs — one incorporated the patentee's invention and the other did not.

Rite-Hite found that nothing in the Patent Act prevented the patentee from pursuing lost profits for lost sales for both devices, stating:

> There is no requirement in this country that a patentee make, use, or sell its patented invention . . . . [The defendant] has thus not provided, nor do we find, any justification in the statute, precedent, policy, or logic to limit the compensability of lost sales of a patentee's device that directly competes with the infringing device if it is proven that those lost sales were caused in fact by the infringement.[56]

---

[52] BIC Leisure Products, Inc. v. Windsurfing Intern., Inc., 1 F.3d 1214, 1218 (Fed. Cir. 1993) (indicating that other means of demonstrating lost profits are not foreclosed by the existence of the *Panduit* test).

[53] *Id.*

[54] *Id.*

[55] *See* Rite-Hite Corp. v. Kelley Co., Inc., 56 F.3d 1538 (Fed. Cir. 1995).

[56] *Id.* at 1548-49.

Rite Hite underscores that a patentee can be compensated for all direct and foreseeable harms that are causally related to infringement.

[B] Spotlight on the Second *Panduit* Factor: Availability of Non-Infringing Alternatives

As previously discussed, a patentee bears the initial burden of demonstrating a reasonable probability of lost sales causally related to infringement. In essence, this showing is a hypothetical reconstruction of the but for scenario to demonstrate sales that the patentee would have made absent infringement.[57] Once the patentee makes this showing, the infringer has the opportunity to demonstrate a lack of causation for some or all of the lost profits asserted by the patentee in this but for world. As one possibility, an infringer might have chosen *not* to infringe the patent. Can this be considered in calculating lost profits?

This issue warrants particular examination of the second *Panduit* factor in detail. Specifically, in *Grain Processing Corp. v. American Maize-Products Co.*, the Federal Circuit considered the infringer's hypothetical actions in the but for scenario. The second factor of the *Panduit* test — the availability of a non-infringing alternative — became the focus of the parties' dispute. In *Grain Processing*, the patentee and the infringer were head-to-head competitors for sales of a chemical food additive. The patentee demonstrated that consumers would have logically purchased the patentee's additive absent the defendant's infringement.

Nonetheless, the district court denied the patentee lost profit damages, based on a failure of the second *Panduit* factor. Specifically, the trial court found that the infringer "could have produced"[58] a non-infringing alternative during the entire infringing period because it possessed all the necessary equipment, know-how, and experience to do so, although the infringer had not actually developed or sold this alternative until years after the litigation began. On appeal, the patentee argued that an infringer "cannot escape liability for lost profits on the basis of a noninfringing substitute that did not exist during, and was not developed until after, the period of infringement."[59]

The Federal Circuit rejected the patentee's argument and affirmed the district court, explaining:

> . . . a fair and accurate reconstruction of the "but for" market also must take into account, where relevant, alternative actions the infringer foreseeably would have undertaken had he not infringed. Without the infringing product, a rational would-be infringer is likely to offer an acceptable noninfringing alternative, if available, to compete with the patent owner rather than leave the market altogether.[60]

---

[57] Grain Processing Corp. v. American Maize-Products Co., 185 F.3d 1341, 1350 (Fed. Cir. 1999) ("Reconstructing the market, by definition a hypothetical enterprise, requires the patentee to project economic results that did not occur.").

[58] *Id.* at 1347.

[59] *Id.*

[60] *Id.* at 1350-51.

Grain Processing found that the evidence supported the district court's conclusion that but for causation failed because the infringer would have likely switched to the noninfringing substitute. Thus, under *Grain Processing*, an infringer can use the existence of a non-infringing alternative that can be readily developed even where that alternative has not been developed or sold in fact.

[C] Lost Profits: Price Erosion

In addition to damages from lost sales, a patentee can also suffer loss from *price erosion*. That is, infringing competition may force the patentee to cut prices below that which the patentee would have otherwise obtained. The patentee bears the burden of demonstrating that but for the infringement, the patentee would have sold products at a higher price.

A proper price erosion analysis must account for the fact that in a market with some elasticity "consumers will almost always purchase fewer units of a product at a higher price than at a lower price, possibly substituting other products."[61] Absent unusual circumstances, a proper price erosion analysis must consider the effect of the higher sales price on a lower quantity that the patentee would have sold in the absence of infringement.

[D] Market Share Calculation of Lost Profits

The inference of but for causation raised by the *Panduit* test rests on the assumption that the patentee and the infringer compete directly in a two-player market. In such a market, it is reasonable to assume that the patentee would have sold products that were sold by a competing infringer so long as there is consumer demand and the patentee is capable of doing so.

Where a market includes additional competitors who are not parties to the litigation, the patentee may still prove lost sales using the *market share* approach. Under this theory, the patentee is entitled to recover the percentage of the infringer's sales which corresponds to the patentee's national market share. The market share theory assumes that the patentee would have made the same percentage of the infringer's sales that the patentee currently earns nationally.

For example, in *State Industries, Inc. v. Mor-Flo Industries, Inc.*,[62] the Federal Circuit affirmed a district court's award of lost profits to a patentee who occupied 40% of the national market. The market included the infringer, as well as a number of others that had not been joined in the case. Thus, in the *State Industries* case, the patentee — who had 40% of the market — was held to properly obtain lost profits on 40% of the infringer's sales.[63] The court determined that the patentee could obtain a reasonable royalty to compensate for the remainder of the infringer's sales.

---

[61] Crystal Semiconductor Corp. v. TriTech Microelectronics Intern., Inc., 246 F.3d 1336,1359 (Fed. Cir. 2001).

[62] State Industries State Industries, Inc. v. Mor-Flo Industries, Inc., 883 F.2d 1573 (Fed. Cir. 1989).

[63] *Id.* at 1579.

An example of the application of the market share rule in graphic form follows. As in the *State Industries* case, assume that the patentee has a 40% share of the market. Further assume that the infringer has 30%, and the remaining market participants non-party A and non-party B (who have not been sued for infringement) have 10% and 20% of the remaining market, respectively:

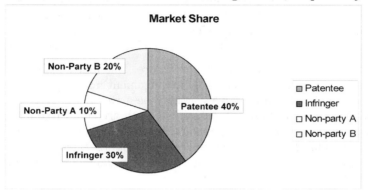

When the market share rule is applied, the patentee obtains lost profits for 40% of the infringer's market share. This result accepts that the patentee would not have obtained 100% of the infringer's sales, as other market participants may have made some of those sales if the infringer was absent from the market.

Once the market share rule applied, the patentee obtains lost profits damages based on 52% of the market, which amounts to 40% of the infringer's market share. In addition, under *State Industries*, the patentee may obtain a reasonable royalty on the infringer's sales in the remaining 18% of the market:

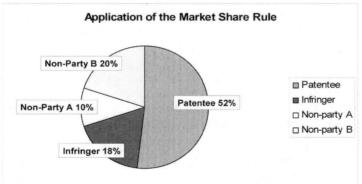

When the market share theory applies, there is no need to determine whether the *non-party's* share is infringing or non-infringing, as long as all of the products are within the same market. This is because the key question is the identification of the patentee's lost sales, and not an accounting of all potentially infringing product throughout.

§ 41.05 MONETARY RELIEF: REASONABLE ROYALTY

35 U.S.C. § 284 authorizes the plaintiff to recover "a reasonable royalty for the use made of the invention by the infringer." Patentees who do not make or sell products in the infringer's market pursue a reasonable royalty because by definition such patentees cannot demonstrate lost sales. In addition, patentees who are unable to prove lost profits under *Panduit* must rely on a reasonable royalty theory to collect damages for infringement. However, *any* patentee may elect to forgo seeking lost profits in favor of seeking a reasonable royalty at trial.

A reasonable royalty can be a lump sum figure. This figure may be based on an assumption that this was the most likely arrangement made by the parties in the hypothetical negotiation. Alternatively, it may be a running royalty that is calculated on an ongoing basis based on actual use. Both are comprised of two discreet parts — the *royalty rate* and the *royalty base*. Essentially, a royalty rate is a percentage of selling price or profit from infringing sales; the royalty base represents the quantity of infringing sales. The damages are calculated by multiplying the royalty rate by the royalty base.

Courts vary in their formulation of the reasonable royalty test. The foundational focus of the inquiry is to determine the value of the invention as implemented by the infringer. The most common reference for the market price of an invention is the result of a *hypothetical negotiation* — that is, the mutually agreeable amount that parties in the litigants' position would have bargained for prior to the time that infringement began.

[A] Established Royalty

An established royalty is one that is an amount "paid by such a number of persons as to indicate a general acquiescence in its reasonableness by those who have occasion to use the invention."[64] Courts have observed that proof of an established royalty for the patent in suit is one of the soundest measures of a reasonable royalty.[65] Thus, even where the patentee's licenses do not meet the "established royalty" standard, such licenses are probative of the market value of the patent.[66] Licenses that are deemed probative for purposes of establishing a royalty must be linked to the infringed technology at issue.[67] Existing licenses must evidence some relation to the litigating parties' actual market positions, as well as the level and type of damages sought in the litigation.[68]

An established royalty is not determinative in all cases. For example, in *Monsanto v. Ralph*, the Federal Circuit affirmed a royalty rate that was significantly higher than the amount stated in the parties' licensing agreement

---

[64] Hanson v. Alpine Valley Ski Area, Inc., 718 F.2d 1075, 1078 (Fed. Cir. 1983) (quoting Rude v. Westcott, 130 U.S. 152, 165 (1889)).

[65] Nickson Indus. Inc. v. Rol Mfg. Co., 847 F.2d 795, 798 (Fed.Cir.1988).

[66] *Nickson Indus.*, 847 F.2d at 798.

[67] *See* ResQNet.com, Inc. v. Lansa, Inc., 594 F.3d 860, 869 (Fed. Cir. 2010); Lucent Tech., Inc. v. Microsoft, 580 F.3d 1301 (Fed. Cir. 2009).

[68] *Id.* at 1331-32.

based on evidence that the patentee would not have permitted the defendant's infringing uses "at any price."[69]

[B]　The Analytic Approach

The analytic approach calculates a reasonable royalty based on the infringer's projected net profit minus a benchmark, such as the net profit in the same industry or the infringer's usual profit.[70] The remainder is the reasonable royalty that represents the premium attributable to the use of the technology.[71] Although broadly discussed, the analytic approach does not appear to have been widely used at trial. Rather, most royalty awards rely on either the established royalty, or an amount derived from the hypothetical negotiation (discussed below).

[C]　The Reasonable Royalty Based on a Hypothetical Negotiation

Perhaps the most common approach to a reasonable royalty is the willing-buyer/willing-seller construct, whereby the parties are assumed to have engaged in a hypothetical negotiation for a license. This method is used to arrive at "the percentage of sales or profit likely to have induced the hypothetical negotiators to license use of the invention."[72] The Federal Circuit has recognized that the term "hypothetical negotiation" is "an inaccurate, and even absurd, characterization"[73] given that the parties are engaged in litigation and cannot agree to a license in fact. To overcome this circumstance, the fact finder must assume the parties' willingness to reach an agreement. Additionally, the hypothetical negotiation must be assumed to occur at the time that infringement began.[74]

The hypothetical negotiation is typically based on one or more factors set forth in *Georgia-Pacific Corp. v. United States Plywood Corp.*,[75] frequently called the *Georgia-Pacific* factors. A comprehensive list follows:

　　1. The royalties received by the patentee proving or tending to prove an established royalty.

　　2. The rates paid for the use of comparable patents.

　　3. The nature and scope of the license, as exclusive or non-exclusive; or as restricted or non-restricted in terms of territory or with respect to whom

---

[69] Monsanto Co. v. Ralph, 382 F.3d 1374, 1385 (Fed. Cir. 2004); *Nickson Indus.*, 847 F.2d at 798 ("a higher figure may be awarded when the evidence clearly shows that widespread infringement made the established royalty artificially low") (dicta).

[70] TWM Mfg. Co., Inc. v. Dura Corp., 789 F.2d 895, 899 (Fed. Cir. 1986) (describing the application of the analytic approach).

[71] *See generally* Lucent Technologies, Inc. v. Gateway, Inc., 580 F.3d 1301, 1324 (Fed. Cir. 2009).

[72] Minco, Inc. v. Combustion Engineering, Inc., 95 F.3d 1109, 1119 (Fed. Cir. 1996).

[73] Rite-Hite Corp. v. Kelley Co., Inc., 56 F.3d 1538, 1554 n.13 (Fed. Cir. 1995).

[74] Applied Medical Resources Corp. v. U.S. Surgical Corp., 435 F.3d 1356, 1361 (Fed. Cir. 2006).

[75] Georgia-Pacific Corp. v. United States Plywood Corp., 318 F. Supp. 1116, 1120 (S.D.N.Y. 1970), modified and aff'd 446 F.2d 295 (2d Cir. 1971).

the manufactured product may be sold.

4. The licensor's established policy and marketing program to maintain his patent monopoly by not licensing others.

5. The commercial relationship between the licensor and licensee, such as, whether they are competitors in the same territory in the same line of business; or whether they are inventor and promoter.

6. The effect of selling the patented specialty in promoting sales of other products of the licensee; that existing value of the invention to the licensor as a generator of sales of his non-patented items; and the extent of such derivative or convoyed sales.

7. The duration of the patent and the term of the license.

8. The established profitability of the product made under the patent; its commercial success; and its current popularity.

9. The utility and advantages of the patent property over the old modes or devices used for similar results.

10. The nature of the patented invention; the character of the commercial embodiment of it as owned and produced by the licensor; and the benefits to those who have used the invention.

11. The extent to which the infringer has made use of the invention.

12. Customary licensing rates in comparable businesses to allow for the use of the invention or analogous inventions.

13. The portion of the realizable profit that should be credited to the invention as distinguished from non-patented elements, the manufacturing process, business risks, or significant features or improvements added by the infringer.

14. The opinion testimony of qualified experts.

15. The results of a hypothetical negotiation between a licensor (such as the patentee) and a licensee (such as the infringer) before infringement began.

A district court has discretion to select only those factors from the entire *Georgia Pacific* test that are relevant to the facts presented.

Minco, Inc. v. Combustion Engineering, Inc.,[76] serves as an example of the application of the *Georgia Pacific* factors. There, the court considered a challenge to a district court's reasonable royalty calculation. The parties were competitors in the market for fused silica. The patentee, who assigned the patent to Minco, developed an improved rotary furnace for fusing the silica. This furnace, which was the subject of the asserted patent, produced a superior product that "enjoyed substantial commercial success."[77] Minco's silica success began to cut into Combustion Engi-

---

[76] Minco, Inc. v. Combustion Engineering, Inc., 95 F.3d 1109 (Fed. Cir. 1996).

[77] *Id.* at 1113.

neering's market, which suffered a 20% reduction in a single year. In response, Combustion Engineering hired an engineer to design new furnaces that could generate fused silica of similar quality to that sold by Minco. In the district court, Combustion Engineering's newly designed furnaces were found to infringe Minco's rotary furnace patent. On appeal, Combustion Engineering challenged the district court's imposition of a royalty rate of 20% on the gross value of the infringing silica sales.

The Federal Circuit affirmed the district court's royalty rate, noting that the district court had properly re-created the parties' hypothetical bargaining positions on the date that Combustion Engineering's infringement commenced. A number of the *Georgia Pacific* factors drove the royalty rate upwards. For example, the parties were head-to-head competitors, a fact which tends to drive the rate upward based on an assumption that a patentee will seek high royalties from a competitor. Additionally, the district court noted that the infringer had an inferior product at the time that infringement began, and therefore would have paid more to obtain the ability to make the improved silica needed to compete with Minco. Further, there were no non-infringing alternatives and the industry overall had high profit margins. Reviewing the record, the Federal Circuit affirmed that "[t]he economic evidence on this point supports the finding that these hypothetical negotiators might have entered a license calculated at 20% of sales" of the silica.[78] Note that such a royalty is called a "reach through" royalty, because the figure is calculated based on the sales of the end product (the silica), rather than the infringing device (the furnace).[79] In other words, the royalty "reaches through" the infringing device to attach to the end product. Imposing a reach through royalty is appropriate where the record establishes that the parties would have bargained for such an arrangement.

In contrast, the Federal Circuit vacated a jury award for a lump sum payment of $358 million in *Lucent Technologies, Inc. v. Gateway, Inc.*[80] The infringed claims were directed to a single feature, a date-picker within Microsoft's Outlook email software, that enabled the user to select the day, month, and year using graphical controls. The *Lucent* court underscored the purpose of the reasonable royalty — that is, to compensate the patentee for pecuniary loss. For damages awarded under a reasonable royalty rubric, this relief allows the patentee to recover "the reasonable royalty he would have received through arms-length bargaining."[81]

The *Lucent* verdict was based on the hypothetical negotiation, an issue of fact that is typically subject to deference on appeal. Nonetheless, the *Lucent* decision determined that the finding that Microsoft would have bargained for a $358 million license was unsupported by substantial evidence. The appellate court observed that the patentee's evidence was limited to a running royalty payment schedule, rather than a lump sum payment. The court observed that the patented feature was a small part of an auxiliary feature of the larger, complex email program. The court noted,

---

[78] *Id.* at 1120.

[79] Donald r. Ware, Research Tool Patents: Judicial Remedies, Ware, 30 AIPLA Q. J. 267, 284 (2002)

[80] Lucent Technologies, Inc. v. Gateway, Inc., 580 F.3d 1301 (Fed. Cir. 2009).

[81] *Id.* at 1324.

"[w]e find it inconceivable to conclude, based on the present record, that the use of one small feature, the date-picker, constitutes a substantial portion of the value of Outlook." Further, the *Lucent* court found that the licenses that had been admitted as evidence were not sufficiently relevant to support the award. Specifically, Microsoft's license agreements with computer makers IBM, Dell, Hewlett-Packard and others were aimed toward PC technology — a broad category that was uninformative of the value of the patent in suit. As one example, the *Lucent* court explained that "the IBM-Dell license agreement for multiple patents to broad, PC-related technologies is directed to a vastly different situation than the hypothetical licensing scenario of the present case involving only one patent . . . directed to a narrower method of using a graphical user interface known as the date-picker."[82]

As the *Minco* and *Lucent* cases illustrate, the reasonable royalty attempts to place the parties in the position just before infringement began to determine the value of the technology as a hypothetically negotiated rate. Thus, this negotiation considers the nature of the patented advance, the infringer's uses of the technology, and other evidence that demonstrates the value of the claim that has been infringed.

§ 41.06   MONETARY RELIEF: ADDITIONAL CONSIDERATIONS

[A]   The Entire Market Value Rule

Many patents cover only one feature of an entire infringing device. For example, an infringed claim for an improved windshield wiper may be sold as part of a car. Should damages be based on the price of the wiper, or on the selling price of the entire car?

The answer depends on whether the *entire market value rule* is applied. When applied, a patentee may recover damages based on the value of an entire apparatus or system containing several features or components when the patent-related feature is the "basis for customer demand"[83] or "substantially creates the value of the component parts."[84] Essentially, this rule permits a patentee to recover for sales of features or components beyond those features specifically set forth in the infringed claim. The entire market value rule has been applied to both the lost profits and reasonable royalty theories of recovery.

An example of the application of the entire market value rule is *Juicy Whip, Inc. v. Orange Bang, Inc.*[85] In that case, the patentee's invention was a beverage dispenser with a transparent container to give the impression that this container stores a beverage purchased by the customer. The invention disclosed that, in fact,

---

[82] *Id.* at 1328.

[83] *Rite-Hite Corp.*, 56 F.3d at 1549. Although the entire market value rule originally applied only to the entire value of a single device, over the years the doctrine has been "extended to allow inclusion of physically separate unpatented components normally sold with the patented components." *Id.* at 1550.

[84] Uniloc U.S.A, Inc. v. Microsoft Corp. 632 F.3d 1292, 1318 (Fed. Cir. 2011).

[85] Juicy Whip, Inc. v. Orange Bang, Inc., 382 F.3d 1367 (Fed. Cir. 2004).

another portion of the device stores flavored syrup that is mixed together with water to create the beverage just before sale. Relying on the entire market value rule, the patentee sought lost profits recovery for both infringing sales of the *patented* devices as well as the defendant's sales of *unpatented* syrup. The district court had rejected the patentee's attempts to obtain recovery on the unpatented syrup, noting that the syrup could be purchased and used independently of the patented device. The Federal Circuit reversed and remanded this ruling, on the grounds that the district court had misapprehended the entire market value rule, explaining:

> . . . Although the [entire market value] rule traditionally had been applied to permit recovery when both the patented and unpatented items were part of the same machine, we recognized that the rule has been extended to allow inclusion of physically separate unpatented components normally sold with the patented components with the caveat that both were considered to be components of a single assembly or parts of a complete machine, or they together constituted a functional unit.[86]

Juicy Whip found that the patented dispenser and the unpatented syrup were "analogous to parts of a single assembly or a complete machine, as the syrup functions together with the dispenser to produce the visual appearance that is central to [the asserted] patent."[87] The entire market value rule permitted the patentee to expand recovery beyond the infringing feature even where the patented feature is not the central reason of the customer's purchase, so long as there is a functional relationship between the patented and unpatented components.

In the previously discussed *Lucent v. Microsoft* case,[88] the Federal Circuit rejected the application of the entire market value rule for a patent claim directed to a feature, the graphical date-picker, which was a small part of the complex and multi-featured Outlook email program. As the court described:

> The vast majority of the features, when used, do not infringe. The date-picker tool's minor role in the overall program is further confirmed when one considers the relative importance of certain other features, e.g., e-mail. Consistent with this description of Outlook, Lucent did not carry its evidentiary burden of proving that anyone purchased Outlook because of the patented method.[89]

Further, the court recognized error in the testimony of the patentee's expert, who had attempted to impose a 1% royalty rate based on the cost of the Microsoft software, as well as the computer on which the software ran. After the district court held that the computer cost could not be part of the royalty base, the expert limited his opinion to the value of the software but increased the royalty percentage to 8%. Finding that the parties would not have negotiated such rates, the appellate court explained:

---

[86] *Id.* at 1371 (quotations and citations omitted).

[87] *Id.* at 1372.

[88] *Lucent*, 580 F.3d at 1336-39.

[89] *Id.* at 1338.

Being precluded from using the computer as a royalty base, he used the price of the software, but inflated the royalty rate accordingly. This cannot be an acceptable way to conduct an analysis of what the parties would have agreed to in the hypothetical licensing context.[90]

As the *Lucent* decision illustrates, patentees who seek to recover for the value of components that are outside the claim scope must provide a proper evidentiary basis. This evidence must reflect rational conduct that approximates the parties' market condition, and accounts for the conduct of consumers operating within that market. Such consumers must be willing to view the patented feature as the basis for demand for the entire product, or to substantially create the value of the non-patented features.

Cornell University v. Hewlett-Packard is a significant district court opinion authored by Chief Judge Rader of the Federal Circuit sitting by designation.[91] In the opinion, Rader formulates a comprehensive set of criteria to support the application of the entire market value rule:

(1) the infringing components must be the basis for customer demand for the entire machine including the parts beyond the claimed invention;

(2) the individual infringing and non-infringing components must be sold together so that they constitute a functional unit or are parts of a complete machine or single assembly of parts; and

(3) the individual infringing and non-infringing components must be analogous to a single functioning unit.[92]

Notably, this three-part test uses the conjunction "and," designating that each of these three elements must exist in order for the entire market value rule to apply. Due to the influence of the opinion's author, this standard is likely to be adopted by other district courts that must consider whether a jury can hear evidence relating to the entire market value rule.

[B]   Patentee Delay and the Ability to Recover Monetary Relief

The Patent Act does not include a statute of limitations.[93] Nonetheless, some time limits on the filing of patent cases exist. Absent unusual circumstances, a patentee who files suit after the patent term expires will be unable to establish any grounds for the prospective remedy of injunction. Additionally, § 286 provides that "no recovery shall be had for any infringement committed more than six years prior to the filing of the complaint or counterclaim for infringement in the action."

---

[90] *Id.* at 1339.

[91] Cornell University v. Hewlett-Packard Co., 609 F. Supp. 2d 279, 286-87 (N.D.N.Y. 2009).

[92] *Id.* at 286-87.

[93] *But see* 28 U.S.C.A. § 2501 (suit against the U.S. government must be brought within six years after accrual of the claim).

In addition, a patentee's monetary recovery may be limited by the doctrine of *laches*. Generally, laches is defined as "the neglect or delay in bringing suit to remedy an alleged wrong, which taken together with lapse of time and other circumstances, causes prejudice to the adverse party and operates as an equitable bar."[94] Laches is an equitable doctrine that assures that claims will be brought expeditiously, while evidence remains accessible and so that any conflict between the parties will be laid to rest. To establish a laches defense that bars past monetary damages:

> . . . a defendant must demonstrate both 1) the plaintiff delayed filing suit for an unreasonable and inexcusable time period, measured from the time the plaintiff knew or reasonably should have known of infringement, and 2) such delay operated to the prejudice or injury of the defendant, either economically or because of a present inability to secure evidence needed for a full and fair defense.[95]

A six (6) year delay from the time that the patentee knows or should know of another's infringement is presumed to be unreasonable.[96] A patentee may rebut a *prima facie* showing of laches by demonstrating a reason to excuse the delay, such as engagement in other litigation, negotiations with the defendant or a dispute over the ownership of the patent.

If the court applies the laches defense, a patentee cannot recover monetary damages for infringement that occurred prior to instituting the lawsuit. Exercising its equitable jurisdiction, court may reject a laches defense where the defendant has engaged in egregious conduct such as copying. Although laches does not bar the entry of injunctive relief, a court might use the fact that the patentee delayed to assess the patentee's assertion of irreparable harm.

[C] Actual and Constructive Notice/Marking

Under 35 U.S.C. § 287, a patentee must mark patented products with the patent number of the invention. If the patentee fails to do so, the patentee is barred from recovering monetary damages unless the patentee has provided actual notice of infringement to the defendant or commences a sufficient marking program. As the statute states:

> In the event of failure so to mark, no damages shall be recovered by the patentee in any action for infringement, except on proof that the infringer was notified of the infringement and continued to infringe thereafter, in which event damages may be recovered only for infringement occurring after such notice. Filing of an action for infringement shall constitute such notice.

---

[94] A.C. Aukerman Co. v. R.L. Chaides Const. Co., 960 F.2d 1020, 1028-29 (Fed. Cir. 1992).

[95] *Id.* at 1032.

[96] *Id.* at 1035-36 (". . . the underlying critical factors of laches are presumed upon proof that the patentee delayed filing suit for more than six years after actual or constructive knowledge of the defendant's alleged infringing activity.").

Marking should be substantially consistent and continuous.[97] One who ships a significant number of unmarked products is said to "mislead[] the public into thinking that the product was freely available."[98] This requirement applies to apparatus and device claims. As a general rule, if the patent includes only method claims, this section might not apply because "where the patent claims are directed to only a method or process there is nothing to mark."[99] There are some notable exceptions to this rule. For example, where a patent includes both method and device claims and both are infringed, the patentee must mark the product.[100] Second, if the method claim is directed to the use of a product, then the patentee must mark that product.[101]

A patentee is entitled to damages that accrue *after* marking has begun and/or after the infringer has actual notice of infringement. Typically, such notice is accomplished by a communication from the patentee that informs the infringer of the asserted patent and the nature of the infringing activity. A patentee's service of a patent infringement complaint is sufficient to trigger actual notice.

A patentee must also take steps to ensure that licensees of the patent comply with marking obligations. Such efforts are assessed based on a rule of reason.[102] Under this standard, the Federal Circuit has affirmed a finding of sufficient marking where the product was marked at least 95% of the time.[103]

§ 41.07 WILLFUL INFRINGEMENT AND EXCEPTIONAL CASES

One who *willfully* infringes a patent might be liable for treble damages.[104]

Formerly, the courts held that one who was on notice of another's patent rights had an affirmative duty of due care to avoid infringement by seeking legal advice before initiating or continuing the allegedly infringing activity.[105] This rule was overruled in the Federal Circuit's en banc decision *In re Seagate Technologies*. Under *Seagate*, the patentee seeking to demonstrate willfulness must show by clear and convincing evidence both: 1) the infringer acted despite an objectively high likelihood that its action constituted infringement of a valid patent; and 2) that the objectively high risk was either known or so obvious that it should have been known

---

[97] American Medical Systems, Inc. v. Medical Engineering Corp., 6 F.3d 1523, 1538 (Fed. Cir. 1993).

[98] *Id.*

[99] *Id.*

[100] *Id.* at 1538-39.

[101] Devices for Medicine, Inc. v. Boehl, 822 F.2d 1062, 1066 (Fed. Cir. 1987).

[102] Funai Elec. Co., Ltd. v. Daewoo Electronics Corp., 616 F.3d 1357, 1375 (Fed. Cir. 2010).

[103] Maxwell v. J. Baker, Inc., 86 F.3d 1098, 1112 (Fed. Cir. 1996); *see also, Funai*, 616 F.3d at 1374 (jury could find that damages could be awarded for products despite the fact that 12% of products sold through a third party were not marked).

[104] 35 U.S.C. § 284.

[105] Underwater Devices Inc. v. Morrison-Knudsen Co., 717 F.2d 1380 (Fed. Cir. 1983), overruled in Sea

to the accused infringer.[106] According to the Federal Circuit, this standard requires at least a showing of objective recklessness.[107]

In *i4i Ltd. Partnership v. Microsoft*, the Court affirmed a jury finding of willfulness under this standard, where the record demonstrated that the infringer was aware that the plaintiff's technology was patented, that the infringer's employees had attended seminars where the technology had been demonstrated, and had discussed the patentee's promotional materials that stated that the "heart" of the technology was patented.[108] In addition, the record demonstrated that Microsoft had designed comparable software with intent to render the patentee's solution "obsolete."[109] Notwithstanding defenses raised by the infringer at trial, the *i4i* court determined that the jury could find that "Microsoft knew or should have know that there was an objectively high risk of infringement."[110]

Some who receive notice of infringement may seek the advice of qualified patent counsel, who examines the infringement allegations and, in some cases, examines whether invalidity or unenforceability defenses exist. Patent counsel's opinions may be set forth in an *opinion of counsel*, sometimes called an "opinion letter." Under the *Seagate* standard, a court may not draw any adverse inference from an accused infringer's failure to obtain on a legal opinion in litigation or to produce one during the discovery phase of patent litigation.[111] In part, this rule was established based on concerns that submitting an opinion letter at trial opened the door to waiver of the attorney client privilege and work product protection, including trial counsel.[112]

If willful infringement is found, a court will determine whether increased damages are appropriate.[113] This assessment is guided by a number of factors stated in the Federal Circuit's *Read Corp. v. Portec, Inc.*:

(1) whether the infringer deliberately copied the ideas or design of another;

(2) whether the infringer, when he knew of the other's patent protection, investigated the scope of the patent and formed a good-faith belief that it was invalid or that it was not infringed; and

(3) the infringer's behavior as a party to the litigation.[114]

In addition, the court may examine other considerations such as the defendant's size and financial condition, the closeness of the case, the duration of the defendant's

---

[106] In re Seagate Technology LLC, 497 F.3d 1360 (Fed. Cir. 2007).

[107] *Id.* at 1371.

[108] I4i Ltd. Partnership v. Microsoft Corp., 598 F.3d 831, 860 (Fed. Cir. 2010).

[109] *Id.*

[110] *Id.*

[111] Knorr-Bremse Systeme Fuer Nutzfahrzeuge GmbH v. Dana Corp., 383 F.3d 1337 (Fed. Cir. 2004); see also 35 U.S.C. § 298.

[112] Seagate, 497 F.3d at 1369-70; see generally, Amy L. Landers, *Intentional Waivers Of Privilege and the Opinion Of Counsel: Can the Scope Of Disclosure Be Managed?*, 20 Santa Clara Computer & High Tech. L.J. 765 (2004)

[113] Spectralytics, Inc. v. Cordis Corp. 649 F.3d 1336, 1348 (Fed. Cir. 2011).

[114] Read Corp. v. Portec, Inc., 970 F.2d 816, 827 (Fed. Cir. 1992).

misconduct, any remedial action by the defendant, the defendant's motivation for harm and whether the defendant attempted to conceal its misconduct. If a court finds a monetary increase appropriate, the award can be increased up to three times the compensatory damages amount. In addition, a court may order the defendant to pay to the patentee's attorney's fees.[115]

Although an opinion letter is not *required* to defend against a charge of willfulness, those accused of infringement might obtain one. The Federal Circuit has observed that such opinions are admissible at trial to demonstrate that damages should not be enhanced under the *Read* factors.[116] An opinion letter may analyze the probability of infringement and consider viable defenses, including invalidity or unenforceability. Under *Seagate*, district courts must presume that trial counsel's privilege and work product has not been waived and permit discovery into such communications and analysis only in "unique circumstances," such as "if a party or counsel engages in chicanery."[117]

§ 41.08 PREJUDGEMENT INTEREST

A patentee may recover as damages "interest and costs as fixed by the court."[118] "An award of prejudgment interest serves to make the patentee whole because the patentee also lost the use of its money due to infringement."[119] Prejudgment interest is ordinarily awarded to a prevailing patentee; however a district court retains some discretion to deny such relief.[120] Generally, limiting or denying such relief should be supported by a justification, such as where a patentee unduly delayed the prosecution of the lawsuit.

§ 41.09 CONCLUSION

The Patent Act provides for both injunctive and monetary relief that can be awarded to patentees and exclusive licensees. Specifically, a court may award preliminary and/or permanent injunctive relief to prevent future uses of the invention. Additionally, a jury may award monetary relief for past infringement, including lost profits and reasonable royalties for use of the invention. A court may increase the monetary award up to three times if the defendant has been found to have acted willfully. In addition, a patentee may seek the award of prejudgment interest and, in exceptional cases, attorney fees. Where no injunction has been granted, a district court has discretion to order payment of an ongoing royalty fixed by the court.

---

[115] 35 U.S.C. § 285.

[116] *Spectralytics*, 649 F.3d at 1348.

[117] *Seagate*, 497 F.3d at 1375-76.

[118] 35 U.S.C. § 284.

[119] Crystal Semiconductor Corp. v. TriTech Microelecs. Int'l, Inc., 246 F.3d 1336, 1361 (Fed. Cir. 2001).

[120] General Motors Corp. v. Devex Corp., 461 U.S. 648, 656 (1983).

Chapter 42

INTERNATIONAL TREATIES AND THE GLOBALIZATION OF PATENTS

SYNOPSIS

§ 42.01 INTRODUCTION

§ 42.02 THE PARIS CONVENTION OF 1883

§ 42.03 COORDINATION OF PATENT APPLICATION FILING: THE PATENT COOPERATION TREATY AND THE EUROPEAN PATENT CONVENTION

§ 42.04 TRIPS: THE WORLD TRADE ORGANIZATION AND THE AGREEMENT ON TRADE-RELATED ASPECTS OF INTELLECTUAL PROPERTY RIGHTS

§ 42.05 CONCLUSION

§ 42.01 INTRODUCTION

There is no single worldwide patent system. The rights granted in each nation are territorial. For example, activity which occurs entirely outside of U.S. boundaries cannot infringe a U.S. patent right.[1] With the exception of treaties that allow for coordinated application filings,[2] one must file for patent protection in each individual country for which protection is sought. However, a number of treaties affect patent practice both within the U.S. and internationally.

The first of these is the *Paris Convention of 1883* (the *"Paris Convention"*). The Paris Convention attempted to negotiate conflicts between member nations' laws and ensure uniform treatment between domestic and foreign patent applicants.

Second, during the 1970's, two systems were created to coordinate patent filings. Specifically, the *Patent Cooperation Treaty* (*"PCT"*) and the *European Patent Convention* (*"EPC"*) allow patentees to commence the application process for several nations with a single filing. Of the two, the PCT's reach is geographically broader, permitting an applicant to seek patent protection in over 100 member nations. However, although the PCT process commences with a single application,

---

[1] For more information about the territoriality of U.S. patent law, *see* Chapter 35 (describing extraterritorial activity that may lead to infringement of a U.S. patent).

[2] *See, e.g.*, the Patent Cooperation Treaty which is described in more detail herein, as well as in Chapters 2 and 18. As an additional example, under the European Patent Convention, also discussed in this chapter, the European Patent Office provides for patent protection within thirty-eight European countries.

ultimately a patentee must obtain individualized approval from each country in which a patent is sought. In contrast, the EPC has one examination process for application that, if granted, results in a single European patent that is enforceable in thirty-four (34) contracting states.

Third and most recently, is the *Agreement on Trade-Related Aspects of Intellectual Property Rights* (the *"TRIPS Agreement"*). Finalized in 1994, the TRIPS Agreement sets comprehensive minimum patent standards that must be enacted by the over 150 World Trade Organization ("WTO") member nations, including the United States. Worldwide, the TRIPS Agreement has provided a significant impetus for enacting or significantly modifying patent law within member nations. Due to its substantive breadth, widespread adoption and enforcement scheme, the TRIPS Agreement has had a momentous impact on international patent practice.

§ 42.02   THE PARIS CONVENTION OF 1883

Prior to the Paris Convention of 1883, no treaties existed to coordinate patent rights internationally. The U.S., which was an active participant in the discussions which led to the treaty, joined the Convention in 1887.[3] The Paris Convention includes two provisions of primary significance to patent practice.

First, the Paris Convention sought to resolve conflicts between members' patent rules that interfered with rights holders' ability to obtain patent protection in multiple countries. As one example of such a conflict, a patentee could not obtain a patent in France if the applicant first filed for a patent in any other country for the same invention.[4] This was resolved by the adoption of Article 4, which provided a six (6) month grace period (in later years, lengthened to its current one (1) year term) for those filing in any member state. In effect, this permits one to initially file in one country and then in other countries within the proscribed grace period without any loss of right or priority. The act of the foreign filing, publication and sales of products incorporating the claimed invention during the grace period do not result in any forfeiture of the patent right.

The U.S. incorporates Article 4 of the Paris Convention in 35 U.S.C. § 119. That section provides that a patent application filed in a Paris Convention country "shall have the same effect as the same application would have if filed in this country" if the U.S. application is filed within the first twelve (12) months after the foreign filing. Under this section, the first foreign filing establishes the priority date for the domestic filing. For example, one who files a patent application in Germany on May 1, 2008 may file a U.S. application on April 30, 2009, and claim priority back to the initial German filing date of May 1, 2008. Publications and sales during May 1, 2008 through April 30, 2009 do not interfere with an applicant's ability to obtain a U.S. patent.

---

[3] *See* H. Kronstein & I. Till, *A Reevaluation of the International Patent Convention*, 12 J.L. & CONTEMP. PROB. 765, 766 (1948).

[4] *See In re* Hilmer, 359 F.2d 859, 873 (C.C.P.A. 1966).

The second significant aspect of the Paris Convention is embodied in Article 2, which was incorporated to ensure *national treatment* of foreign inventors — that is, each member of the Convention must provide the same patent rights to foreign citizens as that country provides to its own. The U.S. did not enact legislation to effectuate this provision, as the U.S. had long granted foreign inventors the ability to obtain a U.S. patent. However, the failure to enact legislation drew criticism. This is because, under a former version of 35 U.S.C. § 104, different priority rules existed for foreign inventive activity. Specifically, former § 104 precluded reliance on conduct undertaken outside the U.S. to demonstrate reduction to practice.[5] Thus, one could not establish that one was first to invent based on non-U.S. work and, instead, was required to rely on the application's filing date as the date of invention. This section had a disparate impact on non-U.S. citizens, who largely created all inventions outside the U.S.[6] Nonetheless, the courts upheld the then-existing statute because, on its face, § 104 treated U.S. citizens working abroad in the same manner as non-U.S. citizens doing so.[7] With the adoption of the TRIPS Agreement, § 104 has been amended to allow foreign activity to establish reduction to practice under U.S. law.

The Paris Convention was a significant first step in international patent coordination. Nonetheless, its impact was limited. As originally drafted, the Paris Convention did not require any country to adopt any patent system.[8] Furthermore, the treaty had no formal enforcement procedures. Finally, the Paris Convention made no attempt to coordinate application filings — that is, one seeking protection in more than one country was required to meet the widely divergent patent requirements for each individual nation in which patent protection was sought.

§ 42.03   COORDINATION OF PATENT APPLICATION FILING: THE PATENT COOPERATION TREATY AND THE EUROPEAN PATENT CONVENTION

Two patent agreements were enacted during the 1970's to assist patentees in filing applications in multiple countries. The Patent Cooperation Treaty ("PCT"), which was enacted in 1970 and became effective in 1978, authorizes a patentee to file a single patent application that can ultimately be designated for patenting in any number of the over 100 member countries. Under the PCT procedures, described in detail in Chapter 2, a patentee has the benefit of an international examination. However, the PCT is not a comprehensive solution. This is because once the international phase is completed, the patentee must pursue patent protection in

---

[5] *See, e.g.*, Shurie v. Richmond, 699 F.2d 1156, 1158-59 (Fed. Cir. 1983).

[6] *See* William LaMarca, *Reevaluating The Geographical Limitation Of 35 U.S.C. § 102(b); Policies Considered*, 22 U. Dayton L. Rev. 25, 40 (1996).

[7] *Id.* at 41 (citing Monaco v. Hoffman, 189 F. Supp. 474 (D.D.C. 1960), aff'd, 293 F.2d 883 (D.C. Cir. 1961) (per curiam) ("A citizen of the United States who lives in Italy and makes his invention there, would be subject to the limitations of section 104 to the same extent as a citizen of Italy.").

[8] *See, e.g.*, R. Carl Moy, *The History Of The Patent Harmonization Treaty: Economic Self-Interest As An Influence*, 26 J. Marshall L. Rev. 457, 486-87 (1993) (noting the example that for some years after the Paris Convention was drafted, "Switzerland could, and in fact did, adhere to the Paris Convention even though it had no patent system whatsoever.").

each country (or, in some cases, region) in which protection is desired. Once the application has completed the international phase, the PCT system requires the expense and time involved in individualized local prosecution.

The European Patent Convention ("EPC") was signed in 1973. As implemented by the European Patent Office ("EPO"), the EPC provides for a single application process for patent protection within thirty-four (34) contracting states. Under the EPC, a patentee's application is examined by the EPO under a uniform substantive patent law that is described in the EPC.[9] If the EPO decides that the application meets the EPC's patentability requirements, third parties are permitted a nine month window to oppose the patent. If the application is ultimately granted, a European patent gives the patentee the same rights as those conferred by the national right available within each individual country that is a member of the Convention.[10] One enforces the patent according to national law in the individual member nation(s).[11] If the application is denied, the patentee may appeal the denial to the Board of Appeals of the EPO.

Alternatively, one can choose to file a PCT application in the EPO. In that event, the first phase of the process is governed by the PCT procedures, and the national phase by the EPO.

§ 42.04   TRIPS: THE WORLD TRADE ORGANIZATION AND THE AGREEMENT ON TRADE-RELATED ASPECTS OF INTELLECTUAL PROPERTY RIGHTS

Today, over 150 members of the WTO are parties to the TRIPS agreement, which requires member countries to establish and maintain uniform minimum standards for intellectual property protection, including patent rights.[12] The TRIPS Agreement provides a minimum level of protection but does not preclude members from enacting more. For example, a member may elect to provide a longer term of protection than the 20 year period mandated by TRIPS.

Some of the most significant terms of the TRIPS Agreement include:

• Members must grant patents for any inventions in all fields of technology without discrimination.[13] Nonetheless, TRIPS includes discretionary exclusions from patentable subject matter. Specifically, a member may refuse

---

[9] Convention on the Grant of European Patents (European Patent Convention), Oct. 5, 1973, 1065 U.N.T.S. 199, *available at* http://www.epo.org/patents/law/legal-texts/html/epc/1973/e/ma1.html.

[10] EPC, art. 64.

[11] For more information on enforcement, *see* Paul A. Coletti, *No Relief In Sight: Difficulties In Obtaining Judgements In Europe Using EPO Issued Patents*, 81 J. PAT. & TRADEMARK OFF. SOC'Y 351 (1999).

[12] For an overview of these provisions, *see* J.H. Reichman, *Universal Minimum Standards of Intellectual Property Protection Under the Trips Component of the WTO Agreement,*" 29 INT'L LAW. 345 (1995).

[13] Agreement on Trade-Related Aspects of Intellectual Property Rights, Marrakesh Agreement Establishing the World Trade Organization, Annex 1C, Legal Instruments-Results of the Uruguay Round, Art. 27, § 1, Apr. 15, 1994, 33 I.L.M. 81, 1869 U.N.T.S. 299, *available at* http://www.wto.org/english/docs_e/legal_e/27-trips.pdf (hereinafter TRIPS).

to grant patents for certain types of inventions, such as (1) diagnostic, therapeutic or surgical methods; (2) plants and animals, and biological processes for the production of plants or animals; and (3) inventions necessary to protect *ordre public* or morality, including the protection of human, animal or plant life or health, or to avoid serious prejudice to the environment.[14]

• Member countries must condition a patent grant on a disclosure that enables those of ordinary skill in the art to carry out the invention. In addition, the invention must be new, involve an inventive step and be capable of industrial application.[15]

• For *product* patents, members must grant a right that allows the owner to prevent others from making, using, offering for sale, selling or importing products incorporating the patented feature;[16]

• For *process* patents, members must grant patents that permit the owner to exclude others from using the process, as well as the right to exclude others from using, offering for sale, selling or importing a product obtained directly from that process;[17]

• Members must establish civil judicial forums for the enforcement of patent rights. These adjudicatory processes must have authority to issue appropriate injunctions and to award damages.[18]

The overall structure of the TRIPS Agreement authorizes members to limit intellectual property protection by adopting "measures necessary to protect public health and nutrition, and to promote the public interest in sectors of vital importance to their socio-economic and technological development."[19] Further, Article 30 states that members may make limited exceptions to patent rights, so long as such exceptions "do not unreasonably conflict with a normal exploitation of a patent and do not unreasonably prejudice the legitimate interests of the patent owner." Taken together, these articles raise questions about members' ability to undertake measures within their borders that may impact patent rights, such as permitting the manufacture or sale of a patented pharmaceutical product without the patentee's consent in order to resolve a public health crisis.

In November 2001, the WTO enacted the "Declaration on the TRIPS Agreement and Public Health" (or "Doha Declaration") to respond to some of these questions by providing interpretative guidance. The Doha Declaration recognized the importance of intellectual property for the development of new medicines as well as

---

[14] *Id.*, § 2 & 3.

[15] *Id.*, art. 27 sec. 1. TRIPS provides that a member may deem the terms "inventive step" and "capable of industrial application" as synonymous with non-obviousness and utility, respectively. TRIPS, art. 27, § 1 n.5.

[16] *Id.*, art. 28, § 1(a).

[17] *Id.*, § 1(b).

[18] *Id.*, Part III.

[19] *Id.*, art. 8.

countervailing concerns about a patent's effects on prices for such products.[20] Among other things, the Doha Declaration confirms that the TRIPS Agreement permits members to enact compulsory licensing in, for example, cases of national emergency or extreme urgency.[21] However, given the complexity of these issues, it is not entirely clear how these provisions will be applied in individual cases.

The TRIPS agreement includes an enforcement mechanism, which empowers the WTO to convene a dispute resolution panel to adjudicate potential violations by members.[22]

The TRIPS treaty has had some impact on U.S. law.[23] For example, the U.S. has modified the patent term to twenty years from the filing date in conformity with the TRIPS Agreement.[24] Other changes include the U.S. expansion of the definition of infringement to include offers for sale.[25] Additionally, as previously discussed, U.S. law was amended to permit citizens from WTO member countries to establish a date of invention based on activity that occurs abroad.[26]

§ 42.05   CONCLUSION

There are four significant treaties that impact international patent practice. Those impacting substantive patent rights in the U.S. are the Paris Convention of 1883 and the TRIPS Agreement. In addition, the Patent Cooperation Treaty and the European Patent Convention provide coordinated systems for those wishing to obtain patent protection abroad. Together, these treaties may be seen as efforts toward worldwide harmonization of procedural and substantive patent law that seek to balance owners and inventors rights with the needs of individual nations.

---

[20] World Trade Organization, Ministerial Declaration on the TRIPS Agreement and Public Health of 14 November, 2001, ¶ 3, WT/MIN(01)/DEC/2, 41 I.L.M. 755 (2002) (also referred to as the 'Doha Declaration'), *available at* http://www.wto.org/English/thewto_e/minist_e/min01_e/mindecl_trips_e.htm.

[21] *Id.* at ¶ 5.

[22] *Id.* at Part V.

[23] *See* Uruguary Round Agreements Act, Pub. L. No. 103-465, 18 Stat. 4809 (1994).

[24] *See Id.*; 35 U.S.C. § 154(a)(2).

[25] *See* Uruguary Round Agreements Act, 18 Stat. 4809; 35 U.S.C. § 271(a), *See also* Rotec Industries, Inc. v. Mitsubishi Corp., 215 F.3d 1246, 1253 (Fed. Cir. 2000) (describing statutory amendment to U.S. patent law pursuant to the TRIPS Agreement).

[26] *See* Uruguary Round Agreements Act, 18 Stat. 4809; 35 U.S.C. § 104.

GLOSSARY

Abandonment	An act which demonstrates that a patent will not be pursued. Either an invention or an application can be abandoned. Abandoning an invention allows the invention to pass to the public domain without a patent being granted. Abandonment of an application can be either intentional or by failure to reply to an office action.
Abstract of the disclosure	Part of a patent application, a brief statement that discusses the gist of the invention. 37 C.F.R. § 1.72(b).
Accused device	The device accused of infringing a patent.
Agent	A professional who is authorized to prosecute patent applications before the U.S. PTO on behalf of others, but who is not an attorney.
Analogous art	Prior art used to determine if an invention is nonobvious. To constitute analogous art, the reference must be either in the same field of endeavor or be reasonably pertinent to the problem to be solved.
Antedates	Refers to circumstances whereby an inventor "swears behind" the date of prior art in conflict with her invention (for reasons of non-obviousness or novelty) to establish an invention date the precedes the asserted art.
Anticipation	Prior art that anticipates the invention and therefore bars patentability for reasons of novelty. The prior art must have strict identity with the invention.
Application number	The U.S. PTO assigns a unique number to each patent application.
Assignment	A transfer of ownership of a patent application or patent from one entity to another.
Best mode	A requirement that compels an inventor to describe the best mode of the invention contemplated by the inventor in the application at the time of filing. 35 U.S.C. § 112, ¶ 1.
Blocking patent	A patent that claims an invention that blocks one from practicing one's improvement patent. This is based on the principle that one patent owner cannot use another's patent without permission or a license from the other. This situation might be resolved through cross-licensing.
Canceled claim	A claim removed from the application by the inventor.

Claim	A single sentence definition of the invention. A patent owner has the right to exclude others from making, using and selling subject matter that is within the scope of a claim.
Claim construction	Interpreting a claim term. Under the U.S. Supreme Court's *Markman v. Westview Instruments*, this operation must be performed by the court.
Combination claim	A claim which combines existing components in a novel and nonobvious way.
Common inventor	Where multiple patents have the same person listed as an inventor.
Composition	A mixture of substances such as chemicals or metallic alloys.
Comprised of or comprising	A transition phrase that is considered "open ended." This means that the claim encompasses implementations that include all limitations of the claim plus an unclaimed feature. For example, a claim for a cup and holder may be infringed by a cup/holder combination that also includes a lid. — compare "consisting of"
Compulsory license	A patent owner's license required by law. Such a license may be compelled with or without the patentee's consent.
Conception	An inventor's mental picture of a complete and operative invention. The idea must be definite enough that one skilled in the art could make and use the invention. Conception does not require reduction to practice. — compare "invention date"
Consisting of	A transition phrase for a "close ended" claim. This means that the claim encompasses implementations that include all elements of the claim but nothing additional. The presence of an unclaimed feature means that the implementation is not infringing. For example, for a claim to a chemical compound consisting of A and B, the presence of C means that the compound is not infringing. — compare "comprised of or comprising"
Continuation	A later application for the same invention claimed in a prior application and filed before the first application becomes abandoned or patented.
Continuation-in-part (CIP) application	An application that encompasses the disclosure of an earlier application and adds new matter. A CIP application enjoys the benefit of the filing date of the earlier patent only for subject matter that was included in the earlier application. The priority date for new matter is the filing date of the CIP application.

Contributory infringement	A form of indirect infringement where an infringer provides a material component part of a patented invention. The component part must be a nonstaple item without any substantial non-infringing uses. For liability to be found, the contributory infringer must act with knowledge.
Critical date	The date upon which a potentially invaliding reference becomes prior art.
Declaration	A statement made under oath.
Definiteness	The requirement that patent claims must "particularly point out and distinctively claim the subject matter which the applicant regards as his invention." 35 U.S.C. § 112, ¶ 1.
Dependent claim	A claim which refers to or depends on an earlier independent claim within the same patent application. A dependent claim inherits all limitations of the independent claim.
Derivation	A patent application must be filed in the name of the true inventor. Derivation represents grounds to prevent or invalidate a patent claim because the applicant is not the true inventor, but rather derived the invention from another.
Derivation proceedings	A procedure instituted by the AIA that allows a patent applicant to petition the PTO to obtain the right to a patent where an earlier-filed application was derived from the applicant.
Design patent	A patent granted for a new, original and ornamental design of an article of manufacture.
Diligence	Continuous work towards a reduction to practice after conception. See 35 U.S.C. § 102(g).
Divisional patent or application	A later application (or patent) for an independent or distinct invention disclosing and claiming part of the subject matter of an earlier parent patent application.
DNA	Deoxyribonucleic acid, a generic term encompassing the many chemical materials that genetically control the structure and metabolism of living things.
Doctrine of equivalents	A judicially created doctrine of patent infringement that was originally promulgated to prevent fraud on the patent holder. This doctrine is used when the accused infringement falls outside the literal scope of the patent claims but is substantially identical to the patented invention.
Drawing	A drawing may be included with the patent application if necessary to understand the invention.

Effective filing date	An earlier filing date than the actual filing date of a patent application. For example, this may occur where one is able to establish priority based on a foreign filing or if the application is a continuation claiming priority to an earlier-filed parent application.
Element	A portion of an accused device, process or method that corresponds to a claim limitation. Also, some sources use the term "element" to refer to a claim limitation.
Embodiment	One manner in which a patented invention may be practiced. Many patents contain more than one embodiment, and some include a preferred embodiment(s).
Enablement	A description in the specification that makes it possible for one skilled in the art to make and use the invention.
Equitable estoppel	A defense to an infringement action. Used when the plaintiff's conduct lead the defendant to believe that the patent would not be enforced. — compare "laches"
Examination	The U.S. PTO's process to determine whether a patent application meets with all requirements for patentability.
Ex parte reexamination	A reexamination proceeding which may be filed by a patentee or a third party, or commenced by the director of the U.S. PTO. If commenced, a third party's participatory rights are quite limited. — *see* "reexamination"
Experimental use	A doctrine that allows an inventor to practice the subject matter of the claims to perfect the invention. An inventor's experimental use will not be counted in determining whether the activity constitutes a statutory bar. Experimental use ends when the inventor reduces the invention to practice.
Federal Circuit	The U.S. Circuit Court of Appeal with nationwide geographic jurisdiction. The Federal Circuit has exclusive federal jurisdiction for patent appeals from cases decided in the U.S. District Courts.
Filing	Submitting an application for a patent to the U.S. PTO or a foreign patent office.
Final office action	The last action taken by the U.S. PTO on a patent application. This action is intended to close prosecution of a nonprovisional patent application by a U.S. PTO examiner.
Foreign priority	A U.S. patent application may obtain an earlier priority date by referencing an application for the same invention filed in a foreign jurisdiction. The U.S. application must be filed within one year of the foreign filing to invoke such a priority date.

Grace period	A one year time period leading to the filing of a patent application. The patent may be practiced by the inventor or third parties during this period without the inventor's loss of an ability to obtain a patent under the statutory bars of § 102.
Independent claim	A claim which stands alone and does not refer back to or depend on another claim.
Inducing infringement	A form of indirect infringement which involves another's encouragement to infringe a patent. To incur liability, the one inducing infringement must act with knowledge. Sometimes called "active inducement."
Inequitable conduct	A defense to infringement suit that relies on a patent applicant's duty of candor during proceedings with the U.S. PTO. For inequitable conduct to take effect the conduct must be material to patentability and the applicant must act with intent to deceive the U.S. PTO. If inequitable conduct is found, the patent is rendered unenforceable.
Information disclosure statement (IDS)	A list included in the patent application of all prior art that may be a bar to patentability. An applicant has a duty to disclose all prior art that are material and known to the patent applicant.
Infringement	For direct infringement, the unauthorized practice of another's invention through the acts of making, using, offering to sell, selling or importing into the U.S. any patented invention either literally or under the doctrine of equivalents. — For indirect infringement, see "inducing infringement" and "contributory infringement"
Inter partes	A U.S. PTO proceeding involving parties other than the patent applicant, such as an interference or an *inter partes* reexamination.
Inter partes reexamination	Similar to an ex parte reexamination but which allows a third party greater participatory rights to submit comments and to appeal an adverse ruling. — *see "reexamination"*
Inter partes review	A limited window of review nine months after a patent is issued instituted by the AIA. This review is restricted to the examination of whether a patent meets the novelty and nonobviousness requirements based solely on prior art patents and printed publications.
Interference	A U.S. PTO *inter partes* proceeding which is used to determine priority to an invention between two or more parties.

Invention date	Under U.S. law, patents are granted to the party who is first to invent. The date of invention is the date upon which the invention is actually or constructively reduced to practice. Alternatively, one who is first to conceive may demonstrate an invention date by demonstrating diligence from a date earlier than the conception by another.
Inventor	One responsible for, or who makes a significant intellectual contribution toward, the conception of an invention. — see also "joint inventor"
Issue date	The date on which a patent is granted and becomes effective for purposes of enforcement.
Joint inventor	An inventor who makes a significant intellectual contribution to an invention. A joint inventor of at least one claim obtains an ownership right and must be named as an inventor to the patent.
Laches	An equitable defense to a patent infringement suit, which allows a defendant to avoid monetary liability when a patent holder has taken too much time to file a lawsuit once becoming aware of the defendant's infringing activity.
License	A contract or agreement with a patent holder that permits the licensee to practice the patented invention.
Literal infringement	When someone makes, uses, sells, offers to sell or import into the U.S. something which falls within the literal scope of a patented claim. — compare "doctrine of equivalents"
Maintenance fees	Fees a patent holder is required to pay to the U.S. PTO for maintaining a patent whose term has not yet expired.
Markush claim	A claim type that permits one to describe a group of component materials or parts named.
Means plus function	A claim type that permits one to define an invention with reference to its function. The use of the word "means" in the claim language may mean that the claim includes a limitation that is written in means plus function terms.
Method claim	A claim type that describes the steps for how a thing is made or used.
Misuse	When the patent holder attempts to assert more than the claim scope. Patent misuse is a defense in an infringement suit. If patent misuse is found, the patent is rendered unenforceable until the misuse is purged.

MPEP	The "Manual of Patent Examining Procedure" is a set of rules and procedures used by the U.S. PTO in examining patent application to determine whether a patent should be granted. This document is available free in electronic form on the U.S. PTO's website.
Multiple dependent claims	A dependent claim which refers back to or depends on more than one preceding independent or dependent claim. A multiple dependent claim may not depend on another multiple dependent claim, either directly or indirectly. — see "dependant claim" and "independent claim"
New matter	In prosecuting patents, new matter is a new invention or a new part of an existing invention which was not originally disclosed either expressly or inherently.
Nonobviousness	A patentability requirement that bars the issuance of patent (or renders an issued patent invalid) if the claimed subject matter is obvious to one of ordinary skill in the art. Unlike novelty, nonobviousness may exist where the reference(s) lack strict identity with the claims.Nonprovisional patent applicationA patent application that establishes a filing date and includes the specification, claim(s), drawing(s) if necessary, oath or declaration and filing fee. A properly filed nonprovisional application is considered a complete patent application. — compare "provisional patent application"
Notice of allowability	Notice issued by the U.S. PTO to a patent applicant that stated that the application has been placed in condition for allowance.
Novelty	The requirement that an invention must be new and previously unknown to the public in order for a patent to issue to the inventor.
Oath	A statement made under penalty of perjury. An *inventor's oath* declares that she is the inventor of the subject matter claimed in the patent application, that she understands the specification and claims, and that she acknowledges the duty to disclose. An inventor's oath (or declaration) must be filed with a nonprovisional patent application.
OED	The Office of Enrollment and Discipline within the U.S. PTO.
Office action	The response made by a U.S. PTO examiner to a patent application. — compare "final office action"

Parent application	The application which preceded a later application disclosing the same invention, and to which a claim of priority is made. This term is used in the context of divisional and continuation applications and patents. — *see* "divisional patent or application" and "continuation"
Patent	A government granted right to exclude others from making, using, offering for sale, or selling a specific invention throughout the U.S. or importing the invention into the U.S.
Patent application	An application to the U.S. PTO for a patent including applications for utility, design, plant, provisional, nonprovisional and reissue patents.
Patent bar exam	An exam administered by the U.S. PTO that determines whether one may practice before the agency.
Patent number	A number assigned to a patent upon issuance.
Patent term	The length of time in which a patent holder has the right to exclude others from practicing the invention. As of June 8, 1995 a U.S. patent term lasts for 20 years from the earliest effective filing date but may be extended upon the satisfaction of certain criteria. Prior to June 8, 1995, a U.S. patent term was seventeen years from the issue date.
Patentee	The patent owner. The inventor is the presumptive owner of a patent. However, an inventor may assign the patent to another.
Patent Cooperation Treaty or PCT	A treaty enacted in 1970 which became effective in 1978. The PCT authorizes a patentee to file a single patent application that can ultimately be designated for patenting in any number of over 100 member countries.
Person having ordinary skill in the art (PHOSITA)	A hypothetical person who constructively knows all that would be expected of a person practicing in the pertinent art. Sometimes called "one of ordinary skill in the art."
Plant patent	A patent granted to one who invents or discovers a distinct and new variety of an asexually reproduced plant.
Post-grant review	A "first window" for third party challenges on any grounds during the first nine months of its term instituted by the AIA.
Preamble	Language that precedes the transitional language in a patent claim. Typically, such terms are not considered limitations unless the terms can be said to be necessary to give life, meaning and vitality to the claim.

Printed publication	Prior art that is a document that is accessed by a member of the public or is publicly accessible to those interested in the art. A printed publication that becomes part of the art prior to a claim's critical date and that discloses the claimed invention may be used to demonstrate a lack of novelty, a statutory bar or nonobviousness.
Prior art	Relevant inventions, discoveries and technology that are used to evaluate the patent application for novelty, statutory bar or nonobviousness.
Priority	A determination of the party who is first to invent a particular invention. 35 U.S.C. § 102(g). The term "priority" also refers to the ability to establish an earlier effective filing date.
Process claim	A claim in a patent or application that recites a number of acts or a series of steps. Such claims are directly infringed by another who performs those acts or steps.
Pro se	An inventor who files for a patent in her own name without the representation of a patent agent or attorney is said to be prosecuting the patent *pro se.*
Prosecution history	A collection of documents which represents all communications and paper generated in the course of a patent prosecution. Typically, such files are available for public inspection.
Prosecution history estoppel	A limit on the doctrine of equivalents based on a patentee's narrowing claim amendment made during prosecution.
Provisional patent application	A patent application that consists of a specification and drawing. Unlike a nonprovisional application, provisional patent applications need not include a claim or an inventor's oath. Provisional patent applications are not examined on their merits but may be used to establish priority for a later nonprovisional filing.
Publication number	An eleven digit number assigned to a published patent application. The first four digits are the year that the application was published.
Reasonable royalty	A form of monetary relief for patent infringement based on the value of the use of the patented invention.
Reduction to practice	For actual reduction to practice, a physical embodiment of the invention such as a prototype. Constructive reduction to practice can be accomplished by a description in a patent application that is filed with the U.S. PTO.

Reexamination	A second examination of an issued patent. A request for a reexamination may be made by the patent holder, a third party or at the direction of the U.S. PTO director. A reexamination may be granted if a prior patent or printed publication demonstrates that there is a substantial question of patentability of at least one of the patent's claims. — see "*ex parte* reexamination" and "*inter partes* reexamination"
Reference	Prior art.
Reissue	An administrative remedy used to correct errors in an issued patent. The error must have been made without deceptive intent and must render the patent partly inoperative or wholly invalid.
Repair/reconstruction	Used in the context of the first sale doctrine, an owner of a product that incorporates a patented invention may repair the invention when broken or replace a part when it is spent without incurring liability for infringement. Because the first sale doctrine does not include the right to reproduce an invention, an owner may be liable for infringement if the invention is reconstructed.
Restriction requirement	A requirement used by the U.S. PTO to restrict a patent application that contains two distinct and independent inventions to a single invention. The applicant elects which invention will be examined and may later claim the other in a divisional application.
Specification	The written description, best mode, enablement and claim(s) of the invention.
Statutory bar	Under 35 U.S.C. § 102, a bar to patentability where either the inventor or third party undertakes certain activities such as a public use, prior printed publication or prior patent that discloses the same invention.
Statutory subject matter	In 35 U.S.C. § 101, Congress defined the scope of patentable subject matter as any "process, machine, manufacture, or composition of matter" or any improvement of these, that fits within the contemplation of the patent system.
Strict identity	The relation between a claim and a prior art reference where every limitation in the claim corresponds to an element disclosed in the prior art reference.
Subject matter	Broadly, the invention. — compare "statutory subject matter"

Supplemental examination	A PTO procedure instituted by the AIA to cleanse any past inequitable conduct. This provides the patentee with an opportunity to present the PTO with material omitted during the initial prosecution will not cloud the patent's enforceability.
Transition phrase	The phrase connecting the preamble to the operative limitations of the claim(s) in the specification. — compare "comprised of or comprising" with "consisting of"
U.S. PTO	United States Patent and Trademark Office.
Utility	In order to be patentable an invention must have specific, substantial and credible use. This includes *general utility*, to achieve some minimum social or human purpose; *specific utility*; be operable and capable of use to perform the functions and secure the result required; and *moral utility*, human purpose cannot be illegal, immoral, or contrary to public policy.
Utility patent	A patent granted to someone who invents or discovers any new, useful, and non-obvious process, machine, article of manufacture, or composition of matter, or any new and useful improvement thereof. — *compare "plant patent" and "design patent"*
WIPO	World Intellectual Property Organization
Written description	The documentation that is part of the patent application, but does not include the claim(s).
WTO	World Trade Organization

TABLE OF CASES

[References are to pages]

A

A.C. Aukerman Co. v. R.L. Chaides Constr. Co..539
A.L. Smith Iron Co. v. Dickson 520
Abbott Laboratories v. Geneva Pharmaceuticals, Inc. 160
Abbott Laboratories v. Sandoz, Inc. 65; 66
Abbott Labs. v. Andrx Pharms., Inc. 526
Abele, In re. 312
Acromed Corp. v. Sofamor Danek Group, Inc. . 229, 230
Adams; U.S. v. 279
Aero Prods. Int'l, Inc. v. Intex Rec. Corp. 329
AFG Industries, Inc. v. Cardinal IG Co. 62
Agawam Co. v. Jordan. 148; 231
Air Products & Chemicals, Inc. v. Reichhold Chemicals, Inc. 354
AK Steel Corp. v. Sollac and Ugine 98
Akamai Technologies, Inc. v. Limelight Networks, Inc. 363
Akzo N.V. v. U.S. Int'l Trade Comm'n. 455
Al-Site Corp. v. VSI Intern., Inc. 407
Alappat, In re. 311
Albright v. Celluloid Harness Trimming Co. 415
Alexander Milburn Co. v. Davis-Bournonville Co. 218–220; 274
Altiris, Inc. v. Symantec Corp.. . . . . . . .357, 358
Amazon.com, Inc. v. Barnesandnoble.com, Inc. . 525
American Bell Tel. Co.; U.S. v. 97; 461
American Cotton-Tie Co. v. Simmons 507
American Medical Systems, Inc. v. Medical Engineering Corp.. 540
Amgen, Inc. v. Chugai Pharmaceutical Co..100; 102; 124; 127; 134; 229; 248
Amgen Inc. v. F. Hoffmann-La Roche, Ltd. . . . 454
Amgen Inc. v. Hoescst Marion Roussel Inc. . . . 111; 119; 393
Anascape, Ltd. v. Nintendo. 116, 117
Andersen Corp. v. Fiber Composites, LLC. 342
Anthony, In re 284
Apotex U.S.A, Inc. v. Merck & Co.. . . . .252; 254
Applegate v. Scherer. 227
Applied Materials, Inc. v. Advanced Semiconductor Materials America, Inc. 32
Applied Med. Res. Corp. v. United States Surgical Corp.. . . . . .328; 405; 533
Arendi Holding Ltd. v. Microsoft Corp.. 348
Ariad Pharmaceuticals, Inc. v. Eli Lilly and Co..110; 113; 120

Arnott, In re 45
Aro Manufacturing Co. v. Convertible Top Replacement Co.. . . . . . . .427; 430; 507; 508
Aronson v. Quick Point Pencil Co. 478
Arris Group, Inc. v. British Telecommunications PLC 425, 426
Arrowhead Indus. Water, Inc. v. Ecolochem, Inc. . 81
Arthrocare Corp. v. Smith & Nephew, Inc.. 45
Asgrow Seed Co. v. Winterboer 74, 75
Ass'n for Molecular Pathology v. United States PTO 306, 307
AT&T Corp. v. Excel Communs., Inc. 311
Atari Games Corp. v. Nintendo of Am., Inc.. . . .485
Athletic Alternatives, Inc. v. Prince Mfg., Inc.. . . 128, 129
Atlanta Attachment Co. v. Leggett & Platt, Inc. . 197
Atlantic Thermoplastics Co. v. Faytex Corp.. . . .64
Auto. Techs. Int'l, Inc. v. BMW of N. Am., Inc.. .99
Autogiro Co. of America v. United States 59
Aventis Pharma S.A. v. Amphastar Pharms., Inc..464

B

B. B. Chemical Co. v. Ellis 434
B. Braun Medical, Inc. v. Abbott Laboratories . .472
Baltimore & Carolina Line v. Redman 323
Barbed Wire Patent. 175
Barker, In re 112
Barmag Barmer Maschinenfabrik AG v. Murata Machinery, Ltd. 284
Bass, In re 227; 274
Bates v. Coe 205
Bauer & Cie v. O'Donnell 358; 361
Baxter Int'l Inc. v. COBE Laboratories, Inc. 170
Bayer AG v. Elan Pharm. Research Corp.. .349; 351
Bayer AG v. Housey Pharms., Inc. 452; 457
Bayer AG & Bayer Corp. v. Schein Pharms., Inc.. . . . . .32; 135; 138; 210
Bayer, In re. 181
BB Chem. Co. v. Ellis 350; 434
Beachcombers v. WildeWood Creative Products, Inc. 173
Beauregard, In re. 316
Beghin-Say Int'l, Inc. v. Ole-Bendt Rasmussen . . 79
Bell & Howell Document Mgmt. Prods. Co. v. Altek Sys. 526
Benger Laboratories Limited v. R. K. Laros Co..134

[References are to pages]

Bernhardt, L.L.C. v. Collezione Europa U.S.A,
    Inc.. . . . . .172, 173
Best Lock Corp. v. Ilco Unican Corp. 72
Beverly Hills Fan Co. v. Royal Sovereign Corp.. .82
Bey v. Kollonitsch. 250
BIC Leisure Products 42; 528
Bicon, Inc. v. The Straumann Co.. 397
Billups-Rothenberg, Inc. v. Associated Reg'l & Univ.
    Pathologists, Inc.. 119
Bilski v. Kappos 298; 307; 314
Bio-Technology Gen. Corp. v. Genentech, Inc. . 452;
                                           454
Biotec Biologische Naturverpackungen GmbH & Co.
    KG v. Biocorp, Inc.. 362
Biotechnology Indus. Org. v. District of
    Columbia. 13
Blonder-Tongue Lab. v. University of Illinois
    Found.. 471
BMC Resources, Inc. v. Paymentech, L.P.. .363, 364
Bogese, In re. 20; 511
Bonito Boats, Inc. v. Thunder Craft Boats, Inc. . 484
Borst, In re. 169
Boston Scientific v. Johnson & Johnson 118
Boyden Power-Brake Co. v. Westinghouse. . . .384
Brana, In re. 284; 289
Bremner, In re 284; 287
Brenner v. Manson . . . 13; 283; 286; 288; 294; 484
Bristol-Myers Squibb Co. v. Ben Venue Laboratories,
    Inc. 153
Brooktree Corp. v. Advanced Micro Devices,
    Inc.. 285
Brown v. Barbacid 196; 249, 250
Brown v. Duchesne 440
Brown v. 3M. 335
Bruckelmyer v. Ground Heaters, Inc. 186; 190
Brulotte v. Thys Co. 478, 479
Burlington Industries, Inc. v. Dayco Corp. 464
Burroughs Wellcome Co. v. Barr Laboratories,
    Inc. 196; 228; 230; 240; 241; 243
Business Electronics Corp. v. Sharp Electronics
    Corp.. 487
Butterworth v. U.S.. 259

C

C.R. Bard. 428
Cal. Motor Transp. Co. v. Trucking Unlimited . . 496
Cancer Research Tech. Ltd. v. Barr Laboratories,
    Inc. 517
Canon Inc. v. GCC Intern. Ltd.. 526
Canton Bio Med. v. Integrated Liner Tech., Inc. . 350

Capon v. Eshhar 110
Carbice Corp. of Am. v. Am. Patents Dev. Corp..474
Cardiac Pacemakers, Inc. v. St. Jude Medical,
    Inc.. 450
Cardizem CD Antitrust Litigation, In re. 494
Carella v. Starlight Archery and Pro Line Co.. . . 168
Cargill, Inc. v. Canbra Foods, Ltd. 197
Carl Schenck, A.G. v. Nortron Corp. 521
Carlson, In re 188; 211; 215
Catalina Marketing Int'l, Inc. v. Coolsavings.com,
    Inc.. . . . . .61; 161; 343, 344
Caterpillar Inc. v. Sturman Industries, Inc.. 230
CCS Fitness, Inc. v. Brunswick Corp.. 401
Centillion Data Systems LLC v. Qwest
    Communications International, Inc.. 359
Central Admixture Pharmacy Services, Inc. v.
    Advanced Cardiac Solutions, P.C.. 44
Checkpoint Sys., Inc. v. All-Tag Sec. S.A.. 232
Checkpoint Sys., Inc. v. U.S. Int'l Trade
    Comm'n. 253
Chef Am., Inc. v. Lamb-Weston, Inc.. 336
Chemcast Corp. v. Arco Indust. Corp.. 135–137
Chesterfield v. U.S.. 415
Chicago Bd. of Trade v. United States 486
Chimie v. PPG Industries, Inc. 392
Chiuminatta Concrete Concepts, Inc. v. Cardinal
    Indus., Inc.. . . . . .405; 407; 410
Christiana Indus. v. Empire Elecs., Inc.. 526
Christianson v. Colt Indus. Operating Corp.. . 78, 79
City of (see name of city). . . . .
Classen Immunotherapies, Inc. v. King Pharms.,
    Inc.. 348
Clay, In re 277
Clement, In re 40
Cole v. Kimberly-Clark Corp.. 402
Coleman v. Dines 241
Comark Communs. v. Harris Corp.. 339
Comiskey, In re 313
Connell v. Sears, Roebuck & Co.. 521
Constant v. Advanced Micro-Devices, Inc.. .78; 184;
                                           339
Cont'l Paper Bag Co. v. Eastern Paper Bag Co..476;
                                           520
Continental Can Co. U.S.A, Inc. v. Monsanto
    Co.. 159
Cooper v. Goldfarb. 244; 247
Cooper Cameron Corp. v. Kvaerner Oilfield Products,
    Inc.. . . . . .115; 117
Cornell University v. Hewlett-Packard Co.. . . .538
Corp. v. Salomon S.A.. . . . . .387; 394

Cortright, In re .286
Cottier v. Stimson 181
Courson v. O'Connor 251
Creative Compounds, LLC v. Starmark Labs. . . . 82
Creo Products, Inc. v. Presstek, Inc.. 362
Crish, In re. .65
Critikon, Inc. v. Becton Dickinson Vascular Access.,
   Inc.. . . . . .464, 465
Crocs, Inc. v. ITC. 72, 73
Cronyn, In re .185
Cross Med. Prods., Inc. v. Medtronic Sofamor Danek,
   Inc.. . . . . .350; 354; 358
Crystal Semiconductor Corp. v. TriTech
   Microelectronics Int'l, Inc.. . . .61; 193; 199; 530;
                 542
CSIRO v. Buffalo Technology, Inc. 523, 524
Cuno Engineering Corp. v. Automatic Devices
   Corp.. 262
Curtis v. Loether. 323
CVI/Beta Ventures, Inc. v. Tura LP 345
Cybersource Corp. v. Retail Decisions, Inc.. . . .302;
               316, 317
Cybor Corp. v. FAS Techs.. . . . .325, 326; 349; 354

D

D.M.I., Inc. v. Deere & Co.. 342
Dabney v. Burrell 84
Data General Corp. v. Grumman Systems Support
   Corp.. 490
Datamize, LLC v. Plumtree Software, Inc. . 126; 128
Davis Harvester Co., Inc. v. Long Mfg. Co. . . . 205
Davis, In re 61
Dawn Equipment Co. v. Kentucky Farms Inc.. . .381;
               406
Dawson Chem. Co. v. Rohm & Haas Co. . 474, 475;
               488
De Forest Radio Tel. & Tel. Co. v. U.S. 502
Decca Ltd. v. U.S.. 442
Deepsouth Packing Co. v. Laitram Corp. . . . 445, 446
DeGeorge v. Bernier. 135
Deuel, In re. 269
Devices for Medicine, Inc. v. Boehl. 540
Di Leone, In re. 121
Diamond v. Chakrabarty . 65; 73; 294; 299; 301–303
Diamond v. Diehr. 307; 310; 316
Digital Control Inc. v. The Charles Machine
   Works 466; 468
Digital Equip. Corp. v. Diamond 463
Dippin' Dots Patent Litigation, In re 328
Donohue, In re 155; 181

Dow Chem. Co. v. Astro-Valcour, Inc.. 242
Dow Jones & Co., Inc. v. Ablaise Ltd.. 282
Dowagiac Mfg. Co. v. Minnesota Moline Plow
   Co.. . . . . .440, 441
DSU Medical Corp. v. JMS Co., Ltd.. 437
Dundas v. Hitchcock 259, 260
Dynacore Holdings Corp. v. U.S. Philips Corp. . 350;
               430
DyStar Textilfarben GmbH & Co. Deutschland KG v.
   C.H. Patrick Co. 267

E

E.E.O.C v. Arabian Am. Oil Co. 440
E.I. du Pont de Nemours & Co.; U.S. v. . . 477; 484
E. Rotorcraft Corp. v. U.S. 245
Earle v. Sawyer. 259
Eastern Railroad Presidents Conference v. Noerr
   Motor Freight, Inc.. 496
Eastman Kodak Co. v. Image Technical Servs.,
   Inc. 477; 484–486; 490
Eaton v. Evans 244
Ecolab, Inc. v. FMC Corp.. 282
Egbert v. Lippmann. 169, 170
Egyptian Goddess, Inc. v. Swisa, Inc. 72
Ehrreich, In re 68
Eibel Process Co. v. Minnesota & Ontario Paper
   Co.. 159
Ekenstam, In re. 188
Elan Corp., PLC v. Andrx Pharms., Inc. 200
Elan Pharmaceuticals, Inc. v. Mayo Foundation for
   Medical Educ. and Research 155
Eldred v. Ashcroft. 13; 91
Electro-Dynamic Co. v. U.S. Light & Heat
   Corp.. 287
Eli Lilly & Co. v. Medtronic, Inc.. . . . . .418, 419
Eli Lilly and Co. v. American Cyanamid Co. . . 452,
               453
Eli Lilly and Co. v. Aradigm Corp.. 230
Eli Lilly and Co. v. Zenith Goldline Pharmaceuticals,
   Inc. 169
Elizabeth, City of v. American Nicholson Pavement
   Co.. . . . . .174; 191
Embrex, Inc. v. Service Engineering Corp.. . . .416
EMI Group North America, Inc. v. Cypress
   Semiconductor Corp.. 153
Engel Industries, Inc. v. The Lockformer Co.. . .381
Environmental Designs, Ltd. v. Union Oil Co.. . .65
Enzo Biochem v. Gen-Probe Inc. . 110; 112, 113; 120
Eolas Techs., Inc. v. Microsoft Corp. 448
Epstein, In re 171

Estee Lauder Inc. v. L'Oreal, S.A.. 246
Ethicon, Inc. v. U.S. Surgical Corp.. 230
Etter, In re. 47
Evans v. Eaton. 109; 111; 124; 147
Exxon Research and Eng'g Co. v. U.S.. . . .124, 125;
128, 129
EZ Dock, Inc. v. Schafer Systems, Inc.. 197

F

Fantasy Sports Props., Inc. v. SportsLine.com,
Inc.. 355
Fed. Trade Comm'n v. Indiana Fed'n of
Dentists .483
Fellowes, Inc. v. Michilin Prosperity Co., Ltd.. . .362
Ferring B.V. v. Barr Laboratories, Inc.. 465
Festo Corp. v. Shoketsu Kinzoku Kogyo Kabushiki
Co., Ltd.. . . . .91; 123; 319; 321; 351; 372; 379;
388–390; 393; 393; 484
Fieldturf Int'l, Inc. v. Sprinturf, Inc.. 360
Fiers v. Revel. 241; 248
Fina Oil and Chemical Co. v. Ewen. 229
Finnigan Corp. v. Int'l Trade Comm'n 177
First Years, Inc. v. Munchkin, Inc. 348
Fisher, In re 105; 284; 286; 289–291
FMC Corp. v. Up-Right, Inc.. 508
Fonar Corp. v. General Elec Co. 139
Forest Labs., Inc. v. Ivax Pharms., Inc.. 40
Fortner Enterprises, Inc. v. United States Steel
Corp.. . . . . .477; 484
Foster, In re. 275
Fout, In re. .67
Franchise Tax Board v. Construction Laborers
Vacation Trust 78
Free Motion Fitness, Inc. v. Cybex Int'l, Inc.. . .320
Freeman, In re 312
Fromson v. Advance Offset Plate, Inc.. 94
Fujifilm Corp. v. Benun 505
Fujikawa v. Wattanasin 118; 194; 252–255
Fujitsu Ltd. v. Netgear Inc.. 426
Funai Elec. Co., Ltd. v. Daewoo Elecs. Corp. . . .540
Funk Bros. Seed Co. v. Kalo Inoculant Co.. . . .299

G

Gambro Lundia AB v. Baxter Healthcare Corp. . 232
Gay, In re. .133
Gayler v. Wilder. 166
Gemstar-TV Guide Int'l, Inc. v. Int'l Trade
Comm'n. 338
Genentech, Inc. v. Chiron Corp.. 247
Genentech, Inc. v. Novo Nordisk A/S 94

Genentech, Inc., In re. 83
General Elec. Co. v. U. S.. . . . . .191, 192
General Electric Co. v. De Forest Radio Co.. . . .299
General Motors Corp. v. Devex Corp.. . . .526; 542
Gentry Gallery, Inc. v. Berkline Corp.. 114
Georgia--Pacific Corp. v. U. S. Plywood--Champion
Papers, Inc.. 533
Gibbs, In re 203, 204; 206
Gillette Co. v. Energizer Holdings, Inc.. 67
Glass, In re 103
Glaxo Inc. v. Novopharm Ltd.. . . . . . . .134; 136
Glaxo Wellcome, Inc. v. Impax Laboratories,
Inc.. 111
Global-Tech Appliances, Inc. v. SEB S.A.. .433–436
Golight, Inc. v. Wal-Mart Stores, Inc.. 361
Gosteli, In re. 140
Gottschalk v. Benson. 63; 308; 310
Graham v. John Deere Co.. . . .6, 7; 10, 11; 84; 257;
263, 264; 484
Grain Processing Corp. v. American Maize-Products
Co.. 529
Grams, In re 316
Granfinanciera, S.A. v. Nordberg 324
Grant v. Raymond. 37; 489
Graver Tank & Mfg. Co. v. Linde Air Prods.
Co.. . . .351; 372; 375, 376; 380; 385; 388; 404
Gray v. James 373
Great Atlantic & Pacific Tea Co. v. Supermarket
Equipment Corp.. 281
Great Northern Corp. v. Henry Molded Products,
Inc. 139
Greenberg v. Ethicon Endo-Surgery, Inc.. 401
Griffith v. Kanamaru. 251
Grip-Pak, Inc. v. Ill. Tool Works, Inc.. 495
Group One, Ltd. v. Hallmark Cards, Inc.. 198
Gulliksen v. Halberg. 182

H

Hafner, In re 156
Hall, In re. .185
Halliburton Energy Services, Inc. v. M-1 LLC. .126
Halliburton Oil Well Cementing Co. v. Walker . 378;
400
Handel, In re. 39
Handgards, Inc. v. Ethicon, Inc.. . . . . . .495; 497
Hanson v. Alpine Valley Ski Area, Inc.. 532
Harries v. Air King Products Co.. 263
Harris Corp. v. Ericsson Inc.. . . . . .359, 360; 434
Hazel-Atlas Glass Co. v. Hartford-Empire Co.. . .461
Hazeltine Research, Inc. v. Brenner . 218; 220; 274

Heard v. Burton 242
Hedgewick v. Akers 232
Henderson, In re 269
Henry v. A.B. Dick Co.. . . . . .472, 473; 484
Hess v. Advanced Cardiovascular Sys., Inc. . . . 229
Hester Indus. v. Stein, Inc. 38
Hewlett-Packard Co. v. Bausch & Lomb, Inc.. . .63;
354; 434
High Tech Medical Instrumentation v. New Image
Industries, Inc. 356
Hilgraeve Corp. v. Symantec Corp. 355
Hilmer, In re 222, 223; 544
Hilton Davis Chem. Co. v. Warner-Jenkinson
Co. 58; 350
Hiniker Co., In re 57; 349
Hitzeman v. Rutter 241, 242; 249
Hobbs v. U.S., Atomic Energy Comm'n 194
Hogan, In re 103
Holmes Group, Inc. v. Vornado Air Circulation
Sys.. . . . . .78; 86
Honeywell Int'l v. U.S. 505
Hotchkiss v. Greenwood 7; 259
Hubbard v. Beatty & Hyde, Inc.. 497
Hughes Aircraft Co. v. U.S. 380
Husky Injection Molding Systems Ltd. v. R & D Tool
Engineering Co.. . . . . .509, 510
Hyatt v. Boone 22; 196; 244
Hyatt, In re 321
Hybritech Inc. v. Monoclonal Antibodies, Inc. . . 94;
196; 228; 244; 247
Hydranautics v. Filmtec Corp.. 499

I

i4i Ltd. P'ship v. Microsoft Corp.. 541
I.C.E. Corp. v. Armco Steel Corp.. . . . . .181, 182
Ill. Tool Works Inc. v. Indep. Ink, Inc.. . . .477; 484;
487; 489
Image Technical Services, Inc. v. Eastman Kodak
Co.. 490
In re (see name of party) . . . .
Incandescent Lamp Patent. 96
Independent Service Organizations Antitrust
Litigation, In re 485; 491
Individual Drinking Cup Co. v. Errett. 434
Innogenetics, N.V. v. Abbott Labs. 525
Instituform Technologies, Inc. v. CAT Contracting,
Inc. 392
Integrated Circuit Systems, Inc. v. Realtek
Semiconductor Co. 328
Intel Corp. v. U.S. Int'l Trade Comm'n. . .349; 354;
355

Intellectual Property Development, Inc. v. TCI
Cablevision of California, Inc.. 520
International Salt Co. v. United States 487
International Shoe Co. v. Washington 82
Invitrogen Corp. v. Biocrest Mfg., L.P. . . . 169; 204
Invitrogen Corp. v. Clontech Labs., Inc. 240
IPXL Holdings, L.L.C. v. Amazon.com, Inc.. . . .188
Israel Bio-Engineering Project v. Amgen, Inc. . . . 230

J

J.E.M. AG Supply Inc. v. Pioneer Hi-Bred Int'l,
Inc.. . . . . .74, 75
Janssen Pharmaceutica N.V. v. Teva
Pharmaceuticals 105, 106
Jazz Photo Corp. v. Int'l Trade Comm'n . . 501; 507
Jefferson County, Ala. v. Acker. 80
Jefferson Parish Hosp. Dist. No. 2 v. Hyde.485, 486;
488
Jim Arnold Corp. v. Hydrotech Sys., Inc. . . . 79, 80
Jockmus v. Leviton. 184
John Mezzalingua Assocs. v. ITC. 86
Johnson & Johnston Assocs.. 395
Johnson Worldwide Associates, Inc. v. Zebco
Corp.. .115; 344
Johnston v. IVAC Corp. 322
Jolly, In re 127
Joy Techs., Inc. v. Flakt, Inc. . . 348; 350; 357; 434;
437; 450
Juicy Whip, Inc. v. Orange Bang, Inc. 177; 284;
293; 536
Jungersen v. Ostby & Barton Co.. 262
JVW Enterprises, Inc. v. Interact Accessories,
Inc.. 66

K

K-TEC, Inc. v. Vita-Mix Corp. 348
Kathawala, In re. 209; 213, 214
Kaufman Co., Inc. v. Lantech, Inc.. 43
Kaz Mfg. Co. v. Chesebrough-Ponds, Inc. 415
Keeler v. Standard Folding Bed Co.. 502
Kemco Sales v. Control Papers Co. 405; 408
Kewanee Oil Co. v. Bicron Corp. . . 13, 14; 91; 212
Kimberly-Clark Corp. v. Johnson & Johnson
Co.. 274
Kimberly-Clark Worldwide, Inc. v. First Quality Baby
Products, LLC. 526
King Instrument Corp. v. Otari Corp.. 245
King Instruments Corp. v. Perego 13
Kingsdown Medical Consultants, Ltd. v. Hollister,
Inc.. . . . . .463, 464; 512

Kinik Co. v. ITC 457, 458

Kinzenbaw v. Deere & Co. 372

Kirk, In re. 105; 289

Klein, In re. 278

Klesper, In re. 220

Klopfenstein, In re 184; 186

Knapp v. Morss 153

Knorr v. Pearson. 243

Knorr-Bremse Systeme Fuer Nutzfahrzeuge GmbH v.
    Dana Corp. 541

Kollar, In re. 199; 356

Kothmann Enters., Inc. v. Trinity Indus., Inc.. . .517

Kridl v. McCormick 243

Kropa, In re 344

KSR Intern. Co. v. Teleflex Inc. . . 17; 65; 269; 270;
    282

Kubin, In re. 269; 272

L

L.A. Gear, Inc. v. Thom McAn Shoe Co. . . . 70; 72

Laboratory Corp. of America Holdings v. Metabolite
    Laboratories, Inc. 302–304

LaBounty Mfg. v. United States ITC 175; 464

Lacavera v. Dudas. 20

Laitram Corp. v. Cambridge Wire Cloth Co. . . .358

Laitram Corp. v. NEC Corp.. 349

Laitram Corp. v. Rexnord, Inc. 129

Lamb-Weston, Inc. v. McCain Foods, Ltd. . . . 227

Larson Mfg. Co. of South Dakota, Inc. v. Aluminart
    Products Ltd. 464

Le Roy v. Tatham. 298, 299

Lear, Inc. v. Adkins 77; 471

Leeds v. Comm'r of Patents and Trademarks. . .124

Leeds & Catlin Co. v. Victor Talking Machine
    Co.. .508

Leegin Creative Leather Products, Inc. v. PSKS,
    Inc.. . . . . .486, 487

Leitch Mfg. Co. v. Barber Co.. 474

Liberty Lake Investments, Inc. v. Magnuson . . . 499

Liebel-Flarsheim Co. v. Medrad, Inc. 99; 155

Linde Air Prods. Co. v. Graver Tank & Mfg.
    Co.. .375

Linear Technology Corp. v. Micrel, Inc. 198

Liquid Dynamics Corp. v. Vaughan Co., Inc. . . . 93

Lister, In re. 188; 190

Litecubes, LLC v. Northern Lights Products Inc..444

LizardTech, Inc. v. Earth Res. Mapping, Inc. . . 92; ;
    113; 121

Lockwood v. American Airlines, Inc.. 171

Loew's Drive-In Theatres, Inc. 312

Loew's, Inc.; U.S. v. 485; 487, 488

London v. Carson Pirie Scott & Co. 389

Loral Fairchild Corp. v. Sony Elecs. Corp.. . . .358

Lough v. Brunswick Corp.. 174

Lowell v. Lewis. 94; 284; 286; 292

Lucent Techs., Inc. v. Gateway, Inc.. .532, 533; 535;
    537, 538

Lund, In re. 225

Lutzker v. Plet 252, 253

M

Macbeth-Evans Glass Co. v. Gen. Elec. Co. . . . 205

Mackay Radio & Telegraph Co. v. Radio Corp. . 308

Madey v. Duke University. 417; 418

Mahurkar v. C.R. Bard, Inc. 246; 248

Mallinckrodt, Inc. v. Medipart, Inc. 505

Manson, In re. 288

Marconi Wireless Telegraph Co. of America v. United
    States 365

Markman v. Westview Instruments, Inc..58, 59; 319;
    322–324; 332; 345

Marvin Glass & Assoc. v. Sears, Roebuck &
    Co.. .206

Mas-Hamilton Group v. LaGard, Inc. 197; 199

Mason v. Hepburn 238

Mattor v. Coolegem 230

Maxwell v. J. Baker, Inc.. . . . . .403; 540

Maxwell v. K Mart Corp. 233

Mayo Collaborative Servs. v. Prometheus Labs.,
    Inc.. . . . . .299; 304

Mazer v. Stein. 15

McGill Inc. v. John Zink Co. 322, 323

McGinley v. Franklin Sports, Inc.. 267

McKesson Information Solutions, Inc. v. Bridge
    Medical, Inc. 464

MedImmune, Inc. v. Genentech, Inc.. . . . .46; 49; 82

Medtronic, Inc. v. Cardiac Pacemakers, Inc. . . . 282

Medtronic Vascular, Inc. v. Boston Sci. Corp. . . . 362

MEMC Elec. Materials, Inc. v. Mitsubishi Materials
    Silicon Corp.. . . . . .360; 437; 443

Mentor Corp. v. Coloplast, Inc.. 40

MercExchange, L.L.C. v. eBay, Inc.. . .521; 522; 526

Merck & Co., Inc. v. Hi-Tech Pharmacal Co.,
    Inc. 513

Merck & Co., Inc. v. Kessler. 20

Merck KGaA v. Integra Lifesciences I, Ltd. . . . 419

Mercoid Corp. v. Mid-Continent Investment
    Co.. . . . . .474, 475

Mercoid Corp. v. Minneapolis-Honeywell Regulator Co.. 474
Metallizing Engineering Co. v. Kenyon Bearing & Auto Parts Co. 172
Metro-Goldwyn-Mayer Studios Inc. v. Grokster, Ltd.. . . . . .427; 437
Meyer, In re 129
Michlin, In re 63
Microsoft Corp. v. AT&T 449
Microsoft Corp. v. i4i Ltd. P'ship. 145
Miller Insituform, Inc. v. Insituform of North America, Inc. 491
Minco, Inc. v. Combustion Engineering, Inc. . . . 533, 534
Minn. Mining & Mfg. Co. v. Chemque, Inc.. . . .168; 433
Minton v. NASD. 200
MIT v. AB Fortia. 184
Mitchell v. Hawley. 501
Moba, B.V. v. Diamond Automation, Inc.. 361
Moleculon Research Corp. v. CBS, Inc. . . 172; 199; 205; 437
Molins PLC v. Textron, Inc.. 470
Monaco v. Hoffman 545
Monks, In re 188; 210; 214
Monsanto Co. v. Bayer Bioscience N.V.. . .463, 464
Monsanto Co. v. Bowman. 507
Monsanto Co. v. Ralph. 533
Monsanto Co. v. Syngenta Seeds, Inc. 285
Morris, In re 321
Morton Int'l., Inc. v. Cardinal Chem. Co.. 124
Morton Salt Co. v. G.S. Suppiger Co.. 474
Mostafazadeh, In re. 40, 41
Motion, Ltd. . . . 357; 359, 360; 441, 442; 450; 452
Motion Picture Patents Co. v. Universal Film Mfg. Co.. . . . . .473; 486
Motionless Keyboard Co. v. Microsoft Corp.. . . .169
Mycogen Plant Science v. Monsanto Co. . . . 159; 228

N

Nachman Spring-Filled Corporation v. Spring Products Corporation 375
Nat'l Soc. of Prof'l Engineers v. United States. .487
National Automatic Device Co. v. Lloyd 292
National Recovery Technologies, Inc. v. Magnetic Separation Systems, Inc.. 94
Nazomi Commc'ns, Inc. v. Arm Holdings, PLC . 341
Nelson, In re 287
Netscape Commc'n Corp. v. Konrad 173
Neugebauer, In re 342

New Process Fermentation Co. v. Koch. 184
New Railhead Mfg., L.L.C. v. Vermeer Mfg. Co..22; 171
Newman v. Quigg 94; 285
Nickson Indus.. . . . . .532, 533
Nikon Corp. v. ASM Lithography B.V.. 328
Nobelpharma AB v. Implant Innovations, Inc. . . 499
Northern P. R. Co. v. United States 486
Northern Telecom Ltd. v. Samsung Electronics Co., Ltd. 134
Norton v. Curtiss 460; 463
Nuance Communications, Inc. v. Abbyy Software House 82; 362
Nuijten, In re 313

O

O'Farrell, In re 269; 273
O'Reilly v. Morse 95; 229
Oakley, Inc. v. Sunglass Hut Int'l . . . 123; 125; 130
OddzOn Products, Inc. v. Just Toys, Inc. . . . 203; 274
Odetics, Inc. v. Storage Tech. Corp.. . . . .405, 406
Odiorne v. Winkley 373
Oetiker, In re 276
Omeprazole Patent Litigation, In re 160
Ortho-McNeil Pharm., Inc. v. Caraco Pharm. Labs., Ltd.. . . . . .331; 344
Ortho Pharmaceutical Corp. v. Genetics Institute, Inc. 520
Orthopedic Equipment Co., Inc. v. U.S.. 267

P

Palumbo v. Don-Joy Co.. 322
Pandora Jewelry, LLC v. Chamilia, LLC 349
Panduit Corp. v. Dennison Mfg. Co. 273
Panduit Corp. v. Stahlin Bros. Fibre Works, Inc..527
Pannu v. Iolab Corp.. 230
Paper Converting Mach. Co. v. Magna-Graphics Corp.. . . . . .353; 355
Parke-Davis & Co. v. H.K. Mulford Co.. 300
Parker v. Flook. 309
Patlex Corp. v. Mossinghoff. 17
Paulik v. Rizkalla. 238; 254
Paulsen, In re. 277
PB Farradyne, Inc. v. Peterson 367
Peeler v. Miller. 253
Pellegrini v. Analog Devices, Inc.. 448
Pennock v. Dialogue 148; 204
Pentec, Inc. v. Graphic Controls Corp.. . . . 67; 279
Permutit Co. v. Graver Corp. 128

Perricone v. Medicis Pharmaceutical Corp.. . . .161
Perrigo, In re 284, 285
Personalized Media Commc'n, LLC v. Int'l Trade
    Com'n 66
Peters v. Active Mfg. Co. 153
Pfaff v. Wells Elecs. 191; 194; 197
Pfizer Inc. v. Dr. Reddy's Labs., Ltd. 419
Pharmacia Corp. v. Par Pharm., Inc. 470
PHG Techs., LLC v. St. John Cos. 72
Philips Electronic & Pharmaceutical Industries Corp.
    v. Thermal & Electronics Industries 182
Phillips v. AWH Corp.. . .59; 91; 110; 320–322; 325;
                327; 332–336; 338, 339; 341; 345
Picard v. United Aircraft Corp. 262
Pilkington, In re 63
Pitney Bowes, Inc. v. Hewlett-Packard Co.. .61; 343
Poppenhusen v. Falke 416; 421
Prasco, LLC v. Medicis Pharmaceutical Corp.. . .81
Prater, In re 129
Precision Instrument Mfg. v. Automotive Maintenance
    Machinery Co. 462
Prestige Pet Products, Inc. v. Pingyang Huaxing
    Leather & Plastic Co.. 349
Prima Tek II, L.L.C. v. Polypap, S.A.R.L. 157
Princo Corp. v. ITC 478; 480
Process Control Corp. v. HydReclaim Corp.. . .106;
                                284, 285
Prof'l Real Estate Investors, Inc. v. Columbia Pictures,
    Inc.. . . . . 496; 497; 499
Prometheus Labs., Inc. v. Mayo Collaborative Servs.
    & Mayo Clinic Rochester 304
PSC Computer Prods., Inc. v. Foxconn Int'l,
    Inc. 396
Purdue Pharma L.P. v. Endo Pharms., Inc. 463

Q

Quanta Computer, Inc. v. LG Elecs., Inc.. . .503, 504
Quantum Corp. v. Rodime, PLC 48
Quantum Patent Mechanics 383

R

Radio Corp. of America v. Andrea 446
Railroad Dynamics, Inc. v. A. Stucki Co.. 323
Randomex, Inc. v. Scopus Corp.. . . . . . .137, 138
Rasmusson v. SmithKline Beecham Corp. . 156; 181
Raytheon Co. v. Roper Corp. 285
RCA Corp. v. Applied Digital Data Systems,
    Inc.. . . . . .153; 156
Read Corp. v. Portec, Inc. 541

Reading & Bates Constr. Co. v. Baker Energy Res.
    Corp. 68
Reazin v. Blue Cross and Blue Shield of Kansas,
    Inc. 484
Reckendorfer v. Faber 261
Recombinant DNA Tech. Patent & Contract Litig., In
    re. 477; 486
Reed v. Tornqvist. 251
Regents of University of Cal. v. Dako North America,
    Inc. 326
Regents of University of California v. Howmedica,
    Inc. 184
Reliance Novelty Co. v. Dworzek. 292
ResQNet.com, Inc. v. Lansa, Inc. 532
Revolution Eyewear, Inc. v. Aspex Eyewear, Inc.. . 82
Rexnord Corp. v. Laitram Corp.. 344
Rhine v. Casio, Inc. 341
Richardson v. Suzuki Motor Co., Ltd.. 521
Rickard v. Du Bon. 293
Ricoh Co., Ltd. v. Quanta Computer Inc.. 429
Rines v. Morgan 251
Rite-Hite Corp. v. Kelley Co., Inc. . . 520, 521; 527,
                            528; 533; 536
Robert Bosch LLC v. Pylon Manufacturing
    Corp.. . . . . .523, 524
Robertson, In re 157
Robotic Vision Systems, Inc. v. View Engineering,
    Inc.. . . . . .139; 196
Roche Products, Inc. v. Bolar Pharmaceutical Co.,
    Inc. 415, 416; 421
Rohm & Haas Co. v. Crystal Chem. Co.. 14
Rosaire v. Baroid Sales Division, Nat. Lead Co.. 170
Rotec Industries, Inc. v. Mitsubishi Corp. . 360; 443;
                            447; 548
Rowe v. Dror. 61; 343
Rubber Co. v. Goodyear. 461
Rude v. Westcott. 532
Ruschig, In re. 111; 112
Ruth v. Stearns-Roger Mfg. Co.. 415

S

Saab Cars U.S.A, Inc. v. U.S. 325
Sage Prods. v. Devon Indus.. . . . . . .66; 396; 402
Sakraida v. Ag Pro, Inc.. 281
SanDisk Corp. v. STMicroelectronics, Inc.. 82
Sanofi-Synthelabo v. Apotex Inc.. 524
Sawin v. Guild. 414
Scaltech Inc. v. Retec/Tetra, L.L.C.. . . . . 194; 199
Schaper Mfg. Co. v. U.S. Int'l Trade Comm'n. .455

[References are to pages]

Scheiber v. Dolby Labs., Inc. 477; 479

Schering Corp. v. Amgen Inc.. 31

Schering Corp. v. Geneva Pharmaceuticals . 156, 157; 160

Schering-Plough Corp. v. Fed. Trade Comm'n. .471; 484

Schiebel Toy & Novelty Co. v. Clark. 375

Schreiber, In re. 160

Schriber-Schroth Co. v. Cleveland Trust Co.. . .111; 113

SciMed Life Sys. Inc. v. Advanced Cardiovascular Systems Inc.. . . . . .340, 341

SCM Corp. v. Xerox Corp. 491

Scott v. Finney. 245

Scott v. Koyama. 247; 250, 251

Scott & Williams v. Aristo Hosiery Co.. 293

Scott Paper Co. v. Marcalus Mfg. Co.. 2

Scripps Clinic & Research Foundation v. Genentech, Inc.. 64; 385

Seagate Technology, LLC, In re 526; 541, 542

Sears, Roebuck & Co. v. Stiffel Co.. . . . . . 11; 13

Seattle Box Co., Inc. v. Industrial Crating and Supply 41–43

Senmed, Inc. v. Richard-Allan Medical Industries, Inc.. 323

Serenkin, In re. 39

Shatterproof Glass Corp. v. Libbey-Owens Ford Co.. . . . . .194; 229

Shepard v. Carrigan 388

Shipp v. Scott Sch. Twp.. 206

Shockley v. Arcan, Inc.. 42

Shurie v. Richmond 545

Silvestri v. Grant. 243

Singh v. Brake 243

Sirf Technology, Inc. v. ITC 317

Sitrick v. Dreamworks, LLC 98

Sjolund v. Musland. 338

Slimfold Mfg. Co. v. Kinkead Indus., Inc.. . . . 416

Smith v. Goodyear Dental Vulcanite Co. . . 261; 278

Smith, In re. 169; 172; 175

SmithKline Beecham Corp. v. Apotex Corp.. .64; 85

Sofamor Danek Group, Inc. v. DePuy-Motech, Inc.. 327

Solomon v. Kimberly Clark 130

Sonoscan, Inc. v. Sonotek, Inc. 194

Sony Corp. of America v. Universal City Studios, Inc.. 425

Sony Elecs., Inc. v. Guardian Media Technologies, Ltd.. . . . . .81, 82

South Corp. v. United States 85

Southwall Techs., Inc. v. Cardinal IG Co.. 319

Space Systems/Loral, Inc. v. Lockheed Martin Corp.. .197

Spectra-Physics, Inc. v. Coherent, Inc.. . . . .103; 135

Spectralytics, Inc. v. Cordis Corp.. . . . . . .541, 542

SRAM Corp. v. AD-II Engineering, Inc.. 325

SRI Int'l v. Matsushita Elec. Corp. of America . 322; 329

SSIH Equipment S.A. v. U.S. Intern. Trade Com'n. 217; 322

Standard Measuring Mach. Co. v. Teague. 415

Star Scientific, Inc. v. R.J. Reynolds Tobacco Co.. 280

Stark v. Advanced Magnetics, Inc. 235

State Indus., Inc. v. A.O. Smith Corp. 14

State Industries, Inc. v. Mor-Flo Industries, Inc.. .527; 530

State St. Bank & Trust Co. v. Signature Fin. Group 312; 366

State Street Bank and Trust Co. v. Signature Financial Group, Inc.. 312

Static Control Components, Inc. v. Lexmark Intern., Inc.. 505

Stearns-Roger Mfg. Co. v. Ruth. 415

Stencel, In re. 61

Stephens v. Tech Int'l., Inc. 348

Stern v. Trustees of Columbia University 241

Stevens v. Tamai. 19

Studiengesellschaft Kohle, m.b.H; United States v.. .361; 489

Sullivan, In re 279

Superior Fireplace Co. v. The Majestic Products Co.. . . . . .37, 38; 44, 45

Surfco Hawaii v. Fin Control Systems Pty, Ltd. . 510

Swartz, In re 284, 285

Symbol Techs., Inc. v. Lemelson Med., Educ. & Research Found., LP 515–517

Syngenta Seeds, Inc. v. Delta Cotton Co-operative, Inc.. 74

Sys., Inc. v. Aarotech Labs., Inc. 360

T

Talbott, In re. 189; 211, 212; 215

Tamoxifen Citrate Antitrust Litigation, In re . . . 494

Tanaka, In re. 39

Taskett v. Dentlinger. 245

Tate Access Floors, Inc. v. Interface Architectural Res., Inc.. 385

Telcordia Techs., Inc. v. Cisco Sys.. 525

Telephone Cases. 97

Tenney, In re. 182

[References are to pages]

Texaco Inc. v. Dagher 486, 487

Textile Prods. v. Mead Corp. 81

Therasense, Inc. v. Becton, Dickinson and Co. . . 54; 463; 465–467

Thomson v. Weston 238

Thomson-Houston Electric Co. v. Ohio Brass Co.. . . . . .423; 434

Thomson S.A. v. Quixote Corp.. . . . . . . .221; 240

Thorpe, In re. 64

Tilghman v. Proctor 158

Timely Prod. Corp. v. Arron. 194

Titan Tire Corp. v. Case New Holland, Inc. . . . 526

Topliff v. Topliff. 37

The Toro Co. v. White Consol. Indus., Inc.. . . .396

Torspo Hockey Intern., Inc. v. Kor Hockey Ltd. . 526

TP Laboratories, Inc. v. Professional Positioners, Inc. 175

Transclean Corp. v. Bridgewood Servs., Inc. . . .157

Transco Products Inc. v. Performance Contracting, Inc. 137

Transocean Offshore Deepwater Drilling, Inc. v. Maersk Contractors U.S.A, Inc. 361; 444

Trell v. Marlee Electronics Corp. 427

Trintec Indus., Inc. v. Pedre Promotional Prods., Inc.. 83

TS Tech U.S.A Corp., In re. 83

Turrill v. Mich. S. & N.I.R. Co.. 341

TWM Mfg. Co., Inc. v. Dura Corp.. 533

U

U. S. v. Line Material Co.. 489

U.S. v. (see name of defendant). . . . .

U.S. Philips Corp. v. Int'l Trade Comm'n. .472; 477

Ultra-Tex Surfaces, Inc. v. Hill Bros. Chemical Co.. 319

Underwater Devices Inc. v. Morrison-Knudsen Co.. 540

Uniloc U.S.A, Inc. v. Microsoft Corp. 536

United Carbon v. Binney & Smith Co. 123

United States v. (see name of defendant). . . . . . .

United States Gypsum Co. v. National Gypsum Co.. 135

Univ. of Rochester v. G.D. Searle & Co., Inc. . . 91; 109; 112; 113; 248

University of California v. Eli Lilly & Co.. . . .112

V

Va. Panel Corp. v. MAC Panel Co. 477; 489

Valley Drug Co. v. Geneva Pharmaceuticals, Inc.. 494

Valmont Indus., Inc. v. Reinke Mfg. Co.. 405

Vas-Cath v. Mahurkar 109; 116

Vita-Mix Corp. v. Basic Holding, Inc.. . . .429, 430

Vitronics Corp. v. Conceptronic, Inc. 322; 333

Voda v. Cordis Corp.. 381

Vogel, In re 58

W

W.L. Gore & Assoc., Inc. v. Garlock, Inc. . 124; 127; 171, 172; 380

Wahl Instruments, Inc. v. Acvious, Inc.. 139

Walker Process Equip, Inc. v. Food Mach. & Chem. Corp.. . . . . .483; 498

Wallace v. Holmes. 424

Walter, In re 312

Wands, In re 100, 101

Wang Lab. v. Mitsubishi Elecs. Am. 502

Warmerdam, In re. 91

Warner, In re 145

Warner-Jenkinson Co., Inc. v. Hilton Davis Chemical Co. . 349–351; 354; 371; 376–378; 380; 388; 396; 400; 405

Warner-Lambert Co. v. Apotex Corp.. 357

Warner-Lambert Co. v. Teva Pharmaceuticals U.S.A., Inc.. 94

Warrior Sports, Inc. v. Dickinson Wright, P.L.L.C.. . . . . .78, 79

Washburn v. Gould. 149

Waterman v. Mackenzie. 81

Waymark Corp. v. Porta Systems Corp.. 359

Webster Elec. Co. v. Splitdorf Elec. Co. 514

Weiler, In re. 38, 39

Weiss, In re 211, 212; 214

Wellman, Inc. v. Eastman Chemical Co. 137

Wertheim, In re 110; 140; 220

Western Marine Elec., Inc. v. Furuno Elec. Co., Ltd. 194

Westinghouse Elec. Corp.; U.S. v.. 491

Wheaton v. Peters. 10, 11

White v. Dunbar. 59

Whittemore v. Cutter. 204; 414

Wilder, In re. 38

Winans v. Denmead 373

Windsurfing Int'l, Inc. v. AMF, Inc.. 471

Winslow, In re 265, 266

WMS Gaming Inc. v. Int'l Game Tech.. 409

Woodbridge v. U.S. 514

Woodland Trust v. Flowertree Nursery, Inc.. . . . 167; 176, 177

[References are to pages]

Wordtech Systems, Inc v. Integrated Networks Solutions, Inc.. 424

Wyer, In re 181; 183; 190

Y

Yamamoto, In re 321

Yoder Bros., Inc. v. California-Florida Plant Corp. 73

Yoo Ja Kim v. ConAgra Foods, Inc. 41; 341

York Products, Inc. v. Central Tractor Farm & Family Center 402

Young Engineers, Inc. v. U.S. Int'l Trade Comm'n. 456

Z

Zenith Laboratories, Inc. v. Bristol-Myers Squibb Co.. 349

Zenith Radio Corp. v. Hazeltine Research, Inc.. .489

Zimmer Holdings, Inc., In re 83

Zletz, In re 125

INDEX

[References are to sections.]

A

ABANDONMENT AND PRE-AMERICA IN-VENTS ACT 35 U.S.C. SECTION 102(C)
Generally . . . 16.01; 16.06
Abandoned invention versus application . . . 16.04
Disclosed but unclaimed subject matter . . . 16.05
Historic background of abandonment . . . 16.02
Patentee delay . . . 16.03

ACTIVE INDUCEMENT
Generally . . . 34.01; 34.05
Conduct that induces infringement . . . 34.03
Direct infringement by another . . . 34.04
Intent to induce infringement . . . 34.02

ADJUDICATION OF PATENT DISPUTES WITHIN COURT SYSTEM
Generally . . . 6.01; 6.05
Declaratory judgment jurisdiction . . . 6.02[C]
District court actions
   Declaratory judgment jurisdiction . . . 6.02[C]
   Personal jurisdiction . . . 6.02[D]
   Standing to sue for infringement . . . 6.02[B]
   Subject matter jurisdiction . . . 6.02[A]
   Venue . . . 6.02[D]
Patent litigation in International Trade Commission . . . 6.04
Personal jurisdiction . . . 6.02[D]
Standing to sue for infringement . . . 6.02[B]
Subject matter jurisdiction . . . 6.02[A]
U.S. Court of Appeals for Federal Circuit
   Generally . . . 6.03[A]
   Jurisdiction of Federal Circuit . . . 6.03[B]
Venue . . . 6.02[D]

AIA (See AMERICA INVENTS ACT (AIA))

AMERICA INVENTS ACT (AIA)
Generally . . . 1.03[C]
Abandonment and pre-America Invents Act 35 U.S.C. Section 102(c) (See ABANDONMENT AND PRE-AMERICA INVENTS ACT 35 U.S.C. SECTION 102(c))
Derivation actions under . . . 19.04
Novelty and . . . 12.04
Pre-America Invents Act
   Abandonment and pre-America Invents Act 35 U.S.C. Section 102(c) (See ABANDON-MENT AND PRE-AMERICA INVENTS ACT 35 U.S.C. SECTION 102(c))
   Section 102, version of
      Historic underpinnings of pre-America Invents Act statute . . . 12.03[B]
      Structure of former version of Section 102 . . . 12.03[A]
Tax strategies . . . 12.07

ANTITRUST LAW
Generally . . . 38.01; 38.07

ANTITRUST LAW—Cont.
First Amendment and *Noerr-Pennington* immunity . . . 38.05[B]
Fraudulent procurement of patent . . . 38.06
Infringement litigation
   Anticompetitive patent infringement litigation: *Handgards, Inc. v. Ethicon, Inc.* . . . 38.05[A]
   First Amendment and *Noerr-Pennington* immunity . . . 38.05[B]
   Noerr-Pennington immunity
      First Amendment and . . . 38.05[B]
      Sham exception to . . . 38.05[C]
Noerr-Pennington immunity
   First Amendment and . . . 38.05[B]
   Sham exception to . . . 38.05[C]
Reverse payment . . . 38.04
Settlements payment . . . 38.04
Tying claims
   Generally . . . 38.02; 38.02[A]
   Evolving jurisprudence of patent tying cases . . . 38.02[B]
   Jurisprudence of patent tying cases, evolving . . . 38.02[B]
   Per se illegality . . . 38.02[A]
   Rule of reason . . . 38.02[A]
Unilateral refusals to license patent . . . 38.03
Walker Process claims . . . 38.06

APPARATUS CLAIMS
Generally . . . 4.04[B]

APPLICATIONS
Earlier filed patents and (See EARLIER FILED PATENTS AND APPLICATIONS)
Patent, for (See UNITED STATES PATENT AND TRADEMARK OFFICE (U.S. PTO), subhead: Applications for patent)

B

BEST MODE
Generally . . . 11.01; 11.05
Application of best mode standard
   Generally . . . 11.03
   Inventor's subjective intent . . . 11.03[A]
   Objective examination of patent disclosure . . . 11.03[B]
Standard
   Generally . . . 11.02
   Application of best mode standard (See subhead: Application of best mode standard)
Violation, impact of . . . 11.04

[References are to sections.]

C

CANONS OF CLAIM CONSTRUCTION (See INTERPRETATION OF CLAIMS, subhead: Canons of claim construction)

CLAIMS
Generally . . . 4.05
Anatomy of claim
    Generally . . . 4.03
    Body of claim . . . 4.03[C]
    Preamble . . . 4.03[A]
    Transition . . . 4.03[B]
Apparatus . . . 4.04[B]
Combination claims, nonobviousness and . . . 21.10
Composition . . . 4.04[E]
Dependent . . . 4.04[A]
Enablement and claim scope . . . 8.03
Historical background . . . 4.01
Interpretation of (See INTERPRETATION OF CLAIMS)
Jepson . . . 4.04[I]
Limitation . . . 4.02
Markush . . . 4.04[H]
Means-plus-function . . . 4.04[G]
Method claims
    Generally . . . 4.04[C]
    Section 271(f), and . . . 35.03[C][3]
Multiple dependent . . . 4.04[A]
Nonobviousness and combination claims . . . 21.10
Procedures for claim construction (See PROCEDURES FOR CLAIM CONSTRUCTION)
Process claims . . . 4.04[C]
Product-by-process . . . 4.04[D]
Types of claims
    Apparatus claims . . . 4.04[B]
    Combination claims . . . 4.04[F]
    Composition claims . . . 4.04[E]
    Dependent claims . . . 4.04[A]
    Independent claims . . . 4.04[A]
    Jepson claims . . . 4.04[I]
    Markush claims . . . 4.04[H]
    Means-plus-function claims . . . 4.04[G]
    Method claims . . . 4.04[C]
    Multiple dependent claims . . . 4.04[A]
    Process claims . . . 4.04[C]
    Product-by-process claims . . . 4.04[D]

COMBINATION CLAIMS
Generally . . . 4.04[F]

CONSTITUTIONAL LAW
First Amendment and *Noerr-Pennington* immunity . . . 38.05[B]

CONTRIBUTORY INFRINGEMENT
Generally . . . 33.01; 33.07
"A material part of the invention" . . . 33.03
Direct infringement . . . 33.06
Knowledge of use for infringement . . . 33.04
Policy issues relating to . . . 33.02
Substantial noninfringing uses . . . 33.05

COORDINATION OF PATENT APPLICATION FILING
Generally . . . 42.03

COURTS, ADJUDICATION OF PATENT DISPUTES IN (See ADJUDICATION OF PATENT DISPUTES WITHIN COURT SYSTEM)

D

DECLARATORY JUDGMENT JURISDICTION
District court . . . 6.02[C]

DEFINITENESS
Generally . . . 10.01; 10.04
Applicant regards . . . 10.03
Inventor's definition . . . 10.03
Particularly point out and distinctly claim
    Claim is definite, assessment . . . 10.02[C]
    Differing definiteness standards . . . 10.02[B]
    Indefinite claim be invalidated . . . 10.02[F]
    Indefiniteness and means plus function claims . . . 10.02[D]
    Issued patents, patent applications versus . . . 10.02[B]
    Means plus function claims, indefiniteness and . . . 10.02[D]
    Patent applications versus issued patents . . . 10.02[B]
    Remedy . . . 10.02[F]
    Rules, general . . . 10.02[A]
    Terms of degree . . . 10.02[E]

DEPENDENT CLAIMS
Generally . . . 4.04[A]

DERIVATION
Generally . . . 19.01; 19.06
America Invents Act, derivation actions under . . . 19.04
Application of Section 102(f)'s two-prong test . . . 19.03[B]
Legal standard for . . . 19.03[A]
Two-prong test, application of Section 102(f)'s . . . 19.03[B]

DESIGN PATENTS
Generally . . . 5.03

DIRECT INFRINGEMENT
Generally . . . 26.03[A]; 27.01; 27.05
Active inducement of direct infringement by another . . . 34.04
Acts that constitute infringement under Section 271(a)
    Generally . . . 27.03
    Imports into U.S. . . . 27.03[E]
    Makes . . . 27.03[A]
    Offers to sell . . . 27.03[C]
    Sells . . . 27.03[D]
    Uses . . . 27.03[B]
Contributory infringement . . . 33.06
Divided infringement . . . 27.04
Multiple infringers . . . 27.04

DIRECT INFRINGEMENT—Cont.
Types of claims and
    Generally . . . 27.02
        Apparatus claim . . . 27.02[A]
        Device claim . . . 27.02[A]
        Process and method claims . . . 27.02[B]
        Product claim . . . 27.02[A]

DISCLOSURE REQUIREMENTS OF SECTION 112
Generally . . . 7.01; 7.04
Adequacy assessment of . . . 7.03
History of . . . 7.02
Policy of . . . 7.02

DISTRICT COURTS (See ADJUDICATION OF PATENT DISPUTES WITHIN COURT SYSTEM)

DOCTRINE OF EQUIVALENTS
Infringement under (See INFRINGEMENT UNDER DOCTRINE OF EQUIVALENT)
Restrictions on (See RESTRICTIONS ON DOCTRINE OF EQUIVALENTS)

DUTY TO DISCLOSE, INEQUITABLE CONDUCT AND (See INEQUITABLE CONDUCT AND DUTY TO DISCLOSE)

E

EARLIER FILED PATENTS AND APPLICATIONS
Generally . . . 18.01; 18.05
Patent Cooperation Treaty, patent applications filed under . . . 18.03
Published patent applications . . . 18.04
U.S. patent applications
    In re Hilmer: prior U.S. patents and foreign filings . . . 18.02[B]
    Origins of U.S. patents as prior art . . . 18.02[A]

ENABLEMENT
Generally . . . 8.01; 8.08
Analysis of
    Generally . . . 8.02[A]
    Bell's telephone patent . . . 8.02[D]
    Edison's light bulb: *Consolidated Electric Light Co. v. McKeesport Light Co.* . . . 8.02[C]
    Historic perspective: *O'Reilly v. Morse* . . . 8.02[B]
Claim scope, and . . . 8.03
Economic considerations . . . 8.07
Modern foundation of undue experimentation: Wands factors . . . 8.04[A]
Priority and timing
    Generally . . . 8.05[B]
    Patent enforcement and enablement . . . 8.05[C]
    Relevant state of art . . . 8.05[A]
Timing (See subhead: Priority and timing)
Undue experimentation . . . 8.04

ENABLEMENT—Cont.
Utility, and . . . 8.06
Written description versus . . . 9.05

EXHAUSTION
First sale doctrine and . . . 39.02
Foreign sales . . . 39.03
Unauthorized sales . . . 39.03

EXPERIMENTAL USE
Generally . . . 32.01; 32.04
Common law
    Current standards . . . 32.02[B]
    Origins of . . . 32.02[A]
Statutory experimental use: 35 U.S.C. Section 271(e)
    Generally . . . 32.03[A]
    FDA approval process and . . . 32.03[B]
    Structure of . . . 32.03[A]
    Supreme Court's construction of, *Merck KGaA v. Integra Lifesciences I, Ltd* . . . 32.03[C]

EXTRATERRITORIAL ACTIVITY AND PATENT INFRINGEMENT
Generally . . . 35.01; 35.06
Exporting components from U.S.
    Enactment of Section 271(f): closing *Deepsouth* loophole . . . 35.03[B]
    Interpretation of Section 271(f): what is component of patented invention
        Generally . . . 35.03[C]
        Designs . . . 35.03[C][1]
        Method claims and Section 271(f) . . . 35.03[C][3]
        Plans . . . 35.03[C][1]
        Tangible items and Section 271(f): software . . . 35.03[C][2]
    Makes and extraterritorial activity: *Deepsouth Packing Co. v. Laitram Corp* . . . 35.03[A]
Importation of products incorporating U.S. patented inventions, Section 271(g) and
    Enactment of Section 271(g) . . . 35.04[A]
    Operation of Section 271(g) . . . 35.04[B]
International Trade Commission, infringement actions before
    Jurisdiction of . . . 35.05[A]
    Patent infringement in, Section 271(g) and . . . 35.05[C]
    Process of . . . 35.05[B]
    Section 271(g) and patent infringement in . . . 35.05[C]
Section 271(a) and
    Generally . . . 35.02
    Infringing uses: *NTP, Inc. v. Research in Motion, Ltd.* . . . 35.02[A]
    Locus of infringing offer to sell and infringing sales
        Extra-territorial activity directed toward U.S. . . . 35.02[B][2]
        Offers for sale . . . 35.02[B][1]
        Sales outside U.S. . . . 35.02[B][1]

F

FDA (See FOOD AND DRUG ADMINISTRATION (FDA))

FIRST AMENDMENT
Noerr-Pennington immunity, and . . . 38.05[B]

FIRST SALE DOCTRINE
Generally . . . 39.01; 39.07
Doctrine of repair/reconstruction
    Analytic framework . . . 39.05[A]
        Sequential replacement of parts . . . 39.05[B]
Exhaustion and . . . 39.02
Foreign sales . . . 39.03
Husky Injection Molding Systems, LTD. v. R & D Tool Engineering Co . . . 39.06
Post sale restrictions . . . 39.04
Replacements that are akin to repair . . . 39.06
Unauthorized sales . . . 39.03

FIRST TO INVENT SYSTEM
Generally . . . 20.01; 20.06
Abandonment, suppression or concealment
    Doctrine . . . 20.05[A]
    Inference of . . . 20.05[C]
    Intentional . . . 20.05[B]
    Patentee
        Delay . . . 20.05[C]
        Resumed activity negating finding of . . . 20.05[D]
    Policy . . . 20.05[A]
Concealment (See subhead: Abandonment, suppression or concealment)
Conception
    Generally . . . 20.03
    Appreciation of invention . . . 20.03[A][2]
    Complete conception . . . 20.03[A], [A][1]
    Corroboration requirement . . . 20.03[A][4]
    Inventor recognition . . . 20.03[A][2]
    Simultaneous conception and reduction to practice . . . 20.03[C]
    Utility not required to establish conception . . . 20.03[A][3]
Operation . . . 20.02
Priority rules under Section 102(g)
    Diligence . . . 20.04[B]
    First to conceive . . . 20.04[B]
    First to reduce to practice has priority . . . 20.04[A]
Reduction to practice
    Generally . . . 20.03[B]
    Actual reduction to practice . . . 20.03[B][1]
    All elements requirement . . . 20.03[B][2]
    Constructive . . . 20.03[B][5]
    Demonstrating that invention works for intended purpose . . . 20.03[B][3]
    Invention's utility, recognition of . . . 20.03[B][4]
    Inventor's appreciation . . . 20.03[B][4]
    Simultaneous conception and . . . 20.03[C]
Structure . . . 20.02
Suppression (See subhead: Abandonment, suppression or concealment)

FOOD AND DRUG ADMINISTRATION (FDA)
Approval process and statutory experimental use . . . 32.03[B]

FOREIGN ACTIVITY (See EXTRATERRITORIAL ACTIVITY AND PATENT INFRINGEMENT)

FRAUDULENT PROCUREMENT OF PATENT
Walker Process claims . . . 38.06

I

INDEPENDENT CLAIMS
Generally . . . 4.04[A]

INDIRECT INFRINGEMENT
Generally . . . 26.03[A]

INDUCEMENT OF INFRINGEMENT (See ACTIVE INDUCEMENT)

INEQUITABLE CONDUCT AND DUTY TO DISCLOSE
Generally . . . 36.01; 36.06
Current standard for
    Generally . . . 36.03
    Intent to deceive . . . 36.03[A]
    Materiality standard, closer examination of . . . 36.03[B]
    Therasense
        Application of *Therasense* standard . . . 36.03[C]
        Intent to deceive . . . 36.03[A]
Development of . . . 36.02[B]
Equity, origins in . . . 36.02[A]
History and policy
    Development of inequitable conduct . . . 36.02[B]
    Origins in equity . . . 36.02[A]
Origins in equity . . . 36.02[A]
Policy, history and
    Development of inequitable conduct . . . 36.02[B]
    Origins in equity . . . 36.02[A]
Regulation of attorney conduct by U.S. Patent and Trademark Office . . . 36.04
Supplemental examination and . . . 36.05
U.S. Patent and Trademark Office, regulation of attorney conduct by . . . 36.04

INFRINGEMENT
Generally . . . 26.01; 26.04
Antitrust law, infringement litigation and (See ANTITRUST LAW, subhead: Infringement litigation)
Contributory infringement (See CONTRIBUTORY INFRINGEMENT)
Direct infringement (See DIRECT INFRINGEMENT)
Divided infringement . . . 27.04
Doctrine of equivalents, infringement under (See INFRINGEMENT UNDER DOCTRINE OF EQUIVALENT)
Foreign activity (See EXTRATERRITORIAL ACTIVITY AND PATENT INFRINGEMENT)

INFRINGEMENT—Cont.
Indirect infringement . . . 26.03[A]
Literal infringement and infringement under doctrine
  of equivalents . . . 26.03[B]
Multiple infringers . . . 27.04
Remedies for (See REMEDIES FOR PATENT IN-
  FRINGEMENT)
Theories
        Generally . . . 26.03
        Direct infringement . . . 26.03[A]
        Doctrine of equivalents, infringement under
          . . . 26.03[B]
        Indirect infringement . . . 26.03[A]
        Literal infringement . . . 26.03[B]
Violation of provisional right . . . 26.02

**INFRINGEMENT UNDER DOCTRINE OF
  EQUIVALENT**
Generally . . . 26.03[B]; 29.01; 29.07
Development of current doctrine of equivalents:
  *Graver Tank & MFG. Co. v. Linde Air Products
  Co* . . . 29.03
Means plus function claims (See MEANS PLUS
  FUNCTION CLAIMS, CONSTRUCTION OF,
  subhead: Infringement of, under doctrine of
  equivalents)
Post-*Warner-Jenkinson* era, tests for infringement in
  . . . 29.05
Putting doctrine together: sample application of
  Warner-Jenkinson standard . . . 29.06
Reverse doctrine of equivalents . . . 29.07
U.S. Supreme Court's refinement of doctrine of
  equivalents: *Warner-Jenkinson Co. v. Hilton Davis
  Chemical Co.*
        Generally . . . 29.04
        Affirmation of doctrine of equivalents, *Warner-
          Jenkinson's* . . . 29.04[B]
        After-arising technology, doctrine of equiva-
          lents and . . . 29.04[D]
        Factual background of *Warner-Jenkinson* opin-
          ion . . . 29.04[A]
        Principle prosecution history estoppel, *Warner-
          Jenkinson* and . . . 29.04[C]
Winans v. Denmead: historic foundations of doctrine
  of equivalents . . . 29.02

INJUNCTIVE RELIEF
Permanent injunctive relief (See REMEDIES FOR
  PATENT INFRINGEMENT, subhead: Permanent
  injunctive relief)
Preliminary injunctions . . . 41.02[B]

**INTERNATIONAL TRADE COMMISSION
  (ITC)**
Infringement actions before (See EXTRATERRITO-
  RIAL ACTIVITY AND PATENT INFRINGE-
  MENT, subhead: International Trade Commission,
  infringement actions before)
Patent litigation in . . . 6.04

INTERNATIONAL TREATIES
Generally . . . 42.01; 42.05
Coordination of patent application filing . . . 42.03
Paris Convention of 1883 . . . 42.02

INTERNATIONAL TREATIES—Cont.
Patent Cooperation Treaty . . . 42.03
Trade-related aspects of intellectual property rights,
  agreement on . . . 42.04
World Trade Organization . . . 42.04

***INTER PARTES* REVIEW**
Generally . . . 3.07

INTERPRETATION OF CLAIMS
Generally . . . 25.01; 25.07
Canons of claim construction
        Generally . . . 25.06
        Additional canons of claim construction
          . . . 25.06[C]
        Construction of terms in preamble
          . . . 25.06[B]
        Doctrine of claim differentiation . . . 25.06[A]
Claim construction
        Analysis together . . . 25.04[A]
        Canons of (See subhead: Canons of claim con-
          struction)
        Former approaches to . . . 25.02
        Validity and . . . 25.05
Current approach: Federal Circuit's en banc decision
  in *Phillips v. AWH Corp*
        Generally . . . 25.03
        Phillips claim construction methodology
                Generally . . . 25.03[A]
                Application of . . . 25.03[B]
Former approaches to claim construction . . . 25.02
History . . . 25.02
Interaction of specification and claim terms
        Canons of claim construction (See subhead:
          Canons of claim construction)
        Claim construction analysis together
          . . . 25.04[A]
        Patentee as lexicographer: *SciMed*
          . . . 25.04[B]
Means plus function claims (See MEANS PLUS
  FUNCTION CLAIMS, CONSTRUCTION OF)
Procedures for interpreting claims (See PROCE-
  DURES FOR CLAIM CONSTRUCTION)

INVENTORSHIP
Generally . . . 19.01; 19.06
Correction of . . . 19.05
Filing patent application . . . 19.02[C]
Inventor
        Oath . . . 19.02[C]
        Patent Act, under . . . 19.02[A]
Joint inventors . . . 19.02[B]
Ownership . . . 19.02[B]

ITC (See INTERNATIONAL TRADE COMMIS-
  SION (ITC))

J

JEPSON CLAIMS
Generally . . . 4.04[I]

[References are to sections.]

JURISDICTION
District court action
    Declaratory judgment jurisdiction . . . 6.02[C]
    Personal jurisdiction and venue . . . 6.02[D]
    Subject matter jurisdiction . . . 6.02[A]
    Venue, personal jurisdiction and . . . 6.02[D]
Federal Circuit, of . . . 6.03[B]
International Trade Commission, infringement actions before . . . 35.05[A]

L

LACHES (See PROSECUTION LACHES)

LICENSES
On-sale activity, and . . . 15.04
Refusals to license and market power under 1988 Amendments to Patent Act . . . 37.04
Temporal scope of patent license, increasing . . . 37.05
Unilateral refusals to license patent, antitrust law and . . . 38.03

LITERAL INFRINGEMENT
Generally . . . 26.03[B]

M

MARKUSH CLAIMS
Generally . . . 4.04[H]

MEANS PLUS FUNCTION CLAIMS
Generally . . . 4.04[G]
Construction of (See MEANS PLUS FUNCTION CLAIMS, CONSTRUCTION OF)

MEANS PLUS FUNCTION CLAIMS, CONSTRUCTION OF
Generally . . . 4.04[G]; 31.01; 31.06
Claim construction under Section 112, ¶ 6, example for . . . 31.03
Infringement of, under doctrine of equivalents
    Comparison of equivalent structure for Section 112, ¶ 6 limitations . . . 31.05[B]
    Functional claims and . . . 31.05[A]
    Literal and doctrine of equivalents infringement . . . 31.05[B]
Literal infringement analysis for
    Generally . . . 31.04
    After-arising technologies and . . . 31.04[B]
    Application of literal infringement standard for claims governed by Section 112, ¶ 6 Governing Rules: *Al-Site Corp. v. VSI Int'l, Inc.* . . . 31.04[C]
    Claims governed by Section 112, ¶ 6, literal infringement of . . . 31.04[A]

METHOD CLAIMS
Generally . . . 4.04[C]
Section 271(f) and . . . 35.03[C][3]

MISUSE
Generally . . . 37.01; 37.07
Common law roots . . . 37.02[A]
Contributory infringement and . . . 37.02[B]

MISUSE—Cont.
Dawson Chemical v. Rohm Haas under 1952 Patent Act . . . 37.03
Mercoid cases: patent misuse and contributory infringement . . . 37.02[B]
1952 Patent Act: *Dawson Chemical v. Rohm Haas* . . . 37.03
1988 Amendments to Patent Act: refusals to license and market power . . . 37.04
Origins of patent misuse doctrine
    Common law roots . . . 37.02[A]
    Contributory infringement and patent misuse . . . 37.02[B]
    Mercoid cases . . . 37.02[B]
Refusals to license and market power under 1988 Amendments to Patent Act . . . 37.04
Temporal scope of patent license, increasing . . . 37.05
Tying and patent pools . . . 37.06

MULTIPLE DEPENDENT CLAIMS
Generally . . . 4.04[A]

N

NONOBVIOUSNESS
Generally . . . 21.01; 21.11
Analytic framework: *Graham v. John Deere* . . . 21.03
Combination claims, and . . . 21.10
Combining multiple references . . . 21.05
Current law: *KSR Int'l Co. v. Teleflex Inc.* . . . 21.06
Determining scope and content of prior art
    Analogous art, reference must constitute . . . 21.08[B]
    What constitutes prior art under Section 103 . . . 21.08[A]
How prior art is used under Section 103 . . . 21.04
Obvious to try: *In re Kubin* . . . 21.07
Origins of nonobviousness requirement
    Former flash of creative genius standard . . . 21.02[C]
    Patentability standards prior to enactment of Section 103 . . . 21.02[A]
    Secondary considerations of . . . 21.02[B]
Secondary considerations of . . . 21.02[B]; 21.09

NON-PROVISIONAL PATENT APPLICATIONS
Provisional versus . . . 2.03[A]
Utility patent applications . . . 2.03[B]

NOVELTY, STATUTORY BARS AND DERIVATION UNDER SECTION 102
Generally . . . 12.01; 12.08
America Invents Act (See AMERICA INVENTS ACT (AIA))
Inherency
    Accidental inherency . . . 12.06[B]
    Definition . . . 12.06[A]
    Knowledge of inherent property . . . 12.06[B]
    New use patents, inherency and . . . 12.06[C]
    Property, knowledge of inherent . . . 12.06[B]

[References are to sections.]

**NOVELTY, STATUTORY BARS AND DERIVA-
TION UNDER SECTION 102**—Cont.
Pre-America Invents Act version of Section 102
    Historic underpinnings of pre-America Invents
        Act statute . . . 12.03[B]
    Structure of former version of Section 102
        . . . 12.03[A]
Strict identity requirement . . . 12.05
Terminology relevant to Section 102 analysis
    . . . 12.02

O

OFFERS FOR SALE, PRIOR SALES AND (See
    PRIOR SALES AND OFFERS FOR SALE)

P

PARIS CONVENTION OF 1883
Generally . . . 42.02

PATENT AND TRADEMARK OFFICE (See
    UNITED STATES PATENT AND TRADEMARK
    OFFICE (U.S. PTO))

PATENT COOPERATION TREATY (PCT)
Generally . . . 42.03
Patent applications filed under . . . 18.03
United States Patent and Trademark Office
    . . . 2.06

PATENT RIGHT (GENERALLY)
Generally . . . 1.01; 1.07
Benefits of patent . . . 1.06
British patent system . . . 1.02[B]
Copyright and patent clause, adoption of
    America Invents Act of 2011 . . . 1.03[C]
    Congressional adoption of patent system
        . . . 1.03[B]
    Patent system and U.S. Constitution
        . . . 1.03[A]
Early European patent systems . . . 1.02[A]
Foundations of modern U.S. patent law
    Generally . . . 1.04
    Appropriation mechanism, patent rights as
        . . . 1.04[B]
    Incentives and patent law . . . 1.04[C]
    Legal foundation of patent rights . . . 1.04[A]
History and origins of
    British patent system . . . 1.02[B]
    Early European patent systems . . . 1.02[A]
    Statute of monopolies . . . 1.02[B]
Right to exclude, operation of . . . 1.05
Statute of monopolies . . . 1.02[B]
U.S. Constitutional basis (See subhead: Copyright
    and patent clause, adoption of)

PCT (See PATENT COOPERATION TREATY
    (PCT))

PERSONAL JURISDICTION
District court . . . 6.02[D]

PLANT PATENTS
Generally . . . 5.04

**PLANT VARIETY PROTECTION ACT CER-
TIFICATE**
Generally . . . 5.05

**POST-GRANT ADMINSTRATIVE PROCEED-
INGS**
Generally . . . 3.01; 3.10
Certificate of correction . . . 3.04
Determining inventorship . . . 3.09
Doctrine of intervening rights . . . 3.03
Inter partes review . . . 3.07
Intervening rights, doctrine of . . . 3.03
Inventorship, determination of . . . 3.09
Post-grant review process . . . 3.06
Reexamination
    Generally . . . 3.05[A]
    Ex parte . . . 3.05[B]
    Former inter partes reexam . . . 3.05[C]
Re-issue
    Generally . . . 3.02[A]
    Error defined for purposes of reissue
        . . . 3.02[B]
    Limitations on
        Rule against recapture . . . 3.02[C][2]
        Two year limit on broadening reissue
        . . . 3.02[C][1]
    Rule against recapture . . . 3.02[C][2]
    Two year limit on broadening reissue
        . . . 3.02[C][1]
Supplemental examination . . . 3.08

POST-GRANT REVIEW PROCESS
Generally . . . 3.06

**PRE-AMERICA INVENTS ACT 35 U.S.C. SEC-
TION 102(C), ABANDONMENT AND** (See
    ABANDONMENT AND PRE-AIA 35 U.S.C.
    Section 102(c))

PRINTED PUBLICATIONS AND PATENT
Generally . . . 14.01; 14.04
Prior patents . . . 14.03
Public accessibility and
    Generally . . . 14.02[B]
    Current standard: *In re Klopfenstein*
        . . . 14.02[B][2]
    Standard development . . . 14.02[B][1]
Section 102, under . . . 14.02[A]

PRIOR PATENTS
Generally . . . 17.01; 17.07
Claim scope and validity of foreign patent
    . . . 17.04
Distinction between Section 102 (d) and patented
    provisions of Section 102(a) (b) . . . 17.06
Foreign invention, patenting . . . 17.05
Foreign patent, claim scope and validity of
    . . . 17.04
Pre-America Invents Act 35 U.S.C. Section 102(d),
    operation of . . . 17.02
Prior art identification that is patented . . . 17.03

[References are to sections.]

PRIOR PATENTS—Cont.
Validity of foreign patent, claim scope and
    . . . 17.04

PRIOR SALES AND OFFERS FOR SALE
Generally . . . 15.01; 15.05
Defining offer for sale . . . 15.03
Licenses and on-sale activity . . . 15.04
On-sale and ready for patenting standard
      Generally . . . 15.02[A]
      Applying Pfaff ready for patenting standard
        . . . 15.02[C]
      U.S. Supreme Court's *Pfaff v. Wells Electron-*
        ics, Inc. . . . 15.02[B]
Sale, definition of . . . 15.03

PRIOR USE RIGHTS
Generally . . . 28.01; 28.03
America Invents Act, implementing prior use rights
   under
      Generally . . . 28.02[B]
      Defense, effect of . . . 28.02[B][3]
      Prior law . . . 28.02[A]
      Subject matter scope . . . 28.02[B][1]
      University exclusion . . . 28.02[B][4]
      Who is prior user . . . 28.02[B][2]

PROCEDURES FOR CLAIM CONSTRUCTION
Generally . . . 24.01; 24.06
Accused device, claim construction and . . . 24.05
Claim interpretation in courts
      Generally . . . 24.03
      Current law: *Markman v. Westview Instru-*
        ments, Inc.
          Generally . . . 24.03[B]
          Markman's aftermath . . . 24.03[B][1]
      Former law . . . 24.03[A]
      U.S. Patent and Trademark Office, versus
        . . . 24.02
Implementing *Markman* . . . 24.04

PROCESS CLAIMS
Generally . . . 4.04[C]

PRODUCT-BY-PROCESS CLAIMS
Generally . . . 4.04[D]

PROSECUTION LACHES
Generally . . . 40.01; 40.04
Delay . . . 40.03[A]
Historic foundations of . . . 40.02
Prejudice . . . 40.03[B]

PROVISIONAL PATENT APPLICATIONS
Non-provisional versus . . . 2.03[A]

**PUBLIC KNOWLEDGE AND USE AS PRIOR
   ART**
Generally . . . 13.01; 13.07
Experimental use exception . . . 13.05
Prior knowledge
      Enabling, knowledge must be . . . 13.03[B]
      Proving prior knowledge and use . . . 13.06
      Publicly known, prior knowledge must be
        . . . 13.03[A]

**PUBLIC KNOWLEDGE AND USE AS PRIOR
ART**—Cont.
Prior use
      Private versus public uses . . . 13.04[B]
      Public use . . . 13.04[A]
Proving prior knowledge and use . . . 13.06
Territoriality restrictions: known or used . . . 13.02

R

REMEDIES FOR PATENT INFRINGEMENT
Generally . . . 41.01; 41.09
Exceptional cases, willful infringement and
    . . . 41.07
Injunctive relief
      Permanent injunctive relief (See subhead: Per-
        manent injunctive relief)
      Preliminary injunctions . . . 41.02[B]
Lost profits
      Infringement, proof of causal relationship to
        . . . 41.04[A]
      Market share calculation of . . . 41.04[D]
      Non-infringing alternatives, availability of
        . . . 41.04[B]
      Panduit test . . . 41.04[A]
      Price erosion . . . 41.04[C]
      Proof of causal relationship to infringement
        . . . 41.04[A]
      Second *Panduit* factor . . . 41.04[B]
Monetary relief
      Entire market value rule . . . 41.06[A]
      Lost profits (See subhead: Lost profits)
      Marking, actual and constructive
        . . . 41.06[C]
      Notice, actual and constructive . . . 41.06[C]
      Patentee delay . . . 41.06[B]
      Reasonable royalty (See subhead: Reasonable
        royalty)
      Recover, ability to . . . 41.06[B]
      Statutory background . . . 41.03
Permanent injunctive relief
      Current standard: *eBay v. MercExchange*
        . . . 41.02[A][2]
      eBay standard, application of . . . 41.02[A][3]
      Former law, statutory basis and
        . . . 41.02[A][1]
      Ongoing infringement, compensation for
        . . . 41.02[A][4]
      Statutory basis and former law
        . . . 41.02[A][1]
Prejudgement interest . . . 41.08
Reasonable royalty
      Generally . . . 41.05
      Analytic approach . . . 41.05[B]
      Established royalty . . . 41.05[A]
      Hypothetical negotiation, reasonable royalty
        based on . . . 41.05[C]
Willful infringement and exceptional cases
    . . . 41.07

**RESTRICTIONS ON DOCTRINE OF EQUIVA-
LENTS**
Generally . . . 30.01; 30.06

[References are to sections.]

RESTRICTIONS ON DOCTRINE OF EQUIVALENTS—Cont.

Additional restriction on . . . 30.03

Equivalent cannot encompass prior art . . . 30.03

Prior art, equivalent cannot encompass . . . 30.03

Prosecution history estoppel: *Festo* cases
    Application of doctrine of prosecution history estoppel . . . 30.02[D]
    Doctrine of prosecution history estoppel . . . 30.02[A]
    Federal Circuit's refinement . . . 30.02[C]
    Ground rules of prosecution history estoppel . . . 30.02[B]
    Putting *Festo* analysis together . . . 30.02[D]

Public dedication rule . . . 30.04

Vitiate an entire claim element, doctrine of equivalents cannot . . . 30.05

S

STATUTORY SUBJECT MATTER

Generally . . . 23.01; 23.05

Abstract subject matter, business methods and software
    Generally . . . 23.03[A]
    Diamond v. Diehr . . . 23.03[D]
    Federal Circuit's restrictive approach . . . 23.03[F]
    Gottschalk v. Benson . . . 23.03[B]
    Parker v. Flook . . . 23.03[C]
    Patentable subject matter at Federal Circuit . . . 23.03[E]

Business methods and software, abstract subject matter (See subhead: Abstract subject matter, business methods and software)

Products of nature
    Generally . . . 23.02
    Claims derived from nature: *Mayo v. Prometheus* . . . 23.02[D]
    Emerging issues: *Myriad* case . . . 23.02[E]
    Natural phenomenon, and . . . 23.02[A]
    Products made from living things: *Parke-Davis & Co. v. H.K. Mulford Co* . . . 23.02[B]
    Products of nature versus living things: Supreme Court's *Diamond v. Chakrabarty* . . . 23.02[C]

Software, abstract subject matter, business methods and (See subhead: Abstract subject matter, business methods and software)

Supreme Court's *Bilski* opinion
    Abstract subject matter, *Bilski* and prohibition on . . . 23.04[A]
    Progeny, *Bilski's* . . . 23.04[B]

SUBJECT MATTER JURISDICTION

District court . . . 6.02[A]

T

TRADE-RELATED ASPECTS OF INTELLECTUAL PROPERTY RIGHTS (TRIPS)

Generally . . . 42.04

TREATIES (See INTERNATIONAL TREATIES)

TRIPS (See TRADE-RELATED ASPECTS OF INTELLECTUAL PROPERTY RIGHTS (TRIPS))

TYING CLAIMS (See ANTITRUST LAW, subhead: Tying claims)

TYPES OF PATENT

Generally . . . 5.01; 5.06

Design patents . . . 5.03

Plant patents . . . 5.04

Plant Variety Protection Act Certificate . . . 5.05

Utility patents . . . 5.02

U

UNITED STATES PATENT AND TRADEMARK OFFICE (U.S. PTO)

Generally . . . 2.01; 2.07

Applications for patent
    Non-provisional
        Provisional versus . . . 2.03[A]
        Utility patent applications . . . 2.03[B]
    Pre-filing considerations . . . 2.02
    Provisional versus non-provisional . . . 2.03[A]
    Secrecy for patent . . . 2.04[A]
    Specification submitted in support of patent . . . 2.03[C]

Communication with . . . 2.04[B]

Examination procedures
    Continuation applications . . . 2.05[C]
    Final office actions
        Allowance . . . 2.05[B][1]
        Appellate option . . . 2.05[B][2]
        Rejection option . . . 2.05[B][2]
    Intake and examination . . . 2.05[A]

Information sharing, patent prosecution and (See subhead: Prosecution and information sharing, patent)

International applications and work sharing . . . 2.04[C]

International considerations . . . 2.06

Non-provisional patent applications
    Provisional versus . . . 2.03[A]
    Utility patent applications . . . 2.03[B]

Patent Cooperation Treaty application process . . . 2.06

Prosecution and information sharing, patent
    Application secrecy for patent . . . 2.04[A]
    Communication with United States Patent and Trademark Office . . . 2.04[B]
    International applications and work sharing . . . 2.04[C]
    Publication for patent . . . 2.04[A]
    Work sharing, international applications and . . . 2.04[C]

Provisional versus non-provisional patent applications . . . 2.03[A]

Publication for patent . . . 2.04[A]

Specification submitted in support of patent . . . 2.03[C]

[References are to sections.]

UNITED STATES PATENT AND TRADEMARK OFFICE (U.S. PTO)—Cont.
Work sharing, international applications and . . . 2.04[C]

U.S. PTO (See UNITED STATES PATENT AND TRADEMARK OFFICE (U.S. PTO))

UTILITY
Generally . . . 5.02; 22.01; 22.06
Economic considerations relating to utility requirement . . . 22.05
Moral utility . . . 22.04
Operable utility . . . 22.02
Specific or practical utility
    Generally . . . 22.03
    Brenner utility standard, subsequent development of . . . 22.03[C]
    Modern utility standard, historical context for . . . 22.03[A]
    U.S. Supreme Court sets Section 101's utility standard: *Brenner v. Manson* . . . 22.03[B]

V

VENUE
District court . . . 6.02[D]

W

***WALKER PROCESS* CLAIMS**
Antitrust law . . . 38.06

WILLFUL INFRINGEMENT
Remedies for patent infringement . . . 41.07

WORLD TRADE ORGANIZATION (WTO)
Trade-related aspects of intellectual property rights agreement and . . . 42.04

WRITTEN DESCRIPTION
Generally . . . 9.01; 9.06
Application of possession test (See subhead: Possession test, application of)
ARIAD: current legal standard . . . 9.03
Enablement versus . . . 9.05
Possession test, application of
    Amendments during prosecution . . . 9.04[A]
    Benefit of earlier filing date . . . 9.04[B]
    Biological and chemical subject matter . . . 9.04[C]
    Chemical subject matter, biological and . . . 9.04[C]
    Earlier filing date, benefit of . . . 9.04[B]
    Prosecution, amendments during . . . 9.04[A]
Principles, general . . . 9.02

WTO (See WORLD TRADE ORGANIZATION (WTO))